W9-ASZ-658

SOCIOLOGY

ACADEMIC REVIEWERS FOR THE FOURTH EDITION

Patricia Allen
Los Angeles Valley College

Robert Antonio
University of Kansas

Howe Barbara
State University of New York at Buffalo

Bernard Beck
Northwestern University

Raymond Bradley
University of Minnesota

H. Wayne Brady
Middlesex Community College

Wilbur Brookover
Michigan State University

Craig Calhoun
University of North Carolina

Al Chabot
Macomb Community College

Daryl E. Chubin
Georgia Institute of Technology

Walter E. Clark
St. Louis Community College at Florrisant Valley

Peter Conrad
Brandeis University

Stephen E. Cornell
Harvard University

Paul DiMaggio
Yale University

James G. Ennis
Tufts University

Michael P. Farrell
State University of New York at Buffalo

James Faught
Loyola Marymount University

Gary Fine
University of Minnesota

Gerald Handel
City University of New York

Christopher Hurn
University of Massachusetts

Satoshi Ito
College of William and Mary

J. Craig Jenkins
University of Missouri

Jack Kamerman
Kean College of New Jersey

Debra Kaufman
Northeastern University

Sherryl Kleinman
University of North Carolina

Robert H. Lauer
United States International University

Edward O. Laumann
University of Chicago

Peter V. Marsden
University of North Carolina

William Martin
University of Wisconsin

Meredith B. McGuire
Montclair State College

W. Lawrence Neuman
University of Wisconsin

William M. Newman
University of Connecticut at Storrs

Elizabeth Nick
Broward Community College

Robert Perrin
University of Tennessee at Knoxville

Charles Perrow
Yale University

Thomas F. Pettigrew
University of California at Santa Cruz

Charles C. Ragin
Northwestern University

Barbara J. Risman
University of Washington

Roland Robertson
University of Pittsburgh

Rachel Rosenfeld
University of North Carolina

William G. Roy
University of California at Los Angeles

James B. Rule
State University of New York at Stony Brook

John Scanzoni
University of North Carolina at Greensboro

Paul T. Schollaert
Old Dominion University

Charles Selengut
County College of Morris

Thomas R. Shannon
Radford University

Paul Schervish
Boston College

Hilary Silver
Brown University

Doris P. Slesinger
University of Wisconsin

William E. Snizek
Virginia Polytechnic Institute and State University

David A. Snow
University of Texas

John R. Stratton
University of Iowa

Joyce E. Teitge
Valparaiso University

Lois Weis
State University of New York at Buffalo

Barry Wellman
University of Toronto

Robert White
Indiana University

David Willer
University of Kansas

John Wilson
Duke University

Richard Zeller
Bowling Green State University

SOCIOLOGY

FOURTH EDITION

Donald Light, Jr.

Suzanne Keller

Fourth Edition
9876543
 Published in the United States by Random House, Inc., and simultaneously in Canada by Random House of Canada Limited, Toronto.

Library of Congress Cataloging in Publication Data

Light, Donald, 1942–
Sociology.

Bibliography: p.
Includes index.
1. Sociology. 2. United States—Social conditions.
I. Keller, Suzanne Infeld, 1927– II. Title.
[HM51.L52 1984] 301 84-17088
ISBN 0-394-33738-7

Manufactured in the United States of America

ACKNOWLEDGMENTS

Chapter opener credits: Chapter 1: Norman Owen Tomalin/Bruce Coleman; Chapter 2: Ron Cooper/EKM-Nepenthe; Chapter 3: J.C. Carton/Bruce Coleman; Chapter 4: Porterfield-Chickering/Photo Researchers; Chapter 5: Ivan Polunin/Bruce Coleman; Chapter 6: Eve Arnold/Magnum; Chapter 7: Michael D. Sullivan; Chapter 8: Mike Mazzaschi/Stock, Boston; Chapter 9: Birgit Pohl; Chapter 10: Richard Davis/Photo Researchers; Chapter 11: Mark Godfrey/Archive Pictures; Chapter 12: Leif Skoogfoors/Woodfin Camp & Associates; Chapter 13: Christopher Springmann; Chapter 14: Ellis Herwig/The Picture Cube; Chapter 15: Craig Aurness/West Light; Chapter 16: David Austen/Stock, Boston: Chapter 17: Steve Weinrebe/The Picture Cube; Chapter 18: Michael D. Sullivan; Chapter 19: Bill Pierce/Rainbow.

Cover art: Sculpture by Jean'Claude Hug, Salon de la Jeune Sculpture, Paris.
Photo by Robert Clark/Photo Researchers.

Cover and text design by Leon Bolognese.

PREFACE

Since its first edition in 1975, Light and Keller's approach has been to reflect the best of modern sociology: a lively blend of important theories and new scientific research interwoven with social topics of great current interest. As always, we have tried in this fourth edition to convey the excitement of sociological discovery and our love for the field. Our goal has been to give our readers provocative sociological insights into the world in which they live and into some major issues of their times.

MAJOR CHANGES IN THE FOURTH EDITION

1. We have brought the text into the mid-1980s by linking theoretical principles and concepts with current issues, including the antinuclear and environmental movements, health and welfare concerns, and the impact of the computer on social phenomena.
2. Recent sociological thinking, such as Theda Skocpol's theory of revolution, has been integrated with material from earlier editions.
3. We have developed the functionalist, conflict, and symbolic-interactionist perspectives with greater rigor and precision. Each perspective is now consistently integrated with the major topics of every chapter.
4. Each chapter ends with an epilogue linking it to others in the text. This helps students to see the way sociological concepts used in the book relate to one another.
5. The number of photographs has been increased by more than 50 percent. Each one has been selected not just to capture student interest, but to illustrate specific sociological points.
6. A program of boxed features introduces students to "The Sociological Eye On . . ." The boxes focus on pertinent sociological issues as well as on careers and the relevance of sociology to the work-a-day-world.

ADDITIONAL CHANGES

In response both to the many sociologists who have used our book before and to the major new developments occurring in the discipline, we have made a number of additional changes in the fourth edition. These can be briefly summarized.

We have turned the sociological eye toward William Foote Whyte's classic study of the "Nortons," looking beyond the individual's personal point of view to consider the broad social patterns and processes not immediately apparent (Chapter 1).

The text uses several key research methods to examine the impact of the Three Mile Island nuclear plant accident on the people who lived nearby. We've also added a unit on historical approaches to the study of special data (Chapter 2).

There is a new major unit on social interaction to

complement the one on social structure. We have also added a section on Erving Goffman's dramaturgical approach as well as a new section on social exchange theory (Chapter 4).

The text expands the treatment of adulthood and aging (Chapter 5).

We have reorganized and tightened the material on gender roles. There is a new focus on the forces bringing about changes in American gender roles, particularly the expansion of the female labor force (Chapter 6).

The conflict approach to deviance has been expanded and strengthened (Chapter 9).

We have enlarged and sharpened the discussion of the conflict and functionalist theories of stratification. There is a new unit on the status attainment process, and an extended discussion of poverty in the United States (Chapter 10).

The problem of illegal immigration to the United States is surveyed. We also examine busing and affirmative action programs as measures to combat institutional discrimination (Chapter 12).

We treat the functionalist, conflict, and symbolic-interactionist approaches to the family. We also expand the cross-cultural treatment of marriage and family patterns as well as the discussion of alternative lifestyles in American life (Chapter 13).

We have added a unit on the New Christian Right (Chapter 15).

The discussion of the Malthus-Marx controversy has been expanded (Chapter 16).

There is a new discussion of social area analysis and a unit on Gemeinschaft and Gesellschaft types of social organization. We appraise the crisis now being experienced by many large American cities and examine a number of programs aimed at contemporary urban problems (Chapter 17).

A new section examines the impact computers are having on American life and the impact of high technology on American jobs (Chapter 19).

PEDAGOGICAL AIDS

To help students more easily identify and understand important terms and concepts, we have paid extremely close attention to how information is organized and presented in the fourth edition. All key terms are boldfaced, clearly defined, and carefully illustrated. A convenient glossary is located at the end of each chapter. There, too, we include a chapter summary and epilogue.

To supplement the pedagogical aids in the text, Theodore C. Wagenaar (ASA Teaching Project and Miami University) and Thomas F. Gieryn (Indiana University) have written an excellent review guide entitled *Reading and Review*. This guide contains learning objectives, chapter summaries, a review of key concepts, review questions with answers and explanations, essay questions, and supplementary readings that pertain to the use of sociology in careers and business.

The instructor has not been neglected either. To aid in the difficult task of teaching introductory sociology, a *Professional Resource Guide* accompanies the fourth edition. This is the only instructor's manual available prepared by many experts in each of sociology's subfields.

A *Computerized Test Bank* has questions that are graduated in level of difficulty. The questions can be selected by computer to provide an almost infinite variety of tests. These tests can also be prepared by our customized test service.

Computerized Activities in Sociology provides simulations of social situations in which the student plays an active role and learns how sociology can be used to understand important everyday experiences. Another instructional aid is *Lecture Launchers*, transparency masters and thought-provoking questions that help introduce the major topic areas of sociology.

THANKS AND APPRECIATION

We are fortunate to have worked with a fine team of editors at Alfred A. Knopf. Barry Fetterolf and Suzanne Thibodeau guided the entire project. Mary Shuford coordinated the development of the manuscript, edited the chapters into their final form, and served as the overall project manager. Anna Marie Muskelly supervised the copyediting process and art program and carried the book through production. We are also grateful to other members of the Knopf staff for their hard work and imagination: Kathy Bendo, photo manager, Sylvia Shepard, assistant editor, and Laura Lamorte, production supervisor. Leon Bolognese is to be credited with the handsome design of the book and cover; Pat Cahalan polished our prose; Cheryl Moch handled the photo research.

We also want to thank those people who helped us with research and essential clerical chores: Mindy Widman, Carol Stamets, and Lynn Groer.

The academic reviewers who are listed facing the title page were extremely helpful in offering their criticisms and suggestions as we planned this revision. We thank them for their time and their insights. We are especially grateful to Craig Calhoun, who sent us materials and answered a number of questions throughout the revision.

CONTENTS

CHAPTER 4

Interaction and Social Structure 77

CHAPTER 5

Socialization 99

BOXES

SOCIOLOGY

PART ONE

THE SOCIOLOGICAL PERSPECTIVE

You are about to take a new look at a very familiar landscape—the social world in which you live. Sociology invites you to step back and view the social forces that influence even the seemingly most private aspects of your life. Whether you complete college, when and whom you marry, how you raise your children, what kind of job you hold, even your political beliefs, your religious affiliation, and how you spend your leisure time are all shaped in large part by social forces beyond your control.

Chapter 1 introduces you to the sociological perspective. It shows how everyday occurrences, such as bowling, take on a new meaning when viewed through a sociologist's eye. Chapter 1 also traces the development of sociological thinking and acquaints you with the major theoretical perspectives in sociology today. Using these perspectives to guide their work, sociologists have dispelled many commonsense myths about how people in social settings behave.

Chapter 2 delves more deeply into the research methods that sociologists use. The application of the scientific method to the study of social patterns requires special techniques, including surveys, laboratory experiments, and systematic observations. The data sociologists collect do not speak for themselves; they must be interpreted. And interpretation is usually influenced by the values a particular sociologist holds. Thus, sociology is not entirely a value-free science, and sociologists; interpretations are at times controversial.

CHAPTER 1

The Sociological Eye

- Very likely you are attending college with the hope of improving your career opportunities. However, a large number of "baby boomers" preceded you in the job market. Does that mean you can expect fewer promotions than in the past, smaller and less frequent raises, harder work, and stiffer demands for good performance?
- Traditionally women, blacks, Hispanics, and other minorities have experienced discrimination in job hiring and promotion. If you are a member of a minority, what are the chances that you will encounter sexism and racism in the years ahead?
- The world is engulfed in a nuclear arms race that has bred antinuclear movements throughout the world. What social forces give birth to social movements? What impact do they have on society and existing social arrangements?
- Over the past quarter century the United States has become much more tolerant of alternative life styles. What options are now available to you in fashioning a comfortable social niche for yourself?
- In recent years many Americans have looked increasingly to religion as an important force in their lives. Can we conclude that a religious renewal is underway in the United States? What impact does religion have on people's lives in modern societies?

Social issues such as these and many more are the subject matter of sociology. They are the focus of what the sociologist C. Wright Mills (1959) called *the sociological imagination*. The **sociological imagination** is a way of looking at our personal experiences in terms of what is going on in the world around us. We come to see that we are more than just actors involved in our own personal dramas. We are also caught up in larger social patterns acted out on a broader social stage. That stage and those social patterns are the subject matter of sociology.

In discussing the sociological imagination, Mills (1959:3, 9) pointed out:

> Nowadays [people] often feel that their private lives are a series of traps. They sense that within their everyday worlds, they cannot quite overcome their troubles, and in this feeling, they are often quite correct.
>
> In these terms, consider unemployment. When, in a city of 100,000, only one man is unemployed, that is his personal trouble, and for its relief we properly look to the character of the man, his skills, and his immediate opportunities. But when . . . [millions] are unemployed, that is an issue, and we may not hope to find its solution within the range of opportunities open to any one individual. The very structure of opportunities has collapsed. Both the correct statement of the problem and the range of possible solutions require us to consider the economic and political institutions of the society, and not

> merely the personal situation and character of a scatter of individuals.
>
> Consider war. The personal problem of war, when it occurs, may be how to survive it or how to die in it with honor; how to make money out of it; how to climb into the higher safety of the military apparatus; or how to contribute to the war's termination. . . . But the structural issues of war have to do with its causes; with what types of men it throws up into command; with its effects upon economic and political, family, and religious institutions, with the unorganized irresponsibility of a world of nation-states.

Viewed in the context of the sociological imagination, we may define **sociology** as the study of human societies and of human behavior in social settings. The sociologist looks beyond individual psychology and unique events to the predictable broad patterns and regular occurrences of social life that influence our individual destinies. In this chapter we discuss some of the ways in which social forces shape our lives. We also examine the development of sociology, its main theoretical orientations, and its uses in today's society. But first we want to explore how your view of an everyday situation would probably be quite different if you were a sociologist.

USING THE SOCIOLOGICAL PERSPECTIVE

The sociological imagination allows us to take a fresh look at the world about us. As the sociologist Peter L. Berger (1963:23) points out, "the first wisdom of sociology" is that "things are not what they seem." We find on close inspection that social reality has a great many dimensions. What distinguishes sociology is that it brings to bear a special form of consciousness in separating these dimensions and examining the "taken-for-granted" ingredients of social experience. "The sociological eye" provides us with a window on those aspects of life that we typically overlook or misinterpret as we go about our daily activities.

As we direct the sociological eye to the human experience we find a recurring theme: *We are ultimately social beings whose attitudes and actions are generated, shaped, and maintained through our interaction with*

People in all societies interact as social beings. Such encounters generate, shape, and maintain our attitudes and actions. (Top, Sepp Seitz/Woodfin Camp; center, Carl Frank/Photo Researchers; bottom, Joel Gordon.)

other people in a group context. How we think, what we feel, and what we say and do derives from what goes on between us as we make our way day by day. This quality, by which we mutually and reciprocally influence one another, constitutes the core of *social interaction* (see Chapter 4). It allows us to enter into patterned and stable relationships with other people to fashion a *group* existence (see Chapter 7).

The sociologist William Foote Whyte (1955) brought the sociological eye to bear upon "Doc and his boys," a group of young men who hung out together in an Italian-American slum neighborhood in Boston. Doc was the twenty-nine-year-old head of the Nortons, the name the group of men applied to themselves. Whyte, then a student working on his Ph.D. in sociology at Harvard, needed a sponsor in the community, and Doc undertook the role. Whyte, an outsider, was able to observe and participate in the group's activities as an insider because he was identified as Doc's friend. In the course of his observations, Whyte gained a good many insights into racketeering, political corruption, and youth gangs.

The Nortons spent a good deal of time bowling. The men engaged in individual matches with one another and also competed in team settings. Whyte was intrigued by an observation that at first did not make sense to him: A man's bowling scores did not reflect his athletic abilities. For instance, on the basis of sheer talent Frank, who had played semiprofessional baseball, should have been the best bowler but was not. Even more perplexing, Frank would make a poor showing when he played baseball with his buddies in the neighborhood.

Alec was another example. He excelled at bowling when he played for the "fun of it" on weekdays. But when the Nortons got together to play one another on Saturday evenings, his game would "fall apart." Yet Doc and Danny, who were only average bowlers, would defeat the other men game-after-game in bowling contests.

As Whyte directed his sociological eye on the events, he too found that "the first wisdom of sociology" is that "things are not what they seem." He discovered that a man's bowling scores were related to the status he held within the group. As shown in Whyte's sketch in Figure 1.1, Doc and Danny enjoyed the highest status and they

FIGURE 1.1 The Nortons: Spring and Summer, 1937

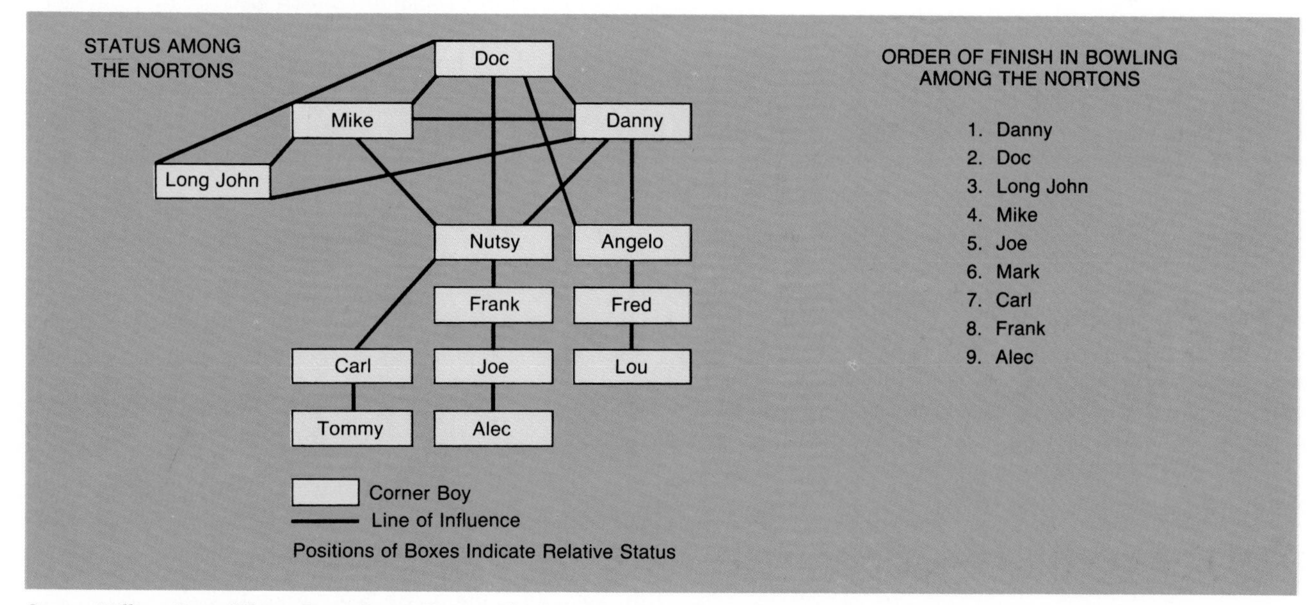

Source: William Foote Whyte, *Street Corner Society: The Social Structure of an Italian Slum* (Chicago: The University of Chicago Press, 1955), pp. 13, 21.

also had the best bowling performance. Frank and Alec, who had the lowest scores, ranked low among the Nortons.

One subtle taken-for-granted expectation of the Nortons was that low-status members should not defeat the top-ranked members. The rule was never explicitly stated, but it was implicit in the men's interaction. Whyte notes that there are many "mental hazards" in athletic performance. An athlete cannot afford to "tighten up" and lose control at critical moments. Self-confidence is crucial to top performance. Viewed from this persepctive, it is hardly surprising that the group's behavior had a powerful impact on a man's performance:

> When Doc, Danny, Long John, or Mike bowled on opposing sides, they kidded one another good-naturedly. Good scóres were expected of them, and bad scores were accounted for by bad luck or temporary lapses of form. When a follower threatened to better his position, the remarks took different form. The boys shouted at him that he was lucky, that he was "bowling over his head." The effort was made to persuade him that he should not be bowling as well as he was, that a good performance was abnormal for him. This type of verbal attack was very important in keeping the members "in their places." It was used particularly by the followers so that, in effect, they were trying to keep one another down. (Whyte, 1955:24)

Based on this and other evidence, Whyte concluded that there is a strong relationship between an individual's performance in social settings and a group's structure. Of equal importance, he found that the men's mental health and psychological well-being were intertwined with their interpersonal relationships. For instance, when Doc suffered a number of setbacks that undermined his role as the group's leader, he began to experience "dizzy spells."

In sum, the sociological eye looks beyond the individual's personal vantage point to consider broad social patterns and processes that are not immediately apparent. In this way the everyday world of the individual is suddenly cast in a new light. Berger (1963:28) puts it well when he says:

> To ask sociological questions presupposes that one is interested in looking some distance beyond the commonly accepted or officially defined goals of human action. It presupposes a certain awareness that human events have different levels of meaning, some of which are hidden from the consciousness of everyday life.

SOCIAL FACTS

As indicated in the opening to this chapter, the sociological imagination implies that much of human experience, no matter how private it may seem, is touched and shaped by social forces not of the individual's making. Emile Durkheim (1938), a pioneering French sociologist of the nineteenth century, emphasized this essential truth when he described what he called **social facts.** Social facts are properties of group life that cannot be explained by reference to the activities, sensibilities, or characteristics of individual persons any more than the properties of the human body can be explained by reference to the workings of individual cells. The social whole, like the biological whole, is not merely the sum of its parts. As each part interacts with and relates to others, new structures, new properties, and new tendencies emerge. Hence, for Durkheim, ultimate social reality resided in the group, not the individual. As we will see in Chapter 15, he viewed religion as rooted in the collective beliefs and practices of a group. Religion thus takes on properties of its own—a tangible form—that constitutes a reality in its own right. Like other institutions, religion assumes an existence apart from given individuals and shapes and constrains people's behavior.

In sum, the social forces that give rise to social facts exist outside the individual and act on his or her behavior. They even determine the course of our inner lives, as illustrated by Doc's symptoms. In order to demonstrate this more fully, we will examine some seemingly very private experiences—sickness and fear of crime.

Being Sick

Surely, it would seem, being sick is an entirely private experience. When we are lying in bed with fever, aches, and pains, absorbed in our personal miseries, how can there be any social forces at work on us? There can be, and there are. How do we know, for instance, that what we are feeling is sickness? In some societies, fever, aches, and pain are considered symptoms of spiritual visitations. The individual plagued with these discomforts is not treated as a sick person but as a person possessed. In our society, however, we treat these symptoms as manifestations of medical diseases. We have learned from our

"Sickness" is defined by what we learn from our social world, not just by the physical discomfort we feel. (Michael Weisbrot & Family/Stock, Boston.)

culture to call ourselves sick when we experience them. A pulled muscle, a broken finger, or poison ivy may make us just as uncomfortable as symptoms of a cold or flu virus, but we do not call them sicknesses. Thus how we know when we are sick is something we have learned from our social world; it is not a property of the physical discomfort itself. In this sense, "sickness" derives from a social definition and as such it is a social fact.

The society we live in also has a widely understood set of rules about how to behave when sick. For certain illnesses we are entitled to stay in bed, free from all obligations that might sap our strength. For others we are expected to continue our daily activities (Jaco, 1979). A sick person who is not terminally ill also has an obligation to behave in a way that will lead to full recovery. Usually this involves following the doctor's instructions about medication, rest, exercise, and interaction with others. When we are sick, we assume a specific role, that of the "sick person," and thereby incur a set of obligations and rights that have been carefully defined for us by society's rules about sickness. Thus there flows from the social definition "sick person" a series of consequences; a reality is fashioned in which the person's social experience is altered and his or her behavior is constrained within certain boundaries.

Society's rules about sickness also tell us who is qualified to heal us. Most patients do not go to medicine men, witch doctors, spiritual exorcists, or mediums for cures (as people in some cultures do). They go to people with scientific training who are licensed by society to heal. Thus being sick is far from a purely private experience. Although the sick role allows a great deal of room for individual expression, the general outline of the role is *socially*, not individually, defined. (Arluke et al., 1979).

Fear of Crime

Fear of crime is likewise not the private experience we often think it is. It cannot be understood without reference to the social context in which it occurs. When we feel fearful walking late at night along deserted city streets, it is largely because the crime statistics tell us that the likelihood of being assaulted is higher in such circumstances than in others. But why is the fear of crime spreading from larger to smaller communities? In 1965, for example, a survey showed that the percentage of people who reported being afraid to walk the streets at night was significantly higher in communities with populations over 50,000 than in communities with fewer residents. But in 1983, people in towns with a population between 2,500 and 49,000 were as likely to be afraid at night as people in larger towns (50,000 to 499,000) were eighteen years earlier, and the gap between these two categories had narrowed considerably (Gallup Poll, 1983; see Table 1.1). Does this mean that the suburbs are becoming as crime-ridden as the central cities?

TABLE 1.1 Persons Afraid to Walk Alone at Night, 1965–1983
By Community Size (in percents)

	Community Size (Population)														
	Total			Under 2,000			2,500 to 49,999			50,000 to 499,999			500,000 and over		
Year	Yes	No	Can't Say	Yes	No	Can't Say	Yes	No	Can't Say	Yes	No	Can't Say	Yes	No	Can't Say
1965[1]	34	63	3	21	77	2	29	67	4	41	54	5	48	49	3
1983[2]	45	55	—	29	70	1	40	59	1	54	46	—	49	51	—

— Represents zero.
[1]The category "Don't know" was used instead of "Can't say."
[2]The category "Under 2,500" was used instead of "Under 2,000."

Source: American Institute of Public Opinion, Princeton, New Jersey, and Gallup Poll Release, 1983.

As you might expect, fear of walking alone at night has risen since the mid-sixties. This fear has increased most in smaller towns and least in cities—to the extent that people feel almost as unsafe in towns over 2,500 as they do in large cites.

Not necessarily. The fear of crime is a social fact. It finds expression in a collective belief that arises in the course of human interaction. As such, it need not correspond to each individual's actual encounters with crime. The collective perception of a crime wave might be created by the local press if it gives top priority to crime when reporting the daily news. Or a marked increase in the fear of crime could be caused by an influx of new residents, prompting people to be less familiar with and more distrustful of their neighbors. The point is that a fear of crime is not caused solely by a person's private experiences and emotional inclinations. Instead, it is very much a community belief shaped by social forces. As you learn more about sociology, you will discover again and again the influence that larger social forces have on individual experiences.

THE DEVELOPMENT OF SOCIOLOGY

Our discussions of the sick role and the fear of crime demonstrate the significant part that social facts play in our daily lives. Yet the extent to which social influences shape behavior has not always been recognized. In fact, many of the important insights of sociology have been made in the relatively recent past. Sociology is a very young discipline; it has developed only in the last century or so. Let us look now at some highlights of that development.

European Pioneers

The sociological imagination sees sociology as relevant in helping us to understand and cope with today's vast social changes. The circumstances that prevailed when the discipline was founded were somewhat similar. Picture yourself living in a European city during the middle of the nineteenth century. Society has undergone startling changes in the last fifty years. The Industrial Revolution has spawned machinery, production processes, and means of transportation undreamed of in your grandparents' day. Cities like your own are burgeoning as thousands of rural workers, no longer needed on the farms, flock to urban factories. Working conditions in the factories are dismal. Men, women, and children toil long hours in unhealthy surroundings for

The Industrial Revolution uprooted a predominantly rural social order. The chaos and misery that prevailed in overgrown cites in the nineteenth century led many social thinkers to try to make some sense of the changes. In this way the discipline of sociology began. (The Bettmann Archive.)

the most meager pay. Church and family are no longer the unquestioned pillars of social life. The traditional values these institutions once instilled seem to be breaking down. Crime is increasing. The destitute are often ignored. In many countries the old political regimes are crumbling or have been forcibly overthrown. It is a turbulent era. Society seems disordered and impossible to understand. In these extraordinary times a handful of gifted thinkers try to make sense of the changes around them, and in so doing they fashion a new discipline—sociology. Chief among these thinkers were Auguste Comte, Herbert Spencer, Karl Marx, Emile Durkheim, and Max Weber (Coser, 1977; Fletcher, 1973).

Auguste Comte

Auguste Comte (1798–1857) was born in France during the tumultuous French Revolution and was raised in its chaotic aftermath. His lifelong preoccupation was grappling with the problem of how society could be totally restructured to meet the demands of an industrial age. The knowledge needed to do so, Comte believed, could be obtained only by applying the methods of science to society. Science, he argued, was the culmination of an inevitable progression in human thought. In the past, people had appealed first to religion (the theological stage) and then to speculative reasoning (the metaphysical stage) in their efforts to impose order and meaning on the social world. But as societies became increasingly complex, especially with the advent of industrialization, these systems of thought proved more and more inadequate. Most important in Comte's view, the theories that religion and speculative reasoning produced could never be checked against observable facts. The only reasonably reliable theories, Comte contended, were those that emerged from careful observation, detailed comparison, and experimentation—in short, those theories derived by employing the techniques of the scientific method.

In addition to formulating the basic approach of sociology, Comte also outlined its subject matter. He believed that two aspects of society lent themselves to scientific inquiry. One was **social statics**—the way in which the various components of society (groups and institutions) are structured, the functions they serve, and how they interrelate. Thus Comte was one of the first observers to describe societies as complex social systems with many interdependent parts. Closely related to the study of social statics was the study of **social dynamics**—the exploration of how the various social patterns in the world have come into existence and how they continue to change. This distinction between statics and dynamics was one of Comte's enduring contributions. Sociologists today still think of their subject as divided in this way.

Comte was not simply a dispassionate observer, spinning out abstract theories and creating new terminology. He wanted to improve society, not just to analyze it. He fervently believed that the application of science to the study of societies could provide a much-needed guide to human action.

According to Auguste Comte, science was the key to understanding the modern social order, and making it better. (The Bettmann Archive.)

Herbert Spencer was unfazed by the social disorder brought on by the Industrial Revolution. A social Darwinist, he viewed such instability as part of an evolutionary process in which only the fittest parts of society would survive and progress. (The Bettmann Archive.)

Karl Marx's views ran counter to those of both Spencer and Comte. According to Marx, society was not formed by survival of the fittest but by the consolidation of those with similar economic interests and experiences, and it could only be changed by class struggle, not by scientific planning. (The Bettmann Archive.)

Herbert Spencer

Herbert Spencer (1820–1903), an English contemporary of Comte's, was also preoccupied with understanding the great transformations occurring in his time. Spencer concluded that the instability in the social order was part of a broader evolutionary process. He argued that the elements of any society are constantly adapting to changing circumstances in order that the society may survive. In this respect, societies resemble the evolving biological organisms that Charles Darwin described. Interestingly, it was Spencer, not Darwin, who coined the phrase "survival of the fittest." By this he meant that through natural selection (a gradual weeding out of the weak and malfuntioning parts), only the optimal social arrangements would eventually remain. This viewpoint led Spencer to adopt a highly conservative, laissez-faire attitude. He believed, for example, that national governments should not attempt to legislate social reforms; they would only interfere with the natural course of social evolution. Thus he strongly opposed such policies as public education, public health care, and laws protecting workers, because he felt that the fittest are capable of fending for themselves. Those who are unable to care for themselves would soon be eliminated. In this fashion, society "progresses" by eliminating its weak links.

It is not surprising that in an age of great colonial expansion and free-wheeling industrialists, Spencer's ideas about social evolution received favorable acclaim. Soon, however, the theory's shortcomings became all too evident, and "social Darwinism" as it came to be called, was widely discredited. Far more enduring in its influence on sociological thought was the work of another nineteenth-century social scientist—Karl Marx.

Karl Marx

Karl Marx (1818–1883) was a philosopher, a political agitator and revolutionary, an economic historian, and a sociologist. He categorically rejected Spencer's notion that what exists in a society without government intervention is what *ought* to be. To Marx (1967; Marx and Engels, 1955), existing social patterns and institutions do not arise through a natural selection of the fittest, but rather through the consolidation of groups of people with similar economic interests and experiences. Marx's view, in short, placed great emphasis on economic factors. He believed that the structure of the economy shaped all other aspects of social life and bred persistent internal strife. In industrial society conflict arose because the **capitalists,** the owners of the means of production (land, factories, machines) were motivated to exploit the **proletariat,** the workers who actually produced economic goods. Marx believed that the conflict between these two classes would continue until the conditions of the workers became so bad that they would unite and overthrow the capitalists. Thus, in contrast to Comte, who maintained that scientific planning would cure society's ills, Marx argued that social change would come about only by a class struggle. Workers had to organize and develop a class consciousness, a sense of their shared interests and plight. Until then, capitalists would use their power to shape the religious beliefs, artistic tastes, leisure activities, and consumer preferences of the oppressed proletariat. This would serve two purposes; first, it would further the capitalists' interests; and second, it would foster a "false consciousness" among the workers so that they would not recognize their own exploited state.

We will discuss Marx's ideas much more extensively in other chapters of this book. Here we simply want to point out his important influence on sociology. Among his many contributions were his penetrating insights into the role of economic factors in shaping social patterns, his awareness of class consciousness and false consciousness, his use of historical research to understand how social structure and institutions change over time, and his deep humanitarian concern for the plight of industrial workers at a time when pay scales and conditions in many factories were appalling.

Emile Durkheim

The French sociologist Emile Durkheim (1858–1917) could not accept Marx's notion that the division of labor in modern societies arose out of perpetual class conflict. He believed that some underlying social forces served to bind individuals together within society. In Durkheim's view, what appeared to be simply rational contracts and agreements (such as "I will work for you if you pay me so much a week") must rest on preexisting mutual trust. Without this mutual trust, each party would waste enormous amounts of time and energy trying to ensure that the other would fulfill his or her commitments. Durkheim referred to this prior trust as "collective conscience," a sense of belonging and mutual obligation that derives from shared rituals, beliefs, and laws.

As a society evolves through time, the nature of its collective conscience changes. Traditional social orders with simple divisions of labor and strongly shared moral obligations give way to a social order bound largely by a complex division of labor and more formal sets of expectations (for example, laws governing minimum wages and working conditions). Compared with tribal or agricultural societies, our society is held together less by common beliefs and rituals than by an elaborate interdependency. Almost everything we want and need is made by someone else, and others likewise look to us to provide for their various needs. Without mutual trust, this elaborate division of labor would fall apart. Thus trust that others will fulfill their economic roles is the glue that binds industrial society together.

Durkheim's interest in solidarity led him to consider how crime and deviance affect the social order. He believed that acts of deviance awaken people to their shared moral bonds and unite them in condemnation of the deviant. Durkheim's interest in deviance led him to conduct a systematic study of suicide in a number of populations, a study that has served as a model of scientific research for other sociologists. (We will describe this study in Chapter 2.) Durkheim's pioneering use of statistics to investigate social life, his insights into the social forces that underlie seemingly individual acts, and his theory of how modern industrial societies work are among his lasting contributions to sociology.

Max Weber

Max Weber (1864–1920), a German sociologist, was less interested in what held society as a whole together than in what united people into *groups,* the basic units of society. Weber argued that economics, politics, and culture are the social forces that divide (and stratify) people into groups and link one group to another.

Like Marx, Weber believed that those who share the same economic fate—whether they be landlords or peasants, workers or industrialists—form distinct social

Emile Durkheim believed that shared social bonds held modern society together. Mutual trust and interdependency created a "collective conscience," or sense of belonging. (The Bettmann Archive.)

Max Weber's interest was in social group patterns formed by economic, political, and cultural forces, and in people's subjective experiences in social life. (Courtesy of the German Information Center.)

classes. And he agreed with Marx that economic forces play a powerful part in shaping the way people see the world and the way they act. But Weber considered politics and culture to be equally important forces. He investigated them by undertaking historical research. For instance, Weber's investigation of capitalism led him to conclude that Protestantism eroded the Catholic traditions,which disallowed receiving interest on loans and established new incentives for saving money and investing it in profit-making ventures. (We will discuss Weber's theory of capitalism in detail in Chapter 11.) In this and many other analyses, Weber employed a concept called an **ideal type**—a pure model of a particular social pattern or process that sociologists use to examine and compare social arrangements in the real world. Ideal types are mental constructs that allow sociologists to highlight the critical properties of a phenomenon. For Weber, capitalism and Protestantism were ideal types, not in the sense that they constituted a desired state of affairs, but in that they were analytical tools for identifying, categorizing, and explaining broad social forces.

Weber's interest in social life extended to the meanings that various behaviors have for the people involved. He stressed that in looking at group patterns, one must not forget that people have feelings, thoughts, consciences, attitudes, and values that affect their relationships. Sociological analysis must include what Weber (1964) called **Verstehen**—an empathic understanding of what people are thinking and feeling. By making inferences regarding the mental states of early Protestants, Weber sought to establish the part that religious motivations played in fostering capitalistlike activities.

Weber's many contributions to sociology are taken up throughout this book. Among other things, he pointed out the importance of people's subjective experiences (**Verstehen**); he provided a major analysis of modern economic arrangements and their impact on society; he developed major theories on stratification and bureaucracy; and he studied the similarities and differences that underlie the institutions of various societies.

Sociology in America

Although sociology began in Europe, it was in America that the new discipline truly flourished. Today, the majority of sociologists are American. How did this tremendous growth of sociology on this continent come about?

During the late nineteenth and early twentieth centuries, the United States was undergoing rapid and very far-reaching change. In the North, industrialization was progressing with unprecedented speed. Rural dwellers, many of them black, were migrating in ever-increasing numbers to the burgeoning industrial cities. So too were immigrants from eastern and southern Europe, seeking economic opportunities unavailable to them in their homelands. Most of these people gravitated to decaying, overcrowded slums, where crime was a persistent problem. The cultural heritages of the newcomers often clashed with mainstream American values and norms. Racial and ethnic conflict were widespread. Observers wondered how these many social ills could best be remedied. The scientific study of society offered the promise of possible solutions.

Lester Ward (1841–1913) was the major figure among the early crusaders seeking the application of sociological knowledge to America's problems. He was a zealous reformer, heavily influenced by Auguste Comte. Like Comte, Ward was convinced that sociologists could play an important role in improving industrial society. Accordingly, he devoted much of his energies to discrediting the laissez-faire notions of Herbert Spencer. Ward strongly believed that it was a terrible error to let social institutions simply take their course. To him, society needed the direction that social science could provide.

It was not until Ward was in his fifties that the first department of sociology was established in the United States. The year was 1893, and the place was the University of Chicago, a recently created institution more open to new lines of inquiry than the older, tradition-bound schools of the East. (It was 1930 before a department of sociology was established at Harvard.) Until World War II, the University of Chicago was the undisputed leader in sociological research. Scholars there viewed Chicago as a "social laboratory" and delved deeply into its social problems. Slum life, crime, juvenile delinquency, prostitution, and drug addiction were all carefully scrutinized. At about the same time, other sociologists at the University of Chicago began to examine the role that social interaction plays in shaping individual personality and behavior. This concern opened a fascinating new field for study. Thus the first half of the twentieth century was an exciting and productive time for American sociology.

After World War II, the interests of American sociologists continued to expand. Some scholars revived the earlier interest in general theories of society. One of these was Talcott Parsons, a sociologist at Harvard. He helped to launch the influential school of thought called structural functionalism, in which the structure of society is described and explained in terms of the functions of its parts, all of which interact in an intricately meshed whole. (We will say more about structural functionalism shortly, when we take up contemporary perspectives in sociology.) Other sociologists turned their attention to sharpening the methods of sociological research, particularly in applying mathematical tools and computers to the analysis of data. In this postwar period of general optimism and faith in technology, social reformers were relatively scarce. All this began to change, however, during the mid 1960s, with the escalation of the Vietnam War and the social criticisms it generated. Gradually, the activist side of sociology reemerged. Today, although most sociologists see themselves as scholars engaged in theory building and basic research, most also feel that their discipline can make an important contribution to improving modern social life.

At the turn of the century, New York City was a beacon for immigrants seeking economic opportunities in the new world. The proximity of so many diverse cultural traditions and practices inevitably led to social conflict. (The Bettmann Archive.)

Lester Ward, a passionate believer in social reform, held that no social problem was beyond the cure of social science. (American Sociological Association.)

Talcott Parsons viewed social problems in the context of general social theories. His structural-functionalist theory defined the structure of society in terms of the functions of its parts. (American Sociological Association.)

THEORETICAL PERSPECTIVES

Through the years, the theoretical streams deriving from the work of European and American sociologists have tended to converge into a few traditions or perspectives. Each perspective rests on its own set of assumptions about the nature of human behavior and the social order. At this point in your introduction to the field of sociology, the importance of these theoretical perspectives may not be apparent. But you will soon discover that the theoretical perspective of particular sociologists greatly influences their view of the social world. It shapes not only the questions that the sociologists ask, but also the answers that they expect to find. But even though they may differ in important ways, all sociological perspectives share the common goal of discovering the basic principles of social life that will allow us to understand the group experience.

Before discussing the most influential theoretical perspectives in contemporary sociology, let us clarify just what a theory is. Quite simply, a **theory** is a systematic explanation of how two or more phenomena are related. In this sense, theory is a tool. It allows sociologists to bind together a good many facts so that they may work with and comprehend them all at once.

Perhaps an illustration will prove helpful. Some social scientists have proposed the theory that if two groups of people are thrown into intense competition for scarce and valuable rewards (land, jobs, income, and prestige) intergroup prejudice will result. Here we have a theory that suggests a direct causal link between two social phenomena: intense competition on the one hand, and prejudice on the other. In short, it attempts to *explain* prejudice by reference to a set of precipitating social circumstances. Note, too, that if this theory is correct, it should be useful in *predicting* behavior. If two groups of people suddenly become engaged in strong competition for scarce and valuable rewards, then prejudice between them is likely, provided counteracting influences do not intervene.

Expressing a theory as an "If/then" statement allows scientists to test it in a systematic manner (assuming, of course, that the phenomena in question can be adequately measured). It is such systematic testing that differentiates scientific research from personal opinion and mere common sense. Testable theories are therefore crucial to science.

Many of the theories discussed in this book are like the one pertaining to competition and prejudice: They attempt to explain a relatively restricted aspect of the social world we live in. They deal with such specific issues as prejudice and discrimination, juvenile delinquency, religious sects, large organizations, and declining population growth. But there are also broader theoretical perspectives that have a strong guiding influence on how more specific theories are framed. Three of the most important of these are the interactionist, the structural-functionalist (or simply functionalist), and the conflict perspectives. These orientations do not exhaust the broad theoretical viewpoints in modern sociology, nor can all specific theories be subsumed neatly under one or another perspective. But together these three perspectives provide an excellent introduction to the general outlooks held by many contemporary sociologists. As you will see, each perspective offers a somewhat different view of our complex social world.

The Interactionist Perspective

As the name suggests, sociologists who view social life from the **interactionist perspective** are interested in how people interact with one another in everyday situations, and how they make sense of their social relationships. As such, they are primarily concerned with human behavior at the person-to-person level. In contrast, the functionalist and conflict approaches focus their attention primarily on the nature and operation of entire societies. Interactionists believe that too much of everyday reality is lost by emphasizing the grand scale. Hence, these sociologists are less concerned than functionalist and conflict theorists with broad social institutions such as the economy, the political system, or the family or with overriding social forces such as stability and change. They criticize theorists of the other two schools for implicitly assuming that social institutions and processes somehow have a life of their own. Interactionists remind us that they do not. Economics, politics, family life, and tendencies toward stability or change are nothing more than creations of people interacting with one another. Understanding the nature of this day-by-day interaction, then, is crucial to sociological knowledge.

Moreover, interactionists take issue with the functionalist view that human interaction involves little more than people acting out roles (parent, child, worker, manager, parishioner, rabbi) based on social scripts, much as theatrical actors take their lines from a play. Instead, interactionists contend that encounters between individuals are almost always ambiguous and uncertain. Consequently, people must constantly devise ways to fit their actions to those of others. They map, test, suspend, and revise their behavior in response to the behavior of others. Participants must constantly read behind each other's words and actions to understand what is being said. The interactionists point out that if sociologists simply studied the roles that people are *supposed* to play, they would get a very unrealistic and lifeless picture of what human interaction entails.

George Herbert Mead (1934), a University of Chicago sociologist, did much to develop the interactionist outlook. He believed that symbols are the very foundations of social life. By this he meant that our thoughts and feelings are not directly accessible to other people. They must first be encoded into symbols—words, gestures, facial expressions, nonlinguistic sounds—which must then be interpreted by others. In fact, Mead argued, it is only through the use of symbols that we "think," in the human sense of the word. This crucial process of symbolic communication came to be called **symbolic interaction,** and it has been central to the interactionist perspective ever since. Although contemporary interactionists may adopt a variety of specific

Everyday human interactions were of major interest to George Herbert Mead. He viewed words, gestures, and expressions as symbols of what we think and feel; these symbols constitute the very foundations of social life. (Courtesy of The University of Chicago, Joseph Regenstein Library.)

approaches, they all revolve in large part around the concept of symbolic interaction.

No aspect of social life is too small for interactionists to study. They turn their social microscopes on the most minute details of everyday life, revealing patterns that most of us merely take for granted. A major concern of interactionists is how people go about fitting their actions to those of others by assigning meanings to their interpersonal relationships. Essentially, the answer entails a process of social exploration and testing.

Think about what happens when you approach your instructor after class with a question. You size up the instructor—what she is saying and doing. You interpret her words and actions (assign meaning to them) and then fashion your own behavior accordingly. If the instructor is talking with another student, you might remain silent, waiting for an appropriate opportunity to ask your question. When you do speak, you monitor your own words and actions and your instructor's reactions to your words and actions. If she seems sympathetic, you are likely to continue. But if she seems angry, you would probably try a new tack. Viewed in this fashion, interaction involves a back-and-forth exchange of tentative cues and feedback as individuals go about fashioning their social behavior. In this way, a shared understanding of the meaning of the particular encounter emerges. Such shared understandings are essential to social life.

The interactionist approach provides sociologists with a powerful tool for exploring the subtleties of human behavior. Consider the relationship between a man and a woman. How do the individuals go about negotiating a shared understanding of each other's role? Linguistic cues play a very important part. For instance, studies have shown that men interrupt women far more frequently than women interrupt men, thus subtly establishing masculine dominance over male-female conver-

Her gestures, posture, expression, and words help this woman to interact intensely with her audience. The other members of the group are responding in terms of their individual interpretations. (Cary Wolinsky/ Stock, Boston.)

sation. A woman is much more likely than a man to use attention-getting linguistic devices, such as prefacing opening remarks with a question: "Did you know . . . ?" "Would you like to hear . . . ?" It is almost as if the woman is apologizing for an intrusion, or asking for permission to speak. In such ways, dominant and subordinate roles between the sexes are often established and maintained, even among people who consider themselves "liberated" (Fishman, 1978). We will say much more about such unconscious processes in Chapter 6, in which sex roles are discussed in detail.

An Assessment

Although the interactionist perspective is a fascinating and powerful tool, it also poses some problems. When conducting research, interactionists often find it difficult to identify the most important variables. Which symbols should be studied, and whose subjective perspective matters at a particular time? In addition, although interactionists provide us with an insightful framework for analyzing interpersonal behavior, they tend to underemphasize the stable patterns and power relations of social institutions. This shortcoming is not shared by the other two major perspectives in sociology—functionalism and conflict theory. These theories take as their central aim the understanding of broad social patterns and processes.

The Functionalist Perspective

Auguste Comte, Herbert Spencer, Emile Durkheim, and Talcott Parsons were pioneers in the functionalist tradition. They sought to depict how society is put together and how it works. Comte and Spencer were especially impressed by the similarities between biological organisms and social systems. Indeed, Spencer pushed the analogy so strongly that in his writings society seemed to emerge as a living, breathing being. Contemporary functionalists are very careful not to go to such extremes. Nonetheless, the notion of a system is central to the **functionalist perspective,** which emphasizes how each part of a society or social institution contributes to the whole. A **system** is a complex of interdependent parts, each tending to fulfill various requirements that contribute to the maintenance of the whole.

Functionalists view society as a system. Among its most important parts are *institutions,* those structures that provide established answers to the recurring problems of group life. Consider our educational system from a functionalist perspective. It performs the vital function of transmitting to young people essential knowledge and skills. In addition, it teaches values considered important in our society, such as competitiveness, orderliness, and respect for authority. In doing so, it also serves as a great blender: It integrates children with somewhat different traditions and outlooks into the mainstream culture.

Even so, the American educational system does not operate in isolation. At the very least, schools depend on families to provide the children whom they teach. And schools depend on the political system to provide their funding. In turn, the political system depends on a healthy economy to raise revenue. In short, these four social institutions—the schools, the family, the political system, and the economic order—are all closely interlinked.

Since all the parts of a society are so intricately intermeshed, a change in one part is likely to reverberate throughout the system. Thus functionalists depict society as a system in delicate balance. In their view, too much change, and especially too rapid change, can cause widespread disruptions.

Functionalists also apply their approach to smaller social units than societies. Consider the family and the traditional divison of labor between husbands and wives. Functionalists argue that this division arose because it had beneficial consequences for the family. Each role provided something important to the survival of the family unit: The husband's breadwinner role contributed essential economic support, while the wife's homemaker role contributed to the successful upbringing of children. The two roles, from a functionalist perspective, are highly complementary. Functionalists contend that it is for this reason that the arrangement has endured so long.

Basically, then, functionalists argue that if we are to understand why a particular social pattern arises, why it persists, or why it breaks down, we must look to the *consequences* of that pattern. Those consequences that are intended and widely recognized are called *manifest functions* and those that are unintended and often overlooked are called **latent functions.** If the consequences of a given social pattern are largely positive, if the pattern contributes more to achieving individual and group goals than it does to impeding them, then that pattern will tend to endure. If, on the other hand, the consequences of a particular social pattern are largely negative, if the pattern hinders the goals of major segments of the population or causes distress to large numbers of people, then that pattern will tend to change. Thus functionalists see social systems as refurbishing many of their own obsolete parts—parts that have become primarily **dysfunctional.** Societies, they say, usually tend toward the restoration of stability and balance on an ongoing basis, or process known as *dynamic equilibrium*.

The changing roles of men and women within the family provides an illustration of functional adaptation. As more and more women have entered the job market for personal fulfillment and economic reasons, the traditional division of labor within the home has become increasingly dysfunctional. The typical working American wife and mother still has the major responsibility for household chores (cooking, cleaning, laundry, child care) in addition to holding down a full-time job. This overload contributes to role strain. As women gain financial resources and reduce their economic dependency on men, they acquire the leverage to alter the traditional division of labor and to fashion more equitable arrangements. In some American households this process of change is already well under way.

An Assessment

The functionalist perspective provides a compelling picture of the way that social systems work. But like the interactionist perspective, functionalism has problems and limitations. For one thing, it has difficulty explaining the rather dramatic changes that occur in a seemingly balanced and harmonious system. The perspective lacks a sense for the sudden twists and turns and explosions of history. If a system is essentially in equilibrium, why would change arise? Second, the functional ist emphasis on social structure leads to a deterministic view of individual behavior. Functionalists tend to see people as rather passive beings who are caught up in established social patterns and who do as the rules of society prescribe. (Thus the interactionist perspective, which sees people as actively constructing and shaping their social relationships, is partly a reaction against functionalism.) Third, functionalism can easily be used to justify existing social arrangemtns. It appears to argue that what exists is functional and therefore should be kept, and that new social patterns are inherently disruptive and therefore should be resisted. This criticism somewhat distorts the functionalist position because functionalists do not assume that the present way of doing things is necessarily the best. Some social change, in their view, can be beneficial, bringing a system that is out of balance back into equilibrium. Nevertheless, many critics take issue with the notion that somehow it is "normal" that social forces operate to produce balance and harmony among the parts making up society. This matter is a major issue over which functionalists and conflict theorists battle, as you will see in the following section.

The Conflict Perspective

The functionalist approach provides us with a rather peaceful and idyllic image of the social world. Not so with the **conflict perspective.** Conflict theorists focus on the interests that divide people within society, leading to domination and exploitation within human relationships (Collins, 1975). They see society as a stage where struggles for power and privilege occur and where elites seek to maintain their advantage by oppressing the disadvantaged.

The conflict perspective traces its roots to the ancient Greek philosophers. However, its most famous writing is found in the nineteenth-century works of Karl Marx, whose views about class conflict in industrial society have already been outlined. In the United States the sociologist C. Wright Mills (1956) did much to popularize the conflict approach and apply it to American society. (His ideas will be considered in some detail later in this book.) Over the past two decades, the conflict perspective has experienced a powerful resurgence both among a new generation of Marxists and among many non-Marxists. And it has had a major impact on the work of such influential sociologists as Jürgen Habermas (1968, 1971, 1975, 1978), Alvin W. Gouldner (1970, 1980), and Theda Skocpol (1979).

Although most contemporary conflict theorists continue to emphasize the importance of class conflict within capitalist states, they also see other kinds of conflict as rooted within modern societies. As we look around us, conflict theorists say, we encounter conflict between racial and ethnic groups, between men and women, between younger and older people, between the Sunbelt states and the Frostbelt states, between nations, between religious groups, and between proponents of different political ideologies. Conflict, it seems, is everywhere. It is an ever-present fact of social life. How, then, conflict theorists ask, can we accept the functionalist assumption that societies tend toward stability and equilibrium?

Conflict theorists offer a compelling explanation of why conflict is so prevalant. They argue that the things people want the most—wealth, power, social prestige—are always in short supply. As a result, individuals and groups necessarily compete over them. As each vies with the other to gain more of society's scarce rewards, conflict is inevitable. By *conflict* these sociologists do not necessarily mean violence. Social conflict can take the form of disputes, dominance, ridicule, and contests, as well as demonstrations, warfare, and revolution.

Conflict theorists also maintain that competition for scarce resources very seldom results in a standoff. Some groups almost always manage to secure more wealth, power, and prestige than others, thus dominating the social order. Society, then, consists of institutions, laws, and practices that dominant groups have established to promote and protect their own privileged status. Although the subordinate groups are hardly docile, they often lack the resources necessary for effective resistance. Also, the values of the dominant culture tend to encourage the view that the existing order is "natural" and "right," thus reducing the likelihood of open rebellion. Even so, an undercurrent of suspicion and resentment usually characterizes dominant-subordinant relationships. This uneasy balance continually breeds conditions that are conducive to social change. Actual change may not come about until access to resources or the means to mobilize them shifts. But the *potential* for change—the dissatisfaction and sense of injustice that can promote it—is never very far beneath the surface.

Given the functionalists' and conflict theorists' contrasting views of the social order, it is not surprising that they ask significantly different questions when analyzing a given society or its components. As we have seen, functionalists ask, "*What consequences* does this particular social pattern have for society or for a particular institution?" They expect to find that most social arrangements make at least some contributions to social integration and stability. Conflict theorists, on the other hand, ask "*Who benefits* from this particular pattern or arrangement?" They expect to find that some group is in a privileged and dominant position. In our own society, conflict theorists argue, those who enjoy this privileged status tend to be white, male, upper class, and of Anglo-Saxon Protestant origins.

Consider once again the matter of sex roles in our society. Conflict theorists see traditional sex roles as an integral part of our social system of inequality and hierarchy. Males, they argue, have taken over society's institutions and have fashioned them to promote their own interests. Men hold most of the top positions of power in America, get the best jobs, escape from much menial household work, and schedule sexual intercourse. Males and females, conflict theorists say, have different life chances, different opportunities for personal fulfillment, income earning, and success. Thus the sexes, in the conflict view, are seen as antagonist factions, with males having the power to exploit and subjugate women.

An Assessment

The conflict perspective can be extremely persuasive, but like other viewpoints it has problems and shortcomings. First, there is the problem of defining just what conflict is. Should mere differences of opinion be considered conflict? Does conflict have to be direct, or can it be indirect? Clearly, if conflict is too loosely defined, conflict theorists can point to the slightest incidents of social disagreement as "evidence" for their view, thus trivializing their perspective. In addition, critics say that conflict theory's major strength—its focus on issues of power and conflict—may simultaneously be a major weakness. Such a focus may impair sociologists' ability to see the underlying harmony and consensus in a social relationship, harmony that enables conflict to occur without destroying that relationship.

The Value of Using Various Perspectives

We will be discussing the interactionist, the functionalist, and the conflict perspectives again and again throughout this book. Sometimes we will highlight the differences among them, and you will be encouraged to consider which one makes the strongest case. But such points of controversy should not lead you to conclude that the three theoretical perspectives are necessarily incompatible. As we have tried to show in presenting their various insights into the subject of sex roles, all three approaches have something important to contribute to our overall understanding. Thus it is often helpful to think of theoretical perspectives not as antagonistic but as complementary. Each sheds light on different aspects of the same social world.

In sum, each perspective provides a tool that allows us to visualize and think about the social experience. Each limits our view and presents a narrow perspective. But each also increases the horizon of what we see, functioning like a pair of binoculars.

THE USES OF SOCIOLOGY

Whatever theoretical perspective sociologists may prefer, their task is always the same: to understand and interpret events and patterns that transcend particular individuals. Unlike psychologists, who are primarily concerned with what goes on *within* individuals, sociologists are concerned with what goes on *among* and *between* people. Hence, sociologists focus on *social* patterns. "Know thyself" becomes, for the sociologist, "Know thy social being." This knowledge leads not only to a better understanding of one's own social behavior, but also to a perspective that penetrates many common-sense myths and stereotypes. Dispelling popular myths, in turn, can help to make the world a better place in which to live.

Making Sense of Common Sense

- TRUE OR FALSE? Most people on welfare are free-loaders who could support themselves if they had to.
- TRUE OR FALSE? Once people become poor they remain poor.
- TRUE OR FALSE? Poor black people leave the South for cities like New York and Detroit because the welfare payments are larger there.

Each of these statements is false, yet millions of Americans persist in believing they are true (Rosenbaum, 1977; Schiller, 1980, 1981). For them, these statements make common sense. When people rely on common sense, they take certain widely shared ideas for granted and make use of convenient stereotypes and generalizations to understand the world. Things we read in the newspaper, hear on TV and radio, learn from discussions with family and friends, or simply instinctively feel to be true strengthen our common-sense notions. But these notions are frequently based on incorrect or imprecise information.

Sociologists get closer to the truth by testing common-sense views. Although they cannot force people to change their minds about welfare and the poor, they can present hard evidence showing that many stubbornly held "truths" are in fact myths. For instance, only about 1 percent of the 11 million people who receive basic welfare payments under the program of Aid to Families with Dependent Children (AFDC) are men. Over 70 percent are children and the remainder are their mothers. Contrary to popular belief, nearly all the people receiving welfare benefits are women, children, and elderly people.

Data also disprove the notion that most poor people have always been poor or will always be poor. Although there is a small category of hard-core poor, most of the families living in poverty differ from year to year. Each year about 10 million people move above the poverty line, and another 10 million drop below it. What's more, the majority of people living in poverty at any given time are hard-working individuals who have experienced a bad break—a prolonged job layoff, a serious illness, or the like.

Sociology likewise dispels the common assumption that southern blacks are lured to northern cities by the promise of fatter welfare checks. A study of six northern cities with large black populations found that "Southern blacks who had migrated there were less likely to be on welfare than were blacks who had been born in the cities" (Rosenbaum, 1977:3).

This book is filled with other examples of this type—examples that show how, through systematic study, sociologists have disproved many common-sense beliefs. In other instances, sociologists have shown that while a common-sense notion may contain a measure of truth, it is frequently overstated. For example, there is a widespread belief that prejudice in this country has significantly declined, almost to the point of being no longer a major social problem. Is that belief accurate? Sociological research shows that a decline in prejudice has indeed occurred, but its magnitude is very often exaggerated. Between 1968 and 1978, the percentage of white Americans who thought that most whites dislike blacks dropped from 72 percent to 40 percent. This decline is substantial, yet we should not overlook that remaining 40 percent, a very large segment of the total population. It suggests that the problem of racial prejudice is still very far from being eliminated (Louis Harris and Associates, 1978).

Thus sociology can do much to make our social evaluations more accurate. And it can also help us to understand why we misassess the facts in the first place. Since common-sense notions are themselves social phenomena, sociologists can shed light on who believes them and why.

Sociology and Other Disciplines

Testing common-sense notions is only one of many uses to which sociology has been put. The discipline has also influenced work in other academic fields. (See boxed insert.) For example, under the influence of sociology, historical analysis has become less elitist. Historians used to focus on the lives of great men (and sometimes women) in the belief that individuals make history. It was sociological research that finally prompted them to look at ordinary people, families, work arrangements, and the patterns of daily life in times gone by. Historians now seek to discover what social forces shaped specific eras and how people living at the time coped with these forces. Statistical procedures borrowed from sociology have helped provide answers to these important questions.

In recent years there has even arisen a distinct branch of sociology called historical sociology, which studies social phenomena in their historical context. This field has increased our understanding of such major institutions as the family, industrialization, education, and bureaucracy. Such a focus is not completely new, of course. The founders of sociology—Comte, Spencer, Marx, Weber—were also trying to understand broad historical trends.

Political scientists, too, have incorporated the sociological perspective. They now focus on such sociological issues as how people acquire different political views, how the political attitudes of parents and children are related, and how the process of formal education contributes to political opinions. These are sociological questions that until the last few decades most political scientists overlooked.

Economics, the most prestigious of the social sciences, is still based largely on models of human behavior that are proving to be overly simplistic. A growing awareness of how social values and group pressures affect economic decisions is leading to a new, more sociological kind of economic analysis. This broader focus may help us to better understand the workings of our highly complex economy.

THE SOCIOLOGICAL EYE ON CAREERS:

Job Market Pay Offs from Studying Sociology

Sociology pays off in the job market in two principal ways. First, there are those jobs and careers that are open to individuals as professional sociologists. Second, sociology affords a variety of skills that find useful applications in other careers and occupations. Let us look at each of these aspects in turn.

The careers and occupations that are available to sociologists typically fall within either the academic or applied realms. About three out of four practicing sociologists are employed by high schools, two-year colleges, four-year colleges, or universities with graduate programs. Most academic positions, particularly those in colleges and universities, require a doctorate degree (Ph.D.) in sociology. A good deal of the three to five years of additional training beyond the B.A. degree is spent in activities that resemble intern programs in law, medicine, and business. In addition to their own course work, graduate students usually find financial support working as teaching or research assistants with established members of the sociology faculty. Thus graduate education marks the first stage in the career of a professional sociologist.

The sociology student who wants to teach at the college level is well advised to obtain a doctorate and to specialize in areas that are in demand today: statistics, population, urban studies, criminology, medical sociology, sociology of the family, and sex roles. Salaries in the academic world are not particulary high compared with those in certain other fields requiring equal years of training. But there are many sources of "psychic income" associated with an academic career, such as academic freedom, a flexible work schedule, the opportunity to satisfy one's curiosity, and the rewards of giving students greater knowledge of social relationships (Wilson and Selvin, 1980). Additionally, many undergraduate sociology majors undertake their graduate work in other fields, including business administration, urban planning, and social work, or go on to medical, law, or divinity school. For lawyers, business people, and health care professionals, sociological training provides a powerful tool for analyzing the social institutions and group dynamics they must deal with daily. Sociology is the only discipline that sytematically studies organizations and the groups within them.

Sociologists are also finding expanding job opportunities in applied sociology. Areas in which sociologists are most commonly employed include survey research, program evaluation, human services planning, corporate marketing, government planning research, health services research, and social and demographic analysis. However, positions in these areas often require a graduate degree in sociology. As yet, few employers seek out sociology B.A.'s in the same fashion that they look for B.A.'s in computer science, electrical engineering, accounting, or nursing. For the most part, sociology B.A.'s find job opportunities in areas similar to those available to other liberal arts students who major in history, political science, psychology, English, and related fields.

Nonacademic jobs in sociology tend to be located in nonprofit organizations (such as the Ford Foundation), federal agencies (such as the Department of Health and Human Services), state and local government agencies (such as city planning councils), business and industry (such as Bell Labs and CBS), and religious organizations. Most nonacademic sociologists are involved in research, but they may also do administering, consulting, planning, writing and editing, counseling, and computer programming. In some instances, sociology majors enjoy a competitive advantage. For example, students seeking business careers would be well advised to take courses in industrial sociology and complex organizations. Students interested in careers with public agencies might concentrate their course work in such areas as race relations, social stratification, urban sociology, and family sociology (American Sociological Association, 1977).

The skills students acquire in sociology courses can likewise prove of value in their jobs and careers. Many college graduates say that they find the insights provided them by sociology immensely helpful in allowing them to work more effectively with other people in interpersonal settings. Sociology majors also gain research skills that enable them to collect and analyze data, adding to their investigative capabilities. Moreover, they find in their sociology courses opportunities to sharpen their problem-solving skills and to cultivate their faculties for critical analysis. When they combine these skills with the unique perspective employed by sociologists for looking at the world, sociology majors have a valuable stock of capabilities for dealing with the challenges encountered in work settings.

Source: Careers in Sociology, Washington, D.C.: American Sociological Association, 1977.

Sociology and Public Policy

Since individuals who have sociological training are found in policy-making positions in both the governmental and private spheres, sociology has had an impact on public policy. Further, sociological findings influence the policies pursued by leaders in various sectors of American life. Significantly, from its earliest beginnings, sociology has been viewed as a way of acquiring a solid, scientific base of knowledge with which to develop social policies. The hope of most of sociology's founders was to create a better, more humane society. This hope is as alive today as it was during the tumultuous period of the French Revolution, which concerned sociologist Auguste Comte (Rossi, 1980; Whyte, 1982). In recent years, American sociologists have conducted policy research

Country club or corporate headquarters? Social science research has shown that productivity in the workplace is directly affected by employee morale. As a result many companies are providing their employees with recreational facilities such as those shown here.
(Peter Menzel.)

for many branches of federal and state governments, including the presidential commissions on pornography, population growth, prevention of violence, and law enforcement.

A recent study by the National Academy of Sciences (1982) concludes that social and behavorial scientists can point to "an impressive array of accomplishments" and that "there is every reason to expect the yield from future research to be at least as great." The change in public perceptions of racial and ethnic minorities has been one of the most noteworthy of these achievements. Classic studies, such as Gunnar Mydral's 1944 report, *An American Dilemma*, did much to awaken Americans to the victimization of blacks by discrimination and racism. The study also credits social researchers with developing information-gathering techniques, including the public-opinion survey, that allow political officials to know what the public really wants. And it finds that social science research has helped to increase national productivity by showing how it is affected by human well-being in the workplace and by organizational structures and procedures. By virtue of these and other findings about child development, alcoholism, mental illness, aging, foreign cultures, and behavioral differences between men and women, Americans today have a very different view of human behavior and social life than did their parents a generation ago.

Yet shaping public policy has never been easy, and sociologists have recently been analyzing why. One stumbling block they have identified is that sociologists have overturned a good many myths and not all people wish to see their myths exploded. Some are threatened by new ideas; others have a stake in preserving existing patterns of social inequality or environmental abuse. Indeed, as conflict theorists point out, competing groups may define social problems quite differently, and some may claim there is no problem at all. For instance, whereas many women view sexist practices as a social problem, some men see "feminists" as the problem.

A second obstacle is that research into social policy is always sponsored by some organization, and the sociologists involved often end up reflecting the perspectives of their sponsors (Horowitz and Katz, 1975). For instance, the social scientists who in the 1960s prepared the Pentagon Papers on Vietnam had become for the most part the servants of the federal defense establishment that employed them. As a result, they failed to analyze the war from a broad enough perspective and therefore overlooked its most disastrous mistakes.

Finally, policy research does not occur in a social vacuum. Its ultimate impact depends greatly on the way in which government officials and the general public receive it. For instance, based on interviews with Germans and Japanese after World War II, sociologists had established that saturation bombing increases rather than diminishes civilian morale and resistance (it knits people together in outrage against the "enemy" outgroup). Yet this insight was largely ignored by American military leaders during the Vietnam War (National Academy of Sciences, 1982). Thus, sociological knowledge is often used only when it suits the political goals of those in power (Scott and Shore, 1979). This means that the policy researchers must be political realists as well as scientists. To accomplish their aims, policy researchers must determine the key issues, identify the aspects that are open to change, and then bring sociological insights to bear on those aspects as forcefully as possible. This approach will give their findings the greatest likelihood of acceptance.

In sum, we have noted in this chapter that the sociological imagination poses a major challenge. It is a challenge to describe, interpret, and predict human behavior and to put sociological knowledge to practical use. The tools for meeting this challenge are the subject matter of our next chapter.

SUMMARY

Sociology invites us to set aside our private view of the world in order to see more clearly and objectively the social forces that shape and control our lives. The sociological perspective allows us to take a fresh look at the world about us and better appreciate those aspects of reality that we typically overlook or misinterpret. We come to recognize that we are ultimately social beings whose attitudes and actions are generated, shaped, and maintained through our interaction with others in a group context.

Social facts are properties of social life that cannot be explained by reference to the activities, sensibilities, or characteristics of individuals. Instead, social facts emerge in the process of human interaction. Sociologists have revealed that many of our experiences are facts of social life. Even our most seemingly private moments are not entirely of our own making.

Sociology is a relatively young discipline. It emerged during the nineteenth century, when a great deal of social change and turmoil raised many questions about the workings of society. Auguste Comte launched the discipline with his call for a scientific understanding of social life. Herbert Spencer is best known for his ideas about social evolution (called social Darwinism) and his laissez-faire notion that social institutions should be permitted to take their own course. Karl Marx rejected that idea, proposing that the only way to overcome the oppression of the working class was through planned social action and revolution. Emile Durkheim examined the "collective conscience" that binds a society together. He was one of the first social scientists to use the empirical approach in studying social phenomena. Finally, Max Weber is important for introducing into sociology an awareness of the subjective nature of social life, for balancing Marx's emphasis on economic forces with an equal stress on politics and culture.

Most sociologists use a variety of theoretical approaches today. An increasingly popular orientation is loosely labeled the interactionist perspective. It focuses on how people interact in everyday situations, and how they make sense of their social relationships. In contrast, the functionalist and conflict perspectives focus on the larger patterns and power relationships of social institutions. The conflict perspective emphasizes competing interests and pressures for change within society, while the functionalist perspective stresses the positive functions served by society's interrelated parts. The theoretical perspective a particular sociologist holds influences the nature of his or her research—both the questions asked and the answers proposed.

Although theory is extremely important to sociological inquiry, there is more to sociology than theory alone. The discipline has many practical purposes. For one thing, it helps to dispel many common-sense myths and stereotypes. For another, it broadens the approaches and understandings of scholars in other fields. Studying sociology can also help prepare a student for a number of different careers. Moreover, sociology can have an impact on public policies. Finally, sociology is useful in understanding one's own social circumstances.

GLOSSARY

Capitalists. The members of an industrialized society who own and control the means of production (the land, factories, machinery, and so forth).

Conflict perspective. A theoretical perspective that focuses on interests that divide people within society, leading to domination and exploitation within human relationships.

Dysfunctional. A term referring to the negative or obsolete consequences of particular social patterns that disrupt social systems.

Functionalist perspective. A theoretical perspective that emphasizes how each part of a society or social institution contributes to the whole.

Ideal type. A pure model of a particular social pattern or process that is used as a basis for comparing social arrangements in the real world.

Interactionist perspective. A theoretical perspective that focuses on how people interact in everyday situations and how they make sense of their social relationships.

Latent functions. The unintended and often overlooked consequences of particular social patterns.

Manifest functions. The intended and recognized consequences of particular social patterns.

Proletariat. The members of an industrialized society who have no control over the means of production—primarily the workers.

Social dynamics. The way in which various social patterns arise and the way in which they change.

Social facts. Properties of social life that cannot be explained by reference to the activities, sensibilities, or characteristics of individual persons; instead, they emerge in the course of human interaction.

Social statics. The way in which the various components of society are structured and interrelated, and the functions they serve.

Sociological imagination. A way of looking at our personal experiences in the context of what is going on in the world around us.

Sociology. The systematic study of human societies and of human behavior in social settings.

Symbolic interaction. The communication between individuals that occurs by means of symbols—such as words, gestures, facial expressions, and sounds.

System. A complex of interdependent parts, each tending to fulfill various requirements that contribute to the maintenance of the whole.

Theory. A systematic explanation of how two or more phenomena are related.

Verstehen. Weber's term for an empathic understanding of what people are thinking and feeling.

CHAPTER 2

Methods and Science In Sociology

Most of us are familiar with Sherlock Holmes, Sir Arthur Conan Doyle's famous fictional detective. Holmes solved the most baffling crimes through his remarkable analytical abilities. One of Holmes's most famous cases involved Silver Blaze, a kidnapped racehorse whose trainer had apparently been murdered. A dog that did not bark provided Holmes with the solution:

> *Inspector Gregory:* "Is there any other point to which you would wish to draw my attention?"
> *Holmes:* "To the curious incident of the dog in the night-time."
> *Inspector Gregory:* "The dog did nothing in the night-time."
> *Holmes:* "That was the curious incident." (Doyle, 1967:277)

Inspector Gregory had overlooked the significant fact that dogs do not bark at people they know.

Like Holmes and other detectives, sociologists must carefully gather and analyze information (Sanders, 1974). But whereas detectives aim to solve crimes, sociologists aim to understand the human experience and social life. Nonetheless, detectives and sociologists approach their tasks in somewhat similar ways. Both formulate theories and devise methods for determining what happened, why it happened, and under what circumstances similar events are likely to happen in the future. In sum, detectives and sociologists seek to establish the facts, explain them, and predict the likelihood of future events.

We too are interested in similar matters. Only by determining what happens and why it happens are we able to predict what is likely to occur—what reasonable expectations we can have for the future. For instance, will attending college and securing a diploma increase our changes for "getting ahead" in life? Will scheduling baseball games between our group and similar groups tend to increase the loyalty and cohesion of our group members? Determining what happens and why it happens allows us to intervene in social processes when doing so will bring about more positive outcomes. In this sense, *knowledge is power.*

In this chapter we consider the scientific method—a marvelous set of rules and procedures painstakingly worked out over the past 250 years to produce valid and reliable knowledge about the world in which we live. We discuss the role of theory in the sociological enterprise and show how the theory one formulates affects what one studies and therefore the methods one uses. We describe the methods that sociologists use to develop knowledge about social behavior. The chapter concludes with a discussion of how values and ethics affect sociological research.

THE SCIENTIFIC METHOD

The **scientific method** is a way of investigating the world that relies on the careful collection of facts and logical explanations of them. Most people think of the scientific enterprise as a very cut-and-dried process—the scientist observes a phenomenon, draws logical inferences from it, and builds a general theory on the conclusions. But, in fact, science often involves inspiration and creative insight. Scientists make use of intuitions, hunches, and leaps of inference as well as carefully measured observations. In the field of sociology, in particular, "one needs ingenuity and imagination to apply the wiles of science to the mysteries of the social arrangement that people contrive" (Wilson and Selvin, 1980:18).

However, to be scientific, hunches, insights, and all other evidence must be subjected to scrutiny and repeated testing by others in order to eliminate individual errors of judgment and to ensure valid results. The goal of any addition to scientific knowledge is for it to be as widely accepted as possible. One noted scientist has maintained that this consensus over the widest possible field "is not a subsidiary consequence of the 'Scientific Method'; it *is* the scientific method itself" (Ziman, 1968:9).

There are ways of knowing the world other than through science. For example, we can know it through law, history, and religion. How does the scientific method differ from the approaches used in these other disciplines? Law is similar to the scientific method in that it uses evidence and logic, but law requires that a dispute be settled in spite of conflicting or incomplete evidence. Under such conditions, those using the scientific method would hold off making a decision.

History, like the scientific method, marshals facts and attempts to explain them. But most of the "facts" of history deal with past events that are open to a number of interpretations. Historians use scientific rules of evidence to verify their interpretations, but they cannot really test them because they are dealing with past events and some degree of speculation.

Religion and science both seek an explanation for things, but the one is based on faith and abstract theological principles and the other on concrete evidence and testable conclusions.

To sum up, then, the scientific method is concerned with digging for information about some observable phenomenon and interpreting the data in such a way that the findings can be tested by others and achieve widespread acceptance.

Steps in the Scientific Method

Emile Durkheim was one of the first sociologists to apply the scientific method to the study of human behavior. Indeed, the publication of his book *Suicide* in 1897 marked the beginning of a revolution in our thinking about social life. In Durkheim's time suicide was thought to be an individual act caused by mental illness, inherited suicidal tendencies, or the effect of climate on a person's reasoning. But if these *were* the causes, then why did suicide rates vary from period to period? And if suicide is caused by forces within individuals, why should the suicide rate be higher in one country than in another? These matters intrigued Durkheim and he undertook an investigation of them.

As we noted in Chapter 1, Durkheim formulated a functional theory that the cement of society is a moral order, or collective conscience, that arises from shared experiences and beliefs. Consequently, he wished to determine whether the social bonds fostered by a moral community influence such seemingly individual acts as suicide. Durkheim thought that people with a web of close, personal social relationships might be less likely to commit suicide than those who are isolated, lonely, or without social ties.

In pursuing his study of suicide, Durkheim shaped sociology as an *empirical* science—with the capacity for analyzing data in an objective fashion. We can simplify this research to show how it followed seven basic steps: defining the problem, reviewing the literature, forming a hypothesis, choosing a research design, collecting the data, analyzing the data, and drawing conclusions (see Figure 2.1).

Defining the Problem

Defining a problem in a precise way—especially key terms and concepts—is often more difficult than one might think. For example, what is suicide? If individuals die because they miscalculate danger or fail to take a necessary precaution, have they committed suicide? Examining the different implications of this word, Durkheim (1897/1951:44) concluded that the term *suicide* refers to "all cases of death resulting directly or indirectly from a positive or negative act of the victim

FIGURE 2.1 Steps in the Scientific Method

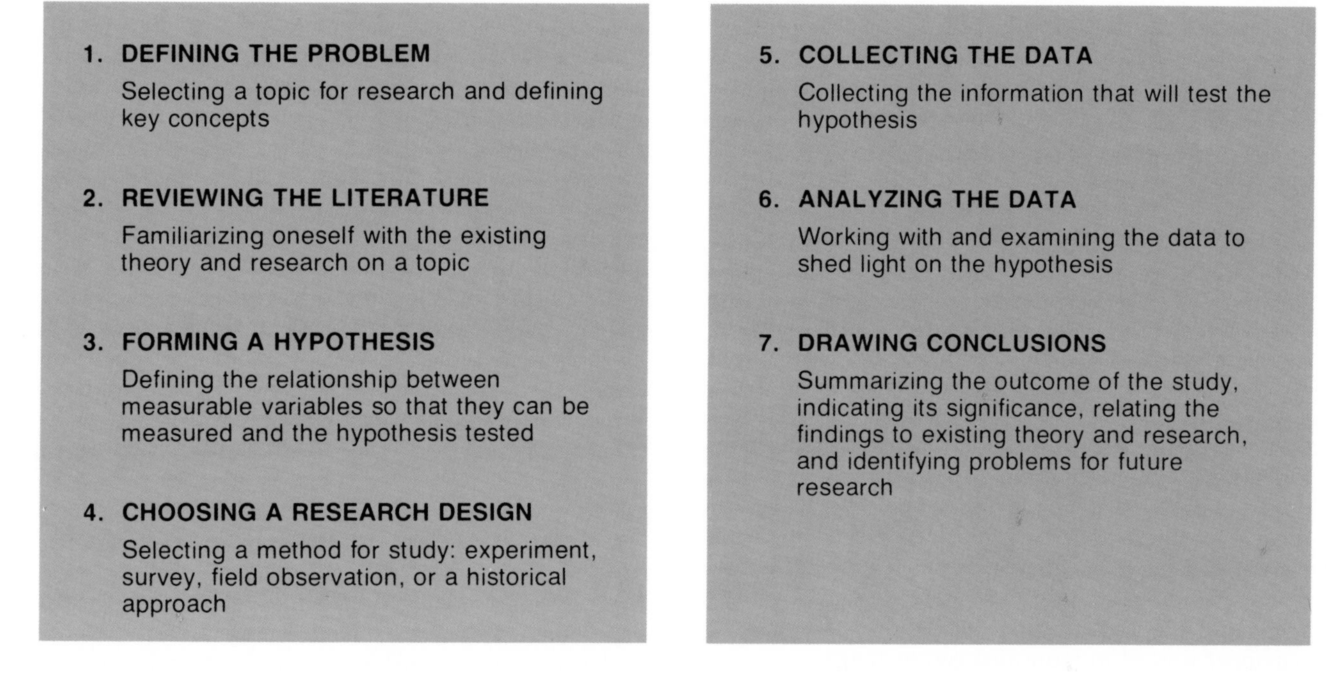

himself, which he knows will produce this result."[1] Further, Durkheim decided to use governmental records listing the cause of a person's death as his source of data.

His next problem was to define in concrete terms the factors he wished to study. When scientists study such abstract concepts as prejudice or economic stability, for example, they must define each idea or aspect in measurable terms. This procedure gives them an **operational definition.** For example, the scientist studying prejudice might define it, for purposes of a specific study, in terms of the percentage of people holding negative attitudes toward blacks or Hispanics; the scientist studying economic stability might define it in terms of fluctuations of the stock market. Durkheim developed several operational definitions of social integration, such as being married (and hence enjoying family ties) and being Catholic (and hence having religious ties).

[1]By "positive act" Durkheim meant such things as shooting oneself or jumping off a bridge. By "negative act" he meant such things as failing to take necessary medicine or not getting out of the path of a moving vehicle.

Reviewing the Literature

Durkheim's next step was to check the writings of knowledgeable authorities on suicide for ideas and research that could provide him with suggestive insights. (Nowadays the task is facilitated by computers. Titles and summaries of research articles are retrievable on computer screens in many modern research and university libraries. Moreover, they are cross-indexed by hundreds of subject categories.) Durkheim also undertook a preliminary review of official records. This survey revealed that suicide rates were highest in countries that had the lowest rates of mental illness, suggesting that insanity alone did not explain suicide. And he could find no consistent differences among "racial" groups in the incidence of suicide. This observation suggested to

Durkheim that hereditary explanations of suicide are inadequate. Nor could he find support for climatic theories of suicide. All that remained was the fact that suicide rates varied from one social group to another.

Forming a Hypothesis

Using this fact as a base, Durkheim (1897/1951:145) concluded:

> We have shown in fact that for each social group there is a specific tendency to suicide explained neither by the organic-psychic construction of the individuals nor the nature of the physical environment. Consequently, by elimination, it must necessarily depend upon social causes and be itself a collective phenomenon.

At this point Durkheim had formulated a proposition: Suicide has some relationship to social causes. A philosopher might stop here, having shown by the logical process of elimination that suicide is related to social causes. But logical deduction is not enough; scientists demand empirical proof. The first step toward obtaining such proof is to translate the problem into a hypothesis, a statement worded in terms that can be tested.

A **hypothesis** is a statement that predicts how two or more variables will affect, or are related to, one another. Durkheim developed several hypotheses, but his major hypothesis was that suicide varies inversely with the degree to which a person is integrated within the social life of society. In Durkheim's hypothesis the two variables are (1) the degree to which a person is integrated within the social group and (2) the suicide rate.

According to his hypothesis, married people would have a lower suicide rate than divorced or widowed people because they were more integrated a social group. In like manner Durkheim hypothesized that suicide rates would be lower for Catholics with their strong church ties than for Protestants, and lowest for Jews because of their tight-knit religious community. He hypothesized that soldiers in their regimented society would be less likely to commit suicide than civilians. And he argued that the suicide rates would be higher in times of economic instability than in times of stability.

Choosing a Research Design and Collecting the Data

Once his hypothesis was formulated and his terms defined, Durkheim had to decide how to collect data that would test the hypothesis. This process involved selecting the group or groups to be studied, evaluating various sources of information, and deciding how to measure the variables. Depending on the problem being investigated, a researcher might design an experiment, conduct interviews, spend time observing the way people interact in certain settings, examine records, or combine these methods. Durkheim chose to analyze official records on suicide from a number of European nations. This method, called **secondary analysis,** involves analyzing data that was collected for another purpose. Sociologists often analyze census and other governmental data as well as historical materials. Nowadays gathering data from many governmental and public sources is expedited by computers. Moreover, because many large studies on a topic such as suicide are available on computer tape, the data collected can readily be used in new ways by other researchers.

Analyzing the Data

In analyzing the data, Durkheim looked for the social conditions under which suicide occurred most and those under which it occurred least often. He found that more Protestants than Catholics and more Catholics than Jews committed suicide. Single people committed suicide more often than married people, and married people with children least of all. Durkheim also discovered that suicide rates rose during periods of sharp economic reversals (inflations or depressions) but fell during periods of political instability. Had he undertaken his research today, Durkheim would have found computers to be of immeasurable assistance in analyzing his data and using the many sophisticated statistical procedures now available. The boxed insert discusses some simple but important techniques.

Drawing Conclusions

Durkheim's analysis confirmed his hypothesis that suicide rates rise when people's attachments to significant groups are weakened and fall when they are strengthened. The stronger the ties people have to social groups, the more they depend on these groups and the more likely they are to take other people into account when making decisions. People who have few ties to their community are more likely to take their own lives than people who are deeply involved with their community.

Classifying Data: Mode, Mean, and Median

Frequently, researchers summarize data on a given population by calculating central tendencies. There are three ways to do this.

The **mode** is the figure that occurs most often in the data. For example, a researcher studies seven families and finds that their yearly incomes are

$3,000	$11,000
$3,000	$15,000
$7,500	$90,000
$9,000	

The modal income in this group of families is $3,000 a year. The mode does not give any indication of the range in data, and it is useful only when a researcher wants to show which statistic appears most often.

The **mean** is what is commonly referred to as the average. To calculate the mean you simply divide the sum of all the figures by the number of items. The mean or average income for the families above is $19,786 ($138,500 ÷ 7). Researchers frequently calculate the mean because it reflects all the available data. However, as the example here illustrates, the mean can be misleading: the fact that one of the families in this group has an income of $90,000 a year obscures the fact that six of the seven families have incomes of less than $19,786 a year. The mean is most useful when the range of figures does not include extremes.

The **median** is the number that falls in the middle of a series of figures—in this example, $9,000 a year. The median is useful because it does not allow extremes (here, $3,000 and $90,000) to hide the central tendency. Frequently, researchers calculate both the mean and the median in order to present an accurate impression of their findings.

This analysis and explanation led Durkheim to introduce a new concept to sociology: *anomie.* **Anomie** refers to a condition within society in which people's integration within the social fabric is weakened and their commitment to societal norms lessened. Durkheim viewed anomie as a major source of society's ills. We will return to the matter of anomie in Chapter 9 when we consider deviance.

Durkheim's study of suicide provided a model of empirical analysis. It is a method that allows us to test the truth of statements regarding various events and happenings. As such, Durkheim provided us with a strategy of explanation and laid the foundations for the science of sociology.

The Science of Sociology

The scientific method is concerned with digging for information about some observable phenomenon such as suicide and interpreting the data in such a way that the findings can be tested by others and achieve widespread acceptance. However, sociology presents the would-be scientist with some formidable research problems, simply because it is necessary to deal with people.

Durkheim's study of suicide highlights some of the problems that sociologists confront when studying social behavior. Like any other scientific study, Durkheim's research must be assessed in terms of its validity and reliability. **Validity** is the degree to which a scientific study measures what it is attempting to measure—for example, the degree to which the suicide rates of different social groups measure their different levels of anomie. **Reliability** is the degree to which a study yields the same results when repeated by the original researcher or by other scientists.

Subsequent studies of suicide rates have shown Durkheim's results to be reliable, but critics have questioned whether Durkheim's data were valid. Might the data have been distorted? Perhaps Catholics appear to have fewer suicides than Protestants because they disguise and cover up their suicides better. A good case could be made for the theory that the better integrated a person is within society, the less likely it is that his or her death will be *classified* as a suicide. For example, officials in a close-knit community might respect a family's wish to avoid embarrassment and record the suicide as a death resulting from natural causes. Or the officials might not suspect suicide because the individual was deemed a leading citizen of the community (Douglas, 1967). Such concerns undermine Durkheim's argument.

Another problem that confronts sociologists is that people, unlike many objects of study in the natural sciences, are not reducible to simple cause-and-effect actions. A meteorologist knows that when air pressure and air temperature mix in a particular way, it will rain. But the social scientist who attempts to predict the effect of a factory's closing on a nearby community's suicide rate has to sort out the many conflicting emotions and motivations of the people who live and work there.

Further, social variables may not remain constant over time or from place to place. The law of gravity and the composition of water are the same everywhere, the same today as they were yesterday. But no two families, for example, are exactly alike, and ideas about what the family should be vary enormously from one culture to another. In the words of Swedish social scientist Gunnar Myrdal:

> The really important difference between [social scientists] and our natural science colleagues is that we never reach down to constants—like the speed of light or sound in a particular medium, or the specific weights of atoms or molecules. We have nothing that corresponds to the universally valid measurements of energy, voltage, ampere, etc. The regularities we find do not have the firm general validity of "laws of nature." (1973)

As we will see later in the chapter, there are limits to how far a scientist can experiment with human beings as subjects. People must be treated with dignity and respect. For example, a sociologist cannot deliberately stage a factory's closing or a failure at a nuclear power plant to determine the effect on the community.

Finally, objectivity is a major problem for all social scientists. It is difficult to study race relations or a nuclear arms race without some emotional involvement. The astronomer who studies the stars and the botanist who experiments with plants are likely to be more objective in their respective fields.

All this suggests that facts do not "speak for themselves." Facts must always be interpreted. Theories allow us to do so. As we noted in Chapter 1, *theories* are statements that describe the relationships between variables. Hence, without a theory, we lack a framework for understanding facts. By the same token, without facts our theories are simply unproven speculations. In sum, the scientific method allows us to arrive at facts that confirm or disconfirm our theories. Our theories permit us to identify relationships among facts so as to give them meaning. Let us turn, therefore, to a consideration of the interplay between method and theory.

The Interplay of Method and Theory in Sociology

Methods in science are not just tools lying around on the workbench, any one of which may be picked up by the researcher. The methods that researchers use to investigate a problem are appropriate to the theories that guide them. In science, a theory is an explanation of something. For instance, based upon his research dealing with suicide, Durkheim developed a theory that may be summarized as follows: Society is not simply a collection of people; it has an existence of its own and influences how people think and act. In other words, a person is a product of the groups to which he or she belongs.

Durkheim took a functionalist approach to suicide (see Chapter 1). To see how methods and theory work together, let us consider an alternative perspective regarding suicide—that associated with symbolic interactionism. Interactionists fault Durkhein for "imposing" his interpretation on the data he analyzed. They say that Durkheim assumed that no matter which groups were being compared, the meaning of suicide was obvious: It reflected a lack of integration into society and it violated norms. Influenced by this theory, his methods did not allow for exploring the possibility that suicide has different meanings for different people. A symbolic interactionist, by contrast, would look closely at how each death occurred and what it meant to those involved. This perspective would complement but not replace Durkheim's approach to the subject.

Interactionists begin with the suicides themselves. These sociologists regard suicides not merely as acts of self-destruction but as socially meaningful actions. The question of why people commit suicide must be answered by a study of what suicide means to the victims and to those immediately involved. Take the example of a man who was known to feel trapped by his suburban and business life. While on vacation in the Bahamas he swims out too far and drowns, even though he was considered a strong swimmer. Did he intentionally swim out too far? Was this a suicide or an accident? A look at his private life might enable us to answer these questions in terms of the man's own perceptions and definitions.

The meaning of a suicide is also a major concern of those authorities who must decide if a suicide has taken place. J. Maxwell Atkinson (1978) examined the ways coroners go about deciding which deaths are suicides.

Finding the social meaning behind a suicide threat is often the key to suicide prevention. These workers at a crisis center talk problems out with troubled individuals. (Paul Fortin/Stock, Boston.)

He found that they typically had no clear, legal definition of suicide in mind. The coroners he interviewed claimed that they "knew" a suicide when they saw one but could not define it or explain how they determined it. However, they interpreted certain signs as indications that a suicide had occurred. Suicide notes and hanging were taken as sure signs and gassing as a fairly certain sign. If the death took place in an improbable, remote place or in an unlikely situation (such as drowning in ten inches of water), coroners are likely to define it as a suicide.

Interactionists examine the meanings embedded in the situation *(situated meanings)* and hence are less concerned than functionalists with generalized data. Instead of imposing a meaning on statistical data, interactionists analyze real-world events to *draw out* their meanings. Only then can they discern patterns and work up to abstract conceptions and theory.

It is clear that this theoretical perspective calls for a methodology different from the one Durkheim chose. Interactionists consider official statistics on suicide by themselves too removed from the event and too filtered of content to be of use in determining why people commit suicide. Instead, interactionists would get down to the details of cases, gradually building up comparative information across social situations. They would analyze such documents as suicide notes and coroners reports, interview people close to the suicide victim, and observe the social context in which the person lived. Interactionists would also assess the impact of a suicide on others. A person who commits suicide often uses the act as a way of communicating a message to someone else in a forceful, dramatic fashion.

Both the interactionist and the functionalist are right, but on different levels: Suicide occurs when people's social bonds weaken, *and* suicide is an event having symbolic meaning.

In sum, one's theoretical perspective influences but does not determine how one goes about doing research. As a functionalist seeking to explain differences in group rates of suicide, Durkheim analyzed large-scale data. As an interactionist examining how people construct a social reality around unnatural deaths, another investigator might instead carry out detailed interviews of the survivors to see how some get called "suicides" and others "accidents." This does not mean that functionalists use only surveys or statistical studies and that interactionists use only interviews, but it does mean that sociological theory affects what questions are asked, and those questions in turn dictate what methods will be most effective in obtaining answers to them. In the section that follows we will look more closely at the various methods available to researchers.

RESEARCH METHODS

Science has evolved as a means of determining what happens and why it happens. Scientists undertake to explain events by establishing cause-and-effect relationships. No matter what the event—an earthquake, the death of an organism, the flow of a river, a race riot, or a crime wave—some order, constancy, or regularity is believed to underlie it. Consequently, under the same set of circumstances, a given action will consistently produce the same effect. Scientists have at their disposal a number of methods for investigating the patterns associated with cause-and-effect relationships.

The Experiment

The **experiment** offers scientists the most effective technique for establishing a cause-and-effect relationship. It allows researchers to test a hypothesis that one variable (X) causally influences another variable *(Y)*. The term **variable** is applied to any factor that is capable of change. In sociology, variables usually consist of some attitude, behavior pattern, or condition that can change. For instance, social scientists may wish to test the hypothesis that people who undergo a severe initiation to gain admission to a group (variable X) develop a strong attachment to the group (variable Y) (Aronson and Mills, 1959; Aronson and Carlsmith, 1968). The logic underlying the experiment is this: If you change one variable *(X)* and another variable *(Y)* also changes, then, if all other factors have been held constant (controlled) the change in Y must have been caused by the change in X.

In order to test a hypothesis, researchers (1) systematically manipulate one variable *(X)* and (2) observe the effect of the manipulation on the other variable *(Y)*. The factor systematically varied is termed the **independent variable;** it is assumed to be the causal factor in the relationship being studied. In our illustration, the initiation condition would be the independent variable. The factor being studied is termed the **dependent variable;** it is the factor that is affected by the manipulation of the independent variable. In this case, the intensity of the subjects' attachment to the group was the dependent variable.

In their experiments, researchers typically assign subjects to matched groups on a random basis. In the illustration discussed above, the experimenters randomly assigned the college-student subjects to three conditions: no initiation, mild initiation, and severe initiation. The no initiation group was the **control group.** Its members were exposed to everything *except* the independent variable (the initiation ritual). The mild and severe initiation groups were the **experimental groups.** The members of these groups actually underwent the experimental conditions and hence they were subjected to the independent variable. The experimenters then compared the responses of the two experimental groups with those of the control group to see if the independent variable made a difference. Thus the control group provided a neutral standard against which the changes in the experimental groups could be measured.

The experimenters devised a rating system to assess the subjects' attachment to their respective groups. The average rating for subjects in the control group was 167; for those who underwent a mild initiation, 171; and for those who underwent severe initiation, 195. The researchers interpreted their results as confirming their hypothesis.

The experimental method enjoys the advantage of permitting researchers to isolate for study one or two variables while holding other variables constant. Further, they can repeat the experiment several times to test their findings. But there is always the danger that experiments employing humans as subjects in a contrived laboratory setting may produce artificial results. A laboratory is one step removed from real life and the setting itself often influences the way people behave. However, experiments carried out in real-life settings do not entirely eliminate this problem, a fact highlighted by a classic **field experiment** conducted by Elton Mayo at Western Electric's Hawthorne plant in Chicago (Roethlisberger and Dickson, 1939).

Mayo wanted to learn how variations in factory conditions affect worker output. Management believed that employees work harder when they are paid in proportion to what they produce. Management also thought that coffee breaks improve morale. But Mayo and his colleagues found that *any* change they made seemed to increase output. Whether management increased or *decreased* the number of breaks, the lighting, or the wage incentives, the workers increased their productivity. Mayo concluded that it was not the changes themselves that made the employees work harder; rather, it was the attention the employees received that made the difference. The bias that researchers unwittingly introduce in an experimental setting, such as giving people extra attention, is known as the **Hawthorne effect.** Sociologists try to design their research to minimize the intrusion of such factors.

Sociologists do not use experimental methods often because they are too narrowing in a complex social world. But the clear logic of experimental design underlies many surveys and field studies. These two methods expand the possibilities for doing creative and imaginative research.

The Survey

A **survey** is a procedure for gathering information from a large number of people. Typically, a researcher interviews people by reading them questions from a prepared questionnaire or mails them a questionnaire and asks them to fill it out and return it. Sociologists use surveys to predict how people will behave (for example, election polls), to test assumptions about behavior, and to measure public opinion. A scientifically conducted survey is a complex undertaking; it involves choosing a sample, constructing and asking the right questions, and analyzing the data.

Choosing a Sample

Although researchers are often interested in learning about large numbers of people, it is not usually practical to study each and every one. For this reason, they choose a sample. A **sample** is a limited number of people selected from the population being studied. If the sample represents the population, the researchers should be able to make reasonably accurate statements about the population as a whole.

There are several kinds of samples, and the one chosen depends on what the researchers are studying. One powerful form is the **random sample.** A researcher in effect puts the names of all people in a barrel and picks as many names as needed, leaving the selection to chance. The more sophisticated and more usual procedure is to assign each person in the population a number and to pick a sample from a table of random numbers. With a random sample each person in the population has an equal chance of being selected. In this manner, researcher bias is minimized. The power of a random sample derives from its ability to represent a population much larger than itself. If you arbitrarily interview the first hundred classmates you meet leaving a campus building about their career plans, you cannot generalize the results to the entire student body, because you do not know how representative they are of the student body. But if you select one hundred people randomly from a student directory, you can generalize your findings to the entire student body.

Most people think a large sample provides more accurate results than a smaller one. This view is not necessarily true. Perhaps the most famous example disproving this notion was the attempt to predict the winner of the 1936 presidential election. A popular magazine, *Literary Digest*, sent post-card ballots to 10 million people chosen from telephone directories and auto registration lists. On the basis of 2 million returns, the *Digest* predicted that Alfred Landon would beat Franklin D. Roosevelt by a landslide. Meanwhile, a young man named George Gallup sampled 312,551 people and correctly predicted that FDR would win.

The editors of the *Literary Digest* were stunned by the election results. How could such a giant survey have gone so wrong? The key to a survey's accuracy is not the *number* of people polled but how *representative* they are of the overall population. Since 10 million people with phones and cars during the Depression did not include a sample of the working class, the survey missed the largest group of Democrats who voted for Roosevelt. Nor was Gallup's success a matter of luck—he had used a random sample that accurately represented the proportion of Republicans and Democrats in the *entire* population of voters. Today, Gallup, Harris, and other pollsters can use a sample of only 1,500 to represent a population of 230 million with a high degree of accuracy.

Constructing and Asking Questions

In order to collect valid information, researchers need to ask good questions. Devising such questions entails careful and precise work. Take, for example, the ques-

Interviewing is a complex process, even when you have a carefully designed questionnaire. What kinds of misunderstandings can arise? (Bohdan Hrynewych/Stock, Boston.)

tion, "Do you think that the government should be more efficient and effective?"

This seemingly straightforward question in fact presents many problems. First, it is difficult to grasp. The question does not provide a standard or reference point for determining what is meant by "efficient and effective." A good question identifies its subject matter with precision, is clearly worded, and elicits meaningful answers. Second, a question must not contain multiple elements; it should address only one idea. The effectiveness of government is not the same as its efficiency (government is effective if it produces the intended result; it is efficient if it accomplishes a job with a minimum expenditure of time and resources). Third, a question should be short so that a person can readily grasp its intent. Finally, the question should be neutral and unbiased. If the question encourages a person to answer one way rather than another, it is biased. For instance, linking an authority figure with a question biases it—"Do you agree with the president that . . ."

A neutral, clear restatement of the original question might be "How efficient do you think the federal government is in collecting income taxes?" "And how effective do you think internal revenue agents are in enforcing the income tax laws?" Having phrased a question, the researcher must next identify the kinds of answers people are likely to give and pretest the question to see whether it elicits accurate information. Only when a researcher has worked out all the problems is a question ready to be used.

Interviewing

Interviewing people is a vital social research skill. The researcher may interview subjects face-to-face or by telephone. Good listeners make the best interviewers. They discern what a person is really saying and are sensitive to a person's feelings. As they conduct an interview, they pay attention not only to what the person says but to how the person says it. Is he upset? Why is she talking in circles? Why am I getting bored? Good interviewers recognize their emotions and use their personal reactions as signals to revise their approach.

In many ways the skills involved in conducting good interviews parallel the skills needed in formulating good questions. The success of an interview depends on the subject's understanding the intent of questions and answering them in a way that researchers can interpret. Moreover, the interviewer must appear neutral and unbiased in phrasing questions and in probing for fuller answers to questions.

A strict adherence to the wording of questions is critical to the **structured interview,** a procedure in which carefully phrased standard questions—often with multiple-choice answers—are asked in a fixed order. Such structuring provides systematic and comparable data and hence facilitates their later analysis. For example, a researcher might phrase the following question: "Do you think homosexuals should be permitted to teach in public schools?" with four possible answers: Yes/No/Uncertain/No opinion. The interviewer asks each person the identical question, and each answer is coded as one of the four alternatives.

In some cases researchers do not seek answers to specific questions. Rather, they wish to explore a broad or subtle aspect of social life, such as how people cope with retirement or how college affects students' relations with their parents. Under these circumstances, they would most likely use an **unstructured interview,** a procedure in which neither the questions nor the answers are predetermined. The unstructured interview allows the interviewer to explore a subject in terms of what the person finds important and meaningful. The major disadvantage of this procedure is that the answers from several unstructured interviews may not be comparable, making the data difficult to analyze.

One solution to the problems of both structured and unstructured interviews is the **semistructured interview.** Here the interviewer works out in advance what areas or specific issues will be covered (structured), but lets the subjects talk about them in the terms most meaningful to them (unstructured). Which technique researchers use in any particular investigation depends, of course, on the kinds of information they are seeking.

An Example: Three Mile Island

Good sampling procedures, good questionnaires, and good interviewing techniques provide the ingredients that make the survey a valuable research tool. We can see how these factors contribute to a successful result by considering an illustration—the information generated by the survey method when it was used by a task force of researchers appointed by a presidential commission to study behavioral effects of the nuclear accident at Three Mile Island (Dohrenwend et al., 1979a; Houts and Goldhaber, 1981). For six days in the spring of 1979 hundreds of thousands of Pennsylvania residents had lived in suspense as their lives literally hung in the balance. Said Louise Hardison, who lived near Three Mile Island, "I just get the feeling we are sitting on a time bomb." Residents had feared that the hot molten core of the reactor would melt down and that a huge bubble of hydrogen gas at the top of the nuclear reactor would escape into the atmosphere. Had this happened, radioactive particles could have contaminated the air, soil, and water and endangered area residents.

Fortunately, engineers were able to shut down the reactor and vent the bubble safely. But what impact did this near-disaster have on the people who lived near Three Mile Island? Would there be long-term behavioral or physiological effects? How would the fabric of social life be affected? These questions echo decades of research in which sociologists have asked what happens

Three Mile Island residents may not know for decades how the nuclear accident there affected their physical health. Social scientists are concerned now with how the near disaster has affected the social health of the community. (Sean Pringle/Photo Researchers.)

when a tornado, a raging river, or an earthquake tears into a community and disrupts people's lives. Within days of the Three Mile Island accident, sociologists had formed teams to study its effect on the people.

The sociologists surveyed four different groups: the general population of male and female heads of households living within twenty miles of Three Mile Island, mothers of preschool children in that area, teenagers in that area, and workers at the Three Mile Island plant. Slightly different procedures were followed for each of these groups, so for the sake of simplicity we will focus on only one of these—the mothers of preschool children. The sample used in the study was randomly drawn from lists of birth announcements in the local papers from 1977 through June 1979.

The researchers set out to assess how the mental health of the mothers had been affected over time as measured by psychological distress, symptoms of stress, and a sense of demoralization. But how were the researchers to know whether the results they obtained from the survey had been caused by the accident or had existed prior to it? To answer this question they decided to survey a similar population of mothers in Wilkes-Barre, a town about ninety miles away, and to employ this sample as a control group. Any significant differences between the two groups could then be attributed to the impact of the Three Mile Island accident.

Another problem confronted the researchers: The task force was not formed until June 1979. The accident occurred in late March. How could the researchers assess the immediate, short-term effects, those that occurred within the first few weeks of the accident? Fortunately, the task force had access to survey data gathered shortly after the accident by researchers from colleges and universities near the site: "Most of these studies employed reliable measures of psychological effects with small but carefully drawn samples of . . . high risk groups such as mothers of preschool children" (Dohrenwend et al., 1979a:1–2). The researchers reanalyzed the previously collected data (a procedure termed secondary analysis).

The sample of mothers selected by the task force was surveyed in July, when the Wilkes-Barre control group was also surveyed. The survey was conducted via half-hour structured telephone interviews with those in the sample. The questions focused on how the mother had felt at the time of the accident, whether she had stayed in the area or left during the time of danger, how demoralized she had been since the accident, whether she thought her family's health was threatened, her attitudes toward living in the area and toward nuclear power, and her trust in authorities. Some questions were direct: "How upsetting was the Three Mile Island incident?" The respondents rated their upset on a scale of 1 to 10, which made the answers easy to score and compare. Other questions had to be more complex. For example, demoralization was scored on the basis of answers to twenty-six questions such as "Since TMI, how often have you felt completely hopeless?" and "Since TMI, how often have you felt confused and had trouble thinking?" All the questions were clear and short, and their answers were easily interpreted. However, note the bias in the use of "how often" rather than a more neutral phrasing such as "have you ever."

In analyzing the data, the researchers were particularly interested in two variables: the effects of living within five miles of the plant site (authorities had advised mothers and preschool children living at this distance from the plant to evacuate the area) versus living more than five miles away, and short-term versus long-term effects. The researchers found that mothers living nearby were more demoralized and more distrustful of authorities than were mothers living in Wilkes-Barre. As for long-term versus short-term effects, the researchers found that demoralization rose sharply after the accident and then subsided after a few weeks. In July the Three Mile Island area mothers were no more demoralized than were the Wilkes-Barre control group. On the other hand, distrust of authorities rose sharply and subsided more gradually in the months that followed (Houts and Goldhaber, 1981). It is also worth noting, as shown in Table 2.1, that people's responses to the disaster varied by age. Thus the older the people were, the more likely they were to pray for guidance and the less likely they were to seek support from friends or relatives. Even so, a good many people, even the youngest, turned to prayer. (The boxed insert will assist you in learning how to read a table if you do not already know how to do so.)

As the Three Mile Island research illustrates, the survey method has both strengths and weaknesses. It is useful for describing the characteristics of a large population and for sampling large segments of the population. It permits a wide range of questions to be asked, which gives researchers some flexibility in analyzing data. The use of standardized questionnaires makes measurement easy.

On the other hand, questions must be phrased so

How to Read a Table

The following steps for interpreting Table 2.1 are general guides that can be applied to any chart or table.

1. Read the title to find out what kind of information is in the table and how it is presented. In this table the data are presented in terms of percentage of the total responses, but this is not true of all tables. Some tables present their data in actual numbers of people responding in various ways.
2. Look for headnotes and footnotes that may explain how the data were collected, why certain variables were studied, and whether data were collected differently for some of the categories. Some tables have a footnote explaining how the data were collected; this provides one way of assessing the quality of the data. This table has no such explanation, and moreover, it does not tell how large the complete sample was. The source of the data, usually given at the bottom of a chart or table, is another measure of quality. For example, the organization that did this survey (a research team from a medical school) probably has good training in research methods. Had the source been a team from a manufacturer of nuclear reactors, you might suspect bias.
3. Read the labels for each column and row to learn exactly what data appear in the table. Here, the column labels indicate that the researchers broke the totals down by age and type of response. These are only two of many responses. Note that the intensity of the response is not measured. Both calling a friend for a brief talk on the telephone and staying up all night sharing fears about a meltdown get measured in the same way.
4. Look at the patterns in the data. Here, praying increases with age while, except for those over sixty, seeking out friends and relatives decreases with age. Another pattern is the range for each type of response: it never falls below 37 percent and never rises above 75 percent.
5. Draw conclusions about the information in the table and consider what other questions it raises. Besides the question of how much people varied in the intensity with which they prayed or sought out friends, an important question is whether the difference exhibited by the different age groups are the result of differences of generation or differences that universally come with growing older. For example, did the younger people pray less because until recently each decade of this century has witnessed a decline in religious activity or because as people grow older they usually become more religious? To find out, the researchers would need a more elaborate design, one that could separate the influence of aging from that of generation. It is important to avoid the common mistake of measuring how people change over time by taking a cross-sectional survey of people in different age categories.

TABLE 2.1 Faith and Friends as Resources in Crisis: Two Responses to the Three Mile Island Meltdown

	Percent Responding by Age				
	Under 30 Yrs.	*30–39 Yrs.*	*40–49 Yrs.*	*50–59 Yrs.*	*60 and Older*
Pray for Guidance	41	48	63	67	75
Seek Advice and Support from Friends and Relatives	63	59	51	37	45
n = 692					

Source: Peter S. Houts, Robert W. Miller, George K. Tokuhata, and Kum Shik Ham, "Health Related Behavioral Impact of the Three Mile Island Nuclear Incident," Pennsylvania State University College of Medicine and Pennsylvania Department of Health, April 1980.

Sociologists conducted a random telephone survey of residents surrounding the Three Mile Island nuclear plant soon after the danger of meltdown.

that they are appropriate to all members of the sample. Consequently, they often tap the least common denominator and are not sensitive to unusual perspectives. Moreover, many surveys do not give researchers an intimate impression of the context of a person's social life. Finally, unlike direct observation, surveys do not measure what people actually do, but only what people *say* they do (Babbie, 1979).

Field Observation

The sociologist as detective has other methods available in addition to the experiment and the survey for investigating the human experience and social life. For example, when the sociologist Edward Walsh (1981, 1983) sought to determine the effect that the Three Mile Island accident had on the mobilization of the antinuclear movement, he employed field observation. In **field observation** researchers deliberately involve themselves in the activity, group, or community they are investigating in order to get an insider's point of view.

Sociologist Edward Walsh systematically observed protest activities such as these to develop a theory of collective action. (Charles Gatewood/The Image Works.)

Walsh wanted to learn more about how ordinary people mobilize themselves into protests and demonstrations such as those surrounding the Three Mile Island episode. The experiment as a method would not have served his purpose because an understanding of a real-life setting was required and because the issues and variables were not clear in advance. Nor was the survey method a practical alternative because he wanted to study social events that were unfolding rapidly and unexpectedly, and he wished to portray all the stages of the developing behavior. Thus he decided on field observation, a method that would permit him to observe the protest activities directly as the social movement evolved. He supplemented his observations with the secondary analysis of newspaper materials and seventy-five hours of taped interviews. Walsh sought to test the hypothesis of a major theory of social movements: that people's preexisting networks and organizational ties are more important factors in mobilizing them for collective action than are their specific grievances and discontent (McCarthy and Zald, 1977).

For several months prior to the accident at Three Mile Island, Walsh had been collecting data on the Environmental Coalition on Nuclear Power (ECNP), an antinuclear group in the area. He attended monthly meetings of the organization as an observer, and he read the literature the group published. When the accident occurred, Walsh was in a good position to study its effect on this and other community organizations. He attended public hearings, rallies, debates, and meetings, in the process collecting hundreds of pages of field notes.

Walsh found that the accident triggered discontent in a large proportion of the local population. In May, two months after the accident, thirty busloads of local residents attended an antinuclear rally in Washington, D.C. People who had never participated in public life began speaking up at hearings. In one small community near Three Mile Island, irate citizens who had no previous organizational ties banded together to form PANE (People Against Nuclear Energy). As Walsh

(1981:3) notes: "The area within a 25-mile radius of the Pennsylvania island has become a symbol for the national anti-nuclear movement; the previously conservative middle-class communities in the vicinity have been transformed into hotbeds of anti-nuclear activism."

Before the accident only two antinuclear organizations existed in the area. One of these, Three Mile Island Alert (TMIA), had the reputation of being a group on the lunatic fringe. The other (ECNP) had little influence. After the accident, seven new antinuclear groups emerged within a twenty-mile radius of Three Mile Island, all linked to one another in various ways. TMIA's structure underwent a complete overhaul as veterans of the antiwar and civil rights movements took over from the local leadership. It grew from a small, local group in Harrisburg to a coalition representing organizations from numerous communities. ECNP also grew in influence as it mobilized people and channeled their distress into organized protest.

Walsh concluded that preexisting community and organizational ties such as those provided by TMIA, ECNP, local churches and universities, and regional and national antinuclear organizations were important in mobilizing the protest. However, they did so only *after* the people in the area had suffered a major catastrophe. Thus discontent played a key role in the mobilization of this particular social movement. (Walsh, 1983).

Field observation requires exceptional self-discipline. First, field workers face the problem of gaining access to the group they want to study and establishing rapport with its members. If researchers reveal their intentions, they risk putting their subjects on guard; if they conceal their motives, they risk assuming an unethical role and living with their false identity for the duration of the study.

Field observation has its advantages and disadvantages as a research method. An important advantage is that it is extremely flexible. For example, in a classic field study undertaken in a low-income, Italian-American community in Boston (see Chapter 1), the sociologist William Foote Whyte (1955:303) found that "as I sat and listened, I learned the answers to questions that I would not even have had the sense to ask." Hence, field observation allows sociologists to gain a deep inner knowledge of group life. They undertake to look behind individuals' public selves in order to discern the relationships between what people say and what they do.

Yet even good field-observation studies present their share of problems. The researcher's observations may not accurately represent the group as a whole. Field workers often find themselves relying on information gained from the more articulate and outgoing members of the group. And at times they misinterpret the significance of certain events. Moreover, a field-observation sample is necessarily small. For these reasons, field-observation studies are generally used to uncover relationships that later can be verified by other research methods. Despite the limitations of such studies, many of the classic works of sociology rest on observational research that uncovered significant aspects of social life. For example, Whyte found that low-income neighborhoods are highly structured communities—not the chaotic places they appear to be to outsiders.

Historical Approaches

Observation can be done only in the here and now. But what is happening in the present can often be understood only in the context of what took place in the past. Moreover, sociologists are concerned with the changes that occur in institutions, groups, and societies across time. Hence, they turn to **historical materials**—data pertaining to acts, ideas, and events that shaped human behavior in the past.

As we noted in Chapter 1 and will detail in Chapter 11, Max Weber (1904–1905, 1930) used historical data to investigate the cultural transformations that were begun by the Protestant Reformation and that encouraged people to engage in behaviors that led to capitalist development. More recently, sociologists have used historical material to gain insight into contemporary transformations in family patterns, gender roles, and childrearing practices. Similarly, research dealing with earlier periods of industrial and technological change is indespensable to understanding the decline of midwestern "smokestack" industries and the emergence of new "high tech" fields (see Chapter 19). Clearly, sociologists cannot ignore the historical context when they study human interaction and group life. Social behavior does not take place in a historical vacuum. It unfolds within the context of historical events such as the Great Depression of the 1930s, World War II, the Vietnam War, the women's liberation and civil rights movements, the

Disenchantment with the Vietnam War and with the American work-success ethic contributed to the formation of a flamboyant youth counterculture in the late 1960s. Sociologists are interested in the interplay of forces that make each historical period unique. (Gregg Mancuso/Stock, Boston.)

nuclear arms race, and the economic changes of the 1980s.

People living in a particular historical period experience a common location in the social and economic process. In response to the circumstances of its era, each generation fashions a unique style of thought and life (Mannheim, 1952; Laufer and Bengtson, 1974). For instance, the events surrounding the Vietnam War and the civil rights movement, coupled with a growing disenchantment with the work-success ethic, contributed to the growth of an anti-establishment, youth counterculture in the late 1960s and early 1970s. This "involved generation's" political attitudes and life styles continue to find expression in the present (Nassi and Abramowitz, 1979). Thus the past is not behind a group but is contained within the group.

Historical material also enables sociologists to study such rare but significant events as revolutions. It makes little sense to postpone research on revolutions until one happens along. And should it occur, conditions similar to those existing during the recent Iranian revolution often make it impractical or unsafe for sociologists to venture a first-hand investigation. But as Theda Skocpol (1979) demonstrated in her comparative analysis of social revolution, sociologists can gain valuable insights from historical materials. In her study, she was able to address the big issues of social change that concerned early sociologists.

Skocpol hypothesized that two conditions underlie revolutions in predominantly agrarian nations: (1) The state collapses under military or economic pressure from stronger nations, and (2) peasants engage in widespread local uprisings. She scrutinized historical materials dealing with three successful revolutions, looking for similarities in their underlying social conditions: the French Revolution of the late eighteenth century, the Russian Revolution of the early twentieth century, and the Chinese Revolution in the first half of the twentieth century. Skocpol then examined data from selected instances of nonrevolutionary change or unsuccessful revolutions, looking at how they differed from the three successful revolutions: England in the seventeenth century (a political revolution), Prussia in the early 1800s and Japan in the late 1860s (change imposed from above by entrenched elites), and Germany in 1848 and Russia in 1905 (revolutions that failed). Through comparative analysis, she identified three stages in successful social revolution: the breakdown of an old regime's governmental apparatus, the mass mobilization of the peasantry into class-based uprisings, and the reconsolidation of political power by a new elite.

The challenge of historical research lies in using data gathered for some other reason and by someone else to find out what one wishes to know. For instance, data collected by governmental agencies can make significant contributions to sociological knowledge. Records on births, deaths, marriages, and divorces provide valuable information on family and population patterns. Statistics on communicable diseases and hospitalizations offer information on a people's health. Property, income, and poll tax records can be helpful in reconstructing patterns of social inequality. And school records reveal trends in education. Durkheim's classic study on suicide, discussed earlier, relied on data derived from governmental archives.

Content Analysis

Sociologists often employ **content analysis** to uncover relevant material in historical and contemporary materials. Content analysis may be applied to almost any type of recorded communication—letters, diaries, autobiographies, memoirs, laws, novels, song lyrics, constitutions, newspapers, even paintings. Such communications can reveal much about people's behavior. This research method provides a way to systematically organize and summarize both the manifest and latent content of communication. The method is especially useful in historical research, because it provides a way for the researcher to systematically organize and summarize data. Here, the computer has proven a powerful tool because it allows researchers to analyze content from many perspectives.

To show how content analysis works, let us suppose that you want to determine the political attitudes that prevailed at the turn of the century in America. One approach to the subject would be to examine newspapers of the period for "conservative" and "liberal" editorials. Since it would be impractical to examine every issue of every newspaper published in, say, a ten-year period, you would have to select a representative sample to study. And within that sample you might select a

THE SOCIOLOGICAL EYE ON:

Content Analysis: John Naisbitt's Trend Report

John Naisbitt is the fifty-three-year-old author of *Megatrends* (1982), the best-selling book that examines the social and economic effects of the shift from an industrial to an information-based economy. In Naisbitt's view the United States is rapidly becoming a knowledge-centered society, a sort of giant university servicing the world. In 1981 he founded TNG (The Naisbitt Group). The firm's chief product is the *Trend Report*, a publication that attempts to let its subscribers know what is going on in the United States by identifying developing trends.

The basic method employed by TNG is content analysis of local newspapers. Articles from some two hundred newspapers are clipped and indexed by NewsBank, a company based in New Canaan, Connecticut. It puts the material on microfiche and sells the service by subscription, mostly to libraries. This raw data is analyzed at TNG by Steven Mendelsohn, a twenty-three-year-old sociology major who graduated from Alfred University. He is one of TNG's eight analysts responsible for tracking developments in agriculture, consumer affairs, energy, environment, and housing. Mendelsohn reads the clips on a NewsBank microfiche and attempts to discern broad themes or patterns in the material that suggest emerging trends. He then writes a summary, which is discussed at a staff research meeting and then incorporated in the quarterly *Trend Report*.

The principal subscribers to *Trend Report* are corporations. Dr. Walter Albers, associated with General Motors's societal analysis department, says, "We used the reports as part of the input to try to identify the trends and emerging issues that go into action points for GM." And John Snow, director of planning and research and of corporate relations at Sears, says, "We are looking at all changes that are taking place in society and trying to make management aware of them. Content analysis is one of many inputs we are using in trend scanning." In 1983 it is estimated that The Naisbitt group did $1.6 million worth of business as an adviser-forecaster-analyst service.

Source: Emily Yoffe, "John Naisbitt's Clip Joint," *Harper's*, September 1983, pp. 18–22.

random sample of editorials. (See the box for a contemporary application of content analysis techniques to newspaper information.)

Content analysis has the advantage of being cheap and easy to use. Anyone can analyze materials for content—no special equipment or outlays of money are required. If you make a mistake, it is easier to redo your analysis than to redo a survey or field research today. No other method lends itself so well to the study of the past. Finally, content analysis is unobtrusive because the researcher does not affect the event being studied. But the method also has disadvantages: One can apply it only to *recorded* communication, and it is difficult to fashion coding methods that produce valid findings (Babbie, 1979).

In conclusion, sociologists use a variety of methods for collecting and analyzing data. As we saw with Walsh's study of antinuclear groups near Three Mile Island, these methods can be used in combination so that the weaknesses of one can be compensated for by the strengths of another. We now turn to the human context and consider how personal values, group behavior, and ethical issues affect the research enterprise.

VALUES AND ETHICS IN SOCIOLOGICAL RESEARCH

The values of researchers intertwine with nearly all aspects of a research undertaking. Such preferences influence the choice of a study problem, the design of the study, the methods of analysis that are used, and the interpretations of the data. For example, an understanding of values can help to explain why those who studied the effects of the Three Mile Island accident chose that topic. Some were concerned about the impact of nuclear power plants on society. In general, they designed their research to show that nuclear emergencies cannot be assessed simply in terms of mechanical defects; the crisis lives on in the minds and hearts of people long after the technical problems have been solved. Other researchers may have had a commitment to a theory of social movements and found that the situation at Three Mile Island presented unique opportunities to test their ideas. Whatever the case, it is important for sociologists to know the values that influence their work (Gouldner, 1962, 1980).

Many individuals are attracted to sociology because they would like to improve human life. They are deeply troubled by poverty, racism, sexism, war, crime, and other social problems. They find inspiration in the writings of such sociologists as C. Wright Mills who, in *The Sociological Imagination* (1959), insisted that sociologists should not define their mission solely as one of developing abstract knowledge. Mills called upon sociologists to shed light on human suffering and to help people free themselves from the "traps" they encounter in their daily lives. He believed this goal could be achieved by linking the "private troubles" of individuals to "public issues," particularly to the structure of society (see Chapter 1).

By analyzing our social experience from the perspective of the sociological imagination, we can begin to appreciate the forces that shape our lives. Much of the power and excitement of sociology comes from its ability to demystify the world. By "telling it like it is"—by stripping away mystery and cant—sociology has a liberating effect. It offers the promise that we need no longer take our circumstances for granted, we can consciously and deliberately intervene in our own destinies. In a world of racial, religious, and national strife, malfunctioning economies, and the impairment of the environment, the cultivation and application of knowledge about social behavior may ultimately determine the survival of humankind.

The recognition that sociological knowledge is useful has led some sociologists to ask, "Sociology for whom?" Sociologists are as much social beings as the people they study. They are caught up in the social demands of university colleagues and administrators, political systems, research organizations and government granting agencies, students, friends, and others. Since values are transmitted and instilled within groups and serve the interests of groups, sociologists must decide whose values and interests their work will serve. Will it be put to the service of jailers or prisoners, whites or blacks, men or women, managers or workers, generals or privates? Such issues are reflected in the theories that guide sociological research, a matter to which we now turn our attention.

Values and Theories

If you were a sociologist, what do you think would make you decide to adopt a particular theoretical perspective?

Sociologists are social beings too. This young man brings certain values to his interview with elders of the Sioux Indian tribe. The crucial question is whether he can recognize his biases and unstated assumptions. (Owen Franken/Stock, Boston.)

To answer this question, you need to examine your values. Do you believe in the individuality of people? Do you think that people can do what they want in their social lives and interact in creative ways? Do you value the importance of others and can you see their point of view? If so, you might well choose the symbolic interactionist perspective. According to sociologist Leon Shaskolsky (1970:17):

> The writings of the symbolic interactionists are permeated with an exhilarating optimism—expressing itself, on the personal level, in the belief in the uniqueness of each member of society and in his freedom to plan and perform his everyday actions in interrelationship with others . . . ; and expressing itself on the societal level, in the belief in an evolutionary process of change built into the system.

Shaskolsky finds this viewpoint particularly well suited to the ideals of American society, which emphasize respect for the individual and the ability to gradually change with society.

But perhaps you put more emphasis on the structure of society than on the individuality of its members. If you believe that the roles of individuals in society are structured and that people internalize society's norms, integrate themselves into the system, and contribute to its equilibrium, then you would be likely to adopt the functionalist perspective.

Functionalism, particularly as set forth by the American sociologist Talcott Parsons and his followers, stresses the importance of social institutions and their basic stability. Because it tends to support the status quo, functionalism is considered to have a conservative bias. Shaskolsky (1970:24) speculates that functionalism became popular in America after World War II because its "reasoned and rational representation of the solid, stable nature of American society" provided a justification for the rejection of "Communist" inroads into American society.

The conflict perspective is likely to appeal to you if you believe that society is basically unstable and torn by conflicting social forces. As we saw in Chapter 1, this perspective is more radical than the other two. It emphasizes countervailing power groups (as in the conflict between classes), and it tends to see the individual as a victim of powerful elites.

The Sociology of Research

Because individual researchers in sociology, as well as those in the natural sciences, subscribe to a certain theory and believe in their view of the world, they form groups with like-minded colleagues. This notion runs counter to the myth of the lone scientist in his or her lab puzzling out a secret of nature. In physics, for example:

> Every scientist sees through his own eyes—and also through the eyes of his predecessors and colleagues. It is never one individual who goes through all the steps in the logico-inductive chain; it is a group of individuals, dividing their labour but continuously and jealously checking each other's contributions. (Ziman, 1968:9)

As in physics, so in sociology, loosely knit communities of researchers work together, compete against other groups, and prefer certain research methods to others. In fact, sociologists are as easily divided by methodological preference—the field workers, the survey researchers, the experimentalists—as by any other factor.

The sociology of scientific research has become a major field of study. Robert Merton (1970, 1973) laid the groundwork for this field by describing how science arose as an institution in response to the needs of others. Merchants needed devices that would enable them to sail their ships long distances in safety; coal mine owners needed ways to mine deeper in order to supply the power needed by industrialization; and nations needed ways to kill greater numbers of enemy soldiers more efficiently in war.

In time, scientific research became highly organized, creating its own norms, values, conventions, and biases. Merton (1973) has identified four major norms that prevail in communities of researchers: impartiality, sharing, altruism, and organized skepticism.[2] **Norms** are rules that specify appropriate and inappropriate behavior. Although norms provide socially shared standards for behavior, they do not necessarily describe what people *actually* do.

Norms of Science

The principle of **impartiality** calls for scientists to judge research according to impartial criteria. They should not consider a researcher's personality, race, nationality, or politics in assessing the validity of his or her work. Nor should such considerations affect a person's career; only talent should matter. Without this norm, society would lack an independent body of valid and objective knowledge.

Sharing means that researchers must make their findings available to the rest of the scientific community. As Merton puts it, there is a moral compulsion to share the wealth of science. Researchers gain recognition by sharing their ideas. However, they usually publicize them only after they have developed the ideas well enough that others will not get the credit for them.

The norm of **altruism** means that researchers should not use or misuse the results of science for personal gain. When coupled with the norm of sharing, this standard provides the basis for a body of public, testable knowledge, the essence of science. This norm found expression in the recent decisions by Harvard, Stanford, and other major universities not to form genetic research corporations, even though the potential profits from such research are enormous. They expressed concern that the formation of corporations would undermine the disinterested pursuit of scientific research.

The norm of **organized skepticism** provides that members of the scientific community should not accept the results of research unquestioningly. Instead, researchers look skeptically at all aspects of a project (using universal criteria to judge it). A scientific claim is not valid until proven so. Like other scientific communities, sociologists carry out this norm by having panels of anonymous readers review research proposals and research papers submitted to scientific journals such as *American Sociological Review* or the *American Journal of Sociology*. The work of faculty members who are being considered for promotion or applying for a position also gets reviewed by anonymous colleagues. At scientific meetings and in the journals, people openly challenge one another's work—a pattern not commonly found in the business community or the clinical professions.

Counternorms of Science

Although these four norms constitute the ideals for scientific research and nearly every researcher pays lip service to them, in practice physicists, sociologists, research engineers, and other scientists often deviate from them. In a study of the Apollo space program, sociologist Ian Mitroff interviewed forty-two moon scientists and found that their behavior was often governed by **counternorms** to those outlines by Merton. He noted that:

[2]Merton termed impartiality *universalism*, sharing *communism*, and altruism *disinterestedness*.

The whole enterprise of scientific research is itself subject to sociological analysis. One can study, for example, the norms and ethics of research, and the question of how far research should go. (Michael Grecco/Picture Cube.)

> No matter what the topic . . . the scientists moved the discussion toward intensely personal matters. They could not discuss the status of physical theory and the scientific evidence bearing on it in purely impersonal or "objective" terms. . . . Some scientists or groups of scientists were clearly associated in the minds of the sample with each theory, serving as its personal advocates and defenders. Hence, the scientists could not react to a theory without reacting simultaneously to its proponents. (1974:585)

One scientist went to so far as to say about another, very distinguished scientist: "X's belief in Q is unshakable. He refuses to listen to reason or to evidence. I no longer regard him as a scientist. He's so hopped up on the idea of Q that I think he's unbalanced" (Mitroff, 1974:586). The attitudes of these scientists did not change over the three-and-a-half years of the study. Yet this counternorm to impartiality has its function, because people who are strongly committed to their ideas and elicit strong reactions to them guarantee that the ideas will get public exposure and scrutiny. And it allows the members of a research group to provide one another with protection and support. Hence, whereas the norms of science promote or advance a discipline as a whole, counternorms serve the interests of particular groups of researchers. The two sets of norms stand today in a delicate balance.

Mitroff identified other counternorms to Merton's dominant norms, all of which have their benefits and liabilities. Sharing is offset by self-protectiveness, altruism by self-interest, and organized skepticism by organized dogmatism (see Table 2.2, p.48).

What social factors encourage the development of these counternorms? Why are scientists so intensely committed to their ideas and suspicious of the ideas of others? Why do they guard their work so jealously? One answer to these questions lies in the reward structure of the scientific community. A scientist does not own a discovery in the sense that he or she can make exclusive use of it or restrict its use by others. Sometimes a discovery is named after the discoverer, as in "Boyle's law" or "Halley's comet," but the name does not imply ownership, nor is there any direct monetary value attached to the distinction. The discovery is the scientist's property only in an intellectual sense, though others recognize that the scientist made it. This recognition and its associated fame are the scientist's principal reward, the main indication that he or she has done a job well. So it is a matter of great importance to prove that one has made a discovery *first* (Merton, 1973). In fact, history is full of fierce battles between scientists over who discovered something first. Galileo took on many opponents in defending his claims to such inventions and discoveries as the geometric compass, the telescope, and

TABLE 2.2 Norms and Counternorms in the Scientific Community

Norm	Counternorm
1. Impartiality A claim is not to be judged on the basis of the claimant's personal or social characteristics.	Partiality A scientist's social and personal characteristics influence how his or her work will be judged, giving some scientists priority over others.
2. Sharing Findings are the property of the scientific community; they should not be kept secret.	Self-Protectiveness A scientist sometimes needs protective control over his or her discovery, necessitating secrecy.
3. Altruism A scientist subordinates self-interest to the interest of the scientific community as a whole.	Self-centered Interest Scientists are expected to serve their specialized communities of interest and themselves.
4. Organized skepticism All scientific knowledge is subject to scrutiny and to doubt.	Organized dogmatism A scientist must be completely convinced of his or her findings, while doubting those of others.

Source: Adapted from Ian I. Mitroff, "Norms and Counter-Norms in a Select Group of the Apollo Moon Scientists: A Case Study of the Ambivalence of Scientists," *American Sociological Review* 39 (August 1974): 579–595, Table 4, p. 592.

the observation of sunspots. Cavendish, Watt, and Lavoisier quarreled over who was first to discover that water was a compound rather than a single element. Today there is a battle over who first discovered interferon, a genetic virus fighter. Such acrimonious disputes over original contributions provide evidence of the personal drive and raw emotion that infuse the scientific realm.

Research Ethics

In the scramble to make an important discovery first and in the competition between research groups, a number of ethical issues can arise. Who should get credit for the work? Were the findings exaggerated or falsified? And were the people being studied abused? Here we have space only to address the last issue of protecting the rights of research subjects.

In the last few decades the issue of protecting people from harm in research has raised new and sometimes disturbing questions: Do researchers have the right to deceive people about their intentions, or expose and hurt them in the name of scientific inquiry?

Federal Regulations

In recent years the federal government has specified regulations on human research, and universities have set up review boards to approve research involving human subjects. The guidelines for this research are clear: explain the experiment or procedure to the subject; do not lie; warn the subject about any hazards; describe how the data are to be used; ensure the subject's confidentiality; make certain that before a subject gives consent, he or she is fully informed about the experiment.

Institutions likewise bear responsibility for protecting the rights and welfare of research subjects. Occasionally, the researcher alone gets blamed for unethical practices when part of the fault also lies with the institution in which the researcher works (Barber, 1980). Many institutions put pressure on researchers to carry out research projects but do not build adequate controls into the research process. For instance, when committees responsible for reviewing research do not insist that consent forms be completed by subjects, researchers often do not bother to have this done (Gray, 1975). Thus, the good will of the researcher is not sufficient; institutional procedures must also be brought into line with ethical principles.

Ethical Dilemmas: A Case Study

Ethical considerations may pose a problem for both researcher and subject. The following example illustrates how ethics enter into research decisions and reactions to those decisions. In the early 1970s Roy Wallis embarked on a sociological study of a religious sect known as Scientology. He was intrigued by the "apparent authoritarianism and even occasional totalitarianism of this movement" (p. 151). Before he began his research, Wallis confronted a moral dilemma. If he revealed the nature of his study to the organization, its leaders would probably prevent him from interviewing members and deny him access to the group's documents. If he did not, he would be deceiving them. Wallis finally decided that covert field work would be ethical, but that if he were asked about his approach he would not lie. Subsequently, however, Wallis shifted tactics: he approached the organization openly as a researcher.

Wallis later wrote up his research for publication as a book. When he had completed his manuscript, he confronted another moral dilemma. Should he send the final draft to the Scientology organization for comments? On the one hand he did not want his work to bring *undeserved* damage to the organization, but on the other hand he did not want to submit to censorship. In the end, Wallis did send the manuscript to the Scientologists, motivated both by a desire to be fair to the group and by fear of a libel suit. Various negotiating sessions resulted in Wallis's making about a hundred changes in his text and incorporating a reply from a Scientologist. In return, the Scientologists agreed not to sue for libel. Wallis feels that this agreement compromised his sociological research but that at least there could be no question that he behaved ethically.

Another ethical issue confronting sociologists is what their role should be in the political process. Should sociologists actively participate in decisions on social policy? Many people believe that sociologists should remain neutral, arguing that to take a stand would contaminate the discipline. But as Robert Lynd suggested in his classic book, *Knowledge for What?*:

> Somebody is going to interpret what the situation (the facts) means. . . . When the social scientist, after intensive study of a problem, avoids extrapolating his data into the realm of wide meaning, however tentatively stated, he invites others presumably more biased than himself—e.g., the National Association of Manufacturers, the American Federation of Labor, the advertising man, the American Legion, and so on—to thrust upon the culture their interpretations. (1946:185–186)

In short, Lynd and many other sociologists argue that social scientists should suggest social policies because if they do not, others wishing to promote their own special interests will do so.

EPILOGUE

The material in this chapter links back to that in Chapter 1 and forward to that in the chapters that follow. In Chapter 1 we saw that sociology examines the social forces and structures that underlie the events and experiences of our lives. Indeed, much of the power and excitement of sociology derives from its ability to lay bare taken-for-granted aspects of the social world. This chapter has described the perspectives and methods that sociologists use to penetrate the surface aspects of life and to arrive at findings that are more valid than those derived by unsystematic observation.

Emile Durkheim's work is a pioneering model. He suspected that many of the intuitive and common-sense notions regarding suicide that prevailed in nineteenth-century France did not conform to the facts. Through research, Durkheim demonstrated that climatic and racial explanations of suicide are invalid. Moreover, he showed how aspects of the social environment render some individuals more vulnerable to suicide than others. In sum, we are reminded that when we turn our sociological eye upon events, we often discover that things are not necessarily what they seem.

The scientific method allows us to generate facts—verifiable observations—about the world. But random facts are meaningless. They take on significance only as we identify relationships among them. Theory provides the vehicle for ordering facts so that we can understand them and use them to make predictions. Hence, the methods we outlined in this chapter provide the means by which we arrive at facts about deviance, race relations, marriage and the family, population dynamics, urban patterns, and other matters we will consider in the chapters that follow. These methods in turn provide us with the building blocks to formulate and test the theories we propose.

As we have pointed out, methods are the tools used to investigate a problem. How we define a problem affects the questions we ask and the methods we use to answer them. Sociologists often distinguish three types of research: basic, descriptive, and applied.

Basic research is concerned with developing and testing theory. Durkheim studied suicide not primarily because he was concerned with suicide per se but because he wanted to formulate and test a theory of social integration. Walsh also carried out basic research. Although he may have had sympathy for the people demonstrating against nuclear power plants, he designed his research to test and improve sociological theory dealing with the rise of social movements. But the boundaries between basic and applied research are often ill-defined. Indeed, whether a piece of research is basic or applied may be in the eyes of the reader rather than those of the researcher.

When sociologists wish to assess the characteristics of a situation or group, they undertake *descriptive research*. They may inquire as to the age distribution, the national or social background, the health or educational levels of a given population. Such studies typically do not involve the testing of a hypothesis. The surveys assessing the behavioral effects of the accident at Three Mile Island illustrate descriptive research.

Applied research attempts to produce information that can be used to change things. It addresses specific, real issues. Many sociologists want their research to make an actual difference in the world. Indeed, people find sociology useful in many lines of work—market research, employee relations, community medicine, all types of social services. No other discipline has developed a body of techniques for analyzing people in groups, organizations, and communities.

But regardless of its nature, each type of research shares a common concern with finding out about something. The perspectives and methods discussed in this chapter provide the basis for the study of social interaction and group life, the subject matter of this text.

SUMMARY

Science is a way of knowing the world that relies on the careful collection and logical explanation of facts. Scientists undertake to explain events by establishing cause-and-effect relationships. In so doing, they assume that events occur in succession. By identifying the cause of an event, we make it intelligible and provide it with meaning.

The scientific method consists of seven steps: defining the problem, reviewing the literature, forming a hypothesis, choosing a research design, collecting the data, analyzing the data, and drawing conclusions. In sociology the scientific method is sometimes strained by the fact that the object of sociological research is people. In their research, sociologists must take account of human changeableness, conflicting emotions, their own emotional involvement, and the need to treat people with dignity and respect.

The chapter examined five methods of conducting research. The experiment offers scientists the most effective technique for establishing a cause-and-effect relationship. A cause-and-effect relationship is said to exist when one characteristic or occurrence (X) determines another characteristic or occurrence (Y). In experiments subjects are exposed to a specifically designed situation, and their reactions are systematically recorded. In the survey, questionnaires or interviews, or both, are used to collect information about how large numbers of people think, feel, or act. In field observation, the researcher is involved in the group he or she is studying in order to get an understanding of the social setting. Historical approaches allow researchers to use data that were gathered for some other reason and by someone else in order to find out what they want to know. Finally, content analysis provides a way to analyze material in order to learn something about a social phenomenon.

The particular approaches chosen by sociologists tend to be suited to the theoretical perspectives that guide them. For instance, as a functionalist, Durkheim compared group patterns of suicide. A symbolic interactionist would be more interested in examining the meanings embedded in individual cases of suicide, gradually accumulating enough data to reveal general patterns.

A researcher's values influence nearly all aspects of research—what to study, how to design the study, what methods to use, and how to interpret the data. Values lead the researcher to choose one theoretical perspective instead of another, and they shape the research that stems from this perspective.

The scientific enterprise is a social one. Researchers build on one another's work, and their scientific community is bound and governed by common norms. Certain ideal norms—impartiality, sharing, altruism, and organized skepticism—are acknowledged by all scientists but are not necessarily followed by every one of them at all times. Counternorms, such as partiality and self-protectiveness, also exist, and scientists may alternate their behavior between these conflicting sets of norms.

A scientist's principal reward comes from the scientific community's recognition of his or her original contribution. This reward structure generates a great deal of competition and many personality clashes in the race to discover something first.

Because they study people, sociologists have to be particularly careful that they protect the rights of their subjects. Federal regulations and university review boards have provided guidelines for research. Another ethical concern is the extent to which sociologists should participate in social policy decisions. Should they remain neutral in controversies over social policy? Or should they interpret their facts before special interests use them to their own advantage?

GLOSSARY

Altruism. A norm of the scientific community identified by Merton that discourages a scientist from using scientific findings for personal interests.

Anomie. A condition within society in which people's integration within the social fabric is weakened and their commitment to societal norms lessened.

Content analysis. A research method that provides a way to systematically organize and summarize both the manifest and latent content of communication.

Control group. In an experiment, the subjects who are not exposed to the independent variable, giving the experimenter a basis for comparison with subjects who are exposed to it.

Counternorm. A shared standard of desirable behavior that runs counter to an identifiable norm.

Dependent variable. A quality or factor that is affected by one or more independent variables.

Experiment. A research method that exposes subjects to a specially designed situation. By systematically recording subjects' reactions, the researcher can assess the effects of several different variables.

Experimental group. In an experiment, the subjects exposed to the independent variable and observed for changes in behavior.

Field experiment. An experiment carried out in a real-life setting.

Field observation. A research method in which researchers deliberately involve themselves in the activity, group, or community they are studying in order to get an insider's view.

Hawthorne effect. The impact that an experiment has because researchers give the subjects special attention.

Historical materials. Data pertaining to acts, ideas, and events that shaped human behavior in the past.

Hypothesis. A proposition about how two or more factors or variables affect or are related to one another.

Impartiality. A norm of the scientific community that calls for judging a scientist's claims according to impersonal criteria.

Independent variable. A quality or factor that affects one or more dependent variables.

Laboratory experiment. Experiment carried out in the artificial setting of a laboratory, where control over variables is possible.

Mean. The average; obtained by adding all figures in a series of data and dividing the sum by the number of items.

Median. The number that falls in the middle of a sequence of figures.

Mode. The figure that occurs most often in a series of data.

Norm. A rule that specifies appropriate and inappropriate behavior; a guideline people follow in their relations with others.

Operational definitions. Measurable indicators for variables in a hypothesis.

Organized skepticism. A norm of the scientific community that calls for the objective analysis of all aspects of nature and society and suspension of judgment until all facts are in.

Random sample. A sample drawn in such a way that every member of the population being studied has an equal chance of being selected.

Reliability. The degree to which a study yields the same results when repeated by the original or other researchers.

Sample. A limited number of people selected from the

population being studied.

Scientific method. A way of investigating the world that relies on the careful collection of facts and logical explanations of them.

Secondary analysis. Reanalysis of previously collected data.

Semistructured interview. A discussion with a subject in which the interviewer predetermines the areas and issues to be covered but lets the respondent answer in terms most meaningful to him or her.

Sharing. An ideal norm of the scientific community identified by Merton that calls for making scientific findings available to other researchers.

Structured interview. A discussion with a subject in which carefully phrased standard questions are asked in a fixed order.

Survey. A method of research using questionnaires or interviews, or both, to learn how people think, feel, or act. Good surveys use random samples and pretested questions to ensure high reliability and validity.

Theory. A statement that describes the relationships between major concepts or variables.

Unstructured interview. A discussion with a subject in which neither questions nor answers are predetermined.

Validity. The degree to which a scientific study measures what it attempts to measure.

Variable. Any factor that is capable of change.

PART TWO

BECOMING A SOCIAL BEING

When we say that humans are social beings, we mean more than the simple fact that they live in close proximity to one another. We also mean that a person's very self—his or her customary way of thinking and acting—is a product of social interaction. Part 2 explores the major components of social life that so influence our behavior.

Chapter 3 begins with a look at what sociologists call culture—the shared set of rules and traditions, passed on from one generation to the next, that shapes the feelings, thoughts, and actions of a group of people. You will discover that our own highly diverse American culture is undergoing significant changes.

Cultural values and beliefs govern the way in which human relationships are structured. The basic elements of that social structure are the subject of Chapter 4. The fact that social relationships are structured in relatively predictable ways raises the question of how free we actually are. Do social roles prescribe the ways we act in different social settings? Or is each human encounter in many respects unique, worked out and mutually understood in the process of interaction?

Chapter 5 then turns to the topic of socialization—the process by which people acquire their culture and internalize their various social roles. You will learn that socialization is a lifelong process in which family, peers, schools, the media, and the workplace all play an important part.

The acquisition of sex roles is an especially good example of socialization, and it is the subject of Chapter 6. Here you will see how traditional myths and stereotypes about male and female behavior tend to become internalized as children grow up.

Buvez
Coca-Cola

CHAPTER 3

Culture

"Come alive with Pepsi" proved a winning advertising slogan in the United States. But some residents of Taiwan found the translation—"Pepsi brings your ancestors back from the dead"—unappealing. General Motors Corporation ran into difficulty in Belgium when the firm promoted its "Body by Fisher" cars that translated into Flemish as "Corpse by Fisher." And some car buyers in Spanish-speaking countries were reluctant to purchase the Chevrolet Nova because *no va* means "it doesn't go." These examples all demonstrate a failure to understand language differences in a foreign environment.

A somewhat different problem arose in Salt Lake City, Utah, when a man came to purchase a Shetland pony advertised for sale. The owner asked what the man planned to do with the horse. "For my son's birthday," was the response. Gratified that the pony was going to a child, the owner closed the deal. But then the buyer took out a two-by-four, clubbed the pony over the head, dumped the carcass in his pickup truck, and drove off. The horrified seller notified the police. When the police arrived at the buyer's home, they found a birthday party underway. The pony was roasting in a "luau pit." The buyer, a recent immigrant from Tonga, a group of Polynesian Islands off New Zealand, explained that the Tongans do not ride horses but eat them. They had acquired their taste for horse meat from European missionaries who found horses the only readily available source of meat on the Pacific Islands (Wells, 1983).

All of the customs, beliefs, values, knowledge, and skills that guide a people's behavior along shared paths are part of their **culture** (Linton, 1947:10). Culture can be divided into material aspects (the products of a people's arts and technology) and nonmaterial aspects (a people's customs, beliefs, values, and patterns of communication). People throughout the world have different cultures. Thus their standards for behavior often differ. We tend to assume that certain behaviors have pretty much the same meaning around the world, and we anticipate that other people will act as we do. But this is clearly not the case. When we are thrust into a different culture, we may find ourselves in situations for which we are unprepared.

Not surprisingly, interaction among peoples of different cultures is often filled with uncertainties and even difficulties. Take the matter of the "language of space," identified by the anthropologist Edward T. Hall (1966). He notes that Arabs tend to get very close to other people, close enough to breathe on them. When Arabs do not breathe on a person, it means that they are ashamed. But Americans insist on staying outside the range of other people's breath, viewing the odor as distasteful. Arabs ask, "Why are Americans so ashamed? They withhold their breath." Americans on the receiving end wonder, "Why are the Arabs so pushy?" Americans typically back away as an Arab comes close, and the Arab follows. Such differences can have serious consequences. For example, an Arab business representative may not trust an American who backs off. On the other hand, the American may distrust the Arab for seeming so pushy.

In this chapter we will first examine the elements of culture and the variety in their expression. Then we will consider how cultural ideas originate and evolve, taking special note of the role that biology is thought to play. Next the basic patterns of American culture and the variations found among subcultures will be examined. We will conclude with a look at the ways culture can work against people.

ELEMENTS OF CULTURE

Culture is a taken-for-granted aspect of life, one we commonly overlook as we go about our daily activities. Yet it touches all aspects of our lives. Alexander Alland, Jr. (1973:227–228), provides the following analogy for culture:

> I remember watching a blind student several years ago walking across the campus of a large state university. He guided himself with a cane, tapping it against the sidewalk which ran in spokes from building to building. Although he knew the campus well, on that particular occasion he became distracted for a moment and wandered onto the grass, where he immediately lost all sense of direction. His movements became disorganized as he searched hopelessly for a bit of cement. He became visibly panicked until a passing student came up and led him back to the appropriate path. Once again he was able to continue toward his class unaided.
>
> I was struck by the similarity of this situation to the situation of all human beings who have grown up within a particular social milieu. Out of an incredibly large number of possible ways of living successfully, all normal human beings operate within a narrow framework of convention. The convention is sometimes limiting and perhaps to certain individuals unsatisfying, but it provides a set of rules which act as guidelines for action.

The anthropologist Edmund Carpenter (1965:55) confronted a situation similar to that described by Alland when he went to live among the Aivilik, an Eskimo people:

> For months after I first arrived among the Aivilik, I felt empty, clumsy. I never knew what to do, even where to sit or stand. I was awkward in a busy world, as helpless as a child, yet a grown man. I felt like a mental defective.

The map of life that underlies both material and nonmaterial culture includes three elements: norms, values, and symbols. Let's consider what each contributes to social life.

Norms

In *Games People Play* (1964:37) Eric Berne describes the greeting ritual of the American:

> "Hi!" (Hello, good morning.)
> "Hi!" (Hello, good morning.)
> "Warm enough forya?" (How are you?)
> "Sure is. Looks like rain, though." (Fine. How are you?)
> "Well, take cara yourself." (Okay.)
> "I'll be seeing you."
> "So long."
> "So long."

This brief exchange is conspicuously lacking in content. If you were to measure the success of the conversation in terms of the information conveyed, you would have to rate it zero. Even so, both parties leave the scene feeling quite satisfied. In using the greeting ritual, they have made social contact and established a friendly atmosphere.

As was briefly discussed in Chapter 2, **norms** are the guidelines people are supposed to follow in their relations with one another; they are shared rules that specify appropriate and inappropriate behavior. Not only do norms indicate what people should or should not do in a specific situation; they also enable people to anticipate how others will interpret and respond to their words and actions. Norms vary from society to society, from group to group within societies, and from situation to situation. Polite and appropriate behavior in one society may be disgraceful in another. For example:

> Among the Ila-speaking peoples of Africa, girls are given houses of their own at harvest time where they may play at being man and wife with boys of their choice. It is said that among these people virginity does not exist beyond the age of ten. [In contrast] among the Tepoztlan Indians

In traditional Japan, bowing is the appropriate social norm for exchanging greetings. (René Burri/Magnum)

> of Mexico, from the time of a girl's first menstruation, her life becomes "crabbed, cribbed, confined." No boy is to be spoken to or encouraged in the least way. To do so would be to court disgrace, to show oneself to be crazy or mad. (Ember and Ember, 1977, p. 277)

Some norms are situational—they apply to specific categories of people in specific settings. We consider it appropriate for a person to pray to God in church, or to speak to people who have long since "gone to the other side" during a séance (even if we think the séance is phony). But we usually find a person "peculiar" if he or she addresses God or invokes spirits on a bus.

Social norms shape our emotions and perceptions. For example, people are *supposed* to feel sad and be depressed when a family member dies. Similarly, people are supposed to pay attention to certain things but not to others. For example, we consider it bad taste to gawk at a couple who is quarreling bitterly or to eavesdrop on an intimate conversation, yet we occasionally do both. Thus we hold norms, but at times we violate them.

Most of the time people follow norms more or less automatically; alternatives never occur to them. This is particularly true of unspoken norms that seem self-evident, such as responding to a person who addresses you. People conform because it seems right, because to violate norms would damage their self-image (or "hurt their conscience"), and because they want approval and fear ridicule, ostracism, or, in some cases, punishment.

Folkways, Mores, and Laws

Norms vary in the importance that people assign to them and the leeway they permit violators. **Folkways** are everyday habits and conventions people obey without giving much thought to the matter. For example, Americans eat three meals a day and call other food "snacks." We have cereal for breakfast but not for other meals; we save sweets for the end of dinner. Even though we could easily begin a meal with cherry pie, we don't. Other customs we observe are covering our mouths when we yawn, shaking hands when introduced, closing zippers on pants or skirts, and *not* wearing evening clothes to class. People who violate folkways may be labeled eccentrics or slobs, but as a rule they are tolerated.

In contrast, violations of mores provoke intense reactions. **Mores** are the norms people consider vital to their well-being and to their most cherished values. Examples are the prohibitions against incest, cannibalism, and sexual abuse of children. People who violate mores are considered unfit for society and may be ostracized, beaten, locked up in a prison or a mental hospital, exiled, or executed. (Hence, most Americans would not condemn an individual who gave a child molester a severe beating.)

Some norms are formalized into laws. A **law** is a rule enacted by a political body and enforced by the power of the state. Whereas folkways and mores are typically enforced by the collective and spontaneous actions of the members of the community, laws are enforced by the police, the military, or some other special organization. Laws may formalize folkways (as some traffic regulations do) or back up mores (as laws against murder and treason do). Political authorities may also attempt to introduce new norms by enacting laws such as those governing the disposal of toxic wastes or the extension of civil rights to various minorities. In general, the laws that are most difficult to enforce are those that are not grounded in the folkways or mores—for example, laws against gambling or the use of marijuana.

Sanctions

Norms are only guides to behavior; by themselves they have no force. It is **sanctions,** or socially imposed rewards and punishments, that compel people to obey norms. Such sanctions may be formal or informal. Examples of formal sanctions that reward people are promotions, medals of honor, and paychecks. Formal sanctions that punish people include jail terms, job dismissals, failing grades, and traffic fines. Informal sanctions are those expressed by behavior in everyday situations—smiles, frowns, friendly nods, gossip, praise, insults, and even attention.

Societies vary in their use of sanctions. For instance, the Amish punish those who violate their norms with shunning, in which no one is allowed to speak to the offender. Such a punishment is less effective in the larger American society. In Japan slurping one's soup

Behavior that deviates from social norms is likely to meet with informal sanctions, such as disapproving looks. (Jean-Claude Lejeune, EKM-Nepenthe.)

loudly is a positive sanction, indicating to a hostess that one has greatly enjoyed a meal. In the United States, such slurping is itself disapproved; instead, Americans are expected to compliment the cook verbally.

Values

Norms typically derive from a people's values. **Values** are the general ideas that individuals share about what is good or bad, right or wrong, desirable or undesirable. These notions transcend particular situations or interactions. Unlike norms (the rules that govern behavior in actual situations with other people), values are broad, abstract concepts. As such, they provide the foundation that underlies a people's entire way of life. Even the games they play reflect their values. A good illustration is formed among the Tangu, a people who live in a remote part of New Guinea and play a game called *taketak*.

In some respects taketak resembles bowling. The game is played with a toplike object fashioned from a dried fruit and with two groups of coconut stakes that look like bowling pins. The players divide into two teams. The members of the first team step to the line and take turns throwing the top into their batch of stakes; every stake they hit they remove. Then the members of the second team toss the top into their batch of stakes. The object of the game, surprisingly, is not to knock over as many stakes as possible. Rather, the game continues until both teams have removed the *same* number of stakes. The Tangu disapprove of winning while favoring value equivalence (Burridge, 1957). The idea that one individual or group should win and another lose bothers them, for they believe winning generates ill will. In fact, when Europeans brought soccer to New Guinea, the Tangu altered the rules so that the object was for two teams to score the same number of goals. Sometimes their soccer games went on for days! American games, in contrast, are highly competitive; there are always winners and losers.

Since values entail broad and abstract cultural principles, we frequently have difficulty identifying them. The sociologist Robin M. Williams, Jr. (1970), in an interpretation of American society, identifies fifteen major value orientations. These include the high value Americans place upon achievement and success, activity and work, humanitarianism, efficiency and practicality, progress, material comfort, equality, freedom, conformity, science and rationality, nationalism and patriotism, democracy, individuality, and racial and ethnic group superiority. Many of these values tend to be interrelated, including those having to do with achievement and success, activity and work, material comfort, and individuality. Others are in conflict, for example, stressing conformity and individuality or equality and racial and ethnic superiority. Moreover, values change. Thus in recent years many of America's more overt racist attitudes have faded. The 1983 annual survey of college freshmen found that, for the first time, a majority supported busing to achieve racial integration in the schools (Astin, 1983). In the same year, 69.3 percent of the freshmen said they believed that being well off was very important; in 1970 the figure stood at 39 percent (see Figure 3.1.) The distinct characteristics of American values become more apparent when we compare them with the values of another culture, such as those of the Japanese, discussed in the accompanying box (p.61).

The Relation between Norms and Values

Values assume considerable importance because norms are usually based on them. Even so, there is not a one-to-one correspondence between norms and values. For instance, some American values favor individuality and competition, yet some norms run counter to these values. Affirmative-action laws, for example, have often allowed minorities to be hired in proportion to their numbers as a matter of fairness, while competitive standards of individual achievement are relaxed. Such a norm attempts to reconcile the values of individuality and competition with the values of justice and equality. Thus conflicts in values are often a source of social change that leads to new norms.

In our daily lives we frequently find that more than one value may also be operating in a given situation. If being honest also means being unkind to another person, we are caught in a conflict of values. You have probably faced situations where the truth will hurt someone and kindness means lying. Hinting gently at the truth or surrounding the hurtful truth with kindnesses or saying nothing at all are norms that attempt to reconcile two conflicting values.

It is important not to confuse norms with values. The distinction is highlighted by a young child's obedience: A child obeys the parent because failure to do so

FIGURE 3.1 Changes in Student Values, 1970-1983

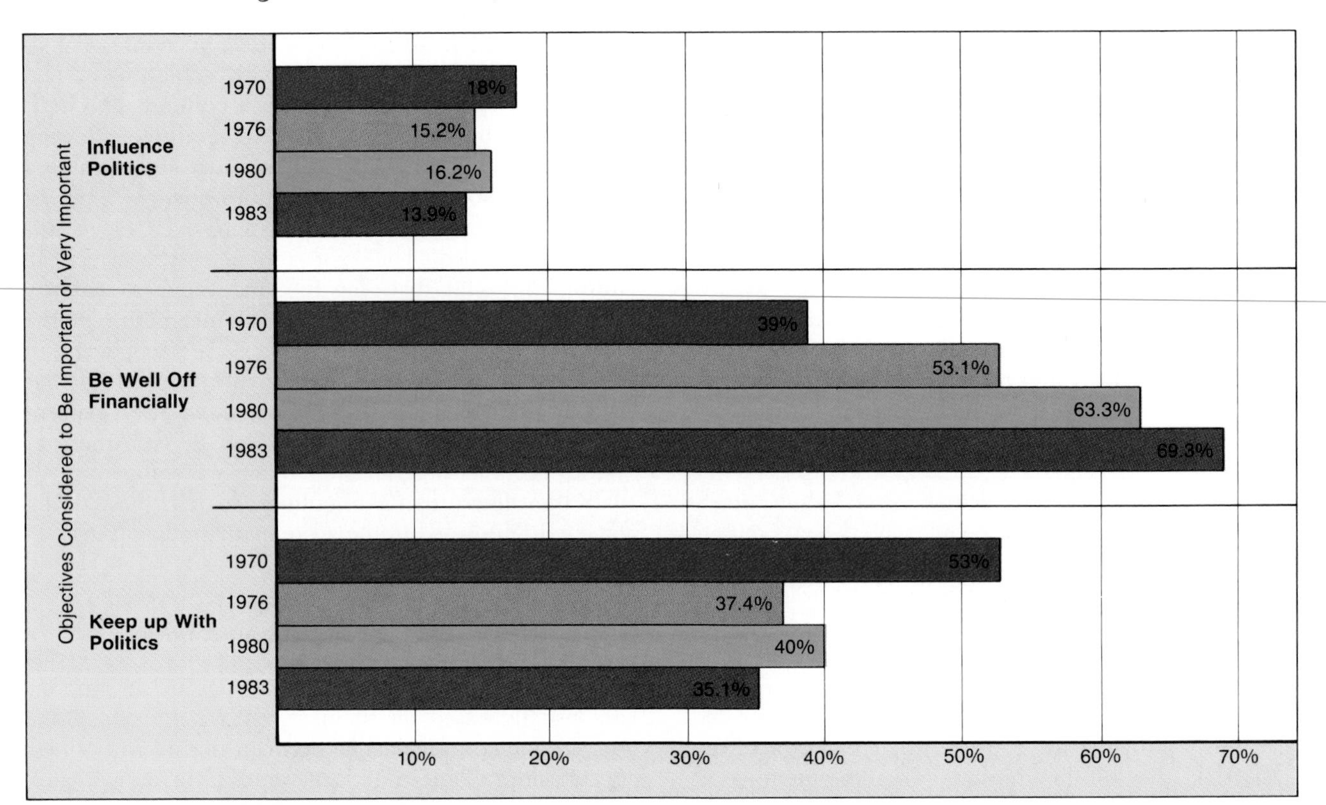

Source: American Council on Education, *National Norms for Entering Freshmen, Fall 1970, ACE Research Reports*, pp. 42–43; and (with the University of California Graduate School of Education, Los Angeles) *The American Freshman: National Norms for Fall 1976, The American Freshman: National Norms for Fall 1980*, and *The American Freshman: National Norms for Fall 1983*.

Every year a sample of new freshmen in 489 colleges and universities completes a questionnaire about their values. The concerns of first-year college students changed considerably between 1970, when the counterculture values of the sixties still predominated, and 1980, when conservative political forces made themselves felt. While the interest in politics fluctuated, the goal of financial success steadily increased in importance.

may result in punishment or jeopardize rewards (a norm). But the child as yet does not judge the behavior as desirable or undesirable in its own right (a value). Likewise, you may stop at a red light even when there is no traffic, yet you do not attach an underlying value to stopping for a red light under these circumstances. In sum, norms constitute rules for behavior; values provide the criteria or standards we use for evaluating the desirability of behavior.

Symbols

The study of the meanings people attach to the things they do and to the things they make is central to the study of culture, as our discussion of values indicated. These meanings may be stored in such *symbols* as the cross, the flag, or even the kiss.

A **symbol** is an object, gesture, sound, color, or design that represents something *other than itself.* For

THE SOCIOLOGICAL EYE ON:

Values in Japanese Life

In recent years Americans have been deluged by television programs, books, and articles acclaiming Japanese business practices and technological capabilities. The journalist Arthur S. Golden (1982) was fascinated by how the Japanese seemed to manage their economic affairs so well. He returned to college to acquire additional sociological and sociologically related skills. He then spent a number of years living in Japan and working in a Japanese company. From this vantage point Golden was able to identify some important values governing Japanese life.

Many of the features of Japanese society that Americans find so impressive—lifetime employment, cooperative management, high productivity, and low crime—emerge from a group consciousness that is central to Japanese values. Whereas Americans typically place a high value on individuality, the Japanese prefer group harmony. Japanese children attend school in uniforms and engage in countless activities that are designed to prepare them for group endeavors. Golden describes a class of third graders who were given pencils and paper and instructed to draw something. The children responded by asking what they, as a group, should draw, and they were unable to begin work until they received the appropriate instruction. Likewise, schooling emphasizes learning by rote rather than creative or innovative thinking. This does not mean that the Japanese do not engage in original thinking. But most Japanese concern themselves more with how the group thinks and feels than with how they as individuals think and feel.

Life in a Japanese company resembles life in the classroom. Employees frequently are expected to wear company uniforms, and they usually work together in a large open room where they are watched by their supervisors. Desks are lined up in double rows, with each desk adjoining another desk face-to-face. Should an employee look up, the worker stares directly at a co-worker. Employees are not addressed by their names but by the title of their positions. These practices emphasize the importance of the group and minimize individuality.

The Japanese also place a premium on hard work. Consequently, workers are often reluctant to ask for an easing of their work loads, even when they are grossly overworked. Golden recounts the case of a recently married young man who clearly had too much to do. His supervisor attempted to redistribute some of his responsibilities among other workers, but the man resisted. He felt that his boss was attemping to shame him by intruding on his work territory. At age twenty-eight the man developed such a severe ulcer that he had to be hospitalized for weeks of treatment. But upon returning to his job, the man resumed his former position, with no change in responsibilities.

Japanese values find expression in their society's norms. A primary Japanese rule is to stick together and not to display aloofness from one another. The Japanese sometimes refer to their society by the term *natto*, a word for a fermented soy bean that sticks together in a gooey lump. At parties Japanese often engage in group singing; they seldom break up into small groups and converse as Americans and Europeans do. Another norm provides that friction be kept to a minimum. Hence they typically hide their feelings, because expressing them can contribute to ill will and dissension.

Because of the economic success of the Japanese system, Americans have looked to Japan for ways to solve their own economic troubles. But the Japanese values of group harmony and hard work allow them to organize their working lives somewhat differently than do Americans. Thus Japanese organizational arrangements and patterns cannot simply be reproduced in an American work setting with its very different values.

Source: Adapted from Arthur S. Golden, "Group Think in Japan, Inc." *New York Times Magazine*, December 5, 1982, pp. 133–140.

example, a circle is nothing more than a closed curve, all points of which are at an equal distance from a point at the center. But for the Oglala Sioux, the circle represents all that they know and feel and believe about the universe.

> The Oglala believe the circle to be sacred because the great spirit caused everything in nature to be round except stone. Stone is the implement of destruction. The sun and the sky, the earth and the moon are round like a shield, though the sky is deep like a bowl. Everything that

In Western society we associate black with mourning, but in Hong Kong white is the symbol of mourning. The traditions and consensus within a society give symbols their meanings. (Brian Brake/Photo Researchers)

> breathes is round like the stem of the plant. Since the great spirit has caused everything to be round mankind should look upon the circle as sacred, for it is the symbol of all things in nature except stone. . . .
>
> For these reasons the Oglala make their *tipis* circular, their camp-circle circular, and sit in a circle at ceremonies. (James Walker, quoted in Dundes, 1968:304)

Like the Oglala's circle, some of the strongest and most pervasive symbols in our cultural life are religious. Think of how many contexts in which you find the Christian symbol of the cross—in everything from jewelry to architecture to rock music.

Symbols do not necessarily look, sound, or otherwise resemble what they stand for. In some cultures black is the color of mourning; in others white or red suggests grief. These colors, like all symbols, derive their meanings from tradition and consensus, not from any qualities inherent in the colors themselves.

People in a society must agree on the meanings of symbols if they are to be understood. A gold band worn on the third finger of someone's left hand tells us that he or she is married *only* because in our culture this is a commonly recognized symbol for marriage. Of course, even though a wedding band is commonly understood to mean the wearer is married, the way the wearer and each of us interprets the condition of marriage has become quite flexible. For some, marriage means a lifelong partnership; for others, it means a commitment as long as it works.

Because symbols are arbitrary, they can be changed. In England two fingers held in a V with the palm in was a rude insult. Churchill turned it around (palm out) during World War II and made it stand for victory in war. Students protesting the Vietnam war made the palm-out V a sign for peace, a symbol of the antiwar movement.

Symbolic interactionists (see Chapter 1) argue that the heart of social life is the interpretation and creation of symbols. They say that humankind's ability to develop culture and to transmit it derives from the human ability to manipulate symbols and to arrive at shared meanings of events. If people are to align their actions with one another they must have common understandings of a situation. Viewed from the symbolic interactionist perspective, culture is nothing more than shared definitions or meanings of frequently encountered events. In this regard, language plays a particularly important part, a matter to which we now turn our attention.

Language

A **language** is a system of verbal and, in many cases, written symbols, with standardized meanings. It is impossible to overestimate the importance of language in the development, elaboration, and transmission of culture. Language enables people to store meanings and experiences and to pass this heritage on to new generations. Through words, we are able to learn about and from the experiences of others. In addition, language enables us to transcend the here-and-now, preserving the past and imagining the future; to communicate with others and formulate complex plans; to integrate different kinds of experiences; and to develop abstract ideas.

The Linguistic Relativity Hypothesis

The Hopi language has no tenses or nouns for expressing time. For the Hopi, life is a continuous present, a continuous movement of becoming. By contrast, the English language has tenses for the present, the past, and the future, and English-speaking people are acutely conscious of time passing. From such observations Edward Sapir (1949) and his student Benjamin Lee Whorf (1956) developed **the linguistic relativity hypothesis;** it states that people adopt the view of the world that is fashioned and portrayed by their language:

> The "real world" is to a large extent unconsciously built up on the language habits of the group. No two languages are ever sufficiently similar to be considered as representing the same social reality. The worlds in which different societies live are distinct worlds, not merely the same worlds with different labels attached. (Sapir, 1949:162)

According to this hypothesis, people interpret the world around them through the categories of their language. In other words, speakers of different languages are said to inhabit different worlds of experience.

A Vehicle for Communication

The Sapir-Whorf hypothesis has made a powerful statement about the influence of language on culture. But recent investigations have discredited the Sapir-Whorf hypothesis that people who speak different languages experience different social realities (Eastman, 1975). It is not that the Hopi ignore time. Rather, their language makes it easier for them to handle time as an ongoing process than as segmented units. By the same token, Americans are not unaware of the continuous flow of time, even though the English language divides time by discrete tenses. In sum, people's capacities to experience various phenomena are not altered by their acquisition of language. It is only that it is easier to communicate about some matters in one language than in another language.

We have just seen that the main elements of culture are its norms and values, symbols and language, each of which has important effects on the way we think and behave. But where did these cultural ideas come from? And how do they change? We will turn now to a consideration of cultural evolution.

BIOLOGY AND CULTURE

Until recently, culture was almost universally thought of as evolving as humans learned to adapt to their environment. Social scientists considered the roles of learning and of language to be essential in this task of adaptation and in the transmission of cultural ideas to succeeding generations. Of course, it was recognized that culture depended in an elementary way on biology as well. For example, early humans could not have made stone tools if they did not have a thumb that could grip things, fingers, good hand-to-eye coordination, and complex brains. In this instance, biological characteristics made cultural development possible. But biology did not directly shape culture.

The Sociobiological View

Over the last decade, a group of biologists led by Edward O. Wilson at Harvard has argued that biology has been the primary force in the evolution of culture (Wilson, 1978; Lumsden and Wilson, 1981). This new perspective, called **sociobiology,** maintains that social groups adapt to their environment primarily by the evolution of genetic traits that shape social behavior. According to Wilson, sociology (and other social sciences) are properly branches of biology.

Darwin's Influence

Sociobiology owes much to the discoveries of Charles Darwin regarding **natural selection,** the process whereby nature favors those best equipped to survive and to reproduce their characteristics by genetic transmission. Take the example of the giraffe, with its long neck particularly well suited for nibbling at leaves in trees. At one time, a chance genetic mutation may have given one giraffe a slightly longer neck than others in the species. Because this genetic trait gave the animal a competitive edge in the fight to survive (in this case, reaching food), it had a better chance to live and pass on the successful trait to its offspring. By contrast, the less fit have a harder time surviving and thus have less reproductive success. Gradually, successive generations of offspring represent in increasing numbers the genetic characteristics that are adaptive. Through this process evolutionary change in the makeup of a species comes about.

The startling claim of sociobiologists is that even human culture and social behavior have largely evolved through natural selection and genetic transmission of traits. To those who insist that our social behavior is learned, they reply that genes may *predispose* us to learn certain things. Consider the following experiment taken from the animal world (Barash, 1977). The experiment requires a dog and a squirrel to move away from food in order ultimately to reach it. A dog fails miserably at the task, while a squirrel solves the problem easily. Why? Although less intelligent than a dog, a squirrel is a member of a species whose nervous system is "wired" to engage in such behavior. In order to reach its food, the squirrel must often jump from tree to tree, choosing a path that takes advantage of branches of adjacent trees that are close together. This approach often entails a circuitous route to the goal. In contrast, a dog must remain on the ground and typically charges straight at its food goal. In the case of the squirrel, natural selection favored the ability to conduct detours and left the squirrel predisposed to learn how to reach the type of goal presented by the experiment. In sum, sociobiologists say that genes construct a brain that is organized in such a way that information is processed more readily in one manner than in another.

Cultural Universals

Wilson (1978:21) asserts that "there are social traits occurring through all cultures which upon close examination are as diagnostic of mankind as are distinguishing characteristics of other animal species." Social scientists define **cultural universals** as those behavior patterns and institutions that are found in all known cultures. The anthropologist George Peter Murdock (1945) identified over sixty cultural universals, such as a system of social status, marriage, body adornments, dancing, myths and legends, cooking, incest taboos, inheritance rules, puberty customs, and religious rituals.

While some social scientists think these "universals" are too vague to have any analytical value, sociobiologists such as Wilson believe they show how much of culture is biologically inherited rather than learned. Wilson maintains that people raised from birth in an environment free of cultural influence would exhibit these cultural universals on their own. He quotes Robin Fox on this issue:

> If our new Adam and Eve could survive and breed—still in total isolation from any cultural influences—then eventually they would produce a society which would have laws about property, rules about incest and marriage, customs of taboo and avoidance . . . beliefs about the supernatural . . . courtship practices . . . gambling of some kind . . . dancing, adultery, and various doses of homicide, suicide, homosexuality, schizophrenia, psychosis and neuroses, and various practitioners to take advantage of or cure these, depending on how they are viewed. (Wilson, 1978:24)

Wilson cites the universal taboo against incest as an example of a cultural universal with a basis in heredity. He says that in avoiding incest, "human beings are guided by an instinct based on genes" (p. 38). Inbreeding, claims Wilson, produces offspring that are genetically less fit than their parents and less capable of producing their own offspring. Darwinian natural selection tends to weed out these individuals while favoring those possessing an inborn mechanism that discourages

Decorating the body, especially the face, is a cultural universal, a behavior pattern found in different forms in all known cultures. (Left, Jack Fields/ Photo Researchers; right, Ethan Hoffman/Archive Pictures)

inbreeding. The transmission of this genetic predisposition through thousands of generations has resulted in a species that culturally proscribes incest.

The Critics of Biological Determinism

The main issue posed by sociobiology is whether culture is a distinctive human creation or the product of genetic programming. Anthropologists such as Marshall Sahlins (1981) maintain that the critical feature distinguishing human beings from other species is the human use of symbols to give meaning to objects and events. More specifically, human beings fashion their behavior according to a meaningful scheme that they themselves have devised. Sahlins says that this scheme—"culture"—does not have its origins in genes, and for this reason sociobiologists have been unable to identify any specific genes for specific behavior.

The sociologist Kenneth Bock (1980) contends that the rapid pace of human history and the wide diversity of human cultures demonstrate that social behavior cannot be explained by biological mechanisms. For instance, in less than two hundred years a revolution has occurred in human modes of transportation, including trains, automobiles, airplanes, and space vehicles. He points out that biology contributes little, if anything, to our understanding of the forces leading to these massive changes.

Likewise, the anthropologist Marvin Harris (1980: 125) argues that the human species is capable of acquiring an overwhelming number of behavioral responses through learning processes, "without the slightest exchange or mutation of genes." These social responses cannot be considered genetically determined because they can be acquired or wiped out in a single generation. For example, influenced by Christian missionaries, some Polynesian peoples gave up their relatively uninhibited sexual ways and took up premarital chastity. And the Mohawk Indians of New York State are well-known for their abilities as construction workers on skyscrapers. "Walking across narrow beams eighty floors above street level, they [are] not troubled by an urge to build wigwams rather than office buildings" (p. 125). Harris insists that the major steps in human cultural evolution—the rise of agriculture, the nation-state, and industrial organizations—have all occurred too quickly for biological evolution to have played a part.

Harris concedes that certain behavior patterns became part of "human nature" because they contributed to the fitness of humans and their reproductive success. But he acknowledges fewer cultural universals than the sociobiologists do. He argues that some traits that the sociobiologists view as universal are not. For example, Harris believes it doubtful that the incest taboo is genetically programmed as a universal trait. He cites practical social and economic reasons for a brother-sister incest taboo in groups that depend on intergroup marital alliances for defense and trade. Similarily, the social fact that both mother and son fear the wrath of a dominant husband and father probably accounts for the rare occurrence of mother-son incest. In contrast, given the greater power and resources of the male, father-daughter incest is *not* rare; an estimated several hundred thousand cases occur each year in the United States alone.

Harris acknowledges that one trait is universal and has a genetic foundation, namely, the human facility for language. Natural selection favored "individuals able to transmit, receive, and store ever-more-complex messages" (p. 123). But Harris points out a paradox here. Language capabilities enhanced our learning and enabled us to acquire and modify behaviors that do not require genes to control them. The learning ability made possible by language helps to account for the enormous variation found in the social behavior of the human species. Hence, critics of sociobiology argue that human behavior is no longer rigidly tied to the gene and cultural evolution has come to be seen as the chief source of behavioral change for human beings.

A Sociological Theory of Cultural Change

In an era of major genetic breakthroughs the debate over the claims of sociobiology will continue. But the idea that cultures evolve may be valid without assuming that genes do the transmitting. Many sociologists have accepted the Darwinian model—the idea that natural selection works through variation and heredity—but have applied it to cultural selection. Genetic mutations are analogous to cultural innovation, and heredity takes the form of **enculturation,** a process by which an initially novel behavior pattern becomes embedded in the lifeways of a social community (Langton, 1979). Enculturation takes place not through the transmission of genes but through learning. What works gets established in a culture, a process that the sociologist John Langton calls **sociocultural selection.** Langton maintains that "there is no valid reason why sociocultural selection, or for that matter social change, cannot be defined in exactly the same way Darwin defined natural selection—as 'the preservation of favorable variations and the rejection of injurious variations'" (p. 302). Of course social change is not neutral. What are and are not favorable variations are subject to social definitions. For instance, the view that mental illness is caused primarily by biochemical imbalances rather than by psychological stress is not only favored but is actively promoted by the drug companies that make enormous profits from this cultural change.

DIVERSITY AND INTEGRATION

Sociobiologists tend to overemphasize the similarities among the world's cultures and to overlook their differences. There is a great deal of cultural variation from society to society. Consequently, different societies tend to evaluate things in different ways. This fact has been the source of considerable misunderstanding and confusion in human history, since most people tend to think their way is the "best" way. Furthermore, *within* a given society, there may be extensive cultural variation. However, most societies are at least loosely integrated. We will examine these ideas in more detail in the following discussions of cultural relativity, ethnocentrism, and integration.

Cultural Relativity and Ethnocentrism

Not all peoples have adopted the same basic values and norms as traditional Western societies. Considerable variation characterizes the cultures of the world. Some groups, such as the Kwakiutl Indians of the Pacific Northwest, competitively strive for social prestige and the individual accumulation of great wealth. Others, such as the Zuñi Indians of New Mexico, favor cooperation, moderation, and the effacement of the individual before society (Benedict, 1946). Individuals from these two societies view aggressive behavior quite differently. Consider another example: One survey of 238 societies found that 193 of them permitted husbands to take plural wives, a practice condemned in Western nations (Murdock, 1949). Consequently, behavior that is deemed appropriate and moral in one society may be deemed inappropriate and even immoral in another. The notion that the elements of a culture should be viewed on their own terms rather than in terms of some assumed universal standard that holds across cultures is known as **cultural relativity.** An understanding of the attitudes and behavior of a people of another culture depends largely on the ability to suspend judgments based on the standards of one's own culture.

Ethnocentrism runs counter to a perspective characterized by cultural relativity. **Ethnocentrism** is the tendency to see one's own way of life, including behaviors, beliefs, values, and norms, as the only right way of living, and to judge others by these standards. It is quite common for the members of a society to believe that they, and they alone, belong to the "best people." Robin Fox (1970:31) has pointed out that "any human group is ever ready to consign another recognizably different human group to the other side of the boundary. It is not enough to possess culture to be fully human, you have to possess *our* culture."

Accounts of the first European contacts with black Africa are a study in ethnocentrism. The letters and journals of fifteenth- and sixteenth-century explorers, merchants, and missionaries overflowed with lurid descriptions of cannibalism, incest, and "unbridled lust." Since the Africans did not practice Christianity, they were labeled "heathens"; since their laws were incomprehensible to the Europeans, they were said to be "lawless"; and since their marriage and family practices differed from those prevalent in Europe, they were judged to be "savages" and "barbarians." The Europeans viewed the Africans as objects of loathing. Ethnocentrism led the Europeans to overlook the accomplishments of great African dynasties such as that of the Sonniki in Ghana, founded in the second century A.D. Not untypical was the following account by a European:

> The majority of them . . . are entirely savage and display the nature of the wild beast . . . and are as far removed as possible from human kindness to one another; and speaking as they do with a shrill voice and cultivating none of the practices of civilized life as these are found among the rest of mankind, they present a striking contrast when considered in light of our own customs. (quoted in George, 1968, p. 25)

Indeed, these accounts tell us more about the biases of the Europeans than about the behavior of the Africans. For most people, culture operates outside their awareness. By virtue of ethnocentrism, they assume that the values and norms of their own society are a part of "human nature." Such attitudes promote group solidarity and loyalty, improve morale, encourage conformity, and foster nationalism and patriotism. But by the same token, ethnocentric sentiments increase hostility toward outsiders, foster conflict among groups, engender racism, and intensify resistance to change. In sum, although ethnocentrism is a source of unity and stability *within* groups, it is a source of misunderstanding and friction *between* groups.

Cultural Integration

A description of the norms, values, beliefs, symbols, and other practices found among a people provides us with only a very limited picture of their social life. A culture is more than the sum of its individual elements, because the parts are interwoven to form a complex whole. The degree to which the parts of a culture form a consistent and interrelated whole is termed **cultural integration.** In a well-integrated culture, there are a few contradictions between the way people think and the way they act; established traditions enable them to make efficient use of the environment and to carry out the daily business of living with minimal inner conflicts. Yet, as the anthropologist Ralph Linton (1947) has emphasized, a highly integrated culture, where religious, economic, and family life are all of one piece, is extemely vulnerable. A people's customs, beliefs, values, and technology are *interdependent.* Changes in one area invariably affect other areas, sometimes throwing the entire system out of balance.

For example, missionaries succeeded in converting large numbers of Madagascans to Christianity. The result? Theft, which was practically unknown in the pre-Christian days, became commonplace and people no longer diligently cared for their homes and villages. The reason? Sanctions against theft and in support of village upkeep lost their power: "The fear of hell and the police are a poor substitute for the fear of ancestral ghosts who know everything and punished the evil doer with sickness on earth and exclusion from the ancestral village in the hereafter" (Linton, 1947:357).

Similarly, the introduction of steel virtually destroyed the highly integrated Stone Age culture of

Japan provides an example of a well-integrated culture that has managed to keep alive its traditions while modernizing society. (J. P. Laffont/Sygma)

aboriginal societies in Australia. To the Europeans who introduced them, steel axes were simply tools that were functionally superior to stone implements. But to the aborigines the ax was more than a tool: relations between families and tribes were based on the ceremonial exchange of cherished stonework. (Arensberg and Niehoff, 1964). These patterns were undermined when the aborigines abandoned their stone implements for those made of steel.

Most cultures are more loosely integrated than were those of the Madagascans or the Australian aborigines; hence, they allow for a certain amount of internal contradiction. This trait is especially characteristic of large industrialized societies where, unlike in tribes, everyone does not know everyone else and people work at different tasks in an elaborate division of labor. Linton (1947:358) writes that "cultures, like personalities, are perfectly capable of including conflicting elements and logical inconsistencies." Such internal differences and contradictions often find expression in subcultures and countercultures.

Subcultures and Countercultures

When the perspective and life style of a group's members are significantly different from the dominant culture of a society, and when they identify themselves as different, we say they belong to a **subculture.** Members of a subculture share a set of norms, attitudes, and values that give them a distinct identity within the society. Subcultures may develop out of occupational groups, ethnic or religious groups, socioeconomic groups, age groups, and so on. Adolescents, for example, build a private world out of their peculiar position as not quite adults and no longer children; medical students share common experiences, goals, and problems, and hence a common viewpoint. Subcultures typically grow among a group of people who find themselves isolated from the conventional world—isolated physically (inmates in prison, soldiers on a base, or poor people in a ghetto), or isolated by what they do and think, by their world of meanings.

A **counterculture** is a subculture characterized by norms, attitudes, and values that clash with or are opposed to those of the dominant culture. The youth movement of the late 1960s and early 1970s had many components of a counterculture. Its members rejected the hard work–success ethic, the materialistic focus, the deferred gratification emphasis, and the sexually restrictive morality of the "establishment." Religious groups like the Unification Church of the Reverend Sun Myung Moon and Hare Krishna likewise have many countercultural overtones.

The Case of the Hispanics

Our discussion of cultural diversity and integration suggests that within modern, complex societies a number of *opposing* forces are at work. Some contribute to diversity and some to integration. Hence, social life is characterized by an interplay of forces advancing, retreating, converging, or diverging in patterns of lesser or greater unity and stability (Simmel, 1955). We can gain an appreciation for these dynamic qualities and processes by considering an illustration, the Hispanic subculture in the United States.

Although Hispanics are often lumped together in the public mind as a single people, they embrace a rich and varied set of cultures. According to the 1980 census, 59 percent of the nation's 14.6 million Spanish-speaking population are of Mexican heritage; 13.8 percent are Puerto Ricans, most of whom reside in New York City; and 6.3 percent are Cubans, most of whom are concentrated in South Florida. These groups use various names to describe themselves. Some use the umbrella term "Hispanic"; others prefer to identify themselves by their nationality—Puerto Rican, Dominican, or Cuban. Still others prefer "Latino," and some Mexican-Americans prefer "Chicano."

The Hispanic population tends to be young and poor, earning half to two-thirds the amount earned by the average American (Canino et al., 1980). Many Hispanics make up a laboring underclass of people who take jobs no one else wants at wages no one else will accept. This structural and economic isolation helps to preserve the subculture from mainstream influences.

Diversity: Distinctive Cultural Patterns

In some respects the perspective and life style of Hispanics differ from those of the dominant Anglo-American culture. Hispanic peoples emphasize the family as a source of comfort, support, security, and identity (Cortés, 1980). Within the dominant society of the United States, the family typically refers to a nuclear unit made up of parents, children, and an occasional grandparent. But among Hispanics, the extended family has flourished—not only parents and children, but grandparents, uncles, aunts, and cousins, by blood or by marriage. An intense sense of family obligation, loyalty, and respect typically cements the individual members to the group. When one individual relocates in the United States, other family members may follow the migrant to the new locale, drawing the family back together again. A strong commitment to mutual assistance within the family often keeps Hispanics from turning to public agencies or social services for assistance in time of need. For instance, elderly Mexicans are seldom placed in nursing or retirement homes, because the elderly enjoy a special status and the traditional family assumes responsibility for them.

Hispanics also place a high value on the inner worth of the individual. They tend to be sensitive to inner dignity and the respect that is owed to others. For this reason they are often particularly sensitive to personal insults or scorn. Spiritual values often take precedence over materialistic values. The Hispanic "tends to think in terms of transcendent qualities, such as justice, loyalty, or love, rather than in terms of practical arrangements which spell out justice or loyalty in the concrete" (Fitzpatrick, 1971:91–92). The Hispanic subculture emphasizes one-to-one relationships more than the American culture does. Impersonal systems or organizations geared to efficiency make many Hispanics feel uneasy. They are used to dealing with others in highly personal ways.

Differences also exist among Hispanic groups. In a recent poll among Spanish-speaking Americans (Russell, 1983), 30 percent said there were significant differences among Hispanic ethnic groups in food and beverage preferences, and 22 percent noted differences in family attitudes; 42 percent cited differences in the way the Spanish language is spoken. Despite these differences, 70 percent said that the Spanish language created a strong common bond among all Hispanics, functioning as a badge of group solidarity.

Most Hispanics in the United States have reached the stage of cultural assimilation: they have adopted many American ways but have kept their own distinct identity. Breaking open the piñata is a traditional highlight of some Hispanic gatherings.
(L. L. T. Rhodes/Taurus)

Integration: Dynamics of Subcultural Change

Subcultures such as those of the Hispanics exist *within* a larger culture, not apart from it. Consequently, subcultures and mainstream culture meet and leave marks on one another at many points. The American culture has been enriched by the introduction of Hispanic food, clothing, dances, and words. The popularity of Mexican restaurants, Caribbean Salsa music, Mexican architecture, and Mexican accents in women's fashion attest to subcultural influences.

At the same time the dominant American culture is profoundly changing the values and behavior of young

Hispanics. English-speaking Americans of European heritage have historically viewed Hispanics from an ethnocentric perspective. Even more significantly, Anglo-Americans have had the power to establish their value preferences as the operating norms of American society. Thus Hispanics have had to make their way in a "foreign" society where English is the language of the workplace, the marketplace, the school, and the political arena. Until recently, Hispanic children in many schools of the Southwest were punished for speaking Spanish in the classroom or on the playground. Even today many Spanish-speaking children are handicapped in classrooms with predominantly English-speaking activities and programs. Further, the realities of American life often force Hispanics into a highly individualistic and competitive environment that in many respects is hostile to the ideals of their traditional culture. In sum, Hispanics have had to relinquish their language and values in order to conform to the dominant Anglo-American culture.

The Hispanic experience is an example of **assimilation,** the process by which a subculture changes through its members' acceptance of the cultural patterns of the larger society. Sociologists have found that it takes about three generations for members of an immigrant group to achieve an identity as Americans rather than as Mexicans or Armenians or Germans or whatever. The sociologist Milton Gordon (1964) has identified three stages of this process. The first stage is **cultural assimilation,** which allows the newcomers to function within the host society by taking on many of its lifeways without necessarily relinquishing their definitions of themselves as a distinct enthic group. Thus Puerto Ricans may learn English, perform their jobs satisfactorily, vote, observe laws and regulations, but still maintain a separate identity as members of a Hispanic subculture.

The next stage (if it occurs at all) is **structural assimilation,** whereby newcomers seek entrance into cliques, clubs, and institutions of the larger society through personal contact with dominant group members. This type of assimilation gradually erodes the unique ties binding individuals within a distinctive subculture. Eventually, it leads to **marital assimilation,** whereby the members of the subculture intermarry on a large scale with members of the larger society. At this point Gordon believes that the subculture has become essentially a historic identity that has little influence on a person's behavior and cultural life.

The assimilation process often brings uncertainty and pain. People may suffer severe identity shocks as they give up old, deep-rooted values for new and often conflicting ones. For instance, the Hispanic value of an individual's inner worth and goodness is not at all the same as the dominant American emphasis on the freedom of the individual to move upward and compete for higher status. As young Hispanics embrace the American ideal of the autonomous individual, they find themselves cut loose from the close-knit, supportive community of their subculture, which they have come to reject as "stifling." But once the young Hispanics have assimilated the American ideal of individual freedom and opportunity, they discover that they are educationally handicapped and that their dream of success remains an empty ideal. The assimilated Hispanic is left stranded —cut off from a traditional culture that offers identity and support and adrift in the new culture. Hence, people may feel themselves out of tune with their culture, a matter to which we now turn our attention.

CULTURE AGAINST PEOPLE

The phrase "culture against people" would seem to be a contradiction in terms. How can culture be against the people who create it, who live in and by it? One answer is that culture exists to civilize raw emotions, to contain desires of passion and violence. Sigmund Freud (1961) believed that conflict was built into the human condition. He argued that people are by nature egocentric, irrational, and antisocial: without coercion, they would never consent to the "instinctual sacrifices" that are necessary in any social order. Thus even while culture's civilizing force enables us to thrive as individuals in a social world, it works against our most primitive impulses and desires.

Another viewpoint holds that some cultures lose touch with basic human needs. Sociologist Philip Slater (1976) believes that American culture neglects our need for community, for engagement, and for dependence. In Slater's view, the high value Americans place on individualism and competition works against the basic human desire for community—"the wish to live in trust, cooperation, and friendship with those around one." We are a lonely people who do not turn to others for help unless we are desperate.

We are also prone to escaping, evading, and avoiding—to what Slater calls the "toilet assumption," the notion that "unwanted matter, unwanted difficulties, unwanted complexities and obstacles will disappear if they are removed from our immediate field of vision" (p. 21). We announce campaigns to clean up the environment, clean out city hall, clear slums, wipe out poverty, mop up wars, and then do very little, as if declaring the problem away, like flushing a toilet, will eliminate it so we can turn our attention elsewhere. As a result we have little experience with the realities of our world. Our basic desire for engagement—"the wish to come directly to grips with one's social and physical environment," the need to understand and feel able to cope with the world we live in—is not satisfied.

As for dependence, American culture emphasizes early self-control. Moreover, Americans believe that each individual is responsible for his or her own destiny. In other societies individuals do not carry the burden of making important decisions and choices alone; choosing a career or a marriage partner without consulting the family or the clan is unnecessary, and even unthinkable. Nor are individuals expected to control their impulses all of the time: the group provides external controls. They can fully vent their anger because they know their friends or family will keep the situation from getting out of hand. Lacking stable communities, constantly moving, living among strangers, Americans cannot count on outside intervention or support. So the desire for dependence—"the wish to share responsibility for control of one's impulses and the direction of one's life"—is not satisfied.

In short, Slater sees our emphasis on individualism, on avoidance of difficulties, and on self-control as contrary to certain basic human needs for social bonds. Others have echoed the view that the culture of competitive individualism has led Americans to self-indulgent excesses and to a narcissistic preoccupation with the self (Lasch, 1978; Veroff et al., 1981). However, Slater also sees evidence that Americans are recognizing the necessity to reconnect with one another and with their physical environment. More and more people are trading in the anonymity of city life for the more intimate ties offered by small communities, both in suburban and rural areas. Many of those who stay in the cities are organizing neighborhood and block associations to address common needs and problems. The number of women who leave the house and enter the workplace increases year by year; for many of these women this is an opportunity to get reconnected with others. And in the process men and women are interacting on a more egalitarian basis. Pollution control, car pooling, and solar heating all reflect a concern for a clean environment and the need to conserve resources. Encounter groups, consciousness-raising sessions, self-help programs dealing with every topic from coping with cancer to investing in stocks wisely, all attest to the desire of people to work together and share information.

On the other hand, reconnection and cultural integration can attain dimensions where they stifle individualism. For example, in the Israeli kibbutz (a communal farm), children, who are raised by the community rather than by their parents, form strong ties with the members of their peer group. The group nurtures and supports the individual, and great emphasis is put on comradeship and caring. The whole community works to help the elderly, the mentally retarded, and the brain-damaged to function within the kibbutz.

The kibbutz therefore satisfies needs for community, engagement, and dependence—but not individualism and autonomy. Those who leave often speak of doing so in order to gain personal maturity:

> Whenever I'm in the city I feel grown up, but as soon as I return to the kibbutz, I feel again as if I were a child. So much is decided for me, so few decisions do I have to make on my own, so guilty do I feel if I do differently from what in kibbutz terms I am supposed to think, do, and feel. (Bettelheim, 1969:272)

The concept of culture, then, presents us with a paradox. We need the skills it gives us to exist as individuals, yet its rules limit our individualism. By its very nature, culture encourages conformity, regularity, and interdependence, yet it provides the context in which we can thrive as individuals. As Robert Frost observed, one moves "easy in the harness."

EPILOGUE

To live is to adapt. This principle underlies all forms of life. Some animals have adapted to their environment by evolving specialized organs and appendages that serve them exceedingly well. For example, evolution has favored the giraffe with a long neck and long legs that allow it to reach vegetation not normally accessible to other animals. But this adaptation has irreversibly chained the giraffe to a particular environment. Should that environment change, the giraffe could find itself as overextended as it looks. Specialization allows an animal to exploit its surroundings more fully. But simultaneously, it limits the animal's ability to survive in new and changing environments.

Like other animals, human beings must also adapt to their environment. We have adapted by remaining in large measure a generalized animal, capable of living in a wide range of environments—witness the nomads of the Sahara Desert and the Eskimo people of the Arctic. Indeed, humans have made their way into outer space, surviving in specially equipped vehicles and walking on the moon in space suits.

The key to these amazing achievements is culture. Unlike animals, whose response to the environment is governed by genetically set and highly specialized patterns of behavior, human beings respond to altered conditions by fashioning new cultural patterns. Cultural evolution can proceed rapidly and innovations are easily diffused. Thus human beings have benefited from a genetic endowment that has freed their brains from set responses and in turn permitted them to develop a flexible list of behavioral responses.

Culture has an additional advantage. It is cumulative, in the sense that each generation need not go through the entire inventive process again. For instance, many techniques had to be mastered and many thousands of years had to pass before human beings learned to make knives out of stone. Even the simplest tool is the result of an extended process of trial and error. But each new generation can learn how to make tools from their elders. The same principle holds for family, economic, and other adaptive group arrangements. Consequently, culture allows each new generation to build on the achievements of the preceding one.

This chapter has provided an overview of culture, the marvelous adaptive mechanism available to human beings. The chapters that follow will examine specific cultural patterns and social arrangements, including the nature of organizations, stratification, and institutions, and will then turn to the subject of cultural change.

SUMMARY

All of the customs, beliefs, values, knowledge, and skills that guide people's behavior along shared paths are part of their *culture*. A culture provides individuals with a set of shared understandings that they employ in fashioning their actions. The map of life that consists of culture has three basic components: norms, values, and symbols.

Language can tell us about a people's view of reality. Sapir and Whorf have theorized that language does not simply reflect culture but actually *shapes* the way we view the world. Other social scientists maintain that people's capacities to experience various phenomena are not basically altered by their use of language. It is merely easier to express certain thoughts in one language than in another language.

How does culture evolve? A recent theoretical perspective, known as *sociobiology*, maintains that social groups adapt to their environment by evolving social traits that are programmed and transmitted by genes. They hold that Darwin's principle of natural selection applies to the evolution of social behavior and cite *cultural universals* as evidence that social traits are hereditary, not learned.

Those who oppose this viewpoint credit learning as the means by which social groups adapt to their environment. These critics downplay the role of genes by pointing out the tremendous variety of social behavior and the fact that many social responses can be acquired or wiped out in a single generation. A sociological theory of cultural evolution holds that cultural traits evolve through learning, but in a process of "survival of the fittest," analogous to Darwin's natural selection.

Customs and beliefs must always be understood in the context of the culture and situation in which they occur. This way of thinking about culture is called *cultural relativity.* In contrast, *ethnocentrism* is the tendency to see one's own ideas, beliefs, and practices as being the only right way of living and the standard by which to judge others.

To the extent that a culture is internally consistent, it is considered integrated. A people's customs, beliefs, values, and technology are interdependent, and changes in one area invariably affect other areas.

American culture is not integrated; it is diverse and inconsistent. Our core values of freedom, equality, and democracy contain contradictions that can lead to confusion and disquiet. One reason for the variations in our culture is the wide range of *subcultures.* Generally, by the third generation, members of an ethnic subculture are assimilated into the larger American culture. But before full assimilation people may suffer identity shocks as old values are given up and new, often conflicting, ones are adopted.

Culture is said by some to work against people. Freud believed that individuals are always struggling against cultural restraints. Slater believes that the accent on individualism and competitiveness in America frustrates needs for community, engagement, and dependence. But a great deal of community, as in the Israeli kibbutz, may stifle individualism.

Culture presents us with a paradox. We need it to exist as individuals, yet by necessity culture limits our individualism.

GLOSSARY

Assimilation. The acceptance of the cultural patterns of the larger society by members of a subculture.

Counterculture. A subculture characterized by norms, values, and attitudes that clash with or are opposed to those of the dominant culture.

Cultural assimilation. The process in which newcomers take on many of the lifeways of the host society without necessarily relinquishing their self-identification as a part of a distinct ethnic group.

Cultural integration. The degree to which the parts of a culture—its norms, values, beliefs, symbols, and their practices—form a consistent and interrelated whole.

Cultural relativity. The notion that the elements of a culture should be viewed on their own terms rather than in terms of some assumed universal standard that holds across cultures.

Cultural universals. The behavior patterns and institutions found in every known culture.

Culture. All of the customs, beliefs, values, knowledge, and skills that guide a people's behavior along shared paths.

Enculturation. A process by which an initially novel behavior pattern becomes embedded in the lifeways of a social community.

Ethnocentrism. The tendency to see the behaviors, beliefs, values, and norms of one's own group as the only right way of living, and to judge others by those standards.

Folkways. Everyday habits and conventions.

Language. A system of verbal and, in many cases, written symbols, with standardized meanings.

Laws. Rules that are enacted by a political body and enforced by the power of the state.

Linguistic relativity hypothesis. The thesis that people adopt the view of the world that is fashioned by their language.

Marital assimilation. The intermarriage of subcultural group members with the members of the larger society.

Mores. Norms people consider vital to their well-being and to their most cherished values.

Natural selection. Darwin's hypothesis of how evolution operates: nature favors those best equipped to survive and to reproduce their characteristics by genetic transmission.

Norms. Shared rules that specify appropriate and inappropriate behavior; the guidelines people follow in their relations with one another.

Sanctions. Socially imposed rewards and punishments that compel people to obey norms.

Sociobiology. A theoretical perspective that holds that social groups adapt to their environment primarily by the evolution of genetically determined traits.

Sociocultural selection. The process by which adaptive social traits are acquired and evolve through social learning principles.

Structural assimilation. Entrance of members of a subculture into cliques, clubs, and institutions of the larger society through contact with new primary groups.

Subculture. A group whose perspective and life style are significantly different from those of the cultural mainstream, and who identify themselves as different; members share norms, attitudes, and values.

Symbol. An object, gesture, sound, color, or design that represents something other than itself.

Values. General ideas about what is good or bad, right or wrong, desirable or undesirable.

CHAPTER 4

Interaction and Social Structure

On a downtown corner in Washington, D.C., is the New Deal Carry-out Shop. It is within walking distance of the White House, if visitors were inclined to walk there, but they never do. On the other three corners of the intersection are a liquor store, a wholesale plumbing supplies showroom, and a dry cleaning shop. Beauty parlors, grocery stores, poolrooms, beer joints, pawnshops, launderettes, and similar establishments abound in the neighborhood. Residential units—typically old, three-story, red-brick row houses long since converted to rooming and tenement units—cluster along the side streets and in the middle of the business blocks. Most of the residents are black and poor.

The carry-out shop is open seven days a week, selling hamburgers, hot dogs, fried-fish sandwiches, cold cuts, ice cream, potato chips, bread, milk, and sundries:

> In this setting, and on the broad corner sidewalk in front of it, some twenty men who live in the area regularly come together for "effortless sociability." They are not, in any strict sense, a group. No more than eight or ten, and usually fewer, are there at any one time. There is nothing to join, no obligations, no one to say whether you belong or do not belong. Some of the men have never spoken to some of the others beyond exchanging a casual greeting. Some are close friends, some do not like others, and still others consider themselves enemies. But each man comes here mainly because he knows others will be here too. He comes to eat and drink, to enjoy easy talk, to learn what has been going on, to horse around, to look at women and banter with them, to see "what's happening" and to pass time. (Liebow, 1967:22–23)

The scene outside the carry-out shop is not too different from that outside "Jelly's," a bar and liquor store located in a run-down building on Chicago's South Side (Anderson, 1978). Middle-class Americans may see these Washingron and Chicago ghetto neighborhoods as grim islands of social chaos. The people seem to be overwhelmed by the social disorganization caused by poverty, unemployment, high crime rates, urban blight, and family disintegration. Yet viewed from the inside, another picture emerges—one of people interacting with one another and, in the course of their daily activities, systematically structuring an ongoing social order.

It is to these matters of interaction and social structure that we turn our attention in this chapter. In the previous chapter we focused on the cultural traditions and rules by which people interpret their experiences and guide their actions. We now consider the people themselves and the web of social relations that they weave with one another. Whereas Chapter 3 dealt primarily with the customs of a people, this chapter describes how they organize their relations with one another.

We will begin by distinguishing between the small-scale, or "micro," and the large-scale, or "macro," levels for examining social relations. We will then focus our sociological eye on social interaction and look at the more immediate, day-to-day activities and relationships of people. In so doing, we will consider the symbolic interactionist, dramaturgical, ethnomethodological, and social exchange approaches to interaction. Then we will turn our attention to the broader structural constraints

Even street corners can be the settings for complex social relationships. On many urban street corners drug users, drug dealers, and prostitutes can be found interacting within their own social structure. (H. Christoph/Black Star)

within which people interact and carry out their daily activities. In so doing we will consider the components of social structure, including statuses, roles, groups, institutions, and societies. Let us begin by returning to Washington, D.C., and "Tally's Corner."

LEVELS OF SOCIOLOGICAL ANALYSIS

Over the course of eighteen months Elliot Liebow (1967) used field-work methods to study the daily routines of two dozen black men who "hung out" on the corner occupied by the New Deal Carry-out Shop. The associations that began on the street corner led Liebow to poolrooms, beer joints, and private houses in the neighborhood as well as to courtrooms, jails, hospitals, dance halls, beaches, and private houses elsewhere in the vicinity of the nation's capital. Two worlds emerged from Liebow's research—and from that of Elijah Anderson (1978) who later undertook a similar study of street-corner life in Chicago.

One world is a view of human behavior at close range, consisting of small-scale structures of human interaction—**microsociology.** At the microsociological level we gain a view of the interpersonal relationships among the men on the street corners. We examine how they see themselves, how they relate to others in face-to-face situations, and how they balance their values and aspirations with their experiences.

The other world consists of a view of the large-scale structures that cumulatively derive from the countless patterned and recurrent activities of the members of society and that in turn shape and channel their actions —**macrosociology.** The macrosociological perspective, which Liebow and Anderson addressed only indirectly, focuses on the organization and distribution of people and resources within the whole of society. These patterns play a powerful role in shaping our lives. For example, the hierarchy of jobs and opportunities, patterns of prejudice and discrimination, and the stereotypes concerning appropriate male and female behavior have an impact on the lives of not only the street-corner men but all of us.

The Microsociological Perspective

The microsociological perspective provides us with the following view of daily life on "Tally's Corner":

> A pickup truck drives slowly down the street. The truck stops as it comes abreast of a man sitting on a cast-iron porch and the white driver calls out, asking if the man wants a day's work. The man shakes his head and the truck moves on up the block, stopping again whenever idling men come within calling distance of the driver. At the Carry-out corner, five men debate the question briefly and shake their heads no to the truck. The truck turns the corner and repeats the same performance up the next street. In the distance, one can see one man, then another, climb into the back of the truck and sit down. In starts and stops, the truck finally disappers. (Liebow, 1967:29)

The truck driver, who is able to recruit only a couple of men from each twenty that he contacts, feels the street-corner men "wouldn't take a job if it were handed to them on a platter." From all appearances, this conclusion would seem to be warranted. But appearances can be misleading, as Liebow demonstrates. In fact, most of the men who refused the driver's offer already have jobs. Sweets, for example, works nights in office buildings, hotels, and other public places, "cleaning up middle-class trash"; Tally, a laborer, has the day off because bad weather stopped construction where he was working. Irregular hours and irregular jobs such as these are the rule in the ghetto. Other men on the street refused work because they were disabled. Some of the men are drawing nearly as much or more money from unemployment compensation then they could earn as laborers. A few are working quite hard at illegal activities —"buying and selling sex, liquor, narcotics, stolen goods, or anything else that turns up" (p. 33). And Tonk is on the corner because he's afraid that if he goes to work, his wife will disgrace him by taking the opportunity to be unfaithful.

Only a handful of the men lingering on the street fit the truck driver's image of them: Arthur has no intention of looking for a job; Leroy is playing pinball instead of reporting to work; last week Sea Cat quit a job without giving notice; and over the weekend Richard drank away his entire paycheck. Why are these men not out working or looking for work? Many people think that the poor do not want to work, that somehow they have never absorbed the work ethic.

The street-corner man, many believe, lives from moment to moment, indulging his whims and giving little thought to the consequences of his behavior or to the future. Working regularly, saving, accepting responsibility for a wife and children, and planning for the future are supposedly alien to him. He does not care about being respectable; in fact, he makes fun of those who are. He lives in a world of gambling, liquor, and drugs, fancy cars and clothes (when he can get them), "fancy women," fast talk, and fast money.

Liebow found this common-sense view to be wrong. The reason these street-corner men live in the present is that the future holds absolutely no prospect for them. Unlike those in the middle and upper classes, they have no investment on which they can hope for a return, no job that promises advancement, no expectation that their children will pursue a higher education. According to Liebow (1967:210–211), the street-corner men should not be regarded as carriers "of an independent cultural tradition," but as a part (the bottom part) of the larger society, which severely limits the extent of their opportunities and chances of success:

> Although he wants to get married, he hedges on his commitment from the very beginning because he is afraid, not of marriage itself, but of his own ability to carry out his responsibilities as husband and father. His own father failed and had to "cut out," and the men he knows who have been or are married have also failed or are in the process of doing so. He has no evidence that he will fare better than they and much evidence that he will not. However far he has gone in school he is illiterate or almost so; however many jobs he has had or hard he has worked, he is essentially unskilled. Armed with models who have failed, convinced of his own worthlessness, illiterate and unskilled, he enters marriage and the job market with the smell of failure all around him. Jobs are only intermittently available. They are almost always menial, sometimes hard, and never pay enough to support a family.

In sum, to understand why these man seemingly fail, why they may refuse work, and why they focus on living from moment to moment, we have to look beyond the street corner to the macrosociological level of social structure.

The Macrosociological Level

Moving back from the close-up view, Liebow analyzes the position of Tally and his neighbors in the American economic system. In so doing, he takes the same behavior that he had examined at the microsociological level and turns a macrosociological eye upon it. The macrosociological perspective directs our attention to the competitive and profit-oriented institutions that dominate American life. It reveals that poverty is profitable—for those on top. The fact that some people live in poverty enables others to live in luxury. The poor do society's dirty work, freeing the well-off from menial tasks (such as mopping floors); provide a market for substandard services and goods (such as day-old bread); and create jobs for others (such as social workers) (Gans, 1973). Tally and his friends perform these functions.

The typically dead-end jobs available to these men include those of unskilled laborer, janitor, dishwasher, elevator attendant, bus*boy*, and delivery *boy*. Not one of these occupations has a "future"—none is the starting point for "moving up the ladder" to a better job. For instance, the positions of busboy or dishwasher in a restaurant do not typically lead to the position of chef or manager. Indeed, the economy is *structured* so that there are several million dead-end jobs. Someone *has* to wash dishes, deliver packages, mop floors—and it is the least privileged who get these jobs. For them it is *structurally* very difficult to move up. Nor is it possible to derive any prestige from these jobs.

> Neither the streetcorner man who performs these jobs nor the society which requires him to perform them assesses the job as one "worth doing and worth doing well." Both employee and employer are contemptuous of the job. The employee shows his contempt by his reluctance to accept it or to keep it, the employer by paying less than is required to support a family. Nor does the low-wage job offer prestige, respect, interesting work, opportunities for learning or advancement, or any other compensation. (Leibow, 1967:58)

Why do Tally and the other men observed by Liebow find themselves in menial, unstable, and unrewarding jobs? Most obviously, they lack the education or training that would qualify them for better jobs. They also lack role models who have achieved success; their fathers held similar jobs, with similar limitations and personal consequences. Most subtly, they lack the contacts in the business world that middle-class people establish while they are growing up and attending school. Being black, Tally and his neighbors have been victims through the years of *institutionalized racism*, a social phenomenon wherein patterns of discrimination become fixed within the social structure (see Chapter 12). Thus, without necessarily intending to be prejudiced, institutions continue to discriminate merely by functioning in established ways. American society, for example, is structured so that blacks and members of other minority groups have trouble getting into the trade unions of skilled labor and thus are excluded from many lucrative jobs. Because school budgets usually are linked to the tax base of the surrounding neighborhood, the educational opportunities of ghetto children are often limited, with poor education leading to poor jobs, and so the cycle perpetuates itself from one generation to the next.

In summary, the attitudes, social relations, and behavior that make up Tally's corner world interact with the macroforces of the labor market, the educational system, and institutionalized racism:

> What lies behind the response to the driver of the pickup truck, then, is a complex combination of attitudes and assessments. The streetcorner man is under continuous assault by his job experiences and job fears. His experiences and fears feed on one another. The kind of job he can get—and frequently only after fighting for it, if then—steadily confirms his fears, depresses his self-confidence and self-esteem until finally, terrified of an opportunity even if one presents itself, he stands defeated by his experiences, his belief in his own self-worth destroyed and his fears a confirmed reality. (p. 71)

SOCIAL INTERACTION

Our discussion of microsociology and macrosociology reveals what can be viewed as two sides of a single coin. Neither aspect can be understood in isolation from the other (Collins, 1981; Wardell and Fuhrman, 1981). Thus the individual worlds of Tally and the other street-corner men were not self-contained, self-generated, or self-sustained. Rather, each man was immersed in an ongoing process of continuous and intimate contact both with his immediate community and with the larger society. As each individual went about his daily activities, he created a social world. But in turn he was shaped and directed by this very world. In this sense, each of the men made his own history and evolved his own unique being as he coped with the requirements of

What's going on here? The woman at right definitely appears to be sizing up the situation. We all continuously define our situations in order to assign meaning to them. (Marilyn L. Schrut)

daily existence. This tie between the individual and society derives from **social interaction,** the process by which people mutually and reciprocally influence one another's attitudes, feelings, and actions. There are several approaches to social interaction, one of the most prominent being symbolic interaction.

Symbolic Interaction

Symbolic interactionists point out that human beings are not the only organisms who live in groups. Wolves, for instance, forage in packs, and ants dwell in colonies. The basis for the wolves' and ants' social existence largely is biological; they are genetically programmed for certain social behaviors. But human beings have benefited from a brain that is capable of fashioning a flexible list of responses. Because they are basically generalized, human beings have been able to adapt to a wide range of environments through external or cultural adjustments.

Human beings, like any other social organism, must "fit" their actions to those of the other members of the group (Blumer, 1969). But without inborn programming, how do people integrate their individual activities so as to achieve *inter*action and enduring relationships? Symbolic interactionists say that the answer lies in the meanings people attribute to various objects and events and to the symbols they employ to convey these meanings to one another. We described the symbolic interactionist approach in Chapter 1. Here we will look at the approach in more detail, focusing on three key concepts: the definition of the situation, constructed reality, and negotiated order.

Definition of the Situation

Sociologist W. I. Thomas (1937) has pointed out that we continuously size up the "here and now" context in which we find ourselves and assign meaning to it. We examine the situation and mentally contemplate various courses of action. Thomas calls this process the **definition of the situation.** The concept draws our attention to the fact that social interaction does not occur in a vacuum. It takes place in specific and concrete settings to which we bring various preconceptions and expectations. For instance, we interpret a wink of the eye not in the abstract but within particular situations (Hewitt, 1979). At a cocktail party or in a singles bar, a wink is often an invitation to another person, a sign saying "I would like to get to know you better." But when used in a classroom by a professor discussing a difficult point, a wink conveys a different meaning. It says, "Aha, clever isn't it!"

In Elijah Anderson's account of street-corner men at Jelly's Bar, he describes how the men go about determining *who* is next to them. Such a definition is of critical importance in this South Side Chicago setting because the person might well be "the law" or, at the other extreme, "the baddest cat in Chicago." Thus before talking to a stranger, a man will try to "read" the person to know how far he can be trusted:

> For this people pay close attention to a variety of symbols the person displays. . . . They listen to the person's language or, as the men say, his "total conversation" and examine it for clues to his residence, associates, and line of work. They check out the way he is dressed. They watch him interact with others. . . . They may even ask someone else, either secretly or publicly, about his trustworthiness. (Anderson, 1978:6)

In this manner the street-corner man seeks to establish what he can expect of the stranger, and what the stranger is likely to expect of him. During this mental process the street-corner man contemplates various courses of action before devising his actual behavior. In brief, he defines the situation.

Viewed from the symbolic interactionist perspective, the behavior people fashion is based on their definition of the situation. But it is not the objects or the events themselves that determine a person's definition (Blumer, 1969). Rather, it is the meanings human beings *impute* to them. Consider, for example, a bank. The meaning we attribute to a bank depends on our viewpoint. It is somewhat different if we are its shareholders, its officers, its examiners, its tellers, its depositors, its loan applicants, Marxists, or bank robbers. And it follows that each person's definition will influence his or her behavior. A shareholder is unlikely to campaign to abolish private ownership of banks, although a Marxist might. A bank examiner scrutinizing a teller's records for evidence of embezzlement is unlikely to view the transactions in the same personal terms that the teller did when dealing with actual customers.

Constructed Reality

Our discussion has suggested that we continually take the stream of information provided by our surrounding environment and make it intelligible through social definitions. In so doing, symbolic interactionists say that we *construct* reality. The sociologist W. I. Thomas was referring to this process when he observed: "If men [people] define situations as real, they are real in their consequences" (Thomas and Thomas, 1982:572). The **Thomas theorem,** as the statement has since been called, suggests that once we assign meaning to a situation, the definition serves to determine not only our behavior but also some of the consequences of our behavior.

The circumstances of the street-corner men studied by Liebow and Anderson illustrate the operation of the Thomas theorem. For centuries whites defined blacks as an inferior people. Since dominant-group whites controlled the critical resources and institutions in American life, they allocated fewer privileges and opportunities to blacks than to members of their own group. Thus, by acting on the basis of their definition, whites *created* a reality in which blacks are disadvantaged: They are less well educated, hold more menial jobs, and have a lower life expectancy than whites. In sum, whites have fashioned a social order characterized by institutional racism (Vander Zanden, 1983; see also Chapter 12)

Negotiated Interaction and Order

The symbolic interactionist concepts of defining a situation and constructing a reality provide us with a dynamic, fluid image of social life. They portray human beings as encountering a world that is often unpredictable and not precise. Hence, individuals must continuously fashion and revise their actions as they define and redefine situations. They constantly "test out" their behavior and modify their actions based on feedback from others. In sum, individuals are said to *negotiate* interaction; that is, they construct their acts and continually "fit" them to the developing actions of others.

Anderson (1978) notes the negotiated nature of a street-corner man's status at Jelly's. His place within the group is always tentative and needs "validation" by others. The men define a person's position by the liberties they allow him and the liberties they take with him. His reactions to this treatment in turn influence their definitions of him. Hence, a man's status is not established once and for all, but is continuously being negotiated in a competitive and precarious context.

The structural functionalists have a sharply different view of social life (see Chapter 1). They do not focus on the continual process of creating and altering social arrangements through symbolic interaction. Rather, they view social order as flowing more or less spontaneously from people's roles and the norms that accompany the roles. Their actions "mesh" with one another because they share a common cultural heritage. For example, having mastered their roles as "men," men know how and when to be lovers, husbands, fathers, and providers, and their conduct is coordinated with that of women and other men (Hewitt, 1979). Viewed in this way, individuals are essentially passive, translating a socially acquired script into overt action. Thus the structural-functionalist perspective emphasizes the structural constraints on human interaction.

Dramaturgy

Over the course of the last two decades or so, several symbolic interactionist theories have emerged. One of the more important is **dramaturgy,** an approach closely associated with the sociologist Erving Goffman (1959, 1974, 1981). Goffman views social interaction from the perspective of a theatrical performance. Life becomes a stage where people interact with one another in the course of their daily activities. Each person is both actor and audience. The parts people play mirror their roles in the larger world. In real life, as in the theater, people "stage" their behavior in ways that they hope will elicit the desired responses from others. Thus social life consists of shaping the impressions that others form of us by the things we do and do not do.

In some ways Goffman's dramaturgical approach differs from more traditional formulations of symbolic interactionist theory. Traditionally, symbolic interactionists have considered each situation to be unique because it includes human activities in different combinations. People must continually "work at" interaction. They must consider, select, and reject various courses of action in order to blend their individual actions with those of other people. In contrast, Goffman attempts to "see behind" these ongoing activities and discern the structures—what he terms *frames*—that invisibly govern them. He concerns himself with the unique features of an interaction only to extract from it the underlying rules people use in staging their performances. In contrast with the traditional symbolic interactionist perspective, Goffman is a structuralist interested in those recurrent, patterned, and tacit understandings—or ground rules—that direct and guide people's public behavior.

Impression Management

Goffman observes that our presentation of self to others involves **impression management**—the manipulation of social impressions. He contends that we have a vital interest in what other people say and do because we depend on them in meeting our biological and social needs. Consequently, in our face-to-face relations in public, we continually monitor or scan individuals for cues that tell us who they really are and what they are really up to. And since other people are also reading us, we have considerable motive to shape their definitions of us, for we can then get them to act as we prefer. Hence, we publicize certain things about ourselves, and attempt to conceal others.

Campus life provides many examples of impression management. College athletes wear their team practice shirts to classes and social gatherings to make everyone aware of their special status. Students "dress up" for on-campus job interviews. At the beginning of the term students undertake to "show" professors how bright they are. And practically no one arrives at a party early or even on time—as it would appear overanxious.

Goffman (1981) finds impression management in many areas of life that we are otherwise inclined to overlook. For instance, it is assumed that universities invite well-known public figures and prominent scientists to deliver lectures to make more information available to the campus community. In point of fact, Goffman says the intent of these activities is to confer the eminence of the speaker on the sponsoring body. The advertising that announces the speaker's appearance is done less to insure an audience than to bring the university to people's attention. Likewise, members of a rock group dye their hair not because it improves the music, but to make their fans feel the show is something exotic and possibly taboo.

Regions

One mechanism for handling impression management is by creating **regions**—places that are separated to some

Through our dress and behavior we create definite impressions of ourselves. (Bernard Pierre Wolff/Photo Researchers)

degree by barriers blocking visibility (Goffman, 1959). There are *frontstage* regions and *backstage* regions. Frequently the performance that people stage in the front region contradicts what they do in the back region. Restaurants, for example, take considerable pains to screen off the backstage dirty work of food preparation—grease, gristle, spoiled food, garbage, flies, and unwashed dishes—from the enticing and appetizing frontstage atmosphere. Backstage the waiters and waitresses drop the facade of geniality that they maintain frontstage in the presence of the customers. On the other hand, some restaurants intentionally display their kitchens to show that they have no backstage, that all is uniformly clean and orderly. Middle-class Americans entertain guests frontstage in living rooms furnished to enhance their status. And backstage in their dorms students ridicule their professors, while backstage in their offices professors joke about their students.

Face-Work

Goffman's (1967) interest in the staging of behavior, especially through glances, gestures, positionings, and verbal statements, led him to investigate face-work. **Face-work** includes the actions people take to convey a positive image of themselves in their dealings with other people. (This research has stimulated sociologists to examine other aspects of interactive rituals such as the gaze or stare discussed in the boxed insert.) In many societies, including our own, people take great pains to avoid "losing face." Through face-work, they seek to control their embarrassment and thus the embarrassment that they and others might have over their embarrassment. Here, too, impression management play a critical part, since "to save face" is to convey a message that one's self-regard is still intact. A "studied nonobservance" of our blunders, errors, and stomach rumblings is one type of face-work. Further, many people deal with threats to face by simply staying away from settings where they are likely to experience humiliation.

When people have lost face, an apology from the offending party may often be necessary to repair the damage. For example, Anderson (1978:199) tells of an incident in a park near Jelly's that involved him in a face-work situation. One of the men, Terry, began "messing" with Anderson in a provocative manner that called upon Anderson to "save face." To resolve the matter, he challenged Terry to an arm-wrestling match. Anderson defeated Terry:

THE SOCIOLOGICAL EYE ON:

Eye Contact and the Social Stare

Consider two strangers seated across from one another in a college library. They look up and their eyes meet. Rather than quickly looking away, they hold each other's gaze as the seconds tick by. What is likely to happen next?

If the two strangers are a man and a woman, the event could mark the beginning of a beautiful romance. But if both are men, they might exchange harsh words and leave the library to begin fighting one another. Allan Mazar, one of a small number of sociologists studying eye contact and social staring, finds that sustained eye contact can mean love, hostility, boredom, or curiosity, depending on the people and the situation.

Much of the behavior associated with the subtle dance of stare and counterstare occurs below the conscious level. Yet at one time or another we all engage in it. Ordinarily, we feel that eye contact between strangers should occur only in a fleeting fashion. To look into another person's eyes and hold the gaze is commonly defined as impolite, even insulting. Hence, in most of us it causes tension. As an experiment, Mazur had his sociology students try staring at other passengers in elevators. (Usually we keep our eyes fixed on the door or the floor indicator). But the staring provoked so much anxiety among the students and the other passengers that Mazur had to discontinue the assignment.

In some settings silent eye contact is viewed as an appropriate form of nonverbal communication. In a bar, silently staring at a member of the opposite sex is a common preliminary to pickups and sexual encounters. It is also permissible to look into another person's eyes if you are well beyond normal conversational distance. Hence, when two people walk past each other on a sidewalk, they might look at one another until they are about five to ten yards apart. Even close friends who have waved or shouted to one another in recognition typically lower their eyes at this distance and do not again gaze at one another until they are close enough to begin talking.

We also use our eyes to show submission, to establish dominance, and to challenge others. Ranking plays an important role. When two people of equal rank converse, the speaker need not look at the listener but the listener is expected to look at the speaker. If the listener holds the speaker in high regard, it is usually thought to be impolite for the listener to look away for even a moment. But if the person doing the listening has the higher rank, he or she can look about at will. Mazur finds it remarkable that eye-contact situations are so well-defined and yet few of us are aware of the explicit rules that govern these behaviors.

Source: Adapted from Glenn Collins, "Stranger's Stare: Baleful or Beckoning?" *New York Times*, April 11, 1983, p. 15.

> Terry looked dumbfounded. The others began to laugh and point at Terry.
>
> Then I said, "Okay, Terry. Let's try it with our left arms? A'right?"
>
> "Okay," said Terry, seeing this offer as an opportunity to save face and redeem himself. The others still looked on, expecting, some even hoping, that I would beat Terry again. But this time I let Terry put my arm to the ground.
>
> As we lay on the ground I said, "Damn, Terry. You stronger than I thought you were!"
>
> "You a pretty strong stud, yourself," said Terry, acknowledging his earlier defeat.

In this manner, Anderson defused the confrontation with Terry and both men avoided "losing face."

The significance of Goffman's work lies in the way he deciphers commonly held assumptions and reveals their underpinnings. His description of how we present ourselves in everyday life demonstrates the subtle qualities we bring to bear in fashioning our behavior. But we also derive from Goffman an overly cynical view of human motivation—he makes social life seem an endless "con game." He emphasizes how individuals use the arts of both concealment and strategic revelation to create impressions that help them to manipulate others. However, critics point out that we in fact experience much of our behavior as "authentic." With our intimate friends and family members we achieve meaningful relationships that are ends in their own right and not merely means to some ulterior goal.

Ethnomethodology

Like Goffman, Harold Garfinkel (1967) focuses attention on the taken-for-granted, routine activities of our daily lives and the understandings that lie behind them. He terms his approach **ethnomethodology.** *Ethnos* is a Greek word meaning "folk" or "people"; *methodology* refers to the procedures used in doing something. Hence, ethnomethodology is a perspective that examines the procedures that people use to make sense of their everyday experience.

Garfinkel and other ethnomethodologists note that people typically experience social life as patterned and continuous. We organize time into days and weeks, with weekends commonly free days and paydays falling at set intervals. The routine of attending college classes differs little whether one is majoring in computer science, physics, or English literature. Traffic regularly flows into cities in the morning and toward the suburbs in the evening. In these and countless other ways life seems to have an orderly and regular cast to it.

Ethnomethodologists suggest that people experience life as having order because they share certain taken-for-granted assumptions. In their daily lives individuals operate on the common-sense notion that society has an independent and objective existence. Linked to this assumption is the belief that society has rules for meething various situations. Yet people are usually hard-pressed to identify the "rules." Indeed, very often the rules are simply background understandings.

Garfinkel (1967) has devised a technique for uncovering these hidden rules: Disrupt people's routine ways of handling situations and see how they handle the disruptions. In one experiment he asked some of his students to act as if they were guests when they returned home to their families. For fifteen minutes to an hour, students maintained the polite distance of guests—speaking only when spoken to, using formal modes of address ("Mr. Jones" instead of "Dad"), avoiding personal exchanges. Two of the forty-nine families thought the students were joking; one ignored the student's behavior; the remainder were upset and annoyed. "Family members demanded explanations: What's the matter? What's gotten into you? Did you get fired? Are you sick? What are you being so superior about? Why are you mad? Are you out of your mind or just being stupid?" (pp. 47–48). In one way or another, the students' families tried to restore "normal" relations and in doing so made explicit some hitherto unstated assumptions about family life.

In other experiments, Garfinkel's students "made trouble" by attempting to bargain for items in a store (something Americans generally do not do); by breaking the rules in a game of tic-tac-toe (erasing the opponent's first move); and by closing in during a conversation so that they were nose to nose with the unsuspecting subject. Each of these violations of the rules of interaction produced confusion and often anxiety (in the students as well as in the "victim") and frequently culminated in an angry rebuke.

By using "upsetting experiments," Garfinkel attempted to understand social settings from "within," as they intuitively seem to the people who live them. He unveiled unrecognized commonplaces by violating them in such a way that they betrayed their presence. The angry and pained responses of people to the "experiments" confirmed for Garfinkel the existence of implicit rules governing social interaction and the tacit structuring of experience by people.

In sum, ethnomethodologists study the unspoken agreements that people use to produce and sustain for one another a sense of social order. They say that these understandings about "reality" are the subjective product of people's interpretative processes. From an ethnomethodological perspective, order is not something engineered by a "society" that functions as an independent entity regulating and mapping human behavior; instead, order arises through processes of everyday life in which people convince one another that "out there" a society "really" exists.

Social Exchange

Both Goffman and Garfinkel study the taken-for-granted and invisible underpinnings of human social interaction. They seek to pull back the veil from social life and lay bare its otherwise hidden rules and mechanisms. We gain a quite different view of interaction from **social exchange** theorists such as Peter M. Blau (1964) and George C. Homans (1974). They portray interaction as a more-or-less straightforward and rationally calculated series of mutually beneficial transactions. Social exchange theory assumes that human beings seek what they perceive to be rewards and avoid what they perceive to be costs. Viewed in this way, everyday social life becomes a "marketplace" where people exchange love, recognition, security, approval, and other intangible gratifications. They make decisions and initiate actions for themselves rather than having their social responses predetermined by cultural scripts.

While symbolic interactionists focus on *process*, exchange theorists focus on *outcomes*. Exchange theorists believe that social interaction depends on receiving rewarding responses from others. When the rewards stop interaction stops and the relationship ends. In a sense, these people engage in a sort of mental bookkeeping, maintaining a ledger of social rewards, costs, and profits. Rewards are positive outcomes. Costs are negative outcomes (physical discomfort, mental anguish, fatigue, concern, and boredom). Profit is total reward, minus costs. Some sociologists (Blau, 1964, 1977) expand the notion of exchange to embrace the complexities inherent in larger social systems such as organizations and societies.

Social exchange theory helps to explain the idea behind the **norm of reciprocity**—the expectation that we should give and return equivalently in our relations with one another. Stated more informally, "One good turn deserves another," or "You scratch my back and I'll scratch yours." Anderson (1978:182) describes the operation of the norm of reciprocity among the men at Jelly's:

> When a regular becomes ill enough to be "off work," group members associated with any of the crowds—wineheads, hoodlum, or regular—will sometimes come to his aid. They contribute out of moral obligation, but also with the hope that their offering will be reciprocated when they are in need. Albert, a regular, became ill and was off work for an extended period. Herman began a collection for him and was able to raise twenty dollars.

And Liebow (1967:161) found that the men on Tally's corner devoted much of their time to "the construction and maintenance of personal relationships." Thus close friends (men who "go for brothers") are expected to help one another out. Failure to assist a "brother" who is in trouble, to share a windfall, or to repay a loan brings friendship to an end.

Exchange principles govern many types of relationships. For instance, sociologists find that individuals tend to pair off with partners who are ranked similarly to themselves in physical attractiveness (Vander Zanden, 1984). Thus attractive people commonly end up with attractive partners and less attractive people with less attractive partners. By following this course they experience the greatest payoff and the least cost. For example,

Does "like attract like"? It has been found that couples do pair off according to how similar in attractiveness each partner judges the other. (Left, Jamie Tanaka/Bruce Coleman; right, Bohdan Hrynewych/Southern Light)

when we try to hold the attention of individuals who are more attractive than ourselves, we often experience considerable anxiety regarding our ability to keep their interest. On the other hand, should we date individuals less attractive than ourselves, we lose reflected prestige among our peers. We avoid complications by associating with individuals who are about as attractive as we are.

Critics of social exchange theory feel that it provides a much too rational and individualistic image of social life. It portrays people as going about life, freely *choosing* among alternative actions based on their individual calculations of rewards and costs. Many sociologists take a different view. They argue that society prescribes through its norms what is and is not appropriate behavior, and thus essentially removes choice and decision from human action. In this sense, critics say that social exchange theory neglects the constraining social elements that affect human behavior. It is to these social elements that we now turn our attention.

SOCIAL STRUCTURE

Our discussion thus far has focused on social interaction. When people interact, many behaviors go on *all at once.* Individuals constantly adjust their actions to fit the changing actions of others. They publicize certain things about themselves and conceal other things as they seek to manage other people's impressions of themselves. They structure their experiences and fashion for one another a sense of social order. And people are engaged in an exchange of activity that they perceive as being more or less rewarding or costly to themselves. Since all these operations cannot be comprehended at once, the aim of using any theoretical perspective is so single out a few attributes for special attention, as we have done in the previous section.

We now shift our sociological eye from the interactive *processes* people use in forming social relationships to the *products* of their interactions. Sociologists employ the concept **social structure** to refer to these products and, more particularly, to the organized relationships that exist among the components of society. In its simplest form, social structure consists of an organization of social positions and the distribution of people in them.

One familiar example of a social structure is the university. Every year a group of seniors leaves and a new group of freshmen enters; some faculty members are replaced; a few new courses are added to the curriculum and a few dropped. Yet despite such changes the structure remains relatively unchanged. Faculty members still design their courses and teach students; students still attend classes and take exams. Of course, change occurs over time. For example, a shift in student interest toward careers in business is likely to cause a shift in the curriculum away from the humanities and toward courses in accounting, management, and finance. And a budget freeze may alter the balance of power between administrators and faculty. But even so, the university remains intact as a unique structure.

The concept of social structure enables sociologists to describe and analyze society as something more than the sum of its individual members. As people carry out their everyday activities, they weave a larger and more inclusive social fabric. Their individual episodes of interaction come together to form a larger whole. Were we to focus only on the events within a single interaction, we would neglect the connections among episodes. It is these linkages that give an additional dimension to social life. From this perspective, society consists of the cumulative outcomes of the individual episodes of interaction that occur among its members. If it were otherwise, social life would be little more than a chaotic collection of people randomly interacting with another.

Social structure can best be understood by breaking it down into its components. At the microsociological level of organization, individual behavior is patterned by statuses and roles; these link individuals to the larger social structure. People in these social positions form groups, which in turn link the microlevel of social structure to the macrolevel, where we find such institutions as the economic system, the political system, and the family. We begin with the first components, status and role.

Status

Ordinarily, we understand the word *status* to mean prestige. However, sociologists use the term somewhat differently. In sociology, **status** refers to a position in the social structure—any position, high or low—that determines where a person fits within the society. For example, Tally, in Liebow's study, was thirty-one years old, black, a school dropout (who could neither read nor write), a construction worker, and an estranged husband and father. All of these statuses affected Tally's life. People would have related to him differently if he had been fifteen instead of thirty-one, a concert pianist instead of a laborer. As this example illustrates, each individual occupies a number of statuses at any given time. Tally was not only a construction worker but also a husband, father, and so forth.

Ascribed and Achieved Status

Some statuses in society are *ascribed*, that is, assigned to a person at birth or at different stages in the life cycle. Being male or female, a Mexican-American, a Rockefeller, a teenager, a senior citizen, are examples of ascribed status. For better or worse, one has almost no control over this kind of status. To be born a Rockefeller in our society guarantees one a high social position; to be born poor and black ensures that one will face obstacles and restrictions. Yet the meanings of these statuses do change slowly. Castes are no longer legal in India, and women have profoundly altered the meaning of their social status in recent years. An **achieved status** is a position a person attains largely through personal effort. Physician, politician, artist, teacher, town drunk, or Boston Strangler—each of these is an achieved status. Thus Tally's age, race, and sex are ascribed statuses; the level of education he has reached, his occupation, and his marital positions are achieved statuses. Yet what Tally, and indeed each of us, achieves is shaped by the **opportunity structure** available to us. In other words, where one is located in the social order determines in large measure what opportunities are available. Tally's children have a different set of achieved roles open to them than the sons and daughters of a successful corporate manager.

Master Status

When one of a person's statuses largely determines his or her social identity, it is called a **master status.** This may be an occupation that takes up most of a person's time and uses most of his or her energy (such as the presidency), or it may be a position of particular symbolic significance. For children in our society, age and gender are the most salient statuses; for example, a child will identify herself as a seven-year-old girl or himself as a five-year-old boy. For adults, occupation is usually most significant. However, a master status may also be an ascribed status such as handicapped, ugly, or beautiful. Today a great effort is being made by certain groups with an ascribed master status—such as women and the handicapped—to weaken the dominance of this status over their lives.

Roles

Every status carries with it socially prescribed **roles**—that is, expected behavior, obligations, and privileges. The difference between status and role is that we *occupy* a status but *play* a role (Linton, 1936). We learn how to perform a role by observing and interacting with others more experienced than ourselves—a process known as socialization (see Chapter 5). For example, from the age of five, American children are taught role behavior associated with their status as students. Raising hands, doing homework, and studying for tests are all aspects of the role that students are expected to play. But these roles are not cast in stone, and individuals alter them as they see fit. Moreover, new roles are constantly emerging as social needs change.

A role exists not by itself but in relation to other roles. Just as the role of daughter cannot be understood except in the context of parents, so all roles have reciprocal relations with certain others: lawyer/client; husband/wife; professor/student; police officer/criminal; and so on. Furthermore, one status typically involves several roles. For example, a medical student fills one role in relation to teachers and others in relation to fellow students, to nurses, and to patients. (See Fig. 4.1, p. 90.) Similarly, an actor relates somewhat differently to other actors, the director, stagehands, the audience, and the press. Thus each status may involve several roles, which are called the **role set** (Merton, 1968).

Role Performance

The expectations we have regarding how a role ought to be played do not necessarily match the way we actually

FIGURE 4.1. A Simplified Illustration of the Role set of a Medical Student

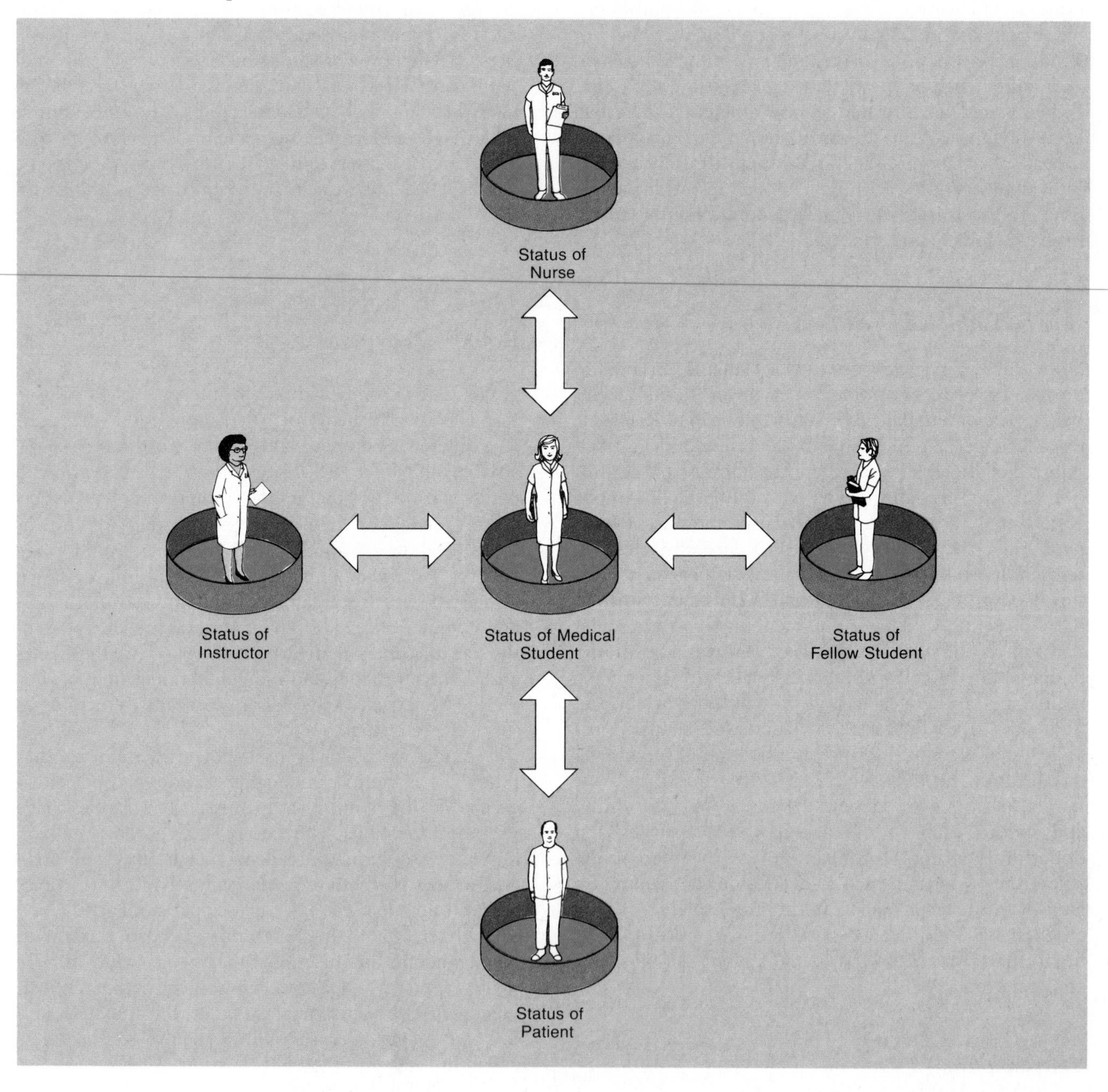

Within the social structure we call "the hospital," a person who occupies the status of "medical student" is tied to other individuals who occupy reciprocal statuses. Thus a status such as that of medical student carries with it a variety of roles termed a role set.

perform the role. Roles provide a social script, but individuals interpret the script in their own distinctive way. Like actors in a play, we need roles and their scripts to participate in social life at all. Without them, human interaction would be chaotic. Yet role expectations typically are loose enough to allow individual interpretations. Even so, there are limits, and people are constantly testing them. To what extent can a police officer, eager to catch a criminal, act unethically or illegally? How far can a father go to demand the "respect" he feels he deserves from his children? How much can you criticize your friend and still be a friend?

When we undertake a new role for the first time, we are likely to be aware of the gaps between the expectations associated with the role and our actual role performance. But although playing a new role may initially involve acting and pretense, people tend to *become* what they play at being:

> One feels more ardent by kissing, more humble by kneeling and more angry by shaking one's fist. That is, the kiss not only expresses ardor but manufactures it. Roles carry with them both certain actions and emotions and attitudes that belong to these actions. The professor putting on an act that pretends to wisdom comes to feel wise. The preacher finds himself believing what he preaches. The soldier discovers martial stirrings in his breast as he puts on his uniform. In each case, while the emotion or attitude may have been present before the role was taken on, the latter inevitably strengthens what was there before. (Berger, 1963:96)

Roles, then, transform both the action and the actor.

Role Strain and Role Conflict

In the course of our daily lives most of us try to bring our role performances in line with the expectations that hold for the role. But this is not always easy or even possible. Sometimes people experience difficulty in meeting the demands of a role. Sociologists apply the term **role strain** to the problems individuals experience in meeting the requirements of a role (Goode, 1960). For example, Liebow (1967:87) found that most street-corner men had married early, with high hopes of being good husbands and fathers. But most failed—at first financially, then emotionally. "Where the father lives with his own children, his occasional touch or other tender gesture is

This policewoman is a strong candidate for role conflict. Her role as a woman and her identity as a black person will not always be in harmony with the duties required of a police officer. (Sepp Seitz/Woodfin Camp & Assoc.)

dwarfed by his unmet obligations. No matter how much he does, it is not enough."

One common source of role strain is **role conflict.** Role conflict ocurs when the carrying out of one role automatically results in the violation of another. A classic example is the situation of black police officers. As blacks, they may feel that the system is weighted against black people; as police officers, however, they are acting as agents of that very same system. Soldiers may also experience intense role conflict. Young men who have been brought up to feel that killing is wrong suddenly are expected to fire guns and drop bombs. Many try to resolve this conflict by not using their weapons. For instance, it is estimated that during World War II, only 25 percent of the soldiers fired back when they were being fired upon (Marshall, 1947).

For the most part, people reconcile themselves to a world in which role strains of one sort or another abound. Yet strains are also a source of structural change. When enough people resist conforming to traditional role expectations, in the case of the women's movements, statuses and roles do change. For example, as a result of the woman's and civil rights movements, structural arrangements of sexism and racism bent and gave.

Social Groups

Roles and statuses are commonly units of social groups. A **social group** consists of two or more people who share a common sense of belonging and who interact on the basis of shared goals and expectations regarding one another's behavior. People are bound together in social groups on the basis of a shared identity and interrelated statuses and roles. Consequently, a social group is more than a mere collection of people who find themselves momentarily brought together in a shopping mall or on a downtown sidewalk. For instance, the men who hang out on Tally's Corner are a group of friends, some of whom call each other "brother."

Groups often form among people of similar status (for example, students getting together for a party or tenants organizing for a rent strike) or a complementary status (for example, a surgical team or an opera company). Some groups are small (a doctor and a patient); some large (a football team). Groups may be formal, such as a board of directors whose members have specific titles and responsibilities and meet regularly, or informal, such as the group on Tally's corner.

Although groups may differ in many ways, their relative size is one aspect that inevitably influences all the others. Size affects not only which individuals within the group will find it possible to interact with one another but also how well the group itself will be able to interact with other groups within the larger society. The sociologist Peter Blau (1977) has shown that the smaller the group, the more integrated it is likely to become. Suppose there is a minority group with ten people and a dominant group with one hundred. If one person from each group become friends, then 10 percent of the minority group but only 1 percent of the dominant group are integrated through friendship. If three from each group become friends, then 30 percent of the minority group but only 3 percent of the dominant group are integrated. If 100 percent of the minority group have a friend in the dominant group, the minority group would be totally integrated, but only 10 percent of the dominant group would be. This is one sociological explanation of why racial integration in the 1950s and 1960s was threatening to many blacks and led to the black power movement: Blacks were afraid they would lose their distinct ethnic identity.

Institutions

Social groups may be thought of as a link between the microsociological and macrosociological levels of analysis. As we progress to the examination of broader and larger-scale processes and structures, we soon discover certain basic needs that every society must confront: (1) organizing activities so that people obtain the goods and services they need to live while the society maintains a balanced relationship with the environment; (2) protecting people from external threats, such as military invasions, and from internal threats, such as crime; (3) replacing people who die or migrate; (4) transmitting a knowledge of statuses and roles, and the skills needed to fill them, to new members (children and immigrants); (5) resolving conflicts; and (6) motivating people to perform their roles by giving meaning and purpose to social activities. According to the structural functionalists (see Chapter 1), these needs must be met in order to ensure the survival of both the people who make up a society and their way of life.

Sociologists use the term **institution** to describe the widely accepted, relatively stable clusters of roles, statuses, and groups that develop to satisfy the basic needs of society and that endure over time. An example is the *family* (see Chapter 13). The family provides solutions to the problems of regulating sexual activity, replenishing the population, assigning responsibility for children and for initiating them into the ways of a society, defining relationships between people in a community (the kinship system), and settling economic questions (such as inheritance). The religious and political institutions sanctify and protect the family.

The more technologically advanced a society is, the more interdependent its members are. Few American families or communities produce everything they need for themselves. Economic institutions such as corporations, organized markets, banking systems, and international trading companies deal with the problems of producing and distributing goods and services. When these institutions fail to provide some people—Tally and his neighbors, for example—with the basic goods, people turn to other, often illegal, means. As the problem grows, new institutions, such as the welfare and penal systems, are developed at the macrostructural level.

Institutions actually serve two kinds of functions: **manifest functions** are those the institutions are openly and specifically set up to perform; **latent functions** are those that are unintended and often unrecognized by-products. Our educational system, for example, has the manifest function of providing opportunity for education to all. But because of differences between schools and selective admissions policies, it has had the latent function of perpetuating inequalities and actually denying some people access to certain opportunities (see Chapter 14). Our economic system is also based on the manifest function of providing equal opportunity for all—we speak of "free enterprise" and "open competition." But in latent ways it protects the advantages of the privileged (see Chapters 10 and 11).

The family, the economic, political, and educational systems, religions, and other institutions are the basic components of social structures around which life in a society is organized. This does not mean that institutions are static. Actually, institutions are quite dynamic, responding to environmental, technological, and cultural changes. Take the example of how remarriage is reshaping the institution of the family. In the past, remarriages nearly always followed widowhood; but today, with the rising divorce rate, more than 85 percent of them follow divorce, and about two-thirds of these remarriages involve children (Cherlin, 1978). Most people have the notion that second marriages are happier and less prone to divorce than first marriages. As Frank Sinatra crooned, "Love is lovelier, the second time around." But sociologist Andrew Cherlin (1978) found that remarried couples are less happy and more likely to divorce than first-married couples. Why? Perhaps because the institution of the family has not caught up with the complexities of stepchildren, stepmothers and stepfathers, and intertwined half-families. The roles and expectations of these new kinds of family members are not well defined. Even language is a problem. Will the father's children allow his new wife's children to call him "Dad" too? Will her children want to call him "Dad"? And who can discipline a misbehaving child? Her stepmother? Her older stepbrother? Or only her biological father? As these families become more common, however, the customs and patterns of family life will change to fit the new and complex relations, and so revamp the family as an institution.

Societies

The most complex macrostructure is a **society**, a comprehensive grouping of people who share the same territory and participate in a common culture. A society is an adaptive mechanism for adjusting to the environment and coping with the basic requirements of social existence. One view, represented by the Lenskis, is that societies evolve from less complex to more complex sociocultural arrangements. As in biological evolution, some societies adapt more successfully to their environment than others. For example, some observers feel that America's evolution from a simple rural network of settlements to a very complex, predominantly urban structure has undermined many desirable social values, including those associated with the hard work ethic and neighborly cooperation. In addition, the economy—particularly, the automotive and steel industries—has

Social structures depend on the complexity of the environment. (Above, Lars Smith/Anthro Photo; below, Larry Lee/West Light)

had difficulty adjusting to changing international conditions and markets. In contrast, some observers point to Japan as an example of a complex society that has adapted very successfully to a modern industrial environment (Vogel, 1980).

Types of Societies

One fundamental way in which societies differ is in their mode of subsistence. The manner in which a society makes its living depends on both its environment and the kinds of technology it has available. The earliest societies were organized around the hunting of animals and the gathering of plants. The members of these societies had to move about in search of game and other food resources that were limited and incapable of supporting large concentrations of people. The hunting and gathering societies typically consisted of small, scattered bands of people. The family fulfilled many of the economic, political, and educational functions that have been assumed by specialized institutions in industrial societies. Social stratification was minimal. Even though subsistence sources were not abundant, people could rather readily meet their needs, allowing considerable leisure time (Lee, 1979).

Pastoral and horticultural societies reversed the relationship with animals and vegetation. Instead of hunting and gathering, they organized animals into herds, and they planted crops. This more powerful strategy for social life allowed much larger societies to develop, and enabled them to stay in one place, until the soil became exhausted. As a result the social organization had to be much more complex, and more elaborate institutions and social statuses evolved.

Not until the invention of the plow several thousand years ago could agricultural societies develop. As they tilled the land more efficiently and learned to replenish the soil's nutrients, people in agricultural societies could settle in one place and support large populations. Cities arose; full-time special roles developed; elaborate political and religious institutions took shape—often together in the form of a king and a state church. Communications became more elaborate in all dimensions, including roads, canals, postal services, written language, and the arts.

Industrial societies are a quite recent development in human history. They are especially powerful because they use scientific technology to overcome shortcomings in the environment and because they have harnessed sources of high energy. We are all intimately familiar with their elaborate institutions. But the question is how long such societies will last as they consume environmental resources and develop weapons that can wipe out entire populations.

EPILOGUE

In this chapter we have considered the building blocks of social life. We began by examining human behavior at close range. At the microsociological level we considered the "small-scale" processes that make up social interaction, scrutinizing the complex web of minute activities that make up people's everyday life. The symbolic interactionist, dramaturgical, ethnomethodological, and social exchange perspectives gave insights into particular aspects of these processes. From them we gained an image of individuals engaged in an ongoing process of creating and changing their social world. These perspectives permitted us to get "inside" people's social experience and grasp how they fashion a meaningful social existence for themselves and others.

We then turned our attention to the macrosociological level. Here we emphasized the "grand scale," scrutinizing broad patterns and forces of social life. This focus derives from the structural-functionalist and conflict perspectives that we considered in Chapter 1. Macrosociological theories approach human behavior in a sweeping fashion, investigating the nature and operation of entire societies. By studying the organized features of social life in this fashion, we see societies as "real in themselves" and as something more than merely the sum of their individual members. We derive an appreciation for "social facts," those properties of social life that cannot be explained by reference to the activities, sensibilities, or characteristics of individual persons. Such social facts exist outside the individual and operate to shape and control his or her behavior (see Chapter 1).

In many respects this chapter is a capsule account of much that will follow. Together with the material in Chapter 1, it puts in place those major perspectives that sociologists employ for looking at social life. And it lays the groundwork for describing and analyzing the structural components that underlie social stratification and various institutional arrangements that are the subject matter of later chapters. Such key concepts as *status*, *role*, *group*, and *institution* will be encountered again and again in the pages that follow. More particularly, the chapter sets the stage for the next chapter, which deals with socialization—the process by which individuals become functioning members of society. In sum, in this chapter we have approached our subject matter much in the manner of prospective home buyers. We gave the "house" a quick "once over," surveying its "rooms" and overall "structure" rather rapidly. We have saved a closer inspection of its parts for later.

SUMMARY

Sociologists approach social life from two levels of analysis. At the level of *microsociology* they study human behavior at close range, examining details of the activities that constitute everyday life. At the level of *macrosociology* they investigate the large-scale structures that cumulatively derive from the countless patterned and recurrent activities of the members of society and that in turn shape and channel their actions.

Operating in a microsociological tradition, *symbolic interactionists* focus on determining how individuals "fit" their actions to those of other individuals. People do so by the meanings they attribute to various objects and events and by the symbols they employ to convey these meanings to one another. Based on their definitions of the situation, they negotiate interaction and construct a social reality. And by defining situations as real, they initiate behaviors that have very real consequences. *Dramaturgy* is one metaphor for looking at interaction in everyday behavior. People "stage" their behavior in ways that they hope will elicit the desired responses from other people.

Ethnomethodologists examine the procedures that

people use to make sense out of their everyday lives. They are especially interested in the taken-for-granted assumptions that people use in finding their way about the world of social experience. By disrupting people's routine ways of handling situations and seeing how they handle the disruptions, ethnomethodologists attempt to identify these assumptions.

Social exchange theorists build their conception of social life from the model of the marketplace: Human beings interact in a series of calculated exchanges to maximize their rewards and minimize their costs. Thus people go about their lives engaged in a sort of mental bookkeeping, maintaining a ledger of social rewards, costs, and profits. *Social structure* refers to the organized relationships that exist among the components of society. The components can be broken down into individual statuses and roles, groups, institutions, and societies. Statuses and roles are the translation of social structure at the personal level. A status is one's position in the social structure—ascribed or achieved.

Social roles are the expected behaviors, obligations, and privileges that are linked to a status. Social roles may be associated with role strain and role conflict.

Individuals in societies gather into *social groups*, two or more people who share a common sense of belonging and who interact on the basis of shared goals and expectations regarding one another's behavior. Groups may be large or small, formal or informal; they may be based on similar or on complementary roles. At the microlevel of society, a family is a group.

We use the term *institution* to describe the widely accepted, relatively stable clusters of roles, statuses, and groups that develop to meet the basic needs of a society. At the macrolevel, the family is an institution.

A *society* is a comprehensive grouping of people who share the same territory and participate in a common culture. Most are classified according to their primary mode of subsistence: hunting and gathering, horticultural, pastoral, agricultural, and industrial.

GLOSSARY

Achieved status. A social position that a person attains through personal effort.

Ascribed status. a social position assigned to a person at birth or at different stages in the life cycle.

Definition of the situation. The meaning people attribute to a social setting; a stage of examination and deliberation in which we size up a situation so as to devise our course of action.

Dramaturgy. A sociological perspective that views social interaction as resembling a theatrical performance in which people "stage" their behavior in such a way as to elicit the responses they desire from other people.

Ethnomethodology. A sociological perspective that studies the procedures people use to make sense of their everyday lives.

Face-work. Those actions that individuals take to achieve or maintain a positive image of themselves in their dealings with other people.

Impression management. The manipulation of social impressions.

Institution. A widely accepted, relatively stable cluster of roles, statuses, and groups that develop to satisfy the basic needs of a society.

Latent function. An unintentional and often unnoticed function of an institution or social pattern.

Macrosociology. That level of sociological analysis concerned with large-scale structures.

Manifest function. An apparent and deliberate goal or outcome of an institution or social pattern.

Master status. One status of a person that largely determines his or her social identity.

Microsociology. That level of sociological analysis concerned with small-scale structures of human interaction.

Norm of reciprocity. The expectation that we should give and return equivalently in our relations with one another.

Opportunity structure. The organization of opportunities available in different parts of society, such as the quality of local schools, the availability of different types of jobs, and the wealth of the area.

Regions. Places that are separated to some degree by barriers blocking visibility.

Role. Expected behaviors, obligations, and privileges attached to a particular status.

Role conflict. A situation where fulfillment of one role automatically results in the violation of another.

Role set. The complex of roles that accrues to a single status.

Role strain. The difficulties individuals experience in meeting the requirements of a role.

Social exchange. A sociological perspective that portrays interaction as a more or less straightforward and rationally calculated series of mutually beneficial transactions.

Social group. Two or more people who share a common sense of belonging and who interact on the basis of shared goals and expectations regarding one another's behavior.

Social interaction. The process by which people mutually and reciprocally influence one another's attitudes, feelings, and actions.

Social structure. The organization of social positions and the distribution of people in them.

Society. A comprehensive grouping of people who share the same territory and participate in a common culture.

Status. A position in the social structure that determines where a person fits in the community.

Thomas theorem. If people define situations as real, they are real in their consequences.

CHAPTER 5

Socialization

At birth we are merely biological organisms, uninitiated in the ways of our society. Through the process of **socialization** we acquire those modes of thinking, feeling, and acting that are necessary to effectively participate in the larger human community. Were it not for socialization, society could not perpetuate itself from one generation to the next, and we would lack a cultural heritage. And without socialization, we could not acquire those qualities that give us our unique nature as social beings. Thus socialization is a twofold process. It is the means by which society transmits its culture to new generations and at the same time the means by which individuals undergo development and change as a result of their social experiences. Through socialization a unique blending process takes place that selectively joins societal patterns of culture to the needs and capacities of the individual organism (Davis, 1949; Gecas, 1981).

As individuals, we experience this blending process in quite human terms. For example, the champion figure skater Emily Greenspan tells how, as a ten-year-old, she confronted the painful aspects of socialization as well as some of its rewards:

> My ten-year-old toes ache from the cold. Only fifteen more minutes until "free style" and I can jump and spin with abandon. . . .
>
> Now almost twenty years later, I remember the tugs-of-war between me and my potential. In my attempt to live up to my athletic promise, I felt considerable pressure from myself, my parents, and my coach. . . . Nevertheless, being one of the kids "with potential," I had the opportunity to develop a love of music, and movement, some degree of discipline, close friendships, early experience with winning and losing, and a feeling—when I walked into school late and my classmates turned in admiration—that I was special. (Emily Greenspan, 1981:59–74)

We encounter the socialization experience in terms of various givens associated with our ascribed statuses. Thus our physique and biological makeup tell us certain things about who we are: male or female, light-skinned or dark-skinned, tall or short. But it is only through our social interactions—with family, friends, teachers, employers, colleagues—that we learn about our *social* identity and internalize the values and roles of our *social* world.

Every society tends to socialize children in its own way. In ancient Sparta young boys were taught discipline, obedience, physical prowess, and self-denial through harsh treatment and deprivation. By contrast, in nearby Athens, parents raised their sons to be aesthetically sensitive and broadly educated as well as athletic. Needless to say, these practices produced quite different individuals (Berger and Berger, 1979). In modern America, middle- and upper-class parents tend to encourage their children to be self-reliant and competitive, whereas lower-class parents foster relatively more submissiveness and obedience.

Four basic elements interact during the socialization process: our biological limitations and potential, the culture and social structure of the society in which we live, the immediate context, and our past experiences. In this chapter we examine the interplay of nature and nurture in determining our social identities. Then we look at some theories on the process of socialization. A consideration of the important agents of socialization comes next, followed by a closer look at socialization early in the life cycle. Finally, socialization in the adult life cycle is described.

SOCIALIZATION: NATURE OR NURTURE?

Social scientists have long debated the issue of how much of what and who we are is determined by our biological makeup (nature) and how much is determined by the social environment in which we live (nurture). In the nineteenth century the scientific community was initially shocked by Charles Darwin's (1809–1882) notion that people and apes share some distant ancestors. Later, though, it largely accepted Darwin's ideas and undertook to extend them to the social domain. Some scholars reasoned that, like other animals, human beings must be born with instincts, or innate predispositions toward certain kinds of behavior. They employed the "herding instinct" to explain the fact that people everywhere live in societies; the "maternal instinct" to explain mothering; the "aggressive instinct," war; and so on. Similar reasoning was used to explain individual differences: one person becomes a thief and another a saint because the first had inherited criminal tendencies and the second had inherited holiness. Nineteenth-century thought was dominated by the notion that human behavior was biologically determined.

Then, near the end of the century, a Russian physiologist named Ivan Pavlov (1849–1936) demonstrated that much behavior is *learned*. Pavlov taught a hungry dog, which salivates instinctively when it sees food, to associate the ringing of a bell with food and to salivate whenever it heard the bell, even if no food was present. Thus his experiment cast doubt on the biological theory of human behavior. Gradually, the medieval idea that a newborn is a *tabula rasa* (blank slate) and that people are *products* of their environment caught on again. The psychologist John B. Watson (1878–1958) proclaimed:

> Give me a dozen healthy infants, well-formed, and my own specific world to bring them up in and I'll guarantee to take any one at random and train him to become any type of specialist I might select—a doctor, lawyer, artist, merchant, chief, yes even a beggarman and thief, regardless of his talents, penchants; tendencies, abilities, vocations, and the race of his ancestors. (1925/1970:104)

The nature-nurture debate goes on, although, in general, the two sides agree that *both* biology and social environment influence development. Sociobiologists, however, argue that many social traits in humans are genetically determined, as they are in ants or other social species (Caplan, 1978; Wilson, 1979). But they argue less from hard data than from analogy to other animals and, in so doing, incite the scorn of many other social scientists, as we have seen in Chapter 3. Most social scientists believe that heredity and learning interact in complex ways, especially in forming our social identities.

Interaction of Heredity and Environment

The number of "personality traits" observed in the first few days of life is surprising. Newborns differ in how energetic or quiet they are, whether they are outgoing or withdrawn, whether they are usually sunny and cheerful or difficult and fussy, and whether they like or dislike stimulation. And these "personality traits" remain stable over a long time (Chess, Thomas, and Birch, 1968; Kagan and Moss, 1962; Willerman and Plomin, 1973).

But the fact that these traits appear shortly after birth does not necessarily mean they are genetically determined; environmental factors such as the mother's diet, her use of drugs, or her degree of anxiety during pregnancy can have an effect on the developing fetus. Most people do not realize that social forces affect our development from the moment of conception (indeed, radiation in the workplace, infectious diseases, and drug use can affect an ovum or sperm prior to fertilization). Nevertheless, the kind of person we end up being is significantly influenced by genetic heritage.

Studies of twins, which attempt to separate the influences of heredity and socialization, show that identical twins are more alike in many characteristics than fraternal twins (Holden, 1980; Farber, 1981). For example, identical twins resemble one another in shyness or wariness toward strangers more than fraternal twins do, suggesting that, in part, shyness may be an inherited trait (Pines, 1982). Yet psychologists are finding that, overall, personality traits seem to be influenced primarily by the environment, with factors outside the home playing a surprisingly large role (Plomin and Foch, 1980; Price et al., 1982).

Although some genes determine very specific characteristics (such as eye color), many genes simply establish a range of inherited potential for various characteristics, which can be developed or stunted by a person's social environment. As Figure 5.1 (p.102) indicates, a child with little innate athletic or musical ability can outperform a potential superstar if the child receives the necessary social supports.

Whatever may be the impact of hereditary factors, their social environment is a powerful influence on development of these Hare Krishna children. (Birgit Pohl.)

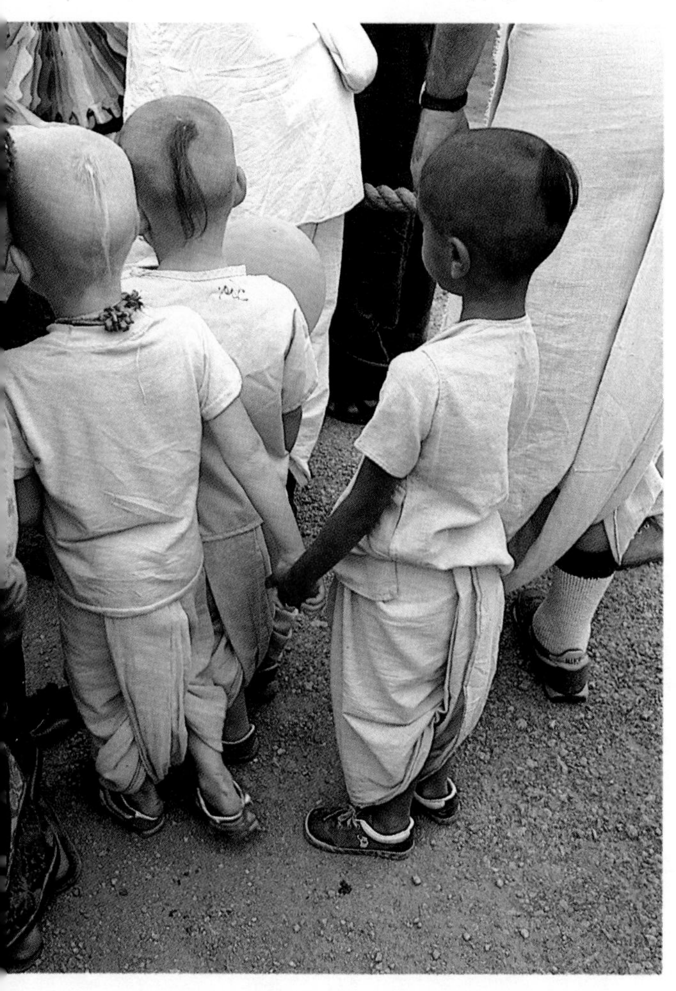

A rich learning environment can stretch genetic potential to its limit, as shown in experiments with chimpanzees, who have been taught to communicate with sign language, play games like blindman's bluff, and function to some extent as socialized members of human families (Temerlin, 1975). But even so, a rich environment cannot overcome the limitations imposed by the genetic endowment. Chimps lack an inherent biological capacity to generate complex sentences and to engage in sophisticated thought. Thus, although the capabilities exhibited by chimps are clearly related to human capabilities, they are not equivalent to human capabilities (Vander Zanden, 1984).

The Effects of Isolation

Socialization also requires an appropriate environment. Consider what happens when a monkey or even a child is fed and cared for in isolation from others. In a classic experiment, the psychologists Harry Harlow and R. Z. Zimmerman (1959) took infant monkeys away from their mothers and raisied them in isolation. Each was given two wire "mothers," one equipped with a bottle, one covered with soft terry cloth. Surprisingly, the young monkeys became attached to the cloth mothers rather than to the mothers with bottles. Clinging to something soft meant more to them than food. Most significant, however, was the fact that *none* of the animals raised in isolation developed normally. When given the chance to associate with others of their species, all were frightened and hostile.

Children and their Caretakers

For obvious reasons, no similar experiments have been performed with human infants. However, we do know of a number of children who during their early years were raised in near-total isolation (Curtiss, 1977). Anna was such a child (Davis, 1949). Because she was born out of wedlock, her mother tried, unsuccessfully, to place Anna in a foster home or an institution. As a last resort she brought Anna home. To avoid the violent disapproval of the child's grandfather, the mother put Anna in an attic room, where she remained for nearly six years. Except for feeding the child just enough to keep her alive, the mother neglected her.

FIGURE 5.1 The Interaction of Inherited Potential and Social Environment

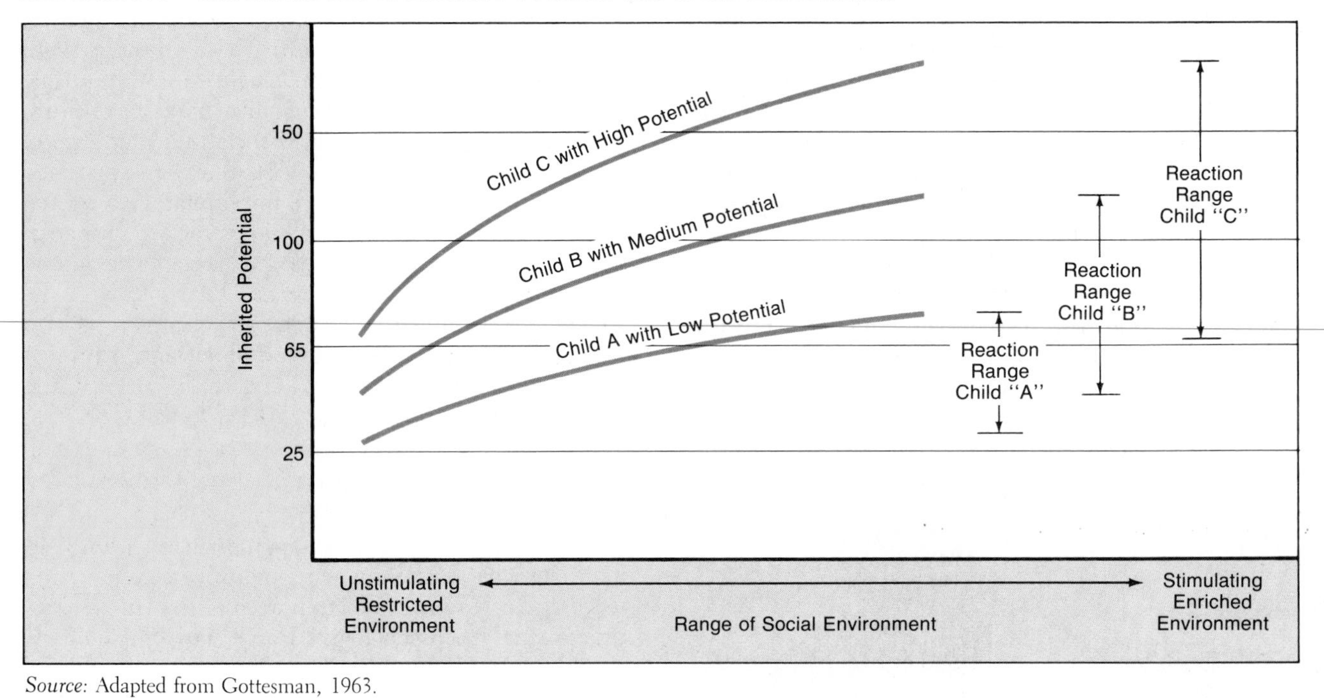

Source: Adapted from Gottesman, 1963.

Although inherited potential establishes the range of socialization, social environment greatly affects the extent to which inherited potential can be realized. This is particularly true for child "C," who has the greatest potential range of the three children in the figure above. With an impoverished environment, "C" would probably develop less than "A," who has low potential, if "A" had an advantageous environment.

When social workers discovered Anna, she could not sit up or walk, much less talk. In fact, she was so apathetic and uncommunicative that they assumed she was deaf, mentally retarded, or both. However, the progress Anna made once she was placed in a special facility indicated that this was not so. With help, she began to talk and eventually learned to care for herself, to walk and run, and to play with other children. What Anna proved in the four and a half years between the time she was discovered and her premature death (from hemorrhagic jaundice) was that practically none of the behavior we associate with human beings arises spontaneously.[1] Clearly, then, socialization is an interactive process. It cannot take place in a vacuum.

[1]Studies of institutionalized children support this conclusion. Even with the best physical care—good food, regular diaper and clothing changes and baths, clean sheets, bright and airy nurseries—infants who are not handled and played with develop slowly, if at all. Mortality rates in orphanages are alarmingly high (Bowlby, 1973; Spitz, 1951).

Any number of psychologists emphasize that we can be optimistic about human development since early maladaptations do not necessarily result in lifelong problems. The psychologist Sandra Scarr (1982:853) observes:

> Human beings are made neither of glass that breaks in the slightest ill wind nor of steel that stands defiantly in the face of devastating hurricanes. Rather . . . humans are made of newer plastics—they bend with environmental pressures, resume their shapes when the pressures are relieved, and are unlikely to be permanently misshapen by transient experiences. When bad environments are improved, people's adaptations improve. Human beings are resilient and responsive to the advantages their environments provide. Even adults are capable of improved adaptations through learning, although any individual's improvement depends on that person's responsiveness to learning opportunities.

Socialization is a reciprocal process in that children also have a profound impact on their caretakers. Mothers of babies with difficult temperaments tend to be "turned off" by them. They stay away from their infants more, look at them less, and interact and play with them less than mothers with "easy" babies do. Since their mothers provide them with less caretaking and stimulation, it is hardly surprising that "difficult" babies later on score lower than other children on IQ tests (Sameroff, 1975). Further, to a surprising degree, parents are the product of the children born to them. Few parents emerge from the experience of raising children without some changes in character, attitude, or behavior. Children's ability to affect parents increases as they gain language competence and encounter new experiences outside the home (Berger and Berger, 1979). For example, when children of immigrant parents attend American schools, they carry back into their homes patterns of behavior that have an enormous impact in hastening the parents' "Americanization."

Another aspect of socialization involves the interaction of siblings in a family. This interaction is especially important because it sets patterns for the way we cope with others later in life. Birth-order position in a family determines to a great extent the type of experiences children will have with other family members. Firstborn children tend to be more strictly disciplined than later-born children and to be more of a focus of parental attention. The appearance of a sibling arouses competitive responses in the firstborn. As a result, firstborns "tend to be more conscientious, achieve higher scholastically, and go to school longer than later-borns" (Forer, 1976: 11). They are also fortune's favorites, more likely than later-borns to be presidents, members of Congress, astronauts, and portraits on *Time*'s cover. Second-borns must learn to work their way around an older, stronger sibling, so they often become adept at diplomacy and negotiation. Parental discipline is usually less stringent in the case of the second-born, which encourages relaxed relationships with people (Snow et al., 1981). The "pioneering" function of older siblings frequently continues across the life span, providing their younger brothers and sisters with role models in coping with divorce, bereavement, widowhood, and retirement (Sobel, 1980). Indeed, because of today's frequent divorces and remarriages, many children form stronger bonds with their brothers and sisters than they do with their parents (Cicirelli, 1980).

Early socialization works both ways. Infants can have a profound impact on the behavior, attitudes, and personalities of their parents. (Elizabeth Crews.)

THE DYNAMICS OF SOCIALIZATION

Three theoretical perspectives—functionalism, symbolic interaction, and conflict theory—have contributed to an understanding of the process of socialization. Functionalism approaches socialization from the perspective of the group rather than the individual (Gecas, 1981). Hence, from it we gain an image of people adapting to the attitudes of others, conforming to role expectations, and internalizing the norms and values of their community. Portrayed in this manner, the object of socialization is to pass on the cultural patterns of a given society or group so that new members can function effectively within it (Elkin and Handel, 1978; Parsons, 1964). This incorporation of values and roles occurs through emotionally significant reactions that are shaped by the social group. The functionalist perspective assumes that small children are relatively unformed; through socialization they develop a social self that reflects the society in which they live. The view we derive of people from functionalism is primarily one of passive beings who are "programmed" in the ways of their society, leading to the criticism that functionalism presents an "oversocialized conception of man" (Wrong, 1961).

We gain a quite different image of human beings as active agents in the socialization process from symbolic interactionist theory. With its concern for how social reality is *constructed* in interpersonal situations, it has been the most influential perspective. For this reason, we will focus on the two great pioneers of symbolic interaction—Cooley and Mead—and then look at the striking contributions of conflict theory to the socialization process.

Cooley and Mead: Identity Through Symbolic Interaction

An analysis of what people say and do is not sufficient to explain behavior. We also need to understand the *meanings* that people attach to their words and actions. In Chapter 4, we discussed the symbolic interactionist position with respect to objects and events. We noted that people employ symbols to convey meanings to one another. In this fashion they define situations, negotiate interaction and order, and construct reality. We now take symbolic interactionist theory a step further and consider its application to the self. According to symbolic interactionists, we not only attribute meaning to other people and the world about us, but we also attribute meaning to ourselves. The self is the notion that each of us has that we possess a unique and distinct identity—that we are set apart from other things and people. It is the cluster of ideas that we employ in defining ourselves. Like other aspects of social life, our self-images and self-conceptions are not givens. Rather, they derive from our interaction with other people. By virtue of the self, we experience ourselves as distinct entities, beings who have continuity across time and who possess individual identities.

Charles Horton Cooley

Adults may take having a sense of self for granted, but we are not born with a sense of self. From observing his own children, Charles Horton Cooley (1864–1929) developed the idea of the **looking-glass self**—in our imagination we mentally assume the stance of other people and look at ourselves as we believe these others see us. We acquire our sense of self by seeing ourselves reflected in others' behavior and attitudes toward us and by imagining what others think about us.

According to Cooley (1956, 1964), the looking-glass self involves three processes; presentation, identification, and subjective interpretation. We start by *imagining* the way we appear to others, then we *identify* with how we imagine others judge that appearance, and finally we *interpret* those judgments for our own self-image. For instance, we imagine how others evaluate our attractiveness and intelligence. Next we conclude that others perceive us as attractive and intelligent (or ugly and dull), and we think of ourselves in similar terms. Then we react to this image—we experience feelings of joy, happiness, and satisfaction (or despondency, sadness, and dissatisfaction). Clearly, the self in this process is not simply a portrait (a mechanical reproduction) drawn on a blank piece of paper by parents or others. The person being socialized acts, interprets, and imagines in response to interactions with others. In sum, the individual imputes meanings to himself or herself.

George Herbert Mead

Moving beyond Cooley's analysis of internal processes, George Herbert Mead (1863–1931) traced the development of self-awareness back to the interaction between parent and child (Mead, 1934). At a very early age, children begin to realize that they depend on other people (usually their mothers) for their comfort, and that their behavior influences the way these people act toward them. Infants learn that crying brings food, smiles bring cuddling, and so on. Gradually, as they explore different ways of arousing desired responses in others, they acquire a vocabulary of **significant symbols**—conventionalized gestures (smiles, screams, and words) that people around them understand. Mead believed that social interaction cannot exist without symbols and that symbols gain significance only in the context of social interaction. In learning to communicate symbolically, children learn to think about themselves and their behavior by reacting to how others respond to them.

Mead was among the first to conceive of individual psychology in social terms. He believed the self was composed of two parts: the active, spontaneous, idiosyncratic self, which he called the "I," and the social self (the internalized social expectations and demands), which he called the "me." The subjective "I" is the product of individual distinctiveness; the objective "me," the product of socialization. Without the "me," orderly social interaction could not occur; without the "I," social interaction would be mechanical and monotonous. With these two complementary parts, we are able to reflect on our own behavior and develop a sense of inner continuity, or identity.

> The self is something which has a development; it is not initially there at birth, but arises in the process of social experience and activity, that is, develops in the given individual as a result of his relations to [the social] process and to other individuals within that process (Mead, 1934:135).

Mead did not resolve the problem of how we gain a sense of I, the subjective sense of self, but the sociologist Norbert Wiley (1979) has offered a solution. Initially, infants have no sense of I. They view themselves simply as part of other objects as they are fed and bathed and changed. Eventually, baby and parent exchange smiles or giggles, and the baby begins to experience a "we" relationship. And in that "we" experience the baby gets a sense of a subjectivity, or an I, from the parent. The baby begins to understand that it too has an ego, or subjective sense of I. It realizes that the parent is reacting to that I, just as the baby is reacting to the parent's I. Thus the I, like the me, is social in origin. A sense of I enables the baby to hold internal conversations with the "me" and thus extend the socialization process. "The development of conscious and moral responsibility seems to require that baby think of himself as having agency, or subject quality, in which responsibility inheres" (Wiley, 1979:96).

With this new sense of self, children begin to take on the social roles they observe around them. For hours on end, two- to four-year-olds play at being mothers and fathers, mail deliverers, and doctors—often embarrassing adults with the accuracy of their imitations. In effect, the child identifies with people who figure importantly in his or her social world, whom psychiatrist Harry Stack Sullivan (1953) called **significant others.** Children at this age seem especially fond of playing mothers fussing over babies who have wet themselves and lecturing make-believe children on their behavior. By enacting the behavior of significant others, they come to incorporate the standards, attitudes, and beliefs of parents and teachers within their own personalities, a process termed **internalization.**

In time children learn to imagine how people will respond to them without actually having to act out the situation. Thus a five- or six-year-old will stop with her hand halfway to the cookie jar and say to herself, "No, you'll spoil your appetite." Mead (1934) conceived of thinking as an internal conversation between the self and others who have become part of the self. Individuals talk and reply to themselves much as they would carry on a conversation with others. They thus become *objects* to themselves, mentally viewing themselves as if they were in the shoes of other people. The subject doing the viewing is the "I" aspect of the self; the object being viewed is the "me" aspect of the self. Thus individuals simultaneously assume a *dual* perspective as both subject ("I") and object ("me"). The individual becomes aware of himself or herself, Mead wrote, "not directly or immediately . . . [but] only by taking the attitudes of other individuals toward himself within a social environment or context of experience and behavior in which he and they are involved" (p. 138).

Imitating adult roles serves an important socializing function. (Patrick Ward/Stock, Boston.)

Gradually, children develop a generalized impression of what people expect from them and of where they fit in the overall scheme of things—what Mead called the **generalized other.** For example, to play baseball, a child must understand the rules of the game and the roles of the players. Similarly, to "play the game of life"—that is, to participate in a given social context—children must know their position in that context and the values and attitudes held by its members must be internalized by the children.

Conflict Theory and Socialization

The conflict perspective puts the experience of socialization in a different light. At the macro level, it takes note of how social customs and institutions are arranged to perpetuate class distinctions. The functionalist argument that socialization is the natural process of teaching children how to be members of their society may appear benign, conflict theorists argue, until you realize that child-rearing practices vary by social class and affect the life chances of those being socialized. As we will see in Chapter 14, a teacher will treat children from different social classes differently, thereby perpetuating the domination of one social class over another in a subtle and powerful way—by subjecting children to it before they are old enough to know what is happening to them. As for the symbolic interaction process, conflict theorists argue that the result is "false consciousness." In the course of their interaction with others in a capitalist society, individuals acquire a sense that they occupy a "natural place" (as a worker, a woman, or a black) without realizing that others have put them there (Bourdieu and Passeron, 1977).

Karl Marx: Legitimizing Oppression

Karl Marx (1906; 1959; 1963) built his theory on the view that capitalist society is torn by a fundamental conflict of interest between capitalists and workers. He then attempted to explain why this rift did not erupt into full-scale warfare and the toppling of capitalist rule. The answer he provided lay in his view that workers are socialized into false consciousness.

Marx contended that institutions such as the educational system and other forms of communication are employed by the capitalist class to foster a false consciousness among the masses. These institutions seek to legitimize social inequality by propagating an ideology that says existing arrangements are right and reasonable. They glorify individual achievement and the pleasure of consumption that capitalism brings. And they foster the workers' hopes for future upward mobility for themselves and their children, fears that representative democracy could be lost in social revolution, and concerns lest their absolute living standards be imperiled by social change. As a result, workers are socialized in traditions that contribute to passivity and compliance (Della Fava, 1980).

Sigmund Freud: Social and Biological Conflict

In his later writing, Freud, one of the giants of modern psychology, also took on a conflict view of socialization. Freud, however, was concerned with conflict not between classes but between society and the primal biological drives of sex and aggression. A contemporary of Mead and Cooley, Freud (1856–1939) believed that every society has to repress and channel the primitive drives of people; otherwise civilization will be destroyed. But by forbidding and punishing behaviors associated with instinctual drives, society gives birth to individual psychological and emotional problems. Although the instinctual impulses are driven from our conscious awareness, they continue to affect our behavior as unconscious motivations, often with bizarre and unhealthy outcomes.

Freud (1977) said that we begin as amoral, egocentric, aggressive, pleasure-seeking infants. He used the word **id** to describe the part of the self that is the reservoir of sexual and aggressive urges, which he believed were inborn biological givens dominated by the pleasure principle. Society—by way of parents—interferes with children's pleasure seeking: parents fail to gratify the child's demands for food at various times; they force the child to regulate bowel movements; and they punish the child for masturbating. As the child struggles to accommodate to these parental demands, what Freud called the ego begins to develop. The **ego** is the rational part of the self that interprets information obtained through the senses and that finds realistic and acceptable ways of satisfying biological cravings. However, the pleasure-seeking infant is not yet "tamed."

Learning to control our physical urges is an important part of growing up. Freud thought that the ego—the rational part of the self—develops as the child learns to adapt to society's demands. (Peeter Vilms/Jeroboam.)

Young children still have powerful sexual and aggressive desires, but realizing that their parents have enormous power over them, they fear being punished for these desires. Children begin to internalize their parents' ideas of right and wrong and so develop a **superego,** or conscience. They learn to repress socially unacceptable desires and, ideally, to redirect their energies into socially approved channels.

Freud's view of the process of human development is thus radically different from Cooley's and Mead's. Cooley and Mead saw socialization as the gradual, complementary merger of individual and society, whereas Freud argued that socialization was forced on small children very much against their will. Freud therefore believed that socialization is never complete. The id continues to press for gratification. The ego's function is to control these lustful and antisocial drives, while at the same time modifying the unrealistic demands of the perfection-seeking superego. Driven one way by biology, the other by society, we are—in Freud's view—subject to continuous torment (Freud, 1962).

AGENTS OF SOCIALIZATION

It is clear that, for the most part, socialization does not simply "happen." It happens because people and institutions "make" it happen. Any person or institution that shapes a person's values and behavior is an **agent of socialization.** Although these agents are particularly important in the early years of the life cycle, socialization is a lifetime process that continues across the entire life span. To be effective, it appears that the socializer must be respected by the person being socialized. The sociologist Morris Rosenberg (1979) has found that for adolescents who did not value the opinions of parents, siblings, teachers, or peers, these opinions had little impact. However, if they considered these people significant others, their opinions mattered. Most of the important socializers in our lives fall into five major categories —the family, peer groups, the media, the school, and the workplace. Each of these categories represents different segments of society, and the relative influence of each changes as we grow older.

The Family

Parents are, for the first few years at least, the primary world to children; they are the mirror in which children begin to see themselves and the source of ideas about what is and is not important. It is from parents and family that children first learn values and behaviors.

Much of a child's socialization in the family is conscious and deliberate. But a great deal of it is not. As we saw earlier, birth order in the family can lead to certain patterns of social interaction that are influential in later life. Moreover, the family is not an autonomous agent; rather, it reflects the attitudes, pressure, values, and folkways of the social class, religion, ethnic group, and region of which it is a part. We will examine the impact of one of these—social class—before we consider various models of parenting.

The Impact of Social Class

The behaviors adults encourage and discourage and the ways in which they discipline children vary with social class. The sociologist Melvin Kohn (1969) found that working-class parents value obedience, neatness, cleanliness, and respect. They want their children to conform to traditional standards of behavior and to do as they are told. They focus on the immediate consequences of a child's actions and tend to use physical punishment to enforce discipline. Middle-class parents, in contrast, are more concerned with children's motives and intentions than with their actions per se. Usually, they attempt to reason with their children, to make them understand why they should or should not do something. These parents value curiosity, happiness, and, above all, self-control. They want their children to be self-directed. Middle-class parents often use psychological punishment—the withdrawal of their love and emotional support—as a means of control.

Kohn (1976) suggests that these different approaches to the raising of children are directly related to the parents' occupations, particularly to three aspects of the job experience: how closely supervised the person is, how routine the job is, and how complex it is. Whereas most white-collar jobs involve some measure of initiative and independence, as well as an ability to get along with people and to manipulate ideas, blue-collar jobs usually consist of carrying out a supervisor's directions. Success in the blue-collar world depends on following rules and orders, and working-class parents tend to train their children to follow orders. In like manner middle-class parents try to prepare children for the reality of middle-class life as they know it.

The sociologist E. E. LeMasters (1975) has also found that the child-rearing practices of blue-collar parents differ from those of white-collar parents. Working-class fathers attempt to transmit to their sons the same code that they themselves employ in regulating their lives: Men ought to demonstrate the strength and "guts" to defend themselves physically, the fortitude to "stand up" to women, the cleverness to succeed in the "big poker game" of life, and the stamina to "tough it out" in the face of adversity. Blue-collar fathers see their parenting task as one of preparing their sons for occupational roles, whereas blue-collar mothers see themselves as socializing their sons for family roles as husbands and fathers. However, working-class fathers are content to leave the rearing of their daughters to their wives. (In the next chapter we will consider how children learn the social roles associated with being males or females and how this affects them throughout life.)

What Is Good Parenting?

Within the United States today many parents preoccupy themselves with being "good" fathers and mothers. They worry about the psychological consequences of their child-rearing practices, as demonstrated by the steady stream of books, pamphlets, and magazines that are read on "proper" parenting. Yet this is a relatively new attitude. The French historian Philippe Ariès (1962) tells us that in the Middle Ages the concept of childhood as we know it was unheard of. Adults regarded children as small adults. Child rearing consisted of letting children participate in adult affairs. And until relatively recently, the lot of children was uniformly bleak (deMause, 1974). Large numbers of children were what today we would label battered children.

One observer of current child-rearing patterns, Marie Winn (1983), contends that childhood is again undergoing profound change. She says that children today lack the innocence that their parents and grandparents had as children. Youngsters once ignorant of adult matters are now made aware not only of sex and violence, but also of drug abuse, injustice, deceit, death, political corruption, and economic instability. This loss of innocence Winn attributes to the sexual revolution of recent decades and to the parade of erotic material on television. Additional factors include the soaring divorce rate and the prodigious increase in the numbers of working mothers. Not only are children provided with less supervision and left to their own resources, they also often become the confidants of their parents, and thus they are brought into intimate contact with adult problems. These changes are attributed to a belief that children should be exposed early to adult experience if they are to survive in a complex and uncontrollable world.

In recent decades psychologists have spent considerable time and energy examining child-rearing issues and debating the relative merits of authoritarian parenting (forcing a child to obey) and permissive parenting (giving a child more or less free rein). As a result of his studies, Gordon Allport (1954) took the side of permissive parenting. He believed that "the child who feels secure and loved *whatever he does* . . . develops basic ideas of equality and trust" (italics added). According to Allport, authoritarian parents give children the impression that power and authority, rather than trust and tolerance, are the basis of human relationships. Other critics of a stern upbringing argue that authoritarian parents may provoke antisocial behavior and rebellion with their sternness or, on the other hand, may generate passivity and dependence, as the child simply gives in (Baumrind, 1966, 1980).

Diana Baumrind (1966, 1980) rejects the idea of permissive parenting. In her studies, she found that children mistake permissiveness and noninterference for indifference. She suggests two ways that permissiveness handicaps children: first, by not letting them learn the costs of nonconforming behavior, and second, by not giving them opportunities to argue and rebel, thereby permitting them to formulate their own positions. In Baumrind's view, parents should be authoritative, not authoritarian—enforcing the child's rights as well as their own "in a rational, issue-oriented manner" so that the child learns how to balance reponsibility and freedom. Authoritative parents see their children as maturing through stages that require a successive transfer of power and responsibility to the children.

Which viewpoint is right? A major study by a group at Harvard (White, Kaban, and Attanucci, 1979) followed children from age seven months to three years and their parents, using both field observation and objective tests. They found that good parenting, at least in the early years, requires a great deal of interaction with the child, along with firm and consistent discipline. "The children who developed the best . . . were in the company of a person who cared very deeply for them for a good deal of their waking time every day" (p. 155). Many of these parents made a point of talking with their children frequently.

A noteworthy, though not unexpected, finding was that mothers spent twice as much time with firstborn children as with later-born children. As a result, at age three the firstborns showed greater early language and cognitive development than did the later-borns at the same age. The mother's level of education and verbal ability did not appear to be important factors. What mattered was how much she interacted with the child, and birth order was a major determinant of this.

A growing body of research points to the conclusion that good parenting cannot be defined by a set of magical recipes (McClelland, 1978; Collins, 1981). Much has to do with the underlying parent-child relationship. In daily life the same parents display a wide variety of behaviors depending on the situation. They may be restrictive or permissive, warm or cold, and consistent or inconsistent. And as we noted earlier in the chapter, a child's characteristics influence the treatment he or she elicits from adults. Moreover, parenting includes not simply what a parent does but also how a child perceives and defines the parent's actions. Consequently, specific practices such as breast feeding, mode of toilet training, and nature of discipline are often less important than how the parent and child *feel* about one another. Increasingly, developmental psychologists are saying that parents can best serve their children by enjoying and loving them.

Peer Groups

The inequality of parents and children enables parents to force children to obey rules they neither understand nor like. But peers are relatively equal. By virtue of their age, sex, and rank (as child and as student), peers "stand in the same relation to persons in authority" and therefore "see the world through the same eyes" (K. Davis, 1949: 217). Among peers, socialization focuses more on the children's own interests and activities than on the priorities of adults. Among their equals, children may learn the meaning of exchange and cooperation. Through peers, and especially friends, children gain insight into other people's feelings, learn how to handle intimacy, and find ways to achieve mutual understanding. These capabilities are the key to interpersonal adjustment not only in childhood but across the life span (Youniss, 1980). And peers share information about such matters as sex and ways to evade and manipulate parents and teachers. But peer groups can also be authoritarian and demand intense conformity from their members.

The importance of the peer group increases as children grow older, reaching its peak when they become adolescents. This coincides with the diminishing of parental influence, as young people attempt to gain independence from adults. Contributing to the waning of parental influence is the overall decline in the influence of the older generation in this century. The pace of social change has been so great that much of what parents know is seen by their children as obsolete or irrelevant (Elder, 1975).

While peer groups are important to all adolescents, they are especially influential when parental guidance, affection, and attention are lacking. As Baumrind (1975) found, alienated and delinquent adolescents are more deeply affected by their peers than are adolescents who are not alienated from their families and do not have a history of delinquency.

In peer groups, young people can defend themselves against the ambiguities of adolescence. In most traditional societies children win adult status early by undergoing rites of passage. When they emerge from such ceremonies, boys are men and girls are women, with all the rights and responsibilities accompanying these roles. In our society, adolescence is a long period of transition. Adolescents are neither children nor adults. Their responsibilites and their capacity and desire for new experiences increase; yet in many ways they are forced to remain dependent. By aligning themselves *with* peers and *against* adults, young people who are still financially dependent on their parents (they may remain so for years if their parents finance college and graduate education) and who are still learning instead of working, can achieve some sense of autonomy.

Yet it is easy to overemphasize the "generation gap" (Troll and Bengtson, 1982). For most teenagers both their parents and the peer group are important anchors

In adolescence, identification with a peer group becomes important. Pressure from such a group may produce a striking degree of conformity. (Nancy J. Pierce/Photo Researchers.)

in their lives. When the issues involve matters of musical tastes, personal dress, entertainment idols, drinking, marijuana use, smoking, and academic cheating, adolescents tend to be most responsive to the preferences of their peers. But when the issues have to do with future life goals and core values, they tend to be most responsive to the preferences of their parents (Davies and Kandel, 1981; Krosnick and Judd, 1982).

In the last decade the importance of peer groups as agents of socialization during post-adolescence appears to have increased, as growing numbers of people consider "singlehood" as a way of life, not just as a temporary condition. (In 1980, 18 million Americans between the ages of twenty and thirty-four were single, an increase of 64 percent over the previous ten years). Many single men and women live in a subculture of their own, built around clubs and apartment complexes, transitory relationships, and the continuing search for identity. To some degree, the peer group—the people who frequent a club or bar, the work or recreational group—becomes an extended family. (For further discussion of this way of life, see Chapter 13.)

The Media

For many children, television has become a major agent of socialization. Indeed, television is the primary babysitter for American children. By nine months many infants are watching television (although not necessarily comprehending it) for an hour-and-a-half a day (Singer, 1983). By three and four years of age, they average four hours a day of viewing (Singer and Singer, 1981; National Institute of Mental Health, 1982). Overall, children in the United States spend more time watching television than they spend in school or, very likely, in direct communication with their fathers and mothers.

Television viewing can have both positive and negative effects. On the good side, experiments show that watching programs that emphasize sharing, cooperation, and self-discipline (such as *Mister Rogers' Neighborhood*) encourages these types of social behavior in children (Cater and Strickland, 1975; Singer and Singer, 1983). Television can also portray good health attitudes, such as not smoking. And for children who live in impoverished environments, television is undoubtedly a major source of stimulation and instruction.

Although the positive socializing effects of television are still unclear, a great deal is known about the effect of TV violence on children. A 1982 report released by the National Institute of Mental Health concluded that there is now "overwhelming" evidence that excessive violence on television leads directly to aggression and violent behavior among children and teenagers. The report was based on about 2,500 studies and publications since 1970. It stated, "Television can no longer be considered as a casual part of daily life, as an electronic toy. Research findings have long since destroyed the illusion that television is merely innocuous entertainment" (p. 87).

A long-term study of children in an upstate New York county found a strong relationship between early viewing of television violence and aggressive behavior in the teenage years. In fact, a preference for violent TV shows was shown to be a more accurate predictor of aggressive behavior than socioeconomic background, family relationships, IQ, or any other single factor (Cater and Strickland, 1975). It is difficult to say which comes first, the aggressive disposition or the preference for violent shows, but the relationship between the two stands. Other research also suggests that the heavy viewing of television in the preschool years puts a child at risk for problem behavior by early elementary school age (Singer and Singer, 1981, 1983).

The television industry has shown a reluctance to clamp down on video violence. For one thing, the responsibility for producing television shows is divided among many groups of people, each of which believes that "forces and factors outside their control dictate what the program fare shall be" (Cater and Strickland, 1975: 66). The writers and producers must please the network executives, who have the final say on what is aired; the networks have to "sell" their programs to the advertisers, who want to back shows with big ratings; and big ratings come with the action-packed shows, which apparently appeal to viewers' desires to see sex and violence, portrayed on the screen (Waters, 1982).

Not everyone, however, feels that viewers, adults as well as children, should be offered this fare of sex and violence on television. Pressure groups, such as the Coalition for Better Television and the Moral Majority, are putting pressure on sponsors to withdraw their advertising from programs that the groups find offensive. It is too soon to tell whether these pressure groups will have an impact on television programming, but it is significant that television's largest advertiser, Procter & Gamble, has refused to sponsor shows it regards as containing excessive sex, violence, and profanity (*The New York Times*, June 17, 1981).

In addition to violence, television tends to promote sex role stereotypes. According to one survey, prime-time male characters outnumber female characters three to one. Women are typically portrayed as weak, passive satellites to powerful, effective men and are most commonly cast as either lovers or mothers. Blacks fare little better. Although a small percentage of black characters emerge as unrealistically romanticized figures, the vast majority are shown in subservient, supporting roles (Waters, 1982).

More subtly, children who spend much of their free time in front of the TV are likely to become jaded. Compared to what they see on television, real life may seem dull, passé. In the words of one child, "I'd rather watch TV than play outside because it's boring outside. They always have the same rides, like swings and things" (*Newsweek*, February 11, 1977:67). Television gives one the illusion of having been places one has not been and having done things one has not done, and thus promotes spectatorship: watching instead of doing. For many children, watching TV has supplanted such traditional activities as playing outdoors, making models, collecting, reading, and perhaps even talking. (Television replaces the "what did you do today" hour in many households.) Television may also give youngsters the unrealistic idea that most problems can be solved in thirty or sixty minutes.

The School

By defining television primarily in recreational terms, we often overlook its socializing functions. In contrast, the school is an institution that is established explicitly for the purpose of socializing people. Indeed, in modern societies the school is the primary agent for weaning children from home and introducing them into the larger society. They may *learn* math and social studies, but they are *socialized* by the role of being a student. Life at school is a drastic change from life at home. In the family, relations are built around emotional ties ("I'm spanking you because I love you"). At school, children are expected to obey not because they love their teachers or depend on them but because rules are rules and must be obeyed.

In most schools students do not participate in decision making about rules or curricula or other issues that affect their lives; they do not even have the right to speak up, move around, or go to the bathroom without permission. An extensive study of today's schools concluded:

> [There] is no more firmly rooted tradition than the one that holds that children must sit still at their desks without conversing at all, both during periods of waiting, when they have nothing to do, and during activities that almost demand conversation. Yet even on an assembly line, there is conversation and interaction among workers, and there are coffee breaks and work pauses as well. (Silberman, 1971:128)

While the official purpose of school is to teach young people technical and intellectual skills, it also serves the function of teaching them cultural values and attitudes and preparing them for their roles as adults in an office or factory. As work and authority relations change in modern society, schools are changing too. In Chapter 14 we examine more fully the functions that education serves today.

The Workplace

At best, schools prepare individuals in only a general way for positions in the workplace. Consequently, when people start a new job, they may go through a formal socialization program, with classes and a set curriculum, or an informal process of "on-the-job" training. Even in an organization with a formal training program, much of the socialization to the organization's values and outlook happens informally. For instance, you interact with your coworkers and boss and you find that some things you say are studiously ignored while others get an enthusiastic response. Thus you undergo a period of initiation during which you learn the skills and vocabulary of your new position, the formal and informal pecking order of the organization, and its written and unwritten rules (see Chapter 8).

Workplaces vary in how much they want to socialize their workers. At one extreme, socialization at IBM, in many fine hotels, in leading acounting firms, or in the State Department touches the most subtle and personal aspects of self. Employees are expected to personify the organization's image every minute of the day. But most companies and organizations demand much less, expecting only that you do your job well.

Whether one is socialized individually or in groups makes a difference. In army boot camp or a large sales training program one goes through the experience with others. Peer relations and group norms become significant sources of sharing and sometimes of resistance to the organization. Being socialized individually makes one more dependent on the superiors who are doing the "breaking in" (Wheeler, 1966; Van Maanen, 1976; Mortimer and Simmons, 1978).

While some careers build on a person's existing qualities, others (such as medicine, law, the military, and police) require **resocialization.** Training programs are designed to strip away the self-images and perspectives that are the results of previous socialization—a process known as **desocialization** —and to replace them with a new outlook and self-image. Resocialization occurs gradually over a period of time and is experienced differently from profession to profession and from individual to individual. The workplace is not the only situation in which resocialization is needed (see box). However, it is possible to identify six stages that most people experience during resocialization (Light, 1980).

During the first stage, recruits are made to feel different. For example, psychiatric residents, who had learned to see themselves as competent young doctors, are told they will go slightly "crazy." Veteran police officers treat rookie cops as novice outsiders who must prove themselves (Light, 1980).

The second stage involves a discrediting process. Military inductees are given haircuts, uniforms, and numbers (on dog tags), and otherwise stripped of their civilian identities. Veterans tell rookie cops to forget everything they learned at the police academy because it

Stripped of their civilian past, these Marine recruits begin the process of resocialization in a highly dramatic way. For most of us, this process proceeds more subtly and gradually. (Thomas B. Hopker/Woodfin Camp.)

will be useless on the streets. Discrediting serves the dual purpose of breaking down the premature image that recruits have of themselves as ready and competent professionals, and of destroying preconceptions about the career so that *re*socialization can take place.

Typically, a period of conflict and confusion follows. Nursing students mutter that school is not what they expected (Davis, 1968: Simpson, 1979). Psychiatric residents wonder if senior staff members really mean it when they tell the residents that a psychiatarist's principal task is not to cure patients but to understand them and to attempt to relieve their symptoms. Rookie cops find their ideas of absolute right and wrong attacked.

Most neophytes do not realize that others are experiencing the same conflicts and uncertainty. The combined effects of feeling different, discredited, and confused lead to despair. The novices are unable to maintain their old sense of self under the onslaught of conflicting norms and values. At this point, some entertain the possibility of dropping out of the program, and a few do so. Others muddle through. They no longer try to understand or justify what is going on; instead, they simply do what is expected of them. In short, they stop resisting.

The more individuals immerse themselves in the behaviors of what they hope to become (whether nurse, psychiatrist, or cop), the more sense the new attitudes and values make. Resocialization occurs in this stage. Nursing students begin to align themselves with their teachers (who conceive of nursing in broad, theoretical terms), against ward personnel (who see nursing in terms of specific tasks). Rookie cops begin to dissociate themselves from the general public on the one hand, and from the police establishment (represented by the "desk jockeys") on the other. "Your only friends are gonna be other cops 'cause they're the only ones who have been there and know the score" (Van Maanen, 1976:53).

A period of self-affirmation follows. Finally, the individuals internalize the world view of the career, and accept its norms and values as their own. Ex-recruits reevaluate past experiences in the new terms, with some amusement about how naïve they were at the outset. The rookie has become a cop; the resident, a psychiatrist; the recruit, a soldier.

STAGES OF SOCIALIZATION

Although socialization takes place across the entire life span, it is experienced somewhat differently by children than by adults. Recently, social scientists have made detailed observations of the psychological and social development of children. The work of Erik Erikson, Jean Piaget, and Lawrence Kohlberg—defining, respectively, stages of psychosocial, cognitive, and moral development—has attracted particular interest. Although Erikson and Piaget emphasize the maturational basis for socialization in the first twelve years of life—a biological clock sets new capacities for social and psychological development in motion at different stages of life—all three have stressed the importance of social context and social interaction in shaping these capacities.

THE SOCIOLOGICAL EYE ON:

Resocialization of Vietnam Veterans

Although the Vietnam War is now more than 10 years behind us, the problems it generated for some of those who fought in it persist. Studies reveal that up to 800,000 Vietnam veterans still suffer varying degrees of difficulty readjusting to peace time. Some psychologists believe that post-traumatic-stress-disorder (PTSD) has afflicted at least half of the combat veterans. Among the problems experienced by the men are guilt, sleep disturbances, impaired memory, identity confusion, cynicism, and loss of intimacy. To many men, coming home did not mean peace but nervous breakdown, suicide attempts, divorces, job problems, and encounters with the law. In a small number of cases, veterans have fled to western states' wilderness areas and Alaska to find sanctuary (Davidson, 1984).

Sociological research has provided insight into some of the problems of Vietnam veterans. A major five-year study of the resocialization of Vietnam veterans found that adjusting to civilian life was not just a matter of individual character but was affected by social circumstances and background. For example, there was a direct relationship between how much combat veterans had seen during their assignments in Vietnam and how large a readjustment they had to face afterward. On returning, veterans with social disadvantages such as a lower educational level, coming from a single-parent home, or being a member of a minority group had a more difficult time resocializing themselves into the values and responsibilities of civilian life. The importance of social supports was highlighted by the success of veterans with supportive spouses. Finally, a factor unique to the resocialization of Vietnam war veterans was the opposition to the war back home after 1968. The study found that veterans who served before 1968 had fewer difficulties readjusting than did those who were in Vietnam after 1968 (Laufer et al., 1981).

No one would expect it to be easy to return from any war—the horrors do not easily vanish. Yet the Vietnam veterans have had more difficulty adjusting to civilian life than have soldiers returning from World War II or the Korean war. For many, socialization to American society has been a process not of reintegration but of estrangement. What has gone wrong?

For one thing, many veterans feel the return to civilian life was too sudden. As one former soldier put it:

> You're in the Army one day and out on the streets the next, bye now. . . . That's it. . . . You really need some pasture time to think about where you've been and where you're going. It just happens *too* quick, you're really not prepared. . . . (Faulkner and McGaw, 1977:309-310).

Many sociologists agree. The new enlistee is carefully socialized into military life. He learns the rituals and behavioral norms that are expected of him. He has time to shed the habits of civilian life before he is sent to war. But he is sent home cold. There is none of the "transition time" so necessary in career changes. "If the full ritual of leave-taking is not allowed, the man may not pass fully into his new status" (Becker and Strauss, 1956, in Faulkner and McGaw, 1977). Vietnam veterans explained the problem this way:

> Guys like me, they come back from Vietnam, bang! Here's civilian life. Now, go out and make a go of it. *It would have been better if they had a true transition period. After four and a half years in the service you become involved in a different society.* [Author's italics] (Faulkner and McGaw: 310–311)

The reversal of norms complicated the veteran's *reentry* into the civilian world. Norms that applied only yesterday in a war are now not only irrelevant but illegal. Where high enemy body counts were once a sign of achievement, violence now is prohibited. "Where drugs were used by many to escape from the harsh realities of war," continued drug use will only create a new problem in civilian life (Faulkner and McGaw, 1977:306). Talking about their experiences and feelings might help, but many veterans find that their war years are essentially unshareable. They find that most people back home do not want to hear about the details of a war they feel uncomfortable about. The Vietnam veteran feels excluded from society. These vets did not return home to fanfare, parades, and celebrations, as did the World War II veterans (and as did the Iranian-held hostages in 1981). Most Vietnam vets feel that the government has not provided the same types of programs and benefits that other veterans have enjoyed. The vets' cumulative sense of injustice, frustration, annoyance, and anger create a sense of anomie: society has lost its familiar norms for them. At this stage the vet is "a marginal man, a person 'in limbo' between two cultural identities—that of the *socialized soldier* and that of the *resocialized citizen*" (p. 316).

FIGURE 5.2 Erikson's Eight Stages of Life

Stages	A Psychosexual Stages and Modes	B Psychosocial Crises	C Radius of Significant Relations	D Basic Strengths	E Core-pathology Basic Antipathies
I Infancy	Oral–Respiratory, Sensory–Kinesthetic (Incorporative Modes)	Basic Trust vs. Basic Mistrust	Maternal Person	Hope	Withdrawal
II Early Childhood	Anal–Urethral, Muscular (Retentive–Eliminative)	Autonomy vs. Shame, Doubt	Parental Persons	Will	Compulsion
III Play Age	Infantile–Genital, Locomotor (Intrusive, Inclusive)	Initiative vs. Guilt	Basic Family	Purpose	Inhibition
IV School Age	"Latency"	Industry vs. Inferiority	"Neighborhood," School	Competence	Inertia
V Adolescence	Puberty	Identity vs. Identity Confusion	Peer Groups and Outgroups; Models of Leadership	Fidelity	Repudiation
VI Young Adulthood	Genitality	Intimacy vs. Isolation	Partners in Friendship, Sex, Competition, Cooperation	Love	Exclusivity
VII Adulthood	(Procreativity)	Generativity vs. Stagnation	Divided Labor and Shared Household	Care	Rejectivity
VIII Old Age	(Generalization of Sensual Modes)	Integrity vs. Despair	"Mankind" "My Kind"	Wisdom	Disdain

Source: Reproduced from *The Life Cycle Completed: A Review*, by Erik H. Erikson, by permission of W. W. Norton & Company, Inc. Copyright © 1982 by Rikan Enterprises, Ltd.

This figure shows the developmental crises that must be resolved at each stage of life and the outcome of successful resolution.

F	G	H
Related Principles of Social Order	Binding Ritualizations	Ritualism
Cosmic Order	Numinous	Idolism
"Law and Order"	Judicious	Legalism
Ideal Prototypes	Dramatic	Moralism
Technological Order	Formal (Technical)	Formalism
Ideological Worldview	Ideological	Totalism
Patterns of Cooperation and Competition	Affiliative	Elitism
Currents of Education and Tradition	Generational	Authoritism
Wisdom	Philosophical	Dogmatism

Erikson: Psychosocial Development

Erikson's central concern is with the feelings people develop toward themselves and the world around them. In *Childhood and Society* (1950), Erikson described eight stages of human development. He refers to these stages as developmental crises—periods when we confront major issues of life. Growth and successful resolution at each stage depend on the growth and degree of resolution at the preceding stage. Thus each of these crises may be partially or fully resolved. And depending on people's makeup and experiences, there is an opportunity to continue resolving earlier crises and to move on to higher stages of psychosocial development. (See Figure 5.2).

Trust Versus Mistrust (Infancy)

During the first year children are totally dependent on adult caretakers. Children whose caretakers respond warmly and consistently to their needs begin to develop feelings of basic trust. Comfort becomes what Erikson calls an inner certainty, and such children come to believe that the world is reliable. If a caretaker is erratic in caring for a child, the child may be afraid to let the caretaker out of sight, fearing that he or she might never return. The quality of care during this first year shapes infants' basic orientation toward themselves and other people.

Autonomy Versus Shame and Doubt (Early Childhood)

For the first two years of life, children spend endless hours trying to make their bodies do what they want them to do. By the age of three, their muscles and nerves have developed to the point where they are capable of grasping, reaching, walking, controlling their bowels, and so on. However, while these accomplishments bring new autonomy, they raise new fears and doubts. A child walks around the corner to another room, then realizes he is alone and cries out. Besides the doubts involved with independence, the child sometimes experiences the shame of losing control, as when a toilet-trained toddler wets a neighbor's rug.

Erikson suggests that to develop self-confidence, children should be encouraged to "stand on their own feet"; however, children should know that their parents are nearby if needed, and they must also be protected from experiences of shame and doubt.

Initiative Versus Guilt (The Play Stage)

At four or five, children begin to extend their mastery over their own bodies to the world around them. In their play and fantasies they begin to act out adult roles, transforming (and hence mastering) the world in their imagination. Most importantly, in Erikson's view, children begin to initiate purposeful activities on their own. Earlier, their play consisted mostly of imitating others and exploring.

Children's feelings of self-worth grow if their parents and other important figures respect their efforts. Ridicule and lack of interest make children doubt the value of their actions and goals; they may punish themselves for their failures. There is a danger, then, of children at this age developing more or less permanent guilt feelings about any self-initiated activities.

Industry Versus Inferiority (School Age)

The social setting now shifts from home to school and the larger community. As they begin to acquire the skills and technology of their society, children come to take pride in being industrious. However, if they find that their race or family background or looks automatically disqualify them in other people's eyes, their experience will be negative. At this stage some children develop a sense of inferiority; they fear that if required to perform, they will fail. One long-term study of inner-city men found that those who learned to work and be industrious during this stage were much more successful in adult life and enjoyed better mental health than those men who did not (Vaillant and Vaillant, 1981).

Identity Versus Role Confusion (Adolescence)

With childhood drawing to a close and adulthood around the bend, adolescents struggle with the question of identity and often experience an identity crisis. They try on many new roles as they begin groping with romantic involvement, vocational choice, and adult statuses. The time has come to draw together the various elements that have made up their lives, to give a more permanent shape to who they are and where they are going as adults. What Erikson (1968) means by **identity** is a sense of continuity about one's past, present, and future, coordinating feelings about the self with the image reflected in the social looking glass. Those who are unable to consolidate their various roles and beliefs into a clear identity will be less able to form intimate relations with significant others—a problem that many college students face.

Intimacy Versus Isolation (Young Adulthood)

Young adults confront the task of reaching out and establishing deep friendships and enduring bonds with other adults. Having emerged from their own search for identity, they must now partially fuse their identity with that of other people so that they are capable of making sacrifices for them. At this time, true sexual love can emerge. The danger is that individuals will isolate themselves from others and fail to commit themselves to loving relationships because of competition or fear.

Generativity Versus Stagnation (Middle Adulthood)

During middle adulthood individuals must come to terms with their place in the larger course of human affairs and embrace the welfare of society and future generations. Failure to achieve this concern leads to stagnation and preoccupation with selfish material interests—the type of outlook exemplified by Scrooge in Charles Dickens's *Christmas Carol*. Simply producing children does not provide people with a sense of generativity. They must see their role in rearing them as a contribution to humankind.

Integrity Versus Despair (Old Age)

The final stage of the life cycle involves individuals in taking stock of their lives. This appraisal should result in a sense of wholeness, of purposes accomplished, and of a life well lived. People should be able to say that if they "had it to do over again" they would make few changes in the choices they made. The major difficulty confront-

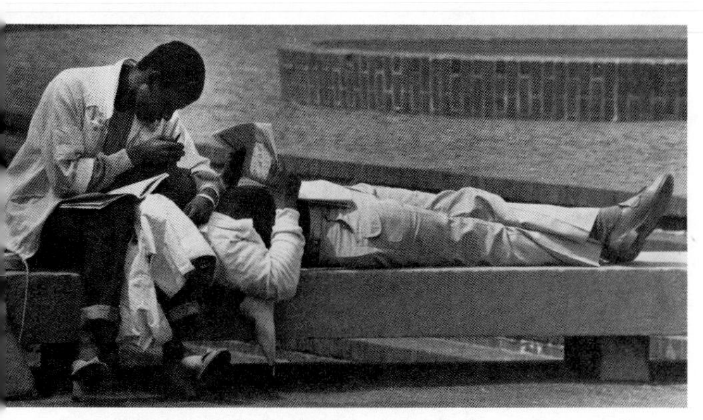

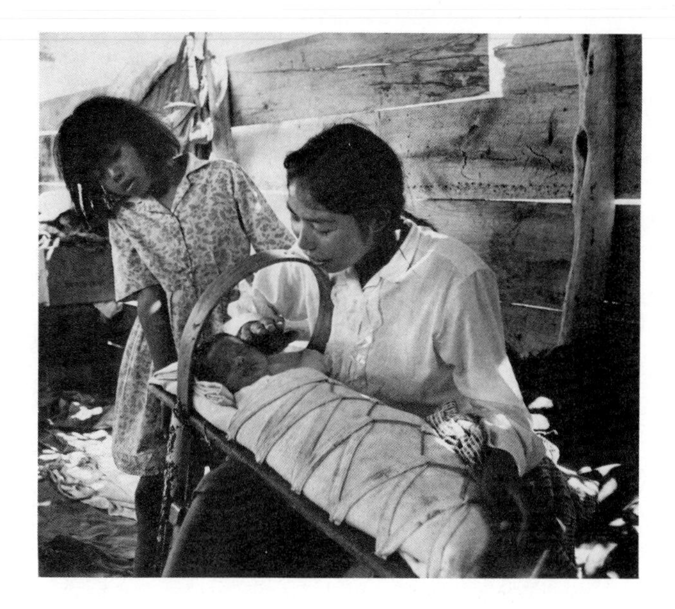

According to Erik Erikson, we pass through several crucial stages of development, starting in infancy and continuing through old age. As infants, we need to learn to trust those around us; as young adults, we need to establish intimate bonds with others. (Above, Ellis Herwig/Stock, Boston; right, Michal Heron/ Woodfin Camp.)

ing individuals in this stage is that they will experience regret and despair over wasted chances and unfortunate choices. People who have a sense of integrity need not fear death and see it as the end of a worthwhile trip.

Jean Piaget: Cognitive Development

Child psychologist Jean Piaget (1969, 1971) was one of the first to recognize that **cognitive development**—the processes of learning to talk, to think, and to reason—is a social as well as a psychological phenomenon. The four stages he outlines complement and reinforce Erikson's and Mead's theories of personality development and add a new dimension to our picture of socialization (see Table 5.1, p. 120).

Sensorimotor

In Piaget's scheme, children during the first year or so of life gradually acquire **motor intelligence**—a physical understanding of themselves and their world. For example, they learn that their hands are part of themselves whereas a bottle is not, and that they can use their hands to grasp a bottle. They acquire **object permanence:** They realize that their parents, toys, and other objects do not dissolve when they are out of their sight. Children begin to appreciate that objects have an independent existence. This cognitive development parallels the emotional development in Erikson's first stage—trust versus mistrust.

Language Acquisition

The next step is the acquisition of *language*, which enables children to communicate with other people, to think symbolically, and to represent internally the external world. Children's use of language and other symbols frees them from a world limited to stimuli in the immediate here and now, enabling them to comprehend and think about the past and the future. Children at this stage can carry out mental experiments and evaluate themselves (by taking the role of another), although they cannot consider more than one point of view. For example, J. L. Phillips, Jr. (1969), asked a four-year-old boy if he had a brother. The child said yes, he had a brother named Jim. "Does Jim have a brother?" Phillips then asked. After pausing a moment, the child replied, "No." This child could recognize that he had a brother (Jim) but he could not put himself in Jim's place and appreciate that Jim also had a brother (himself) as well. Hence, young children have only a limited awareness of other people's points of view.

TABLE 5.1 Developmental Stages of Erikson and Piaget

Age Period	Erikson	Piaget
Birth to 18 months	Trust vs. Mistrust	Sensorimotor stage (birth to two years)
18 months to year 3	Autonomy vs. Shame and doubt	Preoperational stage (language)
Years 3 to 7	Initiative vs. Guilt	Preoperational stage
Years 7 to 12	Industry vs. Inferiority	Stage of concrete operations
Years 12 to 18	Identity vs. Role confusion	Stage of formal thought
Young adulthood	Intimacy vs. Isolation	
Middle adulthood	Generativity vs. Stagnation	
Old age	Intergrity vs. Despair	

Concrete Operations

During Piaget's third stage (the equivalent of Erikson's stage of industry versus inferiority), children's thinking matures markedly. As they approach eight years of age, children learn to manipulate the tools of their culture (what Erikson calls industry) and they begin to understand cause and effect relationships. They also learn to consider other people's points of view and, most important, to coordinate others' viewpoints with their own (the stage at which, as Mead pointed out, children begin to play games). In this stage, children's thinking is **concrete**—that is, they are bound by immediate physical reality and they have difficulty dealing with remote, future, or hypothetical matters. Even so, they begin to appreciate **conservation** processes—the principle that the quantity or amount of something stays the same despite changes in shape or position. Before this stage, children do not realize that if a ball of clay is rolled into a sausage shape, the amount of clay remains the same. Nor do they recognize that ten pennies arranged in a circle and ten pennies laid out in a straight line are the same amount of money.

Abstract Thinking

At age eleven or twelve, children begin to think in terms of abstract concepts, theories, and general principles. This is the stage of **formal operations.** Whereas younger children test their ideas by trying them out, adolescents can formulate hypothetical problems and work on them in their heads. They gain the ability to reason and to generate mentally the various possible outcomes of an event. This development explains adolescents' ability to reflect on their self-image and future hopes. Trying to combine personal desires and social demands, adolescents strive to develop an identity, as Erikson suggested.

Is the development of abstract reasoning (and, by extension, an identity crisis) inevitable? Lawrence Kohlberg, who has devoted much of his career to investigating Piaget's theories empirically, estimates that perhaps 50 percent of Americans never develop formal reasoning (Kohlberg and Gilligan, 1971). Kohlberg's primary interest, however, is in judgment and the development of moral thinking, the third dimension of the process of socialization that we will consider.

Lawrence Kohlberg: Moral Development

Based on Piaget's work, the psychologist Lawrence Kohlberg (1980) has formulated six stages of moral development. According to Kohlberg, a child first judges the morality of an act by its physical consequences. If doing something leads to punishment, then it should not be done. Next, the child begins to realize that conforming to rules can bring rewards, not just the avoidance of punishment. Usually this orientation is quite self-serving and manipulative: "I'll eat my spinach if you give me two helpings of dessert." From this self-centered position, the child progresses to a level known as "good child morality." Children in this stage judge the morality of an act according to how much it conforms to the standards of other individuals, thereby gaining their approval and good will. Gradually, ideas about right and wrong behavior develop. The fourth stage—beyond which many people never progress—emphasizes law and order. Strict conformity to the social order is accepted as right and any deviation as wrong. Emphasis falls on "doing one's duty," showing respect for authority, and maintaining social order.

Cross-cultural studies indicate that the sequence of Kohlberg's stages is universal but that the rate of development and the highest stage reached vary with the social environment. It appears that children who live in industrialized societies and urban settings progress more rapidly and reach higher stages than children in primitive or rural societies (White, Bushnell, and Regnemer, 1978; Colby et al., 1983). These differences may reflect the influence of social interaction in the development of moral judgment.

The last two stages of moral development Kohlberg (1980) described entail fairly sophisticated moral views and are infrequently attained. In the fifth stage the person recognizes that while it is important to adhere to social rules, it is also possible to *change* those rules if such a change would benefit greater numbers of people. Morality is seen as rooted in basic human rights such as life and liberty. In the final stage, a person internalizes ideals of justice, compassion, and equality and conforms both to these ideals and to social standards. On occasions when social standards and internalized ideals conflict, individuals may decide to follow their own ideals (for instance, the Golden Rule and respect for the dignity of each human being). They find it legitimate to break unjust laws because such laws are at odds with fundamental moral principles. Many of those who participated in civil rights and antiwar protests in the 1960s and early 1970s had attained this stage of morality.

Developing moral judgment and acting on it is an important part of socialization. These young people acted on their sense of moral duty by participating in a demonstration against nuclear weapons. (Eric Roth/The Picture Cube.)

Moral Judgment and Moral Behavior

Is it possible to predict how a child will behave by the way he or she judges the morality of an act? Most of the evidence says no. There seems to be little relation between moral *judgment* and moral *behavior* (Blasi, 1980). Our moral behavior is a product of social forces—pressures from peers and parents and the situations in which we find ourselves. For instance, many students who disapprove of cheating will cheat when group pressures encourage it or when the stakes are high. Neither honesty nor deceit are unified personality traits. Most children will deceive in some situations but not in others. Thus morality is not primarily a "character trait" but a function of the social situation in which individuals find themselves (Kohlberg, 1976).

Gender and Conceptions of Morality

Kohlberg's work has consistently shown that on his scale of moral development women score lower than men. This finding led the psychologist Carol Gilligan (1982) to study the developmental stages that characterize men and women across the life span. She concludes that men and women have different "moral domains" and that "women's construction of the moral domain relies on a language different from that of men's" (1982). Men define moral problems in terms of rights and rules—the "justice" approach. For men, independence and competition typically occupy center stage, and morality thus is seen as a system of rules for assigning rights and taming aggression. This domain is captured by Kohlberg's research.

In contrast, women define the moral problem as one of obligation to exercise care and avoid hurt—the "care approach." The woman's sense of morality involves a consciousness or sensitivity that emphasizes protecting the integrity of relationships and minimizing injury. Thus Gilligan challenges Kohlberg's conception of morality with one based on caring and responsibility. This morality is rooted in a psychological concern for human relationships that differs from the formal logic of fairness that permeates the justice approach. Other researchers are finding confirmation of this gender difference in moral construction (Lyons, 1983).

ISSUES OF ADULTHOOD AND AGING

Social scientists used to think that socialization ended with childhood and that adult experiences merely reflected the patterns laid down in the early years. They still believe that childhood development influences how people cope with later life, but they recognize that starting a career, living on one's own, marrying, becoming a parent, changing jobs or neighborhoods or spouses, and growing old all require learning new roles. For an adult, learning new roles often entails learning new ways of expressing existing values. Adult socialization builds on the norms, values, and habits learned in childhood and adolescence (Bachman et al., 1978).

Early and Middle Adulthood

As Erikson's work suggests, individuals undergo change across the entire life span. Two core tasks confront the adult. Sigmund Freud (1935/1960) labeled these tasks *love* and *work*. The first task has to do with establishing and maintaining intimate relationships with others, usually in a family setting. The second task centers on establishing and maintaining a career. For earlier generations of Americans, family and work decisions were often made in early adulthood, and people entered and vacated key statuses in a more or less orderly fashion across the life span. A "social clock" defined the "best age" for a man or woman to marry, to finish school, to settle on a career, to hold a top job, to become a grandparent, and to retire. Individuals tended to set their personal "watches" by the age norms prescribed by this social "Big Ben" (Neugarten, 1968).

In recent decades, however, the possibilities of adulthood have expanded. Events that were not particularly common prior to 1960, including divorce and career change, have now become commonplace. Women's liberation and the sexual revolution have affected how men and women define themselves and each other and, consequently, the statuses they assume and the roles they play. With each year passing, fewer Americans have the same spouse, job, home, or education at age sixty that they had at age thirty.

As we will discuss in Chapter 13, many life-style options are open to Americans. Even so, the overwhelming majority of Americans marry at one time or another in their lives. Once married, couples find that their roles alter over the years. One important source of change is parenthood. Parenthood requires considerable adjustment since adding, or removing, members causes major family reorganization. Many new parents report increased concern about financial matters, difficulties with in-laws concerning "proper" child-rearing practices, and disruptions of plans caused by shifts in the baby's schedule (Russell, 1974). Parenthood signifies adulthood and the passing of youthful roles even more than does marriage.

When children become teenagers, the family structure again changes. As adolescent children struggle to find their places within their own generation, they alter their relationships with their parents. When the children are grown and depart from home, the parents enter "the empty-nest stage." Parents who have a deep involvement with their children may find the adjustment a difficult one. But a surprising number of couples find an overall improvement in marital satisfaction once their children leave home. Retirement of one or both spouses once more confronts a couple with new demands for changing some aspects of the husband and wife roles.

A family's structure is also radically changed by divorce. In the United States children whose parents divorce typically live with their mothers and have only intermittent contact with their fathers. As we will discuss in Chapter 13, a single-parent household is quite different from a two-parent household. But whatever the source of the change, family members undergo changes in their roles across time and must be socialized to the new role requirements.

As pointed out earlier in the chapter, the workplace also involves processes of socialization and resocialization. A person's career normally encompasses four broad stages: (1) selection and entry, (2) adjustment, (3) maintenance, and (4) retirement (Schein, 1978; Santrock, 1983). Entering an occupation signals the assumption of a new status. Individuals must establish themselves in the occupational world and develop a distinct occupational identity. This period of adjustment occupies young adulthood and is discussed in the box (see p. 124). During middle adulthood the emphasis changes to one of bringing idealistic hopes in line with realistic possibilities in light of how much time is left in an occupation. And finally, in later adulthood, a career commonly culminates with retirement.

Of course, not all careers follow such an orderly progression. Many people leave one career for another. Indeed, midlife career change is not unusual. Moreover, not everyone has an occupational career. Some people may remain employed only intermittently or change jobs with considerable frequency. Furthermore, many of the constraints and opportunities that shape career patterns are beyond the control of the individual. Instead, they arise from economic institutions, educational policies, occupational structures, and employing organizations. But the movement of life is constantly forward, propelled by biological aging and cultural norms. Individuals can drift, stall, or stagnate, but there is basically no turning back (Schein, 1978). Thus role changes and the accompanying socialization processes continue across early and middle adulthood and into the later years.

Later Adulthood

No area of socialization is so ripe for controversy and change as is socialization into old age. The ranks of vital, healthy elderly people are swelling, and society's attempts to make them useless are becoming increasingly unreasonable. Despite the fact that aging is continuous, we tend to put people over sixty-five into a separate category from the rest of society. Not all societies treat their elderly the way we in America do. We will consider this and other related sociological phenomena in the following sections.

Aging and the Social Structure: The Functionalist Perspective

From a functionalist perspective the kind of socialization that the older person experiences depends a great deal on the way a society is structured and how it values the qualities and attributes of older people. The biological changes that go with aging—such as a physiological decline in an individual's capacity for physical work and exercise and a decrease in visual and auditory acuity—do not differ from society to society. Societies do differ, however, in how they regard these natural changes. Nomadic peoples, constantly on the move and depen-

THE SOCIOLOGICAL EYE ON CAREERS:

Socialization and the First Major Job

Organizations and people are interdependent. Organizations depend on the performance of people and people depend on organizations to provide them with jobs. Thus the transition from school to career can be viewed from the organization's perspective as one of starting people along an occupational or professional "path" created by the organization. From the individual's perspective it can be viewed as a means of developing one's own life's pattern for work. Entry into an organization is likewise a two-way process. The organization inducts individuals through basic training programs and procedures designed to socialize employees into its core norms, values, and practices. Individuals experience the process as one of breaking in and joining up, of learning the ropes and figuring out how to get ahead.

The overriding feature of entry into one's first major job is "reality shock." Neither schools nor apprenticeship programs totally prepare a person for an occupational role. The initial phase is disconcerting because a person's expectations clash with the realities of organizational life. The major tasks confronting an individual in this early period all arise from the gap between expectations and realities.

The first task is to come to terms with the organization. Many new employees soon discover that other people in the organization frequently constitute a roadblock to what they want to get done. Co-workers do not seem as bright, competent, or productive as they should be. Too often they appear to be illogical, irrational, and unmotivated. The novice must learn to accept the human organization with all its weaknesses. "Selling," "compromising," and "politicking" become essential skills.

The second task is learning to cope with resistance to change within the organization. New employees complain that their "good ideas" are undermined, sidetracked, sabotaged, or simply ignored. They discover that their recommendations, which seem so technically sound, are not implemented for one reason or another. The degree to which new employees learn to cope with resistance to change has important consequences for their future career paths.

The third task is resolving ambiguity in their jobs. Novices find that some aspects of their work are ill-defined. And they have difficulty acquiring the feedback essential for judging their own performance. Thus carving out one's own job is a critical task in learning how to work.

The fourth task is learning how to get ahead. New employees must learn how to relate to their boss, evolving a balance between being too dependent and becoming too independent. Simultaneously, they must learn to decipher the reward system: identifying what is really expected of them, what is really rewarded, and how much they can trust official formal statements.

Finally, individuals confront the task of locating their place in the organization and developing an identity. Many new employees find themselves routed through various training programs or rotated through a series of roles. In the process, individuals must find a proper fit between themselves and the organization and acquire an appropriate identity in it. Of course, all the various tasks are interrelated. They can be viewed as an effort on the part of new members to form "a perspective" toward the organization and toward their organizational roles.

Source: Adapted from Edgar H. Schein, *Career Dynamics: Matching Individual and Organizational Needs.* Reading, Mass.: Addison-Wesley, 1978.

dent on scarce resources, consider old people a burden (Sheehan, 1976). But in agricultural societies the aged enjoy great prestige, derived from their years of experience and wisdom in the ways of planting and harvesting and their accumulation of property over their lifetime. In such a society, it quite literally pays to give deference to the aged.

Modern industrial society grants little status to old people. In fact, such a society has a system of built-in obsolescence. We get educated in our youth, but no formal system exists for continuing our education throughout our life in order to keep up with rapidly changing knowledge. "People whose education and job skills have grown obsolete are treated exactly like those who have never gained an education or job skills and are not encouraged or given the opportunity to begin anew" (Atchley, 1980:16).

As society becomes more highly developed the overall status of older people diminishes (Atchley, 1980; see Figure 5.3). Improved health technology creates a

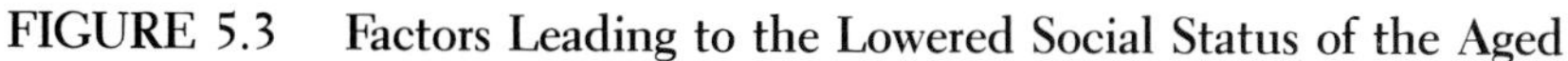

FIGURE 5.3 Factors Leading to the Lowered Social Status of the Aged

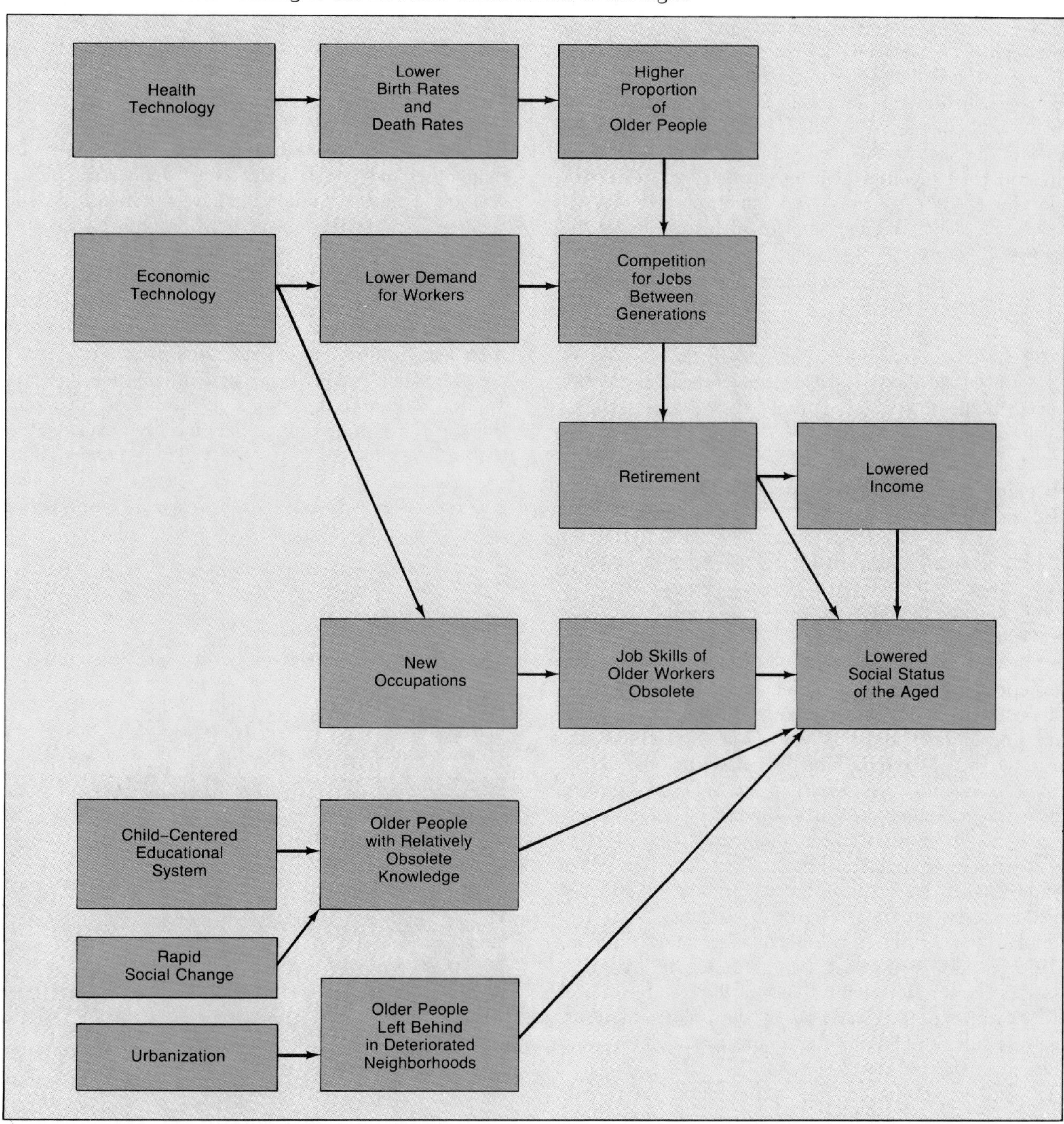

Source: Robert C. Atchley, *The Social Forces in Later Life: An Introduction to Social Gerontology* (3rd ed.). Belmont, Calif.: Wadsworth, 1980, p. 24.

This figure shows how the five indexes of development listed vertically at the left contribute to the lowered occupational, financial, educational, and social status of the elderly.

large pool of old people, who compete for jobs with younger people. However, economic technology lowers the demand for workers and creates new jobs for which the skills of the aged are obsolete, forcing old people into retirement. At the same time, young people are being educated in the new technology and are keeping pace with rapid changes in knowledge. Finally, urbanization creates age-segregated neighborhoods. Because the old live on fixed incomes, they must often live in inferior housing. All these factors—retirement, obsolete knowledge and skills, inferior standard of living—lower the status of the aged in our society.

Yet exceptions exist to the assumption that industrialization and modernization necessarily result in low status for the aged. Cultural traditions play an important part. Hence, in Japan, where the elderly have historically enjoyed an honored status, older people are not assigned the low status of those in Western societies (Palmore, 1975).

Socialization and Stereotypes: The Interactionist Perspective

Given all the obstacles that older people must contend with, how do the elderly experience old age? Here the symbolic interactionist perspective is helpful. People's definitions of themselves and others influence their attitudes and behavior. Thus one factor that affects the experience of aging is the notions the elderly hold about themselves. Many stereotypes about old age apparently do not accurately describe how old people feel and act. Among the more popular sterotypes are that old people value companionship more than sex, are old-fashioned, care little for their appearance, are neglected, are in only "fair" health, and are narrow-minded (Atchley, 1980).

Studies of Americans in the last few decades have shown fairly consistent negative attitudes toward old people; they see them as passive, irritable, and rigid (Golde and Kogan, 1959; Weinberger and Millham, 1975; Waters, 1982). (See Table 5.2). Certainly, television portrays a stereotypical view of the old. Surveys of the portrayal of the elderly on TV show older characters cast as silly, stubborn, sexually inactive, helpless, and eccentric (Harris and Feinberg, 1978; Waters, 1982). The elderly who have authority and esteem are usually senators, congressional representatives, and other public figures. Rarely are older women portrayed as having power or authority, and commercials emphasize the poor health and diminished authority of older women, even for products aimed at older, relatively healthy women.

As might be expected, people over age sixty-five internalize these negative attitudes about old people. But an interesting twist has been noted (Harris, 1981). While people over sixty-five consistently see other people over sixty-five as more passive and useless than the rest of the public, they see *themselves* as more active and useful than other old people. Thus they apply the cultural symbols of old age to others but have a more realistic and accurate view of themselves. This is probably because most people have a fairly strong sense of who they are by the time they reach age sixty-five. Their strong self-image helps to compensate for any loss of roles and resources and explains why many old people manage their socialization into old age rather well.

The ability of old people to maintain such a positive opinion of themselves despite all the negative feedback they get about aging from society has been explained by Paul F. Secord and Carl W. Backman (1964). They theorize that old people *actively* work to maintain congruence with their past self-image in a number of ways: They ignore negative feedback; avoid and devalue

The view that old people are passive, helpless, narrow-minded, and ailing is a stereotype. The elderly do not see themselves in this way, particularly if they are active and have good social relationships. (Abigail Heyman/Archive Pictures.)

TABLE 5.2 Personal Qualities of Older People

Personal Quality	"Most People Over 65" as seen by Public 18 to 64 (Percent)	"Most People Over 65" as seen by Public 65 and over (Percent)	Self-image of Public 18 to 64 (Percent)	Self-image of Public 65 and over (Percent)
Very friendly and warm	82	25	63	72
Very wise from experience	66	56	54	69
Very bright and alert	29	33	73	68
Very open-minded and adaptable	19	34	67	63
Very good at getting things done	35	38	60	55
Very physically active	41	43	65	48
Very sexually active	5	6	47	11

Source: Robert C. Atchley, *The Social Forces in Later Life: An Introduction to Social Gerontology* (3rd ed.). Belmont, Calif.: Wadsworth, 1980, p. 77.

The stereotype the general public holds of old people often does not accord with old people's images of themselves. For example, while only 19 percent of people under sixty-five see old people as very open-minded and adaptable, a much larger proportion—34 percent—of old people hold that others in their age group are. And when old people rate themselves as individuals, an even greater proportion (63 percent) considers themselves open-minded and adaptable.

those who are apt to give it; and adjust certain aspects of their self-image to suit the new circumstances in order to preserve the rest of the aspects.

Dying

Old age is the last phase in life, a period when individuals must face the fact of their own relatively imminent death. People with terminal illnesses are cast into the role of dying person. If the *dying trajectory* (or length of illness before death) is short, not much time is spent in the role and there is little time to adjust to the idea of dying. However, a lingering terminal illness calls for a certain amount of adjustment, and carries with it certain social expectations about how the dying person should behave. Although young people who are dying are expected to fight death and to have as many experiences as possible while they are still alive, older people are expected to accept the idea of death and continue their life style as before (Kalish, 1976).

Elisabeth Kübler-Ross (1969) has studied the process of dying and finds that it typically contains five stages. In the first stage individuals refuse to acknowledge their impending death, a response of *denial.* In the second stage they become *angry.* They resent that they must die and often strike out against family, friends, and medical personnel with little justification. In the middle stage, they attempt to *bargain* with God, fate, or the illness itself, seeking to arrange a temporary truce (for instance, "Let me live long enough to see my daughter married," or "Allow me to get my business in order"). The "bargain" usually falls apart as the illness progresses, leading to psychological *depression.* Finally, in the last stage, the person comes to *accept* impending death and makes peace with it.

Many people assume that this is a progression of stages, whereas in fact a person may experience several stages at once. As a result of this misconception, "People have been chided for not progressing through their own dying on schedule, and dying persons have felt guilty for not having accomplished the various tasks" (Atchley, 1980, p. 202). The experience of being chronically ill or dying depends greatly on both the social situation and its meaning to significant others. Some families are repelled or annoyed by serious illness; others are drawn closer by it. Religious beliefs can play a significant role in the socialization experience at life's end. Finally, the social circumstances of illness or dying—whether the sick person is isolated, receives impersonal professional supervision, or is cared for by loved ones—colors his or her experience. Although death is a biological event, its meaning is a social fact or construction (see Chapter 1).

EPILOGUE

Socialization is an ongoing process of learning new roles, internalizing their norms, developing one's sense of self, and wrestling with conflict in shaping one's identity. Because infants and young children are largely dependent, they cannot originate their own actions in the same sense that adults do. Caretakers thus play a determining role in the way that children develop, influencing and fashioning their intelligence, character, and competencies. Hence, the family (the subject of Chapter 13) plays a vital role in transforming the newborn biological organism into a social being. The core of this socialization process is the transmitting of culture (Chapter 3) and the capacity to employ rules, evolve relationships, and engage in those role behaviors associated with social structure (Chapter 4).

But socialization is more than a passive process in which the human organism is merely shaped and acted upon by others and by environmental factors. As children grow older, they become increasingly capable of selecting their own friends and associates, defining their roles and objectives, and altering their environments. They bring structure to their world, and in the process structure their own actions and construct their selves. As we emphasize in Chapter 4, individuals make their own history—they forge their own personalities and a larger social reality—as they interact with one another in a social context. Such day-to-day shifts in an individual's behavior and self-conceptions lead to substantial cumulative changes across the years and decades.

Many radical transformations are occurring today in the social context in which socialization occurs (Baumrind, 1980). The widespread availability of effective contraception allows recreational sex to be separated from procreational sex. This development has resulted in more liberal attitudes toward homosexuality and abortion because children are no longer viewed as the necessary outcome of sexual relations. Effective contraception has also allowed women to gain greater control of their own bodies. Women can choose whether or not to have children and can space them in ways to accommodate their careers. All this has brought about changes in how people perceive and define children. Simultaneously, the changing gender role definitions that have liberated women from the home have allowed men to enter the home as primary caretakers. Increasingly, the male role is being redefined to include nurturing functions. It is to these matters that we turn our attention in the next chapter.

SUMMARY

Socialization is the process by which we acquire social identities and internalize the values and roles of our social world. Many social traits appear to be inherited, but they will not develop and flourish unless supported and encouraged in social interaction. The importance of social interaction has been demonstrated in studies of children raised in severe social deprivation. The social interaction we have with siblings helps establish patterns for the way we cope with others later in life.

The functionalist perpective contributes to an understanding of the purpose of socialization, the integration of individuals into society. The symbolic interactionist perspective focuses on the process of socialization. Charles Horton Cooley used the image of a *looking glass* to explain how others influence the way we see ourselves. George Herbert Mead has traced the development of self-awareness back to the interaction between parent and child. The socialization process gets extended in play, when children take the roles of others. Gradually, children develop a generalized impression of what people expect from them and of where they fit in their milieu.

The conflict perspective of socialization takes note of how class distinctions get perpetuated and of the conflicts between society and the individual's biological drives. Driven one way by biology, the other by society, we are, in Freud's view, subject to continuous torment.

Socialization is a lifelong process in which family, peers, the media, schools, and the workplace all act as agents of socialization.

Erik Erikson has identified several psychosocial stages, or developmental crises, during which we develop feelings about ourselves and the world. Jean Piaget has analyzed the stages of *cognitive development*. He has shown that very real differences exist in the *way* children think at different ages. These stages unfold as a result of each child's interaction with the world. Lawrence Kohlberg has concluded that as with emotional growth and cognitive skills, moral judgment develops in stages as the child gains experience in the world.

The process of socialization continues during early and middle adulthood as individuals strive to develop intimate relationships to others and to define their life work.

Socialization into old age involves learning to adjust to new roles (such as retired person) and changes in old roles (such as parent). The way a society is structured determines the status of its elderly. Modern industrial society generally diminishes the status of the aged, although older people undergo socialization according to their particular roles and resources.

GLOSSARY

Agent of socialization. Any person or institution that shapes a person's values and behavior.

Cognitive development. The process of learning to talk, to think, and to reason.

Concrete. The term Jean Piaget applies to the reasoning of children between eight and twelve years of age; in this stage children's thinking is bound by immediate physical reality and they have difficulty dealing with remote, future, or hypothetical matters.

Conservation. The principle that the quantity or amount of something stays the same despite changes in shape or position.

Desocialization. The process of shedding one's self-image and values.

Ego. Freud's term for the part of the self that finds socially acceptable ways of satisfying biological cravings.

Formal operations. Piaget's term for the stage when children can think in terms of abstract concepts, theories, and general principles.

Generalized other. A child's generalized impression of what other people expect from him or her.

Id. Freud's term for the reservoir of innate sexual and aggressive urges, as well as for all bodily pleasure.

Identity. A sense of continuity about oneself, derived from one's past, present, and future, from what one feels about oneself, and from the image reflected in the social looking glass.

Internalization. The process by which individuals come to incorporate the standards, attitudes, and beliefs of parents and teachers within their own personalities.

Looking-glass self. Cooley's term to explain how others influence the way we see ourselves. We gain an image of ourselves by imagining what other people think about our appearance and behavior.

Motor intelligence. Piaget's term for children's physical understanding of themselves and their world.

Object permanence. A child's realization that objects exist even when they are not in sight.

Resocialization. Following desocialization, the process of incorporating a new self-image and new values.

Self. The notion that each of us has that we possess a unique and distinct identity—that we are set apart from other things and people.

Significant others. People who are emotionally important in one's life.

Significant symbols. According to Mead, conventionalized gestures acquired in infancy that arouse desired responses in those responsible for child care.

Socialization. The process by which we acquire those modes of thinking, feeling, and acting that are necessary to participate effectively in the larger community.

Superego. Freud's term for the conscience, the part of personality that internalizes the society's views of right and wrong.

CHAPTER 6

Sex Roles

Much has changed since 1963 when Betty Friedan's best-selling book, *The Feminine Mystique*, appeared. It marked a watershed, a response to growing pressures within American society in which traditional conceptions of male and female roles had become increasingly outmoded. In the intervening years women have entered the work force in increasing numbers, finding more careers open to them, and in general, have formed a more equal partnership with men in society.

In 1971, only 4 percent of the nation's lawyers and judges were women; today women account for 14 percent. In 1971 only 9 percent of the country's physicians were women; today 22 percent are. And the proportion of women scientists has risen from less than 10 percent in 1971 to 21 percent today (Prial, 1982).

Attitudes are changing as well. A poll conducted in 1980 found that about half of both men and women preferred a marriage in which responsibility for earnings, housework, and child care is shared. Only two-fifths of those sampled favored the traditional marital arrangement of wife at home and husband as sole provider (Roper Organization, 1980). In contrast, thirty–five years earlier in 1945, three-fourths of all Americans disapproved of married women working. The U.S. Census Bureau has also recognized these changes by abandoning the category "head of household."

Thus it seems that **sex roles**—the idealized and general standards or expectations for the behavior of men and women—are changing and that American society is moving away from traditional sex role expectations. But the change is hardly complete. A Bureau of Labor Statistics survey in mid-1983 showed that the earnings of women who worked full-time were only 66 percent as high as those of men, and that professional women earned only about 71 percent as much as professional men (Rubin, 1984). Further, many occupations are still largely segregated by sex, with women filling more than 90 percent of all secretarial, bookkeeping, and receptionist positions. And there is still resistance to change: The Equal Rights Amendment (ERA) was defeated on June 30, 1982, when it failed to gain ratification by the necessary three additional states.

This chapter examines how the sex-typed behavior, attitudes, and interests that make up sex roles are acquired and what they mean. We will explore some of the "differences" between the sexes, the variation in sex roles among societies, the acquisition of gender identity, the ways that traditional sex roles affect American women and men, and the stratification that sex roles create. Finally, we will see how sex roles are changing in America.

HOW DIFFERENT ARE THE SEXES?

For centuries people have assumed that the differences between the sexes were inborn or "natural," that biology

In early childhood, a girl may play at being a doctor, a boy at being "mommy." But by adolescence, a girl is more likely to be encouraged to pursue an adult role of mother or nurse, and a boy to a career that excludes nurturing behavior. Sex-role training is a big reason for this change. (Left, Charles Leavitt/ The Picture Cube; right, Peter Menzel.)

decreed different interests and abilities for women and men. Men were thought to be instinctively aggressive and women to be motivated to undertake child care by a "maternal instinct." Generations of husbands told their wives not to worry their "pretty little heads" about politics or business, and gallantly protected the "weaker sex" from the "dangers" of the world outside the home. But then researchers discovered societies in which men are passive and vain and women assertive and domineering, and other societies in which there are few differences between the way men and women behave. Consequently, social scientists began seriously to question the biological basis of masculinity and femininity. They asked whether anatomy was destiny after all.

Feminists (both female and male) began to argue that the differences in behavior between males and females are learned, not innate. Little girls are given dolls, little boys trucks and guns, and few of us escape the "blue and pink tyranny" (Reuben, 1972). This view argues for the "nurture" theory. By contrast, there are those who maintain that sex differences are innate, the "nature" argument. We are learning that the truth lies somewhere in between and is more complex than either of these arguments suggests. To sort things out, it is helpful to make a distinction between the meanings of *sex* and *gender*. **Sex** is the biological differentiation of male and female. **Gender** refers to socially agreed upon traits of men and women, particularly those attributes having to do with personal identity, feelings about oneself, modes of dress, attitudes, and interests. This gender differentiation results in cultural ideals of masculinity and femininity.

The Biological Evidence

In most cases the anatomical distinctions between males and females are obvious at birth. Male and female human beings differ as well in their sex chromosome and hormone makeup. Every human being has twenty-three pairs of chromosomes, threadlike bodies in each cell that carry within them the determiners of hereditary characteristics. Female cells have two X chromosomes, male cells an X and a Y. When sperm cells are produced, half of them have an X chromosome, half a Y chromosome. If an ovum (which always has an X chromosome) is fertilized by a sperm with an X chromosome, the child will be a female (XX); an ovum fertilized by a Y-carrying sperm produces a male (XY).

During the first twelve weeks the developing embryo is sexually undifferentiated. Differentiation depends on **hormones**, chemical substances that stimulate or inhibit vital physiological processes. The major sex hormones are estrogen and progesterone (secreted by the ovaries in females) and testosterone and the androgens (secreted by the testes in males). These hormones initiate sexual differentiation in the fetus, and later, at puberty, they activiate the reproductive system and the development of secondary sex characteristics, including breasts in females and beards in males. At some point the male fetus begins to produce testosterone, which inhibits the development of female characteristics. If testosterone is not produced, a female is born.

At times something goes wrong during the prenatal period, and the fetus develops a reproductive structure that has both male and female characteristics. Such individuals are called **hermaphrodites.** At birth the attending physician decides whether the infant is more nearly a boy or a girl. The parents accept the child's sex identification and raise the child as a boy or a girl—whichever they are told. And the child typically grows up to be, in his or her own mind, this sex. Thus, the label "boy" or "girl" directs the socialization of the child by the members of society in the development of its self-conception as being either male or female (Money and Tucker, 1975). In turn, the child typically cultivates those behaviors that match its gender identification.

The Cultural Evidence

Social scientists have found considerable variability from one society to another in the behavior patterns of men and women. This has made them skeptical of claims that biological factors are the primary source of differences between the sexes. For example, American men have used the rationale that women are "fickle," "delicate," and "childlike" to exclude them from traditional male jobs. In contrast, the Tasmanians assigned to women the most dangerous hunting—swimming out to remote rocks in the ocean to stalk and club sea otters. The rulers of the African Dahomeyan kingdom employed women as bodyguards because women were believed to be especially fierce fighters. And among the Arapesh of New Guinea, women regularly carry heavier burdens than men do "because their heads are stronger than men's." Such substantial cultural variation among peoples of the world challenge our beliefs as to what is "natural" and "unnatural" behavior for men and women.

Three Societies in New Guinea

The research of the anthropologist Margaret Mead has done much to foster the view that gender differences among men and women derive primarily from cultural rather than genetic sources. In her classic study, *Sex and Temperament* (1935/1963), Mead described three peoples living within a hundred-mile radius in New Guinea who had quite different notions of what constitutes appropriate masculine and feminine behavior.

The Arapesh What interested Margaret Mead most about the mild-mannered Arapesh tribe was that they seem to have little notion of any temperamental difference between men and women. They expect people to be gentle and home–loving. The Arapesh believe men and women are equally inclined to subordinate their own needs to the needs of those who are younger or weaker, and they derive personal satisfaction from the giving of themselves. Should an infant cry, the nearest man or woman rushes to cuddle and feed the unhappy child. At times relatives borrow a youngster for the sheer pleasure of participating in the child's upbringing. In short, they are what Americans would call a "maternal" culture. "To the Arapesh, the world is a garden that must be tilled, not for one's self, not in pride and boasting, not for hoarding and usury, but that the yams and the dogs and the pigs and most of all the children may grow" (1935/1963:109).

The Mundugumor The neighboring Mundugumor are as fierce as the Arapesh are gentle. The Mundugumor assume that hostility between members of the same sax comes naturally to people and that mistrust should characterize relations between the sexes. They view the birth of a child with mixed feelings. If the child is a boy, the father considers him a rival. Since the Mundugumor obtain brides by exchanging sisters and daughters, a father and his son have an equal claim on the females that are their daughters and sisters, respectively. If the child is a girl, the mother begins worrying that the father will exchange this daughter for a new, rival bride. Children receive only minimal attention and are expected to fend for themselves as soon as they can walk. The Mundugumor apply their aggressive, combative ideal to *both* sexes. Both men and women exhibit what we might call exaggerated **machismo,** or compulsive masculinity.

The Tchambuli Although members of the third tribe Mead studied believe that the sexes are temperamentally different, the roles they prescribe for men and women are the opposite of American sex roles. At dawn Tchambuli women set out for the lagoons to fish and trap, returning at midmorning to work on the crafts they exchange with other tribes. Tchambuli men drift about the fringes of the women's circles, hoping for an approving word, an invitation, or a gift. It is the women who pull the economic strings in Tchambuli society, and the men who devote their lives to self-adornment and the arts of "languishing looks and soft words." Men bicker and pout, exhibiting the emotional ups and downs and employing wiles Americans label "feminine." Mead says Tchambuli women have an attitude of "kindly toleration and appreciation" toward Tchambuli men. They do not seem to take men terribly seriously.

Commenting on these findings, Mead concludes that the characteristics we tend to regard as belonging innately to one sex or the other are "mere variations of human temperament to which members of either or both sexes may, with more or less success in the case of individuals, be educated to approximate" (1935/1963: xvi). Although the nature-nuture controversy is still with us, most scholars feel that neither heredity nor environment can be ignored and that both are involved in gender socialization; that is, biology predisposes but society decrees.

Society, not biology, determines which jobs are women's work. In the Soviet Union, for example, many women hold "men's" jobs—like this Siberian surveyor. (Howard Sochurek/Woodfin Camp.)

Women in Russia

Evidence from the Soviet Union likewise points to the part that culture plays in structuring sex roles. If we were to insist that men are *born* with interests and talents different from those of women, how would we account for the fact that over 70 percent of the physicians in the Soviet Union but only 13.4 percent of their American counterparts are female (World Book Encyclopedia, 1981)? The large number of Soviet women in occupations that are considered male occupations in the United States shows clearly that society, not biology, determines what women can do.

But this is not to say that women's work in the Soviet Union is evaluated in the same way as the work of men. The professions in which Soviet women are most heavily represented, such as teaching and medicine, happen to be at the bottom of the pay and status scales (Daniloff, 1982). Despite Marxist claims about equal pay for equal work and the absence of job discrimination, 74 percent of all Communist party members are male, and men occupy every seat on the all-powerful Politburo and Central Committee. No woman holds a government ministerial post or an ambassadorship. In addition, because Russian men consider housework demeaning, most Soviet women are full-time housewives as well as full-time workers. Women typically spend thirty hours a week on household chores compared to fifteen hours for men. Clearly, the cultural pattern in Russia is one of male dominance.

Subcultural Variation

Sex roles differ not only among various societies; they may also differ within one society. Thus, in the past several years, American television, magazines, and the other media have begun presenting alternative images to that of the man who gets a job, marries, fathers two children, and settles into the comfortable respectability of being a hard worker and a good provider, and the woman who, having had the wedding of her dreams, devotes her life to her husband, her children, and her home. Actually these stereotypes never really applied to many lower- or upper-class people.

In American society the ideal that men should be breadwinners and women homemakers is realized primarily in middle-class settings. Working-class wives believe in this ideal strongly and are more likely than middle-class wives to identify with the role of homemaker, but they are also more likely to have to work to help support the family. Nor does the ideal image fit the upper class, where neither spouse may have to work. Homebound and child-oriented (at least in principle) middle-class wives do many chores that upper-class women leave to hired help. Not surprisingly, these different settings present different definitions of femininity to little girls growing up in them. In one case it means scrubbing floors, washing, ironing, and cooking three meals a day; in the other it means supervising the people who do the heavy work.

Working-class and middle-class marriages present a strong contrast in gender ideals. Research suggests that in the working-class marriage the husband is traditionally dominant. His needs are central, his desires have priority.

With his children his role is more disciplinarian than caretaker. Most working-class men do not consider intimacy or sharing or communication as part of the marriage bond. Here is how one working-class husband describes a typical evening in his home:

> I come home at five and we eat supper right away. Then, I sit down with coffee and a beer and watch TV. . . . Life is very predictable. Nothing much happens; we don't do much. Everyone sits in the same place all the time and does the same thing every night. (Rubin, 1976:123)

In a middle-class marriage, in which the couple is likely to be college-educated, husband and wife are more open and intimate with each other. Most middle-class men and women are in fact motivated to marry by their desire for companionship and intimacy. Middle-class fathers participate more in family life and take more of a role in nurturing the children.

Rubin (1976) attributes these differences in part to the way male children are socialized in middle-class and working-class homes. Boys in the working-class family are taught to be "miniature men"—emotionally controlled, formally correct in manners, disciplined in school. In the middle-class household fewer sex role distinctions are made. "Boys in . . . middle-class homes more often get the message that it's all right to cry, to be nurturant as well as nurtured, to be reflective and introspective, even at times to be passive" (1976:126). Middle-class men, then, tend to be relatively more in touch with their expressive side than working-class men.

Both middle-class and working-class girls grow up encouraged to be emotionally expressive. This upbringing, combined with the rising expectations of women in general today, is putting strains on the working-class marriage. The wives are beginning to yearn for more intimacy and communication, but their husbands do not know what the women want or how to provide it. As Rubin notes, these working-class men do not have "any notion of what is being asked of them. They only know that, without notice, the rules of the game have been changed; what worked for their fathers, no longer works for them" (1976:120).

In sum, comparing sex roles in different societies, and even within the same society, shows that a woman's biological makeup does not determine her worldly achievements. The different rates of women's participation in professional and public life can hardly be attributed to biology, which, as far as we know, does not vary by nation. Moreover, the changes in men's and women's sex roles across historical time point to a similar conclusion.

The Historical Evidence

The sex role differences we currently find in the United States have not always held true. There have been variations in sex role distinctions throughout the history of this country.[1] In Colonial times, for instance, women had a large and visible degree of economic power partly because they were in short supply but chiefly because it was up to them to produce many of the commodities needed by the family. There was no "breadwinner" per se, since the work performed by both men and women was essential to the maintenance of a household, and on the frontier to survival itself.

The advent of industrialism gradually weakened the economic partnership that had formerly existed between husbands and wives. In an economy based increasingly on money and on wage labor, it was typically the husband who worked, and it was his paycheck—occasionally supplemented by children's wages—that supported the family. Long hours of work now separated husbands from wives, and men were likely to spend their leisure hours at a tavern or a gambling parlor. The result was that women gained greater control over domestic matters because they were the ones who were always at home. During the Victorian era, segregation of the sexes was almost complete. The woman's role was primarily that of caretaker of the children, except in those lower-class homes where the wife *had* to work in order to support the family.

If anything, modern times intensified this polarity. As jobs came to require increasing mobility, fathers were often absent from the family while women took care of the children and did the housework. At the same time the housewife's valued position in society was diminished. She had fewer and fewer children and had access to more and more labor-saving devices (Lerner, 1979). Once centers of production, homes became centers of consumption, with many equipped with advanced technological devices such as dishwashers, refrigerators, and vacuum cleaners. Women had more free time, but they were still isolated from the public world of paid employment. Not until significant numbers of women began to enter the work force did these problems receive social recognition.

Sheila Rothman (1978) has traced how the perceptions of what constitutes "proper womanhood" have changed in the last century or so. In the 1880s the notion of "virtuous womanhood" was the ideal: Women were expected to be sexually restrained but to give free rein to maternal instincts and motherly affection. In the early part of this century the emphasis switched from maternal instincts to insights; women were to be educated and trained for the role of motherhood. Another view of womanhood emerged in the 1920s—the "wife-companion." This "romantic and sexual definition, moving women from the nursery to the bedroom even as it kept them at home" (1978:6) came at a time when the birth control movement was just catching on. In the 1950s the concept of "woman as person" began to take root. In this role the woman was to develop her potential outside the home and family.

The situation of American women today is ambiguous, and that ambiguity is reflected in the law: For example, legislation that removes barriers to women's equality exists side by side with other laws or court decisions that seek to protect women as though they were still the "weaker sex." The continued existence of the latter rulings serve as reminders that in many areas Victorian ideals concerning the proper roles for women and men still prevail.

Indeed, even though we can discern some important changes in sex roles, it is still possible to identify certain basic beliefs about men and women that have widespread acceptance and official (legal) support and that affect all Americans to some degree (see Figure 6.1). We will consider these beliefs and practices later in the chapter when we consider sex role stratification.

The Psychological Evidence

Psychologists have also contributed to our knowledge regarding sex differences. Probably the best known study is that by Eleanor E. Maccoby and Carol N. Jacklin (1974). They reviewed more than 2,000 books and articles on sex differences in motivation, social behavior, and intellectual ability. After weighing the evidence, they concluded that the sexes do not differ in sociability, suggestibility, self-esteem, motivation to achieve, ease of rote learning, analytical ability, or responses to auditory or visual stimuli. However, they did find that the preponderance of evidence pointed to four differences between the sexes: Males are more aggressive; males excel at visual-spatial tasks; females show greater verbal ability; and males are better at math.

These conclusions produced considerable controversy and led other psychologists to undertake their own surveys of the gender-related literature. Julia Sherman (1978) and Janet Shibley Hyde (1981) scrutinized the research dealing with verbal, visual-spatial, and mathematical ability. Both concluded that if in fact there are such sex-linked differences, they are at best minimal. (The box on p. 138 examines the matter of sex differences in mathematical abilities at greater length.) And the psychologists Robert Plomin and Terryl T. Foch (1981), both specialists in behavioral genetics, assert that if all we know about a child is the child's sex, we know next to

FIGURE 6.1 Qualities Most Admired in the Sexes

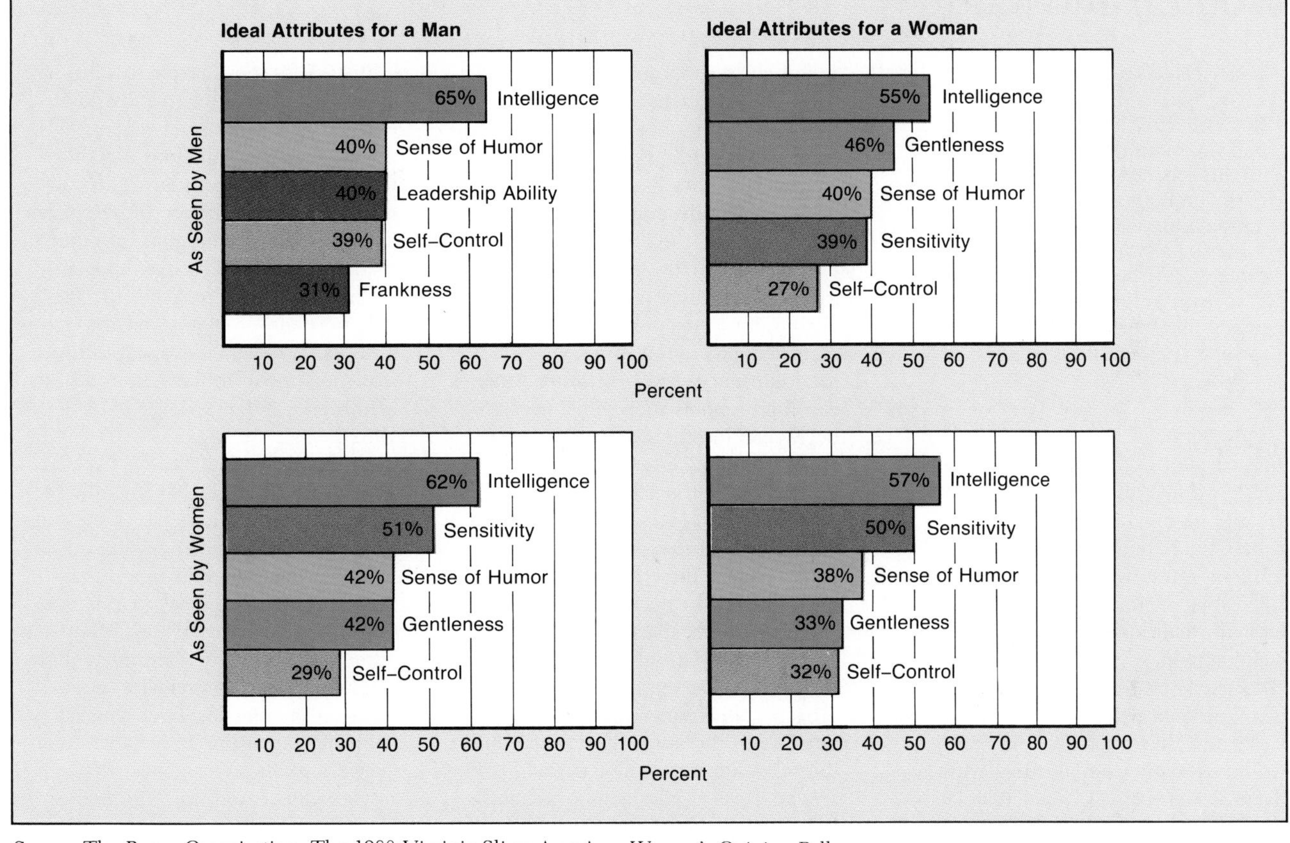

Source: The Roper Organization, The 1980 Virginia Slims American Women's Opinion Poll.

This graph illustrates those qualities most admired in each sex by each sex as reported in a national survey of a cross-section of women and men conducted in 1980 by The Roper Organization. Note that intelligence is the highest rated quality in all four lists. It is also interesting that women's standards transcend gender borders—for women, the qualities they rate highest in themselves are virtually identical with those they most admire in men. By contrast, men ascribe quite different ideals to themselves and to women.

nothing about the child's abilities. If we know about the child's gender, however, we can generally anticipate much of the child's behavior, since the behavior commonly reflects the social expectations for a boy or a girl.

Any number of psychologists have also taken issue with the notion that a biological component underlies gender differences in aggression. For example, Todd Tieger (1980) finds that such differences become observable in children's spontaneous play and behavior only after they are five years old. During these early years, adults encourage boys to display aggression and pressure girls to inhibit it. Hence, Tieger believes that environmental rather than biological factors explain the greater aggressiveness of Western men.

Recently Maccoby and Jacklin (1980) have modified their view. They point out that aggressiveness is not so much a property of individuals as it is a behavior that people are more likely to exhibit in some types of

THE SOCIOLOGICAL EYE ON:

Women and Math

> Today was a day filled with math. First I had to figure out the tip. Boy, I began to feel my palms sweat and my mouth went dry. We didn't ask for separate checks and we had to divide it all up. I was really tempted to say I'd pay for the whole thing so we could only get out of there. . . . I began telling myself that I was a dummy for needing a pencil and paper, but I used one anyway. (quoted in Tobias, 1978: 258-259)

The narrator of this painful story is a young woman attending a clinic for math. She fits the stereotype many people hold about females and numbers—the two simply do not mix. Interestingly, women who have trouble with math often agree with this view, convinced that they lack a mental capacity that males possess. A woman's brain, they argué, must not be "wired" like a man's. Why else would so many women struggle just to balance a checkbook or calculate a tip? Why else when very bright seventh and eighth graders are given the math portion of the Scholastic Aptitude Test (SAT) would twice as many boys as girls score above 500 (Benbow and Stanley, 1980). Why else would women account for less than a fifth of college math majors when they make up more than half of the college population? Why else throughout history would there have been so few outstanding female mathematicians (Kolata, 1980)?

Yet social scientists have strongly challenged the common-sense view that the differences in math achievement between the sexes are primarily a reflection of differences in innate math ability. They begin by pointing to some very important facts. First, sex-related differences in math performance do not begin to appear until the seventh grade. Before then, girls are equal to boys in mathematical skills, or perhaps even slightly better (Meece et al., 1982; Entwisle and Baker, 1983). How could this be if males are innately superior in math? Furthermore, sex differences in math performance are not universal even at the high school level. In some American high schools such differences are negligible; in others they do not exist at all. Also, in certain countries, such as the USSR, the achievement of girls in math and physics is comparable to that of boys (Tobias, 1978). What could explain these findings if males have inherently greather math ability?

The answers, many social scientists say, lie largely in social forces that shape the way men and women approach mathematics. Boys and girls sit together in the same classrooms, but the schooling experience of first-, second-, and third-grade boys differs from that of their female counterparts. The boys' test and aptitude scores in arithmetic do not exceed those of the girls, yet the boys develop higher expectations of their own math performance (Entwisle and Baker, 1983). These estimates reflect parental attitudes. Parents believe their daughters have to work harder than their sons to do well in math. And they believe that taking advanced math is more important for their sons than for their daughters (Parsons et al., 1982). Unfortunately, the failure to take advanced high-school math severely limits the career oportunities of females in fields that offer many of the highest salaries and the greatest prestige.

But even those women who continue to study math generally do less well than their male classmates. Why? Again, social explanations can be found. For instance, many girls may be taught from childhood to be more dependent on the opinions of others than are boys, and so may be less willing to try out creative solutions to difficult math problems and risk wrong answers. And women expect to find math less useful to them than do men (Pedro et al., 1981; Meece et al., 1982).

What all these alternative explanations demonstrate is that it is unwarranted to point to heredity as the most important factor causing women to perform more poorly in math than men. Performance is never a reflection of innate ability alone. Many other factors—learned attitudes, motivations, test-taking strategies, and so forth—also enter in. Thus when it comes to explaining sex-related differences in math performance, these other factors could prove to be the most significant ones.

Sources Camilla Benbow and Julian Stanley. "Sex Differences in Mathematical Ability: Fact or Artifact?" *Science*, Vol. 210 (December 1980), 1262.

Gina Bari Kolata. "Math and Sex: Are Girls Born with Less Ability?" *Science*, Vol. 210 (December 1980). 1234–1235.

Edwin C Lewis. *Developing Woman's Potential.* Ames: Iowa State University Press, 1968.

Sheila Tobias. *Overcoming Math Anxiety.* New York: Norton, 1978.

Women can be aggressive, too, when the social situation permits. (Kenneth Siegel.)

situations than in others. For instance, some researchers have found when physical aggression is private or socially approved, women are just as likely as are men to behave aggressively. In sum, women, like men, inhibit aggression when aggression conflicts with social expectations relating to their gender role, and they exhibit aggression when norms permit or require it (Frieze et al., 1978).

The psychology of gender differences continues to be a much debated topic. Even so, one fact is indisputable. For any trait there exists a wide range of variation in its expression among individuals, male or female, and the ranges of each sex overlap considerably. Not all men are more agressive than all women, nor are all men superior to all women in math skills. And not all women are verbally more capable than all men. The only firm differences between men and women concern primary sexual attributes and functions: Most men have the potential to impregnate a woman, and most women the potential to bear a child. In conclusion, there seems to be little that is either inherently male or female.

GENDER IDENTITY AND SOCIALIZATION

Within American society discrepancies between sex role assignment and the behavior associated with it are strongly disapproved of and even punished. This fact suggests that society has a stake in how individuals perform their roles as men and women. Social agents such as parents, teachers, and other authorities function to transmit the social script outlining gender-appropriate behavior from one generation to the next. In the process each of us acquires a **gender identity**, that is, the conception that we have of ourselves as a man or a woman. It constitutes our inner experience or sense of ourselves as being a male or a female.

Gender Training

Nearly all adults view their gender as unchangeable, but very young children are not so certain. If four-year-old children are asked whether a girl could become a boy if she wanted to, most four-year-olds say that she could. All she had to do is cut her hair and wear boys' clothes (Kohlberg, 1966; Thompson, 1975). It seems that children's sense of gender constancy becomes established between three and five years of age. They then recognize that everyone is either male or female, that boys invariably become men and girls women, and that being a male or a female does not change from one situation to another (Slaby and Frey, 1975).

Gradually, as children learn that being a boy or a girl does not change, most of them identify with their own gender and look favorably on its qualities. Children's acceptance of their gender is reinforced by family, teachers, peers, and the media. They quickly learn that living up to cultural and social expectations of how men and women should behave meets with approval and that nonconformity meets with disapproval.

Sex-typing and sex-role socialization begin at birth (Rubin et al., 1974). Although male and female newborns are indistinguishable except for their genitals, parents (especially fathers) typically describe their daughters as "weak," "soft," "fine-featured," "awkward," and "delicate." In constrast, they describe their sons as "strong," "firm," "large-featured," "well-coordinated," and "hard." Parents decorate the rooms of their sons with animal motifs and provide boys with toy vehicles and guns, sports equipment, and mechanical toys. In contrast, they surround daughters with floral motifs, lace, fringe, and ruffles and with dolls, doll houses, and domestic-related toys (Rheingold and Cook, 1975).

Mothers often rub, pat, touch, kiss, rock, and talk more to male than to female newborns (Brown et al., 1975). And fathers treat their sons differently than they do their daughters. For example, at twelve months of age, fathers are "harder" on their sons than on their daughters. They are likely to punish them more because they believe boys "need" it more (Snow et al., 1983). Clearly, parents play a critical part in socializing their children with respect to their male and female roles. Let us examine this influence more carefully.

The Influence of Parents

During the early years, parents are the primary adults in children's lives. Treating boys and girls differently creates a powerful force to shape children within socially approved modes of gender behavior. Research confirms this. For instance, the developmental psychologist Beverly I. Fagot (1978a) observed twenty-four single-child families whose child was between twenty and twenty-four months old. For one hour on five different occasions she watched how the parents interacted with their child.

Fagot found that boys and girls were often reinforced or punished differently for the same behavior. Parents were likely to react positively to a daughter's requests for help but negatively to a son's requests. Hence girls found that asking for assistance was a rewarding experience whereas boys found themselves criticized or ignored. In this way, the parents subtly fostered dependence in a daughter and independence in a son.

When the child reaches the age of two or three, what were at first casual, half-conscious distinctions become explicit lessons. Parents begin to address the child as "Daddy's little girl" or "Mommy's big boy" and more actively to discourage (or at least ignore) behavior they consider inappropriate. In some ways the change is greater for boys than for girls. Boys are expected to outgrow dependency and clinging, whereas this kind of behavior is encouraged in girls (Bardwick and Douvan, 1971). A mother may begin to ignore a boy's whimpering. If he persists, she may ask him, "Did you ever see your father cry? Do you think Mean Joe Greene cries? Of course not." Gradually boys learn that only girls are permitted to cry. A little girl finds that her parents are genuinely angry when she uses a "nasty" word but chuckle if her brother does. The message is clear. All children develop concrete notions of girl and nongirl, boy and nonboy long before they understand the facts of life. Girls are supposed to be pretty, clean, neat, sweet, and popular; boys are supposed to be clever, strong, and fearless. For most children, striving to live up to these ideals is the path of least resistance.

There are signs that parental training may be changing. Tavris and Jayaratne (1972) found that young, relatively well educated women did not think children of different sexes should be treated differently. Less than 10 percent would encourage aggression in boys and not in girls, and more than 90 percent would have both sexes help with chores around the house. Even so, American parents take greater pains to push their sons toward masculinity than their daughters toward femininity (Lynn, 1976; Langlois and Downs, 1980). They particularly worry lest others view their sons as "sissies."

Today's parents are more likely to treat children of both sexes equally: boys as well as girls may be expected to help with household tasks. (John Lei/Stock, Boston.)

The Influence of Schools

Like parents, teachers seem more concerned with the sex-typed behavior of boys than with that of girls. They allow girls greater latitude than they do boys in trying out the behaviors traditionally associated with the opposite sex. Boys who in make-believe play dress up as girls or who play in the "kitchen" or with dolls are much more likely to receive teacher criticism than are girls who engage in activities stereotyped as masculine (Fagot, 1977).

Teachers also selectively respond to the aggression of boys while paying less attention to that of girls. In so doing, they inadvertently reward boys with attention when they are disruptive and communicate to them the expectation that "boys fight." Simultaneously, teachers encourage girls to be dependent by giving them more assistance than they do boys and by paying them more attention when they remain in the teacher's immediate vicinity (Serbin et al., 1973).

Children are socialized into sex roles in school not only through the behaviors of their teachers and the roles portrayed in learning materials but also by observing adult role models in school. For instance, while 85 percent of elementary school teachers are female, the majority of principals (79 percent) are male (Baker, 1980). Further, schools promote activities that girls typically prefer. In free play girls tend to play with art materials, look at books, and inspect objects whereas boys gravitate to wagons, tricycles, sandboxes, and rough-and-tumble play. A mismatch between boys' inclinations and the early school curriculum may favor girls in the early academic years and foster a dislike of school among boys (Fagot, 1978b). Since the early 1970s, however, parents and educators have organized to combat sexual discrimination in curricula and teaching materials. As a result, schools have opened up home economics courses to boys and shop classes to girls and are providing coeducational team sports.

In school children are also exposed to peer influences. Indeed, as more American youngsters attend day-care centers and nursery schools, the influence of age-mates takes on greater significance in the lives of children. Even three-year-olds know "what boys do" and "what girls do," and they exert pressure on one another to conform to these standards. When children engage in behavior stereotyped as typical of the opposite sex, their peers criticize them, ask them to stop the behavior, divert their attention with another toy or an alternative activity, complain loudly to adults and other peers, or physically attempt to disrupt the behavior. In contrast, they show approval of sex-typed activities with praise, imitation, encouragement, and positive acts (Lamb et al., 1980). In sum, much of the school environment promotes gender training.

The Influence of the Media

Of course parents and schools are not children's only source of information on how they are supposed to act. Lenore J. Weitzman and Deborah Eifler (1972) found that nearly all prize-winning children's books present highly stereotyped and unrealistic images of girls and boys and men and women. Although 51 percent of the population is female, the ratio of pictures of males to pictures of females was eleven to one; and one-third of the books involved *males only*. When girls did appear in the children's books, they were nearly always indoors, helping, watching, or loving the book's hero. One set of books, called *Mommies and Daddies*, was not very complimentary to mothers. "Daddies," the author wrote, "know you're big enough and brave enough to do lots of things that mommies think are much too hard." Not one of the books mentioned mothers who work outside the home or showed fathers helping around the house; not one dealt with death or divorce or any of the real-life problems that might trouble children.

Prime-time television programs and commercials also reinforce sex-role stereotypes. According to the A. C. Nielsen Company, a firm that specializes in gauging the popularity of television programs, the television set stays on an average of fifty-three hours a week in homes with preschool children. On television children observe men and women carrying on their lives in ways that for the most part are consistent with sex-stereotyped roles. Television gives more recognition and respect to men, by casting them in more roles than women and by making their occupational roles more prestigious (doctors, lawyers, etc., as opposed to the female roles of nurses, secretaries, housewives, girlfriends). Joyce N. Sprafkin and Robert M. Liebert (1978:231) conclude that "overall . . . television portrays females as kind and altruistic, and males as aggressive and successful." Moreover, men are still the voice of authority on over 90 percent of the commercials, even when the commercial is directed toward women (Klemesrud, 1981). That children are indeed influenced by the sex role portrayals on television is indicated by research showing that heavy TV watchers (twenty-five hours or more a week) hold more stereotyped sex role values than do children who watch ten hours or less a week (Fruch and McGhee, 1975).

To sum up, then, gender identity does not develop naturally and inevitably as a by-product of physical maturation. It is acquired gradually through experience. It involves an awareness of physical distinctions (anatomy and appearance), a consciousness of sex-specific activities and skills, and a desire to live up to social expectations. These social expectations are embodied in the concept of sex role: the attitudes and behaviors associated with men and women by the societies in which they must function.

SEX ROLE STRATIFICATION

Most societies not only have certain beliefs and expectations about the appropriate conduct and characteristics of men and women but also allocate their privileges and burdens unequally among them. Consequently, one sex is ranked as superior and the other as inferior, a phenomenon known as **sex**, or **sex role, stratification**. If one sex enjoys greater access to wealth, prestige, and power than the other sex, then inequality is built into their relations.

A familiar scene: a man holds center stage while women look on as a silent audience. In our culture, what men have to say is likely to be considered more important and interesting than what women have to say. (Charles Harbutt/Archive Pictures.)

Societies vary considerably in their patterns of sex stratification. For example, the Hopi Indian society of the American Southwest is relatively egalitarian. Each sex is assigned roles that are highly valued:

> The female sphere of activity is the household, and the male sphere of activity is the community. Men and women control different portions of the ceremonial cycle. Each sex has its own tasks—only men hunt, only women grind corn. . . . But . . . the separation of the sexes does not cause the subordination of one and superordination of the other; rather, it permits each sex to fulfill its necessary and equally valued role in the maintenance of the society. (Schlegel, 1977:264)

By contrast, the United States favors men over women in its legal, economic, educational, and political arrangements. These arrangements get support from the ideology of **sexism**, the set of beliefs that supports a system of sexual inequality. In our society the sexist view that men are somehow naturally superior to women is deeply rooted in the Judeo-Christian tradition. Male superiority and female subordination were built into the religion, social structure, and private life of the ancient Hebrews. In the Christian religion exclusion of women from the priesthood and from high ecclesiastical positions in the various denominations reflects a strong bias against females. Sexism is a particularly tenacious ideology because it is not only institutionalized in society but it is internalized by the individual members, including those whom it would keep subordinated. Let us consider these American patterns and their consequences at greater length.

The Legacy of the Traditional Female Role

In American society, particularly among the middle class, inequality between men and women arises from the traditional assignment of an economic-provider role to men and a child-rearing role to women. This division between the public and domestic sectors has permeated the entire social fabric.

In an achievement-oriented society the marketplace and political life afford the primary routes to authority and status. This arrangement places women, who bear and rear children, at a disadvantage. By casting women in the role of mother—and by implication that of wife as well—our society makes it difficult for women to pursue economic success outside the home (Schlegel, 1977). Women may enter the paid work force. But those who have done so have traditionally continued to bear the primary responsibility for household chores and the care of their husbands and children. Consequently, women have lacked the time, energy, and freedom of movement that have been available to men. And since they have not had equal access to the material and social resources of the larger community, women have found themselves vulnerable and dependent in their dealings with men.

Components of the Traditional Female Role

Popular wisdom has traditionally held that all "normal" women wanted to marry and have children and that whatever other interests they might pursue were secondary. Women who did not want to marry or mothers who did not enjoy their children were thought to be unusual or strange. On the whole, a woman's status depended on the men in her life (first her father, then her boyfriends, husband, and sons). Taking her father's name at birth and her husband's name after marriage symbolized this dependency. (For this reason, many women are now keeping their maiden names after marriage.) Society still considers it perfectly legitimate for a woman to depend entirely on her husband for support. Indeed, many a husband still feels that if his wife takes a job it somehow reflects on his masculinity. The value of the unpaid labor that the woman provides in the home (as cook, nurse, maid, seamstress, and governess) has only recently been given some consideration (Lerner, 1979).

Traditional social values encouraged women to share the triumphs and sorrows of their husbands and children, rather than pursuing their own goals. Although the pursuit of self-interest was assumed to be a virtue in the world a man inhabited, a woman was, and in many cases still is, expected to put her family's needs before her own (Bernard, 1971). Displays of self-assertiveness or aggression have been more masculine than feminine. Similarly, women have been discouraged from taking direct initiatives in sexual relations.

A capacity for sympathy, caring, love, and compassion (exemplified in such occupations as nurse and teacher) have been central to the traditional female role in America. Norms have prescribed that women engage in nurturant and life-preserving activities, including bearing children and taking care of the helpless and the ailing. Whereas men have been expected to be achievement-oriented, women have been raised to be people-oriented and to place loyalty to others above other considerations. Finally, women were, and in large measure still are, encouraged (by society in general and the advertising industry in particular) to cultivate beauty and sex appeal and to be concerned with personal adornment.

All these supposedly feminine characteristics, which stem from the different treatment accorded American females, in turn, has led Americans to treat women differently from men (Bernard, 1971). Also, these characteristics have discouraged women from seeking their own achievements; women still tend to bask in the light of successful men they are affiliated with—as daughter, wife, secretary, and so on.

Today there are more and more exceptions to this pattern, which once represented the traditional ideal. Career women, working wives, and working mothers have defied the "rule" that women should be economically dependent on men. Many unmarried women and lesbians have rejected being sexually dependent on men. The women's movement (discussed in Chapter 18) has questioned the entire system of female/male relations. And while many women still conform to the conventional ideals of femininity, a growing number do not.

The Benefits of the Traditional Female Role

The traditional women's role has both benefits and liabilities. Let us first consider these benefits or privileges. Although increasingly large numbers of women are entering the work force all the time, many women are not obliged to work thirty-five or forty hours a week all their lives to provide for others. Furthermore, they have the legal right to claim support from their husbands. In many states a man is liable for his wife's debts, but she is not responsible for his. Until recently, men could not sue for alimony or child support (in the rare case where a divorced man was awarded the custody of his children), but women could. Of course, women do work; but employment, though often an economic necessity and a personal choice, is not yet a *moral* duty for most women.

American values have typically not placed the same

pressures on women to achieve that have been placed on men. Although a women may strive to reach the top of her profession, there is less shame in failure or in achieving only moderate success. Consequently, women may be less prone to fall victim to the career syndrome, which entails almost total devotion to the workplace, often to the exclusion of outside interests and solid interpersonal relationships. Indeed, some women take the view that "any individuals who allow themselves to be so enslaved to the marketplace, with all its destructive side effects, must indeed be inferior to those who have the good sense to stay home" (Forisha, 1978:288).

Women also have more emotional freedom than men; they are permitted to express their doubts and vulnerabilities, and they have more outlets for tension and anxiety. The sphere of intimacy and close human contact is more accessible to women. The expression of nurturance, warmth, and sympathy, qualities which to some extent are denied men in our society, can be most rewarding.

The Costs of the Traditional Female Role

The traditional female role has also had its costs. It has denied women autonomy in most spheres of American life. As noted earlier in the chapter, parents place more restraints on their daughters than they do on their sons. Sex-typed standards dictate that girls are not supposed to be independent or adventuresome. The dependency taught to them as children and experienced as grown women often leads to passivity, timidity, and weakness. (For example, a woman who has not engaged in paid work in ten or fifteen years will think twice before she decides to get out of an unhappy marriage.) This taboo on self-development and self-assertion is especially trying for independent, highly motivated women who are not content with the traditional female role.

Women are treated and institutionalized for certain types of mental illness, such as depression, more often than men are. Perhaps this is because women must repress their hostile and assertive feelings more, because housework does not provide many rewards for educated women, because the housewife feels that hers is an inferior status, and because the role of housewife is unstructured and unsung, leaving much time for brooding—especially when the children have grown up and left home (Gove and Tudor, 1973; Rosenfield, 1980; Scarf, 1980).

Role Conflicts

The benefits and costs of the traditional female role contribute to a number of role conflicts. Women are supposed to depend on men yet be resourceful in times of crisis, to be domestic and also glamorous. Further, many women have to choose between work and family roles. Those women who temporarily drop out of the job market to devote themselves to their children often suffer setbacks in their careers, while those who compete in the workplace must often decide to be childless. Single-parent and working–class women often do not have a choice between working and being a full-time homemaker; their family depends on the income they earn. Most of these women work in nonprofessional, low-paying jobs, with little expectation of climbing a career ladder. Women who seek to commit themselves to both a career and a family frequently find themselves handicapped by the need to be a superwoman who can manage the dual set of responsibilities. For instance, a recent study of women who are physicians found that 75 percent of them did all their own cooking, shopping, money management, and child care (Collins, 1982).

In contrast, men have been able to pursue and enjoy both work and a family life. Indeed, the more successful men are, the more likely they are to marry and have a family. For women the pattern is reversed. Whereas 51 percent of female executives are single, that is true of only 4 percent of male executives. And whereas 61 percent of these women are childless, only 3 percent of the men do not have children (Hull, 1982). Clearly, the choice between career and family is more stressful and the cost more apparent for women than for men (Rubin, 1980).

The Legacy of the Traditional Male Role

In American society, economic rewards, social status, and power have traditionally been greater for the male than for the female role. Institutional arrangements have given social life a decidedly male cast. Male interests and needs have been served, often to the detriment of women. And male values and assumptions have provided the guiding principles that have governed the relationships between the sexes.

Boys are socialized to achieve, girls to be attractive and supportive to the boys (or men) in their lives. The girl who wants to play football rather than cheer the team on from the sidelines is likely to be strongly discouraged. (Alan Carey/The Image Works.)

Components of the Traditional Male Role

The traditional male role has been as deeply tied to the family as has the female role, although the connections are not always so obvious. First and foremost, a man has been expected to be a good provider for his wife and children. Financial idependence has been a prerequisite for manhood in our society; respect has gone to men who were reliable and hard-working. Americans did not think it odd for a man to sacrifice his leisure hours and even his health to a career. His accomplishments and property have been indications of his worth. Initiative, ambition, and strength have been all part of the "masculine mystique." We have seen a man as mature if he accepts obligations for dependents, takes the necessary risks, makes decisions, and provides security and protection for those in his care.

It is no wonder, then, that so many American fathers and mothers encouraged their sons to excel in sports (sometimes ignoring the fact that a boy was not interested in or built for athletics). Sports were not an end in themselves: very few boys went on to become professional athletes, and few fathers expected them to. But team sports teach a boy to be assertive and competitive—which were thought to be essential masculine qualities. These qualities are also, as it turns out, necessary for corporate success at the managerial level. Football, baseball, and basketball were believed to help boys develop personal skills important to a later career: how to compete to win, how to cooperate with those you would not choose as friends to get a job done, how to win and how to lose, how to take risks, how to take criticism, and how to bend the rules (Hennig and Jardim, 1977). These sports taught boys to appreciate the need for teamwork, goals, plans, and leaders. They provided the framework and ground rules for corporate life. And they are rules and skills that women, who tend to participate (if they do at all) in one-on-one or individual sports such as tennis, swimming, or skating, have had less opportunity to learn.

Weakness, doubt, and compromise have been signs of failure for men, who were taught from childhood to conceal or deny such feelings. The taboo on expressing emotions and self-doubt explains the American stereotype of the strong, silent type that historically has been popularized in Western movies. The 100 percent American he-man was happiest when he was with his buddies or alone with his horse. Although courteous to women, he remained detached from them. Impervious to pain as well as to feelings, he was rugged and resourceful and enjoyed going up against overwhelming odds.

Heterosexual prowess has also been essential to American manhood. Stereotypes depict men as possessing a nearly unlimited appetite for sexual adventure and enjoying sex for its own sake (unlike women, who were thought to require at least some romantic feelings). Far more stigma has been attached to effeminate behavior in boys than to masculine behavior in girls, who are permitted to play the role of tomboy. A woman who shows little interest in heterosexual relationships might be labeled prissy or cold; a man has been assumed to be homosexual.

Finally, American men have been accustomed to being in control. When placed in a position subordinate to a female they have often felt uncomfortable. Sharon Mayes (1979) observed the behavior of males in female-led groups at a series of conferences in a university setting. She reported that the males regularly expressed a fear of losing control. Some described women as "plotting against them." They felt threatened when women were no longer subordinate.

Benefits of the Traditional Male Role

Like the female role, the male role has had mixed effects. American men have had access to the pinnacles of institutional power; men (white middle-class men, that is) have controlled the nation's government, churches, corporations, professions, universities—even theaters and art galleries. Men have been free to exercise legal and social powers denied to women and children. With the notable exceptions of the draft registration law and some alimony statutes, neither law nor custom has discriminated against or restricted men solely on the basis of their sex. Men have had more opportunities than women to develop their talents and to acquire special skills and knowledge useful for coping with the world. (If a family has only enough income to send one child to college, in all likelihood it will send the son.) Many more men than women have entered the most prestigious professions.

In general, men earn more than women performing similar kinds of work and are more likely to be promoted to powerful and lucrative executive positions (where they enjoy the ministrations of secretaries, who are nearly always women). The fact that social values have encouraged men to display initiative and independence from an early age must also be counted among the benefits of the male role. Finally, the pervasive myth of male supremacy has buoyed the male ego.

However, even though these potentialities are built into the male role, they have not been equally available to all men. Opportunities for training, economic self-support, and power are clearly more accessible to men at the top of the social pyramid than to those at the bottom. To generalize from the circumstances of the privileged few distorts the actual situation of most men, who are less in control of their lives and fates.

Costs of the Traditional Male Role

The responsibilities attached to the male role in America can be a source of great stress and anxiety as well as a source of satisfaction and pride. Being in a position to make decisions is fine for people who are confident of what they are doing, but it seems less of a privilege to those who are uncertain of themselves. Complicating matters is the fact that men are supposed to maintain the impression of strength and courage at all times. Fear of inadequacy and failure is the dark side of the pressure on men to achieve. What is more, the emphasis men place on strength, toughness, initiative, and superiority can have unintended consequences, including the requirement to test and prove these attributes by engaging in violent exchanges with other men.

Equally costly is the competitive syndrome that asks men to consider all other men as either inferiors or rivals and requires substantial mobilization of psychic aggression. Although men have enshrined the idea of male solidarity, male friendships are not necessarily easy relationships:

> When stripped of male sex role "props," such as baseball scores, automobiles, and masculine sex boasting and fantasy, many men find great difficulty in relating to other men. A man in a group said, "You know, I have a pretty good idea of what I can get in a relationship with a woman; but I just don't know what I could get from a man. I just don't know." (J. Pleck, 1972:8-9)

By defining the expression of warmth, tenderness, and sensitivity as weakness, men limit their relationships with their own children and with women. Further, the separation between work and domestic roles denies many fathers the satisfactions associated with rearing children. Not surprisingly, far too many men find themselves emotionally isolated and alienated from their sons and daughters. And when men define women as sex objects, they simultaneously represent themselves as sex machines, an outlook that can impair sexual functioning and contribute to impotence.

In very concrete terms, men suffer more heart attacks, and their life expectancy is eight years less than

FIGURE 6.2 The Labor Force Participation of Women, 1890–1980

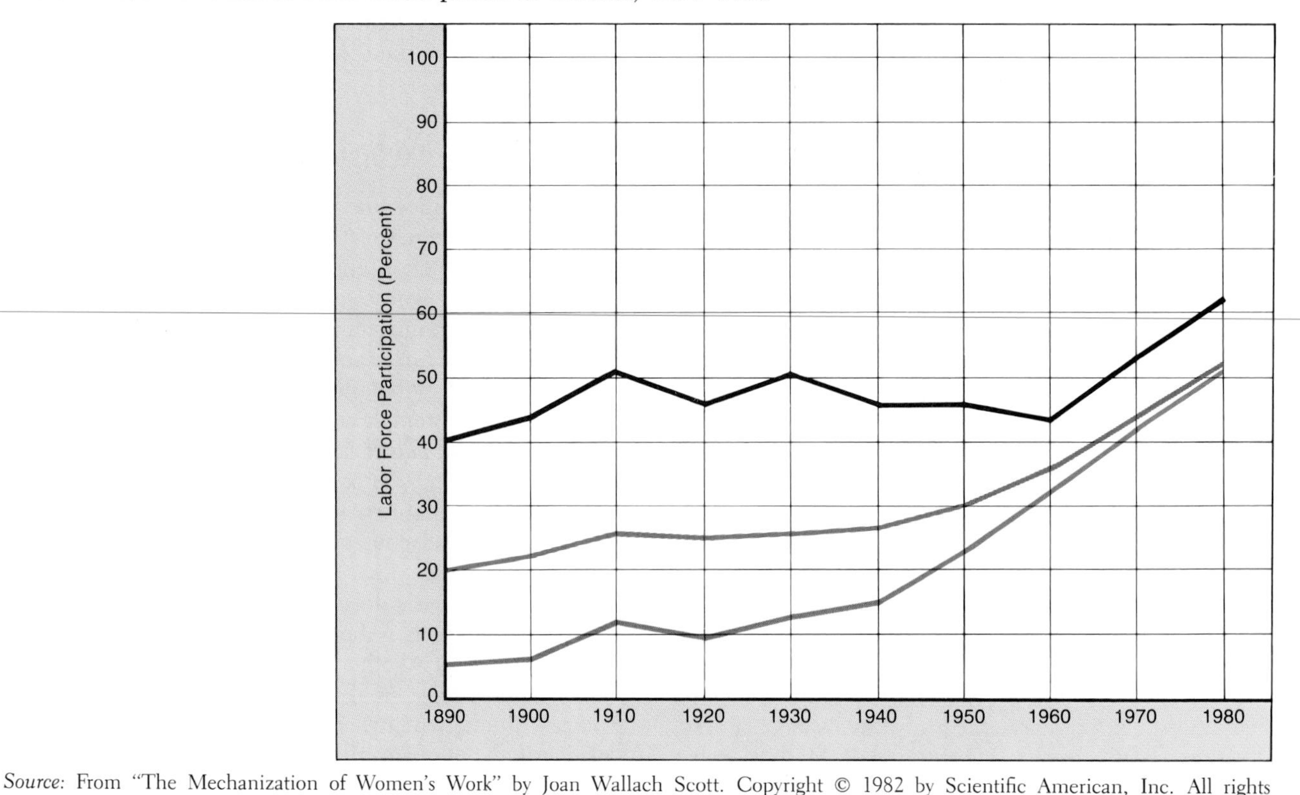

Source: From "The Mechanization of Women's Work" by Joan Wallach Scott. Copyright © 1982 by Scientific American, Inc. All rights reserved.

The percentage of women in the labor force has increased greatly since 1890. The black line shows the labor-force participation rate for single women, the gray line the rate for all women, and the colored line the rate for married women.

that of women. Men also have more psychosomatic diseases, such as ulcers, spastic colon, asthma, and migraine. More males than females suffer from personality disorders marked by aggressive and antisocial behavior (Rosenfield, 1980). The male suicide rate is triple the female rate, and men are fourteen times as likely to become alcoholics. Moreover, men commit 95 percent of all violent crimes and eight times as many murders as women do.

Role Conflicts

Finally, as with the female role, a number of conflicts are built into the male role. Men are supposed to be single-minded in the pursuit of success but not neglectful of their families; they should be simultaneously interested and disinterested in women; and they must be strong, self-reliant, and unemotional, yet require the sympathetic care of a nurturant wife.

As a result, many men find that masculinity is a rather vulnerable and precarious status. The male role is demanding and difficult, and the "failure" rate is high. In American society, as in other industrial societies, few men can hope to achieve the wealth, power, and positions of leadership that social ideals prescribe. *Machismo* may be a last resort for men who accept the traditional masculine role but cannot fill it. Overtly, machismo consists of a show of strength and sexual prowess as well as the denigration, exploitation, and often brutalization of women. Covertly, this display masks fears and doubts about self-worth. In an effort to convince other men, women, and above all himself that he is truly all-male, a man uses machismo as a front for insecurity, self-doubt, and worldly failure (Aramoni, 1972).

Given the contradictions inherent in the traditional male role, many men welcome the changes in the female role as a liberation from the burdens of traditional masculinity. These men seek a new male ideal, less geared toward competition and dominance. Men will be better off, they argue, if they can learn to acknowledge their human vulnerability and limitations and escape the posturing and pretense of the male role. Others see change as a dethronement from a previously privileged status. The more they feel they have to lose, the more likely men—and women—are to resist change. Consequently, anger, conflict, and misunderstandings have often accompanied the social change that has involved traditional sex roles.

Persistence and Change

Despite the persistence of traditional sex role stereotypes, the status of women has undergone major changes over the past twenty-five years (see Figure 6.2). More than half of all American women over age sixteen and nearly 70 percent of all women between twenty and forty-five years of age are now in the labor force (see Figure 6.3). Further, more than half of all women with school-age children are either holding jobs outside the home or looking for such jobs.

The figure shows the percentage of women in each age bracket who are in the labor force compared to all women who are in that age group. As of November 1982, 53 percent of all women sixteen years of age and older were in the labor force.

FIGURE 6.3 Women in the Labor Force by Age, November 1982

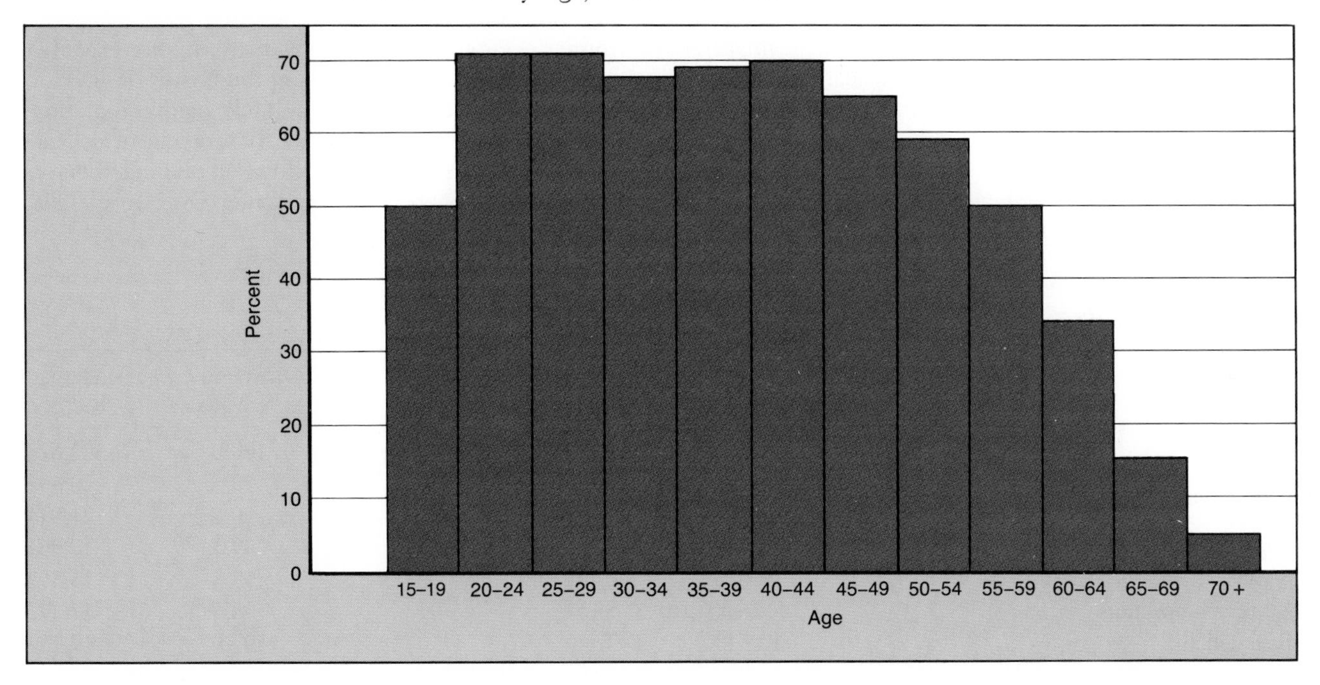

Source: Employment and Earnings, Bureau of Labor Statistics, December 1982.

Many factors have contributed to this expansion of the female work force. Some reflect the changes in the status of women; some reflect economic necessity. Changing attitudes and legislation have broken down many discriminatory barriers and opened new avenues of employment for women. Women have entered college in ever-expanding numbers, increasing the number of women embarking upon careers (whereas in 1972 there were 74 women for every 100 men in college, today there are 108 women for every 100 men). Women are freer to choose careers because of the increasing availability of effective contraception and legal abortion which has permitted them greater control over their childbearing. Economic factors such as the mounting divorce rate have substantially increased the number of households financially dependent on women. Financial pressures associated with fluctuations in the business cycle and inflation have made two paychecks increasingly attractive for many couples as well. The expansion of the nation's service-oriented economy has increased the demand for white–collar workers, providing a broader range of opportunities for all women.

Although the number of women in the work force has increased, little change has occurred since 1900 in the sex segregation of occupations (Scott, 1982). Women have achieved most of their employment gains by displacing men in some low-paying categories and by assuming jobs in the rapidly expanding "pink collar" (secretarial, key-punch, receptionist, and waitressing) occupations. As reflected in Table 6.1, women occupy more than 90 percent of all positions as secretaries, receptionists, bank tellers, telephone operators, and nurses. Many of the jobs open to women in the service industries reflect work traditionally performed by women as homemakers—teaching children, nursing the sick, and preparing food.

Although in recent years women's enrollments in higher education have increased at a faster rate than those of men, women are still concentrated in the traditionally female fields of education, fine and applied arts, foreign languages, nursing and related health care areas, home economics, and library science. Similarly, over half the women at the master's level and over a third at the doctoral level are pursuing degrees in education. Women are also more likely than men to be enrolled on a part-time basis, a pattern that often reflects conflicting demands, more distractions, and delayed graduation (Randour et al., 1982).

Nevertheless, women have made gains in a number of fields traditionally closed to them, including medicine and the law. Women graduating from colleges with degrees in business rose from about 9,000 in 1970 to almost 63,000 in 1980, and those getting engineering degrees increased from 526 in 1970 to 7,669 in 1980. In 1972 women held only one of eight management jobs in companies with one hundred or more employees, today they hold one of five such jobs (see box). However, women occupy only 5 percent of the higher executive positions, and they hold seats on the boards of directors of less than 1 percent of all publicly held corporations (Byrne, 1982). Not surprisingly, 68 percent of college-educated women in a 1982 Gallup Poll said that their sex lacks equal job opportunities with men (*New York Times*, 1982).

TABLE 6.1 Sex Stratification in the Labor Force, 1982

Occupations	% Women	Median Income	Occupations	% Men	Median Income
Secretaries	99.2	$12,636	Railroad switch operators	100.0	$22,828
Receptionists	97.5	10,764	Firefighters	99.5	20,438
Typists	96.6	11,804	Plumbers, pipefitters	99.2	21,944
Registered nurses	95.6	18,980	Auto mechanics	99.1	15,964
Sewers, stitchers	95.5	8,632	Carpet installers	98.8	15,392
Keypunch operators	94.5	12,480	Surveyors	98.5	17,472
Bank tellers	92.0	10,348	Truck drivers	97.9	17,160
Telephone operators	91.9	13,988	Garbage collectors	97.3	12,116

Source: Bureau of Labor Statistics, 1984.

THE SOCIOLOGICAL EYE ON:

Women Managers

One of the most dramatic changes to take place in the American workplace over the past two decades has been the entry of increasing number of women into managerial positions. Since the enactment of the Civil Rights Act of 1964, the number of women managers has grown from less than 15 percent to more than 28 percent. While resistance to women in entry- and lower-level management slots has decreased, women have found it difficult to break through the mid-level management bottleneck and gain the more powerful and lucrative executive positions (Weiss, 1983).

In 1983 *Fortune* magazine found 33 of the 34 women who graduated in the 1973 class of Harvard Business School (MBA program). This was the first class in which at least 5 percent of the students were women (Rowan, 1983). Ten years later at about age thirty-seven, all but one of the women was working full-time; eighteen had married; and fourteen were mothers. The top earner made more than $200,000; four others made at least $100,000. Only nine made less than $50,000. Even so, the women of '73 were making less than their male classmates, 35 percent of whom were earning more than $100,000. Much the same picture emerged for the Princeton undergraduate class of '73—the median salary of men in the class was $46,000 and that of women, $33,000 (Geist, 1983). The Princeton women did not attribute the discrepancy to discrimination but to having changed jobs to accommodate a spouse or having taken time off to have and rear children.

Rosabeth Moss Kanter (1977), who has done extensive research on the corporation, has found that when women make up less than 30 percent of an organization, they encounter the "dynamics of tokenism." Coworkers subject them to unusual scrutiny, considering them "newsworthy" and leading the women to complain of "overobservation." Their performance takes on symbolic significance as to "how women do." Yet simultaneously, their technical abilities tend to be eclipsed by their physical attractiveness. Further, token women seem to heighten male feelings of camaraderie —an "us against them" outlook. Men often respond to the presence of women managers with exaggerated displays of aggression and potency, including episodes of sexual teasing and prowess-oriented "war-stories." And men typically set about "testing" a woman boss, to see if she means "business" or can be intimidated.

Kanter finds that token women are frequently treated in wifelike and datelike ways by their male coworkers. Further complicating their situation, four role traps face the female manager in male groups: "mother"—sympathetic, good listener; "seductress"—the sex object; "pet"—group mascot; and "iron-maiden"—militant and unapproachable. Such attributions and their associated expectations impair a woman's ability to carry out her responsibilities and thus sabotage her rise in the organization.

Kanter suggests that as the proportion of women in management increases, the resistance to their presence should decrease. But an emerging body of research reveals that while this may be true up to a point, it is decidedly not always the case (Weiss, 1983). As the percentage of female managers nears the 50 percent mark, men become increasingly apprehensive and threatened. They attempt to erect new barriers to the advancement of women and intensify their sexual harassment of them. Further, many men do not want to work in units managed by women, an attitude that contributes to the creation of "female ghettos" (see Chapter 6). Sexism plays a large part. But pragmatism also operates. Since women are stereotyped as powerless, men often believe that a female boss will lack the clout necessary to protect and advance their interests. In sum, women managers still confront sizable problems in organizational settings.

According to a recent study prepared for the federal Equal Employment Opportunity Commission, the work women do is paid less than that of men, and the more an occupation is dominated by women, the less it pays (Shribman, 1981). Of interest, 70 percent of working men in the United States and 54 percent of the working women are concentrated in jobs overwhelmingly occupied by members of their own sex. Moreover, despite the changes in the labor market over the past two decades, women still earn less than 70 percent of what men do. Even women with training and credentials equal to those of men earn less than their male counterparts. For instance, women with M.B.A. (Master of Business Administration) degrees average 81 percent of their male

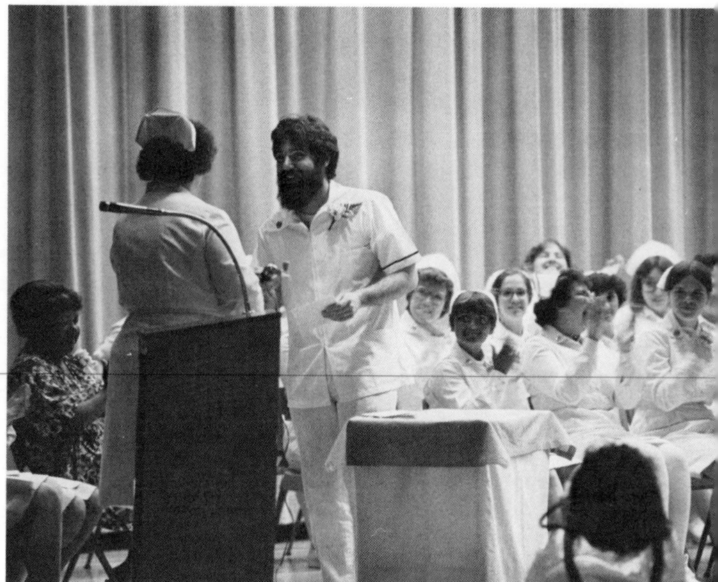

Gender equalization works both ways. Women are beginning to find work in male-dominated fields, like oil drilling; men are entering fields once overwhelmingly female, like nursing. (Left, David E. Kennedy; right, George W. Gardner.)

counterparts' salaries (Wills, 1983). And women on college and university faculties are paid, on average, 85 percent of what their male colleagues receive (Magarrell, 1981).

An influx of women into a previously male-dominated field tends to result in occupational segregation and depressed wages for women. For instance, at one time men outnumbered women in such currently female-dominated occupations as typist, elementary-school teacher, and bank teller (Randour et al., 1982). As men increasingly abandoned these fields, real wages in them declined. One remedy to this dual problem of occupational segregation and low wages would be to revise job-evaluation systems to encompass the "comparable worth" concept. Under this arrangement women would receive the same salaries as men who hold different jobs of comparable value. A secretary, for example, would receive the same pay as an electrician, positions that job evaluators with the Illinois Commission on the Status of Women have found to be of roughly "comparable worth" (in 1982 the monthly salary of secretaries in Illinois averaged $1,486 and that of electricians $2,826) (Gest, 1984). However, determining which jobs are comparable to which others is difficult. Valuation schemes giving points for skills, responsibility, physical and mental effort, and job hazards provoke considerable controversy. Further, by some estimates, it would cost employers $150 billion a year to raise women workers to the wage levels of men who do jobs of roughly "comparable worth" (Lewin, 1984).

EPILOGUE

Few aspects of sociological inquiry are interwoven into the fabric of social experience so intrinsically as our gender roles. In Chapter 3 we considered the shared sets of rules and traditions that shape our feelings, thoughts, and actions as members of society. This chapter, particularly the material on the Arapesh, the Mundugumor, and the Tchambuli, demonstrates anew the importance of culture in providing us with guidelines for our behavior. Culture influences our experiences as men and women by shaping the expectations associated with the male and female roles.

Our gender roles also constitute a key master status integrating us within the larger social structure. As we noted in Chapter 4, our social relationships are patterned in a relatively stable manner. Our beliefs and expectations about the appropriate conduct and characteristics of men and women influence and channel our behavior in recurrent and predictable ways. In turn, our individual episodes of interaction come together to provide a larger and more inclusive social fabric. Thus social life has structure, and society is more than simply a chaotic collection of individuals randomly interacting with one another.

Chapter 5 considered socialization, the process by which we acquire social identities and internalize the values and roles of our social world. The material in this chapter dealing with gender training provides a detailed illustration of one form of socialization. Social agents in the roles of parents, teachers, peers, and the media transmit to us the social scripts that outlines gender-appropriate behavior. In this fashion society perpetuates itself from one generation to the next, and we acquire a cultural heritage. Thus by training us for our sex roles, society prepares us for effective participation in the larger social world. Socialization, then, is a blending process by which societal patterns of culture are selectively joined to our needs and capacities as individual organisms.

The material in this chapter also foreshadows our discussion in Chapter 10 of social stratification. Stratification refers to the division of a society into layers (or strata) of people who have unequal amounts of scarce but desirable resources or rewards. It encompasses not only inequality among individuals, but also inequality among categories of people, such as male and female. In this chapter we have considered sex, or sex role, stratification. We have seen how the benefits and burdens of social living flow unequally to men and women. In the chapter that follows we will explore how individuals carry on their behavior as men and women within group settings and fit their actions together to fashion ongoing relationships.

SUMMARY

Sex roles are the behavior patterns expected of males and females in a society. Although genes and hormones determine sex (that is, male or female biology), they do not determine gender (the set of conceptions that people have regarding "masculine" and "feminine" characteristics). Thus we cannot assume that males and females are born with different abilities and temperaments that make them naturally suited for different sex roles.

The considerable variability that social scientists find from one society to another in the behavior patterns of men and women has made them skeptical of claims that biological factors are the primary source of differences between the sexes. Such substantial cultural variation as that reported by Margaret Mead among the New Guinea people challenge our beliefs as to what is "natural" and "unnatural" behavior in men and women.

In America sex roles vary from one class to another, and they have varied over time, from the Colonial era to the present. Today sex roles in America are undergoing important changes, but it is still possible to identify certain basic beliefs about men and women that have widespread acceptance and legal support.

Psychologists have attempted to identify sex differences in personality and ability. Much controversy surrounds these matters, but one fact is indisputable: For any trait there exists a wide range of variation in its expression among both males and females and there is considerable overlap between the ranges of the sexes. There seems to be little that is inherently either male or female.

Gender identity begins at birth and continues through adolescence into adulthood. Parents give small children both subtle and direct clues to sex-appropriate behavior and feelings. School curricula, learning materials, and administrations have traditionally separated male and female sex roles.

Sex role stratification is the ranking of sexes as superior and inferior. Athough some societies (such as the Hopi Indian) are not sexually stratified, most modern societies, including the United States, are. Woman's biological role as childbearer, her lack of training and tenure in the workplace, the process of socialization into sex roles, supported by the ideology of sexism, all contribute to the stratification of sex roles in this country.

American women were traditionally expected to want marriage and a family and to put the family first; to depend on their husbands, financially and socially; to live vicariously through their husbands and children; to be passive, rather than aggressive and self-assertive, to be loving and sympathetic, and to be glamorous.

American men were expected to be good providers and to be competitive, achieving, self-reliant, and less emotional. Each of these sets of beliefs has certain costs and benefits for each of the sexes, and each involves role conflicts.

GLOSSARY

Chromosome. The material in a cell that carries the determiners of hereditary characteristics.

Gender. Socially agreed upon traits of men and women.

Gender identity. One's psychological identification as man or woman.

Hermaphrodites. Individuals born with reproductive structures that have both male and female properties.

Hormones. Chemical substances that stimulate or inhibit vital physiological processes.

Machismo. Compulsive masculinity, evidenced in posturing, boasting, and an exploitative attitude toward women.

Sex. The biological difference of male and female.

Sex role. The idealized and general standards or expectations for the behavior of men and women.

Sex role stratification. The ranking of one sex as superior or inferior to the other.

Sexism. The ideology that supports a system of sexual inequality.

PART THREE

ORGANIZING SOCIAL LIFE

Place five or ten people together for a day or so, put them on their own or give them a task and one of the first things they are likely to do is "get organized." Each of the chapters in Part 3 deals with the process of organizing social life, the nature of that organization, and the degree to which cultural norms and social structure shape social units.

We begin with the simple fact that much of the drama of human existence is played out in the context of groups. We begin life within a group—the family—and proceed to join and leave many other groups as we mature and age. Indeed, we are so accustomed to group life that we rarely, if ever, stop to ask precisely what a group is and how it affects its members' behavior. Sociologists do ask these questions, and Chapter 7 explores their findings.

Chapter 8 examines formal organizations—groups of people whose activities are deliberately coordinated by means of explicit rules and a hierarchy of responsibility. Bureaucracy is one of the major topics we address here. We will gain insight into the problems of bureaucratic structure, and at the same time better understand its advantages. We will also look ahead to new types of formal organization designed to accomplish the complex tasks of late twentieth-century life.

Any form of organization—be it a family, a business, or an entire society—requires some degree of conformity from its members. But the very processes that encourage conformity can also inspire, or create, deviance. We will explore this paradox in Chapter 9. There, too, we will look at our criminal justice system to see how our society deals with an important category of deviance.

CHAPTER 7

Social Groups

What do you think would happen if thirty boys were to find themselves marooned alone on a tropical island? Perhaps some would try to reestablish the organization adults imposed at home and at school, hold meetings, and delegate responsibility for chores. Some would band together in "war parties," taking advantage of their freedom from adult surveillance to act out their wildest fantasies. Some would whimper for their homes and families and would look for someone to fill the role of older brother. Leaders would emerge, weld together cliques, and vie for power. The group might divide into hostile camps. The boys might get carried away, find themselves swept up by group momentum, and do things they might never have imagined doing as individuals.

This scenario is what happens in William Golding's *Lord of the Flies* (1954), a novel that has proven popular on college campuses. The story opens on an uninhabited tropical island after a plane carrying a load of British schoolboys, ranging in age from six to twelve, makes a crash landing. All the adults are killed, and the boys are left alone to establish an orderly way of life and to try to effect their own rescue. But things do not work out as originally hoped. A rational, democratic group, organized by Ralph, is overcome by an irrational and violent one led by Jack. The boys become consumed by groundless fears, intense competition and hatred, and the drive to experience immediate pleasures. The confusion halts at the end of the novel with the arrival of a British naval ship.

Throughout the story, Golding shows that while we often think we are in command of our personal behavior, the fact is that our group experiences influence us to a remarkable degree. Social groups link our private lives to the larger society. They provide us with security and support. They shape our values, attitudes, and behavior through the influence of others. How we act within a group is seldom how we would act if entirely alone. Because these important sociological insights are dramatically illustrated throughout *Lord of the Flies*, we will return to this novel at various points in this chapter.

In this chapter we direct our sociological eye to social groups, a crucial topic because groups provide the foundations of social order and a social existence. We begin our exploration of social groups by examining their characteristics and functions. We then consider different types of groups. Finally, we conclude with a discussion of the internal dynamics that propel group life.

THE NATURE OF SOCIAL GROUPS

When the boys depicted in *Lord of the Files* crash-land on the uninhabited island, the first to emerge from the jungle are a physically weak, overprotected but intellectual boy nicknamed Piggy and a blond, athletic twelve-year-old named Ralph. At Piggy's suggestion, Ralph summons the other survivors together by blowing into a large conch shell. Small boys, wearing tattered school uniforms, make their way out of the jungle. These boys do not yet constitute a true social group. They are simply an **aggregate** of individuals who happen to be in the same place at the same time, much like pedestrians on the same sidewalk or passengers on the same bus. However, they soon become a group by repeatedly interacting with one another, by developing a structure, by agreeing on norms, and by establishing a feeling of unity and belonging.

Characteristics of Social Groups

A **social group** in its most complete form has four characteristics. First, group members interact on a fairly regular basis. People who do not communicate with one another, who barely acknowledge each other's existence, do not constitute a social group. In *Lord of the Flies* it was only with the blowing of the conch and the calling of the first "assembly" that the ragged collection of survivors started to become a group. Second, the members of a group do not interact haphazardly. Each typically assumes a specific status and adopts a particular role. This structuring of relationships can be seen in Golding's novel. The oldest boys quickly established dominance over the proceedings; they became the group leaders. The youngest boys were deferential and generally obedient; they were expected to follow, not to lead. Third, the members of a group agree to some extent on important norms, goals, and values. A collection of people at cross-purposes is unlikely to form a group. When Golding's assembly of young survivors initially agreed on the need for orderly procedures and the importance of being rescued, they were closer to being a group than they were when the consensus later dissolved. Finally, group members feel a sense of shared identity. They think of themselves as united and interdependent, somewhat apart from other people. This sense of collective belonging quickly emerged on Golding's tropical island, where the boys, separated from all other humans, soon recognized that their fates were interwined. In summary, then, the boys in Golding's novel formed a set of individuals who identified and interacted with one another in a structured way based on shared values and goals—in brief, a *social group*.

Functions of Groups

In order to gain an appreciation for the importance of groups to human thought, behavior, and everyday life, try asking yourself a few questions. Who are you, apart from identification with any sort of group? Could your opinion alone convince your senator to vote for (or against) a gun control bill? Could you alone make up a sorority or a fraternity? Could you have a parade by yourself? Or a party? Can one person fight a war, start a new fad, change a norm, create a new style of living? It takes groups to do all these things.

It is through our association with others in groups—whether it be a college class, a sorority or fraternity, a family, an army, a sports team, or colleagues on the job—that we obtain our social identity. Study after study shows that we act differently in different groups and according to our position in a group. Regardless of personality, most people think and behave differently when they are in the center of a group than when they are on the fringes. When we answer the question "Who am I?," most of us answer in terms of our group affiliations (Kuhn, 1960).

Groups also serve as the medium through which social forces and social institutions influence our behavior. Group norms, status positions, and roles echo larger social forces; they serve to make personal and real that which is impersonal and removed. For example, although on its surface college life appears to be egalitarian, sororities, fraternities, and honor societies separate the more privileged or gifted from the rest, thus replicating the social distinctions and rules of the outside social world. But it takes a sociological eye to see these patterns and forces at work below the surface interaction.

Another function of groups is to give us the influence and power with which to change society. It is unlikely that Congress would have passed the 1964 Civil Rights Act if whites and blacks had not organized group protests in the several years preceding passage of the bill. Less important and far-reaching social changes also begin within groups. Fads start when a group member tries something new or distinctive and the rest of the group follow. Wearing a certain style of clothes or a certain color catches on with one group and then spreads to others if they regard it as the "in" thing to do.

Whether social change is involved or not, groups transform our individual experiences into social experiences. Having lunch alone is not the same as having lunch with a couple of friends; living with others is profoundly different from living alone. Finally, as we will see later, groups serve to contain, manage, and redefine conflicts. Thus, by virtue of their numerous functions, groups are a critical aspect of our social environment.

TYPES OF GROUPS

Human social life clearly depends on the existence of groups. As we consider the nature of these groups we quickly become aware of the diversity among them. In order to make sense of these enormous differences, sociologists distinguish among various types of groups. Let us turn our attention to some of the more important distinctions that sociologists find helpful in describing and analyzing group behavior.

Primary Groups

The most fundamental unit of human society is the **primary group.** The concept originated with Charles Horton Cooley (1909/1929:23), who characterized primary groups as those based on

> intimate face-to-face association and cooperation. They are primary in several senses, but chiefly in that they are fundamental in forming the social nature and ideals of the individual. The result of intimate association, psychologically, is a certain fusion of individualities in a common whole, so that one's very self, for many purposes at least, is the common life and purpose of the group. Perhaps the simplest way of describing this wholeness is by saying that it is a "we"; it involves the sort of sympathy and mutual identification for which "we" is the natural expression.

Breaking Cooley's definition down, we find five interconnected features:

1. Continuous face-to-face interaction
2. Strong personal identity with the group
3. Strong ties of affection
4. Multifaceted relationships
5. A long-lasting group

The nuclear family, at least in theory, is the primary group *par excellence*. Members of the family are frequently in face-to-face interaction; the unit gives them an important source of personal identity and purpose; family members are often bound together by love and affection; family members have many kinds of relationships with one another, ranging from exchange of services—"You set the table, I'll wash the dishes"—to emotional support and physical protection; and finally, the family is enduring (even when members move away, they are still considered part of it).

Our families and similar groups are "primary" in a number of ways. First, they are the principal agents of socialization. Cooley viewed them as the "nursery of human nature" because within them we are initiated into the cultural ways of our society. Thus they serve as a bridge between the individual and the larger community, transmitting, interpreting, and ultimately sustaining a society's critical norms and values.

Second, our family members, friends, and work associates are "primary" because these relationships are the vehicles for meeting our basic emotional and psychological needs. Over 350 years ago, the English poet John Donne (1573–1631) wrote, "No man is an island, entire of itself." His poem describes the profound role that other people play in providing each of us with a sense of love, security, recognition, companionship, and well-being. We discover the central role that primary groups play in our lives when we leave home for college or a new job and experience "homesickness"—nostalgia for a primary group from which we have been set apart.

Third, these groups are "primary" because they are vital agents of social control. In our face-to-face, intimate associations with one another we have unparalleled opportunities to scrutinize one another's attitudes and behaviors and to bring deviants into line. Further, primary groups define "social reality" for us so that we are "culture-bound"—alternative or deviant ways of doing things typically do not occur to us.

The associations among the boys in *Lord of the Flies* revolved about primary groups—initially the orderly, democratic group led by Ralph and later the tyrannical group led by Jack. In the novel Golding portrays human beings as reverting to barbarity, anarchy, and violence when under stress. The situation in Beirut, Lebanon, over the past fifteen years would seem to support

The companionship co-workers provide for each other helps to lighten the day's work. When work associates form a primary group, they meet each other's needs for support with on-the-job and personal problems. (Read D. Brugger/The Picture Cube.)

Golding's depiction. Indeed, Beirut has become a symbol of violence, with warring factions, shelling, and car-bombings commonplace occurrences.

Yet when the normal controls of the larger Beirut society were removed, the hand of each person was not turned against that of every other person (Friedman, 1983). The average resident did not go out and rob the corner grocery store or plunder neighbors. Despite a pattern of apparent lawlessness and anarchy, a remarkable self-imposed lawfulness has in fact prevailed in the city. The reason has to do with primary groups. Beirut is a city of neighborhoods, and the people in each neighborhood are tied together by interlocking family, friendship, ethnic, and religious bonds. These primary group ties have provided a social fabric that has regulated people's behavior and kept individuals' "upright and honest." Further, the primary groups have redoubled their efforts to get the everyday tasks performed. Confronted with disorder, people have become obsessively orderly, undertaking to organize their lives down to the smallest detail. On one block during the height of the Israeli siege of 1982, the children were organized into a work detail to wash the street regularly with detergent.

The difficulty experienced by Lebanon is that its problem and the solution derive from the same social forces. Individuals have achieved a sense of social identity and psychological support from family, neighborhood, and ethnic primary groups but not from the nation as a whole. The civil war has drawn people closer together on the microlevel while tearing them further apart at the national macrolevel. Thus the very bonds that enable the residents of Beirut to cope with the stresses of warfare also interfere with their evolving a more encompassing national identity and government. The feelings generated by a close-knit group bind individuals together so strongly that they override people's other differences while simultaneously creating an inability to belong to any other social grouping.

Secondary Groups

Secondary groups have the opposite characteristics of primary groups:

1. Limited face-to-face interaction
2. Modest or weak personal identity with the group
3. Weak ties of affection
4. Limited relationships
5. Not very enduring

An example of a secondary group is a faculty committee organized to study the curriculum at a large university. Members of the committee meet infrequently and for only a few hours at a time. They do not have opportunities to get to know one another in a variety of situations, as family members or friends do. They get together for an explicit purpose. People view such groups as a means for getting things done, not as ends in their own right. Consequently, members often respond to digressions from a task with impatience and hostility. Although members may hold similar attitudes and values, their basic ties are intellectual, not emotional. Many secondary groups are more casual, such as an amateur sports team in which people are acquaintances —perhaps even friends, but in a quite limited context.

The distinction between primary and secondary groups is not absolute and real groups may have elements of both. For many analytical tasks it is more helpful to view primariness and secondariness as a matter of degree rather than kind. For example, many work groups in businesses, although task-oriented, provide their members with close and warm relationships. But like other distinctions in social science, this one is useful in that it sharpens our focus and highlights dimensions of group life we may not otherwise see.

In-Groups and Out-Groups

Another distinction that sociologists find useful is that between "in-groups" and "out-groups." The terms were first used by the American sociologist William Graham Sumner (1906) in his attempt to describe the feelings of "we" and "they" generated by group membership. An **in-group** is a social unit in which individuals feel at home and with which they identify. An **out-group** is a social unit to which individuals do not belong and with which they do not identify.

In-group and out-group distinctions surround us everywhere. If we are drug users, the out-group is the straight world; if we do not use drugs, users are the out-group. To the wealthy, out-groups are the middle and lower classes; to the middle class, the wealthy and the poor are out-groups. To the residents of ethnic neighborhoods, people of other nationalities, religions, or races belong to out-groups. In other words, any group of individuals who differ from us in significant ways comprises an out-group.

Boundaries

The distinction between in-groups and out-groups draws our attention to *boundaries*—bounds or limits to the flow of social interaction. Without boundaries, there would be no way of setting groups off from one another, of distinguishing members from nonmembers. Boundaries serve a dual function. They prevent outsiders from entering certain spheres of social interaction with insiders. And at the same time, they limit the actions of insiders so that they do not move beyond the confines of the group. In other words, a group's boundaries "encapsulate" individuals so that their lives are focused within a particular social arena. Since a group's boundaries are intangible—a matter of social definitions—people may attempt to give them a more tangible cast through symbolic representations. A fraternity tee-shirt or a college decal placed on a car window announce one's insider status, symbolically telling the world that one "belongs." Forms of slang and specialized languages serve similar functions.

Consciousness of Kind

The distinction between in-groups and out-groups is further clarified by the awareness that members have of their common identity. The tendency of people to recognize others like themselves and to feel a oneness with them is termed a **consciousness of kind.** This consciousness of kind tends to provide a cohesiveness within a group. Thus, groups often attempt to foster and deepen their members' consciousness of kind by rituals, ceremonies, and related measures. For instance, families and cliques often stage birthday parties for their members that serve as occasions for recharging a sense of collective solidarity.

Not surprisingly, in-group and out-group distinctions foster stereotypes about out-group members. People typically see themselves and others in their in-group

Boundaries between in-groups and out-groups distinguish members from nonmembers in many common situations. (Joseph Szabo/Photo Researchers.)

as distinct individuals but view the out-group as homogeneous, as made up of people who are all alike. In other words, we tend to view the behavior and attitudes of a single group member as typical of the group as a whole. Such attitudes feed the ethnocentric tendencies we considered in Chapter 3. In sum, in-group and out-group distinctions not only serve to systematize our experiences; they also influence what we experience.

Group Conflict

Once we recognize that groups are characterized by boundaries and a consciousness of kind, we can begin to ask questions about how these properties are established. One of the most effective ways of creating and maintaining group boundaries and a consciousness of kind is through conflict with outsiders. A common enemy helps draw people together; through confrontation with out-groups, insiders begin to develop a sense of "we-ness." Sports contests between colleges, especially those between "traditional rivals," serve this purpose quite effectively.

In the concluding chapters of *Lord of the Flies*, Jack forms a tight in-group from which Ralph and Piggy are excluded. The members wear war paint, tie their long hair back on their heads, dance and chant together, and build a fortress to keep out "outsiders." Jack actively cultivates and exploits Ralph and Piggy's outcast status as "enemies" so as to unify his band:

> "Tomorrow," went on the chief [Jack], "we shall hunt again."
>
> He pointed at this savage and that with his spear.
>
> "Some of you will stay here to improve the cave and defend the gate. I shall take a few hunters with me and bring back meat. The defenders of the gate will see that the others don't sneak in."

> A savage raised his hand and the chief turned a bleak, painted face toward him.
> "Why should they try to sneak in, Chief?"
> The chief was vague but earnest.
> "They will. They'll try to spoil things we do. So the watchers of the gate must be careful." (Golding, 1954: 145–146)

Georg Simmel (1859–1918), a German sociologist who studied group conflict, suggested: "A state of conflict [with outsiders] pulls the members . . . tightly together. . . . This is the reason why war with the outside is sometimes the last chance for a state ridden with inner antagonisms to overcome these antagonisms" (Simmel, in Coser, 1956:87). Lewis Coser, an American sociologist who elaborated on Simmel's writings about conflict, suggests that white Southerners at the turn of the century exaggerated stories of black crimes against whites to tighten their ranks. Blacks actually committed very few crimes against whites, but stories of rapes, murders, and imminent race wars abounded. Coser contends that the intense fear that whites developed toward blacks derived not from what blacks actually did but from an attempt to maintain a system of white supremacy by rallying all whites around the banner of white racism.

Of course, no amount of conflict with outside groups can sustain a group that is falling apart. Unless a group has some basis for cohesion and consensus, it will tend to disintegrate and will be unable to rally when faced with external attack. During the Great Depression in America, for example, close families become closer and stronger as they united against their troubles, but weak families became weaker and many broke down (Komarovsky, 1940/1971).

Internal Conflict

Like conflict with outsiders, internal conflict may function to define and strengthen a group's boundaries and its consciousness of kind. People typically believe that the best way to deal with those who are at odds with other group members is to try to force them to conform and, if that fails, to expel them. Certainly that is one way of resolving internal conflict and protecting a group's norms. Real-life examples readily come to mind. For instance, someone who disobeys a papal edict may be excommunicated from the Roman Catholic church. And someone who rebels against a school's rules and refuses to attend classes is likely to be expelled from school.

But this solution is not universally imposed. The key variables determining whether a deviant or rebellious member is ejected from a group are the group's cohesiveness, the importance of the issue in dispute, and the magnitude of the disagreement. Other things being equal, as any of these variables (or all three) increase, the likelihood of expulsion also increases. Thus, highly cohesive groups are less tolerant of internal conflict than more loosely knit ones; dissension over a small matter is more frequently accepted than dissension over an important one; and disputes that place antagonists in totally opposite camps are more likely to lead to expulsion of the deviant members than are disputes that leave opposing factions with some common ground. These factors are useful to remember because they can help you to judge what kinds of internal conflict your own groups will tolerate.

Expulsion of deviant members is only one way of dealing with conflict within a group. Another is to exaggerate the prevalence of conflict and, in so doing, to spotlight and reinforce shared norms and goals. A group, after all, must periodically define itself; it must remind its members what the group is all about. As a result, a group may find it expedient not just to permit small acts of deviance within its ranks, but even to magnify and exploit these acts. In doing so, it calls attention to its own aims and values and creates an opportunity for members to reaffirm their allegiance to the group's standards (Dentler and Erikson, 1959). You may have noticed this yourself. For instance, groups sometimes get terribly upset over a member's minor deviation from group norms. Parents are particularly prone to do this as their children grow up and begin asserting their independence. This "overreaction" usually means that the group feels threatened. It makes a large issue of a small transgression in order to communicate to group members the importance of their loyalty to the group and their commitment to its standards.

Reference Groups

Our discussion of group boundaries and of consciousness of kind highlights the importance of our psychological

Being at odds with your reference group can be a source of fun or discomfort, depending on the group and the situation. (Katrina Thomas/Photo Researchers.)

identification with groups. Groups to which we consciously or unconsciously refer when we try to evaluate our own life situations and behavior, but that we do not necessarily belong to, are called our **reference groups.** A student who receives a B on an exam can feel either terrific in comparison to the C students or inadequate in comparison to the A students—it all depends on which category serves as a reference group. But note that the particular reference group a student looks to is not just a matter of whim. The choice reflects the social groups that a student came from and the level of expectation these groups set. Thus, depending on which groups we select to compare ourselves with, we can feel either deprived or privileged, satisfied or discontented, fortunate or unfortunate. Reference groups then serve a *comparison* function; they provide us with standards against which we evaluate ourselves.

Reference groups also have a *normative* function. They provide us with the guidelines we use in fashioning our behavior. Since groups are so critical in meeting our social and psychological needs, we typically wish to achieve a good standing within certain of them. Consequently, we take on a group's lifeways—its dress codes, its fads, its academic expectations, its political views, its drug-using practices, and a host of other behaviors. More than a century ago Henry Thoreau noted that a person who seems to be a deviant—who is out of step with his companions—may merely be marching to the tune of a different drummer (reference group). This observation is useful in understanding the behavior of a reactionary worker, a left-wing corporate executive, a "fallen-away" Catholic, a national traitor, and an assimilated immigrant.

Our reference groups tend to change as our life circumstances change. Going to college, for example, may bring about a change in reference groups, and with it a related change in the way we view ourselves. In a classic study of Bennington College students, Theodore Newcomb (1958: Newcomb et al., 1967) found that the liberal faculty tended to replace conservative parents as a reference group for most students. The longer most students stayed at Bennington, the more liberal they became. The exceptions were those students who continued to lean on their families for guidance. This is a good example of how reference groups affect socialization. Clearly, the processes operating in a group setting are powerful forces in our lives. Let us now examine these processes at greater length.

GROUP DYNAMICS

Earlier in the chapter we noted that recurrent patterns of interaction are one of the chief defining features of a social group. Such patterns are called **group dynamics.** *Lord of the Flies* provides some excellent illustrations of group dynamics at work. By now you are becoming familiar with the story line of the novel, which centers around a struggle for control between the fair-haired, attractive Ralph, who represents civilization with its rules, its structure, its carefully reasoned goals, and Jack, a tall, thin, ugly boy who thrives on excitement and violence and who epitomizes the primitive forces within the group. At first Ralph prevails; the boys are orderly and intent on being rescued. But gradually Jack gains the upper hand. In the end, most of the boys are persuaded to join Jack's "tribe," which then turns on the few remaining "outsiders" and systematically subjugates or destroys them. Ralph is eventually the only advocate of civilization left, and he is hunted down like an animal. The hunt becomes so frenzied that there appears to be no escape for Ralph. But at the last moment a naval cruiser happens by the island, the crew spots signs of the boys' activities, and the adult world intervenes. The important point for our purposes, however, is not the final outcome of the novel but the patterns of group behavior it explores. Group size, conformity to group norms, the quest for status among group members, the emergence of leaders, and the processes of group decision making are all critical forces influencing the boys' behavior.

Group Size

Group size has a profound impact upon social interaction. Ralph's situation early in the novel when he was leading a large group was quite different from that toward the end when he was left with only three followers. As portrayed by Golding and confirmed by sociologists, size is a limiting condition on the amount and quality of communication that can occur among individuals. Thus in group meetings on the island, individual boys had fewer chances to speak when a group was large than when it was small. And rank-and-file boys felt more inhibited in participating in discussions as a group's size increased. Further, very early in his experience on the island, Ralph encountered the sociological principle that a large group has in its membership a greater variety of resources for problem-solving than does a small group. However, the average contribution of each member tends to slacken off as a group becomes larger, and it becomes increasingly difficult to reach consensus on a group solution (Hare, 1976).

The differences between a **dyad** (a two-person group) and a **triad** (a three-person group) are particularly striking. Popular folklore reflects this in the expression, "Two's company; three's a crowd." The existence of a dyad dictates the participation of both members. If either withdraws, the group ceases to exist. A three-person group, however, can survive the loss of a member. Thus, a member of a dyad "is much more frequently confronted with All or Nothing than is the member of a larger group" (Simmel, 1950: 135). Since either member can terminate the relationship and can thus prevent the completion of a task, a dyad often exhibits a high rate of tension; each person has to proceed carefully within certain limits lest the other party pull out (Hare, 1976). Balance theory helps to account for how individuals often make their peace with difficult relationships (see the boxed insert, p. 166).

Another difference between dyads and triads is that participants in a dyad cannot hide their responsibility for events that occur within the confines of the group. If, for example, one of two roommates finishes off the last piece of candy, both know with certainty who did it. When three or more roommates live together, only the person who ate the candy knows for sure. In groups of three or more, one member can also reconcile conflicts between other members. If members of a dyad disagree, there is no insider to act as mediator. On the other hand, dyads do not have to deal with the problem of intruders or spectators. Neither of the two needs to perform for the benefit of a third party; they do not have to worry about giving a third party "air time." Such factors, which are entirely due to the properties of size, have an enormous impact on our experiences in group of all sizes.

The possibilities of building coalitions and creating majorities also distinguish dyads from triads. A coalition and a majority are impossible in a dyad. However, a number of coalitions are possible in a triad, as the sociologist Theodore Caplow suggests in a book aptly entitled *Two Against One* (1969). If A is more powerful than B, and B has the same power as C, then the possibilities for winning coalitions exist between A and B versus C, B and C versus A, and A and C versus B. The

THE SOCIOLOGICAL EYE ON:

Learning to Like Obnoxious People: A Lesson in Group Dynamics

Suppose you learned that you would have to interact closely with someone you found unpleasant and disagreeable. Do you think your negative feelings toward that person would intensify? Common sense certainly suggests they would. Isn't it natural to resent being forced to deal with someone distasteful to you? And wouldn't that resentment only encourage greater antipathy toward the already disliked person?

As sound as this reasoning seems, it does not hold up under scientific scrutiny. Consider an experiment in which researchers asked female college students to participate in three-person discussion groups (Tyler and Sears, 1977). The groups were arranged so that each consisted of two actual subjects and one "confederate"—a person who pretended to be a real subject but who was actually an accomplice of the experimenters. The confederate behaved most disagreeably. She periodically forgot her fellow discussants' names, called their opinions silly and childish, rudely blew cigarette smoke into their faces, snapped her chewing gum, and rocked the table around which they all sat. In short, she was totally obnoxious.

After suffering twenty minutes of this offensive performance, the two actual subjects were ushered into different rooms. One was told that she would soon be continuing the discusion with the same participants; the other was told that she would be switched to another group. Each subject was then asked to rate the other two discussants (including the confederate) in terms of likeability. The top line of the accompanying table shows that those who anticipated continued interaction with the obnoxious accomplice rated her significantly *more* likeable than did those who believed they would be spared another twenty minutes with this highly disagreeable person. This is not what common sense might suggest. How can these rather surprising findings be explained?

Balance theory provides one very persuasive explanation (Heider, 1958). It proposes that people are strongly inclined to seek balance or harmony among their various beliefs, feelings, and behaviors. Thus, if we find that we are going to be in unavoidable contact with someone we regard quite negatively, we tend to increase our liking for that person. In this way psychological balance is restored.

Note that balance theory does not predict a change in attitude when a person is forced to interact with someone already liked. In that case feelings are already in tune with the imposed relationship and no adjustment is required. This is precisely what happened in another part of the experiment just described, as shown in the bottom line of the accompanying table. When a fellow subject was pleasant to begin with, she was rated no more likeable when continued interaction was anticipated than when no further interaction was expected. Thus, balance theory provides a very useful framework for analyzing why our feelings toward others sometimes change and other times do not.

Balance theory can easily be applied to situations in your life. A noisy roommate, a cantankerous in-law, or an overdemanding boss may become more bearable after you acknowledge that the individual will remain a part of your life. Like others, you strive to bring your feelings and relationships into balance with one another. And in so doing you frequently learn to live with even the most disagreeable sorts.

Mean Likeability Scores in Discussion-Group Experiment

Rating of	Anticipated Further Interaction	No Anticipated Further Interaction
obnoxious confederate	15.00	11.22
pleasant fellow subject	19.00	20.56

Note: On the scale used for this rating, a neutral attitude is equal to 16. Values above this indicate liking; values below this indicate disliking.

Dyads and triads are strikingly different. Dyads depend upon the participation of both members, who share an intimate and private bond. Triads allow for shifting alliances, majority and minority opinions, and mediation of disputes. (Above, Cary Wolinsky/Stock, Boston; below, John Launois/Black Star.)

power of majority over minority is particularly marked in a triad because the minority is always a single person who is left potentially isolated and vulnerable. Thus, a three-person situation opens the door to "divide-and-conquer" techniques. Perhaps not surprisingly, in most triads, members tend to switch coalitions from one disagreement to another in order to preserve the group's solidarity and viability (Hare, 1976).

Adding a fourth member to a group again changes things drastically. It opens up new possibilities for coalitions (for example, two versus two; three versus one). As the size of a group grows, the number of possible relationships increases rapidly (see Table 7.1). As a result, a larger group tends to break into subgroups (Hare, 1976).

Although the best size for a group varies with the task, sociologists find that a five-person group constitutes the optimum size for many activities. For one thing, a strict deadlock is not possible with an odd number of members. For another, such groups tend to be large enough so that individuals feel able to express their feelings freely and to risk antagonizing each other; yet they are small enough so that the members show regard for one another's feelings and needs (Slater, 1958). Thus size is a structural property of groups, and it has a considerable influence on the behavior of members regardless of their individual psychological makeup.

Not only does the number of possible relationships increase rapidly with group size, but communication becomes complex. Beyond seven, fewer and fewer people have a chance to talk.

TABLE 7.1 Group Size and Complexity

Size of Group	Number of Relationships
2	1
3	6
4	25
5	90
6	301
7	966

Source: A. Paul Hare, *Handbook of Small Group Research* (Glencoe, Ill.: Free Press, 1976), p. 218.

The size of a group affects the relationships that form within it. In a group of four friends, smaller units may form when group members have different reactions to each other. (Lincoln Russell/Stock, Boston.)

Social Conformity

Initially the band of boys portrayed in *Lord of the Flies* formed a fairly harmonious group. They adopted the familiar norms of the school and adult world they so recently had left. At an early meeting of the group Ralph pointed out:

> ". . . We can't have everybody talking at once. We'll have to have 'Hands up' like at school. . . . Then I'll give him the conch."
>
> "Conch?"
>
> "That's what this shell's called. I'll give the conch to the next person to speak. He can hold it when he's speaking." . . .
>
> Jack was on his feet.
>
> "We'll have rules!" he cried excitedly. "Lots of rules!" (Golding, 1954:31)

The boys initially agreed upon rules concerning where a signal fire would be built, who would keep it burning, how food and water would be obtained and distributed, and so forth. Acceptance of such shared norms help bind a group together. Thus, in everyday life individuals evolve group norms and conform to them to achieve goals. Such rules or standards define the kinds of behavior that are necessary if group tasks are to be performed. Then, by bringing pressure on one another to conform to the norms, individuals achieve concerted action and make group life possible.

Evolving Norms

A classic study by the social psychologist Muzafer Sherif (1936) has shown how individuals evolve group norms in the course of their social interaction. He employed in his research an optical illusion: If individuals are briefly exposed to a dot of light in a darkened room, the dot seems to move about erratically even though it is stationary. When Sherif showed a lone individual the light over a number of episodes, the person would evolve a rather fixed estimate of the distance of the apparent movements.

Sherif then assembled a number of people who, in the solitary sessions, had arrived at quite different estimates. In the group setting they were again exposed to the light and asked individually to report aloud the distance the light moved. Their assessments tended to converge toward a group standard. Furthermore, individuals retained the group norm when they observed the stimulus alone at a later time. Of equal significance, the majority of individuals insisted that they had arrived at their conclusions before their peers had spoken and that they had *not* been influenced by the others.

Conformity to an Incorrect Majority Opinion

Another social psychologist, Solomon Asch (1952), was intrigued by Sherif's findings. He wondered what would happen if he were to confront individuals with a situation in which the other members of a group were obviously wrong. Accordingly, Asch devised an experiment that is also now regarded as a classic. He would seat seven or eight individuals side by side in a classroom with two large cards propped up in the tray of a chalk-board. Asch then would explain to the subjects that they were to match the length of the line on the first card with one of the three lines of the second card. There were eighteen comparisons and the subjects were instructed to give their answers aloud, each in turn.

In the experiment all but one of the subjects were coached confederates of Asch. These confederates were instructed to agree on an obviously incorrect answer for twelve of the comparisons. In nearly one-third of the sessions, the uncoached subjects responded with answers identical to or in the direction of the rigged errors of the majority. Furthermore, 74 percent of the subjects conformed to the incorrect majority view at least once. Group opinion clearly was influential enough in some cases to cause people to deny their correct perceptions of reality. But the study also revealed that individuals differ enormously in their willingness to yield to majority opinion.

Obedience to Authority

The social psychologist Stanley Milgram (1974) added a new dimension to conformity research. He asked how it was possible for many Germans during the Nazi period to obey orders to kill Jews and millions of other human beings. To explore this question, he devised a procedure, presented as a study dealing with memory and learning, in which an experimenter ordered a subject to administer electric shock to a victim. Each subject was told to press a switch to a simulated shock generator when the "learner" gave a wrong answer. The switches had labels ranging from "Slight Shock" to "Danger: Severe Shock," and finally, one simply labeled "XXX."

According to plan, the "learner" (a Milgram confederate) gave the wrong answers on occasion, and Milgram would tell the subject to administer a given level of shock. As the subject activated the switches indicating ever higher shock levels, the learners responded with cries of anguish, shrieks of torment, and pleas to stop. Eventually the "learner" would complain that his heart was bothering him, and then he would cease responding altogether. Even so, and despite their own often agitated state, 65 percent of the subjects gave the "learner" the maximum shock voltage. Milgram concluded from his research that obedience does not primarily depend on people's moral qualities, but on the situation in which they find themselves. In other words, the subjects' inclination not to harm others was overridden by their tendency to obey a person whom they defined to be a legitimate figure of authority.

It should be emphasized that Milgram's research has generated heated debate regarding its ethics. Not only were the subjects falsely led to believe that they were participating in a learning study, but they were ordered to engage in behavior that they perceived as being sufficient to injure or kill a person. Clearly, many subjects were exposed to severe psychological trauma, though follow-up studies showed that they recovered. Under the current guidelines for research, Milgram's study would no longer be considered legitimate (see Chapter 2).

Leadership

Milgram's research reveals how susceptible many people are to obeying authority, even if it means carrying out atrocious acts. The mass suicide led by Rev. Jim Jones in 1978 at the People's Temple settlement in Guyana provides a vivid reminder of the coercive qualities of blind obedience. The stark brutality of the boys in *Lord of the Flies* under Jack's leadership contained similar elements. Indeed, the power struggle that arose between Ralph and Jack (and that later turned into an all-out war) illustrates some key points about leadership.

Leadership Depends on the Situation

As the boys' situation on the island changes, so does Ralph's ability to lead. At first he appears to have some sort of **charisma,** a special quality that causes others to accept a person's authority. Not only was he one of the older and larger boys, but he had an attractive appearance and had taken the initiative in calling the boys together for the first time. Further, he was the only one with the insight to recognize Piggy's intelligence and the independence to befriend him. Even though he could not quite understand Simon, a quiet, introspective boy whose mystical intuitions baffle the others, Ralph included him in his plans. Ralph's easy self-assurance earned him the respect of all the boys. They applauded when he was elected chief, and they looked to him to call meetings, establish the rules, and assign tasks. In other words they accepted him as their leader, at least in the beginning.

As the story unfolds, however, it becomes increasingly clear that in large part circumstances have forced the leadership role on Ralph—his being a bit older and a bit abler than most of the others, his desire for order and eventual rescue, and his happening to be the one who finds and first blows the conch. Far from being a natural leader, he is uncomfortable with the attention and the responsibility and is often at a loss as to what to do next. It is not too long before Jack emerges as the leader who appeals to the boys' need for adventure and emotional release.

This gradual shift in influence from Ralph to Jack illustrates a basic fact about leadership—one that contradicts a widely held view. Most people believe that leaders have special traits that make them different from nonleaders. But attempts to isolate those traits have been disappointing. Few traits emerge repeatedly from studies of actual leaders. And those that do turn out to be common among many nonleaders as well. Such traits include intelligence, enthusiasm, dominance, self-confidence, and involvement (Hare, 1976). Thus, attempts to distinguish natural leaders from natural followers on the basis of personality traits alone have consistently failed (Secord and Backman, 1974). Leadership depends more on the situation than on the person. "The pilot of a bomber crew, for example, who is an excellent leader for the group while the plane is in the air, may be a most inadequate leader if the plane crashes and the crew is faced with the task of surviving or finding its way to safety" (Cartwright and Zander, 1968:495). In short, many people are capable of leadership if the needs of the group fit their skills. The person deemed most appropriate to lead at any given moment may change as the situation changes.

Leadership Roles: Task and Emotional Support

By carefully watching groups in the process of formation, Harvard sociologist Robert Bales and his students observed that groups need leaders for two basic purposes: to direct various tasks and to provide support to group members (Secord and Backman, 1974). On the island, the boys elected Ralph their overall leader, just as in most groups one person at first is the source of both direction and group support. But, as often happens, a division of labor emerges and two people begin meeting these separate functions. Hence, Ralph appoints Jack as task leader to organize the hunting of wild pigs for food.

The act of directing a group toward its goal is known as **task leadership,** and the act of maintaining good spirits and relations within a group is known as **socioemotional leadership.** The socioemotional leader is usually a well-liked person. Ralph has the qualities of a good socioemotional leader: he values harmonious and democratic social relations, he protects Piggy and other underdogs, and he listens to everyone's ideas and needs. But he becomes so intent on the task of keeping a smoke signal going in hope of rescue that he begins to neglect the socioemotional needs of the group.

> "Look at us. How many are we? And yet we can't keep a fire going to make smoke. Don't you understand? Can't you see we ought to—ought to die before we let the fire out?"

> There was a self-conscious giggling among the hunters. Ralph turned on them passionately. . . .
> "And another thing."
> Someone called out.
> "Too many things." . . .
> There was a row immediately. Boys stood up and shouted and Ralph shouted back. (Golding, 1954:73).

Jack, who is greedy for power, senses the unmet needs of the group and moves to fill the gap that Ralph has created by making a single, very tedious task assume overriding importance. While Ralph concentrates on keeping the fire going, Jack offers fun and adventure to those who will leave Ralph.

> "Bollocks to the rules! We're strong—we hunt! If there's a beast, we'll hunt it down! We'll close in and beat and beat and beat—!"
> He gave a wild whoop and leapt down to the pale sand. At once the platform was full of noise and excitement, scramblings, screams and laughter. (p. 83).

Thus, the leadership roles on the island shifted over time, although the task and socioemotional needs of the group did not.

Group Decision Making

The boys on Golding's island have no idea why events take the course they do. Things just happen; decisions get made. However, sociologists who have studied group interaction have identified some of the ways that groups make decisions. Whatever the group's composition or the task at hand, the group typically goes through four distinct stages in arriving at its choices (Bales and Strodtbeck, 1951).

The first stage is devoted to orientation. Members analyze the task before them, exchange data, and offer possible solutions. In the second stage, the group evaluates the information it has collected. A scene early in the novel illustrates both these stages in the decision-making process.

> Ralph cleared his throat.
> "Well then."
> All at once he found he could talk fluently and explain what he had to say. He passed a hand through his fair hair and spoke.
> "We're on an island. We've been on the mountain top and seen water all round. We saw no houses, no smoke, no footprints, no boats, no people. We're on an uninhabited island with no other people on it. . . .This is our island. It's a good island. Until the grownups come to fetch us we'll have fun."
> Jack held his hand out for the conch.
> "There's pigs," he said. "There's food; and bathing water in that little stream along there—and everything." (pp. 30–32).

Tension mounts as the group moves toward the third stage, reaching a decision. The members decide to put aside their fears and misgivings and instead concentrate on making the best of things. Once a decision is made (in this case to remain on the island and await rescue), the group moves toward the fourth stage—restoring equilibrium. A period of joking and informal banter draws dissenters into the fold. In various ways, members stress the importance of group solidarity.

> Ralph lifted the conch again and his good humor came back as he thought of what he had to say next.
> ". . . This is what I thought. We want to have fun. And we want to be rescued."
> The passionate noise of agreement from the assembly hit him like a wave and he lost his thread. He thought again.
> "We want to be rescued; and of course we shall be rescued."
> Voices babbled. (pp. 34–35)

Groupthink

In *Lord of the Flies* the boys' decision to remain on the island and await rescue was the best one possible under the circumstances. Even should the youngsters have fashioned a makeshift boat, venturing out on the ocean would have courted sure disaster. Not all decisions are this sound, however. Even when a group of highly intelligent adults are analyzing sound data, serious errors in judgment can occur. When are groups most prone to poor decision making? Social scientist Irving Janis (1972) believes the small, highly cohesive group with forceful and respected leaders are especially likely to produce decisions that have critical flaws. Such groups, according to Janis, can give rise to a process he calls *groupthink* —the tendency for members to be so intent on maintaining group unanimity that they overlook or dismiss as

The nature of the interaction within a group varies with its size. Thus the optimal group size for a task depends on the decision-making demands of the situation. (Above, Bill Gallery/Stock, Boston; below, Bohdan Hrynewych/Stock, Boston.

unimportant the major problems with the choices they make. Victims of groupthink collectively rationalize their decision in order to discount warnings about it. They suppress their own doubts and the doubts of others in the group. They insulate themselves from the opinions of knowledgeable outsiders, while negatively stereotyping those views at odds with their own. As a result, they convince themselves that their decisions are undeniably sound and that their designated courses of action will inevitably bring success. Needless to say, they are often unpleasantly surprised.

A classic example of a groupthink-induced fiasco is the Bay of Pigs invasion that President John F. Kennedy and his advisers decided on in 1961. The plan called for 1,400 CIA-trained Cuban exiles to land in Cuba and overthrow the Castro regime with covert United States support. The invasion was a disaster. It embarrassed the United States and solidified the Cuban-Russian alliance.

In making their decision, the group considered only two plans and chose one of them. They failed to reconsider the second plan when the flaws of the first became apparent, did not consult with a wide range of experts, ignored contradictory information brought to their attention, and did not provide for adequate contingency plans. The same pattern unfolded again as President Lyndon Johnson's inner circle of advisers steadily escalated the Vietnam War. Janis argues that in both cases the major reason was a strong compulsion, common in small, closely knit groups, to maintain unity and agreement at all costs—in short, not to rock the boat.

This tendency can also be seen in *Lord of the Flies*, when the boys persistently ridicule and suppress any views that contradict majority opinion. Consider this scene in which Simon attempts to warn the others that the "beast" they are dismissing as nonexistent may actually lie within themselves (the "beast" does not exist independently in the world, but is a mental creation that reflects the boys' own destructive potential).

> "Maybe," he said hesitantly, "maybe there is a beast."
> The assembly cried out savagely and Ralph stood up in amazement.
> "You, Simon? You believe in this?"
> "I don't know," said Simon. His heartbeats were choking him. "But. . . ."
> The storm broke.
> "Sit down!"
> "Shut up!"
> "Take the conch!"
> "Sod you!"
> "Shut up!"
> Ralph shouted.
> "Hear him! He's got the conch!"
> "What I mean is . . . maybe it's only us."
> "Nuts!" (P. 80)

Simon never publicly expressed his view again. Given such strong group pressures toward conformity, it is not surprising that the boys failed to confront the problem of the "beast" until it was too late, and they became consumed by violent impulses. Such pressures toward conformity are common in small, cohesive groups.

Janis points out, however, that group cohesiveness is a necessary but not a sufficient condition for groupthink. If groups are aware of the groupthink potential and encourage independent critical thinking, high quality decision making can emerge from cohesive groups, because the members are comfortable enough with one another to say freely what they think. Members of noncohesive groups, on the other hand, may be prone to conformity when they are too timid or too unfamiliar with other members to express their own views or to dissent with another's.

Janis also suggests other techniques to avoid groupthink. He advises group members and leaders to include practices in their deliberations that lead to an open consideration of alternative viewpoints. He suggests that they invite outside experts to critical meetings and encourage the experts to challenge the views of the core members, or that they assign an individual the task of acting as devil's advocate. And Janis recommends that when vital national interests are at stake leaders reassemble for a "second-chance" meeting with the specific purpose of expressing their doubts and redefining the issues.

Group Polarization Effects

Groupthink can contribute to the unsettling tendency of some decision-making groups to become increasingly out of touch with reality. As a result, they arrive at poor or erroneous conclusions. Much the same outcome can be produced by **group-polarization effects.** Social scientists have found that in the course of group discussions individuals tend to arrive at decisions *more extreme* than the ones they initially held (Deaux and Wrightsman, 1983). Thus, if the group members were mildly in favor of a particular position prior to the group discussion, they come to favor the position even more strongly in the course of the group meeting. Similarly, if they were mildly opposed to a particular position prior to the group discussion, they come to oppose the position even more strongly.

Group polarization effects are found in many settings. For instance, jury members typically start with an initial, and somewhat hazy, tendency to hold a defendant guilty or innocent, and then, based on their discussions, move toward an increasingly firm confirmation of their views (Kalven and Zeisel, 1966). Likewise, group discussion leads highly racist high school students to become more racist, whereas groups composed of low-prejudice members shift toward even less prejudice (Myers and Bishop, 1970). And in a crowd, individuals often become more extreme, although in the same direction, than they were in the precrowd context (Johnson et al., 1977). It seems that the dominant values of the reference group can intensify the feelings of individuals, whether or not they consider themselves "members." Members shift more extremely than they would individually toward either a risky or cautious approach depending upon the option dictated by the group's values (Myers and Lamm, 1976).

EPILOGUE

In the course of the chapter we illustrated important sociological concepts and principles about groups with material from Golding's novel, *Lord of the Flies*. Admittedly, we gain a rather negative image of the human experience from this work. But groups are central to human social life; thus it is not surprising that they should have an enormous potential for evil. By the same token, however, they have an immense capacity for good. For instance, self-help groups like Alcoholics Anonymous, Parents Without Partners, and Weight Watchers achieve their benefits through group interaction. Yet, whether we perceive the activities of this or that group as good or bad is not the central point. The fact remains that groups constitute the core of social life.

Since groups are so central to the human experience, they touch the material in every chapter of this text. We may view culture as the product of group life—those shared definitions of various kinds of situations that allow us to make sense of our experience and guide our behavior. Similarly, we may conceive of socialization as the process that prepares and equips us for group life. Further, we may think of deviance as deriving from group definitions of people's behavior when judged by group standards. And we may characterize social stratification as the ranking of people in a group context and the unequal allocation among people of group rewards and burdens.

We extend our treatment of groups in the next chapter with a discussion of large-scale organizations. We will see that primary groups such as work cliques provide an essential bridge between the individual and these formal organizations—indeed to the larger society as well.

SUMMARY

A social group is a set of individuals who identify and interact with one another in a structured way based on shared values and goals. Groups perform vital functions. They provide us with our social identities, serve as the medium through which social forces and institutions influence our behavior, arm us with the influence and power with which to produce social change, transform individual experiences into social experiences, and help to manage conflict.

In order to make sense of the great diversity that we encounter among groups, sociologists distinguish among different types of groups. The most fundamental unit of human society is the primary group. Such groups are "primary" in a number of ways. First, they are the principal agents of socialization. Second, they are the vehicles for meeting our basic emotional and psychological needs. Third, they are vital agents of social control.

Primary groups are characterized by several interconnecting features: continuous face-to-face interaction, strong personal identity with the group, strong ties of affection, multifaceted relationships, and group performance. Secondary groups, on the other hand, are characterized by opposite features: limited face-to-face interaction, modest or weak personal identity with the group, relatively weak ties of affection, limited relationships, and less permanence.

Boundaries, a structural component of groups, create feelings of "we" and "they." An in-group is a social unit in which people feel at home and with which they identify. An out-group is a social unit to which people do not belong and with which they do not identify. One effective way to create and maintain group boundaries and a consciousness of kind is through conflict, for it brings members together in the face of a common enemy. Internal conflict may also strengthen a group.

Reference groups are groups against which we evaluate our life situations and behavior, but to which we do not necessarily belong. Thus reference groups serve a comparison function, providing us with standards for self-evaluations. They also have a normative function, providing us with guidelines for fashioning our behavior.

The recurrent patterns of interaction that occur within a group are called group dynamics. Group size has a profound impact upon social interaction. The differences between dyads (two-person groups) and triads (three-person groups) are particularly striking. Since in a dyad either member can terminate the relationship and thus prevent the completion of a task, dyads often exhibit higher rates of tension than do triads. Another difference is that participants in a dyad cannot hide their responsibility for events that occur within the confines of the group. Finally, a coalition and a majority are impossible in a dyad.

In the course of their group experiences, individuals evolve norms and conform to them to achieve goals. However, individuals are not usually aware of the group's impact on them. In some cases, group opinion is strong enough to cause people to deny their correct perceptions of reality.

Leadership also emerges from group interaction and from the particular situation the group faces. At first the group welcomes an effective task leader, but it needs socioemotional leadership as well.

Group decision making involves four stages: orientation, evaluation, making the actual decision, and restoring equilibrium. Groupthink is a tendency for members of small, cohesive groups to be so intent on maintaining group unanimity that they overlook or dismiss as unimportant major problems with the choices they make. In many cases individuals make more daring decisions when they are in groups than they would alone, a product of group-polarization effects.

GLOSSARY

Aggregate. Individuals who happen to be in the same place at the same time.

Balance theory. The theory that people in small groups tend to make their beliefs, feelings, and behaviors compatible with their interpersonal relations.

Charisma. A special quality that causes others to accept a person's authority.

Consciousness of kind. The tendency of people to recognize others like themselves and to feel a oneness with them.

Dyad. A two-person group.

Group dynamics. Recurrent patterns of interaction that occur within groups.

Group-polarization effects. The tendency of groups to make more extreme decisions than those toward which their individual members were initially leaning.

Groupthink. The tendency for members of small cohesive groups to be so intent on maintaining group unanimity that they overlook or dismiss as unimportant the major problems with the choices they make.

In-group. A social unit in which individuals feel at home and with which they identify.

Out-group. A social unit to which individuals do not belong and with which they do not identify.

Primary group. A group characterized by continuous face-to-face interaction, permanence, ties of affection, and multifaceted and long-lasting relationships.

Reference group. A group or social category that an individual refers to in evaluating himself or herself, but does not necessarily belong to.

Secondary group. A group characterized by limited face-to-face interaction, modest or weak personal identity with the group, weak ties of affection, and limited and not very enduring relationships.

Social group. A set of individuals who identify and interact with one another in a structured way based on shared values and goals.

Socioemotional leadership. Leadership with the function of maintaining good morale and relations in a group.

Task leadership. Leadership with the function of directing a group toward its goals.

Triad. A three-person group.

CHAPTER 8

Organizations and Bureaucracy

As you make your way through a typical day, what organizations do you encounter? Your college? The firm you work for? A supermarket or drug store? The U.S. postal service? The local newspaper? The electric company? A sports club? A large oil company? You probably can come up with a list containing a substantial number of **formal organizations**, that is, human collectivities whose activities are consciously designed for the purpose of achieving specific goals.

A century or so ago Americans lived much of their lives in primary groups centered in the family, a village, a small church congregation, and the one–room school. But with the accelerating pace of urbanization and industrialization, more relationships occur within large-scale secondary groups. We are born in big hospitals; educated in huge educational complexes; employed by mammoth international corporations; governed by countless local, state, and federal agencies; and buried by large mortuary firms. Indeed, most of the crucial decisions affecting the lives of Americans—especially those having to do with our economic circumstances and issues of war and peace—are made by large organizations. And many of the decisive interactions occurring in our society take place between powerful organizations, each with its own specific concerns. It is little wonder that our modern society has been termed the "organization society" (Presthus, 1978).

By turning our sociological eye on contemporary formal organizations, we gain important insights for understanding modern society. In this chapter we will consider the nature of formal organization and the different forms in which it finds expression. We will look at how formal organizations coordinate the activities of scores of people and pursue various goals. We will examine how organizations develop and work and how they have changed over time. And we will consider the ways careers are affected by formal organizations.

ORGANIZATIONAL STRUCTURES

Although formal organizations play a central role in contemporary societies, they are hardly a modern invention. The ancient civilizations of Mesopotamia and Egypt relied on well-developed organizations to carry out economic, political, military, and religious functions. The construction of the Egyptian pyramids, for example, required the coordination of large numbers of workers, the transportation of building materials from distant locations, and the provision of food and other essentials on a regular basis. Likewise, the emperors of early China developed comprehensive organizational arrangements for the administration of agriculture, national defense, government financing, and the education of scholars. And the early popes turned to formal organization for spreading the new faith and winning converts to Christianity. Why should formal organization have proven itself so attractive as a social tool for mobilizing human beings and coordinating their activities? The answer lies in the characteristics of formal organization.

The Nature of Formal Organization

Formal organization has evolved as a social device that enables people to pursue a variety of goals. It has allowed work to be broken down into tasks or routines according to a comprehensive division of labor. And each job can be governed by rules designed to make every worker's behavior predictable. The various jobs and people within an organization can be arranged in a hierarchy of authority and responsibility so that everyone knows who is responsible for what and to whom. Most commonly, power is concentrated in the hands of leaders or executives who control the activities of the organization (Etzioni, 1964).

In contrast to the small groups that were our principal focus in the preceding chapter, organizations tend to be self-perpetuating. Their procedures and goals do not change whenever an established member leaves or a new one arrives; members are usually expected to fit themselves into a structure. Organizations thus develop an existence apart from their members. They do not arise casually or spontaneously, as many primary groups do, but typically are set up to achieve specific goals. And organizations resemble secondary groups in that face-to-face interaction within them is often limited, ties between people are based on exchange functions rather than affection, and relationships are task-oriented and nonpermanent. Indeed, the sheer number of participants and the scale of operations preclude primary-type relationships among most members. The term "formal" organization reflects the fact that roles and relationships are arranged in an explicitly defined pattern.

Types of Formal Organization

Although formal organizations share many characteristics, they also differ from one another. The sociologist Amitai Etzioni (1964) distinguishes among organizations based on the factors that lead people to join them. Some organizations are *voluntary*; individuals enjoy considerable freedom in determining whether to join or withdraw from them. Political parties, religious groups, hobby clubs, and fraternities and sororities are examples of voluntary organizations. Other organizations are *coercive*; people are compelled to enter them. Examples include prisons, concentration camps, custodial mental hospitals, and military institutions based on a draft. Still other organizations are *utilitarian*; people join them for practical reasons. Business and work organizations are illustrations of utilitarian organizations. Let us consider each type of organization more carefully.

Voluntary Associations

A **voluntary association** is a formal organization that people join primarily because they have a personal interest in its goals and norms. Voluntary associations have long been a part of the American scene. When the French writer Alexis de Tocqueville visited the United States in 1831, he remarked on both the wide variety of voluntary associations he saw and the broad range of personal needs they seemed able to meet. In recent years many Americans seem to have rediscovered voluntary associations as a means of controlling aspects of their own lives or environments that previously appeared uncontrollable. The present trend can be traced back to the early 1960s, when the civil rights movement and organizations such as the Southern Christian Leadership Conference offered people a way to work for social change. Today, some voluntary associations like the Sierra Club or the National Organization of Women (NOW), pursue various social programs while others, like Parents Without Partners or tenants' councils, help people cope with their problems (see Chapter 18).

One organizational quality of voluntary associations is that they often keep going even when they accomplish their goals (Sosin, 1981). For example, the March of Dimes originally mobilized citizens against polio. When the development of a polio vaccine eradicated polio, the organization did not fold. In a classic organizational study, David Sills (1961) described the process of *goal displacement*, whereby the March of Dimes shifted its goals to embrace other health issues and thus perpetuated the organization.

Sociological research has shown that voluntary

These men, enjoying St. Patrick's Day festivities, belong to a voluntary organization of Irish Americans. They will stay in the organization as long as they share its goals and norms. (Alan Carey/The Image Works.)

associations have many positive results. Almost uniformly it has pointed to favorable personal consequences for their members (Knoke, 1981). Voluntary group members typically show higher levels of morale, self-esteem, political effectiveness, and community orientation and lower levels of alienation, apathy, and social withdrawal than nonparticipants. Sociologists also find that voluntary associations assist in the integration of society by providing people with additional sources of social cohesion and alternate means for achieving social change (McPherson, 1981; Pollock, 1982).

Coercive Organizations

Coercive organizations typically take the form of a **total institution**—an organization that deliberately closes itself off from the outside world and minimizes variation in its own internal environment. All organizations are coercive to a certain extent, but coercion is highlighted in the extreme case of total institutions. In these institutions, people lose all control over and all responsibility for their lives.

The sociologist Erving Goffman (1961) refers to total institutions as "asylums." He defines an **asylum** as a place where a large number of like-situated individuals are cut off from the wider society for an extended period and lead an enclosed, formally administered round of life. In asylums, control over the internal environment is carried to its extreme.

Inmates are segregated as completely as possible—emotionally, mentally, even physically—from other environments. In time, the organization becomes the only, or at least the dominant, reality for its members. Once a

There is no more coercive organization than a prison, where the prisoners' every move is subject to scrutiny. (Michael O'Brien/Archive.)

person is admitted to a total institution, the process that Goffman calls **mortification** begins. Individuals are methodically stripped of the clothes, adornments, and personal possessions people use to define themselves in everyday life. In exchange, they receive standard, nondescript, and often ill-fitting attire—a uniform or hospital robe. They may be disfigured as well, as in the case of the military or prison haircut. The new member's spirit is also mortified. The institution designs exercises to break the will: It compels individuals to perform meaningless acts, to submit to arbitrary and unreasonable commands, and to endure personal abuse (verbal or physical). Finally, it deprives people of their privacy: They must initially undergo a debasing physical examination and they must sleep, shower, and eat with a group. They are under constant surveillance, with every moment of every day planned by others.

These procedures destroy people's feelings of self-worth and train them for deference. Thus total institutions foster psychological regression; they promote feelings of helplessness so that the members become dependent on the organization. At this point individuals are ready to be resocialized to a new role, one the organization has designed.

Goffman attributes the extreme environment of total institutions to a number of factors. First, the inmates have low status. Second, a few staff members must control large numbers of inmates. And third, means tend to become ends; finishing the day's work becomes more important than meeting the institution's goals, which are often themselves only poorly defined. "Keeping the lid on" mental hospitals, prisons, and the military currently occupies thousands of bureaucrats and uses up vast financial and human resources.

Utilitarian Organizations

Utilitarian organizations play a particularly significant role in American life. Most of the important organizations in our society fall within this category. They include corporations, unions, colleges, most hospitals, and government agencies. Utilitarian organizations tend to be neither entirely voluntary nor entirely coercive. Thus, although we typically are not forced to work, if we are to support ourselves, we must secure a job.

As organizations become larger and more complex, and particularly utilitarian organizations, they require a special structure to direct, coordinate, and control the activities of the many people engaged in a great variety of tasks. Sociologists term such a structure a **bureaucracy**, a hierarchical arrangement in which the parts of an organization are ordered in a pyramid-shaped structure based on a division of function and authority. Since the bureaucracy is such a critical organizational structure, let us consider it at greater length.

BUREAUCRACY

Bureaucracies are created to provide a structure that will allow the organizations to reach their goals. If bureaucratic organizations work well, they serve three main functions: (1) they maximize *effectiveness* for accomplishing a particular goal, whether it be making profits or providing education; (2) they maximize *efficiency* by getting the most done at the least cost; and (3) they *control* uncertainty by regulating workers, supplies, and markets. Thus, in many respects, the sociological meaning of the term *bureaucracy* is quite different from its popular connotations of inefficiency, red tape, busywork, and rule-conscious, officious administrators.

In a utilitarian organization relationships are neither as free as they are in a voluntary organization nor as rigid as they are in a coercive organization. Although the shop foreman (right) may disagree with the plant super (left) from time to time, both know who is in charge. (David Powers/Stock, Boston.)

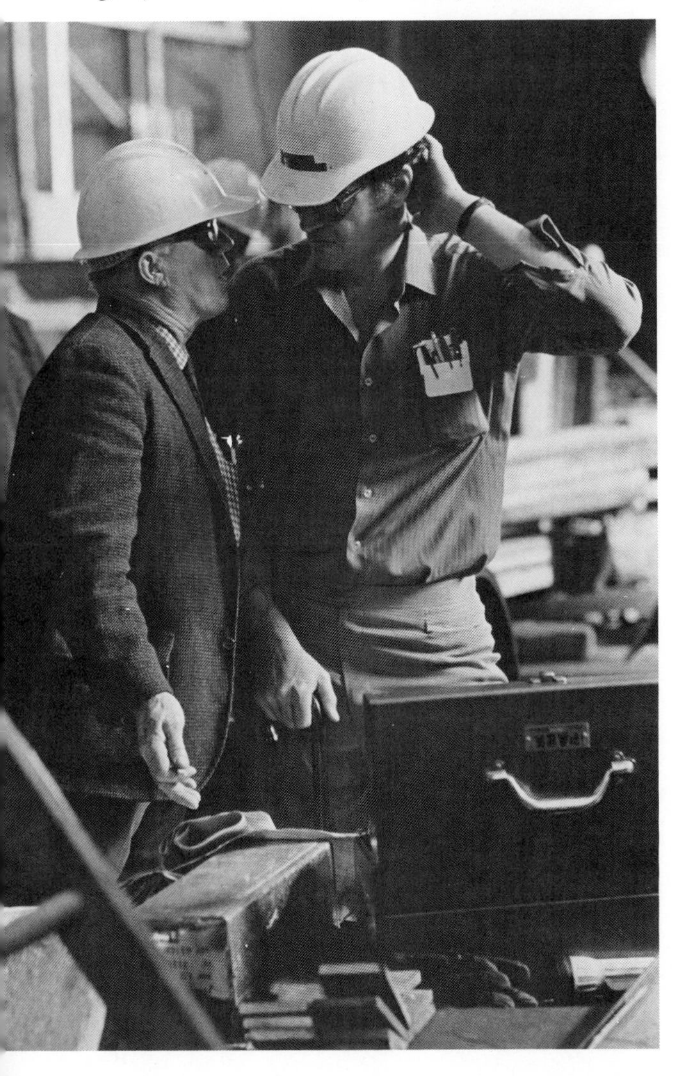

Within modern societies many of us have become accustomed to thinking of a bureaucracy as forceful, willful, all-powerful, almost as if it had a mind of its own. We tend to forget that a bureaucracy is just a human invention created to cope with uncertainties both inside and outside the organization. Although bureaucratic organizations have been around since ancient times, it was not until industrialization swept through the nations of Europe in the nineteenth century that bureaucracy developed into a powerful tool that could maximize effectiveness, efficiency, and control as never before.

What brought about this change? The early civilizations had not developed bureaucratic organization to its fullest extent because slave labor was abundant, technology was not advanced, and there was no capitalist drive to make profits and produce surplus goods. The industrialists of the nineteenth century, on the other hand, had to take account of hired labor, rapidly evolving technology, and the need to accumulate capital and produce for mass markets (Braverman, 1974; Presthus, 1978). Tough, disciplined management and control were top priorities of this new order. The logic of mechanics, which so excited popular imaginations during the nineteenth century and that had resulted in the invention of the steam engine, the cotton gin, and the locomotive, was applied to the organization of the manufacturing process as well.

Each operation of the manufacturing process was dissected, and then each part was assigned to a different worker. In this way, one skilled worker who could do the whole operation was replaced by a number of unskilled workers, each of whom could do only one part of the operation. The result was a bureaucratic organization that might be thought of as a human machine. Indeed, bureaucracy represents the application of mechanical principles to the organization of human activities.

The advantages of the bureaucratic division of labor were that more work got done at much lower wages, and the manager (rather than individual craftsman) controlled the whole process (Braverman, 1974). The increased profit and control for the owners of companies were first noted and appreciated by the conflict theorist, Karl Marx. But Marx also saw how the new work organization alienated workers, leaving them with no

In the early days of automobile manufacturing the task of assembling a car was broken down into many small tasks, each performed by a separate worker. Such bureaucratic division of labor enabled automobiles to be produced quickly and economically, but its effects on workers were as yet unforeseen. (Courtesy General Motors.)

sense of accomplishment and systematically destroying their crafts. Bureaucratic principles soon spread to public institutions as well, replacing madhouses with asylums and jails with prisons where reformers hoped that inmates would learn the benefits of rational, orderly life. It was not long, though, before this organizational machine was used to cut costs and more completely control inmates as it had workers (Rothman, 1971, 1980).

Weber's Model

Max Weber's analysis of bureaucratic structure—written long before "red tape" and "bureaucrat" became acknowledged social problems—remains the classic work in the field. Although Weber recognized and regretted its dehumanizing side effects, he believed bureaucracy to be *technically* superior to other forms of social organization as a means of achieving specific objectives by coordinating the activities of large numbers of people. "Precision, speed, unambiguity, knowledge of files, continuity, discretion, strict subordination, reduction of friction and of material and personal costs—these are raised to the optimum point in the strictly bureaucratic administration" (Weber, in Gerth and Mills, 1946:214). To emphasize the differences between bureaucracies and other structural arrangements, Weber defined bureaucracy in terms of five characteristics and tried to show how each of them functions to further the goals of the organization. Together, these characteristics make up an *ideal type* against which the realities of actual bureaucracies can be measured. An ideal type is not a description of any existing structure nor does it portray total "reality." Rather, it is a descriptive and analytical tool that allows sociologists to abstract features commonly found in large-scale organizations. However, each particular organization will reveal its own unique properties. Weber's ideal type of bureaucracy has five characteristics:

1. *Specialization.* Bureaucratic organization rests on the precept that the most efficient way to do complex work is to break it down into a clear-cut *division of labor* and have individuals specialize

in performing one task or another. For example, one person working alone might spend months to produce a single automobile, but a team of workers, each performing a single task, can produce many cars in a day. In a bureaucracy, workers in each area are familiar with and responsible for only one part of the bureaucracy's administration or its production process.

2. A *hierarchy of offices.* Once an organization's operation is divided into smaller and more manageable tasks, the various activities must then be integrated—the gears of the machine must mesh. If they do not, experts in one department might design a bolt that is one-eighth of an inch larger than the nut designed in another department (Blau and Meyer, 1971). The solution is to organize workers into a **hierarchy**, with each person responsible to the person directly above in the chain of command and responsible for the actions of those below. A hierarchy is typically pyramid-shaped, such as in military organizations, with rank and authority increasing as one moves up the pyramid.

   Organizational hierarchies consist of positions or offices, not of people. Each office carries with it specific duties, responsibilities, and privileges, as well as a specific salary. Authority rests in the office, not in the person who occupies it.[1] In addition, the authority of bureaucratic officials is clearly defined and limited. Although they have the power to recommend that individuals be promoted or fired, supervisors have no formal authority over the personal lives of their subordinates.

3. *Rules.* Activities and relationships among officers in a bureaucracy are governed by explicit rules. In this way, each bureaucrat knows (at least in general terms) what is required of him or her in the way of performance, and how his or her decisions will be carried out. Rules make the workings of even a complex bureaucracy orderly and predictable. And they allow for the continuity of operations despite changes in personnel.

4. *Impersonality.* Weber argued that because personal emotions impede efficiency, they have no place in a bureaucracy. Personal detachment promotes rational decision making. Impersonality toward both coworkers and those who do business with the organization assures the equitable treatment of all individuals and the subordination of personal considerations to organizational goals. If officials make a practice of promoting subordinates because they are friends, or of awarding contracts to companies owned by relatives, the organization will eventually suffer.

5. *Sphere of competence.* Positions in a bureaucracy are awarded on the basis of technical qualifications (as measured by tests, college degrees, or other standardized procedures), and people are paid for their work. Weber also felt that people should be guaranteed a job as long as they perform their duties adequately. Promotions and raises handed out on the basis of merit and/or seniority were seen by Weber as essential not only to motivate individual effort but also to keep up a bureaucracy's *esprit de corps.* Weber maintained that the more complicated and specialized work became, the greater would be the need for a bureaucracy of "personally detached and strictly 'objective' experts." In sum, bureaucratic offices would become filled by technically competent individuals who would view their employment in the organization as a "career."

[1]Weber called this *rational-legal authority,* to distinguish it from the links of authority one finds in older, more traditional societies. We will return to this distinction in Chapter 11.

Shortcomings and Limitations of Bureaucracy

As we suggested above, Weber's model is an ideal type that calls attention to significant characteristics of bureaucracies by emphasizing certain of their general properties. But actual bureaucracies do not in fact conform entirely to Weber's model. Studies of business firms in 150 societies and an analysis of organizations in this country suggest that the five bureaucratic traits do not always emerge or necessarily appear together (Udy, 1959; Hall, 1963–1964; Zey-Ferrell, 1981). Wide variations are found in degree of specialization, in hierarchical organization, and in adherence to rules, both within and between companies. The fact that an organization relies on specialization does not guarantee that employees are arranged in a hierarchy or that their relationships are impersonal. Moreover, professionals within organizations may possess a degree of authority that is based on their expertise and that is not necessarily indicated by their position in the hierarchy. And authority may rest not only on one's office but on personal charisma, such as that enjoyed by Lee Iacocca at Chrysler Corporation.

Furthermore, while bureaucracy may be the solution to some problems, it is often the cause of many others. The bureaucratic structure has some side effects on workers that Weber did not consider important or simply did not consider. Moreover, modern research has shown that many of Weber's most cherished assumptions —that rules always help organizations achieve their goals, for example, or that job security promotes expertise and efficiency—must be taken with a grain of salt. Let us examine some of these assumptions and fallacies.

Formal Versus Informal Structure

All organizations seek to define members' responsibilties and regulate their activities. The explicit rules defining each person's duties, organizational charts, and a system of rewards and punishments (for example, salary increases, promotions, and demotions) constitute the organization's **formal structure**. However, any time people join forces to accomplish a task, friendships, antagonisms, and power relationships develop, and with them come cliques, factionalism, grapevines, and the like. Some people wield more influence—and others less—than their job titles indicate. Thus there evolves alongside the formal structure an **informal structure**: procedures that enable people to solve problems not covered by the formal regulations, to eliminate unpleasant or unnecessary work, and to protect their own interests. An informal organization sometimes promotes and sometimes hinders the achievement of the formal organization's goals.

Informal structures often emerge as a means of dealing with problems or situations either not covered or caused by organizational rules or procedures. For example, when a respected professor faces a two-day deadline in submitting a federal grant application and its approval at five levels of the university bureaucracy normally takes a month, everybody signs the application on trust as it is rushed around from office to office, by-passing normal protocol. Further, to avoid the "red-tape" and "busywork" found in bureaucracies, workers often reach informal understandings and agreements with one another.

Informal structures also emerge in part because of the values of the larger society: "In a democratic culture," write the sociologists Peter M. Blau and Marshall W. Meyer, "where independence of action and equality of status are highly valued, detailed rules and close supervision are resented" (1971:58). Thus workers will often organize their own informal groups and establish strict standards and procedures to which they adhere (Burawoy, 1979; J.R. Blau, 1982; Hollinger and Clark, 1982). Elaborate patterns of "goldbricking," unauthorized work breaks, pranks, drug use, gambling, and mutual assistance often operate in conjunction with informal social relationships. Indeed, the very impersonality of the formal organization encourages individuals to seek warm, congenial relations with their coworkers. Individuals look to their peers as an important source of emotional and psychological support (Evans, 1983). Moreover, friends informally organize birthday parties and baby showers and perhaps bowl together on a company team. Thus formal organization breeds informal organization.

The informal structures that develop in a formal organization help to meet the emotional needs of group members. Here, members of a corporate running team enjoy posing for a group picture. (Courtesy of Jennifer Brennan, Random House, Inc.)

Ritualism

Do rules and regulations facilitate rational decision making and maximize efficiency, as Weber suggested? In a famous essay on the bureaucratic personality, the sociologist Robert Merton (1968) came to the conclusion that when people become devoted to procedures, as bureaucrats tend to do, they may lose sight of why those procedures were established in the first place. They end up performing them simply as acts of **ritualism**. Bureaucratic managers often encourage a ritualistic approach to the job, because rituals are efficient. They keep workers from questioning why they must follow procedures and rules. But sometimes, when rituals become a blind obsession, they prevent people from recognizing and dealing with new conditions and problems. Officials may become rigid and inflexible. In such a situation organizational efficiency and goals may be undermined.

The Negotiated Order

Symbolic interactionists have gone one step further than Merton by arguing that organizational behavior is largely a matter of **negotiated order**—the processes of bargaining, diplomacy, and give-and-take whereby people at various levels of the organization together solve work-related problems. Certainly, rules and bureaucratic procedures exist, but studies point out that these are further areas for negotiation rather than inflexible rules. In his view, *all* organizational behavior is largely informal and subject to change—a far cry from the bureaucratic model. In the classic study of this process, Anselm Strauss and his colleagues (1964) discovered many kinds of negotiations taking place. In hospitals, doctors often had to negotiate to get their patients into certain wards and to get cooperation and information from nurses and aides; nurses had to bargain with doctors to get certain treatments for patients instituted or changed; and the patients devoted considerable effort to haggling for privileges, drugs, placement in certain wards, and information concerning the length of their stay and their progress in the hospital. While negotiations go on in all organizations to some degree, they are most prevalent in ones where work cannot be routinized.

Parkinson's Law: Waste Making

Although Weber portrayed bureaucracies as particularly efficient structures for getting tasks performed, critics point out that they tend to contribute to waste making, an outcome captured by **Parkinson's law**: "Work expands to fill the time available for its completion" (Parkinson, 1957). Take, for example, bureaucrats who want to appear busy to justify their job. They create extra tasks for themselves but soon find they need assistance to handle all the work. Suppose they hire two assistants

Bureaucracies, once considered highly efficient, can also create work and increase the need for employees to perform it. The people in the picture were hired by Kaiser Aluminum Co. to do work mandated by federal regulations. The cartons contain the paperwork representing one year of compliance. (John Marmaras/Woodfin Camp & Associates.)

each (two being safer than one since one might become a competitor). In all likelihood, they will reserve the power to make decisions for themselves, thereby adding supervision to their original workload. If all goes well, however, in a year or two their assistants will need assistants, and there will be five or even seven people to do the work that one did. But the ritual of holding conferences and shuffling paper back and forth among seven people will by itself keep them all *demonstrably* busy.

Peter F. Drucker (1983), an authority on management, points out that colleges and universities are no exception to Parkinson's law:

> A liberal arts college I know had, in 1950, a president, a dean, an assistant dean of students who handled admissions and a chief clerk who kept the books. Enrollment has doubled, from 500 to 1,000; but administrative staff has increased six-fold, with three vice presidents, four deans and 17 assistant deans and assistant vice presidents. . . . Five secretaries did the same work now being done by seven or eight deans, assistant deans and assistant vice presidents—and did it very well.

The force of Parkinson's law was seen during the severe recession of the early 1980s. By December 1982 there were nearly 9 percent more managers and administrators in the American economy than in January 1980. In contrast, during the same period overall employment fell 1 percent and blue-collar jobs dropped 12 percent (Arenson, 1983).

Protection of the Inept

Weber believed that bureaucratic organizations encourage the optimal use of available talent, weeding out deadwood as a matter of course. However, the sociologist William Goode (1967) called attention to the fact that companies are typically reluctant to demote or otherwise discredit incompetent employees. By protecting its less able employees, an organization builds loyalty. Since low morale and personnel turnover are disruptive and expensive, the organization benefits from a benevolent approach.

Managers also tend to promote individuals who display superior performance in their present jobs. But this rational procedure can have an irrational consequence. People who prove capable of handling their new assignments are advanced again and again—until they finally reach their level of *in*competence! Thus individuals eventually reach positions that exceed their abilities and talents. Laurence Peter and Raymond Hull termed this **the Peter principle** (1969). Good teachers who become good principals may be promoted to district superintendent. But should they perform poorly at this new level, they remain in the post, continually disguising their incompetence. For instance, they may bury themselves in rules and regulations. Meanwhile, the real work is carried out by those employees who as yet have not reached their level of incompetence.

Michels' Iron Law of Oligarchy

Weber thought that a major advantage afforded by bureauratic organization is that authority rests in the office, not in the person who occupies it. Moreover, the authority of officials is prescribed by clearly defined rules and procedures. But as we will see in Chapter 11 in our discussion of power, Robert Michels (1915/1949) concluded that bureaucracy has quite the opposite result. According to Michels, bureaucracy invariably leads to the concentration of power in the hands of a few individuals who use their positions in the organization to advance their own private interests, an outcome he termed the *iron law of oligarchy*. He cited the history of European labor unions and socialist parties as evidence that leaders seldom promote the democratic aspirations espoused by their organizations. Instead, they entrench themselves in office and pursue their personal growth and financial gain at the expense of the membership.

In sum, this discussion suggests that bureaucracies, while providing a social mechanism for integrating and coordinating the activites of large numbers of people, also have shortcomings and dysfunctions. These limitations—from ritualism to inept bureaucrats to negotiated arrangements—reflect less the personality of individual bureaucrats we encounter than tendencies inherent in organization. As such, bureaucracies have consequences for us and our careers, matters to which we now turn our attention.

Bureaucracy and Careers

Many people think that if they can just get that first good job, they can work themselves into the career position

TABLE 8.1 The Impact of Organizational Structure on Career, Attitudes, and Behavior

Opportunity	
Positions low in opportunity tend to make people:	*Positions high in opportunity tend to make people:*
Have limited aspirations	Have high aspirations
Have low self-esteem	Have high self-esteem
Gripe rather than take direct action to seek change	Have an action-oriented approach to change
Power	
Positions low in power make people:	*Positions high in power make people:*
Exhibit authoritarian behavior; rigidly control subordinates	Be flexible; delegate control to subordinates
Restrict talented subordinates	Encourage talented subordinates
Rely on coercive more than persuasive power	Use persuasive power
Proportions of Types of People	
Being represented in small proportions makes people:	*Being represented in high proportions makes people:*
Be highly visible and thus try to become socially invisible	Fit into groups easily
Feel pressure to conform	Be preferred for high-communication managerial jobs
Lack "credibility" in the organization	Enjoy high "credibility"

Adapted from Rosabeth Moss Kanter, *Men and Women of the Corporation*. New York: Basic Books, 1977, pp. 246–249.

When working people find themselves becoming irritable and bossy on the job, they tend to blame themselves or those close to them. Rather than automatically blaming themselves, Rosabeth Moss Kanter contends that they should see to what extent the structure of opportunity and power in their workplaces is contributing to their behavior.

they desire. But things do not always work that way. Bureaucratic organizations channel careers along certain paths, opening some doors while closing others. Hence, individuals are wise to find out the best route to a desired career before committing themselves to an organization. Otherwise, they may find that the organization is moving them along in an undesired direction toward an unchosen career. Consequently, when sizing up a job, it is important to consider not just the individual position but also the organizational career chain in which the position is embedded (Stewman and Konda, 1983).

While upward mobility in a career depends on the structure of opportunity in an organization, two other factors come into play. The first is the distribution of power. How free are you to act within the organization, and what resources are at your disposal? The second factor is the proportion of people who fall into one or another category within the organization. If you are one of a small minority of women or blacks at a given level of the company, you can expect to be perceived as different. As we will see, this can be a handicap if you aspire to a high-level position. The various consequences associated with each of these organizational dimensions are described in Table 8.1. Let us now look more closely at some of these matters.

Impact of Bureaucracy on Managers and Executives

Among the managers and executives at the upper levels of most organizations, strong pressures operate to produce a high measure of conformity. Social skills, predictability, and reliability are considered essential attributes in most managerial ranks. "Outsiders" are not appreciated.

Why should such homogeneity be encouraged? Perhaps because there is the most uncertainty at the top of the organization. The higher the position, the more unstructured it is; it involves more uncertainty, more

In the upper levels of most organizations, managers tend to share many traits with each other. If a company's top executives are reliable, the company can attend to the external environment. (Charles Harbutt/Archive Pictures.)

nonroutine tasks, and greater discretionary power. From management's point of view, it is important to fill those positions with people who can be trusted (Kanter, 1977*a*). If a company can reduce internal uncertainty by relying on pressures to conform, it can be freed to focus on uncertainties in the *external* environment.

Impact of Bureaucracy on Workers

Far below the managers and executives are the clerical and service personnel who do office work. Most of these workers are powerless and can go nowhere in the organization because their career ladders have few, if any, rungs.

In the last century, as office work has expanded and has become increasingly mechanized, clerks have in effect been downgraded from assistant managers to unskilled workers, overseen by a few highly skilled managers. In other words, the bureaucratic model of the human machine has been applied to office work in the extreme.

Secretaries have always held an unusual place in the bureaucratic organization because their career is tied to a boss. The boss, not bureaucratic rules, defines the role that the secretary is to play. As the sociologist Rosabeth Moss Kanter points out:

> . . . bosses make demands at their own discretion and arbitrarily; choose secretaries on grounds that enhance their own personal status rather than meeting organizational efficiency tests; expect personal service with limits negotiated privately; exact loyalty; and make the secretary a part of their private retinue, moving when they move. (1977*a*:73)

Kanter views the secretary-boss relationship as a throwback to the prebureaucratic model of patrimony. Secretaries owe whatever status and power they have to the status of the boss; their duties are at the discretion of the boss, and they are rewarded for loyalty and devotion to the boss.

Humanizing Bureaucracy

More and more workers are dissatisfied with the idea of routine jobs that lead nowhere. Even middle-level managers are finding their work life unsatisfying as they take on jobs with responsibility but not authority. Such dissatisfaction can lead to lack of commitment, hostility, and stress, all of which impair effective behavior at work. So it is in the interest of both the workers and the organization that steps be taken to improve the career pattern. But what can be done?

Kanter (1977*a*) traces most personnel problems to the organizatinal problems of *limited opportunity*, *limited power*, and *unbalanced numbers*. She has outlined various methods to alleviate these problems.

Broadening Opportunity

The opportunity structure in organizations needs to be redesigned to provide more entry levels and niches in career ladders. Job descriptions of clerical positions would make it possible to identify those who are competent at their jobs and perhaps ready to move on. Bridges between job ladders could be created to allow, say, a secretary to move into a technical job or managerial job. And new jobs could be designed to allow people in low-status, dead-end jobs to make a gradual entry into higher-status positions.

Feedback from supervisors and a regular system of performance appraisal would boost a worker's sense of his or her skills and allow that person to see areas of improvement. This kind of system requires that managers be skilled in human development. The organization might even make some provision for training managers in these skills and rewarding those who develop the talent and increase the opportunity of subordinates.

Job rotation would increase skills, provide more varied work, break down parochialism, and increase commitment to the larger organization. It would also serve as a way of showing that opportunity can involve lateral moves as well as vertical ones. Rewarding length of service instead of just position in the hierarchy would also help broaden the definition of mobility.

Another way to open up opportunity is to decentralize the organization. If larger units were broken up to make smaller units, more direct-level managerial positions might be created.

Finally, flexible work hours (flextime) would allow employees to acquire skills and still meet family responsibilities.

Increasing Workers' Power

Kanter believes that the principal way to go about increasing the power of workers is to flatten the hierarchy —remove levels of management and spread authority downward. In this way organizations can make tasks less routine and more discretionary. Decentralization also functions to empower workers if it creates work units that have autonomy and influence. Reducing the number of people who can impose vetoes adds to worker power and improves effectiveness.

A person's sources of informal power in an organization also need to be enhanced. Workers can be given more access to the power structure by opening up channels of communication, educating them about the system (budget, salary ranges, fringe benefits, and perquisites), and providing sponsors for them among the senior members of the organization.

Achieving Balance

Unequal numbers of different categories of people, such as women executives or black managers, can be gradually balanced by hiring minority members in batches instead of one by one, and initially clustering them in a number of departments rather than spreading them thinly throughout the whole organization. This procedure allows the minority members to develop networks in which they can give each other feedback and support. Of equal importance, they can serve as role models for new recruits.

Organizational reform of the magnitude suggested by Kanter does not appear to be just around the corner. There are formidable obstacles. To work well, each reform needs to be accompanied by a number of other supporting changes. But large organizations are typically unwilling to run the risks associated with large-scale reform. If the organization decides to try comprehensive reform in just one unit of the organization, the experiment is likely to fail because of rivalries with other units and because the dynamics of a complex organization are just too overwhelming for an experiment on a small scale.

Kanter feels that ultimately it is necessary to rethink the basic questions of how labor is divided and how power is concentrated, and to find alternatives to large, overly hierarchical organizations. But until then she thinks it is worthwhile to pursue gradual reform. Those who bear the burden of waiting for fundamental change are . . .

> not the well-off . . . it is the people without advantage who continue to lose out: the women who find doors closed to them in certain jobs; the people stuck in dead-end positions, whose lack of opportunity depresses their aspirations and sense of self; the powerless who bear the frustrations of trying to manage without any real resources or influence; the token women or token minorities who suffer from their isolation. (Kanter, 1977*a*:287)

We can gain an appreciation for the complexities involved in altering bureaucracies by examining the dynamics of organizational life.

DYNAMICS OF ORGANIZATION

Our discussion has alluded to the requirement that all organizations must cope with the external environment —the physical, social, and political surroundings— within which they exist. Each organization must also devise ways to cope with its own internal environment— the activities and attitudes of its own members. Because these environments are constantly changing, every organization that wishes to survive must maintain a balance between stability and flexibility, between concentration on its own goals and awareness of what is happening in the world outside.

Sociologists have therefore begun to look at organizations not as unchanging structures but as people continually solving problems and organizing. In this section we will look at this process of problem solving in the context of how organizations interact with their environments. We will then explore some of the major sources of change in organizations.

The Internal Environment

No organization can survive for long if its members fail to perform their jobs adequately. An organization must therefore have control over its **internal environment**— over its members and the jobs they do. To achieve control, most organizations rely on a system of rewards and punishments, including such incentives as raises and promotions on the one hand and the ability to fire an ineffective worker on the other. In addition, organizations attempt to regulate their internal workings through recruitment and socialization.

Recruitment

Every organization has jobs or tasks that must be performed in a certain way. Thus, if a law firm hires a tax lawyer with eight years of experience, it will not have to acquaint the individual with the fundamentals of tax law. The more selective an organization is in recruiting people who possess not only the skills but also the attitudes that the organization feels are desirable, the less it will have to socialize its members to conform to organizational requirements. Not surprisingly, the organization selection process favors individuals who fit the existing organizational profile. This tendency has operated to the disadvantage of women and minorities (see Chapters 6 and 12).

Socialization

Every organization has a spoken or unspoken "system" that new employees must learn if they are to succeed.

These recruits at a job-training session will assess their employer, but they will also be assessed. Employers want people who fit in—people whose skills and attitudes are deemed right for the company. (Ellis Herwig/ Stock, Boston.)

School equips people with some of the traits expected in the working world. For instance, schedules and deadlines, assignments and reports, and pressure to adhere to norms of punctuality and respect for superiors are features of the classroom that prepare us for similar demands in the office. But the organization also functions in its own right as a miniature social system and socializes its members in its approved ideals, attitudes, and behavior (Presthus, 1978). Each organization possesses a somewhat unique "culture" that ties employees together and gives meaning and purpose to their day-to-day activities. Organizations with "weak cultures" lack clear values or beliefs that can inspire and motivate their members. In contrast, organizations with "strong cultures" lead their members to believe that "we'll succeed because we're special" (Deal and Kennedy, 1982).

The External Environment

Although organizations often appear to be self-contained entities, they are all involved in more or less constant interaction with the **external environment**—the surrounding system of resources, other organizations, clients, markets, transport facilities, and governments within which an organization operates. For instance, the movements of the 1960s and early 1970s greatly modified the context in which many organizations operate. Demands by women and minorities for affirmative action in hiring and promotions have altered traditional employment arrangements. Simultaneously, those on the lower rungs of bureaucracy have begun demanding greater participation in workplace decisions. And consumer movements have placed limits on the policy actions of large corporations (Presthus, 1978).

Some organizations must survive in and interact with several different environments simultaneously. For example, many American firms do business in other countries, where business norms are different from our own. While giving bribes to improve business is considered an illegitimate form of interaction in the United States, in many foreign countries under-the-table payoffs are a time-honored custom. Thus different external environments lead to different expectations, demands, and ways of doing business.

For some organizations, the external environment is reasonably stable. For example, companies that market food staples, work on long-term contracts, or sell insurance can count on a relatively steady market for their services or products. But many organizations find the

During the 1970s, American automobile manufacturers lost millions of dollars due to changes in the external environment. Higher prices for gasoline made fuel-efficient cars like these Japanese models very attractive to Americans. (J.P. Laffont/Sygma.)

external environment unstable and unpredictable. New technologies or products may appear; natural resources may run out; consumer tastes may shift.

American auto firms provide a good illustration of organizations that have had difficulty handling forces of external change (Bluestone and Harrison, 1982). In 1970 General Motors reported profits of $609 million; in 1980 it reported losses of $763 million. The same pattern held true for the two other major car manufacturers—Ford and Chrysler. What brought about this collapse? Perhaps most important was the sixfold increase in the price of gas between 1970 and 1980. As a result, some Americans curtailed their use of cars. Others traded in their big cars for economy cars—small cars with high gas mileage. Because American manufacturers did not provide subcompact and compact cars until recently, foreign manufacturers moved into the market. In 1980 foreign cars accounted for more than 26 percent of all car sales in America, up from 15 percent in 1970. In spite of import curbs on foreign cars, American car manufacturers have not been able to offer competitive quality or prices on small models. Compounding matters, inflation drove up the price of the steel used in making cars and the wages of automotive workers. Retooling to make smaller cars proved costly. And government regulations for safety and pollution control further added to the cost of design and manufacture. Thus, such external forces as the oil squeeze by OPEC, inflation, shifting consumer tastes, and government regulations all contributed to the decline of what once seemed to be an invincible industry. Although the American auto industry made a comeback in 1983, in part protected by import curbs on the fiercely competitive Japanese cars, price increases had frozen an estimated 750,000 potential new-car buyers out of the market. The American manufacturers staked their recovery on a strategy that conceded a quarter of the U.S. auto market to foreign producers and aimed at higher profits on lower volume (Nag, 1983). This strategy has worked for the companies—profits are up sharply. But costs are significantly higher than for Japanese cars, and quality is still lower.

Major Sources of Change

We have noted that the internal and external environments of formal organizations are constantly changing. Sociologists have identified three major sources of change: new technology; growing professionalism within organizations; and management's respect for worker autonomy.

Technological Change

Organizations in which tasks are routine, predictable, and repetitive usually have considerable bureaucratic efficiency. But when new technology is introduced, making old ways obsolete, efficiency suffers until the new methods are successfully integrated into daily routines. Consider the impact such inventions as transistors, optical fibers, microchips, and computers have had on

THE SOCIOLOGICAL EYE ON:

Computers and Power in Organizational Structures

In 1980 the sociologist Amitai Etzioni was a senior advisor at the White House. He spent a much of his time trying to develop a computer program for the President. The purpose of the program was to track the directives issued by the president to the White House staff and to heads of federal agencies. The computer files would provide, upon request, status reports on actual work undertaken on presidential instructions. Although the management computer system was never set up, Etzioni drew a number of conclusions about the introduction of computer systems in organizations from his White House experience.

First, Etzioni found that computers are not introduced in a vacuum. They have wide-ranging consequences for organizational structure and, more particularly, for the distribution of power. As noted in this chapter, bureaucracies are characterized by a division of labor and a hierarchy of authority. Within such arrangements, information is a major source of power. Since computers store, retrieve, and analyze information, those who have access to the computers have a power advantage over those who lack such access. Moreover, the information provided by computers can give rival managers a competitive advantage. For instance, competing division leaders can determine who is behind schedule and who is meeting organizational goals. Thus Etzioni found considerable opposition, from both White House Aides and heads of federal agencies, to efforts to have computers track their performance—although they were quite willing to have computers monitor their rivals. In sum, government officials perceived the projected plan as altering the Washington power structure, and they succeeded in killing it.

Second, Etzioni found that tracking performance by computers raised another issue, namely, what is information? More specifically, the matter became one of defining what is and is not a directive of the president. Very often a president prefers that his instructions remain rather vague so that they can be applied to some situations and ignored in others. For instance, if a president says in a speech to a joint session of Congress that he favors appointing more women and minorities to federal positions and increasing expenditures for child care, he may not wish his aides to take his remarks too literally. Indeed, a president makes endless gestures, promises, and threats that vary greatly in their intensity. These subtleties in human interaction are difficult to capture in a computer program.

Finally, Etzioni discovered that accountability is not a simple matter. Often a high-powered accountability system leads to the faking of results. For example, when the head of one government agency required that all letters to his agency be answered within ten days, the agency became a model of performance in meeting the deadline. However, many answers read, "We received your letter of ____________. We are looking into the matter and will be back in touch as soon as possible." Many White House aides preferred an informal approach to accountability. Thus the sociological focus of informal communication and power hierarchy—two elements in any organization—won out over plans to computerize the White House.

Source: Adapted from Amitai Etzioni, "A Top Management Computer." *Behavioral Science*, 28(1983):1–3.

industry. Companies adopting these technologies have found that their introduction requires long hours of employee training and initially results in confusion, waste, and unpredictable output (see box, p. 193). In the process of incorporating technological change into an organization, routinization often goes out the window, and so to a certain extent does organizational efficiency. To minimize this problem, firms now define technological change as a continuous process with which they must come to terms on an ongoing basis. Companies like Wang Laboratories, Warner Communications, and Sony have attempted to establish organizational routines that encourage technological breakthroughs, that enable production personnel to manufacture "high-tech" products and sales staff to market them, and that keep the public informed about the new technology. This requires a well-paid, highly motivated staff, but clearly it can be done.

Professionalism

Accompanying rapid technological change is the increased need for highly trained professionals—researchers with Ph.D.'s, salespeople with advanced technical training, and managers with degrees from business schools. Professionals see themselves as having autonomy over their own area of expertise, which creates pressure to get away from the classic bureaucratic model. Moreover, as Charles Perrow (1979:162) notes, nonroutine units or organizations are difficult to bureaucratize:

> More discretion must be given to lower-level personnel; more interaction is required among personnel at the same level; there must be more emphasis upon experience, "feel," or professionalization. If so, it is difficult to have clear lines of authority, a high degree of division of labor, rules and procedures for everything, exact specification of duties and responsibilities, and so on. There is more craft, or art, or esoteric skill (in the case of professionals) involved.

Worker Autonomy and Control

Managers are not the only ones seeking more control over their work lives. In many organizations today, workers at the lowest levels are demanding increased power and control over their work situations. Generally speaking, the more control workers have over their time, physical movement, and pace of work, the greater their job satisfaction (Gruenberg, 1980; Zeitz, 1983). Over the past decade or so, in both the United States and Europe, traditional structures of authority in many industrial organizations have had to give ground to work-centered strategies of participation and control (Jain and Jain, 1980; Stephens, 1980). The style of organizational management based on the assumption that people hate work, want to avoid responsibility, and must therefore be coerced into productivity is giving way to one that sees people as eager to be creative, assume responsibility, and work willingly under the right circumstances (Dickson, 1975; Whyte, 1982).

Some workers in the United States are gaining the chance to participate more fully in the organizations they work for through employee stock ownership plans (ESOPs). ESOPs were given legislative approval in the mid-1970s. They provide financial and tax incentives to encourage organizations to expand stock ownership to their employees, either through bonus plans or purchases. Many companies have adapted such plans as an incentive to encourage greater worker productivity. In practice, however, the programs have provided more symbol than substance. Ownership does not ensure worker control so long as the day-to-day running of a company remains in the hands of professional managers (Whyte and Blasi, 1980; Woodworth, 1982).

In Sweden, the motive behind worker-participation programs were industrial peace and the extension of the welfare state. A look at SAAB and Volvo manufacturing plants demonstrates the Swedish philosophy in action. The automotive firms have eliminated the most grueling, monotonous aspects of the assembly line. At SAAB, workers finishing rough engines divide into teams of four, and each team *decides for itself* whether to work alone, in pairs, or together. In addition, work is structured so that ideally each group can feel it has done a complete job, such as installing a motor or an electrical system. Giving workers such opportunities for decision making and sense of achievement are unheard of in traditionally organized automobile plants.

Although the new system complicated some factory processes and required more time to complete an engine, SAAB's management expected several benefits, including less absenteeism, high quality work, better worker attitudes, and better public relations. Less than two years after the new process began, the plant was meeting all its production targets, and SAAB was firmly committed to the new system (Dickson, 1975). SAAB's experience confirms what other studies have shown—autonomy is related to job satisfaction (though neither necessarily improves productivity).

A study of organizational hierarchies in five countries (Italy, Austria, the United States, Yugoslavia, and Israel) has revealed that the closer a member is to the top, the greater the person's motivation and initiative (Tannenbaum et al., 1974). Similarly, in four of the countries, a positive correlation existed between an individual's position in the hierarchy and that person's psychological adjustment. These findings suggest that worker satisfaction in organizations with little hierarchy tends to be higher than in organizations with steep, all-pervasive hierarchies. In fact the researchers found that the highest degree of alienation—the strongest feelings of powerlessness, meaninglessness, and social isolation—were found among workers in a rigidly hierarchical Italian industrial plant where members were allowed very little participation in decision making. By contrast, the least alienation was found among the members of an Israeli kibbutz, an organization based on common ownership and formal participation of members in setting organizational policies and goals. The *most* alienated workers in the kibbutz, in fact, were still more satisfied, on the whole, than the *least* alienated Italians.

Organizations generally find it necessary to exercise some control over the behavior of their members. Those in charge need to be sure that the organization's interests have priority over individual interests. They can do this in three ways: (1) **direct control**, which makes use of rules, direct orders, and surveillance; (2) **bureaucratic control**, which relies on specialization, standardization, and hierarchy to monitor the behavior of workers; and (3) **control of premises**, or the motives that underlie actions, which involves socializing the workers so that they internalize the organization's sense of right and wrong (Perrow, 1979).

A system of direct control is expensive, especially in large organizations, and workers dislike it. Bureaucratic controls are more efficient but somewhat inflexible. The most effective system is the control of premises, because the worker *voluntarily* complies. It is, however, the most difficult type to achieve. In recent years, the changes taking place in the internal and external environments of organizations have made direct and bureaucratic controls less workable. More and more organizations are now aiming for premise control by concentrating on building an *esprit de corps*, long a centerpiece of many Japanese organizations.

The Japanese Organization

In 1945 Japan floundered in the ruins of wartime defeat; within three decades it had become one of the top industrial nations of the world. Despite the fact that Japan must import 30 percent of its food supplies and 85 percent of its energy resources, it now has a stable, growing economy. Japanese industry in highly competitive with other nations in shipbuilding, steel, autos, electronic equipment, cameras, motorcycles, sports equipment, watches, and textiles. And the quality of life in Japan today is exceptionally high. Teamwork between industry and government has maintained an unemployment rate of less than 3 percent, the lowest of any major developed country (Lohr, 1983*a*). Ezra Vogel (1979), who has studied Japanese culture for many years, regards Japan as the prime example of a nation able to cope with the problems of the postindustrial era.

How can we explain the phenomenal success of the Japanese? Part of the answer lies in cultural traits of industriousness, patience, self-discipline, and sensitivity to others. Whereas American society extols individualism, Japanese society emphasizes group spirit and common effort (Sayle, 1982). But a fuller answer to Japan's industrial success can be found by examining how Japanese organizations incorporate these traits and put them to work on a large scale.

Organizational Features

The Japanese approach to work organization contrasts sharply with that traditionally found in the United States. William G. Ouchi (1982) calls the techniques used by Japanese managers "Type Z." Type Z control is characterized by relatively low task specialization, low job turnover, and primary relationships in the work setting. Ouchi labels the approach found in the United States "Type A." Type A control entails highly specialized tasks, relatively high job turnover, and impersonal, contractual relationships between employers and employees.

The Japanese organization functions as a benevolent patron that hires workers for life. Ceremonies—for example, singing the company song at this electric plant—open each work day. (©Hiroji Kubota/Magnum.)

An important feature of the Japanese work organization and Type Z management style is a system of permanent employment. Some Japanese workers are hired for life, and they need never fear layoff or dismissal. Companies cannot fire employees because they are losing money. When industries require paring back, workers are retrained and reassigned. Moreover, every employee can expect to move steadily up the corporate ladder; rank automatically comes with seniority. This means that all members of an age group move up to the next level together. There are few, if any, wage distinctions among members of an age group. However, highly valued employees can expect to receive higher bonuses, extra sick leave, and use of company facilities.

Another even more distinctive organizational feature is the emphasis on group achievement rather than individual achievement. Companies tend to be divided into sections of eight to ten people, headed by a section chief. The section members share tasks and cooperate in order to turn in a good group performance. Within the section those who are more talented are assigned the more difficult tasks. Thus, tasks are assigned not by rank but according to ability to do the job. It matters little if a section is headed by a mediocre boss because section chiefs know that it is to their advantage to make the best use of each worker's talents.

Organization by sections also allows for "bottom up" authority. Each section is given wide latitude to come up with original ideas, identify problems, work out solutions, and consult with other sections. Many decisions by company officials are simply ratifications of intitiatives taken by the sections. This system of worker participation in decision making contributes to positive morale.

Employee morale and company spirit are boosted in numerous other ways as well. Each firm has its own uniform, badge, song, motto, and daily opening ceremonies. The company commonly provides resort houses, dormitories and apartment complexes, recreational facilities, and team sports. It gives its employees gifts, semiannual bonuses, and parties to celebrate important occasions, and in general acts as a benevolent patron.

The Japanese organizations are able to commit themselves fully to the security of their employees because they themselves are secure. Most of them are backed not by fickle stockholders, but by banks, which are, in turn, backed by various government institutions. Because the Japanese businesses are so important to the economic health of the nation, the government nurtures fledgling industries. It determines the industries most likely to contribute to Japan's future prosperity, organizes research projects, and provides seed money. In declining industries, the government decides how sacrifice will be allocated among various companies (Lohr, 1983*b*).

Consequences

A worker who is assured of a job for life and participates in decision making is willing to accept reassignment and retraining for new tasks, and companies can justify the expense of retraining. Thus technological change and the innovations it brings hold little threat to the Japanese worker. Instead, the worker realizes that such change is good for the long-term growth of the company. In this way Japanese companies gain flexibility in the use of their employees, and the employees themselves enjoy varied work.

Because all members of an age group move up in the organization together, effective communication commonly prevails among the heads of various divisions. It also means that high-level officials of the company have links with former classmates who have been advanced to similarly responsible positions in other companies and in government bureaucracy.

Unlike their American counterparts, Japanese companies feel free to make long-term plans and investments in auto design or microchip technology. Secure financial backing and a reliable, steady, and loyal labor pool encourage this orientation to the future. For their part, employees are not reluctant to devote themselves to long-range projects because they know they will be with the company until retirement and they will advance regularly during that time. Employees who are advanced on merit and liable to dismissal at any time most likely would be more interested in reaching short-run goals.

The emphasis on group participation enhances cooperation within the company. And the warm, supportive, noncritical atmosphere provided by the Japanese work organization defuses tensions among employees and intensifies their commitment to the company. Japanese workers are prepared to put in extra time without pay and to take on extra tasks. They are absent less and strike less than American workers. Because union relations with management are cordial and for the most part noncontroversial, labor unrest is not the problem in Japan that it is in many Western nations.

Despite glowing reports on Japanese organizations, they too have their drawbacks. They are the benevolent complement to Goffman's total institution and provide little individual choice. Although employees have life tenure, they cannot switch companies, and the tight integration of social and personal life with work can be suffocating.

EPILOGUE

Organizations play a vital role in contemporary societies because they allow large numbers of people to mesh their activities to achieve a variety of social, political, and economic goals. Without the framework provided by the organization, such institutions as the contemporary nation-state, corporation, university, church, hospital, farmers' cooperative, and labor union would not be possible. This chapter has detailed how formal organization is a response to these realities.

As we have seen, organizations come in a great many different forms. Bureaucracies, for instance, have evolved as a means to bring to human enterprise the rational, efficient, and technical competence found in the machine. Yet the ideal model of bureaucratic structure outlined by Max Weber is seldom encountered in the real world; all sorts of anomalies exist in practice. Bureaucracy also entails high human costs. Indeed, as we have noted, primary groups arise within formal organizations to provide elements of human warmth in people's working lives.

A consideration of formal organization links back to the concepts of social structure in Chapter 4 and to socialization in Chapter 5. Status, role, and group are the "stuff" of which organizations are made. And socialization is the process by which people are prepared for life within ongoing social systems. Our discussion of formal organization also directly relates to later chapters on political, economic, educational, and religious institutions. In the next chapter we examine deviance and social control. Here, too, we encounter formal organization, especially in "organized crime" and in the "organized response to crime" found in the criminal justice system.

SUMMARY

Formal organizations are human collectivities whose activities are consciously designed to achieve specific goals. As urbanization and industrailization accelerate, increasingly more relationships occur within large-scale secondary groups. Indeed, most of the crucial decisions affecting the lives of Americans are made by large organizations.

Formal organization has evolved as a social device that enables people to pursue a variety of goals. It has allowed work to be broken down into tasks according to a comprehensive division of labor. Unlike other kinds of social groups, formal organizations are *self-perpetuating*: Members may come and go, but procedures and goals remain. Relationships within formal organizations are based on exchange functions rather than affection.

Although formal organizations share many characteristics, they also differ from one another. Some organizations are *voluntary* in that individuals are free to decide whether to join or withdraw from them. Others are *coercive* in that people are compelled to enter them. Still others are *utilitarian* in that people join them for practical reasons.

Most formal organizations have a bureaucratic structure—they consist of interrelated parts with separate functions. Although bureaucracies are not a modern invention, they did not develop to their fullest extent until the nineteenth century. Max Weber identified the distinguishing characteristics of bureaucracy as (1) specialization (the division of production into small tasks); (2) a hierarchy of offices (each individual being responsible to the person above and for the people below; authority vested in the office, not in the individual); (3) adherence to specific rules and regulations; (4) impartiality; and (5) technical competence. Weber described a model or ideal type: In reality the completely bureaucratic organization does not exist.

Organizations have both a formal and an informal structure. The explicit rules defining each member's duties, organizational charts, and a system of rewards and punishments constitute the *formal structure*. The *informal structure* consists of a loose network of procedures that facilitate problem solving, eliminate unnecessary work, and protect the interests of individual workers.

Bureaucracy does not always promote efficiency. Overemphasis on rules results in *ritualism*. When rituals become a blind obsession, bureaucrats lose sight of goals and the ability to deal with new problems. Employees also tend to protect inept coworkers.

Three structural forces within an organization affect the course of an individual career: (1) the structure of opportunity for a given career; (2) the distribution of power; (3) the proportion of different types of people in the organization.

Because positions in the managerial ranks have a high quotient of uncertainty, strong pressures to conform are brought on those in the upper reaches of an organization. Controlling internal uncertainty by filling those positions with people who can be trusted frees an organization to focus on external uncertainties.

The impact of the organization on office workers is to keep then in dead-end jobs. Over the years office work has become increasingly mechanized, reducing tasks that were once semimanagerial to low-skill status.

Career paths in large organizations can be improved by addressing the problems of limited opportunity, limited power, and unbalanced composition. Some ways of alleviating these problems include broadening opportunities, improving feedback on job performance, increasing workers' power, and hiring minorities in groups.

Organizations do not exist in a vacuum: They must cope with their internal and external environments, both of which constantly change. Three major sources of change are (1) new technology, (2) growing professionalism within organizations, and (3) managers' respect for worker autonomy. In recent years American managers hvae taken particular interest in the Japanese organization as a model for improving relations between management and labor.

GLOSSARY

Asylum. Goffman's term for a place where a number of like-situated individuals, cut off from the wider society for an appreciable length of time, together lead an enclosed, formally administered round of life.

Bureaucracy. A hierarchical arrangement in which the parts of an organization are ordered in the manner of a pyramid based on a division of function and authority.

Bureaucratic control. The control an organization has over its members by means of specialization, standardization, and hierarchy.

Control of premises. The control an organization has over its members by influencing the motives that underlie their actions.

Direct control. The control an organization has over its members by means of rules and regulations, direct orders, and surveillance.

External environment. For an organization, those resources, other organizations, customers, transport systems, governments, and so on within which it operates.

Formal organization. Human collectivity whose activities are consciously designed for the purpose of achieving specific goals.

Formal structure. In an organization, the elements of formal structure include the explicit rules defining each person's duties, organizational charts describing relationships among members, and a system of rewards and punishments.

Hierarchy. In bureaucracies, a chain of command, with each person responsible to the person directly above and responsible for the actions of those directly below.

Informal structure. In an organization, the informal structure consists of the procedures that enable people to solve problems not covered by the formal regulations, to eliminate unpleasant or unnecessary work, and to protect their own interests.

Internal environment. For an organization, its members and the jobs they do and attitudes they hold.

Mortification. Goffman's term for the process of stripping a person of his or her civilian identity and physical integrity in preparation for indoctrination into a total institution.

Negotiated order. The process of bargaining, diplomacy, and give-and-take whereby people at various levels of an organization together solve work-related problems.

Parkinson's law. Parkinson formulated his law to explain why bureaucratic employees often appear busier than they should be: "Work expands to fill the time available for its completion."

Peter principle. Attempting to account for the incompetence characteristic of many bureaucratic employees, Peter and Hull suggest that "in a hierarchy, every employee tends to rise to his [or her] level of incompetence."

Ritualism. Merton's term for following rules and regulations without regard for the original goals or the consequences of one's actions.

Total institution. An organization closed off from the outside in which inmates lose nearly all control over and responsibility for their own lives (Goffman).

Voluntary association. An organization people join because they support its goals and values.

CHAPTER 9

Deviance and Social Control

For twenty-seven years Paul Arthur Crafton was a professor of engineering administration at George Washington University in Washington, D.C. But at Millersville State College, 118 miles away in southeastern Pennsylvania, he was known as Peter Hector Pearse, an associate professor of economics. And at Shippensburg State College he masqueraded as John Byron Hext, an instructor of mathematics and computer science. Complicating matters, at Towson State University he passed himself off as David A. Gordon, a part-time instructor in business administration. He juggled his class schedules by dint of frantic commuting and supported his multiple indentities through the use of fake credentials. In March 1983 the professor was tripped up by his colleagues at Millersville and arrested by authorities. He was convicted of impersonating a professor at two colleges and sentenced to three to nine months in jail.

In 1980 a scandal swept through the athletic programs of a number of the nation's leading universities. During an inquiry into illegal gambling in the Southwest, the Federal Bureau of Investigation stumbled on the faking of college credits for football and basketball players. Hundreds of college athletes, often with the help of their coaches, had managed to remain in good standing as students by having fraudulent academic credits transferred from summer and extension programs offered by other schools. In commenting on the revelations, Charlie McClendon, who for eighteen years had served as football coach at Louisiana State University, noted: "Football and basketball are the income producers, and if you don't sell tickets, you're out of a job. So a coach who needs a player real bad will bend the rules a little to keep him eligible. Once you bend them a little, you bend them a little more." And Darryl Rogers, then head football coach at Michigan State, said that the scandal reminded him of an old rule in college coaching: "They'll fire you for losing before they'll fire you for cheating" (Toubman, 1980).

Princeton University has long prided itself on its honor code. Upon admission, all students must sign a statement indicating that they understand the code and pledge to abide by it. It was little wonder that the university community was shocked in 1979 by the results of a survey conducted by the *Daily Princetonian*, a campus newspaper: More than a third of the students admitted to cheating on an examination at least once during their college careers.

As we have stressed in earlier chapters, members of groups and societies share various expectations about how people should behave. Yet at times, the behavior of some people goes beyond that permitted by the prevailing norms. Our illustrations above highlight this fact. In this chapter we consider these matters. We also examine the nature and importance of social control for group life. Then we turn to some explanations of deviance. Among other things, we explore how people get labeled as deviant and what the consequences of this labeling process are. Finally, we look at deviant acts that are considered criminal and examine the criminal justice system. But first, we want to provide a clearer idea of the nature of deviance.

THE NATURE OF DEVIANCE AND SOCIAL CONTROL

On an unusually hot summer day police officers in one of the nation's larger cities brought a man to a psychiatric center. When interviewed by a psychiatric worker, the man's responses did not seem out of the ordinary until the following exchange occurred:

> Q. How did you happen to come here?
> A. I don't know. I was just minding my own business.
> Q. Who brought you here?
> A. The police.
> Q. What had you been doing?
> A. Nothing. Just minding my own business.
> Q. What were you doing at the time?
> A. Just walking along the street.
> Q. What street?
> A. (He gave the name of one of the busiest streets in the city.)
> Q. What had you done just before that?
> A. It was hot, so I took my clothes off.
> Q. All your clothes?
> A. No. Not my shoes and stockings.
> Q. Why not those too?
> A. The sidewalk was too hot (Slotkin 1950: 70–71).

In a way, the man's behavior seemed to make more sense than did that of other pedestrians who sweltered in their clothing on a blistering, hot day. However, when measured against prevailing standards, his behavior would be judged deviant. Indeed, on the basis of that behavior and other responses, the man was diagnosed as schizophrenic and placed in a mental institution. This illustration highlights for us the nature of deviance. Sociologists view **deviance** as any behavior that the members of a social group define as violating their norms. As used by sociologists, *deviance* is a relatively neutral term. Yet, in everyday usage, *deviance* has taken on negative connotations of crime, mental instability, or immorality. Let us cast a sociological eye on some of these popular notions of deviance.

Even the appearance of violating a social norm, occasions at least an amused second look. (Birgit Pohl.)

Some Myths About Deviance

One popular myth holds that certain acts are inherently deviant. But sociologists point out that deviance is defined by social norms, and since norms are relative to time and place, so too is deviance. Even killing another person may be considered normal and right if the people involved are wearing soldiers' uniforms and are fighting for their countries. (We never say that a soldier *murdered* one of the enemy.) Thus one person may be honored with the Congressional Medal of Honor while another is sent to prison for committing the same act. And behaviors that qualify one person for a mental asylum, prison, or execution in one historical period may qualify the same person for sainthood in another. For instance, among the reasons given by fifteenth-century authorities for burning Joan of Arc at the stake was that she claimed to hear the voice of God speaking to her. Later, many French people accepted this same assertion as evidence to support her elevation to sainthood in the Roman Catholic church. In contemporary France a young peasant girl claiming to hear supernatural voices would very likely be hospitalized for psychiatric observation. In sum, because people's norms differ from one society or social situation to the next, what they regard as deviant also varies (see Table 9.1).

Not only do we fall into the trap of talking about certain acts as if they are inherently deviant, we also tend to think of deviance as whatever is uncommon or atypical. Of course, many deviant acts are characteristic of only a minority of the population. However, the uncommonness of a behavior is not sufficient to determine whether it is considered deviant. Many uncommon acts are not deviant, and some deviant acts are rather common. For example, skydiving is uncommon but not deviant, while speeding is deviant (in the sense of being illegal) but common.

A third myth holds that certain categories of people —so-called "nuts, sluts, and perverts"—do all the deviating. However, most "normal" people also engage in deviant acts, even though their deviance goes largely undetected. For example, how many people do you know who have never stolen anything? Or run a red light? Or told a lie? Or cheated on their income taxes? Clearly, people other than socially labeled deviants violate norms.

A fourth myth asserts that deviant individuals willfully break social norms. Yet a consideration of the people stopped by police officers for speeding shows that this is not always the case. Although some people do deliberately drive above the speed limit, others may be unaware of the posted speed, and still others may unintentionally drift into speeds that exceed the limit. And some, particularly owners of "hot rods," may be stopped for "speeding" even when they are obeying the law: Police officers commonly define these individuals as "speeders" and they act on their definitions by giving

Studies that ask national samples of people in different cultures the same questions about the same behaviors are rare. In this major study, note that Americans are far more tolerant of protest and homosexuality than any of the other cultures, with Iran being the least tolerant. On the other hand, condemnation of air pollution is uniformly high—a global norm that did not exist a generation earlier.

TABLE 9.1 The Cultural Relativity of Deviance

Type of act	Percentage who think act should be prohibited by law*				
	India	*Iran*	*Italy (Sardinia)*	*U.S.*	*Yugoslavia*
Homosexuality in private between consenting adults	74	90	87	18	72
Public, nonviolent political protest	33	77	35	6	46
Failure to help another person in danger	45	56	80	28	77
Air pollution caused by a factory	99	98	96	96	92

* Percentages have been rounded off.

Source: Adapted from Graeme Newman. *Comparative Deviance: Perception and Law in Six Cultures.* New York: Elsevier, 1976, p. 116, Table 4.

them tickets even without cause. Under these circumstances, the police enjoy the power to translate their definition of "speeder" into social reality—they have the ability to make their charge of "speeding" stick.

The Role of Power and Social Definitions

It should now be clear from the discussion that *deviance* is defined by the values and norms that prevail among people in a particular place at a particular time. In other words, a social audience determines whether an act is or is not deviant. Of course certain acts, such as murder, rape, theft, perversion, and mental pathology, would occur whether or not we define them as deviant. But by defining them as deviant, we set in motion a series of events that would not otherwise take place.

Consider the matter of drug use. Americans have long encouraged the use of caffeine, a mild stimulant, and alcohol, a central nervous system depressant, is a common "social lubricant" on business and recreational occasions. But marijuana is a different story. Many scientific authorities consider marijuana, a mild hallucinogen, no more dangerous to health than tobacco and less so than alcohol. Nonetheless, in many American communities its use is punishable by fine or imprisonment.

Apparently, marijuana was openly smoked during the nineteenth century by artists and writers in urban centers. Doctors used it widely as a painkiller and antidepressant. The push to make the drug illegal only came about in 1937 when Harry J. Anslinger, head of the Federal Bureau of Narcotics, needed an issue to galvanize public opinion and the Congress against further cuts in his agency's budget. Claiming that marijuana was the "assassin of youth," Anslinger organized a national campaign against the "crazed drug fiend." Congress duly responded with antimarijuana legislation, and a healthy increase in his budget to stamp out marijuana use (Becker, 1963).

Shifting public attitudes toward marijuana use highlight the point that deviance is not a property inherent in particular behaviors. Rather, it is a property that people *confer* on some forms of behavior by their social definitions. Viewed in this manner, groups create deviance by making rules (Schur, 1980). Given that deviance is relative to the values and norms that prevail at a particular time and place, a key question becomes *whose* values and norms are being violated and *who* has the power to identify and punish violators?

By way of illustration, consider abortion. The voluntary termination of a pregnancy violates the moral principles of some groups who equate abortion with murder. However, many women's groups strongly believe that every woman should have the right to exercise control over her own body and hence should be able to end an unwanted pregnancy if she chooses. The issue that then arises is whose values should prevail? As will be discussed in Chapter 11, power decides which group is able to make its value preferences the operating norms for all members of society. Through the manipulation of rewards and the imposition of penalties, some individuals and groups can make their standards prevail even when others object.

Within the United States many behaviors that not too long ago were defined as deviance are now being contested in the political arena. Traditionally, a "nonpolitical" or "welfare" approach was taken to such "problems" as homosexuality, unwanted pregnancies, poverty, alcoholism, and mental illness. Americans deemed these matters to be the province of social workers, psychiatrists, psychologists, and other "professionals." But increasingly, individuals who fall within these "problem" categories are establishing their own constituencies. Gay organizations have formed in response to the harassment of homosexuals and as vehicles to promote gay rights. Women's groups have likewise mobilized in support of legalized abortions. Poor people have contested many prevailing welfare approaches and have championed new policies. And individuals plagued by alcoholism and mental illness have in some cases demanded programs better suited to their needs.

Viewed from the perspective of conflict theorists, deviance is a contest between those who have power and enforce their rules and those who lack power and violate these rules. In this view, elitist groups define as deviants those who challenge or interfere with their goals. But the victims, those who see themselves as being exploited and abused by prevailing institutions, view matters quite differently. They define elitist groups and dominant institutions as the sources of social problems. We will return to this matter later in the chapter when we examine various theories of deviance.

Whether abortion is considered to be deviance or not depends on whose values or norms are being violated. (Left, Alan Carey/The Image Works; right, Mark Antman/The Image Works.)

Social Control

In no society is deviance left totally unrestrained. If it were, the foundations, norms, and values on which a society is based, and in which many people have a vested interest, could quickly disintegrate. Thus, in all societies, people are subject to various forms of **social control**—those mechanisms used to uphold social norms and restrain their actual or potential violation. Social control implies power—at times coercion—to regulate the behavior of individuals and groups. Consequently, in examining deviance from a sociological perspective, we need to ask who is controlling whom, by what means, under what circumstances, and for what reasons (Schur, 1980).

Internalization

Mechanisms of social control operate on both an internal and an external level. On the internal level, social control rests on socialization, the process by which a society transmits its values and norms to its new members (see Chapter 5). Sociologists use the term **internalization** to describe the process by which cultural standards become part of a person's personality structure. Through internalization people thoroughly accept certain norms and values. They abide by these rules not because they fear punishment but because following the rules seems "natural"—deviance does not even come to mind. As members in good standing within a group, people simply do what other group members do. Further, deviating from the group's norms makes most people feel guilty and disoriented. In an important sense, internalized norms and values form the basis of social order, for people police themselves. Social control becomes self-control.

But socialization is never perfect; people may not internalize all the rules that society deems "proper" and "right." (See boxed insert on ethical behavior on the job.) Moreover, many situations that arise are not

THE SOCIOLOGICAL EYE ON:

Ethical Standards and Behavior on the Job

According to the National Institute of Justice, about one-third of the nation's employees steal from the workplace. The institute's director, James K. Stewart, estimates that such theft costs American business between $5 billion and $10 billion a year. Further, roughly two-thirds of employees admit to sick-leave abuse, drug or alcohol abuse, or other misconduct that results in "counterproductive behavior" on the job.

The findings are based on surveys carried out in the Dallas–Forth Worth, Minneapolis–St. Paul, and Cleveland areas by the Department of Sociology at the University of Minnesota. A total of 9,175 randomly selected employees at forty-seven business organizations responded anonymously to a mailed, self-administered questionnaire (a 54 percent response rate) provided by the Minnesota researchers. Included in the survey were sixteen retail-department-store chains, twenty-one general hospitals, and ten electronic-manufacturing firms. Employee theft consisted of "borrowing" money from cash registers; padding expense accounts; stealing company tools and supplies; taking consumer items such as televisions, fur coats, and patio furniture; and misusing a store's discount privelege by allowing others to make purchases with it. The sociologists found that "those employees who felt their employees were genuinely concerned with their workers' best interests reported the least theft."

The Gallup Organization uncovered somewhat similar patterns in 1983 when it undertook personal in-home interviews with a nationally representative sample of 1,558 adults. For sensitive questions on personal behavior, respondents received a separate answer sheet, checked off answers, and sealed the sheet in an envelope. Gallup simultaneously polled a sample of 396 middle-level large-company executives, employing confidential mail questionnaires. The results of these polls are shown in the table below.

Ethical Behavior on the Job

	Percent Who Have Ever Done Each Activity	
Reported Behavior	Business Executives	General Public
Taken home work supplies	74%	40%
Called in sick to work when not ill	14	31
Used company telephones for personal long-distance calls	78	15
Overstated deductions somewhat on tax form	35	13
Driven while drunk	80	33
Smoked marijuana	17	25
Used cocaine	2	8

Source: Reprinted by permission of *The Wall Street Journal*, © Dow Jones & Company, Inc., 1983. All rights reserved.

As reflected in the table, the general public and the executives differed in their reported behavior. While 40 percent of the public said they had taken home work supplies, 74 percent of the executives admitted to having done so. However, only 14 percent of the executives said they had falsely called in sick, while 31 percent of public acknowledged having done the same.

The Gallup surveys revealed that the behavior of younger Americans differed considerably from that of older Americans on ethical matters. Only 26 percent of those over age fifty admitted to taking home work supplies, but 50 percent of those in their thirties and forties confessed to the practice. And while only 18 percent of those over fifty said they had falsely called in sick, 40 percent of the group under age fifty acknowledged having done so.

The Gallup Organization also found that women consistently reported more ethical behavior than did men. While 47 percent of the men admitted that they took home work supplies, 33 percent of the women admitted to doing so. However, religion seemed to have only a marginal effect. Some 37 percent of those who attended church or synagogue or felt a religious affiliation said they had taken home work supplies, whereas 43 percent of those who did not attend religious services said they had done so. Overall, the Gallup surveys suggested that a widespread double standard prevails among Americans: People who condemn taking advantage of an individual often shrug their shoulders over doing the same thing to an employer.

covered by the rules, and people must improvise new behaviors. Because socialization is not adequate to ensure conformity, external contraints are required. Sociologists term these constraints **sanctions**—rewards for conforming to a social norm or penalties for violating it.

Informal Social Controls

Some sanctions are applied informally. **Informal social control** involves subtle and unofficial pressure to conform to norms and values. It is effective because people want to live up to the expectations of others, even in ways they do not always consciously or explicitly recognize. Positive informal sanctions include a smile, praise, and a kiss; negative informal sanctions, ostracism, ridicule, and verbal and physical threats.

In his studies of how people interact with one another, the sociologist Erving Goffman (1967) found that informal controls often take the form of "ritual exchanges" that make things run smoothly and according to expectations. For example, in our everyday conversations we employ ritual exchanges to handle awkward moments and to minimize deviant behavior. We expect that each person will attempt to avoid conversational lulls and will focus attention on the speaker, refrain from rude interruptions, control emotional displays, and tactfully end the conversation. Similarly, we hold in reserve a variety of rituals that help us repair serious breaches in conversational behavior. We expect the offending party to offer an excuse or apology, the injured party to then bestow forgiveness, and the offender to conclude with an expression of gratitude. Such measures allow both parties to feel that social order has somehow been restored.

Embarrassment plays a particularly powerful role in the workings of informal social control. Goffman believed that the discomfort we feel when we are embarrassed creates a strong motivation to avoid engaging in behavior that again will produce social disapproval.

In Goffman's view, informal social controls satisfy the basic social requirement that people be able to predict one another's behavior. The obligations and expectations associated with roles achieve this end (see Chapter 4). You are obligated to conform to the rules associated with a particular role and others expect you to conform. When rules are broken, both parties in a reciprocal role relationship are discredited. Hence, it is to everyone's advantage to obey the rules.

Nonconformity can incur informal penalties ranging from mild disapproval to differential treatment. For example, patients who conform quietly to hospital norms and procedures typically receive better care than those who interrupt well-established routines by arguing with staff members and by complaining excessively about pain and discomfort. These latter individuals acquire the label "problem patients." Consequently they may encounter deliberate neglect, early discharge, or referral to a psychiatrist. Word about "problem patients" travels quickly through hospitals, and thereafter staff members are less likely to define their complaints as legitimate (Lorber, 1975).

Formal Social Controls

Formal social control involves direct and official pressures to conform to social norms and values. Some control is the product of special organizations such as police departments, legislatures, courts, prisons, juvenile facilities, drug rehabilitation centers, and settlement houses. It tends to be coercive. The medical system, especially psychiatry, also operates as an agency of social control by defining who is "sick" and then by managing "illness." Likewise, the welfare system, particularly as embodied in the activities of social workers, defines who is eligible for various benefits and polices conformity to the rules for welfare assistance. Further, viewed in Marxist terms, the entire corporate system dominates the economy, deciding which activities in the production and distribution of goods and services are legitimate and which are deviant.

Other formal controls are built into the organization itself. Consider how your college rewards you for behaving in accordance with its standards of excellence and punishes you for noncomformity. Indeed, all organizations dictate the goals that their members will pursue; determine which behaviors are permissible and which are not; and structure who does what, when, and where. Hence, the skills we have come to identify as "management skills" revolve about socializing people in an organization's goals, motivating people to carry out various organizational tasks, and minimizing deviance as defined by organizational rules.

The Marxist sociologist Michael Burawoy (1979) provides one example of how organizations produce conformity. He gathered his data while working as a machine operator in a Chicago plant. During this time,

Burawoy was impressed with the seemingly furious pace with which the workers carried out their tasks. This observation led him to ask, if Marx was right and workers are alienated from their work, why do they push themselves so hard working for employers? Indeed, he recounts that he was also drawn into the process: "But it wasn't long before I too was breaking my back to make out, to make the quota, to discover a new angle, and to run two jobs at once—risking life and limb for that extra piece. . . . Why was I actively participating in the intensification of my own exploitation and even losing my temper when I couldn't?" (1979:xi).

Burawoy found that workers perceived their livelihood as dependent on the survival and growth of their capitalist employer, and they defined capitalist profit as being legitimate. Moreover, the machine operators consented to exploitative capitalist relationships by treating activities on the shop floor as a kind of competitive game. For example, the company paid their employees on the basis of a piece-work system that allowed them to earn incentive pay. This arrangement led the workers to define the labor process as a competitive contest in which they pitted themselves against technology and company regulations. For instance, they would look for "angles" that enabled them to finish quickly so that they could accumulate time for relaxing later. Finding angles also challenged their ingenuity and relieved their boredom. Making games out of who could find the best angles got workers to accept the capitalist work arrangements. In sum, organizations, by channeling and patterning activities along some lines rather than others, determine the alternatives for behavior and, by doing so, are able to structure conformity. Let us examine more closely how organizations and societies undertake to achieve conformity.

Deviance, Control, and the Social Order

The boundaries between acceptable and unacceptable behavior are usually not hard and fast. Societies typically permit a "permissive zone of variation" around even strongly supported and rather specific norms. In addition, most norms are not expressed as firm rules or official codes. Consequently, a rule becomes defined only in the course of people's day-to-day activities.

Deviance plays a double role, both clarifying norms and contributing to social order. First, in defining certain kinds of behavior as deviant, a group or a community also defines what behavior is acceptable.

The boundaries between acceptable and unacceptable behavior are usually not hard and fast. (Abigail Heyman/Archive.)

Second, in uniting against the deviant, that group or community comes together and reaffirms its common bonds. Thus, when people in the old West formed a posse, when parents unite to fight porno shops in their neighborhoods, when citizens vote for a new, more trustworthy politician, they owe a debt to the "deviants" who brought them together—the outlaw who stole their horses, the adult bookstore owner who opened the shop, the corrupt politician who accepted bribes. Not only do they reaffirm the norms and values that were threatened; they also strengthen other values, work together, and pour energy into shoring up the social order they believe in.

The sociologist Kai T. Erikson (1966) provides an illustration of the functional contributions that deviance makes to social order in his study *Wayward Puritans*. In 1630 when Anne Hutchinson began to proclaim that Boston's ministers did not have the exclusive right to interpret the Bible, she drew large audiences, angering the Puritan ministers who ruled colonial Boston. The ministers claimed that she was undermining church authority, which they equated with civil authority. Yet Mrs. Hutchinson was an upright and law-abiding citizen, and therefore they lacked a "handle" for defining her behavior as deviance. To meet her challenge, they wrote a law that made what she was doing illegal, found her guilty, and banished her from the colony. "I desire to know wherefore I am banished," she said. Governor Winthrop gave her this answer: "Say no more, the court knows wherefore and is satisfied." "And that was exactly the point," writes Erikson (1966:100–101)

> The court *did* know why Mrs. Hutchinson had to be banished, but it did not know how to express that feeling in any language then known in New England. The settlers were experiencing a shift in ideological focus, a change in community boundaries, but they had no vocabulary to explain to themselves or anyone else what the nature of these changes were. The purpose of the trial was to invent that language, to find a name for the nameless offense which Mrs. Hutchinson had committed.

Thus, without realizing it, Anne Hutchinson helped the Massachusetts Bay Colony to redefine the limits of acceptable religious belief. And somewhat ironically, she also contributed to the social solidarity of the community she left behind.

In addition to helping people define the contours of their social order, deviants often serve as agents of social change. For example, the unwillingness of blacks to comply with segregation laws during the 1950s—considered serious acts of deviance at the time—gave rise to a new legal and moral code. And during the past decade or so, efforts by women to achieve equality have also involved behavior—such as the refusal to relinquish their own last name upon marriage—that initially appeared, or may even still be thought of by some people, as deviant.

Such observations suggest that deviance is a *normal* part of social life. We commonly think that it is the task of the police to eliminate crime and for federal agencies such as the Federal Drug Administration (FDA) to eliminate such deviant practices as producing and distributing harmful substances. But sociologists find that typically these organizations and agencies seek not to eradicate deviance but to contain it within "reasonable" bounds (Schur, 1980). In fact, individuals and agencies engaged in monitoring and curtailing deviance would find themselves out of work were deviance eliminated. Consequently, agencies of social control convey a double message in their annual budget requests: We are doing a great job controlling deviance but there is much more that must be done.

Unless societies are prepared to devote a large portion of their resources to policing people's behavior, they must decide which deviant behaviors they will ignore and which they will attempt to control. Excessive control can sometimes amplify the very deviance that is the target of control. For instance, as the Internal Revenue Service (IRS) cracks down on income tax evaders, it encourages the development of the "underground economy"—moonlighting, gross-receipt skimming, working "off the books," and bartering goods and services to evade the payment of tax. The IRS estimates that Americans dodge some $100 billion in income tax each year through such devices. In sum, societies find they must live with a good deal of deviance.

EXPLANATIONS OF DEVIANCE

Although groups and societies differ in the behaviors that they define as being acceptable and unacceptable, all nonetheless attempt to secure the conformity of their members to basic norms. But why are social controls needed? Why do some people break the rules of their group or society? Three basic types of explanations have been advanced: Some scholars have explained deviance in terms of the biological characteristics of the deviant. Others have sought an answer in psychological factors, especially a person's personality problems. And still others have scrutinized the social environment of the deviant.

The biological and psychological approaches focus on the deviant and ask how offenders differ from nonoffenders. This perspective attempts to identify the "kind of people" who become deviant and to show the factors that contribute to their becoming deviant. In contrast, those scholars who look to the social environment assume that deviants and nondeviants are essentially the same "kind of people." They seek to explain deviance by situational and social factors that lead ordinary people to break the rules. Let us consider these differing approaches more carefully.

Biological Explanations

Why do some people turn to crime and others not? Cesare Lombroso, an Italian criminologist of the nineteenth century, believed that he had discovered the answer while examining the skull of Villela, a master criminal.

> At the sight of that skull, I seemed to see all of a sudden, lighted up as a vast plain under a flaming sky, the problem of the nature of the criminal—an atavistic being who reproduces in his person the ferocious instincts of primitive humanity and the inferior animals. Thus were explained in the enormous jaws, high cheekbones, prominent superciliary arches . . . found in criminals, savages, and apes. (Lombroso, in Cohen, 1966:50)

Lombroso and his students took dozens of measurements of the heads and bodies of many prisoners and "found" that they *all* fitted the "animalistic" pattern. Lombroso concluded that some people—people who physically resemble the "early" and "savage" ancestors of modern humans—are *born* criminals.

But Lombroso made one serious error: He measured only criminals. When Charles Goring, a British physician, measured the skulls of a large sample of both criminals and ordinary citizens, he found no physical differences between the two groups (Goring, 1913). Lombroso's famous theory was dashed. But this failure has not dissuaded later scientists from searching for other biological foundations of deviance. Researchers are finding mounting evidence that biological malfunctioning in the brain's chemistry is associated with schizophrenia, manic-depressive disorders, and a host of other mental illnesses (Wender and Klein, 1981). Moreover, psychiatric drugs can bring the symptoms of some severe mental illnesses under control. Today, of course, the tools and approaches of biological researchers are much more sophisticated than they were in Lombroso's day.

One question twentieth-century investigators have asked is whether criminal behavior might have a genetic basis. Much attention has been paid recently to the so-called XYY syndrome, the possibility that the presence of an extra Y sex chromosome in some men might predispose them toward deviance. (A normal man has an XY chromosome pattern; a normal woman has an XX pattern.) When researchers found that a greater percentage of XYY men than XY men were in prison for crimes, it lent support to the idea that the extra Y chromosome makes a man more aggressive and therefore leads to increased criminal behavior (Witkin et al., 1976). But like Lombroso's work, the research was based on a sample composed only of prisoners. A later Danish study comparing prisoners and nonprisoners also found a significant difference between the percentage of XYY men and that of XY men who had been convicted of one or more crimes (Witkin et al., 1976). But there was little evidence linking criminality with increased aggressiveness. Instead, the researchers found that men with an extra Y chromosome were appreciably less intelligent than were XY men. This fact led the researchers to speculate that the XYY men were merely easier for the police to catch—which would explain why more XYY men end up in jail.

The application of biochemical knowledge to criminology is still in its infancy. But new theories and research are gaining public interest and attention (Van Dusen, 1983; Wilson, 1983). The sociologist Lee Ellis (1979) suggests that the future of this work is still too uncertain to predict. Even so, Ellis contends that the theoretical understanding of deviance is "ultimately impossible without understanding, first and foremost, how the neurological processes directly controlling such behavior operate, and, second, how these neurological processes are, in turn, controlled by the impact of the major environmental factors in interaction with the overall biochemical blueprint" (1979:372–373).

Psychological Explanations

While some scientists have looked to the biological characteristics of people to explain deviant behavior, others have turned their attention to the psychological make-up of individuals. Psychologists following in Sigmund Freud's psychoanalytic tradition maintain that all people have deviant impulses toward sexuality and aggression. However, in the process of growing up, most of us learn to inhibit these inclinations. Freud argued that through identification with their parents, children acquire a superego, or conscience, that forbids deviant kinds of behavior, and an ego that enables them to deal realistically with internal drives and social demands. Psychoanalytic theory suggests that acts of wanton cruelty and crimes committed without apparent motives may indicate an underdeveloped superego. Conversely, an *overdeveloped* superego may also lead to deviance. People who are repulsed by their own urges may commit deviant acts to provoke the punishment they feel they deserve for hating their parents or for having sexual fantasies.

The popularity of Freudian theory has faded in recent years, and many psychologists have looked to alternate explanations of deviance. Some contend that deviance, like any form of behavior, is learned from those around us. In a classic study, Albert Bandura and Richard H. Walters (1959) compared groups of delinquent and nondelinquent white boys from financially stable homes. They found that the most aggressive youngsters typically came from families in which the parents urged or condoned aggression. This and other research by Bandura also reveals that punishing children for aggression results in more, not less, aggressive behavior:

> Indeed, parental modeling behavior may often counteract the effects of their direct training. When a parent punishes his child physically for having aggressed toward peers, for example, the intended outcome of this training is that the child should refrain from hitting others. The child, however, is also learning from parental demonstration how to aggress physcially and this imitative learning may provide the direction of the child's behavior when he is similarly frustrated in subsequent interaction. (Bandura, 1967:43)

In sum, Bandura (1973; 1977) contends that exposure to models of violent behavior and reinforcement for aggressive acts explain why people so often attack one another.

Still other psychologists maintain that deviance cannot be fully understood if the focus of inquiry is limited to influences during early childhood. They argue that deviance should instead be viewed as part of a life-long developmental process in which one type of deviance leads to another. For instance, in a thirty-year study that traced black men from their childhood to their adult years, Lee Robins and Eric Wish (1977) found that early deviant acts like truancy in the first grade, drinking and sexual relations before the age of fifteen, drug use, and alcohol problems were all good predictors of subsequent deviant behavior. They concluded that both the kinds of deviant acts and their frequency affect the likelihood that individuals will engage in later deviant behavior.

Structural Stress Theory

Although psychological theories of deviance provide insights into *individual* cases, they do not explain why *rates* of deviance (the number of deviant acts per unit of population) vary from group to group and from neighborhood to neighborhood. Consequently, sociologists seek answers to the question of deviance in the larger social environment. One sociological approach looks to the part that social structure plays in producing stresses that prompt people to engage in deviant behavior. According to this view, when conformity to the prevailing social norms fails to satisfy a person's legitimate desires, the person will be forced to seek satisfaction through deviant means.

The work of Emile Durkheim highlighted the part that social factors play in deviant behavior. In his 1897 study of suicide rates (see Chapter 2), Durkheim (1897/1916) introduced the concept of **anomie**. Through the years sociologists have come to view anomie as a

FIGURE 9.1 Merton's Five Modes of Social Adaptation

Modes of Adapting	Accepts Culturally Approved Goals	Accepts Culturally Approved Means
Conformist	Yes	Yes
Innovator	Yes	No
Ritualist	No	Yes
Retreatist	No	No
Rebel	No (Creates New Goals)	No (Creates New Means)

Source: Adapted from Robert K. Merton. *Social Theory and Social Structure.* New York: Free Press, 1968, p. 194.

This figure illustrates the five patterns of coping with social expectations specified by Robert K. Merton. While conformists accept both culturally approved goals and means, deviants reject either these goals or these means, or both.

condition within society in which individuals find that the prevailing social norms are ill-defined, weak, or conflicting.

The sociologist Robert K. Merton applied the concept of anomie in an American context to explain the different ways in which people adapt to the discrepancy between expectations and opportunities. He used stress theory to account for varying crime rates in different social classes (1938/1957) and linked high rates of deviance to anomie. For example, people may expect to have a job, but the economy may not provide enough jobs to go around. From a functionalist perspective, Merton reasoned that to some degree all people internalize the goals considered worth striving for in their culture. Everyone also internalizes the norms governing proper and legitimate ways of striving for these goals. But when opportunities for achieving highly valued goals (as the culture defines them) do not exist, people may seek alternative ways to reach those goals, or they may abandon the goals altogether. Thus, "some social structures exert a definite pressure upon certain persons in the society to engage in nonconforming rather than in conforming behavior" (Merton, 1938/1957:132).

Exactly what courses of action can people take in response to these pressures? Merton identified five possibilities (see Figure 9.1). One is **conformity**. A person faced with a discrepancy between expectations and opportunities can nevertheless continue to seek culturally valued goals by culturally approved means. When opportunities are severely limited, the same person could choose to adopt one of various forms of deviance. What Merton calls **innovation** is the pursuit of culturally approved goals by culturally *dis*approved means. For example, office workers who earn a subsistence wage may pilfer company funds to supplement their income. Another way for these individuals to resolve the conflict between their goals and their limited opportunities is what Merton calls **ritualism**: abandoning the goals denied them but rigidly adhering to the socially prescribed means for achieving the goals. Thus, they might immerse themselves in their work, following the company's rules and procedures religiously while simultaneously resigning themselves to low-paying, dead-end jobs. Yet a fourth course of action is **retreatism**, which involves abandoning both culturally and prescribed goals *and* means. In this case, the officer workers might simply decide to quit their jobs and go on welfare. They see no point in continuing to pursue the culturally valued goal of getting ahead, and they no longer find it intrinsically worthwhile to follow the norms of hard work and employee loyalty. Perhaps still later, alienated from both traditional goals and norms, they may turn to new ideals and unconventional ways of pursuing them. For example, they might embrace the goal of creating an egalitarian society and help to organize a commune that adopts such a life style. Merton calls this course of action, in which new goals and means come to replace old, **rebellion**.

Since its publication in 1938, Merton's theory has been highly praised for its logical tightness, but it has also been widely criticized for making some false assumptions. For example, the theory assumes that most people try as best they can to adopt conventional goals and means, when in fact the acceptance of social conventions varies with the situation. As the sociologist Albert K. Cohen (1965, 1966) points out, people do not work out a solution to their stressful circumstances all by themselves in a social vacuum. Rather, they take into account what other people are doing. In turn these perceptions influence the social framework they use in defining whether particular actions are appropriate or inappropriate. Merton also assumes that people deviate when they cannot attain their goals through legitimate means. But Travis Hirschi (1969) contends that this is not always the case. He finds little research evidence to support the hypothesis that delinquency arises in response to the frustration of having one's efforts to succeed blocked. And critics say that Merton overlooks the part that socialization processes play in producing deviance, a factor highlighted by cultural transmission theory.

Cultural Transmission Theory

In the 1920s Clifford Shaw and Henry McKay found that high crime rates had persisted in the same Chicago neighborhood for over twenty years. Yet during this time, different ethnic groups had come and gone. Obviously, ethnic cultural traditions could not explain the crime rate. In one of the classic studies of deviance, Shaw and McKay (1969) found that newcomers were continuously learning deviant ways from established residents, primarily in juvenile play groups and teenaged gangs. Once the newcomers had absorbed the neighborhood norms and values, they in turn passed them on to the next wave of immigrants.

Shaw and McKay's study was supported by the work of Edwin Sutherland. Sutherland's book, *Principles of Criminology* (1960) written with Donald Cressy, contains an explanation of how this **cultural transmission**—the process by which deviance is learned through the transmission of norms within a community or group—takes place. Everyone is exposed to different and conflicting definitions of right and wrong. The standards people eventually adopt as their own are learned through **differential association** with others. If they spend more time with deviants and have more intense relations with them, those influences will outweigh nondeviant influences. Through the transmission of norms within a community or group, people can be socialized to the drug subculture, the homosexual subculture, the radical subculture, and so on. Thus some communities offer young people opportunities for education, role models of

Through the process of cultural transmission the members of this street gang will pass along its values and norms to younger members. (Ed Lettau/Photo Researchers.)

people who have achieved success by established means, and contacts with people who can help advance their careers through conventional channels. In contrast, other communities offer opportunities for learning how to hustle and evade authorities, role models of people who have achieved success as gamblers and pimps, and contacts with people who control underworld career opportunities.

In a classic participant-observation study of lower-class young men, the sociologist Walter Miller (1958) found that delinquency was greatly encouraged by the subcultural values that prevailed in the urban neighborhood. These values centered on *trouble* (with the law and with women); *toughness* (physical prowess and playing it cool); *smartness* (being able to outsmart and con others, as well as a respect for verbal quickness and ingenuity); *fate* (a sense that many forces are beyond one's control, that success is a matter of luck); and *autonomy* (a resentment of outside controls—"No one's gonna push me around"). Such delinquent acts as drinking or stealing cars, Miller concluded, are expressions of these underlying subcultural concerns. Thus he viewed delinquency as "a directed attempt . . . to adhere to forms of behavior and to achieve standards as they are defined in that community" (1958:5).

But subcultures do more than simply transmit values that direct their members' behavior. They also offer emotional support to people who share in their somewhat unique experiences and circumstances. Contact with the members of a subculture may help a person adopt a new and more fulfilling identity. Take the case of Carla, a young woman who grew up in a small Iowa town, believing she was the only lesbian in the community. When she was eighteen, she hitchhiked to San Francisco, where she made contact with gay organizations. For Carla, "it was as if I had come home" (Lewis, 1979:156). Another lesbian found that not until she immersed herself in the gay subculture was she able to overcome mainstream cultural prejudices about lesbians and find role models that were appealing to her. The emotional support and the role models provided by a subculture hold true for all sorts of stigmatized groups—including "little people," the retarded, and the handicapped.

Subcultures serve another important role by providing members with a system of beliefs that explains and justifies their deviance. Homosexuals, for instance, believe that their persuasion is as natural for them as heterosexuality is for others (Simon and Gagnon, 1970). Subcultures may even develop a public collective identity to fight against society's discriminatory ways: think of gay liberation and of the organizations dedicated to bettering the lot of ex-convicts or the aged.

In sum, cultural transmission theory describes how deviance is learned from others and supported by a sympathetic subculture. This is unquestionably an important insight (Matsueda, 1982). Yet it also has limitations. For one thing, cultural transmission theory does not explain why a sizable number of people in a community where deviant norms prevail do *not* become deviant. For instance, two persons may be exposed to criminal patterns, yet only one of them become a criminal. Moreover, the theory does not apply to some types of crime, primarily those in which neither the techniques nor the attitudes need be acquired from others. Examples include violations of financial trust, situational offenses, nonprofessional shoplifting, and "crimes of passion." Hence, by itself cultural transmission theory is incomplete.

Conflict Theory

The theories of deviance that we have considered thus far treat deviance as if a social consensus prevails within society. Presumably, such a consensus defines desirable and moral behaviors as well as undesirable and immoral ones. Conflict theory departs from this perspective. Its proponents contend that there is no consensus within society as a whole and that most social rules are not neutral. Rather rules embody the value preferences of one or another group and derive from the group's concept of moral order. Take questions as to which sexual practices, family arrangements, or chemical substances are acceptable and which are not. The answers to these questions ultimately rest on which party will have sufficient power to enforce its will upon others. To an even greater extent, the criminal justice system reflects the values of those who hold power through their control of the legislative, policing, and criminal labeling processes.

Viewed from a Marxist perspective, law is "first and foremost a reflection of the interests of the governing class" (Chambliss, 1974:34). This image of law sharply contrasts with that depicted in such doctrines as "the rule of law," "equality before the law," and "the separation of powers." Indeed, Marxists say that such doctrines obscure the underlying reality of open or hidden conflict between social classes. They portray the legal order as serving the interests of a ruling class and not the collective will or the general social good. The state designates acts as criminal because they run counter to the interests of those who have power at their command (Quinney, 1979). For instance, throughout the nineteenth and early twentieth centuries the criminal justice system supported, often with violence, the interests of capitalists attempting to block the formation of labor unions. And for seventy-eight years the Constitution sanctioned racism and racist practices through its legalization of slavery. Likewise, whites who murdered and subjugated native Americans were supported by countless legal stratagems (Michalowski and Bohlander, 1976).

Marxists point out that the nation's policing efforts are directed toward controlling the crimes of the disadvantaged—burglary, theft, robbery, vandalism, drug use, public intoxication, and traffic offenses. Violations against consumers or the commonwealth, such as water or air pollution, are typically handled by regulatory agencies that enjoy little power and minimal funding. The Federal Bureau of Investigation, for example, routinely records every murder, rape, assault, and auto theft reported in the nation. Law-enforcement agencies also log embezzlements and thefts from corporations. But no agency tracks crimes committed by the corporations themselves.

Of equal significance, laws often do not cover the damage caused in the pursuit of corporate profits. For example, no law barred the Ford Motor Company from positioning gas tanks in their automobiles where they provided a high risk of explosion in a rear-end collision. Although the faulty design resulted in hundreds of fatalities, Ford reasoned that design changes were unwarranted because their cost would exceed the "cost" of the lives lost (Michalowski and Bohlander, 1976; Kelly, 1982).

One study found that 60 percent of the nation's largest corporations were involved in regulatory or criminal offenses in 1975 or 1976 (Clinard and Yeager, 1980) And since 1976, over half of the nation's largest corporations have been linked to some form of serious misbehavior. Authorities agree that these figures reveal only the tip of the iceberg (Kelly, 1982).

In addition, compared with the penalties meted out to robbers and muggers, corporations and their executives get off lightly. For example, when FMC, a large producer of chemical products, was caught fouling West Virginia's Kanawha River with carbon tetrachloride, a harmful substance, it paid the top fine of $35,000 and agreed to provide $1 million to study the effect of water pollution on health (a penalty amounting to less than 1 percent of the firm's 1982 profits of $150 million). And when Westinghouse Electric Company pleaded guilty in 1978 to charges of bribing Egyptian officials, it was assessed the maximum fine of $300,000 (1 percent of the value of the $30 million contract realized by the bribery). Some corporate figures even flourish after their convictions. In 1978 David Begelman stepped down as president of Columbia Pictures after admitting that he forged $40,000 in Columbia checks. The court placed him on probation. One year later Metro-Goldwyn-Mayer hired him as its chief executive, and he later became president of United Artists (Kelly, 1982).

The conflict approach draws our attention to the partisan nature of social institutions. Yet it is often difficult to determine from conflict literature, particularly its Marxist versions, which specific individuals and groups are covered by such phrases as "capitalist elites" and "governing classes." Indeed, one often gets the impression that the legal system and the state are instruments that can be manipulated at will by the capitalist class or segments of it. But this picture hardly conforms to reality. Many state policies do not advance the interests of capitalist groups. For instance, welfare legislation supports unemployed and nonproductive workers, and rent controls inhibit a landlord's ability to receive full market rents. In many situations the "state apparatus" in fact exercises a relative autonomy from the interests of outside groups (Beirne, 1979).

The Labeling Perspective

Among sociological explanations of deviance, the labeling perspective offers a unique approach. It focuses on the process by which some individuals successfully define other individuals as deviants rather than upon the deviants themselves. The perspective traces its origin to the distinction between primary deviance and secondary deviance made by the sociologist Edwin M. Lemert (1951). He defined **primary deviance** as the pure and simple violation of a norm. This definition involves no inferences about motives or about the person who acted in a given way. Distinct from this initial, pure act is **secondary deviance**, in which people come to define themselves as deviants and undertake life patterns as a reaction to their being labeled as deviant by others. The distinction between the two forms of deviance is crucial when you consider that most primary deviance leads to no social reaction. For example, nearly everyone violates the penal code at one time or another, but little or nothing comes of it. An exhaustive study found that nearly one in five people interviewed in a random sample had serious emotional and psychological problems, but none of them was confined in a mental hospital (Srole and Fisher, 1978).

Lemert departed from traditional approaches to deviance in that he did not ask why some people break the law or succumb to deviant acts while other people do not. Instead, he asked how some individuals get singled out; labeled as "criminal," "schizophrenic," "homosexual," or whatever, and processed by social-control agencies. Thus, the labeling perspective focuses on how society's reaction to certain behaviors contributes to their being defined as "deviant." The approach relies heavily on the insights afforded by symbolic interactionist theory for its understanding of deviance.

The sociologist Howard S. Becker points out in *Outsiders* (1963) that people may perform deviant acts for various reasons. They may do so unwittingly; they may do so knowingly but not care; they may drift into deviance; or they may calculate that deviance is instrumental in achieving their goals. Whatever the reason, however, their fate depends not on their original motive but on whether they are caught and publicly *labeled* deviant.

The sociologist William J. Chambliss (1973) found the labeling process at work in the case of two gangs at "Hannibal High School," the Saints and the Roughnecks. The eight members of the Saints came from upper-middle-class families. They were good students and active in school affairs. On weekends and on days when they would sneak out of school, the Saints amused themselves with various forms of delinquency: heavy drinking, reckless driving, petty theft, vandalism, and games of "chicken." One of their favorite pastimes was to remove the wooden barricades and lanterns from street repair sites and watch unsuspecting drivers cruise into the hole. In spite of these hazardous activities, the people of the town considered them good boys who were sowing a few wild oats. The police did not arrest one Saint in the two years Chambliss spent at "Hannibal High" as an observer.

In contrast, the six Roughnecks were constantly in trouble with the police, and the townspeople considered them good-for-nothings. The Roughnecks came from lower-class families and were not particularly good students. Most weekends they could be found hanging around the local drugstore, drinking from concealed bottles of alcohol. About once a month they got into some sort of fight—usually among themselves. The Roughnecks also engaged in petty theft. Even so, Chambliss estimates that property damage done by the Saints cost the townspeople *more* than the Roughnecks' thefts. And although the Saints rarely fought, they endangered their own and other people's lives nearly every time they got behind the wheel of a car.

Why did the townspeople excuse the Saints but condemn the Roughnecks as delinquents? One reason was that the Saints had cars and left the immediate community for their drinking bouts. The Roughnecks, too poor to own cars, were more visible. In addition, the police knew from experience that the Saints' upper-middle-class parents would cause trouble if their children were arrested. The Roughnecks' parents lacked the power and influence to protect their children. Finally, the Saints dressed nicely, drove good cars, and spoke politely to teachers, police, and other authority figures. Anyone could see they were "good boys," tomorrow's leaders. The Roughnecks were different: "Everyone agreed that the not-so-well-dressed, not-so-well-mannered, not-so-rich boys were heading for trouble" (1973:27). In short, the community's social structure protected the Saints but not the Roughnecks. Through selective perception and labeling, the visible, poor, undiplomatic "tough kids" were noticed and identified as "delinquents." But the equally delinquent middle-class youth went unnoticed.

Typically, people who are labeled delinquent and criminal, declared mentally ill, and so on are excluded from mainstream life. Because the delinquent behavior of the Roughnecks was reinforced by the police and the community, in some cases their lives were steered into deviant careers. Several of the boys were arrested a number of times, and two were sentenced to six months' incarceration in boys' schools. In contrast, the Saints left adolescence, moved along middle-class pathways, and remembered their youthful flings fondly.

Thus deviant labels tend to become self-fulfilling prophecies. For instance, Chambliss found that with few

The attitudes of police are influenced by how they label groups or individuals. (Right, George W. Gardner; below, Charles Gatewood.)

exceptions, the Saints and Roughnecks lived up (and down) to community expectations. In other words, one response to being labeled deviant is to embrace the role (Goffman, 1963b:30).

This is the final step toward a **deviant career**, the adoption of a deviant life style and identity within a supporting subculture. Cut off, the addict begins to associate almost exclusively with other addicts, the prostitute with other prostitutes, and so on. Gradually they learn from more experienced offenders the various techniques for deviating. Equally important, they learn rationalizations for deviant behavior. For example, prostitutes grow to regard their work as a social service and consider those who condemn sex for money as hypocrites. The deviant subculture begins to play an increasingly central role in the person's identity and life style. As one addict told a researcher, she realized she was addicted when she noticed that all her friends were junkies (Becker, 1963). In sum, by labeling certain people deviant and shutting them out of conventional life, society virtually *ensures* the behavior it is trying to prevent.

While this description of the drift into deviant careers is compelling, it may overstate the facts. Labeling theorists imply that the people who fill the wards of mental hospitals, for example, are there because someone more or less arbitrarily decided to label them sick and subject them to the consequences. They tend to ignore the fact that most of the people in mental hospitals were unable to cope with their lives and their problems outside. Sociological studies have found that both families and authorities usually consider commitment to a mental hospital as a last resort (Gove, 1975, 1979).

Labeling theorists also tend to pay relatively little attention to the fact that not all labeled people accept their stigma passively. Mentally retarded people who have been released from institutions, for instance, go to great lengths to hide their stigma not only from others but also from themselves (Edgerton, 1967).

It is also true that some labels can be shed. Many alcoholics, for example, have been able to delabel themselves by joining Alcoholics Anonymous, an organization that makes it possible for problem drinkers to replace their stigmatized deviant status with a socially acceptable "repentant role" (Trice and Roman, 1970).

All this is not to say that labeling theory is "wrong," but that it only partly explains deviant careers. It does not explain why people violate rules in the first place or why some people are able to resist or overcome the stigma of deviance. When coupled with the conflict perspective, labeling theory helps us to focus on the social structure of power behind the rules. What really matters, in this view, is who makes the rules and who has the power to make various labels stick.

CRIME AND CRIMINAL JUSTICE

The type of deviance that most concerns Americans is crime. **Crime** is any act that is illegal. Like other forms of deviance, crime is not an absolute; what constitutes a crime changes with the times. Some crimes once considered serious, such as the smoking of marijuana, are now receiving less and less attention. Others once neglected, such as the dumping of industrial wastes in unauthorized areas, are receiving much more attention than before. Sometimes what was formerly believed a crime is no longer classified as such. For a long time alcoholism was treated as a criminal offense, but today it is widely viewed as a disease.

Changing definitions of crime are prompted not only by changes in norms and values; social-control agencies also help to shape the formulation of laws. They have contributed to the redefining of many former crimes as "medical problems" (Conrad and Schneider, 1980). The first shift probably occurred more than a century ago, when the courts began regarding juvenile delinquency as a psychiatric-social problem, and so assigning delinquent youths to "treatment." As we have seen, delinquency can be explained biologically, psychologically, or sociologically, and there was no overwhelming evidence at the time supporting one view over another. Thus, the reclassification of delinquency tells us more about society and the interests of its social-control agencies than it does about delinquency itself. Further, we commonly differentiate among various types of crime, a matter to which we will now turn.

Types of Crime

There are many types of crime. Perhaps the crime with which we are most familiar is **index crime**—those crimes that the Federal Bureau of Investigation cites in its annual *Uniform Crime Reports*. Local and regional police agencies are required by law to submit data to the FBI on two types of offenses, Type I and Type II crimes. Type I crimes, those with criminal intent, include both crimes against people—murder, rape, robbery, and assault—and crimes against property—burglary, theft, auto theft, and arson (see Figure 9.2, p. 219 and Table 9.2, p. 220). Type II crimes include white-collar crime, prostitution, sex offenses, gambling, vandalism, and receiving stolen property. In reporting Type I crimes to the FBI, police agencies include data on *all crimes* known to them as well as the number of arrests made, number of people charged, weapons used, and so on. For Type II crimes only *arrests* are reported (*Crime in the U.S.*, 1982).

Statistics on crime are quite unsatisfactory. Not all agencies required to report to the FBI do so, and the FBI makes estimates when it publishes its annual crime reports. Moreover, when a criminal incident involves more than one crime, such as a robbery that results in a death, only the most serious crime (murder, in this example) is counted (*Crime in the U.S.*, 1982). Local politics can also have a profound impact on the reporting of crime to the FBI. If a local police department is

FIGURE 9.2 Crime in the United States

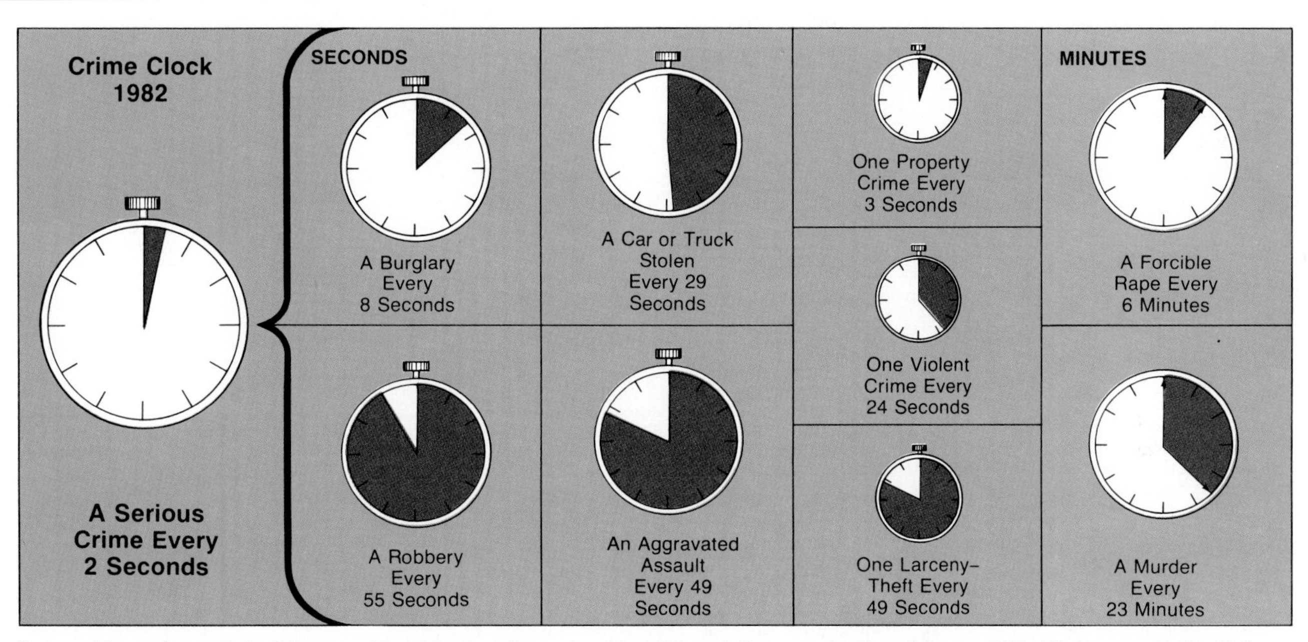

Sources: News release, Federal Bureau of Investigation, September 11, 1983, and *Crime in the United States, 1981*. Washington, D.C.: U.S. Department of Justice, Federal Bureau of Investigation, 1982.

seeking a substantial budget increase, for example, it may exaggerate either the extent of crime in its area or the number of people it has arrested, depending on which will justify the largest budget increase. However, most official statistics underestimate crime. Some crimes are never detected: Others are detected but not reported. According to estimates by the U.S. Department of Justice, only 30.7 percent of all motor vehicle thefts, 58.5 percent of all rapes, and somewhat less than half of all robberies, aggravated assaults, and burglaries are reported to the police. At 72.5 percent, larcenies and thefts are most likely to be reported (*Criminal Victimization*, 1980).

What reasons do people give for not reporting crime? Some feel either that nothing could be done, that the offense is not serious enough to report, or that the police do not want to be bothered. Some find it too inconvenient or feel that the matter is private or personal. Some fear reprisals, and still others report the matter to someone else (*Criminal Victimization*, 1980).

Crimes Without Victims

We typically think of crime as having an identifiable victim who suffers as a result of another person's criminal behavior. But there are some crimes that lack victims—**victimless crime**. Victimless crime includes prostitution, illegal sexual acts among consenting adults, illicit drug use, gambling, and drunkenness (see Table 9.3, p. 220). The laws that prohibit these behaviors are intended to regulate people's personal lives in a manner that is consistent with certain moral standards. The community as a whole, or powerful groups within the community, regard the acts as morally repugnant. In

TABLE 9.2 National Crime Rate, 1981, and Percent Change Since 1977

Index Crime	Number Reported	Rate per 100,000	Percent Increase since 1977
Violent Crime			
Murder and non-negligent manslaughter	22,500	9.8	2.8%
Forcible Rape	81,540	35.6	.8
Aggravated Assault	643,720	281.0	4.1
Robbery	574,130	251.0	7.6
Total	1,321,890		
*Property Crime**			
Burglary	3,739,800	1,632.0	3.9
Larceny-Theft	7,154,500	3,122.0	3.6
Motor Vehicle Theft	1,074,000	469.0	1.2
Total	11,968,300		
Total Index Crime 13,290,190			

* Figures for Arson unavailable

Source: *Crime in the United States, 1981*. Washington, D.C.: U.S. Department of Justice, Federal Bureau of Investigation, 1982.

TABLE 9.3 Arrests for Crimes Without Victims, 1981

Crime	Estimated Number of Arrests
Prostitution and commercialized vice	103,000
Drug Abuse Violations (all)	587,000
Illegal Gambling	41,000
Drunkenness	1,089,000
Curfew, Loitering (Juveniles)	91,000
Runaways (Juvenile)	145,000

Source: *Statistical Abstract of the United States, 1982–1983*. Washington, D.C.: U.S. Department of Commerce, Bureau of the Census, 1983.

recent years some individuals and groups have advocated decriminalizing the activities associated with victimless crime. They question whether government should be in the business of legislating those forms of morality, and they believe that including them in the penal code taxes an already overloaded police and court system.

Often the people who engage in victimless crime do not regard their behavior as immoral. For instance, protitutes and their customers, gamblers, and pornography buyers and sellers do not necessarily accept the codes that make their behavior illegal. Consequently, a significant body of consumers exists who desire goods and services prohibited by law. In large measure, organized crime in the United States owes its existence to this fact.

Organized Crime

Organized crime consists of organizations that are structured in a bureaucratic fashion (see Chapter 8) to provide illegal goods and services that are in high demand. They resemble legitimate business organizations except that their activities are illegal and they depend on extralegal violence and intimidation to control their clients and their own members.

An Italian-based crime syndicate has operated for some decades in the United States. Called La Cosa Nostra by many criminal groups and the FBI—the Mafia by the media—it is a loose confederation of local and regional organizations. These groups apparently cooperate on such projects as Las Vegas gambling, although they operate independently in their home localities elsewhere in the nation. But organized crime is hardly an Italian monopoly. Black syndicates operate in New York and Philadephia; Chinese gangs shake down San Francisco merchants; the self-proclaimed Israeli Mafia extorts money in Los Angeles; and Colombian and Cuban rings supply drugs in Florida (Press, 1981).

White-Collar Crime

It is not organized crime but white-collar crime that is the principal source of economic crime. The term **white-collar crime** was first used by the sociologist Edwin Sutherland (1949:9) to refer to "a crime committed by a person of respectability and high status in the course of his occupation." Through the years sociologists have extended the concept to include corporate crime and crimes such as embezzlement, stock manipulation, and bribery that are undertaken by high-status people for their own personal benefit. White-collar crime includes individual and corporate violations of laws and regulations—everything from tax evasion and price fixing to bribing foreign officials and dumping toxic wastes in rivers.

In our discussion of conflict theory earlier in the chapter, we noted the magnitude of white-collar crime. During the decade from 1971 through 1980, some 2,690 American corporations of all sizes were convicted of criminal offenses (Kelly, 1982). Although the prosecution of corporate executives involved in crime is increasing, only a fraction are charged with crime, and of those charged and convicted, even fewer spend time in prison. Even then, according to the sociologist Marshall B. Clinard (Clinard and Yager, 1980), the average prison stay for a convicted corporate criminal is 2.8 *days*. Also noteworthy, bank embezzlers steal an average of $23,000 each, while bank robbers steal only one-eighth as much. Yet while only 17 percent of bank embezzlers end up in prison, 91 percent of bank robbers go to jail.

The Control of Crime

From almost any perspective, it would appear that crime in the United States is out of control. In 1981, 69 percent of those queried in a Harris survey felt that crime had been increasing in their area (*Sourcebook*, 1982). Crime has increased steadily throughout this decade (see Figure 9.3, p. 222). There are as many murders in Manhattan alone as in all of England and Wales, more burglaries in Chicago than in all of Japan, more drug addiction in Los Angeles than in all the countries of Western Europe combined (Radzinowicz and King, 1977). Between 1960 and 1976 one's chances of being murdered, robbed, raped, or assaulted in America nearly tripled (Silberman, 1980).

One disturbing trend is that more and more violent crimes are being committed by people who are strangers to the victims. The result is that in certain high-crime neighborhoods people do not know whom to trust. A major cause of the increase in crime is that the informal controls that restrain people have broken down with the fragmentation of society (Silberman, 1980).

In part, the high rate of crime among Americans may reflect Merton's argument about resorting to deviant means when desirable goals are out of reach. In a major study of crime, Charles Silberman puts it this way: "In the United States, the premium placed on winning —on success—encourages people to violate rules that get in the way, and to feel justified in doing so" (1980:50). Those who are poor and those who are discriminated against have good reason to believe that they will not achieve "success" except through unlawful means. As criminal activities become an established part of the social environment of poor whites and blacks and Hispanics, children are socialized into that life style, and crime gets culturally transmitted from one generation to the next.

How do we break this vicious circle? According to Silberman, it will require nothing less than "the elimi-

FIGURE 9.3 Selected Crime Rates: 1971 to 1981

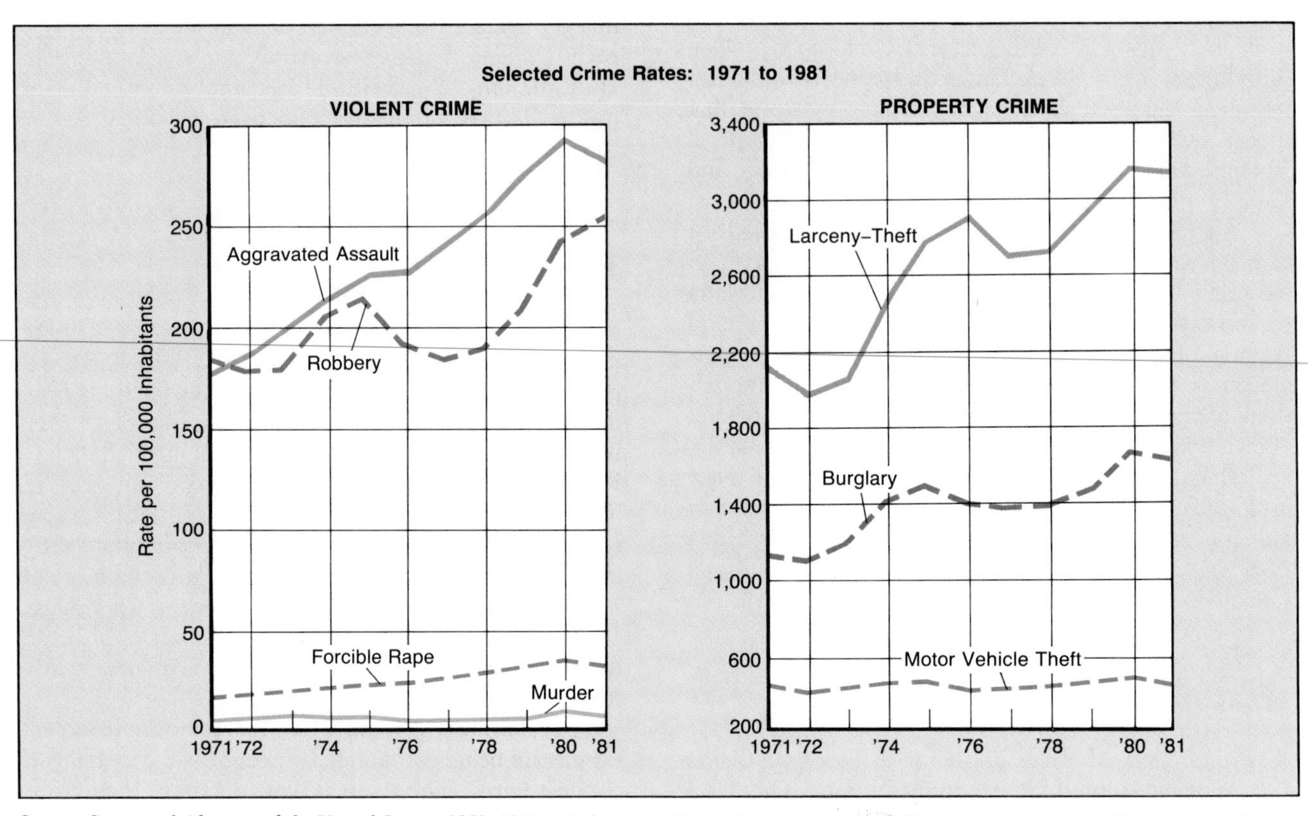

Source: Statistical Abstract of the United States, 1982–1983. Washington, D.C.: U.S. Department of Commerce, Bureau of the Census, 1983, p. 173.

nation of poverty, inequality, and racial discrimination as significant factors in American life" (1980:227). Until we reach that goal, if ever, we are dependent on institutional means of social control to check crime and punish the criminal. We therefore conclude this chapter with a look at the control functions of the police, the criminal justice system, and prisons.

Police: Key Agents of Control

While the police are set up as a formal means of control, their most important work consists of informal control. Just seeing a uniform affects a person's behavior and sense of security. Moreover, it is generally true that talking, coaxing, threatening, encouraging, and just watching are more effective means of shaping behavior than search, seizure, arrest, and the other more formal and forceful means at the police officer's disposal.

The best indication of what can be accomplished by the police is the example of Japan. Until recently, Japan was notable among industrialized nations for its *falling* crime rate. From 1949 to 1973 the crime rate was cut in half (Vogel, 1980). Lately the crime rate has been rising, but it is still very low by our standards. One factor contributing to this excellent record is the nature of the Japanese police station. This system is organized around a network of mini-police stations (called *kobans*) staffed by police officers who are trusted members of the neighborhood. The *koban* is accessible to the public at all times and serves a variety of neighborly purposes—giving directions, settling disputes, lending carfare, find-

In Japan, the police are easily accessible to the public, and officers become well acquainted with local residents. As a result, the Japanese public and police enjoy a close and trusting working relationship. (©Rick Smolan/Contact.)

ing hotels for strangers, even warming baby bottles and repairing broken zippers. The officers stationed at the *koban* make frequent rounds of the neighborhood and become intimately acquainted with its residents.

As a result of this close relationship, the Japanese public trusts and respects the police. Japanese citizens readily call on their police and are cooperative in investigations. Offenders are often encouraged by their families to turn themselves in; full confessions are routine. The residents of neighborhoods and villages also band together in crime-prevention associations, which work closely with the police in preventing and solving crime. It should be pointed out, too, that gun laws in Japan are extremely strict, reducing the number of violent crimes considerably.

The proof of the system's effectiveness lies in these statistics: in 1980, 60 percent of all reported crimes in Japan were solved, and 99 percent of those arrested were convicted. In the United States in 1979, police arrested only 20 percent of the suspects of reported crimes and less than 1 percent of those were convicted (*Christian Science Monitor*, March 11, 1981). The conviction rates in America are another story. We'll turn now to an examination of what might be called the criminal justice funnel.

The Criminal Justice Funnel

The best studies of how the criminal justice funnel works have focused on particular cities and their justice systems. One study was carried out in New York City. It examined all the 1979 felony cases—offenses punishable by more than a year in prison. In that year, approximately 829,000 felonies were committed in the city. About 104,000 people were arrested, 16,000 were indicted, and 1,000 were imprisoned (*New York Times*, January 4, 1981; see Figure 9.4., p. 224)

What are we to make of these figures? Does the criminal justice system simply not work? Actually, there are a number of valid reasons for the dwindling numbers before prosecution and conviction. It is not simply a question of overcrowded and underfunded courts, as is commonly believed.

A study by the Vera Institute of Justice (1977) has found that many felons are never prosecuted or convicted because their victims or the complainants refuse to testify against them. When people call the police, they often do so to frighten the offender and show their anger; they cool off when it comes to giving testimony that will send the person to prison.

Another explanation for the funnel effect is that felonies may get reduced to misdemeanors (less serious offenses) through **plea bargaining**. Plea bargaining is the process in which the district attorney offers to reduce charges if the suspect will plead guilty and relinquish the right to a trial. Plea bargaining saves the state time, expense, and trouble, but it pressures some innocent people to plead guilty, and it puts some serious offenders back on the streets in less than a year.

As a result of the way the criminal justice system works, almost half of the people in jail have not been convicted of a crime; they are being held for trial (*Stastistical Abstract*, 1983). Malcolm Feeley (1979) contends that for many felons, these pretrial procedures constitute a punishment in itself, sometimes even more

FIGURE 9.4 The Criminal Justice Funnel: New York City, 1979

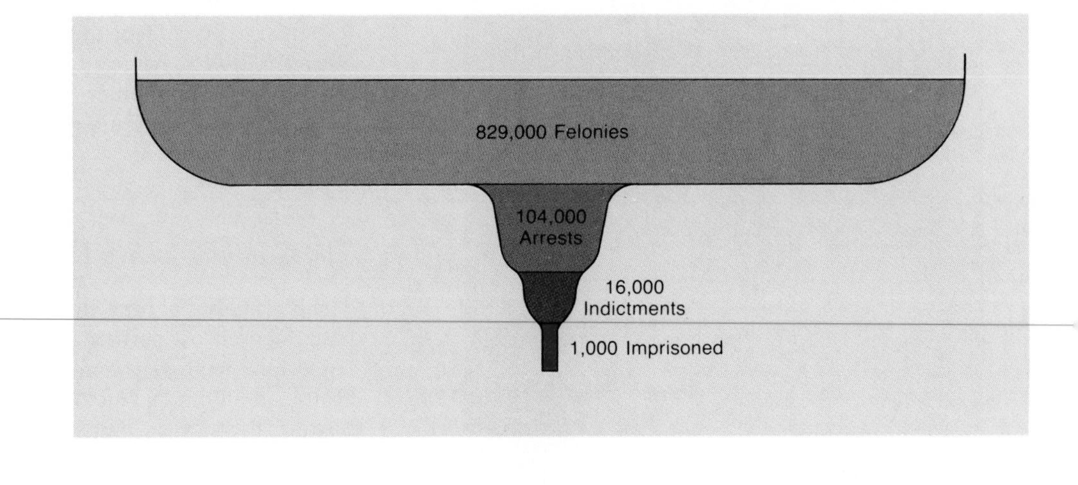

As this figure shows, only a very small percentage of the felonies committed in New York City in 1979 resulted in arrests, and less than 1 percent of the people arrested were actually convicted and sent to prison.

severe than an actual sentence or fine. He believes that these conditions induce the accused to waive a trial and plead guilty: they will do anything to minimize the pretrial costs to themselves.

Generally, it is the poor nonwhite who gets funneled into the prison system. All along the way formal controls work in discriminatory ways, intentionally or not. First, the police use their judgment to decide who is a danger to the community and threatening to police authority. We have already seen how the police harassed the lower-class Roughnecks while tolerating delinquent acts of the smoother middle-class Saints. All this has implications for the functioning of prisons, a matter to which we now turn our attention.

How Well Do Prisons Function?

Each year, we spend an average of $11,012 for each male and $9,919 for each female confined to prison. This comes to a total of $2.5 billion annually (*Sourcebook*, 1982). If the cost of police, courts, prosecutors, and public defenders is included, the total cost of the American criminal justice system is $25.9 billion (*U.S. News & World Report*, November 1, 1982:36). Are we getting our money's worth? The answer is not all that clear.

Prisons are supposed to punish criminals, protect the public by taking known deviants off the streets, act as a deterrent, and rehabilitate offenders. These different goals conflict with each other, and in the end prisons do not achieve any of them very well.

In the first place, prisons do not protect the public. Most criminals are never imprisoned: arrests were made in only 16 percent of the more than 13 million crimes reported to the FBI in 1982–83 (*Statistical Abstract*, 1983). Only 3 percent of the people known to have committed crimes ever go to jail (only 1.5 percent if we include unreported crimes). Moreover, most prison officials estimate that only 15 to 25 percent of inmates are actually dangerous. Studies suggest that fewer than 10 percent of criminals commit nearly 30 percent of crimes (Moore, 1983).

The harsh conditions found in prisons (overcrowding, lack of sanitation, neglect, and brutality by guards) combined with the humiliating conditions of living in a total institution (constant supervision and regulation, degradation, loss of personal identity and personal possessions) make the prison, in Charles Silberman's words, "a crucible of intimidation and conflict." The only way an inmate can achieve status or identity is to put someone else down "verbally, physically, financially, or sexually. . . . there is exaggerated emphasis on toughness: the ability either to victimize others or to withstand victimization" (1980:523). This kind of prison culture is hardly conducive to rehabilitation. After their release, at least a third of former prison inmates end up back in prison. Indeed, prisons may socialize people *to* deviance. Many observers consider them "schools for crime," where first offenders learn the tricks and rationalizations of deviant careers.

What are the prospects that our social control agencies can be more effective in reducing crime? The answer depends in large part on our attitudes. Many people are ambivalent about prisons and controlling crime. On the one hand, they want swift and effective action against criminals. But on the other hand, they do not seem willing to take some of the steps that might help to bring down the crime rate. For instance, they do not want police to invade private life to the extent they do in a country like Japan, even though the Japanese record on crime prevention is far superior to ours. Nor are most Americans willing to legislate enough money to create well-staffed prisons with good facilities and programs. This ambivalence places police and prison officials in a difficult position: They are given the task of reducing crime but not all the means to do it. Particularly important from a sociological viewpoint, the social control of deviance cannot be effectively accomplished when distrusted outsiders serve as the agents of control. Yet in the eyes of the people they are assigned to regulate, police and prison officials are often viewed as just that—remote and distrusted outsiders imposing rules through force.

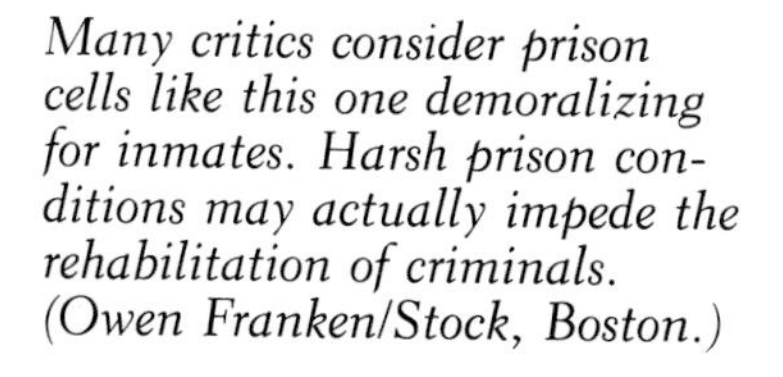

Many critics consider prison cells like this one demoralizing for inmates. Harsh prison conditions may actually impede the rehabilitation of criminals. (Owen Franken/Stock, Boston.)

EPILOGUE

In the preceding chapters we examined the relatively patterned and orderly characteristics of social life. In Chapter 3 we focused on culture—the traditions and rules by which people interpret their experiences and guide their actions. In Chapter 4 we turned our attention to social interaction and social structure. In Chapter 5 we considered how human beings acquire through socialization those modes of thinking, feeling, and acting essential for effective participation within society. And in Chapters 7 and 8 we scrutinized the dictates and ramifications of group and organizational life. In so doing, we focused our sociological eye on the broad social fabric, stressing the rather regular and predictable aspects and processes that underlie the human experience.

But our treatment of social life would be incomplete were we to ignore the fact that human interaction does not always proceed smoothly and that people often violate social norms. Even so, deviant behaviors are "social" in that they arise in a social context and have social consequences. Indeed, as we have pointed out in the chapter, deviance is a necessary and regular part of the social order. Because social factors have so important an impact on deviant ways of thinking and acting, they are best studied through the discipline of sociology.

In considering deviance, we are reminded of the critical link that exists between the private troubles of people and the features of the society in which they live. As stressed by the sociologist C. Wright Mills (1959), the essence of the sociological imagination is the ability to see the relationship between individuals' private troubles and public issues. People who have problems typically view them as rooted in their own personal lives. They fail to see the connection between their own difficulties and the larger social context. Hence, in this chapter we have considered not only individual behavior but also the social world that influences, shapes, and channels what people say and do.

In the next several chapters that deal with social inequality and power, we return to the insights afforded by the labeling and conflict approaches to deviance. We note that power is distributed unequally within society. Some people have more influence than others in defining which behaviors and which people are considered deviant and in determining public policy toward deviance.

SUMMARY

Deviance can be defined as behavior that the members of a social group define as violating their norms. Whether an act is considered deviant or not depends on who commits the act, on where and when they do so, and on who is doing the judging.

Social control entails those mechanisms used to uphold social norms and to restrain their actual or potential violation. It implies power—at times coercion—to regulate the behavior of individuals and groups. Consequently, we need to ask who is controlling whom, by what means, under what circumstances, and for what reasons. Mechanisms of social control operate on both an internal and an external level. On the internal level control rests on socialization, particularly internalization. On the external level, it relies on the application of informal or formal sanctions.

The boundaries between acceptable and unacceptable behavior are usually not hard and fast. Deviance plays a double role in clarifying norms and contributing to social order. First, in defining certain kinds of behavior as deviant, a group or community also defines what behavior is acceptable. Second, in uniting against the deviant, the group or community comes together and reaffirms its common bonds.

Various explanations have been offered for deviance. These include biological and psychological theories as well as sociological ones. Among the sociological theories, four are widely recognized. One is the *structural stress theory*, which argues that deviance arises when conformity to social norms fails to satisfy a person's legitimate desires. Another is the *cultural transmission theory*, which holds that people learn deviance when they are immersed in a deviant subculture. Still another is the *conflict theory*, which portrays the criminal justice system as serving the interests of particular groups and not the collective will or public good. And finally, the *labeling approach* focuses not on why some people break the law or commit other deviant acts in the first place, but on how a few among them are singled out, labeled as deviants, and processed by agencies of social control.

Which acts are considered crimes and which of those are considered serious change over time. These changes are prompted by shifts in social norms and values and in the interests of agencies of social control.

What happens to known lawbreakers? The police and courts exercise considerable discretion in making arrests and applying the penalties available under the law. Only a very small percentage of the people known to have committed crimes are arrested, tried, and sent to prison. These people are predominantly poor and nonwhite.

The functions of prison include punishing lawbreakers, protecting the public, deterring other potential offenders, and rehabilitating prisoners. But it is doubtful how well all these functions are being served.

GLOSSARY

Anomie. A condition within society in which individuals find that the prevailing social norms are ill-defined, weak, or conflicting.

Conformity. Seeking culturally approved goals by culturally approved means (Merton).

Crime. Any act that is illegal.

Cultural transmission. The process by which deviance is learned through the transmission of norms within a community or group.

Deviance. Behavior that the members of a social group define as violating their norms.

Deviant career. The adoption of a deviant life style and identity within a supporting subculture that provides techniques for breaking rules and rationalizations for nonconformity.

Differential association. The process by which individuals are socialized into the group with which they spend the most time and have the most intense relationships.

Formal social controls. Official pressure to conform to social norms and values specifically enforced by organizations such as police departments, courts, and prisons.

Index crime. Those crimes that the Federal Bureau of Investigation annually cites in its *Uniform Crimes Reports*.

Informal social controls. Unofficial pressures to conform, including disapproval, ridicule, and the threat of ostracism.

Innovation. Pursuing culturally approved goals by deviant means (Merton).

Internalization. The process by which cultural standards become part of a person's personality structure.

Labeling. The assigning of a deviant status to a person, which then dominates his or her social identity.

Organized crime. Organizations that are structured in a bureaucratic fashion to provide illegal goods and services that are in high demand.

Plea bargaining. In a criminal trial, a defendant's agreeing to plead guilty to a lesser charge rather than risk conviction and a more severe penalty.

Primary deviance. The initial violation of a social norm, about which no inferences are made regarding motives or the character of the person who committed the act.

Rebellion. Creating new goals and new means for pursuing them (Merton).

Retreatism. Abandoning culturally prescribed goals and means (Merton).

Ritualism. Adhering rigidly to norms, yet abandoning related goals (Merton).

Sanctions. Rewards for conforming to a social norm or penalties for violating it.

Secondary deviance. A pattern by which people come to define themselves as deviants and undertake life patterns as a reaction to their being labeled as deviants by others.

Social control. Those mechanisms by which social norms are upheld and by which their actual or potential violation is restrained.

Victimless crime. Crimes that lack victims, except perhaps the people who commit them.

White-collar crime. Crime committed by corporations or by individuals of high status in the course of their occupations.

PART FOUR

STRATIFICATION AND INEQUALITY

A corporate executive for a large manufacturing firm earns several hundred thousand dollars a year. A public school teacher, who has equal years of education and devotes equal hours to the job, is paid less than a tenth that much. The mayor of a large city, regardless of abilities or personal traits, is accorded substantial prestige in our society. A farm hand, despite honesty, competence, and diligence at his work, receives very little social status. Such patterned inequalities exist in virtually all human societies. The basic questions sociologists ask are how social systems distribute valuable rewards such as wealth, power, and prestige, and why those patterns of distribution prevail.

Chapter 10 begins with a look at the extent, consequences, and relative permanence of social stratification in the United States. It also attempts to explain inequalities from two sociological perspectives.

Chapter 11 then turns to one of the key dimensions of any stratification system—an unequal distribution of power. Here we focus on the two major institutional centers of power in American society, the political and the economic. "Who runs America?" is our fundamental question.

Finally, Chapter 12 concludes with an exploration of an age-old form of social stratification—inequalities based on racial and ethnic differences. Why does racial and ethnic prejudice arise? What have been its consequences? Can institutionalized discrimination ever be eliminated? These are critical questions in a world marked by racial and ethnic strife.

CHAPTER 10

Class, Status, and Mobility

Zhang Longquan, a twenty-five-year-old Chinese farmworker, recently got himself into a good bit of trouble in Shanghai. It seems that Mr. Zhang, having tired of his ordinary status, masqueraded for several months as the son of Li Da, a top Chinese general. Although supposedly a "classless" society, the People's Republic of China is in fact ruled by a political elite. Ranking state officials and army officers have access to spacious housing, cars, first-class accommodations on trains, theater seats, the nation's best food, and other priveleges. These benefits also flow to the wives and children of the political elite by virtue of their ascribed status (see Chapter 4). Until the police caught up with him, Mr. Zhang was showered with gifts and dinners by Communist party officials and others seeking favors. He even gained use of an official's personal car (Ching, 1979; Butterfield, 1981).

Brother Clovis and some forty-nine other Trappist monks live in isolation in a 125-year-old American abbey. They have forsaken the world to lead a life of prayer and work in obedience to a call from God. Brother Clovis, like the other monks, owns no property, not even his own clothes. The monastery permits no economic distinction among its members. Even the abbot sleeps in the same kind of bed in the same kind of cell and eats the same food as the other monks. The monks support their absolute material equality with a strong egalitarian ideology. However, some measure of inequality characterizes the relationships of Brother Clovis and his fellow monks. The differences in rank arise from differences in individual compliance with the ideals of the community, which include love, friendliness, simplicity, humility, spirituality, and integrity (Della Fava and Hillery, 1980). A person's rank derives from achievement. Further, the benefits stemming from higher rank are reflected in prestige rather than in money or material possessions.

Mary Blake is a thirty-one-year-old secretary in Milwaukee. She is divorced and has two school-aged children. When asked by a poll taker to discuss American classes, Ms. Blake becomes confused. Like many Americans, she has difficulty describing the nation's class system. Americans are aware, of course, that some people earn more and live more luxuriously than others. Yet they do not necessarily equate higher annual incomes with a higher class status. But when the pollster asks Ms. Blake to indicate the class to which she belongs, she replies "middle class." Her answer is quite typical. Not too many Americans acknowledge membership in either the "upper class" or the "lower class." In response to a carefully worded question, however, some Americans will assert that they belong to the "working class."

As these examples show, in one way or another all human groups are characterized by some degree of inequality, even if they pride themselves on their egalitarianism. The ranking of people is the essence of **stratification:** the division of a society into layers (or strata) of people who have unequal amounts of scarce but desirable resources or rewards. Stratification refers not only to inequality among individuals, but also to inequality among categories of people, for instance, people with similar levels of education or in similar occupations. These inequalities are built into the social structure and may persist from generation to generation. As we will see later in the chapter, societies differ considerably in the possibilities they provide individuals for moving up or down the stratification hierarchy by their own efforts.

In this chapter we will look at several aspects of unevenness in human affairs. We begin by exploring the nature of stratification, looking at variations in wealth, power, and prestige. Then we examine how stratification affects our personal lives. Next we turn to the question of why social stratification arises, comparing the views of conflict theorists and functionalists. Then, after examining social mobility in America, we conclude with a discussion of programs to reduce inequality.

DIMENSIONS OF STRATIFICATION

If someone were to ask you where you ranked in the stratification system, what would you answer? Most Americans would not be able to give a precise answer, because there are so many criteria—birth, wealth, occupation, education, prestige, power, life style—to choose from. In other societies it would be easier to identify distinct social layers because the criteria of rank are few. For example, a caste system utilizes birth as the key criterion of rank, although there are gradations within each caste.

In American society we generally think of the different layers of the stratification system as **classes,** groups of people who are on the same rung of the economic ladder. As emphasized by the sociologist Max Weber, social stratification is not simply a question of wealth, because money is not synonymous with prestige or power. There are obvious differences, for instance, between people who earn $50,000 by drawing a salary, by collecting interest from an estate, by selling heroin, by winning a Nobel Prize, by holding public office, or by winning the lottery. Someone who wins the lottery has acquired wealth but not prestige. Someone in the clergy may have prestige but not wealth. Someone who makes decisions about allocating large sums of government money possesses power but not necessarily prestige or wealth. In short, income contributes to but does not completely determine prestige and power. Family name, ethnic and religious background, age, sex, education, occupation, life style, club membership, neighborhood —even grammar and diction—all influence a person's social rank.

Although wealth, power, and prestige constitute distinct dimensions of social ranking, in practice they typically coincide, reinforcing and sustaining one another. The reason for this is that individuals and groups can often translate any one of these dimensions into the others (Goode, 1978). Take power. Communist leaders like Stalin, Mao, Tito, and their successors have used the leverage inherent in their political positions to gain the prestige and privileges associated with high office. Similarly, those who enjoy wealth can often acquire power and the trappings of eminence. And sports and television celebrities can frequently employ their prestige to acquire wealth and influence. As in many other societies, wealth, power, and prestige are distributed quite unequally within the United States, a matter to which we now turn our attention.

Wealth and Income

One question of timeless interest is who gets what share of the goods and services produced by an economic system. The answer not only influences an individual's chances for material well-being and opportunities for earning and learning, but it also has implications for a society because it shapes people's motivations to work and their willingness to support existing social arrangements.

Economic stratification is based on what people own (wealth) and what they earn (income). *Wealth* refers to what people *have;* it consists of the value of everything a person or group owns. *Income* refers to how much people *get:* it is the amount of money a person or group receives. For example, one person could earn a high annual salary and spend it all; he would have little wealth. Another person could own much productive property and receive little income. Most people get income from wages or salaries; relatively few people get income from property.

Economists view wages and salaries as a return on labor, and they view interest, dividends, and rent as a

The question of who gets what share of wealth and income is closely related to the issues of status, power, and occupation. (Robert V. Eckert, Jr./EKM-Nepenthe.)

return on property. Interest income derives from bonds and bank accounts; dividend income, from the ownership of stock; and rental income, from payments for the use of property. Both income and wealth are distributed unevenly in our society, but to different degrees. Within the United States there is a greater concentration of wealth than of income.

Wealth

Information about the wealth of Americans, especially the affluent, is not readily available. It is generally agreed that information about the concentration of wealth is much harder to secure than information on earned income. However, the available data suggests that most Americans have little wealth; about half the population owns assets such as stocks, real estate, houses, cars, and savings worth less than $5,000 (Page, 1983). Great wealth is typically either inherited or obtained by capitalizing on a valued resource like land or mineral rights or a new product.

In 1978, 2,041 Americans reported to the Internal Revenue Service that they had incomes over $1 million. Only 16 percent of the income they reported came from wages or salaries; the remainder came from the ownership of property. Other data reveal that 1 percent of Americans hold 33 percent of the nation's total wealth and 62 percent of all the corporate stock (Page, 1983).

Wealth confers distinct advantages to individuals beyond the availability of such essentials as food, shelter, and health care. The very wealthy also have access to services, travel, and hobbies not available to less advantaged individuals. Moreover, substantial wealth often brings income, power, and independence.

Income

A common way of examining the distribution of income is to divide the population into fifths and compare each segment's share of the total national income. Table 10.1 provides this information for 1980. It shows that the

TABLE 10.1 Percentage of Aggregate Family Income Received by Each Fifth and Highest 5 Percent, 1980

All families	Percentage of aggregate income
Lowest fifth	5.1%
Second fifth	11.6
Middle fifth	17.5
Fourth fifth	24.3
Highest fifth	41.6
Highest 5 percent	15.3

Source: U.S. Bureau of the Census, *Current Population Reports*, "Money Income and Poverty Status of Families and Persons in the United States: 1980." Washington, D.C.: Government Printing Office, 1981, Table 5, p. 15.

FIGURE 10.1 Distribution of Income in the United States in 1981

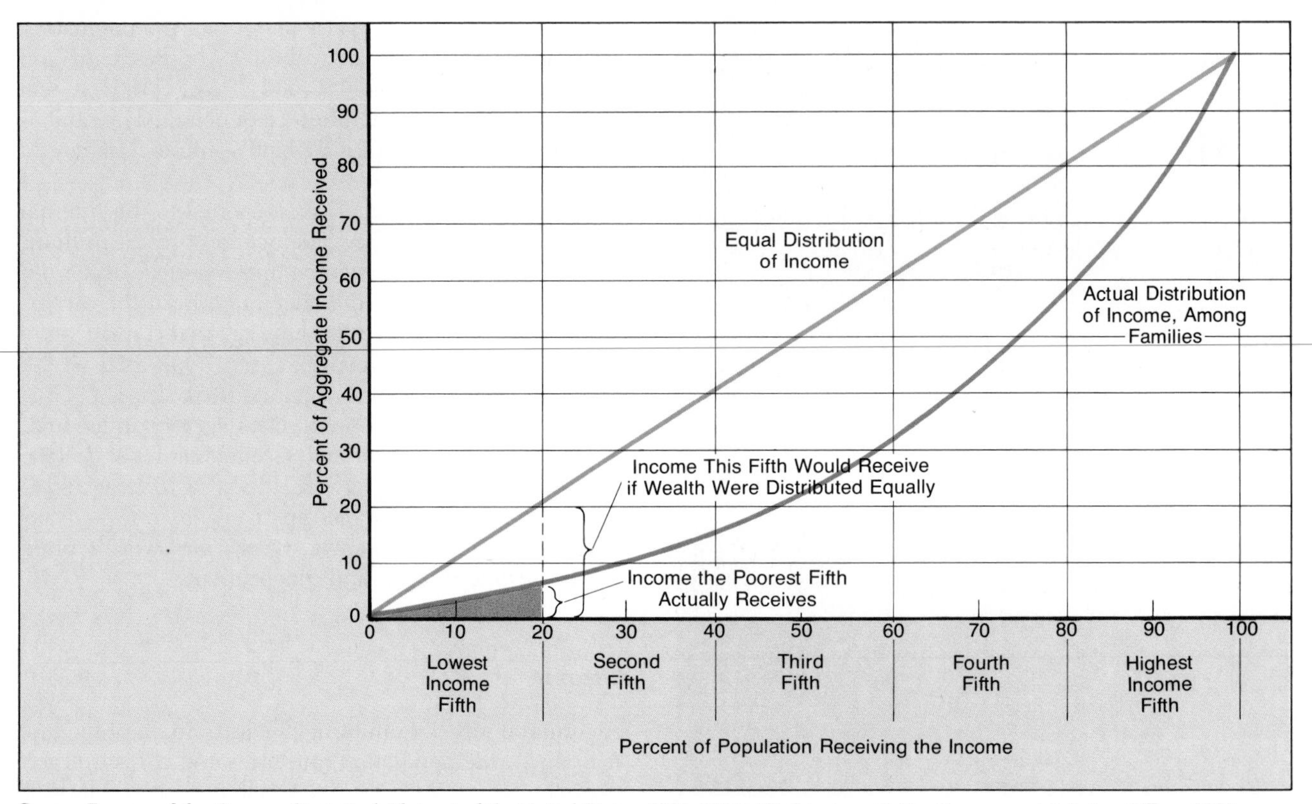

Source: Bureau of the Census, *Statistical Abstract of the United States: 1982–1983*. Washington, D.C.: Government Printing Office, 1983.

This graph is constructed by plotting the amount of income realized by various percentages of Americans. An equal distribution would produce a straight diagonal on the graph: 20 percent of the population would earn 20 percent of the income, 40 percent would receive 40 percent, and so on. However, the actual distribution of income in the United States (represented by the curved line) is quite different. The lowest 20 percent receive about 5.1 percent of the total income; the lowest 40 percent receive a little more than 15 percent; and so on.

lowest fifth of American families received 5.1 percent and the highest fifth received 41.6 percent of all income. It also reveals that the top 5 percent of families received 15.3 percent of the nation's total income, three times the share they would receive if all Americans were to receive an equal income. In monetary terms, the bottom fifth of American families had incomes of less than $10,000, and the top fifth had incomes over $35,000.

The distribution of income is dramatically illustrated by the graph in Figure 10.1. The percentage of the population is plotted on the horizontal axis, and the percentage of total personal income along the vertical axis. If each group were to receive exactly the same proportion of total income—that is, if personal income in the United States were distributed equally—the income distribution curve would rise at a straight 45-degree angle (like the straight line in Figure 10.1). Any deviation from this 45-degree angle indicates some inequality in income distribution; the more bowed the curve, the more unequal the distribution. The arched line in Figure 10.1 represents the actual distribution of income in the United States. As you can see, it deviates substantially from the 45-degree line. The curve illustrates the facts presented in Table 10.1. The poorest 20 percent of Americans earned about 75 percent less than what their share would be if income were distributed equally, while the wealthiest 5 percent earned 15.4 percent, about three times more than an equal share. These portions have remained quite stable over the past thirty years.

A few Americans earn substantial incomes. For example, in 1982 twenty-nine top corporate executives earned in excess of $1 million and another 254 executives earned more than $500,000. In addition to their salaries, some corporate officers also receive several million dollars in gains from various stock options and other long-term financial agreements (Bronson and Morse, 1983). Indeed, with the growth of multinational corporations, we can no longer understand stratification only in terms of personal inequalities of wealth and income. We also have to look at how large economic and political organizations influence people's life chances and their standard of living, a matter that brings us to an examination of power.

Power

The word *power* has a generally negative connotation (Marger, 1981). We talk about people being "power mad," "power hungry," or "only out for power." And we often associate power with tyrants, dictators, and the leaders of totalitarian regimes. Yet the notion that evil is imposed by power while good flies on its own wings is untenable. Power can also be used to combat sexism, racism, and tyranny.

Power is a fundamental and inherent element in all human interaction at every social level; it can be used for constructive as well as selfish ends. **Power** is the capacity to get others to act in accordance with one's wishes even when they prefer not to do so. Wherever we look in human affairs, be it families, juvenile gangs, or nation-states, we find that some people get their way more often than others. The Women's Liberation Movement has focused attention on the ways in which power pervades even one-to-one relationships and contributes to women's receiving fewer of the benefits and more of the burdens from many relationships than do men.

Power is exercised at both an *interpersonal* level and a *societal* level (Marger, 1981). At the interpersonal level, power operates in direct face-to-face relationships such as those between husbands and wives, supervisors and subordinates, and teachers and pupils. For the most part, the use of power within these contexts has immediate consequences only for the individuals involved. But when individuals or groups bring power to bear in situations that affect many, if not all, elements of society, the power is societal. The presidency of the United States is an example of societal power. The decisions the president makes are not like those of other people: few of us think in terms of billions of dollars, of millions of people, or of triggering a nuclear war.

Although we will explore the concentration of power in America more fully in Chapter 11, the highlights of that discussion are relevant here. Power is an important dimension of social stratification, and there is no doubt that it is unequally distributed in this country. The question sociologists debate, therefore, is not *whether* the possession of power is unequal in America, but *how* unequal it is. Is power monopolized by a small group of people who share the same interests and goals, or is it more broadly dispersed?

C. Wright Mills (1956) held the former view. He argued that the heads of government, the military, and business in this country constitute a **power elite,** a handful of like-minded people who make the decisions that determine how the rest of us will live. G. William Domhoff (1967) has tried to determine the validity of Mills's hypothesis. Using various socioeconomic critera (wealth, education, club membership, and so forth), Domhoff identified a group consisting of about one half of one percent of the United States population, which he labeled a "governing class" because it shares disproportionately in the nation's wealth, income, and positions with decision-making power.

But not all sociologists agree with Mills and Domhoff. David Riesman is one. Where Mills saw a single cohesive elite, Riesman (1953) sees many competing elites whose varied goals and interests prevent them from coalescing their power. Riesman believes that power is fairly widely dispersed in our society, with no one group in command.

But not even Riesman would argue that power in America is distributed in a truly democratic fashion. Far from it. At best, power is dispersed among many elites. As Roderick Martin has commented:

> Contemporary capitalism is not dominated by a small, cohesive power elite. But neither is it ruled by the

> popular will, as understood in the doctrine of popular sovereignty. The characteristic political structure of contemporary capitalism is rather one of democratic elitism. (1977:160)

Thus, no matter what view one takes of power in America, the fact emerges that the vast majority of Americans, the masses, have very little power. As Mills wrote, most Americans cannot control "great changes" that affect their behavior and outlook. These changes are largely the result of decisions made by powerful others whom the majority of Americans may not even know.

Prestige

The third dimension of stratification is prestige. **Prestige** is "the esteem, respect, or approval that is granted by an individual or a collectivity for performances or qualities they consider above the average" (Goode, 1978:7). As such, it provides people with a sense of worth and respect, a feeling that somehow they are admired and valued by others.

Societies differ in what attributes they attach prestige to. In a society preoccupied with religion, holiness and zeal may be the most important attributes for

TABLE 10:2 Prestige Ranking Of Occupations In The United States, 1963

	Score		Score
U.S. Supreme Court justice	94	Owner-operator of a printing shop	75
Physician	93	Farm owner and operator	74
Nuclear physicist	92	Reporter on a daily newspaper	71
Scientist	92	Bookkeeper	70
Government scientist	91	Carpenter	68
State governor	91	Mail carrier	66
Cabinet member in the federal government	90	Automobile repairer	64
College professor	90	Barber	63
U.S. representative in Congress	90	Garage mechanic	62
Chemist	89	Truck driver	59
Lawyer	89	Streetcar motorman	56
Diplomat in the U.S. Foreign Service	89	Singer in a nightclub	54
Dentist	88	Dockworker	50
Architect	88	Railroad section hand	50
County judge	88	Taxi driver	49
Psychologist	87	Farmhand	48
Minister	87	Janitor	48
Member of the board of directors of a large corporation	87	Bartender	48
Mayor of a large city	87	Clothes presser in a laundry	45
Priest	86	Soda fountain clerk	44
Head of a department in a state government	86	Share-cropper—one who owns no livestock or equipment and does not manage farm	42
Sociologist	83	Garbage collector	39
Accountant for a large business	81	Street sweeper	36
Public school teacher	81	Shoe shiner	34
Author of novels	78		

Source: Adapted from Robert W. Hodge, Paul M. Siegel, and Peter H. Rossi. "Occupational Prestige in the United States." *American Journal of Sociology* (November 1964).

prestige; in a military setting, physical courage is often what counts the most; people in the film or the fashion fields often equate status with talent or good looks. In America we bestow prestige according to how people earn their money (their occupation), how they spend it (their mode of consumption), who they are (their ancestry), whom they know, and how successful or well known they are. Being a neurosurgeon, earning several hundred thousand dollars a year, owning a large yacht, having an Ango-Saxon surname, belonging to the "right" clubs, and having friends in positions of power are all sources of prestige in our society. However, the main general determinant of prestige appears to be one's occupation. As reflected in Table 10.2, Americans rate most highly those jobs that afford political power, require professional skills, and provide high income. Supreme Court justices, doctors, scientists, governors, and cabinet members are at the top; garbage collectors, street sweepers, and shoe shiners at the bottom; schoolteachers, builders, farmers, and police officers in between. But there are some surprises. Americans are not as anti-intellectual as they are sometimes depicted: college professors rank eighth (well ahead of bankers), and movie actors rank well below teachers.[1]

Prestige is a subjective matter, one that is more intangible than tangible. However, since prestige is such an important part of social relations, people give it a more tangible cast through symbolic representations. Titles ('Sir," "Mr President," "Your Royal Highness," "Doctor," "Professor"), honorary degrees, seats of honor, medals, badges, trophies, and displays of deference are symbolic expression of prestige.

Corporate life provides countless clues to a person's rank in the prestige hierarchy. A corner office on a top floor, for example, is one sign of success. Bank of America employees know that they have made it when they are given stationery with the bank's logo in gold rather than black ink. The Ford Motor Corporation has a very elaborate system of status classification. Employees are graded on a scale of 1 (clerks and secretaries) to 27 (chairman of the board). Grade 9, the lowest executive level, includes the right to an outside parking place; Grade 13 brings a larger office, windows, plants, an intercom system, and a secretary. Those who reach Grade 16 receive an office with a private lavatory, signed Christmas cards from the chairman, an indoor parking space, and company cars.

While such corporate perquisites do not affect the lives of most Americans, social stratification does have widespread consequences for people's life chances. It is to this matter that we now turn our attention. In particular, we will look at what it is like to be poor.

[1]The occupation of movie actor appeared on an extended scale, and drew a rank of forty-four, compared with eighty-one for a public school teacher (Tumin, 1973).

LIFE CHANCES

The term **life chances** refers to the distribution within a social system of opportunities that affect people's health, survival, and happiness. People's life chances differ from one nation to another. Industrial nations tend to be wealthier than agricultural and preindustrial nations. Moreover, the gap between rich and poor nations is widening. The United States, the world's richest nation, emerged from World War II with a decided advantage. While most of the developed nations were cleaning the rubble from their bombed out factories and cities, the United States turned its economy from war production to consumer goods, creating a standard of living that for a time was unprecedented in history. But by 1979 many industrialized countries had achieved higher absolute income levels than the United States (see Table 10.3, p. 238). Moreover, as revealed in Figure 10.2 (p. 258), the United States ranks near the bottom of Western industrial nations when egalitarianism is measured by the distribution of income. Only France and Canada provide approximately the same small share of their national income to those at the bottom of the economic scale. The lowest 10 percent of families in Japan, West Germany, and the Netherlands receive about double the share of national income received by the bottom 10 percent in the United States (Magaziner and Reich, 1983).

While most Americans have access to such essentials as food and shelter, those at the top and bottom of the social hierarchy—the rich and the poor—have their life chances enormously increased or decreased simply by virtue of their class. Thus the poor have a sharply decreased chance of reaching their first birthday, of getting an education, of being able to afford adequate nutrition, decent housing, and health care, and of

TABLE 10.3 Gross Domestic Product Per Capita as Percent of U.S. Gross Domestic Product Per Capita

	1960	1963	1970	1975	1979
Switzerland	57	66	70	118	139
Denmark	46	53	67	104	119
Sweden	67	75	86	118	115
Germany	46	53	64	95	116
Iceland	49	56	51	82	103
Norway	45	50	60	99	106
Belgium	44	47	55	90	107
Luxemborg	59	57	66	89	109
Netherlands	47	55	58	90	101
France	47	55	58	90	100
Canada	79	72	81	101	91
Japan	16	22	41	63	82
Finland	40	45	48	82	82
U.K.	48	50	46	58	67

Source: Excerpted from *Minding America's Business* by Ira C. Magaziner and Robert B. Reich. Copyright © 1982 by Law & Business, Inc. Reprinted by permission.

FIGURE 10.2 Distribution of Income in Western Industrial Nations: After-Tax Income Shares

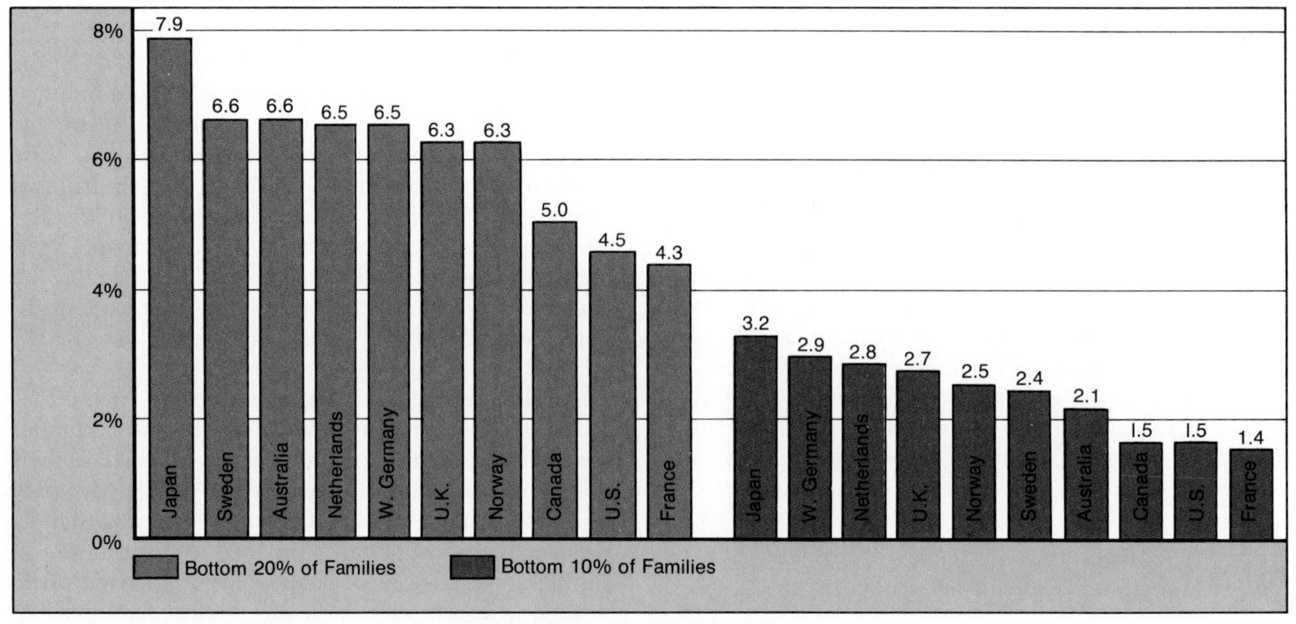

Source: Excerpted from *Minding America's Business* by Ira C. Magaziner and Robert B. Reich. Copyright © 1982 by Law & Business, Inc. Reprinted by permission.

rounding out their days in dignity and comfort. And the poor enjoy far fewer options than the rich in how they will lead their lives or spend their time. Let us examine the situation in the United States more carefully.

Life Expectancy

In all industrialized nations, the lower one's social class, the greater the risk of death at birth or from occupational hazards, and the shorter one's life span (Gortmaker, 1979). The effects of stratification are seen most clearly in occupationally related deaths (such as the miner's black lung disease). But the poor also suffer more from chronic and infectious diseases than the rest of the population, usually because of substandard housing and unsanitary living conditions. And when illness does strike, the poor have less access to superior health care than the affluent. Moreover, many working-class people put off treatment of health problems in order to stay on the job and bring home the paycheck.

It is hard to specify exactly what role poverty plays in adult mortality because certain behaviors that result in death (such as smoking or reckless driving) are not related to socioeconomic status. However, the effects of poverty on mortality can be seen quite clearly in *infant* mortality rates. Infants are helpless beings, dependent on a healthy environment for their survival. Here the hazards of poverty—inadequate housing, poor sanitation, insufficient nutrition, inadequate postnatal medical care—can be crucial. Within the United States the risk of death for infants born into poverty is 50 percent greater than that for other infants (Gortmaker, 1979). (We will discuss health problems of the poor in detail in Chapter 16.)

Nutrition

The poor spend a much greater proportion of their incomes on food than other Americans do: 35 percent for families earning less than $5,000 per year, compared with 15 percent for families with incomes of $20,000 to $30,000 per year (Gallo et al., 1980). Often the poor pay more for less: ghetto merchants justify high markups on the grounds that they take high risks working in the area; small local groceries charge high prices and extend credit. The poor not only pay more but also receive poorer quality goods. For instance, chain stores unload day-old bread and other leftovers in low-income neighborhoods.

The low food budgets of the poor usually require that they subsist on the cheapest, most filling commodities available. Millions of Americans (mostly children) live on white rice, spaghetti, macaroni, beans, white bread, and other high carbohydrate foods. When money runs short, many poor people turn to pet food.

From 30 to 50 percent of poor children suffer from protein, iron, and vitamin deficiencies. Malnutrition stunts children's growth and makes them more vulnerable to disease, but that is not all. There is a growing body of evidence to suggest that severe protein deficiency during the first twelve to eighteen months of life causes irreparable damage to the brain and the nervous system. In addition, hungry children are apathetic, lethargic, unable to pay attention for more than very brief periods, and often irritable and agitated (Winick, 1980). In short, hunger interferes with learning and intellectual development.

Housing

Many of the housing units of the poor sections of America's large cities are in disrepair; some are condemned and abandoned. In 1976, 6.2 million families (disproportionately black and poor) lived in physically inadequate housing (Holleb, 1981). Significantly, the poor spend proportionately more of their income on rent than others do—71 percent of households earning $3,000 or less per year pay over 35 percent of their income for rent, compared with 19 percent of those earning $20,000 to $25,000 per year (U.S. Department of Housing, 1978). These economic pressures are forcing increasing numbers of people to seek housing assistance. For instance, some 10 percent of Boston's population live in government-financed housing. Another 7,000 Bostonians are on waiting lists (Lodge and Glass, 1982). Yet in Boston 4,000 public housing units stand vacant; they are uninhabitable, derelict shells (Lodge and Glass, 1982).

The people living in these two communities have very different opportunities in life. Those who live in the middle class suburb have better health care, more nutritious diets, higher quality educations, and even a longer life expectancy than the people living in poverty. (Above, Michael D. Sullivan; right, Mark Antman/The Image Works.)

Mental Health

Studies suggest that mental disorders are more common among the lower strata of society than they are among the upper ones (Goodman et al., 1983). Indeed, a classic study conducted in New Haven, Connecticut, during the 1950s found that the ratio of lower-class to upper-class mental patients was a startling 40 to 1 (Hollingshead and Redlich, 1958). Similarly, community surveys reveal comparatively higher rates of psychological distress among individuals in the lower than in the upper strata (Kessler and Cleary, 1980; Kessler, 1982).

Many factors interact to produce the negative relationship between socioeconomic position and psychiatric symptoms and distress. First, people with chronic mental-health problems often "drift" downward in status or find their upward ascent impeded because their disorder interferes with their gaining or holding many jobs (Eaton, 1980). Second, evidence suggests that the lower strata are more exposed to unemployment and other stresses that are known to precipitate emotional difficulties than are people in the upper strata (Myers et al., 1974). And third, their socialization and educational experiences provide them with fewer of the skills and social competencies that are necessary to cope with life's stresses (Kessler and Cleary, 1980).

Criminal Justice

The poor are also the losers in the criminal justice system. Residents of low-income neighborhoods are more likely to be arrested for drunkenness, gambling, and such ambiguous crimes as vagrancy, which together account for about 60 percent of all arrests. The poor, too, are less likely to be released on their own recognizance and they are more likely to be sent to jail if convicted (Cratsley, 1972; Berk et al., 1980; Thomson and Zingraff, 1981). And since poor neighborhoods are more often high crime areas, their residents are more likely to be victims of "street crimes" than people in middle-class neighborhoods (Roncek, 1981).

In summary, then, the poor have far fewer opportunities to enjoy a long, healthy, comfortable, and secure life than do people in higher social strata. That is true not simply because the poor have less income and wealth than others do. The life chances of the poor are also restricted because they lack access to the important resources of power and prestige.

Matters have been complicated over the past fifteen years as the affluence that the United States enjoyed during the two decades following World War II began to decline. Impoverishment of public goods has become a growing concern—air pollution, inner-city decay, health hazards in the workplace, and the decay of mass transit systems. In some areas of American life the actual amounts of goods and services produced has declined. As the economic pie becomes smaller, it is more difficult to find an equitable way of sharing the nation's resources (Magaziner and Reich, 1983). All this raises a more basic question: why should there be such differences in life chances and why should social life be characterized by stratification? Two very different explanations have been advanced.

TWO THEORIES OF SOCIAL STRATIFICATION

Most sociologists trying to account for the unequal distribution of wealth, power, and prestige in human societies lean toward one of two theories. On one side are the conflict theorists. They maintain that stratification is the result of the struggle among people for scarce rewards, and that it persists in society because the "haves" are determined and equipped to preserve their advantage by dominating and exploiting the "have-nots." Conflict theorists consider stratification unjust and unnecessary. On the other side are the functionalists. They argue that stratification is necessary—in fact, inevitable—in order to channel suitable individuals into various occupations and hence to insure that the essential tasks of group life are performed. As we will see, both sides of this fundamental and far-reaching debate have their strengths and their weaknesses.

Conflict Theory

As the name implies, conflict theory stresses the link between stratification and an ongoing struggle among competing groups and classes over a limited supply of rewards and resources. From this point of view, the winners gain a disproportionate share and resolutely undertake to defend and enhance their positions of privilege. Thus the rich stay rich or get richer while the poor stay poor or get poorer.

Marx and the Theory of Class Conflict

As we noted in Chapter 1, conflict theory has a long history. However, it received its most powerful impetus from the work of Karl Marx (1818–1883). Marx believed that all of history has been the story of class conflict over material privilege and power. One group, the exploiters, strives to maintain its advantage over subordinate groups, the exploited. In industrial society this struggle takes place between those who own the means of production —the capitalists, or **bourgeoisie,** as Marx called them— and those who sell their labor to the owners—the workers, or **proletariat.** According to Marx the bourgeoisie maintain their position of dominance by controlling the economic life of a population. Through their ownership of the factories, mines, large farms, and other sources of subsistence, the bourgeoisie strategically position themselves between the proletariat and the means by which the proletariat meet their social and biological needs. By gaining mastery of a society's critical resources, the bourgeoisie gain mastery of its people, rendering the masses vulnerable and susceptible to their control. Moreover, dominating the means of communication, the schools, and other key institutions, the bourgeoisie seek to socialize the proletariat with conventional opinions and ideas so that they cannot easily develop an accurate awareness of their exploited condition. As a result, workers develop a "false consciousness."

Marx saw the nation-state as an instrument of oppression, religion as a method of diverting and controlling the masses, and the family in its nineteenth-century form as a device for keeping wealth and education in the hands of the few. He predicted that as the ranks of the industrial workers swelled, they would become more and more conscious of their exploited condition and of the increasing disparity in wealth between owners and workers. This consciousness would spark open warfare between the classes. The victory of the proletariat would usher in first a socialist society in which the means of production would be publicly owned under a benevolent dictatorship of the proletariat, and ultimately a classless communist society, in which all would be united in a plentiful, cooperative, "full community."

Updating Marx

Until recently, America's social scientists largely ignored Marx's theories, in part because his theories seemed less relevant than they were in other societies. The United States was historically a frontier society whose economy absorbed vast numbers of immigrant workers with diverse languages and backgrounds, and the nation held a dominant role in the world capitalist system. As a result, American society did not evolve a rigid class system nor did its members develop a sharp class consciousness. Writing about the United States, Marx (1963:25) himself noted, "Though classes, indeed, already exist, they have not become fixed, but continually change and interchange their elements in the constant state of flux."

But the neglect of Marxism can be attributed to other factors as well, including the hostility with which leading sociologists of the 1950s and 1960s viewed Marxist thought. For instance, Talcott Parsons (1967), the most prominent sociologist of the period, dismissed Marxism as "obsolete," merely a vestige of nineteenth-century thinking. Parsons and other sociologists emphasized that the experience of the major Western capitalist nations had proven most of Marx's predictions false. Instead of the working class growing at the expense of the middle class, the middle class has grown much larger, and the poor actually had improved their situation under capitalism. Moreover, the socialist revolutions that did take place were in societies more agricultural than industrial (Cuba, China, Russia), and their results did not conform to Marx's expectations. Perhaps most devastating of all, Marx's thinking came to be equated, in some respects unfairly, with the totalitarian regimes of the Soviet Union and Eastern European nations.

So long as the American economy seemed to prosper and widespread confidence in America's institutions prevailed, it was easy to ignore Marxist theory. But as the political divisions of the late 1960s and early 1970s began to wrack the nation, as the Vietnam War was lost, as the Watergate revelations exposed corruption and deceit in high governmental circles, and as inflation eroded living standards, the old optimism faded. Many younger sociologists saw much that was valuable in Marx's work, and it stimulated their research. They insisted that Marxist thinking did not stop with Marx (Szymanski and Goertzel, 1979; Burawoy, 1982). Rather, they saw as a central tenet of Marxist thought the notion that theory and practice are linked and that theory must undergo continual reconstruction.

Today, Marx's ideas about the relationship between stratification and social conflict, and his perception of state power and ideology as the servants, justifiers, and defenders of the interests of the dominant class, are widely recognized as keen insights. These Marxist notions are at the heart of modern conflict theory, and a growing number of studies that employ Marxist thinking are being undertaken. For instance, Erik Olin Wright and his colleagues (1982) have used data from a national sample of the working population to investigate the class structure of American life from a Marxist perspective. According to their interpretation, the working class is the largest of the classes, comprising 44 percent of the white and 64 percent of the black population. They include the lower-status white-collar occupations in the working class since they "are virtually as proletarianized as manual occupations" (p. 709). Overall, women and minorities make up the majority of the American working class. Thus, conflict theorists emphasize that not only do class divisions wrack American society, but there are also divisions based on other characteristics including gender and race.

In sum, Marx continues to provoke controversy about how the rewards and burdens of society should be distributed. In the 1980s the debates about fair shares of the economic pie, the responsibility of government to aid the unemployed, sex discrimination in the workplace, and the rights of minorities attest to the continued relevance of the questions posed by Marx more than 100 years ago. However, we gain a quite different perspective on these same issues from functionalist theory.

Functionalist Theory

The idea that stratification serves an important function in society was first elaborated by Kingsley Davis and Wilbert E. Moore (1945, 1953) in the *American Sociological Review*. Davis and Moore reasoned as follows: If all the positions that have to be filled in a society were equally important and everyone were equally capable of doing these jobs, there would be no need for stratification. But this is not the case. Some tasks are clearly more necessary than others, and some require a great deal more talent and training. For example, almost anyone can learn to dig ditches in a day or two, but it takes years of schooling to become a physician. Medical school is demanding. For a year or more, medical students must devote their time to the business of memorizing endless facts of human anatomy. Young interns are expected to work long hours, sacrificing their nights and weekends and social life. Many interns go into debt to finance their education. And the job of physician itself is demanding of time, energy, and compassion. How many people would choose to spend their lives confronting life and death issues if they were not amply rewarded in money and respect?

This argument is the key to Davis and Moore's position. Societies must motivate people to seek socially important positions and to fill these positions conscientiously by rewarding those who do so with more of the things that contribute to sustenance and comfort, humor and diversion, self-respect and ego expansion. In other words, societies have to entice people into jobs that are essential and difficult to fill by special rewards.[2] Otherwise, many essential tasks would not get done. Therefore, social inequality is both necessary and constructive. Since stratification serves the interests of the society as a whole, functionalists argue, coercion is not required to maintain social stability. Most members of a society accept the system and cooperate in preserving the existing distribution of rewards and opportunities. In the long run, the entire society benefits.

One Critique

But Melvin Tumin, a conflict theorist, and others have challenged the functionalist position. Tumin (1970:380) begins by pointing out the difficulty of even defining what is and is not functionally important: "In the long run, *some* labor force of unskilled workmen is as important and indispensable to the factory as *some* labor force of engineers." He also questions Davis and Moore's proposition that only a limited portion of the population has the necessary talents for essential positions. Tumin believes that the stratification system, instead of facilitating the filling of those positions, actually prevents the discovery of talented members of the society because access to education depends on access to wealth. What's more, a stratification system passes on its inequalities from generation to generation because those seeking higher education generally must depend on their parents to pay for it. In addition, one's motivation to succeed is lessened or enhanced according to what one's parents have achieved and can afford. Thus talent is socially constrained. Elite groups tend to restrict access to their privileged position in order to preserve their prestige and power. For example, each year medical schools turn down hundreds of thousands of qualified applicants. Physicians protect their incomes by limiting their numbers. In sum, as the British sociologist T. B. Bottomore (1966:11) observes, "It would be a more accurate description of the social class system to say that it operates, largely through the inheritance of property, to ensure that each individual maintains a certain social position,

[2]As the argument goes, important jobs that are easy to fill do not call for such high rewards. In technological societies, for example, teachers may be as important as doctors, but more people have the talent, training, and desire to teach than to practice medicine. As a result, teachers receive more modest compensation than doctors.

This business consultant, working at home, has achieved a high degree of success, and is being amply rewarded for whatever struggles he might have undergone on his way to the top. The Chicano farm laborers, however, may work hard all of their lives, but, due to the way society distributes its rewards, they may never achieve the status and wealth of the businessman. (Left, Will McIntyre/ Photo Researchers; right, Stephanie Maze/Woodfin Camp & Associates.)

determined by his birth and irrespective of his particular abilities."

Tumin further maintains that, looked at in the long run, the sacrifices that Davis and Moore ascribe to those who train for important positions are *not* true sacrifices. A doctor who must struggle for the first ten years or so of practice to pay for years of training is more than rewarded in the next twenty to thirty years for his or her services. Moreover, the person who fills an important position in society enjoys many psychic and spiritual rewards—high prestige, self-development, access to leisure and freedom denied less privileged persons.

Tumin disputes the idea that the inducements for taking on essential functions must involve access to scarce rewards. Instead, he suggests the motivation to take on such jobs might be joy in work or social duty and service. In short, Tumin argues that far from being functional, social stratification is dysfunctional. It restricts talent and by doing so limits the productive capacity of a society. It legitimates the status quo, however right or wrong it might be. It distributes favorable self-images unequally among the population. It functions to make the less privileged hostile and suspicious, thereby preventing full social integration. It makes some people feel insignificant in the system as a whole, thereby diminishing their satisfaction, loyalty, and active participation in social life.

Combining the Two Theories

The differences between the functionalist and conflict theories appear profound and in many ways irreconcilable. Perhaps the most fundamental question at issue has to do with why people work. The functionalists argue that people need monetary or other incentives to be motivated to do demanding work. The conflict theorists argue that the concrete rewards for work provided by the present social system are disproportionate to value and effort and that this basic injustice stems from a social system organized around inequalities of wealth and power. Therefore, the goal must be to create public awareness of this injustice and to work for a more humane system based on community and cooperation rather than competition and exploitation.

Both theories have obvious strong points. Increasingly sociologists are emphasizing the similarities in the two approaches. In his influential work *Power and Privilege* (1966), Gerhard E. Lenski takes a major step toward a workable synthesis of the two perspectives. Lenski bridges one of the gaps between functionalist and conflict thought by noting that on the one hand, stratification may actually serve a purpose in society along the lines suggested by the functionalists. But on the other hand, forms of stratification will tend to persist long after they have ceased to be functional, which supports many of the claims advanced by the conflict theorists.

Theodore D. Kemper (1976) finds common ground between Marxist and functionalist explanations of social stratification in two areas. Both theories recognize that social power plays a part in determining the unequal distribution of rewards, and both theories acknowledge that the evaluation of the contribution a job makes to society also helps determine unequal rewards. The extent to which each theory favors each determinant varies widely, of course. Marxist theory leans heavily on the significance of power in the distribution of resources, while the functionalists emphasize the necessity of assigning some positions or work higher status than others. Accordingly, each has a different opinion about the need to mitigate the effects of stratification and the inequalities it engenders. Still, the theories are not entirely incompatible.

THE LAND OF OPPORTUNITY: AN EVALUATION

Leonard Stern's father came to this country from Germany several decades ago. When his textile business got into trouble, the elder Stern and a friend decided to import canaries. They were moderately successful, but then their canary business also fell into debt. Meanwhile, Leonard had gone to college and acquired an M.B.A. at record speed. He took over the business in 1959. The younger Stern built the family's Hartz Mountain Corporation into a $150-million-a-year enterprise, and by the time he was thirty-five he had amassed over a half a billion dollars (Louis, 1973).

This rags to riches success story typifies the American dream. The belief that any person who gets an education, works hard, and takes advantage of opportunities can "get ahead" is central to that dream—and it is one reason why American workers have failed to develop a sharp class consciousness. The data from recent national surveys presented in Figure 10.3 (p. 246) provide evidence that the majority of Americans still see the United States as a land of opportunity. However, many Americans have reservations as to whether or not hard work necessarily leads to success. Is this country truly a land of opportunity? Have we moved closer to the ideal of equal opportunity in the last decade? Can we move closer to it?

To answer these questions, we must first determine the degree of social mobility that exists in this country. By **social mobility,** we mean the movement of people from one social position to another. The term **vertical mobility** refers to upward or downward changes in a person's status, as shown in the case of Leonard Stern. The term **horizontal mobility** refers to changes in position that do not appreciably alter a person's status, as when a top oil company executive becomes the Secretary of Transportation.

FIGURE 10.3 Americans Assess Opportunity

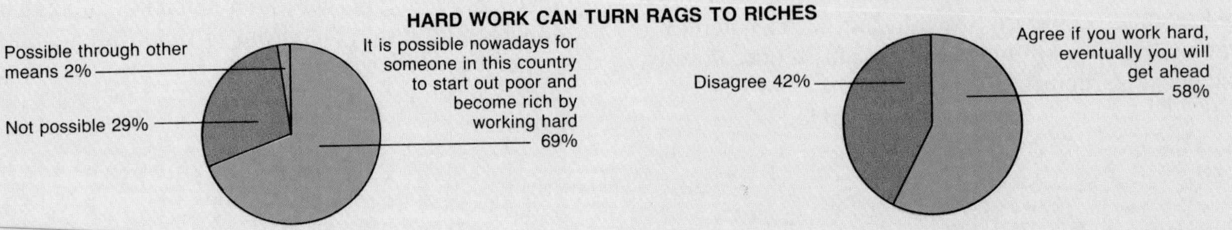

HARD WORK CAN TURN RAGS TO RICHES

Possible through other means 2%

Not possible 29%

It is possible nowadays for someone in this country to start out poor and become rich by working hard 69%

Question: Do you think it's possible nowadays for someone in this country to start out poor, and become rich by working hard?

Disagree 42%

Agree if you work hard, eventually you will get ahead 58%

Question: I'm going to read you a few statements. For each, please tell me if you tend to agree or disagree with it. . . . It is true in this country that if you work hard, eventually you will get ahead.

Note: In March 1981, 63% agreed to the ABC News/*Washington Post* question, 37% disagreed.

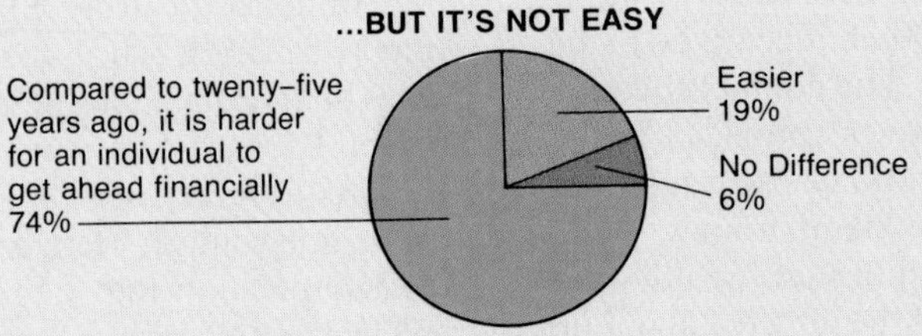

...BUT IT'S NOT EASY

Compared to twenty-five years ago, it is harder for an individual to get ahead financially 74%

Easier 19%

No Difference 6%

Question: Compared to twenty-five years ago in this country, do you think it is easier or harder for an individual to get ahead financially?

Source: From *Public Opinion*, Vol. 5, No. 3 (June–July 1982), p. 23.

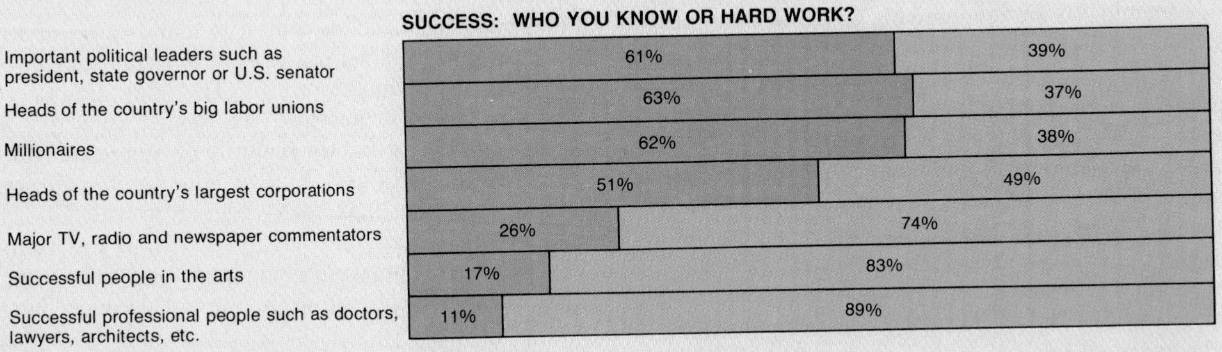

SUCCESS: WHO YOU KNOW OR HARD WORK?

	Who they are, who they know	Hard work
Important political leaders such as president, state governor or U.S. senator	61%	39%
Heads of the country's big labor unions	63%	37%
Millionaires	62%	38%
Heads of the country's largest corporations	51%	49%
Major TV, radio and newspaper commentators	26%	74%
Successful people in the arts	17%	83%
Successful professional people such as doctors, lawyers, architects, etc.	11%	89%

Note: Responses recalculated for comparison purposes. The largest "don't know" was 11 percent.

Question: I'm going to read a list of some of the top positions in our society (Card shown respondent). For each one, would you tell me the reason you think most people reach them—is it because of chance, say the type of family you're born into, whom you know, etc., or is it more due to talent, hard work and a strong will on the part of the individuals to reach those positions in spite of chance? First, do you think more people get to be important political leaders such as president, state governor or U.S. senator because of who they are and who they know, or more get there because of hard work, talent and strong will?

Success more due to: ▭ Who they are, who they know ▭ Hard work

Source: From *Public Opinion*, Vol. 4, No. 4 (August/September 1981), p. 33.

Open and Closed Systems

There are two analytically distinct types of stratification systems—open and closed. A truly **open class system** has few impediments to social mobility; positions are awarded on the basis of merit, and rank is tied to individual achievement. Because status depends on what individuals can do by their own effort, it is said to be *achieved* (see Chapter 4). Family origins, race, creed, color, sex, and other *ascribed* characteristics do not matter. Anyone with talent and ambition can advance. Therefore, there is a wide range of status positions, and class lines are blurred. This is not to say that an open society is an equal society. There is a difference between **equality of opportunity** (when the members of a society achieve different standards of living based on their different talents and contributions) and **equality of results** (when all members of a society have the same standard of living). Open systems simply provide people with an equal chance to succeed. Whether they do or not greatly depends entirely on them.

A closed or **caste system** is the opposite: Status is ascribed—that is, determined at birth—and people are locked into their parents' social position. In caste systems, ascribed characteristics determine social position, and individuals' opportunities are limited accordingly. Caste lines are clearly defined, and legal and religious sanctions are applied to those who attempt to cross them. The South African apartheid system (which is euphemistically described as "separate development") comes close to exemplifying a true caste system. In South Africa, blacks, Asians, and whites live in separate neighborhoods, attend separate schools, obey separate laws, endure different punishments. In India, there was long a rigid caste system. Today it is illegal, but strong vestiges of the system remain.

Most societies, including the United States, fall between the two extremes of open and closed stratification systems. Forty or fifty years ago, the social structure of the South was more castelike than it is today. Jim Crow laws prevented blacks from crossing racial lines, and many preachers taught that black skin was a curse. Today, federal law explicitly forbids racial discrimination, and there are signs that the Civil Rights Act of 1964 has worked to break down many traditional barriers to black advancement. But the extent to which racist arrangements remain a problem in contemporary American life is a hotly debated issue, as we will see in Chapter 11.

Classes in the United States

The first social scientist to explore in any depth the system of ranking in modern communities was W. Lloyd Warner. His study of "Yankee City" (Newburyport, Massachusetts) yielded a six-class model based on wealth, life style, possessions, and participation in community life and private clubs (Warner et al., 1949). (Note that Warner was using the term *class* in a broader sense than Weber.) Warner's six classes broke down as follows: upper-upper (1.4 percent), lower-upper (1.6 percent), upper-middle (10 percent), lower-middle (28 percent), upper-lower (33 percent), and lower-lower (25 percent).

Warner undertook his research prior to World War II. More recently Richard D. Coleman and Lee Rainwater (1978) have investigated the class structure of urban America by sampling residents in Boston and Kansas City. Class emerges from this research largely as a matter of wealth and income, especially as these are translated into a life style based on housing, cars, appliances, and leisure activities. When asked to describe differences between status groups in their communities, the individuals portrayed a many-layered system of social strata, all with rather fuzzy boundaries. However, a rough ranking arrangement on the following order emerged:

- *People Who Have "Made It."* The individuals of this level constitute an elite group of wealthy members of the old rich (the Rockefellers), the celebrity rich (television personalities), the anonymous rich (owners of oil wells, shopping centers, and other properties), and the run-of-the-mill rich (well-heeled professionals).
- *People Who Are Doing Very Well.* For the most part this level consists of corporation officers and professional people. They live in large, comfortable homes, belong to country clubs, occasionally vacation abroad, and send their children to prestigious large state universities or private colleges.
- *People Who Have Achieved the Middle-Class Dream.* Americans of this level enjoy the "good life" but they lack many of the luxuries of those in the higher levels. They are the nation's suburbanites residing in three-bedroom homes with a family–TV room.
- *People Who Have A Comfortable Life.* Although a step removed from those who enjoy the "good life,"

these individuals nonetheless live a "comfortable" existence in the less fashionable suburbs.

- *People Who Are Just Getting By.* Both husband and wife are typically employed—the husband in a blue-collar job and the wife as a secretary or salesclerk. They rent an apartment or own a small home but simply "getting by" places a strain on their financial resources.
- *People Who Are Having A Difficult Time.* Unemployment often stalks couples on this level but the husband and wife usually manage to "scrape by." Many single-parent families fall in this category as well. Although these individuals have a difficult time, they are proud that they are not on welfare.
- *People Who Are Poor.* These individuals constitute an "underclass," many of whom are on welfare.

Many sociologists prefer to simplify the division of Americans into upper, middle, and lower classes. Adding more refined occupational- or income-based criteria yields a more accurate but also a more unwieldy scheme. And some sociologists find the term *class* too partisan and politically charged. They prefer the more neutral terms *stratum* or *socioeconomic strata*.

Horatio Alger: Myth or Reality?

The stories of the nineteenth-century writer Horatio Alger exemplify the American dream: a poor immigrant boy—like Leonard Stern—works hard, has some luck, and becomes rich. How much truth is there to this tale?

Some sociologists argue that mobility in America has historically been upward. Our labor market has grown dramatically since the turn of the century, with the total number of jobs more than doubling and the number of white-collar jobs skyrocketing. Technology has opened whole new fields, expanding the career opportunities open to technicians, managers, and professionals. (See the box.)

Large scale immigration has also provided an impetus for occupational advancement. An influx of unskilled and semiskilled laborers, such as occurred in this country during the late nineteenth and early twentieth centuries, frees experienced workers to move up the occupational ladder. (For example, an artisan who once did all the work in the shop can hire assistants, expand operations, become a white-collar worker.) The fact that white-collar workers tend to have fewer children than workers in other categories further stimulates upward mobility. Quite simply, white-collar workers do not produce enough children to refill their ranks, which gives individuals from the other groups a chance to move up.[3] Thus changes in the birth rate, improved technology, and migration historically have acted to expand and change the United States labor market.

But even though upward mobility tends to outweigh downward mobility, the extent to which a given person rises on the social scale is usually limited. One way sociologists measure individual mobility is by comparing fathers' and sons' jobs (intergenerational mobility). Using this measure, Peter M. Blau and Otis Dudley Duncan (1967) have concluded that Americans as a whole are upwardly mobile, but that most individuals move only a step or two up the ladder. Thus family status plays an important role in determining occupational status.

David L. Featherman (1979), using the same research approach, concludes that upward social mobility is very much a part of our national image. He found that while educational mobility at the college level seemed to be at a standstill, there had been a large increase in access to a high school education over the preceding few generations. And there had been more upward than downward job mobility across generations. Using U.S. Census surveys of the male labor force, Featherman compared sons' and fathers' occupations in 1962 and 1973 and found in both years that 49 percent of the sons were upwardly, while only 17 percent were downwardly, mobile in 1962 and 19 percent in 1973. Featherman maintains that the opportunities for social mobility have increased more for blacks than for whites, in large part reflecting the fact that more and more types of jobs have opened up to blacks.

Sociologists at the University of Michigan's Institute for Social Research have taken a somewhat different approach to the study of social mobility (Duncan, 1982). These researchers have followed the economic fortunes of a large, representative sample of American families since 1967. Each time a family member leaves one

[3]Changes in the death rate may have a similar effect. One reason why women in the U.S.S.R. have achieved more high-level positions than women have elsewhere is that so many Soviet men were killed in World War II.

THE SOCIOLOGICAL EYE ON CAREERS:

The Shift from a Blue-Collar to a White-Collar Job

Frank LaRose is a twenty-three-year-old former steelworker now employed as a computer programmer. He grew up in Weirton, West Virginia, and on graduating from high school, secured a job in one of the city's giant steel mills. Mr. LaRosa worked in a section of the plant called "the hole." He and three other men banded hot strips of steel on a rolling machine. The hole was so hot that the men wore cotton long johns under their clothing to protect themselves from the intense heat.

With the downturn in the economy in the early 1980s, Mr. LaRosa was laid off from the mill, and he realized that it was only a matter of time before the mill permanently closed. Concluding that he had no future as a steelworker, he obtained a $5,000 student loan, added $2,000 of his own savings, and enrolled in a fourteen-month program at a Pittsburgh computer systems institute. He observes that he was only four years out of high school and "hadn't forgotten how to study like some of the older guys who were trying to retrain." He graduated with a straight A average and received an associate degree in computer programming.

He is finding the shift from a blue-collar to a white-collar job a difficult one. Indeed, some days he feels like a refugee trying to adjust to a new country: "In the mill you put in your eight hours, said whatever you felt like saying and then went out with your buddies for a beer. But if you're white collar and trying to get ahead, you've got to present yourself just so. And your work is always on your mind even after work." He finds relationships with coworkers and supervisors appreciably different. And there is no union that spells out his job duties. Further, although his current job is generally considered more prestigious than that of a steelworker, it pays only two-thirds as much as he earned in the steel mills.

Mr. LaRosa says that his current work is more "challenging" than that in the mill, but it also requires more concentration. He feels under continuous pressure to "move, move, move from one thing to the next." In the mill, he says, "my brain was in neutral all the time. Here you've got deadlines and clients to please, and everybody wants everything done yesterday."

Mr. LaRosa is also learning about white-collar status symbols. He notes that if he were higher up in the ranks of management he would have a private office with a door and a window. But he would have to exchange his shirt and slacks for a suit. He feels that his background as a steelworker has placed him at a disadvantage: "They think, 'Once a laborer, always a laborer.' I'm going to have to show them how smart I am." On his first day at work, his boss told him that he would have preferred to hire a college graduate and that Mr. LaRosa would have to prove himself: "I felt lower than most everybody else here." Yet he is optimistic about his future: "Someone may have more seniority than me, but maybe they're just making lateral moves and I can jump around them. As a programmer, nobody is stopping me but me."

Source: Condensed from Carol Hymowitz, "Culture Shock Affects Steelworker Who Switched to White-Collar Job." *Wall Street Journal*, June 1, 1983, P. 31.

household to form another, the new household is added to the sample. They find that Americans move up and down the economic ladder with considerable frequency. For instance, only about a half of the individuals who in 1971 were living in households with incomes in the bottom fifth were still at the bottom in 1978. Moreover, less than half of the individuals in the top fifth in 1971 had stayed on top. The individuals most affected by these changes were women and children under age fourteen. The divorce or marriage of a woman profoundly influenced her fortunes and those of her dependent children. Divorce had a particularly devastating economic impact, not only because women typically earn less than men do, but also because children usually remain with the mother (see Chapter 6). This research suggests that changes in household composition predict change in economic status better than any of the variables commonly thought to determine success or failure, including intelligence, achievement motivation, education, and future orientation.

Featherman's conclusions and those of the Michigan researchers are challenged by conflict theorists who are more likely than other sociologists to view class in terms of people's ownership or nonownership of the means of production. For instance, Sidney M. Willhelm (1979:17) claims that mobility and opportunity are under the control of corporate America, which has "transformed great numbers of people from property owners to propertyless individuals." People are not really free to move up or down the scale; instead, they are molded into the type of person who can fill a certain position predetermined by corporate needs. Thus a move from a blue-collar position to a white-collar position is not truly indicative of upward mobility: "That many persons come to shed blue for white collars cannot hide the reality that collars still remain around our necks and, indeed, do what all collars must do: constrain our lives" (pp. 12–13). According to Willhelm, Featherman and many other sociologists make the mistake of emphasizing life style in their analysis of what constitutes mobility, whereas the real issue is who controls wealth and production. Willhelm also downplays Featherman's findings of increased intergenerational job mobility among blacks as compared to whites. At most, blacks have been able to achieve occupational stability among their own kind and in the lower-level occupations. Whites have increased their control of the "supposedly superior" white-collar categories.

These differences in defining what constitutes social mobility affect the way sociologists answer the question of whether the United States offers greater opportunities for advancement than do other nations (Tyree et al., 1979; Smith, 1981). Many sociologists conclude that the industrialized nations of the world are surprisingly similar in their rates of social mobility (Hope, 1982). This conclusion holds for Communist nations as well (Connor, 1979). Apparently, rates of social mobility are less a function of political systems and social values than of structural factors associated with technological innovations and industrialization. In most nations the shape of the occupational structure has been shifting from a pyramid (a triangle with most occupations concentrated at the bottom) to an oval (with more occupations concentrated in the middle). Such changes increase the proportion of individuals who attain a higher status than their parents. Among the factors contributing to this shift in Western nations are the replacement of family-owned enterprises by public corporations, the bureaucratization of corporate life, the recruitment of management personnel from the ranks of college graduates, and the awarding of high positions on the basis of competitive promotions (Lipset, 1982).

Status Attainment Processes

Sociologists are interested not only in the extent of social mobility within a society, but also in the factors that underlie status transmission and attainment. William H. Sewell and his colleagues at the University of Wisconsin (Sewell and Hauser, 1976; Hauser et al., 1982, 1983) have contributed greatly to our understanding of these matters. They followed, at periodic intervals, some 10,000 people who graduated from Wisconsin high schools in 1957. The researchers sought to determine how one's social background influences one's later career and what mechanisms intervene between one's social origins and one's later placement.

The Wisconsin sociologists concluded that educational and occupational attainment are the outcome of two related processes: those that shape a person's status aspirations and those that convert the aspirations into a new status ranking. Practically the entire effect of a family's class position on a child's later attainments is the result of the personal influences that family members bring to bear on the child's status aspirations during adolescence. Parental and teacher encouragement to attend college and the college plans of the adolescent's best friend also influence an adolescent's status aspirations.

From that point on, the impact of the parent's social background becomes inconsequential. The level of a person's schooling then becomes the principal influence. Viewed in this fashion, occupational attainment is shaped by many intervening or mediating links in a chain extending from birth across the life span: Parental status colors the adolescent's aspirations; aspirations contribute to the individual's educational attainment; educational attainment influences the person's first occupational placement; and one's first job affects one's later occupational opportunities (thus, the lower people begin on the occupational status ladder, the higher they have to rise, and the less likely they are to reach the top positions).

Research by Christopher Jencks (1972, 1979; Jencks et al., 1983) comes to similar conclusions. Jencks depicts

The aspirations parents have for their children during the adolescent years greatly affect later attainments. (Frank Siteman/ EkM-Nepenthe.)

the United States as a class-ridden society where being born into the "right" family is vitally important, especially because of its impact on educational attainment. Education is typically crucial to "getting ahead" in America. Successful early experiences in school shape people's aspirations as well as the expectations of others. But what counts most is not what one learns in college but the fact that one completes college and acquires the proper credentials. Hence, the factors making for success are interrelated: An individual who comes from the "right" family is more likely to acquire high aspiratons, have high academic test scores, complete college, and have the personality attributes associated with success.

REDUCING INEQUALITY

The Declaration of Independence forthrightly declares as a self-evident truth that "all men are created equal." Yet as our discussion above has shown, inequality is a fact of life in the United States. How do Americans reconcile the dream of social equality with the reality of social inequality? How can the nation's disadvantaged be expected to give their allegiance to a system that provides them with less than their proportionate share of America's wealth?

Part of the answer lies with American conceptions of equality. According to the American dream any poor child can get ahead, just as a rail-splitter named Abe Lincoln could become president. But this promise has been based on the principle of equality of *opportunity*, not equality of *results*. The object of equality of opportunity is to free individuals from discrimination based on race, family, religion, gender, or community so that they might rise in society according to their own merits. In an order characterized by *distributive justice*, rewards are apportioned among individuals in accordance with each person's contribution to the group (Homans, 1974). Those who do more or invest more receive more than those who do less or invest less. This *contributive standard* is rooted in the capitalistic ethic. But if some people become "winners," gaining wealth and high status, others—at least by implication—become losers: Equality of opportunity produces inequality of results. The American dream has never been one of a classless society in which all individuals enjoy equal wealth, power, and prestige. It is instead a dream of a class society in which people have equal access to the top positions.

The doctrine of equality of opportunity assumes that all men (and recently also women) are created equal. If they are not in fact created equal, it is society's responsibility to make them more equal at the outset so that all people can begin from the same starting line. This argument had provided the rationale for the creation of the nation's public school system and the enactment of compulsory school attendance laws. Nevertheless, Americans have not enjoyed equal opportunities for getting ahead. Chapter 6 detailed how sexism has handicapped women and Chapter 12 discusses how racism has victimized blacks. President Lyndon B. Johnson, in his June 1965 address at Howard University, noted that much injustice was left untouched by civil rights legislation: "You do not take a person who for years had been hobbled by chains and liberate him, bring him up to the starting line of a race and . . . say, you're free to compete with all the others, and still justly believe that you have been completely fair."

While not abandoning allegiance to the value of competitive success, President Johnson nonetheless alludes to other American values, namely justice and fairness. These values have suggested to some Americans that because the nation had not accorded all its citizens equality of opportunity, it has acquired an obligation to equalize more of the benefits and rewards of the system. They have advocated affirmative action programs for minorities, school busing, and welfare programs financed by taxes on higher-income groups.

Recognizing that the contributive standard associated with the principle of equality of opportunity has produced inequality of results, some Americans have looked to other standards for distributing rewards. One of these is the *needs standard* that is expressed in the slogan of pure communism, "From each according to his ability, to each according to need." However, this standard does not just apply to communist ideology. Norms of social responsibility within the Western world have historically dictated that people's needs should influence how rewards are distributed. Hence, the sick, the infirm, the elderly, the very young, and others have had a social claim on a portion of a nation's resources.

Another standard for distribution is based on the *equality standard.* This approach has a long history, dating back into antiquity. Many people view a system that allocates its rewards unequally as inherently insensitive and unjust. Instead they favor an arrangement based on the credo, "To each, equally." This type of distributive system is most commonly encountered within families and closely knit in-groups.

The tension in American life between the principle of equality of opportunity and that of equality of results often finds expression in the debate between what is a "right" and what is a "privilege" (see Figure 10.4). In general, political conservatives have favored domestic programs fostering equality of opportunity whereas political liberals have favored programs promoting equality of results. Let us examine these matters more closely, particularly as they bear on poverty within the United States.

Who Are the Poor?

When the plight of the poor in the United States became a national issue in the 1960s, President Lyndon Johnson responded in 1964 by launching a "war on poverty." The Johnson administration undertook to define poverty in terms of a dollar amount that established a line between the poor and the nonpoor. The poverty line was—and continues to be—based on the minimum amount of money families need to purchase a nutritionally adequte diet, assuming that they spend one-third of their income for food. Defined in this fashion, poverty in the 1960s was concentrated among the elderly, large families, Appalachian whites, white and black rural southerners, and minorities in the cities (Hess, 1983).

The programs inaugurated as part of President Johnson's War on Poverty contributed to a decline in the proportions of families and individuals below the governmentally defined poverty level: from 19 percent in 1959 to 11 percent today of all American families, and from 22 percent to 14 percent of the total population. Most notably, poverty among the elderly has been more than halved—from over 35 percent in 1959 to 15 percent today. The liberalization of Social Security benefits and the introduction of Medicare (relieving the elderly of the full burden of medical care) played an important role in this decline. But not all the reduction in poverty can be attributed to public programs. For example, much of the reduction of the poverty in the South resulted from the movement of rural southerners to urban centers and to the North and the West. Similarly, the decrease in large families accounted for part of the decline in the proportion of children in poverty from almost 27 percent of all children in 1959 to about 20 percent today.

Despite the gains of the past quarter-century, nearly 32 million Americans still fall below the poverty thresh-

FIGURE 10.4 Notions of Rights and Privileges

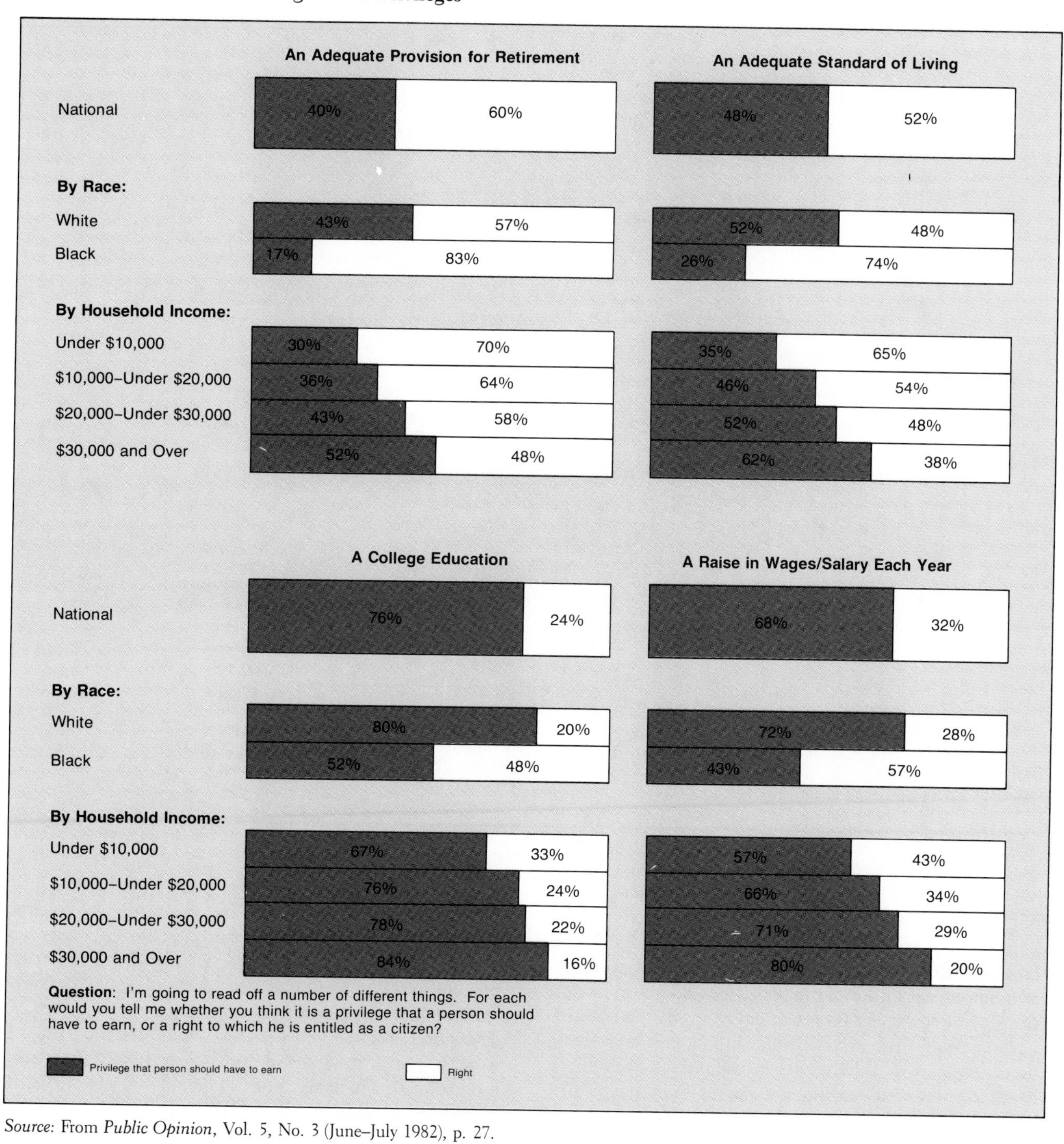

Source: From *Public Opinion*, Vol. 5, No. 3 (June–July 1982), p. 27.

FIGURE 10.5 Who the Poor Are, 1981

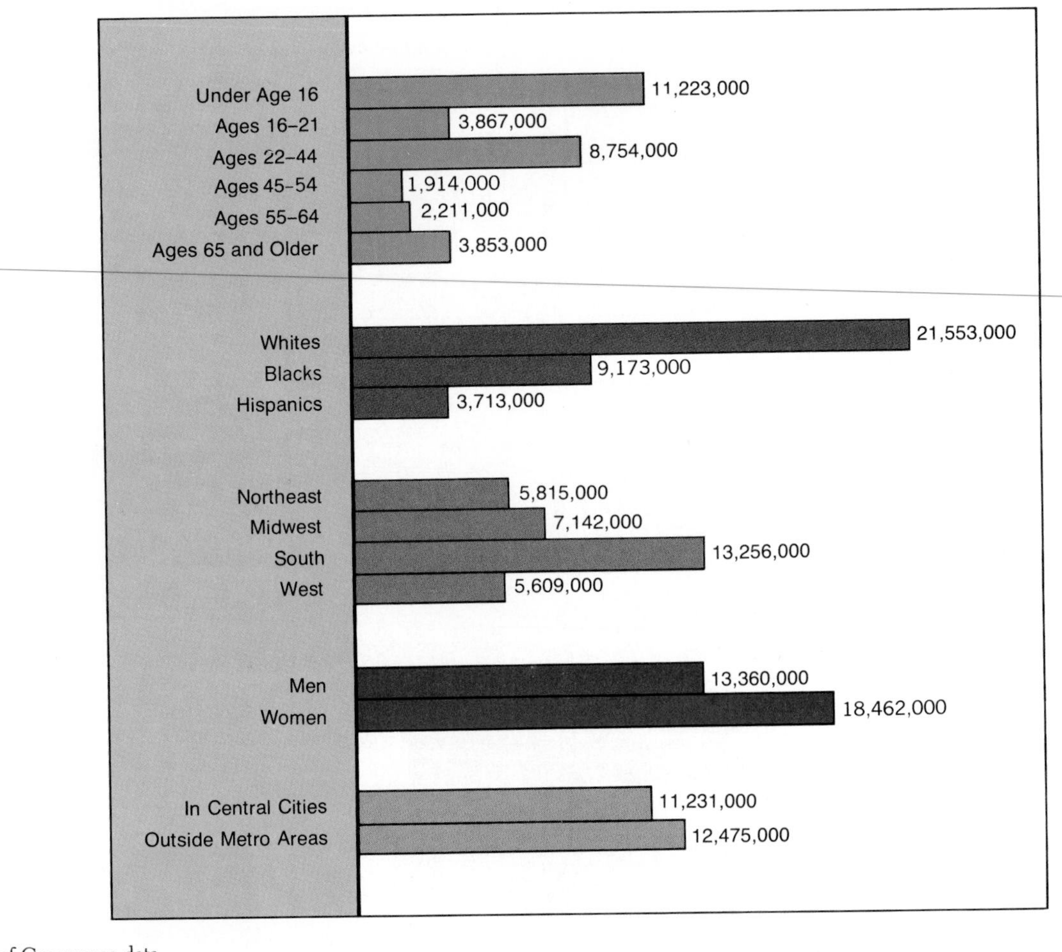

Source: U.S. Department of Commerce data.

old, and another 8 million constitute the "near poor" (see Figure 10.5). Roughly 29 percent of the poor are black and 12 percent of Spanish origin. About half of all families below the poverty level are headed by women, and more than a third of the poor are children. Whereas twenty-five years ago poor women were likely to be the wives of impoverished men, today they are more likely to be on their own. When a relationship ends because of death, divorce, or desertion, a woman's income typically declines drastically. Conversely, a man's financial status is often enhanced because he has fewer people to support (Hess, 1983).

Of course, how we define poverty influences our judgments of its extent and the government's role in alleviating it. For instance, a study by the U.S. Census Bureau suggests that the poverty rate would drop from 11 percent to 6.4 percent if noncash governmental benefits were included in income calculations (Smeeding, 1982). The study says that between 1965 and 1980 the value of in-kind transfers—housing subsidies, school lunches, food stamps, Medicare, and Medicaid—rose from $2.2 billion to over $72.5 billion. These in-kind transfers to low-income Americans exceed cash public assistance by more than two to one. Even so, the current definition of poverty includes only money income. By counting the market value of all cash benefits, for example, the number of elderly below the poverty line would drop from 4.1 million to 1.3 million, a 70 percent reduction produced simply by changing the measurement technique. Hence, some people believe that the extent of poverty in the United States is exaggerated by not including in-kind transfers. Others contend that the noncash benefits have had only a marginal effect on real poverty. They say that the officially defined poverty threshold is unreasonably low, especially in major urban areas, where most of the poor are concentrated.

Income Redistribution Programs

As our discussion above suggested, the government has undertaken a variety of programs to combat poverty within the United States. In one way or another these programs are intended to reduce inequality through *income redistribution*. The government uses three primary methods to alter the distribution of income: income taxes, transfer payments, and subsidies for goods and services.

Taxes

How does taxation affect distribution of income? The federal income tax is meant to be a **progressive tax**—the more money a person earns, the higher his or her rate of taxation. For example, in 1984 married couples filing joint returns were taxed at a rate of 11 percent for incomes between $3,400 and $5,500, 25 percent for incomes from $24,600 to $29,900, and 50 percent for incomes over $162,400. But some claim that progressive taxation is less effective than it was intended to be. President Reagan's tax bill, passed by Congress in 1981, substantially lowered the progressive tax rates—by 5 percent in 1981 and by 10 percent in 1982 and 1983. Moreover, many provisions of the tax law enable upper-income groups to reduce their taxes substantially. For example, interest earned on state and municipal bonds is not taxed, capital gains are taxed at low rates, and depreciation allowances can be taken on income-producing property. Such provisions are of little use to those whose incomes are limited to wages and salaries. The Reagan tax program further weakened the progressive effect of the income tax by extending such "loopholes."

Also some kinds of taxes that Americans pay are regressive—that is, the poor actually contribute a greater proportion of their income than middle- and high-income people do. The federal payroll (Social Security) tax, state and local sales taxes, and property taxes are all regressive. Although the original intent of the American tax system was to reduce inequality, these taxes combined with tax laws that may be manipulated in favor of wealth- and property-owning people, ensure that the tax system fosters some gross inequalities.

Transfer Payments

Another approach to income redistribution are various transfer payment plans. **Transfer payments** include cash welfare benefits that are designed to raise the income of the poor, the unemployed, the aged, and the blind. Money is transferred from one sector of the economy to another without a corresponding contribution to current production. Over half of all transfer payments are for Social Security; beneficiaries typically receive considerably more over the course of their retirement than they contributed to the system while they worked. The size of a person's Social Security check is determined by his or her prior tax contributions and earnings, not by need. Thus, these recipients are distributed throughout the income scale and are not concentrated among the lowest income groups.

Another transfer program is Aid to Families with Dependent Children (AFDC). This program provides payments to parents who lack other sources of income. In most cases the mother is the only parent in the household and she receives the payment on behalf of her children. In 1981 AFDC payments were made to 3,842,534 families, consisting of 7,599,376 children and the 3,501,733 parents who cared for them. Some 12.2 percent of all American children under eighteen years of age were in families receiving AFDC assistance. In 1981 the typical monthly payment came to $288.77 for a family consisting of one parent and an average of 1.9 children. AFDC payments go almost entirely to low-income families.

Government Subsidies

Government subsidies of goods and services are closely related to transfer payments, except that they consist of

THE SOCIOLOGICAL EYE ON:
Fact and Fiction about Welfare

Do you agree or disagree with the following statements?

- The eligibility requirements for welfare in this country are far too lenient. A large number of people who could live all right without public assistance are nevertheless receiving it.
- The majority of welfare recipients are shirking the responsibility to earn their own living. They are able-bodied people, but they lack the motivation to work. Instead, they freeload off the government.
- One of the problems with the current welfare system is that it enables recipients to live too well for nothing. Why should people find a job if they have everything they need without working?

The chances are you suspect there is some truth to one or more of these common assumptions. Indeed, many people harbor unfavorable impressions of welfare recipients, as the accompanying graph indicates. Does sociological research substantiate the statements listed above? The answer is a definite no.

First, the Census Bureau's "poverty thresholds," widely used to help estab-

"What Is Your Impression Of Welfare Recipients?"

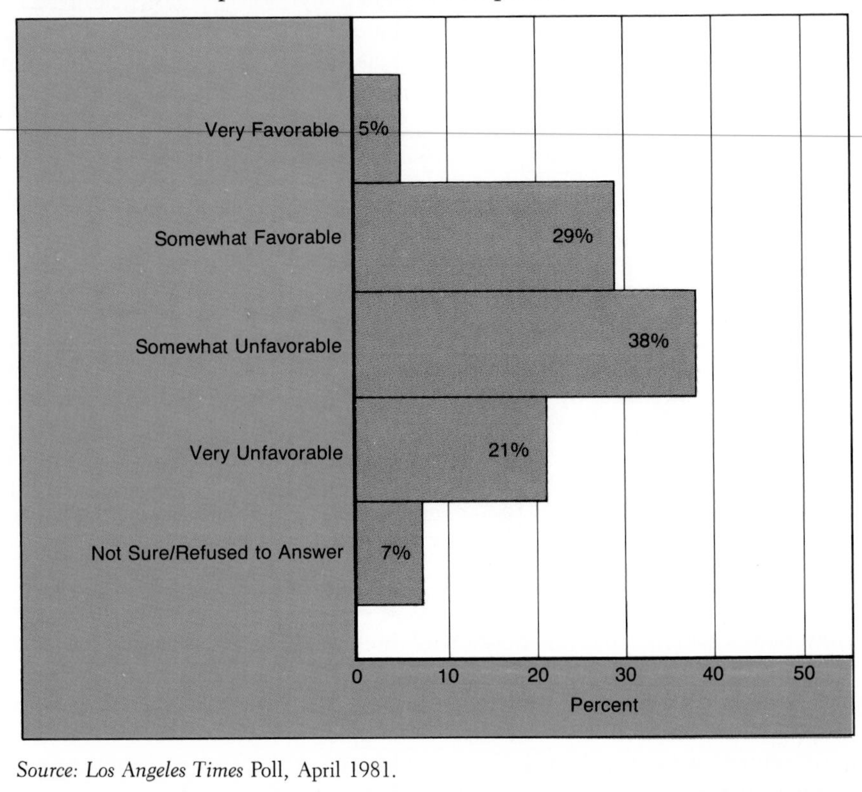

Source: Los Angeles Times Poll, April 1981.

in-kind transfers, not cash benefits. The food stamp program is an example of an in-kind transfer. In 1981, 6,769,000 American families (8.2 percent) received food stamps at some time during the year. Another example is subsidized housing. Of the 26,487,000 families living in rental premises in 1981, 2,777,000 (10.5 percent) resided in subsidized or publicly owned housing. However, not all government subsidies favor lower-income groups. Many state-supported public services, including higher education, highways, airports, and boat facilities, although legally available to all citizens, primarily benefit the affluent classes rather than the disadvantaged ones.

Federal programs have helped to fill basic needs. The beneficiaries of such programs have been primarily the elderly and mothers and their dependent children. Yet, as pointed out in the box, Americans have many lish eligibility for welfare, are hardly what could be called generous. For instance, in 1981 the poverty threshold for a nonfarm family of four was $9,287. These thresholds are partly determined by the U.S. Department of Agriculture estimates of the minimum amount of money needed to keep different-sized families decently fed. But the department's own studies show that only about 10 percent of people spending so little can manage to provide a diet rated as fair or better.

Second, the majority of people on welfare are not shirking the responsibility to earn their own living. Many are either too young or too old to work. (Nearly half of the poor are children under sixteen or people over sixty-five. Hence, a good many of the poor are not even of the appropriate age to be seeking full-time jobs.) As for the able-bodied men that many Americans believe their tax dollars are supporting, they are excluded from most public assistance programs (with the exception of food stamps) no matter how low their incomes are.

Third, individuals do not typically reduce their work effort or quit their jobs in order to get or retain welfare benefits (Pear, 1983). For instance, people removed from the welfare rolls by the Reagan administration generally stayed off the rolls and did not leave their jobs in order to qualify for public assistance payments. Further, many of those who lost their jobs and returned to welfare soon found other employment, leaving the welfare rolls once more. Indeed, one factor in the higher unemployment rates of disadvantaged groups is their tendency to turn over jobs more rapidly than the better-off.

Why do so many Americans hold such erroneous views about the welfare system? Part of the reason is their overly idealized image of America as the land of unlimited opportunity. Thirty-two million Americans living in poverty—fully 14 percent of the population—is too discordant a statistic for many people to believe. Consequently, some Americans assume that the majority of those receiving welfare benefits must simply be defrauding the system. Others conclude that those in poverty must somehow "deserve" their fate. The poor must lack motivation and ambition, the argument usually goes. If poverty can be attributed to the shortcomings of individuals, then they do not merit public assistance—"idlers" should not be able to enjoy that for which others work so hard. This rationalization is called blaming the victim, and it is clearly spurious. Willingness to work hard does not guarantee escape from poverty. For instance, a woman with two children, working forty hours a week for fifty-two weeks, at minimum wage, would have an annual income below the poverty threshold, plus the expenses of child care and travel to and from work (Hess, 1983). Thus the tendency to blame the victims of poverty for their own plight ignores the fact that poverty is not just an individual matter. It is the result of a system of social ranking that offers those at the bottom society only menial, low-paying jobs or often no jobs at all. Poverty is largely the product of forces beyond the control of its victims—the shift from labor-intensive to capital-intensive (particularly from "smokestack" to "high tech") industries, dual labor markets, the flight of the middle classes to the suburbs, banking and real estate practices, extended life expectancies, and changing patterns of family life, especially the rise of single-parent homes (Hess, 1983).

misconceptions about programs to assist the poor. Further, the hidden costs of poverty—wasted lives, illness, alienation, and degradation—are often overlooked. An estimated 10 million Americans have come to constitute what some have called an "underclass" (Lodge and Glass, 1982). Disproportionately black, Hispanic, and young—although by no means exclusively—its members are more or less permanently unemployed and poor. They live in desolate urban neighborhoods characterized by high rates of drug addiction, street crime, arson, and vandalism. Many residents find themselves cut off from the legitimate economy, the world of work, and political power. Ties to the larger society have weakened or been severed. A national failure to address these situations can only serve to feed crime, violence, unemployment, drug addiction, and inner-city instability.

EPILOGUE

The evidence suggests that inequality will persist in American society. Some visionaries have dreamed of bringing about an egalitarian society guided by humanitarian and cooperative principles. Yet any number of sociologists, including functionalists like Kingsley Davis and Wilbert E. Moore (1945, 1953), have raised the possibility that a classless society may not be feasible. They suggest that true classlessness would require doing away with situations in which people are differentially evaluated and rewarded for what they do and say. Pessimists point to the failures of past utopian experiments and to the fact that nations like Cuba and China have increasingly had to resort to material incentives to increase productivity. But even if material inequality could be overcome, unequal power and prestige would remain. Both can involve as much—perhaps even more—suffering and degradation as do inequalities of wealth and income.

Although we may not be able to eliminate inequality, we can work to reduce the degree of inequality in American society by eliminating both excess privilege and abject poverty. Perhaps the first step is to recognize that the *system* (not the poor individual) is responsible for most of the poverty that exists today.

The sociologist Herbert Gans (1973) points out the many ways that poverty actually is functional for our social system. The poor make possible the existence of many "respectable"positions—crime experts, prison officials, social workers, public health workers. The poor provide a pool of labor for doing the "dirty" work of a society at low cost. Their low wages subsidize the activities of the affluent, as in the case of poorly paid domestic workers who free their employers for professional, cultural, social, and civic activities. The "deviance" of the poor provides a way of justifying the dominant norms of hard work, thrift, honesty, and so on. And the poor can provide emotional satisfaction to the rest of the population by evoking their compassion and charity. The poor serve as a measuring rod of status, particularly for members of the working class. There are, of course, alternatives to these functions, for example, social workers could counsel the rich instead of the poor. Although Gans does not claim that these considerations by any means justify poverty, he finds that most of these functions would be replaced only at higher costs to other people, especially the affluent. He concludes, therefore, that poverty is likely to persist.

Stratification pervades all areas of human life. Not only is there class stratification, but also stratification based on gender (Chapter 6) and race (Chapter 12). Consequently, social rewards and burdens are distributed unequally among the members of a society. Such inequalities have implications for institutional functioning. Indeed, as detailed in the next chapter, stratification systems play a powerful role in shaping the governmental institution while in turn being influenced by its actions.

SUMMARY

This chapter examines stratification: the way societies distribute desirable resources and rank their members. Although stratification affects all members of society, it creates special suffering for the poor, whose chances of leading long, healthy, comfortable, and secure lives are far lower than those of more affluent people.

The three dimensions of stratification are income and wealth, power, and prestige. The distribution of income is unequal in this country: the poorest 20 percent of Americans earn only 5.1 percent of all income, while the wealthiest 5 percent earn 15.3 percent. Wealth is even more concentrated than income: 1 percent of the population dominate the ownership of corporate stock.

Power is the capacity to get others to act in accordance with one's wishes even when they prefer not to do so. Although sociologists debate just how concentrated power is in our society, there is widespread agreement that it is unequally distributed. The majority of Americans are relatively powerless.

Prestige is the esteem or approval granted to those whose traits or actions are deemed above average. It is a subjective matter, one that is more intangible than tangible. Consequently, people often seek to give it a tangible cast through symbolic representations. Prestige is a function of occupation, ancestry, consumptive class, success, and fame, among other things, but the most important of these is probably occupation.

Two main theories attempt to explain the determinants and consequences of stratification. According to conflict theory, the rich excercise a monopoly over society's resources and systematically deny opportunities to the poor. In contrast, functionalists argue that stratification exists because societies must entice people into important and difficult jobs by rewarding them more highly than others.

The American dream of Horatio Alger, the poor boy who becomes rich, is something of a myth. Although Americans as a group are upwardly mobile, most move up only a step or two. Status at birth plays an important role in determining occupational status. It seems that the industrialized nations of the world are surprisingly similar in their rates of social mobility.

The American dream has resided in the principle of equality of opportunity, not equality of results. The object of equality of opportunity is to free individuals from discrimination based on race, family, religion, gender, or community so that they might rise in society according to their own merits. To some extent equality of opportunity produces inequality of results. But not all Americans enjoy equality of opportunity. And some Americans view a system that allocates its rewards unequally as insensitive and unjust. All this has contributed to a tension in American life between the principle of equality of opportunity and equality of results.

The government has undertaken a variety of programs to combat poverty within the United States. In one way or another they have been designed to reduce inequality through income redistribution. The primary methods for altering the distribution of income have been income taxes, transfer payments, and subsidies for goods and services. However, recent cutbacks in government social welfare spending has cast doubt on whether the lives of the poor will be improved in the near future.

GLOSSARY

Bourgeoisie. The term Marx used to denote the owners of the means of production.

Caste system. A system of social inequality in which status is determined at birth, and people are locked into their parents' social position.

Class. A term Weber used to refer to people who occupy the same rung on the economic ladder.

Equality of opportunity. The members of a society achieve different standards of living based on their different talents and contributions.

Equality of results. The members of a society enjoy the same standard of living.

Horizontal mobility. A change in a person's position that does not alter the person's rank.

Life chances. The opportunities to realize health, long life, and happiness in a social system.

Open class system. A class system in which there are few obstacles to social mobility; positions are awarded on the basis of merit, and rank is tied to individual achievement.

Power. The capacity to get others to act in accordance with one's wishes even when they prefer not to do so.

Power elite. Mills's term for a concentrated group occupying the command posts of society and determining its direction.

Prestige. Status resulting from the possession of attributes that are regarded as admirable, and perhaps enviable, by people in a specific social setting.

Progressive tax. A tax rate that increases as a person's income increases; the opposite of a regressive tax.

Proletariat. Marx's term for the class whose members sell their skills to the owners of the means of production.

Regressive tax. A tax that takes a larger share of a poor person's income than of a rich person's; the opposite of a progressive tax.

Social mobility. The movement of people from one social position to another.

Stratification. The division of a society into layers of people who have unequal amounts of any given scarce reward or resource.

Transfer payments. Cash welfare benefits that are designed to raise the income of the poor, the unemployed, the aged, and the blind.

Vertical mobility. Upward or downward changes in a person's status.

CHAPTER 11

Power, Politics, and Economics

Whenever we have to deal with any form of organization—whether a church, a government bureau, a university committee, an army platoon, or a hospital admitting office—one of the first things we want to know is who is in charge. Once we know that, we then want to know the qualifications or credentials of those who are in command. We next attempt to establish the basis on which they exercise command (Galbraith, 1978). These and other characteristics of power touch all aspects of our social lives. Although power has many forms, the term most often calls up images of individuals who are larger than life, who may hold the destinies of millions in their hands. Such individuals may be tyrants or saints, birthright rulers or elected leaders.

One question that has intrigued laypeople and scholars alike is, "Why do people seek power?" Some psychologists say that the drive for power arises from deep-seated personality needs. Presumably those who seek power derive great satisfaction from the act of controlling others (Kipniz, 1976). But sociologists also stress a different motive. They point out that the possession of power bestows very valuable rewards (Lenski, 1966). Power can be used to acquire both wealth and prestige. For instance, the ancient Persian emperor Xerxes commanded a yearly tribute in gold bullion that today would be worth $35 million. During the late Shah of Iran's reign of thirty-seven years, he and his family amassed a fortune estimated at $3 billion! The office of the United States presidency does not bring great wealth, but it does bestow honor and respect. And comparatively speaking, the honor accorded an American president is modest. Many rulers, from Roman emperors to Japanese shoguns, have been revered and treated like gods. Even the highest-ranking nobles and ministers of state had to grovel in the monarch's presence.

It is easy to think of the enormous power of kings, emperors, or czars in highly personal terms—as if their exercise of power largely arose from their own personal attributes. This, however, is seldom the case. Power is as much a social construct as it is a personal trait. Societies create positions of power that individuals fill. The most obvious are political offices that bestow the power to make and enforce laws, redress grievances and settle disputes, carry on relations with other nations, and so forth. But power also resides outside the political sphere. Depending on the society and the era, power can accrue to other institutions as well. In a highly religious age or nation, the church and clergy will be a dominant force. In our business-oriented society it is not surprising that our economic organizations and their leaders wield much power.

In this chapter we will focus on the two major institutional centers of power in American society—the political and the economic—which, we will see, are closely interlinked. We will ask a number of key questions. What is power? What are its sources in the political and economic realms? How is power distributed in our society? Is it highly concentrated or reasonably diffuse? What broad changes are taking place in the exercise of power in this country and the world? And how do such changes affect people's lives?

THE NATURE OF POWER

What is power? What is it that an emperor, an ayatollah, and a large corporation share? **Power** is the ability to control other people's behavior—to get them to act in accordance with one's wishes even when they prefer not to do so. An individual, group, or organization that can achieve its goals, regardless of what others might want, has power.

As we saw in Chapter 10, one of the enduring features of power in almost every society is its unequal distribution. Throughout the world some individuals, some groups, some organizations wield considerably more power than others. Why is power usually distributed unequally? Essentially, social scientists have offered two opposing answers, one deriving from the functionalist and one from the conflict perspective. Each rests on a very different view of power's social role.

The Social Role of Power

Although disagreeing about why power is distributed unequally, functionalist and conflict sociologists agree that the *formal* organization of power is a relatively recent development in human history. Ten thousand years ago, when humans lived in small, homogeneous hunting-and-gathering bands, no exercise of power was required beyond the informal leadership of those with special knowledge or skills. The fact that everyone engaged in the same activities (hunting game, gathering edible plants, fashioning a few simple tools) meant that everyone shared essentially the same outlook. And because people were constantly on the move in search of their next meal, they could own only what they could carry with them. As a result, conflicts over ownership of property seldom, if ever, occurred.

With the advent of agriculture, however, all this changed. Control of the food supply through the cultivation of crops and the domestication of animals meant that not everyone needed to be involved in immediate subsistence activities, that some could be supported by the surplus produced by others. Changes in social organization rapidly followed. For one thing, populations became much larger. Permanent villages and even cities arose. For another, societies became more diverse with more elaborate divisions of labor. Since the entire population was no longer needed for food production, other full-time occupations began to emerge—warrior, artisan, healer, and so forth. And finally, the increased level of productivity and now settled way of life made the accumulation of wealth possible. Some people could hope to acquire more land, more cattle, more luxuries than others. According to both functionalists and conflict theorists, the stage was now set for the development of inequalities in the distribution of power. But each school of thought sees a different set of catalysts at work. Whereas functionalists see power as a means for achieving group ends, conflict theorists view it as a means certain people use to acquire and hold wealth and to prevent others from getting it.

The Functionalist Perspective

From a functionalist point of view, a complex society requires an unequal distribution of power if it is to survive. The reason involves the need to accomplish various communal tasks, maintain order, and unify society. Given the relatively large size, economic diversity, and potential for conflict over property in agricultural societies, far more coordination and control were needed to run them than had been required in hunting-and-gathering bands. So full-time political leaders began to emerge. They were granted the power to make and enforce the rules for the community, to redress grievances and settle disputes, and to carry on relations with other societies, including the conduct of war. Gradually these positions of leadership became institutionalized and an unequal distribution of power became a permanent feature of society. Thus the functionalists contend that it is by necessity, not by force, that some members of society hold authority over others. They argue that some inequality in power is needed to preserve, protect, and coordinate the complex social order. The alternative, according to functionalists, is chaos.

The Conflict Perspective

Conflict theorists answer that the functionalist explanation is not enough. While acknowledging that some inequality in decision making may be necessary in all but the simplest societies, they point out that leaders tend to accumulate far more power than is strictly necessary from an administrative standpoint. Conflict theorists see the amassing of great power as a result of a drive for privilege and self-aggrandizement. When advances in technology make surplus wealth possible, some people will invariably try to secure an unusually large share for themselves. Gradually a privileged elite emerges, whose wealth, power, and prestige are passed on to its descendents. Social institutions become shaped so as to support and justify this established order. From a conflict perspective, then, the major social role of power is not to preserve and protect society as a whole, but to preserve and protect the interests of a privileged few.

We will say more about these competing views of power later in this chapter. The main point to remember now is that both functionalists and conflict theorists contribute something important to an understanding of power. To fully comprehend why an unequal distribution of power arose, we must consider both the need to coordinate a complex social structure and the human desires for wealth and privilege.

Legitimacy and Authority

People comply with the wishes, requests, and orders of others for a great many reasons. But whatever the reasons, they find that in some situations they enjoy greater leeway than in others for determining whether or not they will obey. At the one extreme, people obey commands voluntarily because they believe that it is appropriate that they do so. At the other, they submit because they are coerced. **Coercion** is power that rests on the threat or use of force.

The sociologist Max Weber (1918/1949) built on the differences between these two sources of compliance in distinguishing between *legitimate* and *illegitimate* power. Legitimate power is power that is exercised with the social approval of most individuals in a group or a society. In contrast, illegitimate power is exercised without such social approval. Thus Americans may turn over their wallet to a mugger at the point of a gun because they fear they will be harmed if they do not do so. This is an example of illegitimate power. On the other hand, Americans typically pay their local taxes each year when billed by their county or city auditor. It is not that Americans enjoy paying taxes. Rather, they consider the auditor's exercise of power to be "right." Having voted to impose school and related tax levies on themselves, they view the auditor's action as legal and appropriate—as the use of legitimate power.

Weber termed legitimate power **authority**—power to which people willingly submit. Thus, if power is the *ability* to control other people's behavior, authority is the *right* to do so. Weber identified three types of authority: legal/rational, charismatic, and traditional. Each is characterized by a different base on which legitimate power rests.

Legal/Rational Authority

Legal/rational authority derives from a system of explicit rules or laws that define legitimate uses of power. Authority is vested in offices or positions, not in the people who temporarily occupy them. Thus, legal/rational authority is viewed as "a government of laws, not of people." Authority is also limited to "official business." For example, bosses have considerable authority over the way employees spend their working days, but not over how they spend their weekends. Under legal/rational authority, an officeholder can exercise power only within specified limits. People view the officeholder as carrying out his or her responsibilities within the context of a "rational" system defined by rules and regulations.

Charismatic Authority

Charismatic authority is the opposite of legal/rational authority. It derives from exceptional personal qualities that people perceive as a "gift of grace," capabilities that seem superhuman or supernatural. People follow a charismatic leader out of personal devotion. But Weber (1918/1949:249) observed: "The charismatic leader gains and maintains authority solely by proving his strength in life. If he wants to be a prophet, he must perform miracles; if he wants to be a war lord, he must perform heroic deeds." Because charismatic leaders have unique qualities, successors are not easily found. For this reason, charismatic authority is inherently unstable and does not endure for long. Examples of charismatic leaders in recent history are Mahatma Gandhi, who led the nonviolent struggle for independence in India, Martin Luther King, Jr., and Malcolm X, both black leaders in the United States, and César Chavez, a forceful spokesperson for Mexican-American farm workers.

Traditional Authority

Traditional authority lies somewhere between legal/rational authority and charismatic authority. In tradi-

The priviledged elite that emerge from an unequal distribution of power display their wealth and status in many ways, depending on the culture to which they belong. Such ceremonies, which are often elaborate and steeped in tradition, serve as symbols of elevated position. (Left, Patrick Ward/Stock, Boston; below, Wendy Watriss/Woodfin Camp.)

tional societies people tend to regard the way things have always been done as sacred; kings, queens, chiefs, priests, councils of elders, and the like are part of this sacred order. Although traditions may limit the authority of kings or queens or chiefs, these leaders do have some latitude in making decisions. Positions are typically hereditary and people feel a sense of personal loyalty to the occupants.

In practice the three types of authority Weber identified may overlap. John F. Kennedy, for example, had rational/legal authority by virtue of his election to the presidency; he also had the traditional authority that surrounds the office of the presidency and the power of charisma as well. In any given instance of legitimate power, however, authority often rests primarily on one or another of these three foundations. As we will see in the sections on economic and political power, rational/legal authority predominates in most modern industrialized states.

ECONOMIC POWER

All economic systems face the same basic problem: how to satisfy potentially unlimited human desires with limited resources. There is only so much land, water, fuel, money, labor, and talent. How resources get allocated and whose desires are satisfied reflect the distribution of power in the economic system.

Industrialization promotes the development of complex economic systems. It involves a shift from muscle power (human and animal) to machines powered by fossil fuels; from reliance on traditional ways of producing goods to the application of technical and scientific knowledge. In nontechnological societies families and villages are largely self-sufficient, but in industrial societies individuals are drawn into an intricate economy in which they are dependent on others for most of their needs. Work becomes separated from family life; people produce goods for sale to others rather than for their own use. Work also becomes more specialized: Hundreds, even thousands, of individuals play small roles in creating a single product (such as a car). The more specialized the division of labor, the more interdependent members of a society become. Traditional methods of distributing goods and services, based on reciprocal obligations between family groups, no longer suffice.

Such changes have had a profound impact on society. The scale and significance of the economic sector in modern industrial societies has taken on enormous dimensions. Power is now acquired by large corporations and their leaders to an unprecedented degree. The economist John Kenneth Galbraith (1978) points out that not until the past century and a half was economic activity thought to produce great power. Firms were small and no single firm could control the market or set prices, wages, interest rates, and costs. But by the middle of the last century, production had become dominated by those who control and supply capital.

Given the massive changes in the economic structures of modern life, an economic system has to supply answers to four major questions: (1) What goods and services should be produced (for instance, private cars or tanks), and in what quantities? (2) How should they be produced? (3) Who should receive what share of the economic pie? (4) What proportion of earnings should be spent now, and what proportion reinvested in production (building new factories, improving technology through research, and so on)? How these questions are answered depends on how economic decision making is structured. There are essentially two major types of economic systems dominating the world today—the capitalist market system and the socialist command system. To understand where economic power lies in any given society, we must understand the ideologies underlying these two economic orders. An **ideology** is a set of ideas that explains and justifies a social order.

Economic Ideologies

There are two principal economic arrangements in the world today—the capitalist market system and the socialist command system. In actual fact, however, no nation strictly follows one system or the other. All economies incorporate elements of both to different degrees. Nevertheless, it is useful to consider the ideologies underlying capitalism and socialism in their "pure" form before examining how they find expression in specific nations.

The Capitalist Market Economy

The **capitalist market economy** is recognized by friend and foe alike as a system that has created unprecedented wealth:

> The bourgeoisie . . . has accomplished wonders far surpassing Egyptian pyramids, Roman aqueducts, and Gothic cathedrals. . . . The bourgeoisie cannot exist without constantly revolutionizing the instruments of production. . . . The bourgeoisie, during its rule of scarce one hundred years, has created more massive and more colossal productive forces than have all preceding generations together.

These words might have been written by a publicist for the Chamber of Commerce or the National Association of Manufacturers. In fact, they were written by Karl Marx in *The Communist Manifesto* (Marx and Engels, 1848/1967). Although he believed that capitalism exacted a very high cost in human misery and had outlived its historical usefulness, Marx nonetheless credited capitalism with enormous vigor, particularly in its early stages. Today, proponents of capitalism insist that Marx's observation about the productive capacity of capitalism still holds true. They point to the success of capitalist economies whose output is measured in hundreds of billions of dollars. What has generated such enormous expansion of economic capacity? What is the ideology that gives capitalism its impetus?

One of the basic principles of capitalism is the concept of *private property*. In a pure capitalist system all the means of production—from farm lands to oil refineries to factories producing ball-point pens—are owned by private individuals rather than by the state. Why this stress on private ownership? Capitalist ideology holds that private property is an inalienable, almost sacred right. People in a capitalist society define fulfillment and success largely in terms of the ownership of property. And it is private ownership of the means of production that provides capitalism with its driving force—the *profit motive*.

Capitalist ideology contends that owners of businesses are strongly motivated to maximize profits. The reason is simple. By increasing profits, they also increase their own wealth and prestige. Thus it is easy to understand why being able to own productive property and earn a profit is highly desirable from the capitalist's viewpoint. But why would society in general also endorse the profit motive? The answer is less obvious but equally compelling. Capitalist ideology holds that the drive for ever-greater profits ensures that entrepreneurs will produce only the goods and services consumers want the most and at the lowest possible price. Entrepreneurs who persist in producing things that consumers do not want will soon be driven out of business. And if the cost of producing a certain good is higher than the price that consumers are willing to pay for it, then no profit can be earned and production methods must be reassessed. The result is that capitalists are constantly looking for both new markets to enter and new technology to lower their manufacturing costs. From society's standpoint, therefore, resources are used with the greatest possible efficiency. Hence everyone benefits, not just the entrepreneur. When people are permitted to pursue their self-interest, society achieves its greatest good.

But what is to prevent an enterprising capitalist from charging exorbitant prices in order to maximize profits? Capitalist ideology says that because a capitalist market economy is characterized by *free competition*, no one entrepreneur is able to earn more than a "normal" profit. If one firm's products are overpriced, consumers will simply reject them in favor of similar products produced by other firms. The same competitive forces presumably operate in the market for productive resources. If one firm tries to augment its profits by paying workers less than the going wage, its best employees will find work elsewhere, resulting in the lowering of the quality of the firm's product. In the end, such a firm may be driven out of business, or at least be forced to pay higher wages. The result, of course, is that everyone else benefits. Products are priced fairly, workers are paid fairly, resources are used efficiently, and capitalists earn a normal profit.

Does a capitalist market economy, in its idealized form, exist anywhere today? The answer is a simple no. Although the United States is generally considered the prime example of such a system, the American economy actually contains many features that do not conform to the pure capitalist market model.

First, the means of production are not always privately owned. The Tennessee Valley Authority (TVA), the mammoth public utility that supplies electric power in portions of the Southeast, is a good illustration of an enterprise owned and operated by the government. Likewise, a number of businesses (such as the Communications Satellite Corporation) operate under joint government/private ownership. And government's indirect involvement in business is even more widespread.

Competition will influence the success of every shop in Detroit's Fairlane mall. Those retailers who offer the goods consumers want at prices they are willing to pay will succeed, while those who cannot market their products competitively will not. (Donald Dietz/Stock, Boston.)

Research and the defense, electronics, and oil industries are heavily dependent on government expenditures. In effect, the government has become their silent partner. One result is that American tax dollars often support projects that ordinarily might not be profitable in a pure market economy but that the public nevertheless wants. In sum, the American economy is not a system based strictly on the profit motive.

In addition, the fact that most business corporations today are owned by a large number of stockholders, rather than by a single entrepreneur, may also undercut the profit motive. Because those who manage the nation's productive assets are not necessarily those who own them, the drive to earn the greatest possible profit may not be so powerful. In fact, some have argued that in a modern capitalist economy the goal of corporate growth frequently supersedes the goal of maximizing profits. We will say more about the effects of the separation of corporate ownership and management later in this chapter.

Another feature of the American economy that does not conform to the pure capitalist model is that entrepreneurs are not always free to enter any markets they please. Part of the reason is strictly financial. Business firms in some industries have grown so huge that it is almost impossible for an entirely new company to enter the field on a reasonably competitive footing. The start-up costs are enormous. Too much time is needed to construct factories and assembly lines before any revenue can be generated. In addition, government has restricted entry into certain potentially lucrative markets. For instance, banks, television stations, and some other institutions must be chartered by governmental agencies before they can operate. And government also severely limits entry into other markets through licensing, manufacturing restrictions, and various regulatory conditions.

Just as American entrepreneurs are not always free to enter any markets they please, so too American consumers are not always free to purchase whatever products they desire. Part of the constraint on the freedom of consumers comes from limited purchasing power. In a pure market system, all people can presumably "vote" with their dollars for the goods and services they want. In this way their economic voices are heard. The poor, however, with their subsistence incomes, have little to say in such a system. And in the United States, where some 32 million people live below the poverty level, this is a substantial number of economically "disenfranchised" (see Chapter 10). And even for those who do have the money to "vote" in the American marketplace, consumer choice may be constrained. For instance, many critics say that with the advent of huge firms and their enormous advertising budgets, much of consumer demand is artifically created. It is seldom the buyers who initiate the desire for a new toothpaste or a new detergent; it is usually the firms that manufacture

Many forces, including advertising, make the model of the pure market system more of an ideal than a reality. (Nancy Pierce/Photo Researchers.)

these products who promote them through well-financed advertising campaigns.

Finally, contrary to the model of a pure market system, the forces of supply and demand do not always set prices in the American economy. When only a few large firms control an industry, they may agree to set prices at whatever the market will bear. Under this agreement, termed **oligopoly** by economists, consumers have little recourse because of the absence of other supplies. Within Western industrial nations, the oligopolistic sector is the dominant power in the economy. In addition, government also regulates pricing. It imposes a minimum wage, for example, and in some industries sets price ceilings.

Yet despite these departures from the philosophy of a strictly market economy, the United States still strongly adheres to the basic values of capitalism. Private ownership, free enterprise, and the profit motive are all widely accepted as basic cornerstones of our economic system. An alternative arrangement is the modern command economy.

The Command Economy

The modern command economy arose in response to some of the abuses and excesses of nineteenth-century industrial capitalism—long hours, low wages, dangerous work conditions, and child labor. Particularly influential were the criticisms raised by the social philosopher Karl Marx. Marx believed that far from promoting the greatest good for society as a whole, capitalism benefits mainly the owners of the means of production, the capitalists. He argued that the capitalists were motivated only by the desire to maximize their profits and so had no reason to pay workers more than the minimum needed to keep them at their jobs. And when machines are widely used and few skilled jobs are available, this amount can be extremely low—sometimes only enough to keep the workers and their families alive at the barest subsistence level. Thus the economic freedom that nineteenth-century capitalists extolled was to Marx simply a means of exploiting the workers (the proletariat) to the advantage of the bourgeoisie (the capitalists).

Marx believed that through a long process of self-awareness, discussion, and organization on their own behalf, workers would eventually rise up against the capitalists and wrest control of the means of production. In Marx's vision, capitalism would ultimately be replaced by a classless society. Although he did not describe in detail the economic system that would bring about this egalitarianism, he did propose its basic elements. First, it would be socialistic, meaning that all the means of production would be collectively owned. And second, it would be what economists have come to call a **command economy,** meaning that economic decision making would not be left to the vagaries of the market but would be placed in the hands of a central planning board. This board would have the enormous task of determining what goods society would produce and in what quantities, and where and how it would produce them.

The first modern command system was established in the Soviet Union after the Bolshevik Revolution of 1917. Many other socialist societies have since emerged, but the U.S.S.R. is still the country that most immediately comes to mind when many Americans think of a socialist state. The Soviet Union, however, does not adhere strictly to the model of a command economy, just as the United States does not strictly follow the capitalist market model. For example, although virtually all the means of production and capital assets are state-owned in the U.S.S.R., housing is not. About half of all urban homes and almost all rural ones are privately owned. Nor is the market mechanism of supply and demand completely absent in the Soviet Union. For example, a small "capitalist" sector is permitted in which peasant farmers can sell what they have grown on small private plots of land. And doctors, lawyers, carpenters, and others conduct private practices. Finally, the Soviets have found that sizable incentives are needed to attract people to positions of responsibility. As a result, the U.S.S.R. has a privileged managerial class that closely resembles those in capitalist states (Davies and Shaw, 1978; Hecht, 1978).

Yet in spite of these deviations from strict socialist philosophy, the Soviets adhere to very different economic values than we do under capitalism. They value collective (not private) ownership of the means of production, centralized planning for the collective good (not decentralized planning by individual firms and consumers), and an ultimate vision of a truly classless society (not simply the equality of economic opportunity that we value). Many Americans do not understand the ideological appeal of the Soviet system and believe that military power is the Soviet Union's sole source of strength. However, close observers of the Soviet people note that the communist ideology provides Soviet citizens with a consistent view of history and of world events and makes them feel that life has a basic, underlying meaning (Satter, 1983). In the section that follows, we will explore the kind of economic sytems to which our own capitalist values have given rise.

Modern Capitalism in Action

In 1912 over 170,000 Model-T Fords rolled out of the Ford Motor Company's streamlined new factory in Highland Park, Michigan. This was six times the output of any other car maker and nearly ten times Ford's own output just three years earlier. The secret was Ford's introduction of numerous labor-saving techniques—from a machine that drilled 45 holes in an engine block in one precision movement, to an automated device that painted 2,000 tire rims a day. The result was that the price of the Model-T fell dramatically, putting it within the reach of millions of Americans. Ford's achievements were considered a milestone in modern production methods. But they were only a beginning. In the years that followed, capitalist nations made countless other technological strides. They invented radio, television, and other advanced means of communication. They developed computers so sophisticated that they could process and store more information than an army of mathematicians. They designed automated factories that could make, package, and ship a staggering number of products. Today a single automotive plant can turn out hundreds of thousands of cars and trucks a year.

The Corporation

This impressive technological progress was inevitably accompanied by a transformation in the structure of business. To produce such sophisticated equipment in such enormous quantities required economic organization on an unprecedented scale. Thus arose the giant capitalist corporation. A **corporation** is an organization created by law that has an ongoing existence and powers and liabilities that are distinct from those of its owners and employees. For example, if you have an accident because the steering mechanism on your new car jams, you sue General Motors, not the engineer who designed the car or the mechanic who neglected to tighten a bolt. A corporation, in other words, is a legal entity in its own right. Individual personnel—even corporation presidents—come and go but the corporation lives on. This fact gives the corporate form of business organization many advantages. Perhaps most important, it enables corporations to raise huge sums of working capital. As a legal entity, a corporation can sell shares in its ownership. And because the liability of corporate owners is limited—because lawsuits or bankruptcy cannot touch their personal assets—investment in a corporation is highly attractive. Many corporations are owned by literally thousands of stockholders. The collective resources provided by these investors are immense. Thus the ability of the corporation to raise large sums of capital makes it well suited to an era of large-scale industry.

An examination of the actual resources controlled by the thirty largest American corporations indicates how enormous many modern corporations have become (see Table 11.1). Specifically, Exxon, the largest Ameri-

TABLE 11.1 The 30 Largest U.S. Industrial Corporations, Ranked by Sales, 1983

Rank	Company	Sales	Assets		Net Income (Profits)		Employees	
1983		$ Thousands	$ Thousands	Rank	$ Thousands	Rank	Number	Rank
1	Exxon	88,561,134	62,962,990	1	4,977,957	2	156,000	9
2	General Motors	74,581,600	45,694,500	2	3,730,200	3	691,000	1
3	Mobil	54,607,000	35,072,000	4	1,503,000	11	178,100	7
4	Ford Motor	44,454,600	23,868,900	9	1,866,900	6	380,077	2
5	International Business Machines	40,180,000	37,243,000	3	5,485,000	1	369,545	3
6	Texaco	40,068,000	27,199,000	5	1,233,000	12	54,683	62
7	E.I. du Pont de Nemours	35,378,000	24,432,000	7	1,127,000	13	159,231	8
8	Standard Oil (Indiana)	27,635,000	25,805,000	6	1,868,000	5	56,734	55
9	Standard Oil of California	27,342,000	24,010,000	8	1,590,000	8	40,091	92
10	General Electric	26,797,000	23,288,000	10	2,024,000	4	340,000	4
11	Gulf Oil	26,581,000	20,964,000	13	978,000	14	42,700	83
12	Atlantic Richfield	25,147,036	23,282,307	11	1,547,875	9	49,693	70
13	Shell Oil	19,678,000	22,169,000	12	1,633,000	7	35,185	113
14	Occidental Petroleum	19,115,700	11,775,400	21	566,700	25	41,369	87
15	U.S. Steel	16,869,000	19,314,000	14	(1,161,000)*	489	98,722	19
16	Phillips Petroleum	15,249,000	13,094,000	18	721,000	18	28,400	143
17	Sun	14,730,000	12,466,000	19	453,000	34	37,804	104
18	United Technologies	14,669,265	8,720,059	32	509,173	28	193,700	6
19	Tenneco	14,353,000	17,994,000	15	716,000	19	97,000	20
20	ITT	14,155,408	13,966,744	17	674,510	21	278,000	5
21	Chrysler	13,240,399	6,772,300	38	700,900	20	81,478	29
22	Procter & Gamble	12,452,000	8,135,000	34	866,000	17	61,700	50
23	R.J. Reynolds Industries	11,957,000	9,874,000	26	881,000	16	96,228	21
24	Getty Oil	11,600,024	10,385,050	23	494,314	29	19,440	192
25	Standard Oil (Ohio)	11,599,000	16,362,000	16	1,512,000	10	44,000	77
26	AT&T Technologies	11,154,700	9,087,500	30	50,700	229	142,000	11
27	Boeing	11,129,000	7,471,000	36	355,000	44	84,600	28
28	Dow Chemical	10,951,000	11,981,000	20	334,000	47	54,500	64
29	Allied	10,351,000	7,647,000	35	98,000	145	117,750	15
30	Eastman Kodak	10,170,000	10,928,000	22	565,000	26	125,500	14

* Loss rather than profit

Source: Reprinted from the FORTUNE Directory by permission;

can corporation on the basis of its sales and assets, had profits of nearly $4.2 billion in 1982, more than the gross national products of Nepal, Bolivia, Panama, Iceland, Zambia, and a number of other nations. Its sales (more than $97 billion) exceeded the gross national products of most nations of the world. Corporate control of such enormous resources has vast ramifications for national life. Thus when hard times hit the automotive industry in the spring of 1980, General Motors (GM) laid off a total of 155,000 workers within a single week—a number equivalent to the population of many small American cities! Thus the corporation has become the main locus of economic control in the United States.

The National Power of Large Corporations

There is no disputing the fact that a small number of large corporations control a disproportionate share of the American economy. In 1982 the top 500 companies accounted for nearly $2.4 trillion in sales, equal to about 78 percent of the gross national product of the United States. Moreover, the largest 808 firms employed 21.6 million people, or one out of every five working Americans. Of these 21.6 million workers, 20 percent were employed in ten firms (*Forbes*, 1983). Of the nation's industrial firms, 259 corporations own 65 percent of all corporate assets and account for nearly 70 percent of all profits (U.S. Bureau of the Census, 1983) There is no sign that the economic share of the largest corporations is decreasing. In fact, the last several decades have seen a steady trend towards greater and greater concentration of wealth and earnings in the hands of a relatively few firms.

As noted earlier in the chapter, many American industries are *oligopolies*—industries dominated by only a few very large firms. In the manufacture of products as diverse as automobiles, chewing gum, tennis balls, razor blades, cigarettes, detergents, steel, canned soups, and cameras, the four largest firms are responsible for over 80 percent of total United States output. Overall, about 60 percent of manufacturing in this country is oligopolistic. In addition, there are signs that the trend toward increasing concentration is now spreading to the economy's service sector (those firms that provide the public with services rather than tangible goods). The fifty largest banks in the nation employ about a third of all banking personnel, and about half of all those in the insurance industry work for the fifty largest insurance firms (Heilbroner, 1976). In short, the trend toward oliogopoly seems likely to continue, at least into the near future.

Size and wealth in and of themselves do not guarantee power. The issue is whether large corporations are able to make decisions that significantly affect others. There are reasons for thinking that they do.

First, economists point out that when a few corporations provide nearly all of a particular product, those companies are virtually free from the restraints that exist in a competitive market. They can charge as much for the product as consumers will pay before they turn to less desirable substitutes. And through extensive advertising, corporations can often ensure that demand for their product will remain high despite an inflated price tag. In addition, by taking out patents, controlling raw materials, and either convincing the government to suppress competition or colluding with other corporations, oligopolies can prevent new firms from entering the market. They can also buy up other companies—competitors, suppliers, manufacturers of related or different products—and become a **conglomerate**, thus controlling even larger amounts of resources and greater numbers of jobs through subsidiaries.

Second, huge corporations have the power to influence a large number of people because they decide when and at what pace to invest, thus determining the rate of growth not only of their own corporations but of related industries as well. For example, reluctance to modernize steel production facilities in this country caused shortages in the 1950s and again in the 1970s. Our mills are outdated (in comparison with those of other nations), and we now import much of our steel—which affects employment rates, the price of anything made with steel, and even taxes (because steel is vital in the manufacture of defense equipment).

Third, large corporations are free to decide what new technologies to explore through research and development and what innovations will be translated into new products and services. Technology has a profound impact on all aspects of social life (as we will see in Chapter 19). If, for example, Ford and General Motors had put all of their assets into developing high-quality public transportation (such as electric trains) instead of private automobiles, this country's settlement patterns, dating habits, and even foreign policy (in particular, American relations with oil-producing nations) would be quite different from what they are today.

The power of giant corporations is not confined to the economy. Corporations wield considerable political power as well. On the state and local levels, national firms can promise to build or expand in a given area, or to withdraw from that area if legislatures do not pass the taxes, zoning regulations, and road plans that suit them. They can, with certain restrictions, also help finance the election campaigns of public officials—an especially effective tool today when media advertising is so essential to reaching voters, and so costly.

The growth of the automobile industry during this century has had a profound impact on American life. The Los Angeles freeway system shown here, for example, developed in response to a life-style based on quick, readily available personal transportation. Had public transportation taken precedence over the automobile, the landscape of L.A. and most other American cities would look quite different. (Craig Aurness/West Light.)

At the national level, corporations also use campaign contributions to influence politics, but they employ several other tactics as well. For example, most giant business concerns hire full-time lobbyists to persuade Washington officials that certain legislation should or should not be passed. In fact, many members of Congress and the federal bureaucracy depend heavily on the voluminous information that Washington lobbyists provide. In addition, a number of large corporations have established very close relationships with the federal agencies that hire them to provide goods and services. Such relationships are symbiotic: both the corporate executives and federal officials recognize their common interests. Since each could not exist without the other, they tend to see things eye to eye. The most widely publicized example of such intimate ties are those that exist between firms producing military equipment and the U.S. Department of Defense, which annually awards military contracts in excess of $100 billion. President Dwight D. Eisenhower warned in his "Farewell Address" in 1961 that this "military-industrial complex" might some day grow beyond the bounds of democratic control. Finally, corporate leaders can influence national politics through outright bribery and collusion. Although many observers feel that such corruption is more prevalent at the local level, federal officials are certainly not immune from it. In 1980, for example, seven members of Congress were indicted and later convicted for accepting bribes from FBI undercover agents posing as the representatives of a phony Arab oil sheik—the famous Abscam cases.

The Global Power of Multinationals

As large, profitable, and powerful as American-based corporations may be, the scope of these organizations seems limited indeed when compared with that of the multinationals. A **multinational corporation** is a private business firm with operations and subsidiaries in many different countries. Crossing national boundaries to obtain raw materials and to market goods is a tradition that dates back to the Phoenician glass merchants and even earlier. But the actual integration of peoples from all lands into a world economy began with the expansion and conquests of European nations in the fifteenth century. Colonial territories exported spices, coffee, tea, and tobacco to Europe. Later they became suppliers of agricultural and mineral raw materials. However, today's multinational corporations are not simply buying and selling abroad; they are actually *producing* there. For instance, Exxon, the world's largest oil company, operates approximately 70 refineries in 37 countries. In 1981, 70.1 percent of its total revenues and 56.7 percent of its profits derived from sources outside the United States (see Table 11.2).

Not all multinational corporations are American. European and Japanese multinational companies include the mammoth Royal Dutch/Shell Group (oil—Netherlands/United Kingdom), Mitsui (wholesaler—Japan), and the Volkswagen Group (automotive—Germany). Multinational corporations do not consider foreign factories and markets as adjuncts to home operations. Instead, they view the entire world as a single economic system.

Critics charge that multinationals are too big, too rich, and too powerful. It is nearly impossible for many national governments to impose control over such enormous firms. The annual incomes from sales of big oil firms such as Exxon, Mobil, and Texaco and big auto

TABLE 11.2 The 30 Largest U.S. Multinationals, 1981

Rank	Company	Foreign Revenue as Percent of Total Revenue	Foreign Profits as Percent of Total Profits
1	Exxon	70.1%	56.7%
2	Mobil	62.9	63.1
3	Texaco	67.0	59.7
4	Standard Oil Calif	53.9	39.9
5	Ford Motor	48.4	NA
6	General Motors	25.0	NA
7	IBM	48.1	37.1
8	Phibro-Salomon	53.3	97.4
9	Citicorp	62.0	54.0
10	Intl Tel & Tel	47.3	58.8
11	Gulf Oil	36.7	47.0
12	BankAmerica	52.7	55.1
13	Chase Manhattan	65.0	60.0
14	E.I. Du Pont de Nemours	29.5	17.0
15	General Electric	20.9	17.9
16	Dow Chemical	47.9	38.2
17	Standard Oil Indiana	16.4	34.0
18	Occidental Petroleum	31.7	79.8
19	J.P. Morgan	63.3	67.4
20	Safeway Stores	24.7	76.4
21	Sun Co	25.6	0.6
22	Manufacturers Hanover	53.3	47.6
23	Eastman Kodak	38.0	21.7
24	Xerox	44.5	42.2
25	Procter & Gamble	32.8	19.5
26	Goodyear	41.0	38.3
27	Phillips Petroleum	21.3	51.1
28	F.W. Woolworth	40.9	48.6
29	Union Carbide	31.4	27.6
30	Colgate-Palmolive	58.7	63.2

NA = Not available

Source: Forbes, July 5, 1982, pp. 126–127. "The Largest U.S. Multinationals, 1981."

Not only can the financial resources of multinational companies affect a country's economy, but the products themselves may also have an enormous impact on a country's culture. This process has been called "cocalonialism." (Owen Franken.)

companies such as General Motors exceed the gross national products of most nations in which they do business. Indeed, the financial resources of major multinational corporations are so large that these companies often can manipulate the economies of the nations in which they operate. For example, should a multinational decide that a country's currency is overvalued or unsafe, they can shift to another country's currency. Or if they believe that a particular nation is politically unsympathetic or unstable, they can take their investments elsewhere. Such decisions have a profound impact on the wealth of nations.

Furthermore, by shifting assets and operations abroad, they are able to avoid government regulations, high taxes, and labor unions. For example, by selling to their own divisions, they can take a loss in countries with high taxes and show a gain in countries with low taxes.

Moreover, global corporations often have a significant impact on the political and social institutions of the countries in which they operate, especially developing nations. For instance, when multinationals become extensively established in a developing country, equality of income distribution frequently declines and overall economic development often lags (Bornschier and Ballmer-Cao, 1979; Bornschier and Hoby, 1981). The reason has to do with the efforts of multinationals to further their own growth. These giant corporations may use their substantial economic and political influence to keep taxes and wages low and to foster other conditions that increase their profitability (Chase-Dunn, 1975). At their most blatant and aggressive, such efforts may involve bribery and other illicit dealings, as well as deliberate attempts to topple unsympathetic regimes. The most highly publicized example of the latter was ITT's spending of $1 million to overthrow Chile's socialist president Salvador Allende. As a result of the embarrassment such disclosures have caused, some multinationals have established specific policies trying to limit their involvement in a host country's politics (U.N. Commission, 1978).

But such gestures on the part of multinationals only indicate that a new economic power structure is emerging—one that transcends the political power of nations. Increasingly, the managers of GM, IBM, Pepsico, General Electric, Pfizer, Shell, Volkswagen, Exxon, and perhaps a hundred other global corporations influence the prosperity, balance of payments, and political strength of the countries in which they operate. Yet even so, corporate managers do not have a completely free hand. Workers have organized themselves into labor unions as a counterbalancing force to the growth of mammoth corporations. And governments in Western nations have placed curbs on the unrestricted use of corporate power. However, the emergence of gigantic multinational corporations has provided new dimensions to the exercise of power by organizations pursuing economic gain. This has raised the question of who controls the corporations.

Who Controls the Corporations?

Who precisely are the decision makers who apparently wield so much power in the capitalist world? Has the growth of giant corporations created a new group of powerholders?

In a classic work entitled *The Modern Corporation and Private Property* (1932/1968:vii–viii), Adolph Berle and Gardiner Means proclaim that:

> The translation of perhaps two thirds of the industrial wealth of [a] country from individual ownership to ownership by the large, publicly financed corporations vitally changes the lives of property owners, the lives of workers, and the methods of property tenure.

In the "old days" (the early nineteenth century), owner-entrepreneurs ran their own businesses, made all key decisions, and reaped the profits or suffered the losses of their economic policies. With the rise of the corporation, however, ownership became divorced from management.

The modern corporation collects wealth from small and large investors who are willing to take risks for a profit-making enterprise, and it turns the actual operation of the firm (setting policy and making daily decisions) over to professional managers. As a result, ownership is said to have become diffuse and passive. The thousands of people who own stock in IBM, for example, do not know one another or meet regularly. Moreover, they lack the technical and legal expertise necessary to make decisions for "their" company. So long as the company makes a profit, the managers (who have the cohesion and know-how stockholders lack) are free to do what they think best. And what they think best may entail "feathering their own nests" with substantial bonuses, stock-option rights, and lavish offices and expense accounts (Bronson and Morse, 1983). Largely freed from the dictates of stockholders, the overriding concerns of management become organizational interests rather than profits. In sum, the owners do not manage, and the managers do not own (although managers receive substantial salaries and may own some stock). Hence, according to Berle and Means, corporate ownership and corporate control are two very different things.

Many social scientists disagree, however. An accumulating body of evidence suggests that profits do remain the primary concern of corporate managers. Despite the growth in their size and complexity, corporations still continue to be basically capitalist in goal and in practice (Herman, 1981). And profit performance remains the primary standard for judging corporate officials. A decline in profits over a number of years is a strong predictor that an executive will be fired (James and Soref, 1981). Indeed, a frequently heard criticism of large corporations is that their managers are too oriented to short-term profits and that they neglect long-term research, development, and plant modernization (Bluestone and Harrison, 1982; Magaziner and Reich, 1982). A key reason is that managers change jobs so often that they need concern themselves only with short-range programs.

Other constraints also operate on corporate managers so that the capitalist character of large corporations is not altered (Useem, 1980). Some stockholders are far from passive bystanders in the running of the modern corporation. As noted in Chapter 10, 1 percent of the American population dominates the ownership of corporate stock. And a few thousand investors have huge economic holdings. Institutional stockholding by mutual funds, pension funds, and bank trust departments has emerged in recent decades as a particularly powerful force influencing corporate policies. Portfolio managers for these institutional investors control more than 50 percent of the nation's corporate assets. Today, private pension assets alone exceed $750 billion and are expected to grow to $3 trillion by 1995 (Wallace, 1983). Similarly, mergers and conglomerate expansions have brought many companies under the control of other companies (Mintz and Schwartz, 1981*b*). Thus many corporations that appear to be directed by their managements are significantly influenced by outside institutions.

Another source of nonmanagement influence derives from **interlocking directorates**—networks of people serving on the boards of directors of two or more corporations. Such director exchanges promote economic dependency among the corporations and facilitate social relationships that produce cohesion among corporate leaders. In particular, major New York financial institutions (for instance, Citicorp, Chase Manhattan, and J.P. Morgan) are the hub of many corporate interlocks (Mintz and Schwartz, 1981*a*, 1981*b*). Large banks also control the credit lines so essential for the funding of corporate operations (Useem, 1980; Glasberg, 1981; Gobel and Koenig, 1981).

In summary, then, Berle and Means are probably

The people who sit in boardrooms such as this often have extensive interlocking connections with each other and with other corporations. For example, the twenty-two Citicorp directors elected to that board in 1984 also sat on the boards of over fifty major corporations. A third of Citicorp's directors hold graduate business or law degrees from Harvard, and half of them belong to the Washington-based Business Council. (Jacques Charlas/Stock, Boston.)

right that in today's corporations a great deal of authority rests in the hands of professional managers. But this does not mean that capitalists—owners of the means of production—are now passive and powerless. "The fact that the king allows his chief minister to govern while things are going well," writes French sociologist Maurice Duverger (1974:121–122), ". . . does not mean the elimination of the power of the throne." In much the same way, there is little doubt that capitalists still play a powerful role in the modern market economy. Moreover, it is likely that capitalist political organizations will be closely involved in shaping our economic future. It is to these political organizations, therefore, that we now turn.

POLITICAL POWER

A political system consists of the individuals, groups, organizations, and procedures responsible for "making and carrying out . . . binding policies related to crucial problems facing a society" (Andrain, 1975:49). All political systems, at all times and in all places, confront four basic problems. The first is *creating a common political identity*. The many civil wars that have erupted in sub-Saharan Africa, where tribal loyalties are often stronger than nationalism, suggest how difficult this can be. The second problem is *establishing power*. A government that is unable to implement its policies—to secure compliance from its citizens—is no government at all. The third problem is *legitimizing power*—that is, establishing authority. No political system can long rely exclusively on force. Leaders have to justify their decisions and gain acceptance for their policies. Fourth is the crucial problem of *producing and distributing goods and services*. As we pointed out earlier, this problem is not solved solely by the economy. Governments set broad economic policies, regulate business practices, and control the use and distribution of a great many resources. For this reason politics is sometimes defined as the method by which society determines who gets what, when, and how (Lasswell, 1936). And this is why businesses seek to influence and control government decision making.

Political Ideology and the State

In any political system the center of power is the **state.** The state differs from other organizations in a society in that it sucessfully "claims the monopoly of the legitimate use of physical force within a given territory" (Weber, 1918/1949:78) such as in forcibly arresting, jailing, and in some cases killing people. This monopoly on the legitimate use of force is what defines the state.

There are great differences in how states exercise their power and in the role the people play in directing state policies. In a **democratic state,** authority ideally derives from the law, rooted in the consent of the people. But the rulers and the ruled ideally believe in the principle of due process. The government has the power to implement its policies (opposition groups do not succeed in immobilizing the government), but that power is limited. Individuals or parties are granted only temporary authority. Other groups have the right and also the resources—including numbers of people, organizations, knowledge, and private property—to challenge government decisions. The government guides but does not control the economy; private firms compete in a market system. Politics is based on the belief that power should not be used in capricious or arbitrary ways, and on adherence to the democratic rules of the game—such as the holding of free and open elections, acceptance of the will of the majority, and respect for the right of minorities to work within the system in an effort to change policies they dislike. The democratic state does not claim exclusive, unquestioning loyalty (Andrain, 1975). If the state oversteps the powers people have entrusted to it, the people have a right—even a duty—to oppose it.

In contrast, in a **totalitarian state,** the centralized government does not recognize or tolerate parties of differing opinion. Authority rests on ideological and/or personal grounds. Leaders justify their right to rule by claiming that they embody an ideological cause. Power tends to be concentrated in the hands of one ruling party, which is permanently identified with the government: The party and the state are one. The government ideally directs all economic activity. It also seeks to create ideological uniformity by controlling education, the mass media, and the arts and literature. The power of authorities is so great that it may be exercised in capricious and apparently arbitrary ways. The resulting atmosphere of anxiety and insecurity compels citizens to demonstrate active loyalty to the state (Andrain, 1975).

The contrasts between these two systems are obvious, and we are accustomed to think of states as *either* democratic *or* totalitarian. However, many nation-states are neither one nor the other. Most "rulers know," writes Barrington Moore (1980:18), "that there are certain bounds to their power beyond which they cannot expect compliance. . . . And to remain rulers, they require [compliant] subjects." Thus efforts at totalitarianism are seldom as complete as our definition of the term suggests they might be. Whenever rulers consistently overstep the limits of their authority—when they seek personal gain to the detriment of the social order—they are frequently challenged and even overthrown. The late Shah of Iran is a good example. He amassed an incredible fortune at the expense of society. He misused the state's instruments of violence against Iranian subjects, and he challenged the religious order that mobilized opposition against him until he was driven from power.

In much the same way that totalitarian regimes are seldom completely totalitarian, democratic regimes are seldom completely democratic. Even states that we tend to consider highly democratic usually lack at least some of the elements included in a strict definition of democracy. The American political system is a case in point, as we will see in the following sections.

Political Power in America

The term *democracy* derives from the Greek words *demos* meaning "the people" and *kratis* meaning "authority"—hence the classic definition of democracy as government by the people. Most Americans consider their own political system to be a prime example of democracy. Yet there is a wide gap between the ideal of government by the people and the reality of popular participation in American politics. Traditionally, there have been three major channels of public participation in American politics: individual participation through voting, and group participation through political parties and through interest groups. Let us consider the extent and type of participation that actually occurs through each.

The American Voter

The American political system is based on mass participation through periodic elections. Ideally, the principle of one person, one vote offsets inequalities of class, sex, and race in our society. But because many Americans fail to vote, the validity of this assumption is question-

TABLE 11.3 Percent of Voting Age Population Voting for President

1932	52.4%
1936	56.9
1940	58.9
1944	56.0
1948	51.1
1952	61.9
1956	59.3
1960	63.1
1964	61.8
1968	60.7
1972	55.4
1976	54.4
1980	53.9

Source: U.S. Bureau of Census.

able. Whereas in Western Europe 80 to 90 percent of the voters regularly turn out for elections, only 53.9 percent of Americans eligible to vote did so in the 1980 presidential election. And 1980 was not an unusual year. Voter participation has been declining since 1960 (see Table 11.3). The turnout for off-year (nonpresidential) elections is lower: In 1982 it was 48.5 percent.

Polls show that the people least likely to exercise their right to vote are the poorly educated, those with low incomes, and those who are unemployed (Clymer, 1983*a*). Thus, to the extent that the political preferences of these categories of people differ from those of other Americans, their views are not being adequately represented at the ballot box. If America has a government "by the people," it is clearly only by some of them.

Why the Low Voter Turnout?

Several explanations of low voter turnout have been proposed. Some political observers have suggested that a majority of Americans feel that their votes do not matter, that things will go on much as they are whether or not they vote. Recent polls suggest that there may be some truth to this assertion (See Figure 11.1). But a majority of Americans believes that it does make a difference which candidates are elected and to which political party a candidate belongs. Moreover, individuals are more likely to vote and participate in politics when they feel their interests are at stake. Hence, youth increased its political involvement in the late 1960s and early 1970s as did the unemployed in the 1982 election (Beck and Jennings, 1979; Clymer, 1983*a*). People seem to vote their resentments and fears; when there is a dearth of each, they are less likely to vote (Adelman, 1980).

There is probably no single reason for the relatively low voter turnout found in the United States. Yet, by itself, a large voter turnout does not necessarily signal a strong, healthy democracy. Voter turnout in totalitarian nations such as Romania, Albania, and East Germany hovers somewhere over 99 percent. And Sierra Leone set a "world record" in June 1977 when 2,215,586 votes were cast by an electorate of 2,152,454, a stunning 103 percent turnout.

Class Voting

But what about those Americans who do go to the polls? How do they make their political choices? According to the profile of voters that emerged from studies conducted during the 1940s and 1950s, American voters paid little attention to political events, had little understanding of the issues, and felt removed from the political arena. They voted less for a principle than for "their" group—social, religious, ethnic, racial, or regional. An individual's political preferences were usually solidly group-anchored. For instance, they often voted the way trusted members of their social class voted, which usually meant consistently voting "the party." Everybody knew the Republicans were for big business, the Democrats for the underdog. Voting was an exercise in party loyalty, and party membership was determined largely by social class.

Then, during the turmoil of the 1960s, this began to change. Studies suggested that social class was no longer a decisive factor in American elections. In 1972, for example, Democrats attracted only 5 percent more blue-collar voters than Republicans did. However, the 1976 election presented a different picture. The Democratic candidate Jimmy Carter bested the Republican Gerald Ford among blue-collar voters, 57 percent to 41 percent. Then in the 1980 presidential election, the Republican Ronald Reagan narrowly carried the blue-collar voters, 47 percent to 46 percent (Clymer, 1980*b*). The switches in voting patterns from one election to the next have led some political observers like Gerald M. Pomper (1975) to conclude that Americans vote by class when, and only when economic issues are at stake. Otherwise they vote for the *candidate*.

FIGURE 11.1 American Beliefs Regarding the Significance of Elections

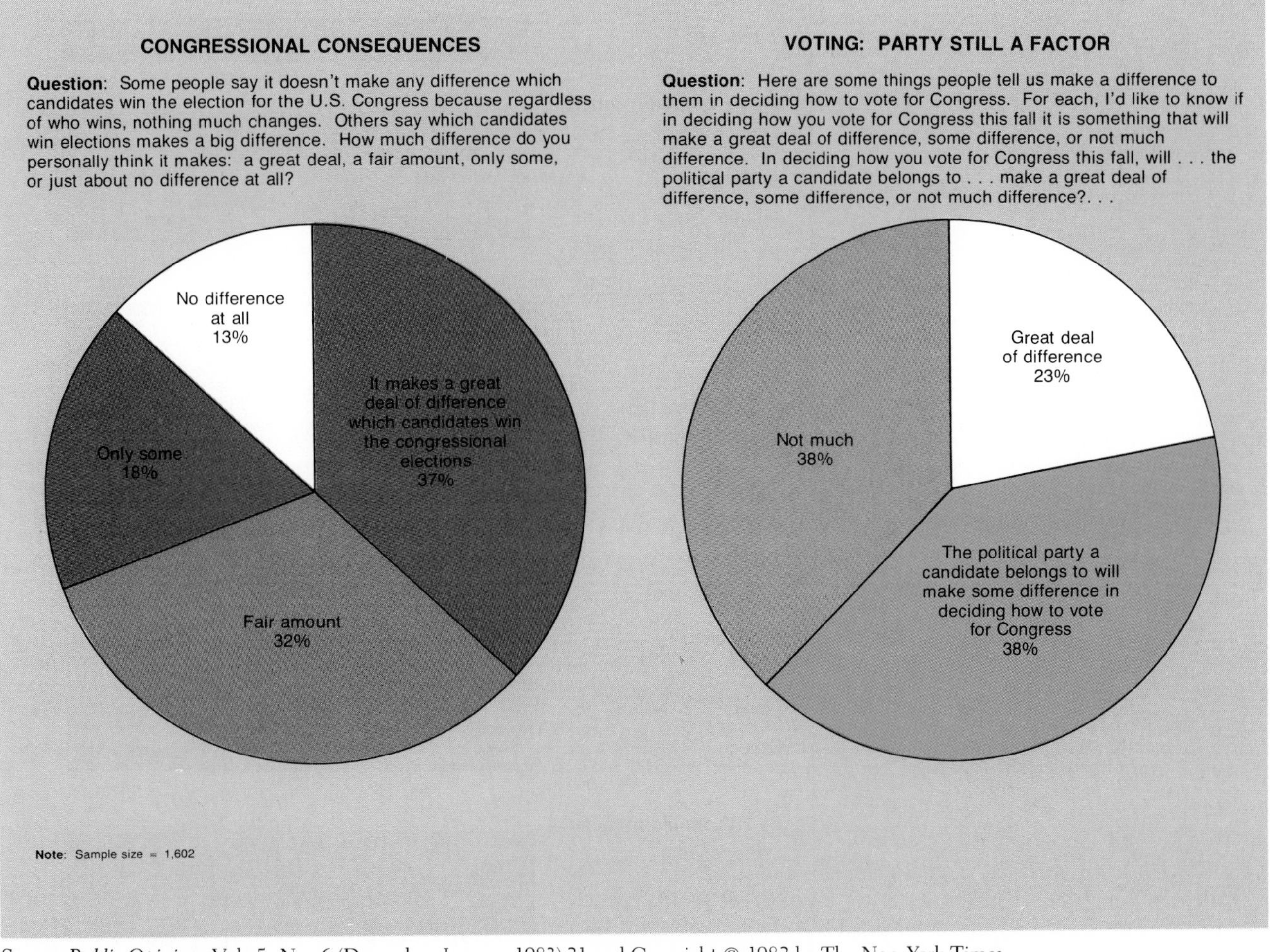

Source: Public Opinion, Vol. 5, No. 6 (December–January 1983):21 and Copyright © 1982 by The New York Times Company. Reprinted by permission.

But the extent to which class loyalty to a particular party is actually breaking down still remains uncertain. Some evidence suggests that class voting is more persistent than observers like Pomper believe. For instance, household income is still closely associated with voting behavior, a fact highlighted by the results of the 1982 congressional elections (see Figure 11.2, p. 280). Similarly, when sociologist Thomas Guterbock (1980) studied voting choices in "Middletown" (Muncie, Indiana), a community that Robert and Helen Lynd had investigated in the 1930s, he found that the influence of social class had not diminished at all. In fact, class voting had actually increased slightly, due primarily to a rise in black support for the Democrats. (During the 1930s, in contrast, many blacks were still loyal to the Republican party, viewed as the "party of Lincoln.")

What can explain the discrepancy between Guterbock's findings and the findings of earlier studies? Guterbock says that the earlier studies may not have used a sensitive enough measure of class. They may, for exam-

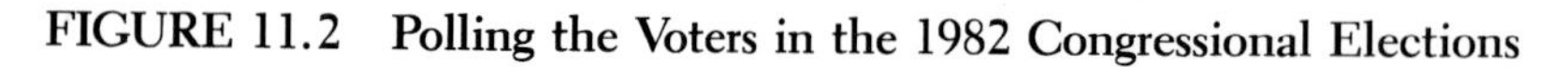

FIGURE 11.2 Polling the Voters in the 1982 Congressional Elections

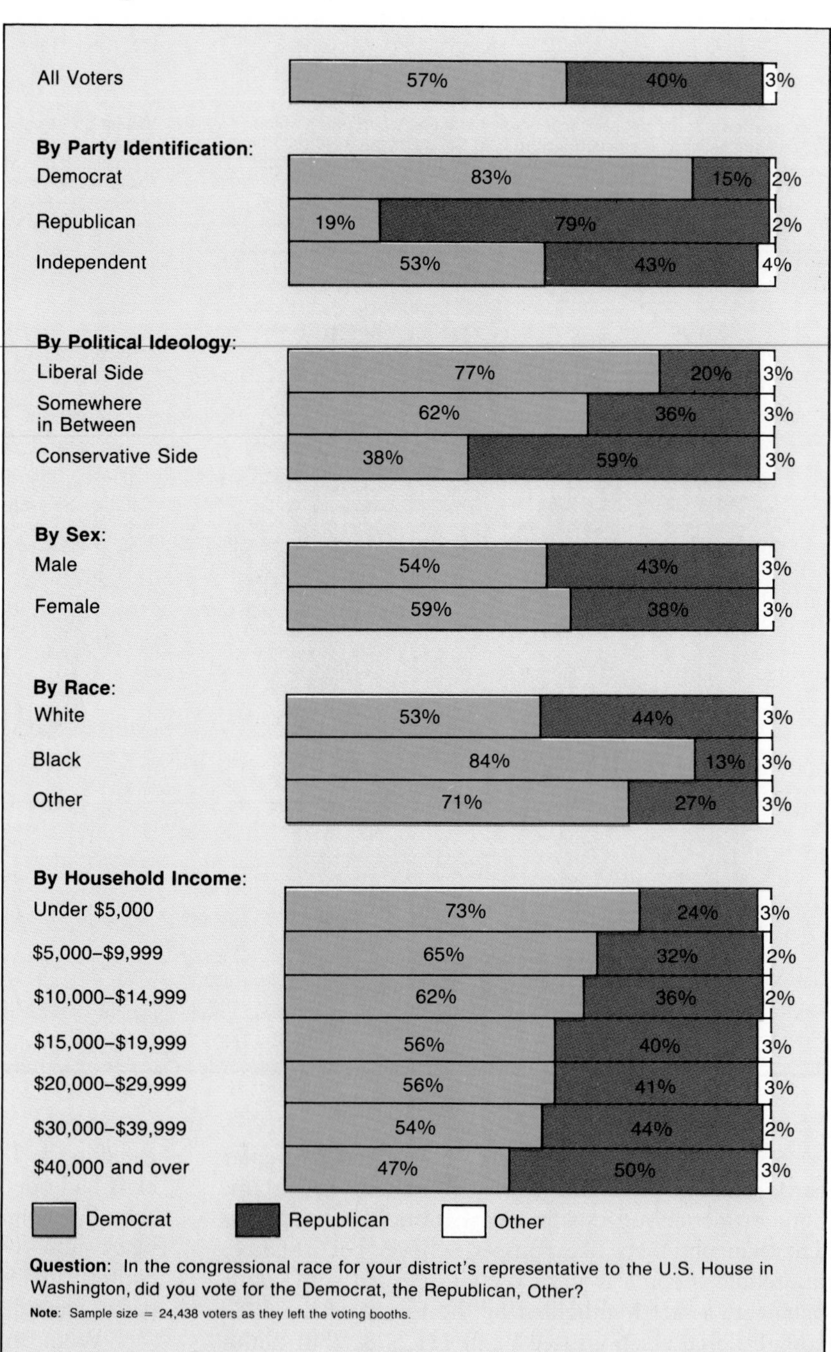

Question: In the congressional race for your district's representative to the U.S. House in Washington, did you vote for the Democrat, the Republican, Other?

Note: Sample size = 24,438 voters as they left the voting booths.

Source: Public Opinion, Vol. 5, No. 6 (December/January 1983):29.

ple, have determined class strictly by occupation, ignoring other yardsticks such as family background and education. If so, this alone could explain the divergent findings. In addition, the earlier studies may have focused on elections that were in some way unusual. For instance, in 1972, when so many blue-collar workers voted for Republican Richard Nixon, their preference may not have reflected a breakdown in class voting as much as a distrust of the antiwar Democrat George McGovern. In short, Guterbock feels that class-based voting is as strong as it was in the 1930s but that specific issues or the personalities of candidates sometimes encourage voters to abandon temporarily their traditional party loyalties.

Whether or not class voting is in fact breaking down is more than just an academic question. An eroding of class-based loyalties could have a very marked effect on the workings of our political system. For instance, if traditional patterns of class voting are indeed disappearing, our political parties will be forced more than ever to appeal to people with very divergent political views. As a result, voters may be left with no ideological choice regarding candidates. This is a common problem in many two-party systems, and one we will now explore.

The Two-Party System

The kinds of choices our electoral system offers are closely related to the nature of our political parties. Traditionally, political activity in America has centered around parties. For most Americans, politics boils down simply to choosing between the Republicans and the Democrats. In 1915 Robert Michels (1915/1949:134) defined a political party as a "society of propaganda and of agitation seeking to acquire power." Although these are not the words contemporary Americans might choose, this definition is essentially correct. A **political party** is a collectivity designed for gaining and holding legitimate government power.

Parties perform several crucial functions in large, complex political systems. Ideally, they link the people and the government, transmitting public opinion up to where decisions are actually made, thereby converting public opinion into legislation. They mobilize grass roots support for policy decisions made at the upper level. They also serve as a link between different branches and levels of government (executive and legislative, federal and state) and between official (government) power structures and unofficial (nongovernment) ones. On the practical level, parties play a dominant role in recruiting personnel for elective office (Dowse and Hughes, 1972).

Although we are accustomed to thinking in terms of two main parties, in some countries there are five or more parties, in others only one (and the struggle for power takes place within the party rather than between parties). Why is this? Why does the United States consistently generate two parties, while Italy consistently generates several? The answer lies in the structure of a country's electoral system.

French sociologist Maurice Duverger (1954) argues that two-party systems emerge when there can be only one candidate from each party and the winner of the election takes all. This simple-plurality system discourages third parties, because a vote for a minor party is in effect a wasted vote. There is almost no chance that the third-party candidate will win. In contrast, in proportional-vote systems like Italy's a party receives the same percentage of representatives as of votes in the election. In this kind of electoral system, a vote for a minority-party candidate is not wasted, for even if the party receives only 10 percent of the votes, it receives a tenth of the seats in the legislature.

The simply-plurality system determines not only the number of parties in the United States, but also their character. To win state and national elections, American parties must embrace diverse kinds of people and a wide range of interests. Differences of opinion must be settled before elections. Critics like Duverger argue that the American system forces parties into bland positions and prevents many groups from being represented. Both the Democratic and the Republican parties must lean toward the center and create policies that sound attractive to everyone and offend no one. Duverger's analysis suggests that politicians cannot be blamed for political double talk; the social structure of American parties forces them to generate it. However, Duverger points out that the simple-plurality system is more stable than proportional representation, where coalitions must be formed issue by issue in the legislature.

There are signs that the party system in America is changing. The media—in particular, television news—have taken over some of the functions formerly performed by political parties: scouting for talent; informing voters about what candidates are saying; predicting which way the election will go. In some cases newscasters act as self-appointed public defenders, exposing the frailties of candidates and fixing blame for breakdowns in the system. Partly as a result, parties cannot organize and mobilize the electorate as effectively as they once did (Ladd and Hadley, 1975; Lipset and Schneider, 1983).

Another factor straining political party alignments is the contradictory attitudes Americans hold toward the federal government and its social programs (Ladd, 1983). While three-fourths of all Americans say tax money spent for human services is poorly used, three-fourths argue that the federal government should provide medical care and legal assistance to those who cannot afford them. Although seven in ten people think that government has gone too far in regulating economic life, the same proportion believes that government should assure everyone a good standard of living. Three-fifths of the public—including solid majorities at all educational, income, and occupational levels—indicate that they do not believe that the "federal government over the last 20 years has gone too far in trying to help the poor." These contradictory attitudes toward government make it difficult for political parties to develop coherent, articulate ideological positions.

Still another factor influencing changes in the American party system has been the growth in the proportion of voters who identify themselves as Independents (see Figure 11.3). According to some forecasts, within twenty years, the Independents may become an absolute majority (Madron, 1979). Many observers of American politics do not view this trend very favorably. Some say that loss of party ties reduces electoral stability. Presumably, people without party affiliation are more readily influenced by immediate and transitory issues (Nie et al., 1976; Pomper, 1975). Walter Dean Burnham (1970) suggests that the eroding of party loyalties may actually herald the collapse of the entire party system. And Pomper (1977) associates such an outcome with the loss of democracy itself. Why such gloomy predictions related to a decline in party politics? One reason is that a decline in party strength and influence will benefit special interests (Madron, 1979). Without parties there would be no buffer between interest groups and elected officials. So the most powerful interest groups would be in an excellent position to control public policy. And in a stratified society such as ours, the most powerful interest groups represent only a small percentage of the people.

How likely is it that these pessimistic warnings will come true? No one knows for sure. Some clearly think that the potential threat is great. But others are not so certain. For example, Bruce Keith and his colleagues argue that many of the voters who classify themselves as Independent are in fact "hidden partisans." When they actually enter the voting booth, they vote for one or the other party with nearly as much loyalty as people who call themselves Democrats or Republicans. In short, many self-professed Independents are not truly independent at all. The increase in genuine Independents, these researchers say, has actually been rather modest. Consequently there is little reason to fear the collapse of the entire party system because of a small increase in the proportion of true nonpartisans. In fact, recent polls suggest that the increase in true Independents is now leveling off (Clymer, 1981).

The historian Arthur Schlesinger, Jr. (1979), reminds us that American political parties have always been somewhat unmanageable. He points out that over 140 years ago the French writer Alexis de Tocqueville, writing about democracy in the United States, noted that this difficulty stemmed from the dependence of legislators on their constituents:

> A representative is never sure of his supporters, and, if they forsake him, he is left without a resource. . . . Thus it is natural that in democratic countries the members of political assemblies should think more of their constituents than of their party. . . . But what ought to be said to gratify constituents is not always what ought to be said in order to serve the party to which representatives profess to belong.

Thus, difficulty in functioning of political parties, far from being a novelty of our times, is one of the conditions that American democracy has confronted from the beginning.

Interest Group Politics

In a sense, interest groups counteract the broad, coalition-building nature of political parties in the United States. An **interest group** is an organization created to influence political decisions that directly concern its members. They range from business associations (such as the National Association of Manufacturers) to labor unions (most notably the powerful AFL-CIO), agricultural groups (including the National Milk Producers Association), professional associations (the American Medical Association, the American Bar Association),

FIGURE 11.3 Increase in Independents among American Voters

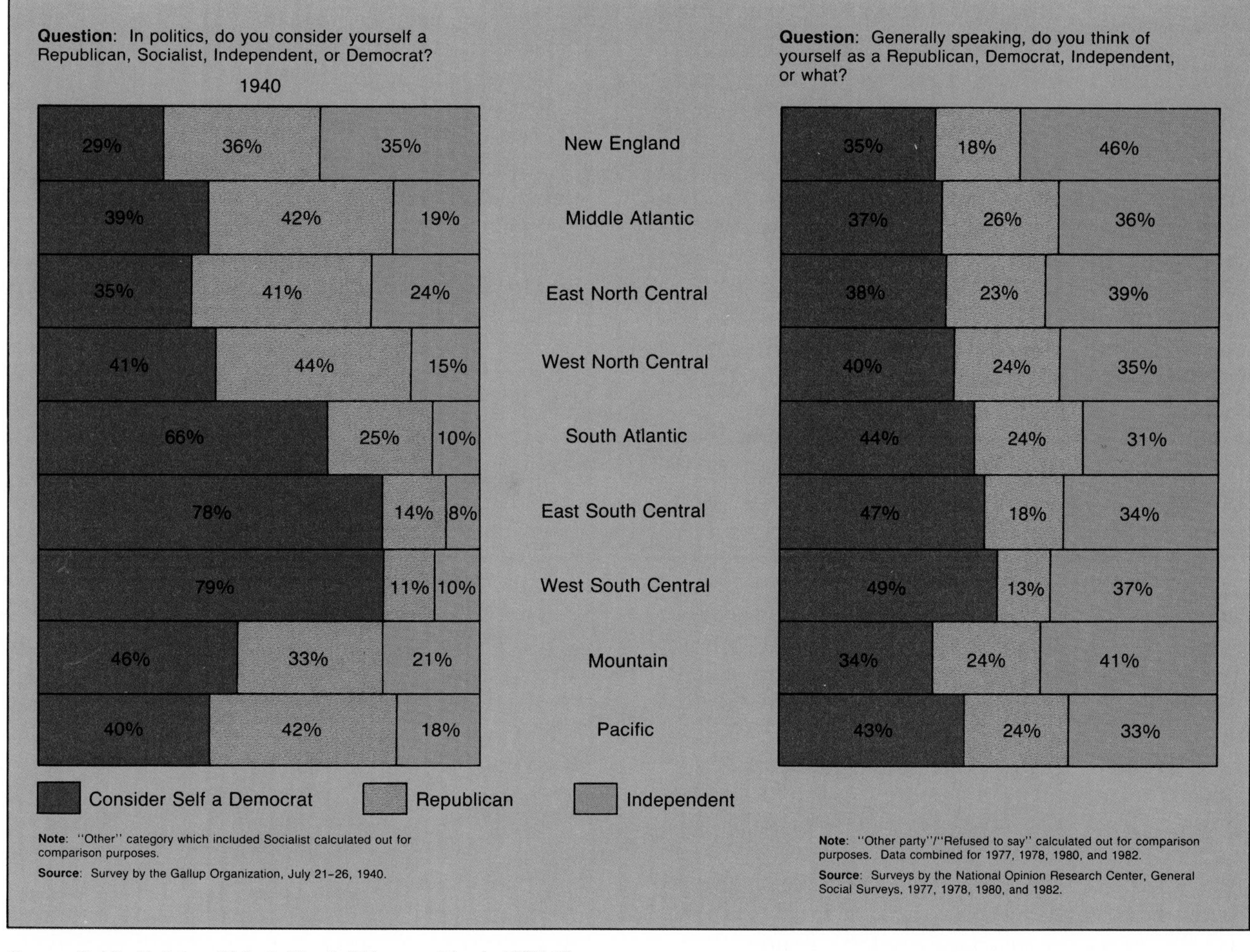

Source: Public Opinion, Vol. 6, No. 1 (February–March 1983):30.

civil rights groups (The National Association for the Advancement of Colored People), political groups (Americans for Democratic Action, the John Birch Society), the single-issue groups (such as the right-to-life movement). Corporations may form their own lobbies, the most notorious example being ITT's attempt to gain a favorable settlement of an antistrust suit by offering to underwrite the 1972 Republican National Convention. In addition, agencies and departments within the government may lobby, using their resources and spokespeople to influence Congress. For example, members of the Defense Department regularly testify in favor of increased military spending. Foreign governments also maintain lobbies in Washington to look out for their interests.

When Americans are asked by pollsters why they think our system of government does not work better than it does, they cite by a hefty margin "too much influence on government by special interest groups and lobbies" (Etzioni, 1982). Yet special interest groups and lobbies are hardly new to the national scene. They have been with us ever since we have had a Congress (Schlesinger, 1979). Indeed, private-interest lobbies were never more powerful than in the years following the Civil War. Nor are contemporary single-issue movements—antiabortionists, anti-gun-control groups, antinuclear groups, and environmentalists—a modern innovation. They have been a part of the political landscape since 1789, raising such issues as the elimination of Freemasonry, the abolition of slavery, the issuance of greenbacks, the free coinage of silver, the restriction of immigration, or the enactment of prohibition.

The campaign finance reform laws passed by Congress in the mid-1970s sought to relocate political power by taking it from the monied interests and dispersing it to the grass roots (Alexander and Haggerty, 1981). The measures restricted the role of large contributors, particularly large corporations, labor unions, and special interest groups. Yet, paradoxically, the laws have served to increase the role played by special interests by sanctioning the establishment of political action committees (PACs). A PAC is typically organized by a business, labor, professional, farm, environmental, or issue group to raise money from numerous individuals so that small contributions can be aggregated into large amounts to support the campaign of favored candidate or political party.

Although labor-sponsored PACs have steadily increased the amounts of money they raise and spend on behalf of candidates, they have been outstripped by corporate and business-related PACs. And while the number of labor PACs has not increased notably, those sponsored by corporations rose from 89 in 1974 to 1,415 in 1982 (Alexander and Haggerty, 1981; Etzioni, 1982). Single-issue PACs, such as gun groups and antiabortion advocates, have also become forces to be reckoned with in the electoral process. In the 1982 elections PACs gave $10,870,509 to Republican Senate candidates and $10,794,796 to the Democratic Senate candidates. The Democrats in the House of the Representatives got quite a bit more than did the Republicans because PACs prefer to support incumbents and the Democrats had more of them: Democrats received $31,824,711; the Republicans, $25,629,386 (Clymer, 1983*b*). Many PACs switch sides after the votes are counted, providing postelection gifts to help the winners cut their campaign debts (Jackson and Fialka, 1983).

The 1970 campaign finance laws establishing PACs have had a number of unanticipated consequences (Alexander and Haggerty, 1981). By broadening the financial base for candidates and parties, PACs have taken over some of the functions of the traditional large fund raiser. PACs can organize dinners, cocktail parties, and direct mailings to raise money, and at no cost to candidates. In some cases PACs have also increased the participation of people in the political system by organizing their membership to campaign for the candidate they support. But simultaneously PACs have made candidates less dependent on political parties, and they have weakened political allegiances among elected officials. The result has been the fragmentation of legislative processes and the strengthening of single-issue politics.

Although special interest groups have acquired a bad reputation, many social scientists believe they fulfill some useful functions (Etzioni, 1982). For one thing, they provide a mechanism for political input that supplements the electoral process. For another, the various groups operate as a check against one another and create numerous cross-currents in American politics. People are often active in more than one group, so that those with different outlooks may sometimes join forces. For example, in her support of women's rights, a conservative Southern Democrat may find herself aligned with outspoken liberals. The sociologist Seymour M. Lipset (1963) suggests that diverse and conflicting interests, which prevent the formation of solid political blocs, are essential to modern democracies. If interests and affiliations did not overlap, the country might split in half, as the United States did during the Civil War. Hence, multiple loyalties prevent the polarization of society into rigidly hostile groups.

But just because interest groups create cross-cutting affiliations does not mean that the sum of their efforts adds up to an accurate reflection of the popular will. Not all people are represented by interest groups. In fact, most probably are not. And even when a person is associated with an interest group, there is no guarantee that lobbyists in Washington will be voicing that person's views. In most cases lobbyists work for the elite of an organization. They are hired by the leaders of a union, for example, not by the rank and file, and they are accountable to those leaders. Finally, interest groups are certainly not equal in the degree of influence they exert. Some have far more resources at their disposal than others and consequently wield far more power. Thus interest group politics in America cannot be viewed as simply another form of popular representation.

Special interest groups, like these farmers, supplement the electoral process by communicating their wishes clearly and directly to legislators. (Paul Conklin.)

HOW CONCENTRATED AND STABLE IS POWER?

In exploring power in our economic and political systems, we have found that it is distributed unequally. But how extreme is this inequality? Is power concentrated in the hands of a small minority, or is it broadly shared?

As we suggested earlier in this chapter, social scientists have offered several answers. Some claim power is concentrated in the hands of a select few who dominate and manipulate the many. This position is evident in the writings of Karl Marx. Marx believed that in a capitalist society power rests with the owners of the means of production, who use it to promote and protect their own class interests. All social institutions—from the political to the religious—support and reflect the capitalists' dominant role. And the capitalists, for their part, consistently act to preserve these institutions, which underlie their power. But Marx was not the only observer to argue that power in society is highly concentrated. A group of scholars collectively called **elite theorists** contend that power is monopolized by those relatively few people who occupy the top positions in our organizational hierarchies (Field and Higley, 1980). These **elites,** they say, are of similar backgrounds and share similar interests and goals. Their aims are reflected in virtually all our important public policies. In sharp contrast to Marxists and elite theorists, social scientists who adopt a **pluralist** position believe that a variety of groups and interests compete for power in American society, with more or less success. In short, they see power as far more dispersed than either the Marxists or the elite theorists do. Instead of one they see many centers of power in a modern democratic state (see Figure 11.4, p. 286).

In addition to their differing views on the distribution of power, these three schools of thought also differ on the question of how stable the existing power structure is. Marxists see the current distribution of power as less stable than elite theorists do because they believe that capitalism contains inherent conflicts that will eventually lead to its downfall. Thus Marxists believe that power is potentially available to the working class if it develops enough class consciousness to join forces and take control of the means of production. In contrast, elite theorists generally maintain that an unequal distribution of power is self-perpetuating. Finally, like Marxists, pluralists see power structures as inherently unstable

FIGURE 11.4 Elitist and Pluralist Views of the American Power Structure

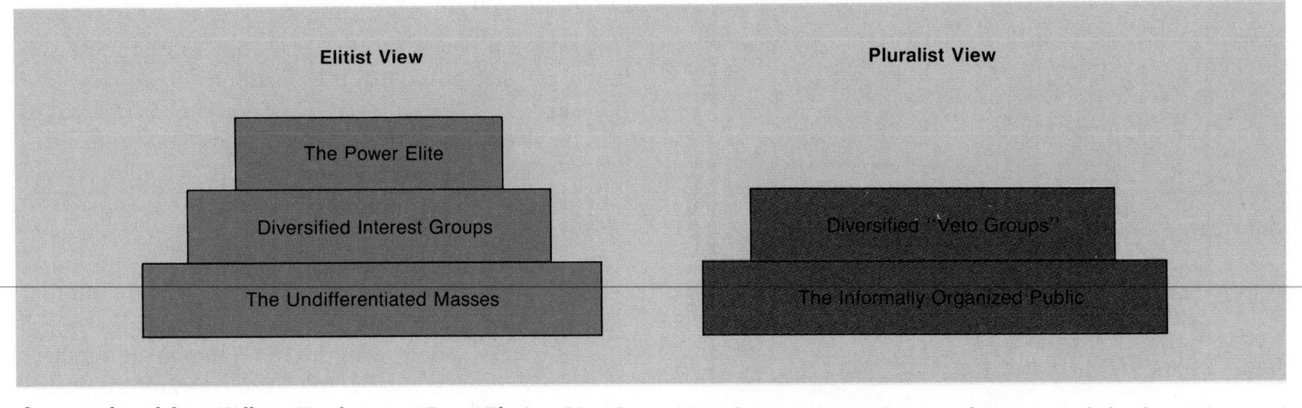

Source: Adapted from William Kornhauser, "'Power Elite' or 'Veto Groups'?" in Seymour Martin Lipset and Leo Lowenthal, eds., *Culture and Social Character* (Glencoe, Ill.: Free Press, 1961), pp. 525–567.

The primary difference between elitists and pluralists is that while the former see a unified elite at the top of the power structure, the latter do not.

but believe the instability results from constantly shifting alliances rather than from internal conflict. Keeping in mind these broad differences among Marxists, elite theorists, and pluralists, let us look at these three schools of thought more closely.

The Marxist View

Before Marx, political philosophers more or less assumed that social power resided in the state and in such related organizations as the military. Their discussions of power centered on government. Marx added a new dimension to political theory by drawing attention to the economic roots of power. The people who own the means of production (the factories, the land, and the mines) control the members of society through their domination of subsistence activities. The dominant class employs the force of the state to subdue domestic unrest and to promote its interests in the international sphere.

According to Marx, each historical period is characterized by a predominant mode of production, a way of obtaining a livelihood, such as manufacturing. Each mode of production creates its own power hierarchy, or in Marx's terms, a ruling class and an oppressed class. Under the earliest class system, slavery, the ruling class consisted of slaveowners; the oppressed, the slaves. Later, under feudalism, the ruling class was made up of landowners; the oppressed class, serfs. Still later, under industrial capitalism, the ruling class is the bourgeoisie (the owners of industry); the oppressed class, the proletariat (propertyless wage earners). Because the ruling class owns and controls the means of production, it directs not only economic activity but also the institutions shaping the moral and intellectual life of the workers, including law, government, art, literature, science, and philosophy. Thus the ruling class directs all of society's institutions, and in doing so, it ensures its own fortunes and the subjugation of the populace.

Any number of social scientists have focused their attention on the question of *who* occupies powerful positions and on *how* these individuals are linked with one another in an inner group. However, Marxists argue that it matters little who makes the decisions in a capitalist order. They insist that so long as an economic system is based on private ownership, the range of decisions that any politician or any other leader can make is restricted by the requirement that corporations generate profits.

Marx believed that capitalism, like all previous

economic orders, contained the seeds of its own destruction. By this he meant that certain contradictions were inherent in a capitalist economy that would eventually bring about its overthrow. In particular, the relentless drive of capitalists to maximize profits would progressively worsen the circumstances of the working class, intensify the crippling effects of the business cycle, and deepen international tensions. Ultimately conditions for workers would become so deplorable that the workers would band together and overthrow their exploiters. In short, the downfall of capitalism in Marx's view was inevitable because the system gradually forces its people into abject poverty and degradation, circumstances that eventually become intolerable. This exploitive system, Marx believed, would be replaced by a socialist order that in time would give way to communism, a classless society.

The Power Elite View

Marx's focus on economics and his predictions about the coming of a classless society did not long go unchallenged. Two Italian social philosophers, Vilfredo Pareto (1848–1923) and Gaetano Mosca (1858–1941), saw inequalities of power as inherent in any social order. A classless society was in their view impossible. Pareto (1916/1935) began with the simple observation that some lawyers are sharper, some royal mistresses more influential, and some thieves more successful than others. These are the **elites** of their respective fields—members of that small minority who lead because they are more gifted than other people. The same holds true for society as a whole. Throughout history, small governing elites—individuals distinguished by talent and organization—have ruled the masses by virtue of their social superiority. This both Pareto and Mosca (1939) believed was an inevitable pattern—indeed, a desirable one.

Writing in the first decades of the twentieth century, the German economist and sociologist Robert Michels claimed that power tends to fall into the hands of a small group of leaders in *all* organizations, whatever their goals and ideology. After studying the labor and socialist movements of his time, Michels (1915/1949) concluded that as organizations grow in size and complexity, the need for leadership becomes more and more pressing. Informal decision making in which all members participate becomes impractical. There are too many issues to resolve. Further, the organization must present a united front to the outside world. Leaders chosen for their special talents in administration and public relations gradually take command. In time, these leaders develop a vested interest in maintaining their positions. A combination of admiration and apathy in the rank and file accelerates this concentration of power in the hands of a few. The ruling clique becomes conservative, seeks compromises with its enemies, avoids risk taking, and erects barriers to challenges by opponents—measures designed to protect their positions and advance their fortunes. Nowhere is this process more obvious than it is in successful radical political movements. Revolutions, Michels argues, are little more than the replacement of one elite by another. In Michels' view, "Who says organization says **oligarchy**"—rule by the few. The chain of events Michels portrayed as leading to the concentration of power in the hands of the few has become known as his **iron law of oligarchy.**

Among twentieth-century American sociologists, C. Wright Mills (1959) took the lead in postulating the existence of an American **power elite,** a coalition of military leaders, government officials and business executives that effectively rules our capitalist society. According to Mills, this small group makes the major decisions that affect the lives of Americans, especially those relating to matters of war and peace. He began with the fact that many people who occupy high positions in government have also held high positions in corporations or the military and seem to move back and forth between these centers of power. America's governing elite, wrote Mills, is "a coalition of generals in the roles of corporation executives, of politicans masquerading as admirals, of corporation executives acting like politicans" (1959:278). Tracing their personal histories, Mills found that by and large these people come from white Anglo-Saxon Protestant, old American backgrounds, attend the same Ivy League schools, belong to the same exclusive clubs, and visit the same resorts. Thus, if the president of an oil company does not know the federal "energy czar" personally, he surely knows someone who knows him (and can place a confidential call, if necessary). Through their social similarities, the power elite's coinciding interests are reinforced, and something like a ruling class emerges.

Mills argued that the different branches of the elite are interlocking. Congress approves billions of dollars in military appropriations every year, dollars that go more

Many government and military leaders are also closely connected with major corporations. For example, of the participants in this MX Missile Commission meeting, Casper Weinberger (Secretary of Defense) and George Shultz (Secretary of State) were both top-level executives of the Bechtel Corporation, a construction and engineering firm with enormous government contracts. (J.L. Atlan/Sygma.)

or less directly into corporate pockets. Why does Congress make these appropriations? In part for national defense, in part because military contracts create jobs, and in part because business leaders are important campaign contributors. Thus politicians tend to support big business, and business leaders often support politicians. All three sectors—economic, political, and military—have a vested interest in what Mills calls "military capitalism."

Mills believed the trend toward centralization of power would continue unabated. "The top of modern American society is increasingly unified, and often seems willfully coordinated: at the top there has emerged an elite whose power probably exceeds that of any small group of men in world history" (quoted in Olsen, 1970:261). Mills (1958:29) summed up his views with these words: "I should contend that men are free to make history, but that some men are indeed much freer than others."

G. William Domhoff (1978) has attempted to collect evidence for such an elite, although he does not think it is as unified or coordinated as Mills believed. He concludes that half of 1 percent of the United States population controls a large share of the country's wealth and holds a disproportionate number of high-level positions in government and business. Members of "the governing class" attend the same schools, belong to the same clubs and civic associations, and intermarry, producing a tightly knit central circle (see box).

Similarly, the sociologist Michael Useem (1979, 1980) says that the primary owners and top managers of America's major corporations constitute an "inner group." By virtue of their multiple corporate connections, their common social networks, and their commitment to the capitalist system, they share a similar perspective on contemporary political issues and problems. They bring this outlook to bear in government through their participation in top political and decision-making circles and in their direction of key nonprofit organizations and foundations.

The Pluralist View

But in fact are America's political, military and corporate chieftains all of one mind and do they cooperate with one another? Is not the reverse a more accurate portrayal—they see one another as rivals? This is the question pluralists ask. They agree with Mills that some people are freer to make history than others and that

THE SOCIOLOGICAL EYE ON CAREERS:

Dressing for Success and Authority

When we consider special power, we once again encounter the sociological axiom expressed by the Thomas Theorem that if people define situations as real, they are real in their consequences (see Chapter 4). Sociologists point out that in human affairs it is often not so much actual resources that count as the beliefs that people have regarding these resources (Wrong, 1968). Of particular importance in this respect is the ability of individuals and groups to project the appearance of power. To successfully manage the impression that one has power and is prepared to use it may be as effective as actually having the real thing (Kaplowitz, 1978). Hence, superpowers place their forces on "alert" or sent a naval fleet to foreign waters as a "show of force" with the expectation that such displays will achieve some political outcome.

Success in a career also entails making the right impression and projecting the appearance of power. Within patriarchal societies, authority is depicted and enshrined as male; it is wrapped in male trappings and judged by male standards of voice, styles of speech, behavior, and dress. This fact is particularly important for women who aspire to achieve success in business, politics, and academic life. They must not only exhibit the proper qualifications and credentials but also the proper image. Accordingly, some consultants have urged women who wish to succeed to dress for the part. John T. Molloy (1977), who calls himself a "wardrobe engineer," contends that women can increase their chances for promotion in corporate, political, and academic arenas by dressing for authority. He observes, "Women who want to be taken seriously and who want to succeed must dress in a way that says, 'I am important. I am a business professional and don't you dare send me for coffee'." (pp. 26–27).

Molloy says that by designing clothes that impede women in getting ahead, the fashion industry helps those who would keep women from the centers of power. By featuring women as alluring and sexually attractive, designers reinforce the image of women as sex objects rather than as competent professionals. According to his guidelines, women must adopt a business or professional uniform, much in the manner that men have done. Solid, conservative suits, as opposed to frilly dresses, give women the aura they need to give orders and have the orders carried out. Likewise, neutral grays, beiges, and tweeds are preferable to pastel blues and pinks. And glasses and attaché cases (rather than handbags) are further accessories of authority.

Molloy (1975) contends that *men* should also "dress for success." He finds that suits are positive authority symbols worn by people who make important decisions. Customers, clients, and subordinates seem more likely to believe, respect, and obey men who wear suits than men who do not. Here too solid, conservative suits and neutral grays and beiges seem to be the best choices. Of equal importance is the tie. Men opting for the authoritative look would do well to select ties in deep colors such as navy blue or burgundy with small, quiet patterns.

It should be stressed that Molloy's recommendations constitute guidelines and do not guarantee success and authority. From a sociological perspective, the main point is that power has a socially stereotyped image. And how one appears and dresses are important, even critical, ingredients of this image.

unorganized individuals (the masses) are relatively powerless. But they do not see a single ruling clique, a power elite at the top of the power structure in this country. Rather, pluralists argue that social power is dispersed among a variety of competing interest groups—the oil industry and the coal industry, car manufacturers and ecologists, union and business associations, hunters' lobbies and wildlife foundations, the Navy and the Air Force, and General Motors and Ford. All these groups control resources and activities at different times with varying degrees of success, but no one group is in command. In most cases they can do little more than veto programs that threaten their interests. As the sociologist David Riesman (1951:242) has said, "Today we have substituted for [centralized, mercantile-aristocratic] leadership a series of groups, each of which has struggled for and finally attained a power to stop things conceivably inimical to its interests and, within far narrower

THE SOCIOLOGICAL EYE ON:

Studying Community Power

Consider the following approach to studying the structure of power in a typical American community. A team of researchers administers a questionnaire that begins by asking, "Who dominates decision-making in this community?" Ideally, a list of key powerholders will emerge. If it does, the researchers then explore the extent to which these influential people control a disproportionate share of resources related to power—resources such as money, social standing, esteem in the community, control over financial credit, jobs, or earnings, and so forth. At the same time, they interview the members of this dominant group to determine whether they hold the same views on community issues, interact on a regular basis, and frequently join forces in pursuit of common goals. Common sense suggests that there will be a single local power elite. Many social scientists have found otherwise.

These critics contend that what common sense labels a sound research strategy in fact has serious flaws. For one thing, the wording of the very first question presumes that *some* group necessarily dominates community life. As a result, respondents may take this as a cue to what they are "supposed" to answer. They may report that certain local residents (usually those with wealth and prestige) wield more power than they actually do.

Nelson Polsby has proposed one way of avoiding all such leading questions. He advises researchers to focus their attention on how actual community decisions are made—who shapes them and who benefits. Only when the same group of people repeatedly dominates important decisions for their own ends can an enduring power elite be said to exist.

Does the evidence show this pattern to be common? Polsby, like other pluralists, is skeptical. In his view even the evidence some elite theorists offer has many contradictions. For instance, in their classic study of "Middletown" (a fictitious name for Muncie, Indiana), Robert and Helen Lynd (1929, 1937) concluded that the city was controlled by a small group of wealthy manufacturers, bankers, corporate managers, and successful attorneys—in short, a local business-class elite. Yet there were occasions on which other community groups dominated public policy, even over the opposition of the business class. A case in point was the inability of business-class residents to get the city to clean up pollution in the White River, along which their expensive houses were built. Apparently, working-class members of the city council saw no advantage to themselves in making the sizable outlay of funds required. What sort of power elite is it, Polsby asks, that can't impose its will on public officials regarding an issue that so greatly affects its members' lives? Can this group rightly be said to "run" the community? In the view of Polsby, no.

There is much merit to Polsby's analysis of approaches to studying community power. Researchers *must* guard against inadvertently biasing their results. To this end, Polsby recommends that social scientists concentrate on studying actual decision making about key local issues, either witnessed first hand or reconstructed through public documents, newspapers, and reliable informants.

Source: Nelson W. Polsby, *Community Power and Political Theory.* New Haven: Yale University Press. 1980, pp. 112–121.

limits, to start things" (see also Dahl, 1961; Keller, 1963; Kornhauser, 1961). Economist Lester Thurow (1980) has made this point even more forcefully. He argues that "too much" pluralism may be the reason why we cannot solve some of our major social and economic problems. With many interests competing for a voice in public policy, decision making often becomes hopelessly deadlocked, or legislation is filled with so many compromises that it is totally ineffectual.

In summary, then, elite theorists like C. Wright Mills believe that coinciding interests, reinforced by social similarity, bind America's leaders together into a single cohesive power elite. In contrast, pluralists like David Riesman maintain that diverse, often conflicting, interests preclude united policy or action. Mills argues that members of the power elite settle important questions among themselves, behind closed doors. Riesman disagrees, arguing that fundamental issues are decided through bargaining by and among interested parties, and that the parties who exercise power vary with the issue. (The National Rifle Association, for example, is not interested in farm subsidies or endowments for the arts.)

Mills laments the erosion of democracy, the loss of responsible and accountable centers of power, and the alienation of the powerless many. Riesman deplores the dearth of leadership and the lack of direction in American politics.

In *The Power Structure* (1967), the sociologist Arnold Rose concludes that the two sides of this argument are not necessarily mutually exclusive. What exists in our society may be a complex mixture of both. Rose concedes that foreign affairs seem to be dominated by a small group of people who resemble Mill's power elite, but he suggests that the growth of the federal government and the emergence of new pressure groups (such as civil rights organizations) have undercut the power of big business. In his view, there are many power structures in America, not just one, and nationwide decisions are made through a process of bargaining among them (the pluralist view). However, the power structures themselves (political parties, government agencies, legislatures, businesses, and so on) tend to be dominated by ogilarchies (the elitist view). In sum, Rose sees the American power structure as a complex plurality of elites.

Other social scientists who have studied the way our policy decisions are actually made have found Rose to be at least partially right. For instance, sociologist J. Allen Whitt (1979) recently investigated the making of a number of key decisions regarding mass transit in California. (The box discusses how sociologists go about investigating community power.) He found that depending on one's viewpoint and how carefully the evidence is sifted, support for all three theoretical positions might be found. Thus different interest groups (the highway lobby versus central-city businesses, for example) *did* compete with one another to some extent in their positions on public transportation, just as pluralists would predict. And as elite theorists would argue, business leaders *were* highly involved in all of these decisions, and a great deal of cooperation did occur among them. Likewise, as the Marxists would contend, the very need for mass transit *was* in part related to the capitalist quest for ever-increasing profits. Thus Whitt concludes that an integration of all three approaches may broaden our understanding of policy making in the United States.

EPILOGUE

The sociologist Amos Hawley (1963:422) points out that "Every social act is an exercise of power, every social relationship is a power equation, and every social group or system is an organization of power." Indeed, one cannot be powerful alone. Being powerful is a part of social interaction. It is a matter of outcomes—the ability of one party to translate its preferences into social reality. In other words, some individuals and groups are better able than others to structure institutional arrangements in ways they deem desirable and beneficial.

This chapter has stressed how power provides an answer to the question of who shall get what, when, and how. As such, power relates to the issues of social stratification discussed in Chapter 10. Even in a society such as that in the United States where positions are, in theory, open to all individuals on the basis of merit, talent, and capabilities, some people begin with a headstart. By virtue of their race, gender, or family background, they enjoy substantially greater opportunities. But this is not all. Their group's privileged position allows it to screen off others from access to critical knowledge, skills, and resources. Institutional racism is one such mechanism, a topic we will consider in the next chapter.

Power also provides an answer to the question of which group will make its value preferences the operating norms for society. In Chapter 9 we pointed out that deviance is a matter of values; being able to make one's values stick in the definition of deviant behavior is a function of power. Similarly, in Chapter 3 we discussed how dominant English-speaking Americans have insisted that Hispanics relinquish their traditional language and behavior for that of the Anglo-American culture and have extracted from Hispanics a high measure of conformity ("assimilation"). The evolution of the state has had important consequences for dominant-minority relationships. The anthropologists Charles Wagley and Marvin Harris (1964:242) note:

> Only with the development of the state did human societies become equipped with a form of social organization which could bind masses of culturally and physically

heterogeneous "strangers" in a single social entity. Whereas primitive peoples derive their cohesion largely from a common culture and from kinship and other kinds of personal ties, state societies are held together largely by the existence of a central political authority which claims a monopoly of coercive power over all persons within a given territory. Theoretically, with a sufficiently strong development of the apparatus of government, a state society can extend law and order over limitless subgroups of strangers who neither speak the same language, worship the same gods, nor strive for the same values.

But if power is as unequally distributed as sociologists suggest, what influence can the rank and file exert? Can their voices be heard at all? The answer is partly related to a point we stressed earlier in the chapter: In no system does the dominant group have absolute control. There are always certain boundaries in the exercise of power beyond which those without power will protest. A **protest movement** may be defined as the mobilization of previously inactive, unorganized constituency to challenge established practices or policy. Such movements have occurred at various times throughout history. (Chapter 18 examines collective behavior and social movements.) Perhaps the classic example of a protest movement in recent times is the civil rights movement. Given the importance of power to an understanding of racial and ethnic relations and to the civil rights movement, we turn our attention in the next chapter to these matters.

SUMMARY

Power is the ability to control other people's behavior, while authority is the exercise of power in a way that people consider legitimate and right. The power that makes a real difference in the way social life works is the power that flows from the dominant organizations and institutions. The two major institutional centers of power and authority in America are the economic and the political. They are closely interlinked.

All economic systems face the same basic problem: how to satisfy potentially unlimited human desires with limited resources. There are two principal economic systems in the world today. The capitalist market economy rests on the concept of private property and has profit as its primary motive. The socialist command economy rests on the collective ownership of property and the centralization of economic decision making in the hands of the state.

A relatively small number of large corporations dominates the American economy. They exert considerable power, both economic and political. But the power of American-based firms is dwarfed by that of the giant multinational corporations, which view the entire world as a single economic system.

Who controls America's large corporations? Some argue that a group of top executives and managers set corporate policy. In this view, the owners of the corporations (the stockholders) are diffuse and largely passive. But others strongly disagree. Since only 1 percent of the American population owns most of the nation's corporate stock, and since a significant number of these large stockholders are represented on corporate boards of directors, a reasonable case can be made that America's largest firms are dominated by a ruling capitalist class.

Although most Americans believe that their own political system is a prime example of democracy, there is a wide gap between the ideal of true government by the people and the reality of popular participation in the United States. First, only a relatively small percentage of Americans turn out for elections. Usually, those with low incomes and poor education are the least likely to vote. Second, the fact that the major American political parties generally adopt positions at the center of the political spectrum means that the views of many groups are inadequately represented. And third, interest group politics in America tends to be dominated not by the rank and file but by elites.

One of the enduring features of power in almost every society sociologists study is its unequal distribution. But how extreme is this inequality? And how stable is it? There are different views. Marxists believe that power in our society is lodged in the hands of the capitalists, who dominate and manipulate the workers in pursuit of their own class interests. They also contend that this power distribution is inherently unstable because it generates class conflict that will eventually lead to its downfall. Elite theorists also believe that power in America is monopolized by a relative few, but they maintain that this pattern is self-perpetuating and therefore unlikely to change. Finally, pluralists see power as more broadly dispersed than Marxists and elite theorists do. They also believe that the distribution of power is constantly shifting, as groups compete with one another for influence and alliances are formed and broken.

GLOSSARY

Authority. Power to which people willingly submit; power exercised in a way people consider right and legitimate.

Capitalist market economy. An economic system based on the principles of private ownership of the means of production, the use of productive assets to maximize profits, and free competition among business firms.

Charismatic authority. A type of authority (identified by Weber) that derives from public recognition of exceptional personal qualities.

Coercion. Power that rests on the threat or use of force.

Conglomerate. A company consisting of a number of subsidiaries in a variety of industries.

Corporation. An organization created by law that has an ongoing existence, powers, and liabilities distinct from those of its owners and employees.

Democratic state. A state in which authority derives from the law, rooted in the consent of the people.

Elite theory. The view that society is dominated by the relatively small number of people who occupy top positions in organizational hierarchies.

Elites. Influential, expert, or powerful groups.

Ideology. A set of ideas that explains and justifies a social order.

Interest group. An organization created to influence political decisions that directly concern its members.

Interlocking directorates. Networks of people serving on the boards of directors of two or more corporations.

Iron law of oligarchy. The view of Robert Michels that large organizations inevitably produce a concentration of power in the hands of the few, who use their positions to advance their own fortunes and self-interests.

Legal-rational authority. A type of authority (identified by Weber) that derives from a system of explicit rules defining the legitimate uses of power. It is vested in positions, not in specific individuals.

Multinational corporation. A giant, usually diversified, corporation with operations and subsidiaries in many countries.

Oligarchy. Rule by a small group of powerful leaders.

Oligopoly. An industry dominated by only a few very large firms.

Pluralism. The view that the political power structure is composed of a variety of competing elites and interest groups.

Political party. A collectivity designed for gaining and holding legitimate government power.

Power. The ability to mobilize collective resources, to accomplish things, to overcome opposition, and to dominate others—to get people to act in accordance with one's wishes even when they prefer not to do so.

Power elite. A coalition of military leaders, government officials, and business executives united by common interests and social affinity. In C. Wright Mills's view, this coalition rules America.

Protest movement. The mobilization of a previously unorganized constituency to challenge established practices or policy.

Socialist command economy. An economic system based on the principles of collective ownership of the means of production and the centralization of economic decision making in the hands of the state.

State. According to Weber, the one organization in a society that has the authority to employ physical force.

Totalitarian state. A state in which the centralized government does not recognize or tolerate parties of differing opinion.

Traditional authority. A type of authority (identified by Weber) that stems from sacred traditions of loyalty to monarchs, chiefs, and priests.

CHAPTER 12

Racial and Ethnic Relations

Whether one is called Ricardo Rodriguez or Richard Rodriguez may seem rather inconsequential. But for the son of Mexican immigrants growing up in Sacramento, California, it was a matter of two worlds, the one Mexican and the other Anglo-American. Indeed, it was more: it was a matter of two beings—two identities tugging for ascendancy. Spanish was the language of the home—of warmth, intimacy, and rootedness. English was the language of "gringos"—of indifference, aloofness, and alienation. And in the larger community it was a matter of separateness, rejection, humiliation: "Hey, Greaser! Hey, Pancho!" and "I pee on dirty Mexicans" (Rodriguez, 1983).

Bloke Modisane is a black South African journalist. Until he left South Africa, his home was the Johannesburg slum called Sophiatown. Like all South African blacks, Bloke Modisane was required by law to live in a racially segregated area regardless of his income or preferences. Like all South African blacks Bloke Modisane was also required to carry with him at all times an official document called a Reference Book. Among other things it contained a stamp granting him permission to remain in Johannesburg as long as he was employed there. As a black he lived and worked in Johannesburg solely at the discretion of the white government (Modisane, 1963).

Vladimir Ostrovsky sits at a kitchen table in his small Jersey City apartment, leafing through a Russian-English dictionary. He, his wife, their two daughters, and his elderly mother-in-law have been in the United States for less than a year. "There is no future for a Jew in Russia," Mr. Ostrovsky says. He tells of Jews being unable to obtain better jobs, of a new government policy making it difficult for Jewish children to go to college, and of losing his job after asking Russian authorities for permission to emigrate. Now, with more than 1,000 other Russian émigrés in Jersey City, he speaks of revitalizing a neighborhood that less than two years earlier was a model of urban blight. "I have," he says, running his finger down a page in the dictionary and finding the word he wants, "hope" (Geist, 1982).

Although Richard Rodriguez (as he now calls himself), Bloke Modisane, and Vladimir Ostrovsky lived more than 10,000 miles apart, each suffered restrictions and humiliations that the other would find familiar. Because of their national origin, race, or religion, a dominant group had marked them as different; and they faced prejudice and discrimination.

Understanding such patterns of discrimination is the task of sociologists who study racial and ethnic relations. They ask questions about why and how certain groups come to be stigmatized and maltreated. For example, can any generalizations be made about how societies respond to encounters with new and different groups? Why do racial and ethnic diversity lead to coexistence in one instance but to a rank order of superior and inferior in another? Why do some minority groups become assimilated into a dominant society more rapidly than others? What changes in racial and ethnic relations have occurred in this country in the past 30,

50, 100 years? What future trends seem likely? These are some of the issues we will explore in this chapter.

MINORITY GROUPS

Richard Rodriguez, Bloke Modisane, and Vladimir Ostrovsky are members of what sociologists call **minority groups.** The term *minority* is something of a misnomer, for often the so-called minority group actually outnumbers the majority. In South Africa, for example, nonwhites constitute 80 percent of the population, yet they are treated as a minority by whites, who have the power of a majority. A minority group, then, is one that, because of the power differences among groups, is singled out for unequal treatment in the society. As minorities, these people are the victims of collective discrimination—in some cases even segregation, oppression, and persecution. In many societies, including our own, children (who have virtually no legal rights), the aged, and women (who make up 53 percent of the American population but occupy few positions of power) also have some of the characteristics of a minority. Most societies contain racial or ethnic minorities; these groups are the subject of this chapter.

Conflict among racial and ethnic groups is a worldwide problem. It occurs not only in our own country, and in South Africa and Russia, but in other countries as well. In Great Britain, for example, tension has arisen over recent immigrants from Pakistan, Kenya, Jamaica, and other former crown colonies in Asia, Africa, and the Caribbean. These nonwhite peoples, who now make up 3.7 percent of the population of the British Isles, are subject to growing prejudice and discrimination, as the riots in a number of English cities in 1981 demonstrated. Interracial conflict has been even greater in Uganda, where the black government actually confiscated the property of its Indian citizens and expelled them from the country. This drastic step was taken despite the fact that many of these people had never lived outside Uganda: they were "Indian" only by ancestry, sometimes two or three generations removed. Blacks in other east African nations, such as Kenya, likewise resent their Asian minorities. In these cases the people doing the discriminating are black. People of Chinese ancestry living in several nations in Southeast Asia also find themselves the victims of discrimination and prejudice at the hands of other Asians. So do Central American Indians in Mexico, Koreans in Japan, Hungarians in Romania, gypsies in Greece, Armenians in Turkey, Aborigines in Australia—the list could go on and on. In today's world, it appears, interracial conflict is less the exception than the rule. In view of the widespread nature of such discrimination, it is useful to examine the concepts that underlie it—race and ethnicity.

Race and Ethnicity

Biologically, a **race** is a population that through generations of inbreeding has developed distinctive physical characteristics that are transmitted genetically. In principle, it should be relatively simple to divide the human species into distinct racial categories. In reality, it is not.

Suppose we begin with the three groups most people identify as races—the white or Caucasian race, the yellow or Mongoloid race, and the black or Negroid race. Few of us have any difficulty telling Africans from Asians or Europeans. But where do we put the peoples of southern India, who have black skin but straight hair and Caucasian features? And do we classify the San (Bushmen) of southern Africa, who have yellowish skin and epicanthic folds (which make the eyes appear slanted), as Mongoloid?

In an effort to define racial categories, physical anthropologists have long studied physical differences between groups of people. But these studies have not led to clear racial distinctions. The anthropologist William Boyd (1950), for example, attempted to classify populations according to blood types. He discovered, among other things, that a high percentage of the people who live in sub-Saharan Africa have the so-called *cDe* gene. However, the same gene is also found in Europeans, in Asians, and in Navajos. Moreover, blood types do not correlate with outward appearance. The Papuans of New Guinea look very much like Africans; they could easily disappear into the crowds of Nairobi or of New York's Harlem. But the "Negroid gene," *cDe*, is exceedingly rare in New Guinea. In short, it is impossible to say biologically where one race stops and another begins. As the geneticist Theodosius Dobzhansky (1973) has pointed out, there is as much variation *within* one or another of the so-called races as there is between them.

Nevertheless, people perceive and react to racial differences, and this is why sociologists study them—not because skin color, hair texture, or other physical characteristics are intrinsically significant, but because people *think* they are. Thus a sociological definition of a *race* is a group of people who *perceive* themselves and are perceived by others as possessing certain distinctive and hereditary physical traits. These physical traits, in turn, are *assumed* to be related to a number of moral, intellectual, and other nonphysical attributes (Van den Berghe, 1978). As a result, the members of a race tend to consider themselves different from all other groups of people, and other groups tend to treat them as if they were.

You can see from this definition that race in the sociological sense is a social construct—a notion regarding group differences that has evolved across the centuries and that in turn has consequences for one's behavior. A race's existence lies only in the perceptions and beliefs of its beholders. For example, members of the Watusi tribe of central Africa consider themselves racially distinct from their Bahutu neighbors. Both have black skin, similar hair texture, and similar facial features, but the Bahutu are short and stocky while the Watusi are tall and lean, a fact of great social significance to the Watusi and Bahutu.

Like the concept of race, the concept of *ethnicity* is also a socially defined label. But there is an important difference between the two. Whereas race is a label based on perceived physical differences, ethnicity is a label based on perceived cultural differences. An **ethnic group,** in other words, is a category of people who perceive themselves and are perceived by others as possessing shared cultural traits—traits such as language, religion, family customs, and food preferences. Polish Americans, French Canadians, Jews, Puerto Ricans, and Navajo Indians are all examples of ethnic groups. Note that the extent to which ethnic group members actually share unique cultural traits is less important than that they, as well as others, *believe* they are ethnically distinct. Thus, ethnicity, like race, is a label that people create and apply.

As important as it is to define the concepts of race and ethnicity, it is equally important to understand their social consequences. One such consequence is the provision of what has been called a sense of "peoplehood" (Gordon, 1978). By this we mean a sense of identification with a relatively small segment of the world's population—those who by virtue of common ancestry or heritage we consider "our own kind." Although we may live and interact with people of other racial and ethnic backgrounds, we continue to feel that they are somehow "different" from us. Notions of race and ethnicity provide a consciousness of oneness, an

Although these paraders live and participate in the dominant American culture, one way they maintain their ethnic identity is by celebrating Norwegian Constitution Day. (Katrina Thomas/Photo Researchers)

ingroup feeling that "I am one of these" and "not one of those."

Why this compelling sense of racial and ethnic identity? One answer is that it satisfies an important psychological need. As Erich Fromm wrote in 1941:

> This identity with nature, clan, religion, gives the individual security. He belongs to, he is rooted in, a structuralized whole in which he has an unquestionable place. He may suffer from hunger or suppression, but he does not suffer from the worst of all pains—complete aloneness and doubt. (quoted in Isaacs, 1975)

This comforting sense of belonging may be one reason why racial and ethnic identities have persisted in spite of the homogenizing impact of modern industrial life. But there is also another reason. Social solidarity with others perceived as similar to oneself may serve important economic and political interests. Thus the belief in a superior "white" race that accompanied colonial expansion did much to fuel and justify economic exploitation. Similarly, shared racial consciousness among twentieth-century Africans did much to unite previously warring tribes in the struggle for independence. From this perspective, therefore, racial and ethnic bonds can be instrumental in achieving economic and political goals.

Prejudice and Discrimination

Prejudice and discrimination have taken on a strongly negative cast. We find it disconcerting to be accused of either. Indeed, to suggest that a person may be prejudiced or may discriminate is to raise doubts not only about the individual's essential morality but also about his or her patriotism and commitment to democratic principles. Hence, most of us take considerable pains to distance ourselves from public perceptions that we may be "bigots."

Prejudice is a categorical like or dislike of a group of people based on real or imagined social characteristics, usually associated with their race, religion, ethnic group, sexual orientation, or perhaps occupation. When people are so convinced that all members of a group are immoral, violent, and backward (or moral, peace-loving, and brilliant) that they cannot see them as individuals and ignore evidence that refutes their convictions, they are prejudiced. Because of their attitude, they "prejudge" all the individuals of a group from an inflexible perspective.

Discrimination refers to the act of disqualifying or mistreating people on the basis of their group membership. Whereas prejudice is a state of mind, discrimination is actual behavior. Discriminatory behavior does not necessarily indicate that a person is prejudiced. For example, a black store owner may decide not to hire Jews, not because he himself is prejudiced against Jews, but because he believes his customers are. However, discrimination tends to create and support prejudice by keeping people apart and limiting opportunities to disprove rumors and stereotypes. Conversely, prejudice also tends to create and support discrimination. When minority group members are viewed as inferior and unsuited to higher-status occupations, discrimination against them seems appropriate. Thus prejudice and discrimination work hand in hand to create and sustain racial and ethnic stratification.

The distinction between prejudice and discrimination is important. We often hear it said, "You cannot legislate against prejudice." This argument has been advanced by those who claim that laws are ineffective weapons for combating racism. What the argument overlooks is that such laws are designed primarily to deter discrimination. Just as laws against murder and theft are designed not to root out people's desire to kill or steal but to prevent these desires from finding expression in actual behavior, antidiscrimination laws are aimed at preventing certain kinds of behavior. Yet people often bring their attitudes in line with their actions. As discriminatory barriers have been legally broken down, people of different groups have begun to interact with one another in new and unimpeded ways and many of their prejudiced attitudes have been undermined.

The focus of prejudice and discrimination falls on what people as individuals think and do in their day-to-day interactions with others. The study of prejudice and discrimination is obviously useful. But it is also necessary to investigate **institutional discrimination**—how policies and programs are structured so as to systematically deny opportunities and equal rights to members of particular groups. Conflict and Marxist theorists have stressed that social arrangements in the United States have insured that critical decisions are made, issues defined, and resources allocated in ways that work to the advantage of whites while working against the interests of blacks and Hispanics (Carmichael and Hamilton, 1967; Friedman, 1969).

The concept of institutional discrimination draws our attention to the fact that schools, hospitals, factories, banks, and other key institutions do not have to be staffed by prejudiced people in order to bring about discriminatory results. For instance, employers typically require a certain level of formal education, such as a high school diploma or a college degree for certain positions. But when these standards are uniformly applied to all job applicants, individuals who did not have an equal opportunity to gain the necessary credentials are often automatically excluded. If members of minority groups have systematically been provided with less than adequate schooling, they enter the job market educationally handicapped; they cannot successfully compete with those who have the proper test scores, diplomas, degrees, and certificates (McLemore, 1983).

Another form of institutional discrimination occurs when members of a minority lack a qualification because of prior discriminatory practices. Some police and fire departments, for example, require a person to have worked in a job for ten or more years before becoming eligible for certain promotions. Even if minority members gain entry-level positions, they often find their opportunities impaired because they have been unable to acquire the years of seniority needed to qualify for the promotion. As we will see later in the chapter, affirmative action programs are designed to combat such types of institutional discrimination.

WHEN DIFFERENT GROUPS MEET

Viewed from one perspective, human history has consisted of a long series of contacts between different racial and ethnic groups. Archaeological evidence shows that, long before the dawn of history, human populations were on the move. The migrations of the early Hebrews recounted in the Old Testament were hardly unique (Berry and Tischler, 1978). Such contacts were marked by curiosity, conflict, accommodation, and occasionally fusion into new physical and cultural types (Shibutani and Kwan, 1965). These basic patterns are still being repeated, even though our time frame is usually too narrow for us to witness the broad, cyclical changes. Instead, our attention is often drawn to the most salient features of intergroup encounters—the misunderstandings, the conflicts, the exploitations, the cruelties, and the injustices.

Sociologists who study racial and ethnic relations have asked whether any generalizations can be made about the many instances of intergroup conflict. And they have found that several specific patterns have occurred repeatedly throughout recorded history. We will discuss some of the most common ones here by considering, first, patterns of conflict and domination, then, patterns of accommodation.

Patterns of Conflict and Domination

When people of different racial and ethnic groups come into contact with one another, they tend to view their own way of life, including their behaviors, beliefs, values, and norms, as the only right way of living, and they judge others by these standards. As pointed out in Chapter 3, sociologists term this process *ethnocentrism*. When people are strongly ethnocentric, they are distrustful of outsiders, seeing them as symbols of strangeness, evil, and danger: Their rituals seem sacrilegious; their customs, uncivilized; their laws, incomprehensible; and their gods, pagan. Intense glorification of the ingroup and loathing of the outgroup provides a fertile soil for prejudice and racist attitudes (Noel, 1972; Vander Zanden, 1983).

When ethnocentric attitudes are coupled with *intergroup competition* for territory and scarce resources, an explosive social mix results. When two groups both strive for the same things—and each perceives its claim to be mutually exclusive and legitimate—the stage is set for conflict. As pointed out in Chapter 11, when groups disagree as to whose values will prevail in channeling and regulating behavior and who will receive more of the benefits and fewer of the burdens of social living, *power* is the deciding factor. In modern societies, the state has become the vehicle that enables one group to dominate and keeps another group subordinate. In sum, competition supplies the motivation for systems of stratification, and ethnocentrism directs competition along racial and ethnic lines, but power determines which group will subjugate the other (Noel, 1972; Barth and Noel, 1975).

Were the Andean villagers of Urubamba, Peru and the Dogon people of Mali to observe each other's religious rituals, each group would find the other strange, perhaps even threatening or barbaric. The view that one's own cultural and religious traits are superior to others is an aspect of ethnocentrism. (Above, Paul Conklin; right, Eugene Gordon/Photo Researchers)

Economic and Political Subjugation

The economic takeover of one nation by another more powerful one and the subsequent political and social domination of the native population is called **colonialism.** It often begins when one group of people needs more labor, raw materials, and markets to fuel a growing economy. European colonialism, which began in the fifteenth century, is a prime example. The colonial powers wanted gold, silver, petroleum, and tin, which were not abundant in western Europe. They also wanted the tropical lumbers, mahogany and teak; warm-weather crops such as sugar, rubber, cotton, and tobacco; outlets for their surplus capital; and strategic military and naval bases. These they found in many areas of Africa, the Middle East, Asia, South America, and the Caribbean.

Initially, contact with the peoples of these areas was limited to a relatively small number of traders. Relations between them and the native population were often amicable, for the traders appeared to pose no serious threat and expanded the array of available goods. But as trade grew and profitable businesses were established, the governments of the European nations wanted to ensure that this lucrative commerce would continue indefinitely. They declared the areas in which they had established their economic holdings to be "colonies." Because of their great technological superiority, and because they soon came to control most of a colony's resources, the Europeans found that they could maintain their power with a relatively small number of administrative and military personnel.

Under economic colonialism the hard and dirty work—janitor, field hand, ditch digger, garbage collector, porter, street sweeper—is invariably delegated to the natives. This division of labor plus the mass organization of natives for work in the mines and fields results in a system of racial stratification. Usually, it is rigid. Natives can seldom rise out of the lowest stratum. Why is the system of rank ordering so inflexible? Part of the answer may lie in the fact that the colonialists are so greatly outnumbered. As a result, they may feel that a tight monopoly on the sources of power is essential to maintaining control (Shibutani and Kwan, 1965).

We are most familiar with overseas colonialism. But colonialism can also occur within a single state—**internal colonialism.** According to the sociologist Michael Hechter (1975), internal colonialism typically begins when different segments of a country industrialize at different rates. As a result, two distinct groups are formed—one relatively advanced and the other less so, each economically and spatially segregated from the other. It is not long before the more advanced group seeks to institutionalize its advantages through policies that perpetuate existing social inequality. Gradually, it becomes the dominant, or *core, group,* while those in the less developed areas become the subordinate, or *peripheral, group* (Blauner, 1972). Economically, the core exploits the periphery. The economy of the periphery is little more than a complement to the core; frequently, it rests on a single agricultural or mineral export. This economic subjugation is reinforced by political domination (Hechter, 1975).

Blacks in the United States have many of the earmarks of an internally colonized group, even though they are not geographically isolated (Clark, 1964, 1965; Franklin and Resnik, 1973). (Blacks, however, *are* residentially isolated.) For generations American blacks have been exploited as a source of cheap labor and as a group to fill the most menial jobs. And until the middle of the twentieth century, various voting restrictions also denied them access to political power, especially in the South. The civil rights movement of the 1950s and 1960s did much to remove the *legal* barriers to black equality. But this is not yet a racially integrated society. With a few exceptions, there is no easy and fluid mixture of blacks and whites in social cliques, intimate friendships, marriage relationships, or private organizations (Gordon,

South Africa is one of the most rigidly segregated nations in the world. For example, blacks and whites may not mingle on this staircase. (Peter Jordan/Liaison Agency)

1964). In many respects, the problems of blacks have been unique and not typical of immigrant groups with European backgrounds (Willhelm, 1970, 1980).

An inevitable accompaniment to all systems of colonialism and racial stratification is **segregation**—the physical and social separation of the races through custom or law. (**Integration,** in contrast, is the absence of this separation between the races.) In a segregated society, only certain types of contact between the dominant group and the minority group are permissible. Members of the subordinate group cannot live where the colonialists live, they cannot join the same clubs and organizations, and they are often prohibited from using the same public facilities (including everything from drinking fountains, restaurants, and movie theaters to restrooms and park benches). Segregation reinforces inequalities in income, power, and prestige. It usually finds its most extreme expression when the dominant group perceives the minority as a potential threat to the established order (Berry and Tischler, 1978).

Displacement of a Native Population

Economic and political subjugation of a minority population by a more powerful group is not the only pattern of conquest that occurs when different racial and ethnic groups meet. For instance, when a weaker group occupies a territory that a stronger group wishes to inhabit, and when there is not enough land to accommodate the two, the stronger is likely to displace the weaker. This displacement sometimes occurs through attrition: Members of the weaker group may die of starvation or disease. At other times the displacement takes the form of population transfers: Native peoples are either forcibly expelled from the area or leave voluntarily because life there becomes so hard for them. In the most extreme cases, a weaker group may be deliberately and ruthlessly exterminated *(genocide)*. Examples of all three means of displacement can be found in the pioneers' treatment of Native American groups, as well as in the European settlers' handling of native populations in Australia and New Zealand.

Displacement of native populations is typically found in areas rich in natural resources and similar in geography and climate to the homeland of the invading group (Lieberson, 1961; Van den Berghe, 1978). These traits make permanent settlement there appealing. At the beginning, contact between the newcomers and the native population may be tolerant or even friendly, because the newcomers are few in number. But as the size of the settler population increases, and more native land is encroached upon, intergroup conflict erupts. This pattern occurred on the American frontier. The Native Americans did not think of land as a commodity to be bought and sold. Consequently, they did not realize that white occupation of a piece of land meant a monopoly on its use. By the time this became clear, the Native Americans' very survival was threatened. They began to resist white expansion, but by then it was too late. The Native Americans were no match for the endless influx of white settlers with their vastly superior weapons (Spicer, 1980).

At first the whites attempted to "resolve" the conflict by moving the Native Americans west of the Mississippi. For example, in the 1830s the Cherokees, among others, were forced to march from their homelands in Georgia to an arid reservation in Oklahoma. As many as 4,000 Native Americans died on what came to be known as the Trail of Tears. By the early 1840s only a few Native Americans were left in the eastern United States. Later, on the Great Plains, whites destroyed the Native Americans' principal means of survival—the buffalo. Diseases introduced by the white settlers, for which the Native Americans lacked natural immunities, also decimated large segments of the native populations. Smallpox, for instance, completely annihilated the Missouri Indians. Sometimes whites intentionally left clothing infected with a deadly disease in places where Native Americans were sure to come upon them. The Native Americans, of course, continued to fight back, but this only convinced the white population that the two groups could not live together. A program of mass extermination began. Land, cattle, and other interests were only too happy to champion the cry, "The only good Indian is a dead Indian." In the end, about two-thirds of the Native American population was wiped out. The survivors were either relegated to the lowest rungs of the larger society or placed on poverty-stricken reservations run by the federal government (Shibutani and Kwan, 1965).

Unfortunately, the white settlers' treatment of the Native American was not a unique occurrence. Similar patterns have been repeated many times, in many places, and under a variety of circumstances. During World War II, for instance, the Soviet Union seized the opportunity to reduce interethnic conflict by expelling "disloyal nationalities"—the Volga Germans, the Chechen-Ingush, the Crimean Tartars, and the Kalmuks

—from their homelands. Genocide has also been practiced throughout history. The British settlers in Tasmania hunted the natives there for sheer sport. When the natives fought back, fierce warfare resulted. The British, of course, had the upper hand, and before long only a few hundred Tasmanians remained. These were herded onto a native reserve where the population gradually died out. In our own time the Nazi murder of 6 million Jews is yet another example of annihilation as the "final solution" to ethnic conflict. Thus sociologists have found that genocide and mass expulsions are not limited to instances of territorial expansion. In general, they occur when the dominant group perceives the threat posed by a minority as too great to be endured, when assimilation of the minority into the dominant group is viewed as impossible or undesirable, and when minority group members are not considered essential for their labor, knowledge, or skills.

The Creation of Racial and Ethnic Myths

One important question is how acts as inhumane as genocide and forced expulsions can be practiced by so many ordinary human beings. The answer lies partly in the creation of very powerful racial and ethnic myths. When people behave in ways that can be viewed as cruel or unjust, they tend to develop beliefs to justify those actions, and these beliefs then become widely dispersed. For example, the fact that members of the lowest caste in India (the untouchables) were once treated like social lepers was justified by age-old religious doctrine. The Hindu religion holds that a person's present station in life is a result of his or her conduct in the life directly preceding (Hindus believe in reincarnation). A person of low status, in other words, has *earned* that low status through unworthy deeds in the past. Such a belief clearly makes social distance from untouchables seem much more appropriate, even "right."

This same type of belief system frequently arises to justify racial and ethnic stratification. The most common example in recent times is the doctrine of **racism**—the belief that some human races are inherently inferior to others. Racism provided a convenient justification for European subjugation of other peoples. For instance, the Englishman Sir Harry Johnston, a well-known colonial administrator and presumed "authority" on Africa, argued that blacks were by nature a docile and cheerful people, quick to forget injustices and cruelties, always grateful for any kindness (Shibutani and Kwan, 1965). In short, blacks in the view of Johnston and many other eighteenth-century Europeans were simple and childlike. These qualities, they concluded, made them biologically suited to be the servants of whites. Precisely the same reasoning justified black slavery in the southern United States. Harsher views have justified even harsher treatment. For example, the belief of many settlers that Native Americans were savages, little more than wild beasts, justified their extermination.

Racist views are still common today, although they are often much more sophisticated. For instance, in 1969, Arthur Jensen, an educational psychologist at the University of California at Berkeley, published an article on race, heredity, and intelligence in the *Harvard Educational Review*. The average score for black Americans on IQ tests, he reported, is ten to fifteen points lower than the average score for whites. Reviewing the literature on this subject, Jensen concluded that "it [is] a not unreasonable hypothesis that genetic factors are strongly implicated in the average Negro-white intelligence difference" (1969: 82).

Was Jensen right? Are there biologically based differences in the intellectual capabilities of the average black and the average white? Very few sociologists think so. Instead, they feel that Jensen's reasoning reflects age-old racial myths—this time cloaked in the legitimacy of modern scientific research. Sociologist Melvin Tumin (1973) holds this point of view. He argues that the high levels of prejudice and discrimination in this country make it impossible to equate blacks and whites, even if their incomes and educations are alike. If we could find people whose experiences were identical, only at that point could we make valid racial comparisons, concluding that whatever differences we found were innate. But we cannot.

Most social sicentists reject Jensen's interpretation of racial differences in IQ test performance (Scarr, 1981). For example, recent research demonstrates that basic mathematical ability develops in a robust manner among both white and black preschoolers (Ginsburg and Russell, 1981). Although their academic achievement later diverges, both groups *enter* school with the intellectual capabilities for adequate performance in school arithmetic. And the psychologists Sandra Scarr and Richard A. Weinberg (1975, 1976) find that most of the IQ gap between blacks and whites is closed among black children who are adopted by white middle-class foster parents.

Differences in IQ between black and white children are not biologically determined. The gap that exists between the two groups arises from unequal educational and social opportunities. (Charles Gupton/Southern Light)

In sum, most social scientists have concluded that if there are IQ differences between blacks and whites, they exist largely because these groups have not had and still do not have the same opportunities. The significant differences are not biological; they are socially created and maintained. Indeed, the psychologist Leon J. Kamin (1974) asserts that IQ tests are simply devices employed by elites to justify inequality and racism. If, as elites claim, IQ is a matter of genes, then little can be done environmentally to improve people's abilities. And if people's abilities cannot be improved, then inequalities in power and rewards are inevitable, and the existing stratification structure is fixed. Viewed in this manner, the use of IQ tests for educational and job placements ensures that the children of elites—having gained the "proper" IQ credentials—will secure the best positions.

Patterns of Accommodation

Although we hear so much about interracial and interethnic conflict and oppression, it is important to recognize that race and ethnic relations can also be characterized by tolerance and accommodation. Sometimes this accommodation follows a period of severe conflict. At other times initial conflict may hardly arise at all. Sociologists are particularly interested in knowing the conditions that underlie various forms of accommodation among members of racial and ethnic groups. We will explore some of those conditions here.

The Melting Pot Concept

One form that interracial and interethnic accommodation can take is for majority and minority to intermarry and for their various customs and values to blend, thus creating a new cultural hybrid. This is what the early-twentieth-century writer Israel Zangwill (1909:198–199) had in mind when he described America as a *melting pot* in his popular play concerning the life of a young Russian-Jewish immigrant: "There she lies, the great melting pot—listen! Can't you hear the roaring and bubbling? Ah, what a stirring and seething—Celt and Latin, Slav and Teuton, Greek and Syrian, Black and Yellow—Jew and Gentile." In Zangwill's romantic plot, the poor Jewish boy marries the beautiful Christian girl, all animosities between their families disappear, and the couple lives happily ever after. Such a cultural and biological blending—in which the customs and values of both groups are to some extent preserved—is, of course, possible. It is probably most likely to occur when power among various racial and ethnic groups is relatively equal and when relations among them are more cooperative than competitive. Blending also is more likely when ethnocentrism is not strong and when group members do not perceive themselves as having a large stake in preserving traditional ways.

Although the melting pot concept is frequently lauded in our political speeches, it is not a very accurate description of what actually happened to those who immigrated to the United States. Sociologist Milton Gordon (1978) writes:

> There is no reason to suppose that these men [the nation's founding fathers] looked upon their fledgling country as an impartial melting pot for the merging of the various cultures of Europe, or as a new "nation of nations," or as anything but a society in which, with important political modifications, Anglo-Saxon speech and institutional forms would be standard. (p. 185)

John Quincy Adams expressed the sentiment in the early nineteenth century:

> To one thing they [immigrants to America] must make up their minds, or they will be disappointed in every expectation of happiness as Americans. They must cast off the European skin, never to resume it. They must look forward to their posterity rather than backward to their ancestors; they must be sure that whatever their own feelings may be, those of their children will cling to the prejudices of this country. (Quoted in Gordon, 1978: 187)

Thus, from the earliest days of this country, newcomers were expected to adopt Anglo-Saxon customs and values.

Assimilation

The adoption of prevailing norms and values is part of the process of **assimilation**—the incorporation of a minority into the culture and social life of the majority such that the minority eventually disappears as a separate, identifiable unit. Assimilation is another form that interracial and interethnic accommodation can take.

Assimilation has two faces: It leads to a merging of different customs and traditions to produce a common culture having the attributes of both groups. However, it often brings with it pressure to adopt new culture and leave the old behind. If success or upward mobility can be achieved only by shedding the old culture, then the new culture begins to seem "superior"—and the old "inferior" by comparison.

The sociologist Robert E. Park was one of the first to describe the assimilation process as a cycle of stages through which each new immigrant group to the United States presumably passed (Park, 1925). The process begins with the newcomers competing to gain a foothold in their newly adopted nation. But because they do not know the dominant culture, the immigrants can only manage to secure what others do not want—the poorest land, the worst housing, the most menial jobs. As a result, they find themselves scorned and ridiculed, looked down upon by better-established people. Most gravitate to separate ethnic enclaves (often city slums) where they can feel secure and at ease. Eventually, however, these immigrants, and especially their children and grandchildren, begin to acquire the culture of the dominant group. Their original struggle for survival is converted to a struggle for respectability, better living conditions, and higher-paying, more prestigious jobs. This struggle is not an easy one. But gradually more and more members of the ethnic group achieve upward mobility, remnants of their traditional culture fade, and intergroup marriages occur. The result is complete assimilation.

A look at the racial and ethnic groups that have come to the United States reveals that Park's description applies better to some than to others. The Scottish and Scandinavians, for instance, have been assimilated quite fully, the Italians somewhat less so, and the Puerto Ricans hardly at all. What can explain these differences in the speed and degree to which groups have been absorbed into the larger society?

One factor is simply differences in the amount of time different groups have been here. Most northern European immigrants, for instance, arrived before the turn of the century. In contrast, the influx of immigrants from Puerto Rico has occurred only since World War II, so not surprisingly they are less assimilated. However, the time factor cannot explain all differences in current levels of assimilation. Why, for example, are blacks, who have been here for several hundred years, still excluded from the mainstream of American life? The answer has much to do with a deep ethnocentrism among many Americans of white Anglo-Saxon Protestant heritage. In general, this ethnocentrism has meant that the invitation to participate equally in American society has been offered very selectively. People whose cultural background and physical appearance are most similar to those of the dominant group have had by far the easiest time. The dominant group may also discourage rapid assimilation because they derive economic benefits from another group's minority status. For example, the building of the railroads across the West—and the amassing of gigantic fortunes by railroad magnates—was fostered by the availability of a large underclass of Chinese laborers who would work for subsistence wages. Finally, different rates of assimilation are also related to an immigrant group's own *desire* to assimilate. Some ethnic groups have felt more ambivalence than others toward certain aspects of American culture. Many Hispanic Americans, for instance, question the white middle-class custom that parents and their children live apart from other kin (even thousands of miles from parents, siblings, grandparents, aunts, uncles, and cousins). Instead, they value the warmth and security of a large extended family. Such ambivalence toward some of the customs found in the United States could make an immigrant group reluctant to abandon its own cultural ways.

Pluralism

Because of all these factors, and probably several others, the pattern of racial and ethnic assimilation in the United States has been uneven. In reality, there is considerable cultural and structural **pluralism.** In a pluralistic society, each group retains its own language, religion, and customs, and its members tend to interact socially (date, marry, form close friendships) primarily among themselves. Yet all jointly participate in the economic and political systems. A prime example of such an arrangement can be found in Switzerland. There, people of German, French, and Italian heritage preserve their distinct cultural ways while coexisting peacefully and equally. No one group enjoys special privileges or is discriminated against.

In the United States pluralism does not exist to the same degree. White Anglo-Saxon Protestant customs and values still largely predominate. But many members of racial and ethnic minorities—from blacks to Italians to Chinese to Hispanics—do seem to wish to preserve at least some of their cultural identities. What's more, for most such minorities there is a network of organizations and relationships that permits members to live their lives within the confines of the group. In short, largely because of ethnic exclusiveness among minorities as well as the dominant group, pluralism has been an important part of American racial and ethnic experience (Lieberson, 1980).

New York's Chinese community maintains its cultural identity through shared language, customs and religious festivals. Here, a costumed "dragon" walks through the streets of Chinatown as part of the traditional Chinese New Year celebration. (Rick Winsor/Woodfin Camp & Associates)

A CLOSER LOOK AT RACIAL AND ETHNIC STRATIFICATION

We have explored the broad patterns of racial and ethnic relations—the historical trends, the various modes of conquest, domination, rejection, and accommodation. Now it is time to switch lenses and take a closer look at systems of racial and ethnic stratification. Can any generalizations be made about why such systems arise? Why do prejudice and discrimination arise in the first place? And why are they directed more against some groups than against others? These are key questions in the study of race and ethnic relations. We will discuss some of the answers that social scientists have proposed.

The Psychological Perspective

Suppose a man works five or six days a week in a factory, trying to support his family, but never seems to be able to make ends meet. Given his circumstances, he might blame the well-to-do generally and his employers specifically for failing to pay him an adequate wage. But these people have the power to cut off his income; to oppose them openly could be counterproductive. He might also blame himself for his financial problems, but this is likely to make him uncomfortable. So he looks for another source of blame. Mexican immigrants have begun working in his factory. He does not really know them, but he suspects that they are willing to work for low wages and that many Mexicans are eager to take his job. By a process of twisted logic, he perceives the Mexicans as responsible for his poverty. Soon he is exchanging derogatory stories about them with his cronies and supporting efforts to close the border. Hating Mexicans makes the man and his friends feel a little better.

This psychological portrait of prejudice is based on the **frustration-aggression hypothesis.** According to this view, people are goal-directed creatures who become angry and hostile when their desires are frustrated. Consequently, they lash out. But at whom do they strike? Presumably, if people do not know who or what is blocking their ambitions or believe the obstacle is too threatening and powerful to attack, they look for some person or group on which to vent their feelings. Frustrated and angry, they often displace their hostility on a substitute target—a **scapegoat.** Usually, the scapegoat is readily accessible and, conveniently, too weak to retaliate.

Once they find a group to serve as a scapegoat people justify their irrational feelings and behavior by "discovering" evidence that the outgroup is indeed wicked and inferior. In this way, people can maintain some feeling that they are reasonable and kind. But the catch is that in verbally or physically attacking Mexicans, Jews, blacks, or members of any other group, prejudiced people avoid confronting the true sources of their problems. Consequently, their situation does not change, and frustration and hostility grow.

The Role of Intergroup Conflict

As intriguing as psychological perspectives on prejudice and discrimination may be, they do not seem able to provide a full explanation. Why, for example, is one minority singled out for the most intense bigotry and hatred even though other subordinate groups would be equally powerless to retaliate? One very persuasive answer is that the degree of prejudice and discrimination depends heavily on the level of conflict between groups. When the dominant group perceives a given minority as particularly threatening to its established position (or to its desire for *more* income, power, and prestige), a great deal of prejudice and discrimination will result. From this perspective, therefore, prejudice and discrimination are very effective weapons in intergroup conflict: Discrimination injures or neutralizes the other group, while prejudice justifies discrimination (Newman, 1973). Prejudice and discrimination arise, in short, because in certain situations they prove useful.

At times, however, it is difficult to ascertain which is cause and which effect: Does social and economic conflict cause prejudice and discrimination or is it the other way around? There are many historical cases in which intergroup conflict appears to have arisen first. For example, when the British first established themselves in India, they showed little bigotry toward the native population. The colonizers even encouraged intermarriage. All this changed, however, when the offspring of mixed marriages began to outnumber the Europeans and to compete for managerial and administrative jobs. Then Indians and so-called mixed bloods became the targets of intense discrimination, justified by a strong belief in their racial inferiority.

A key question in analyses of prejudice and discrimination is: Who profits from it? Is it primarily elites within the dominant group whose economic and social interests are served? Marxists say yes. They see racial and ethnic prejudice as arising from a calculated effort on the part of capitalists to keep large segments of the population easily exploited, subject to subsistence wages (Reich, 1981). And Marxists say that blacks and immigrant workers make an ideal "reserve labor force." During times of labor strife or high production, they can be readily hired. Then, when the economy contracts, they can be as readily released into the ranks of the unemployed without any unsettling effects. Moreover, Marxists point out that racial hatred, when it permeates society, is an effective way to divert the attention of workers from the true cause of their plight. In short, they believe racism is deliberately fostered by the ruling class to create discord and antagonism *among* workers, thus helping to safeguard the capitalists' privileged position. It is a strategy of "divide and conquer" that deflects a united working-class challenge to capitalist rule.

In support of this view Marxists point to a variety of historical incidents. For example, in the early twentieth century in California, there was a great deal of hostility toward Japanese farmers, even though the Japanese held only a tiny fraction of the arable land. Whites who owned small farms became convinced that the Japanese were driving agricultural prices down by their practice of using the entire family as a source of cheap farm labor. (In truth, the Japanese probably held too little land to have any effect on prices.) Eventually, the California legislature passed the Alien Land Acts, which denied Japanese immigrants the right to buy additional land in the state. Now, on the surface, this conflict appears to be strife strictly among small farmers, divided along racial lines. But a deeper look reveals that this was not the case. The real organizers behind the anti-Japanese protest turned out to be the owners of the huge California agricultural estates. According to George E. Simpson and J. Milton Yinger (1972: 118):

> These men certainly did not fear the competition of the few Japanese farmers with their relatively small holdings. What they did fear was the opposition of the small white landowners who found it difficult to compete with the estates, the struggles for improvement of their very badly paid field hands, the traditions in favor of family-sized farms and homesteads, and federal legislation that prevented them from monopolizing the water supplied through governmentally sponsored irrigation projects. If they could divert attention from their own control of the land by attacking the Japanese farmer as the cause of everybody's difficulties, they might funnel off some of the hostility to which they were vulnerable and get political support for laws favorable to them.

It is just this kind of manipulative behavior on the part of capitalists that Marxists believe fosters racial and ethnic prejudice among members of the working class.

Others, however, strongly disagree. They say that the conflicts between workers of different races and ethnic backgrounds are not always this contrived. For instance, after the Civil War, when white craftspeople (blacksmiths, carpenters, and the like) found themselves in direct competition with former slaves trained in these skills, very real conflict over jobs erupted. The outcome was a great deal of hostility toward blacks among working-class whites. The sociologist Edna Bonacich (1972, 1975) says that as a result, a "split labor market" has grown up in the United States—an "aristocracy"of higher-paid labor (mostly white) and a lower layer of cheaper labor (largely black). She says business pays blacks lower wages not because it is sinister, but simply because it pays labor as little as possible, regardless of race or ethnicity. Consequently, higher-paid workers are motivated to resist capitalist attempts to undercut their wages and jobs, and they do so by instituting a "caste system" (erecting social and legal barriers to the employment of blacks, disfranchising black voters, and setting up a system of segregated, inferior schools for blacks). Hence, Bonacich places the responsibility for racism on higher-paid workers rather than on capitalists. The antagonism of white workers toward black workers may help explain why, in most tests to measure prejudice, lower-class and working-class whites score higher on average than upper-class whites. It is noteworthy that a study of the Ku Klux Klan found the majority of members to come from the working and lower middle classes (Vander Zanden, 1960). Racism among the lower classes, critics of Marxism say, cannot *all* be the result of upper-class cunning and lower-class gullibility.

Our discussion has stressed the central role conflict plays in breeding prejudice, discrimination, and racist institutions. On this matter sociologists are in agreement. They differ, however, in their appraisal of the extent to which the fundamental conflicts within society are *between* classes and the role of various classes in generating racism. Even so, sociologists emphasize that some individuals and groups have a stake in racist ideologies and arrangements and that some benefit more than others. Further, once embedded within a society's culture, racism gains a momentum of its own, a matter to which we now turn our attention.

The Cultural Factor

Although conflict theories of prejudice and discrimination, like psychological theories, are very compelling, they cannot explain everything. Why, for example, do bigotry and hatred frequently remain even after the conflict that originally caused them has long since disappeared? An exploration of the cultural side of prejudice and discrimination can shed some light on this question.

In ethnically stratified societies, prejudice becomes part of the culture, a social habit handed down from generation to generation. Children learn to value their whiteness or blackness and to avoid or defer to members of different races and ethnic groups, much as they learn their gender identity and sex role. Children learn from parents, siblings, friends, and, of course, television, which until recently indirectly taught young Americans that black people are like Amos and Andy, and that Native Americans are hostile, ignorant savages. With such early training, it is not surprising that prejudice toward minority groups would seem as "natural" as love of competition, respect for private property, or any other attitude deeply embedded in American culture.

But how can people continue to hold racial and ethnic prejudices when these prejudices are based on such gross overgeneralizations, if not complete inaccuracies? Part of the answer is that many people seldom come in contact with members of the disparaged minority, so they have no chance to have their traditional stereotypes disproven. Moreover, when people do encounter members of a disparaged group, their very prejudice tends to distort their view to conform to their negative preconceptions. They "see" the people of their stereotypes—they "check out" the people based on their cultural definitions and "lock onto" those traits that confirm their pre-existing notions. For instance, a dominant-group member who "takes a break" is defined as "resting"; a minority-group member who does the same is perceived as "shiftless." The result is that prejudice is very difficult to undo.

Even traits normally considered virtues become vices when perceived through a prejudiced eye. The sociologist Robert K. Merton (1957:428) observes:

> Did Lincoln work far into the night? This testifies that he was industrious, resolute, perseverant, and eager to realize his capacities to the full. Do the out-group Jews or Japanese keep these same hours? This only bears witness to their sweatshop mentality, their ruthless undercutting of American standards, their unfair competitive practices. Is the in-group hero frugal, thrifty, and sparing? Then the out-group villain is stingy, miserly and penny-pinching. All honor is due to the in-group Abe for his having been smart, shrewd, and intelligent and, by the same token, all contempt is owing the out-group Abes for their being sharp, cunning, crafty, and too clever by far.

Finally, people are adept at using the *consequences* of prejudice and discrimination to "prove" that their negative evaluation was right. Blacks on average *do* live in poorer houses than whites, they *do* hold lower-paying jobs, they *do* have fewer years of schooling. But rather than being any justifiction for prejudice and discrimination, these conditions are the *result* of prejudice and discrimination. Yet whites turn around and use these facts as evidence that blacks are inferior to whites (see Figure 12.1, p. 310). Through such illogical reasoning prejudice can survive even if most people derive little concrete benefit from it.

CONTEMPORARY AMERICAN RACE AND ETHNIC RELATIONS

Targets of prejudice and discrimination are frequently condemned to the lowest rungs of the social hierarchy, and this in turn limits their basic life chances. Substandard housing, malnutrition, inadequate health care, a greater likelihood of suffering divorce, serious crime, physical and mental illness, and an early death all come with being at the bottom of the social order. These outcomes were discussed in detail in Chapter 10 and so will not be repeated here.

Living in a society that preaches equality and practices discrimination also has its psychological costs.

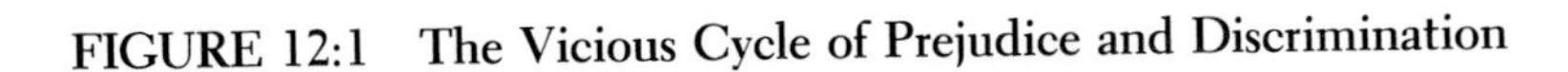

FIGURE 12:1 The Vicious Cycle of Prejudice and Discrimination

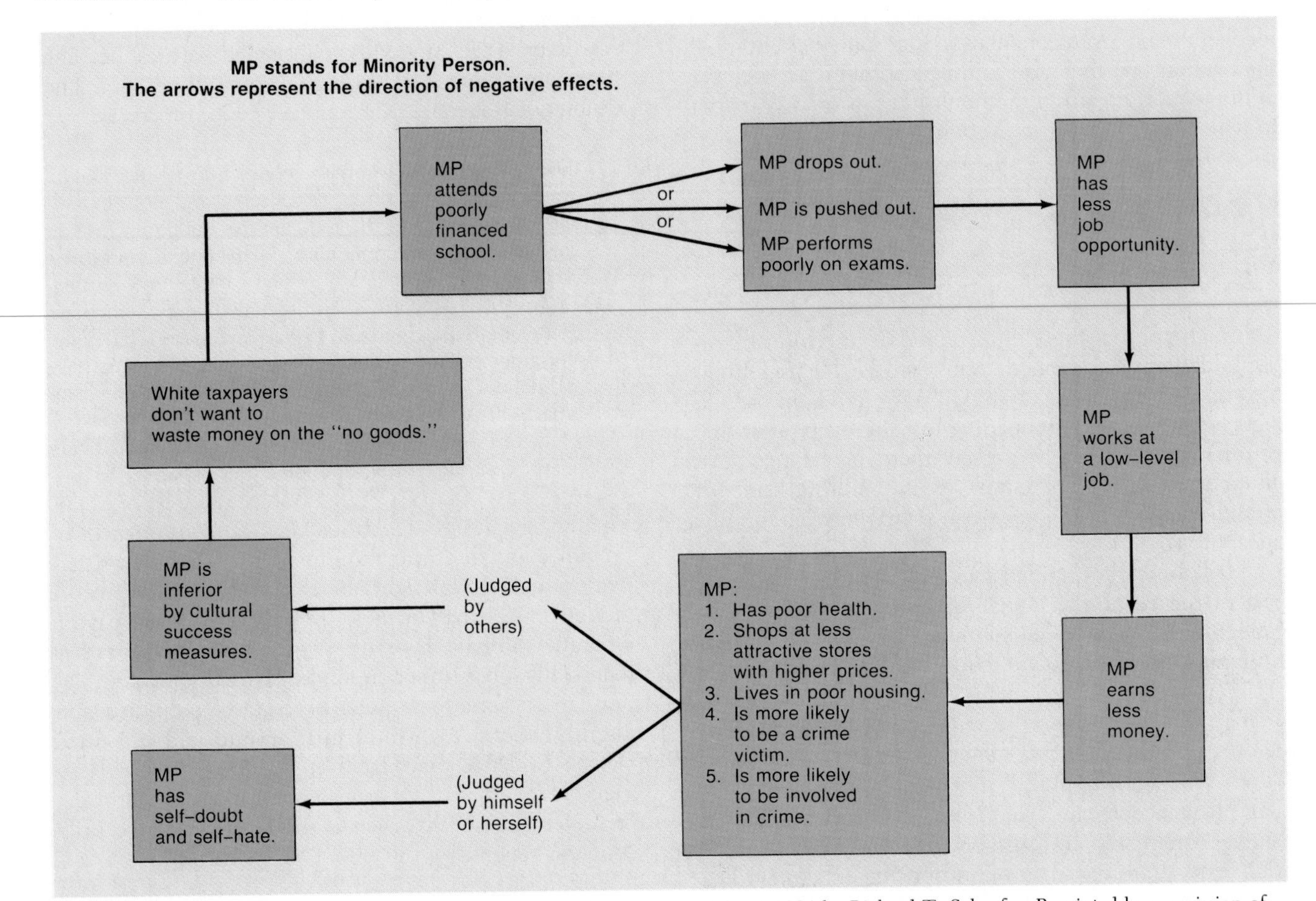

Source: From Richard T. Schaefer, *Racial and Ethnic Groups*, 2nd ed. Copyright © 1984 by Richard T. Schaefer. Reprinted by permission of Little, Brown and Company.

This figure illustrates the vicious cycle that is created by prejudice and discrimination. The outcome of this system—members of minority groups are judged inferior by cultural standards—then becomes the rationale for future discrimination and prejudice.

In *Dark Ghetto,* the psychologist Kenneth B. Clark (1965:63–64) argues that chronic social injustices

> corrode and damage the human personality, thereby robbing it of its effectiveness, of its creativity, if not its actual humanity. . . . Human beings who are forced to live under ghetto conditions and whose daily experience tells them that almost nowhere in society are they respected and granted the ordinary dignity and courtesy accorded to others, will, as a matter of course, begin to doubt their self-worth.

Here we will review the circumstances of a number of American minority groups, consider minority responses to racism, and examine several programs to combat institutional racism.

American Minority Groups

It is often said that the United States is "a nation of immigrants." There is much truth to this statement. Even so, at the very time in 1886 that the nation was preparing to unveil the inscription on the Statue of Liberty inviting to America "your huddled masses yearning to breathe free," Congress had already enacted the Chinese Exclusion Act. And some immigrants have been more welcome than others (see Figure 12.2). (The boxed insert discusses current immigration to the United States.) It is also true that Americans of African ancestry

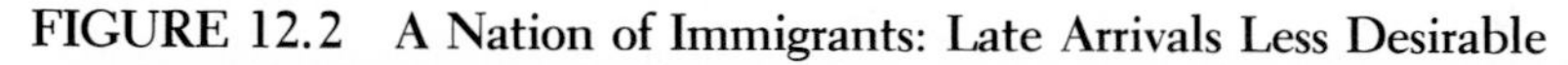

FIGURE 12.2 A Nation of Immigrants: Late Arrivals Less Desirable

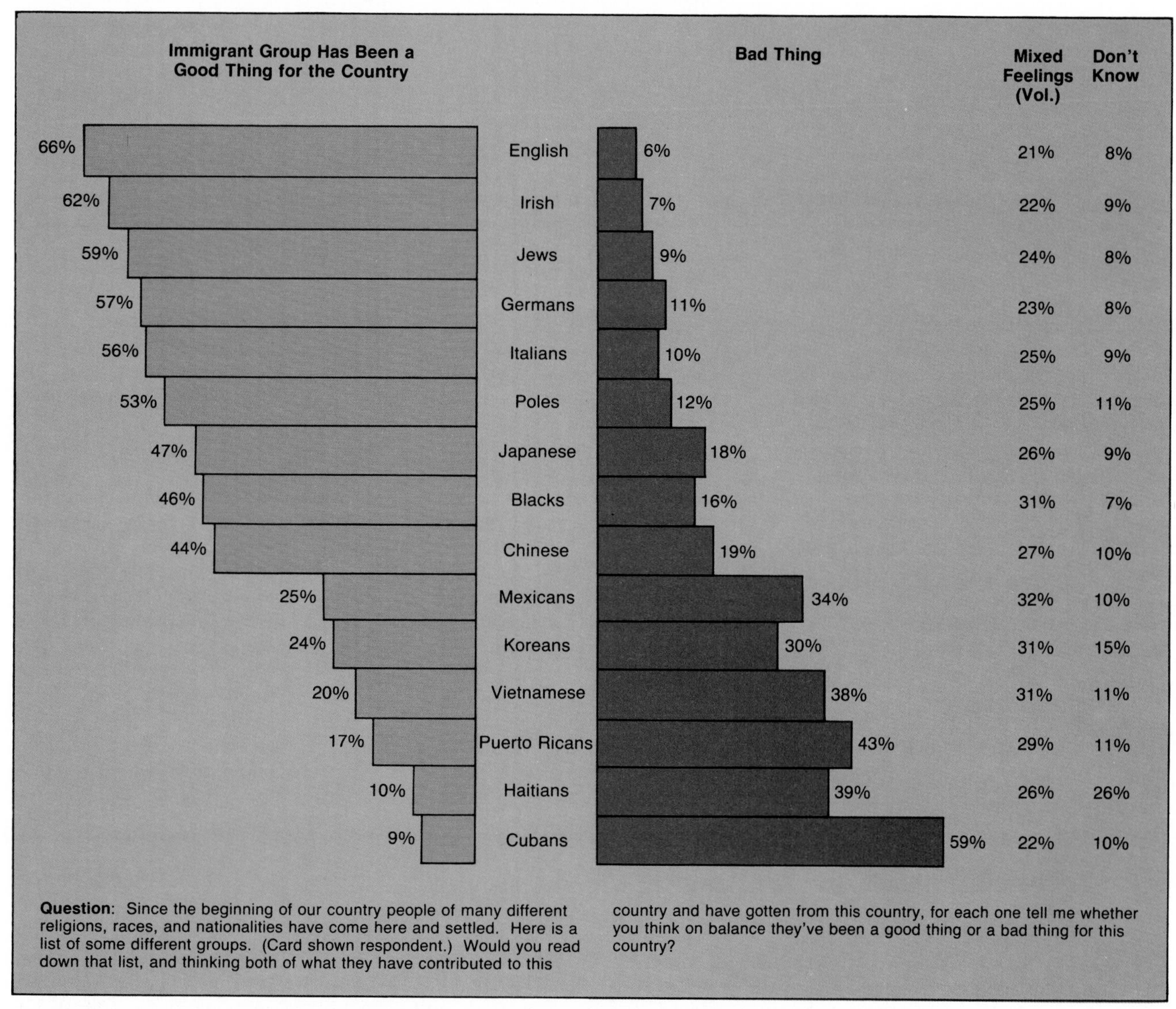

Source: Survey by the Roper Organization (Roper Report 82–4), March 20–27, 1982; *Public Opinion*, Vol. 5, No. 3 (June–July 1982):34.

THE SOCIOLOGICAL EYE ON:

United States Immigration Today

In the early years of the twentieth century, millions of immigrants arrived in America. They came mostly from eastern Europe and Italy, and many of them settled in the eastern states and in New York City. Like the waves of Irish and Scandinavians who preceded them, these newcomers were predominantly poor and uneducated. They spoke little or no English and their customs and traditions were strange to the established American population. Predictably, they met with discrimination and prejudice. Even though the immigrants were not typically welcomed to American shores, their children learned English, became educated, and entered the American mainstream.

Over the past two decades, immigration to the United States has once again sharply increased, reaching levels not seen since the first two decades of this century (Massey, 1981). During the 1960s more than 3 million people legally immigrated to this country, and during the 1970s more than 4 million arrived. These trends have accelerated in the 1980s.

Three major developments have shaped immigration to the United States since 1960 (Massey, 1981). First, the Immigration Act of 1965 (the Hart-Celler Act) abolished the discriminatory national-origins quota system and replaced it with an ethnic-blind system. Second, large numbers of refugees from Cuba and Vietnam fled to this country when the pro-American governments in their homelands fell. Third, the migration of labor between low- and high-income nations gained momentum. Let us consider each of these factors in turn.

Immigration to the United States went largely unregulated until 1882. In that year Congress enacted the Chinese Exclusion Act, which for the first time prohibited immigrants from a specific nation from entering the United States and declared them ineligible to become citizens. In the 1920s new legislation established a national-origins quota system that gave preference to immigrants from northern European nations. Underlying the arrangement was the notion that some racial or ethnic groups were preferable to others. The significance of the Immigration Act of 1965 is that it abolished the national-origins quota system. The new program allowed 120,000 entrance visas annually for individuals living in the Western Hemisphere and 170,000 visas for those living in the Eastern Hemisphere. (In 1977 the number of entrance visas for immigrants from the Western Hemisphere was increased to 170,000.) Overall, the new legislation gives preference to applicants with family ties to other Americans and with essential occupational skills.

The military and political upheavals in Cuba and Indochina have brought over 1 million Cubans and 400,000 Indochinese to the United States (Massey, 1981). Many of the Cuban immigrants had been professionals, managers, landowners, and business owners. Initially, they experienced sharp downward occupational mobility in the United States, but in recent years their talents and skills have enabled many of them to achieve substantial upward mobility. Most of the Vietnamese immigrants also enjoyed higher status in Vietnam than in the United States, but they too give evidence of upward mobility.

Immigration from third-world nations to higher-income nations has also increased in recent decades. Economic and political difficulties in their native lands, coupled with job opportunities and freedom in the United States, have encouraged many foreign nationals to enter the United States illegally when they cannot attain legal admission. Just how many illegal aliens are in the United States is not known. Some estimates place the figure in excess of 12 million. However, the Census Bureau concludes that 2 million illegal aliens were included in the 1980 census and that the total number is under 4 million. (It estimates that 6 million aliens were legally in the country.) Of the undocumented aliens counted in 1980, the Census Bureau estimates that 45 per-

came to the New World involuntarily as slaves. Moreover, some Americans were conquered by English-speaking "outsiders," namely the Native American (Indian) peoples and the Mexican and Spanish peoples of the Southwest. Table 12.1 (p. 314) portrays the racial and ethnic makeup of the nation's population as ascertained by the 1980 census. A number of population experts predict that by the year 2080 whites of European ancestry will be a numerical minority. The biggest shifts will be in the growth of the Hispanic and Asian populations (Coates, 1982).

Closing the open door

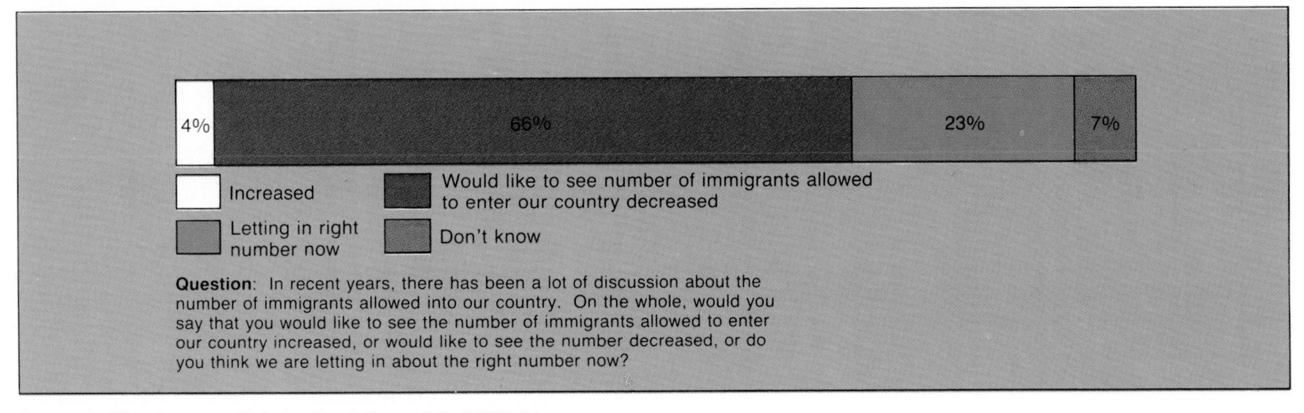

Source: Public Opinion, Vol. 5, No. 3 (June–July 1982):34.

cent were from Mexico, 17 percent from Central America and the Caribbean, 12 percent from Europe, 12 percent from Asia, 7 percent from South America, 5 percent from Africa, Australia, and the Pacific Islands, and 2 percent from Canada (Pear, 1983).

On the whole, Americans would like to see the number of immigrants allowed to enter the United States decreased (see figure). Some labor leaders express concern that immigrant labor takes jobs from citizens, holds down wages, and impedes efforts to improve working conditions. They add that the fear of deportation makes illegal aliens vulnerable to intimidation and cuts them off from government remedies. But some economists say that while aliens take jobs, they also make jobs. For example, truckers and workers in processing plants are "supported" by migrant workers who pick the vegetables and fruit that they transport and handle. And the money the aliens earn generates demand for other goods and services. Moreover, immigrants often do not compete with citizens for jobs. Immigrants have helped to revitalize the garment industry in New York City and Los Angeles, although admittedly at high human cost to the alien workers. And many nursing homes in the United States are made economically viable by the availability of cheap labor. Further, contrary to popular belief, many studies have found that illegal migrants pay more in taxes than they consume in government services. Indeed, they are unlikely to apply for Social Security and welfare benefits (Keely, 1982).

Black Americans

The 26.5 million Americans who trace their ancestry back to Africa through 360 years of poverty, exploitation, and violence are this country's largest racial minority. As late as World War II, 80 percent of black Americans lived in the South, where they functioned in large part as farm workers. Today, nearly half of the nation's black population live outside the South, and 74 percent live in metropolitan areas (U.S. Bureau of the Census, 1980).

Many of the first Africans to come to America came

TABLE 12.1 Racial and Ethnic Categories, 1980 Census

White	188,341,000
Black	26,488,000
Hispanics*	14,600,000
American Indian, Eskimo, Aleutian Islanders	1,418,177
Chinese	806,000
Filipino	775,000
Japanese	701,000
Asian-Indian	362,000
Korean	355,000
Vietnamese	262,000
Hawaiian	167,000
Samoan	42,000
Guamanian	32,000

*Due to a peculiarity of the 1980 Census form, many Hispanics were additionally counted in the "white" or "black" categories.

Source: U.S. Bureau of the Census, *Statistical Abstract*, 1980.

not as slaves but as indentured servants—people who contract to work for a given number of years, after which they receive their freedom. For a time it even seemed as if slavery might not flourish in the newly established colonies. By the end of the seventeenth century, however, nearly all blacks and their descendants had been relegated to perpetual servitude under the law. The reason was primarily economic: Southern planters found slavery highly profitable. With the invention of the cotton gin and the tremendous increase in cotton production it unleashed, slavery came to be seen as vital to the prosperity of the South. Before slavery was abolished, nearly half a million blacks had been forcibly brought to this land, where they were viewed purely as property. They were bought, sold, used, and abused at the will of the white majority. The belief in black inferiority that developed to justify slavery continues to influence black-white relations to this day.

Slavery was abolished in 1865, but white terrorism and discrimination were not. **Jim Crow laws,** which barred blacks from public facilities, and periodic lynching kept blacks "in their place." That "place" meant continued economic exploitation and political exclusion.

A decisive battle against segregation began in the South during the 1960s, with boycotts and nonviolent demonstrations. Blacks marched, picketed, and sat in at "white only" restaurants. Not long after, blacks began to win civil rights victories in the courts and in Congress. At the same time, they continued to migrate to Northern cities, as they had been doing in increasing numbers since before World War I. (By the late 1970s, however, the trend had reversed: More blacks were moving South than were leaving.) Northern ghettos grew, and there arose a new generation of black leaders, street-wise and uncompromising, who stopped looking to white America for answers.

Urbanization, political awareness, and social and economic mobility have made black Americans a growing force to be reckoned with. In such key states as New York, California, Illinois, and Texas, there are at least 1 million potential black voters per state; in Michigan, New Jersey, Ohio, and Pennsylvania there are enough black voters to be decisive in any election. All told, some 220 electoral votes could depend on how the black vote swings. In 1984, there were 254 black mayors, 20 of them running cities with populations over 100,000. Additionally, 21 members of the House of Representatives, 347 state legislators, and about 5,000 local elected officials were black.

Blacks today are also better educated, better off financially, and have better job prospects than their parents (or even older siblings), but they are still not even with whites in these areas. For example, only 8 percent of black adults currently have college degrees, compared with 18 percent of whites (Reid, 1982). Blacks are still likely to attend racially imbalanced schools. In the 1980–1981 school year, almost half the black students in the northeastern states attended schools where at least 90 percent of the students were members of minority groups. By contrast, only 23 percent of the black students in the South attended such schools (Pear, 1982).

Economically, blacks have made gains, but they remain substantially worse off than whites. The ratio of black family income to white family income increased from 44 percent in 1970 to 64 percent in 1975, then it fell back to 56 percent in 1981. Further, the personal wealth—or accumulated assets—of black families is only 36 percent that of white families. Although black households make up 12 percent of all households, they hold only 4 percent of the combined wealth of blacks and whites (Shellhardt, 1983). Housing for blacks and whites is still strongly segregated, and the white exodus to the suburbs seems to be increasing de facto residential segregation in the central cities. By **de facto segregation** we mean racial separation that results from unofficial social patterns, as opposed to segregation imposed by law **(de jure segregation).**

In 1981 the income of 30.8 percent of black families fell below the poverty level, 3.5 times the number of white families classified as poor by the Census Bureau (Reid, 1982). Black poverty is in part a consequence of black unemployment; the unemployment rate for blacks has run around double that of whites since the Korean War. In 1982, the total black unemployment rate was over 20 percent, that for black teenagers, nearly 50 percent. If we count those blacks employed but earning less than the poverty-level income and those working part-time but wanting full-time jobs, we discover the subemployment rate, which is at least double the rate of those completely unemployed. In human terms, these figures are staggering, for they depict a group of people who have little hope for a decent living and for whom jobs are a source of frustration rather than of satisfaction (Liebow, 1967).

How is the past progress and current status of blacks viewed by white and black Americans? Not surprisingly, their outlooks are quite different. A 1980 Gallup poll showed that while 75 percent of whites think the quality of life for blacks has improved over the last decade, only 44 percent of blacks feel this way. Furthermore, while only 20 percent of whites think that blacks are currently treated not very well or badly in our society, nearly half of blacks (46 percent) feel they are mistreated. Most whites, in short, seem to feel that blacks today are doing fairly well and are no longer the targets of great discrimination. This idealized view may be one of the reasons why increasing numbers of whites are reluctant to support the efforts needed to achieve further integration. Even so, white attitudes toward blacks continue to become more favorable (see Figure 12.3, p. 316).

Hispanic Americans

Spanish-speaking Americans, or Hispanics, are the second-largest minority group in the United States. The 1980 Census counted 8.7 million Mexicans, 2 million Puerto Ricans, 803,000 Cubans, and 3.1 million "other Spanish." Three out of four Hispanic immigrants from Mexico live in either California or Texas. About half the Hispanics from Puerto Rico live in the New York City area, and 59 percent of Hispanics from Cuba live in Florida (Russell, 1983). An estimated 2 to 10 million live in the nation's fifty largest metropolitan areas. Additional Hispanics live and work in the United States illegally. The Hispanic population is overwhelmingly urban. Eighty-eight percent live in metropolitan areas, as compared with 75 percent of the population as a whole. Hispanic Americans are also our fastest-growing minority. Between 1970 and 1980 their numbers increased 61 percent. The people who make up this group have several important things in common: the Spanish language, the Catholic religion, and the Hispanic culture, which places great value on family ties (see Chapter 3). But each subgroup also has its own unique history and heritage.

Before New England was colonized, the Spanish had settled in what is now the American Southwest. However, it was not until 1848, following wars and conquest, that they and their land became part of the United States. Soon after, English-speaking settlers began edging the Hispanics out: When all else failed, they were "sent back" to Mexico. Except in New Mexico, where Hispanics were able to hold their ground, most withdrew to rural towns and mining camps. When they went into areas dominated by English-speaking settlers to work as migrant laborers, they were housed in segregated camps; when they moved into the big cities, they lived apart from other groups.

Beginning about the turn of the century, a new group of Mexican nationals entered the United States to harvest cotton in East Texas. After the harvest, they would return to their homes in Mexico. As the years passed and cotton production expanded into West Texas, agricultural interests in the Southwest became increasingly dependent upon Mexico's vast army of migratory workers. The Mexicans have entered the United States legally under periodic agreements with the Mexican government and illegally by swimming or wading the Rio Grande. In recent years, the smuggling of aliens has become highly organized, with a network reaching from professional smugglers through labor contractors to American growers and manufacturers dependent on cheap labor. Increasingly the aliens are bypassing the farms and ranches of the Southwest, their traditional sources of employment, for urban jobs elsewhere in the nation's construction, manufacturing, and service industries. Mexican nationals are particularly susceptible to exploitation and abuse because they fear being apprehended and returned to Mexico, or fired. Employers often short-change the alien workers by paying them less than the federal minimum wage, by not providing them

FIGURE 12.3 White Attitudes Toward Blacks Now More Favorable

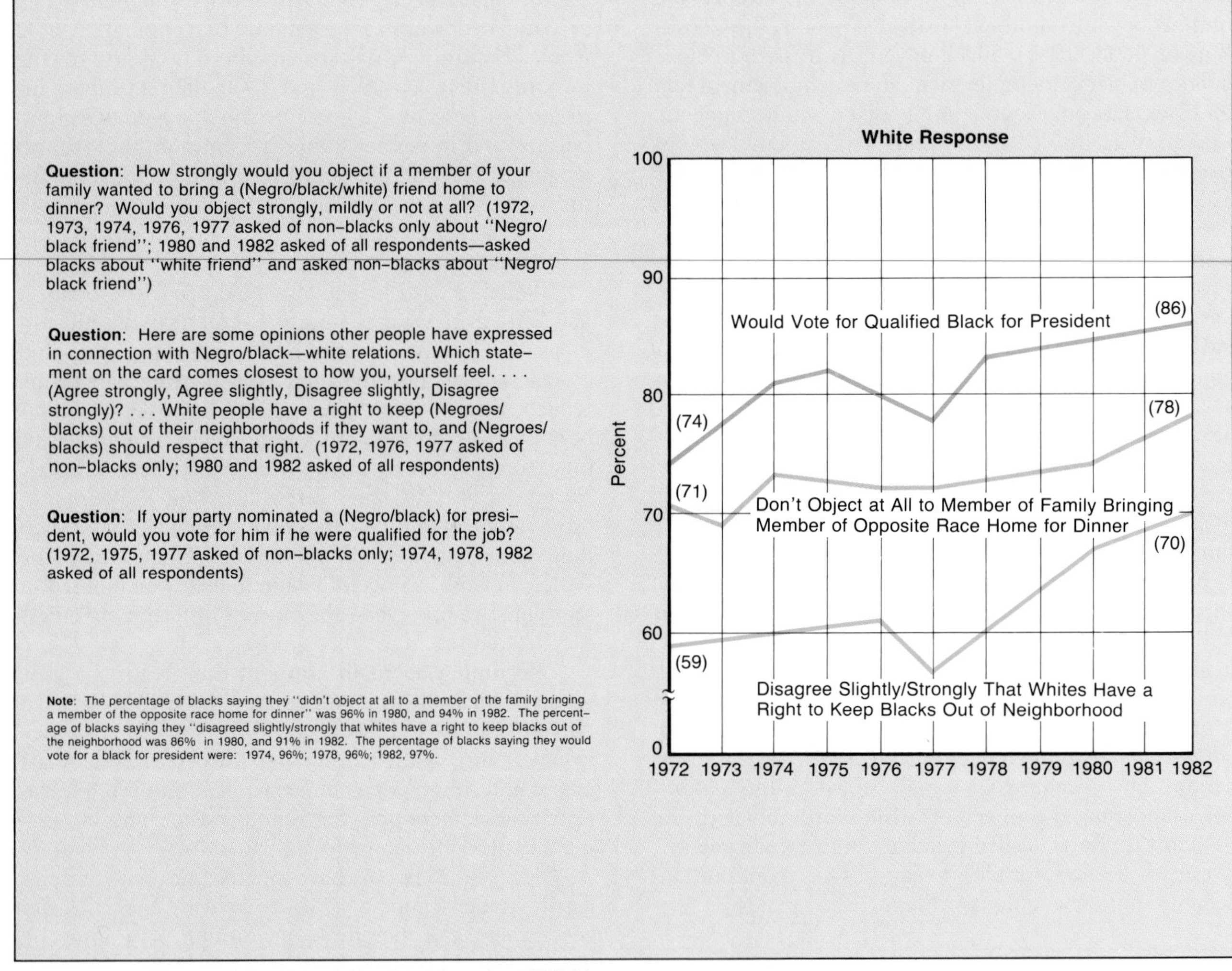

Source: Public Opinion, Vol. 5, No. 5 (October–November 1982):34.

with overtime pay, and by short-counting the hours they work.

Population pressures in Mexico and economic opportunities in the United States have encouraged Mexicans to come to the United States. Comparable factors have contributed to the migration of Puerto Ricans to the mainland of the United States, particularly to the New York City area. Their influx there is relatively recent. The United States acquired Puerto Rico in 1898, and in 1917, all Puerto Ricans were declared American citizens. Mainland companies began to open branches on the island but were met with violent nationalist resistance. A compromise was reached, granting Puerto Rico aid for modernization and economic development as well as commonwealth status. Most Puerto Ricans did not benefit from economic expansion, however, and

These Mexicans have been hampered in their attempt to enter the United States illegally. Many who do make it across the border are often subject to economic exploitation. (Stephanie Maze/Woodfin Camp & Associates)

when the airlines introduced low fares after World War II, increasing numbers left the island to seek their fortune in New York.

In New York City, Puerto Ricans suffer acute education and health problems. They have the highest school-dropout rate of all ethnic groups and a higher mortality rate from drug addiction, alcoholism, accidents, homicides, and diabetes.

In city ghettos Puerto Ricans are often forced to endure double discrimination—discrimination due to their language and due to their color (the skin color of Puerto Ricans may be black or white or any shade in between, but Puerto Ricans are usually labeled nonwhite). What makes the Puerto Rican situation unique is that immigration is a two-way street: The island is close enough for immigrants to return home, and most do, temporarily or permanently. As a result, most have less incentive to learn American ways and English.

Like blacks, Hispanic-Americans are underrepresented in high-skill, high-income jobs, especially white-collar positions, and are overrepresented in low-skill, low-paying jobs, though Hispanics have been more likely to be blue-collar or farm employees than blacks. Hispanic median family income languishes at 74 percent of the average in the United States.

Native Americans

Native Americans are the poorest minority group in America. Their past and present are experiences of lies, corruption, and abuse. The wars against the Native Americans reached a peak toward the middle of the nineteenth century, when the eastern United States was becoming crowded and the transcontinental railroad made travel easier. During this period, gold was discovered in the Black Hills of South Dakota and on other Native American lands, and adventurers could still make a profit from buffalo hides. Over 500,000 Indians died before the century was over. The 300,000 who survived war, disease, hunger, and bounties ($25 to $100 per scalp in many places) were forced onto inhospitable reservations that were administered by the notoriously corrupt Bureau of Indian Affairs (BIA).

Today, only 38 percent of the 1.4 million Native Americans live on reservations recognized by state or federal government officials. The remainder are scattered across the United States, nearly 50 percent in urban areas. Forty-eight percent of Native Americans on reservations live below the poverty line, and their unemployment rate exceeds 40 percent. Some 55 percent of those on reservations live in substandard housing, and 70

FIGURE 12.4 The Disadvantaged Circumstances of Native Americans

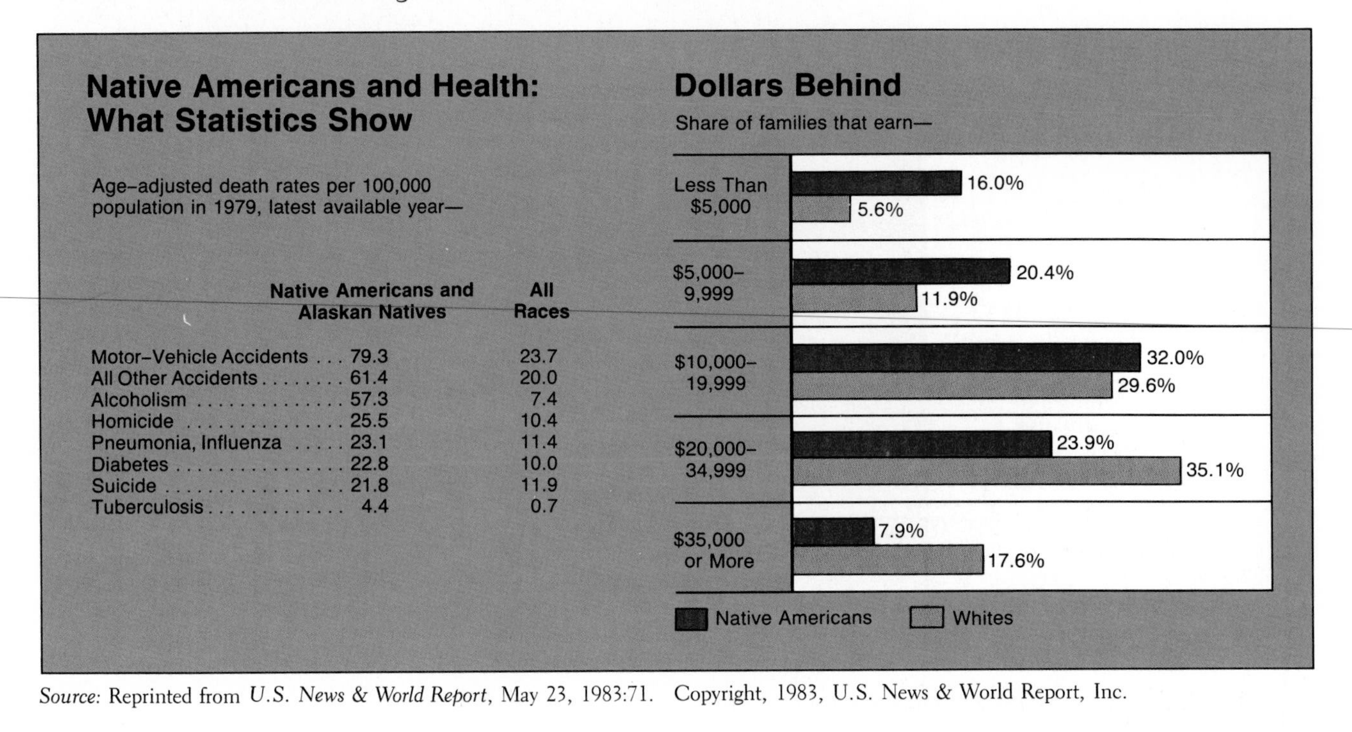

Native Americans and Health: What Statistics Show

Age-adjusted death rates per 100,000 population in 1979, latest available year—

	Native Americans and Alaskan Natives	All Races
Motor-Vehicle Accidents	79.3	23.7
All Other Accidents	61.4	20.0
Alcoholism	57.3	7.4
Homicide	25.5	10.4
Pneumonia, Influenza	23.1	11.4
Diabetes	22.8	10.0
Suicide	21.8	11.9
Tuberculosis	4.4	0.7

Source: Reprinted from *U.S. News & World Report*, May 23, 1983:71. Copyright, 1983, U.S. News & World Report, Inc.

percent must haul their drinking water a mile or more (frequently drawing it from unsanitary sources). Fifty-eight percent of reservation children drop out of school before completing eighth grade. Thirty-six percent of all Native Americans have a yearly income of $9,999 or less, as compared with only 17 percent of the United States population as a whole. They also have unusually high rates of accidents, homicide, suicide, alcoholism, pneumonia, and diabetes (see Figure 12.4). Overall, they have the highest infant mortality rate and the lowest longevity rate of any American minority group.

During the early 1970s, as militancy among many black Americans grew, Native Americans also became more forceful and insistent in their demands that past wrongs be redressed. Several of their demonstrations—such as the occupation of Alcatraz Island and the demonstration at Wounded Knee—made national and international headlines. In addition, Native American leaders brought their grievances to the courts. In 1980, for example, three Native American tribes were awarded $81.5 million for 12.5 million acres of land in the northern part of Maine, land that was illegally taken from them over 150 years ago. An even larger settlement ($122.5 million) was recently granted to eight tribes of the Sioux nation in compensation for the United States seizure of the Black Hills of South Dakota. (A treaty that had given the land exclusively to the Sioux was broken when gold was discovered there.) Such suits mark progress in the acknowledgment of the injustices Native Americans have suffered.

Chinese Americans

The Chinese began immigrating to the West Coast in the middle of the eighteenth century. Laboring on the railroad, washing, and cooking, they earned a reputation as hard workers. But when the railroad was finished and unemployment began to rise, white workers turned on the Chinese. The Chinese Exclusion Act of 1882 halted

In 1978 a coalition of 100 Indian groups, organized by leaders of the American Indian Movement, marched 2700 miles from Alcatraz, California to Washington, D.C. Of the original 250 Indians who began the "Longest Walk," 20 completed the entire journey. The symbolic march ended with peaceful demonstrations in Washington. (Gianfranco Gorgoni/Contact Stock Images)

further immigration, and denied Chinese the right to become naturalized citizens or to own land. In most places the Chinese were also denied schooling, jobs, and housing. They withdrew to ethnic enclaves (termed "Chinatowns"), keeping largely to themselves until anti-Chinese feelings started to subside. In 1943, under the impact of war conditions, the Chinese Exclusion Act was repealed and a quota for Asian immigrants was established. The number was meager, however—only 105 Chinese were permitted to enter this country annually. Finally, in 1965, national origins quotas were abolished, and for the first time Chinese immigrants were treated on a par with other nationalities (Wong, 1982). By 1980 there were 806,000 people of Chinese ancestry in the country, an increase of 85.3 percent since 1970. Enclaves in four major United States cities —New York City, Los Angeles, San Francisco, and Boston—have absorbed most of this increase, which has come from Taiwan and Hong Kong.

The traditional power structures in these communities are being eroded and challenged by culturally assimilated second-generation Chinese Americans and by younger, more militant immigrants and third-generation Chinese Americans. Dissatisfaction has grown with the substandard housing and education in the Chinese ghettos and the high rate of unemployment in these areas. Under these pressures, the social order in the Chinatowns across the United States is crumbling. Crime and other indications of social pathology have been on the rise. Many immigrant youths have had to cope with language problems, unemployment, low-paying jobs, and estrangement from the larger American society. These tensions are transforming the traditional Chinatown from an urban ethnic ghetto into an "interest group based on a common culture" (Wong, 1982:108).

Japanese Americans

The Japanese came to America about two decades after the Chinese. They established groceries, flower shops, and other small businesses and took jobs as truck farmers and laborers in the lumber mills and fish canneries all along the West Coast. But anti-Oriental sentiments ran high, and in 1924, all East Asian immigration was halted. Then, during World War II, 110,000 Japanese, including 70,000 who were American citizens, were rounded up and placed in "relocation centers," even though the vast majority supported the Allies. In part, this reflected anti-Japanese prejudice whipped up by the attack on Pearl Harbor. During their internment, Japanese families lost an average of $10,000 each (in terms of the 1941 value of the dollar).

With each generation the Japanese-Americans have become more assimilated (Woodrum, 1978). The *Issei*—the first generation—were mostly agricultural laborers who spoke little English. Their children—the *Nisei*, typically born between 1910 and 1940—were considerably more assimilated than their parents, having attended

American schools. The *Sansei*—the third generation, most of whom were born after World War II—have become even more acculturated to American patterns. Even so, the *Sansei* have retained some elements of the traditional Japanese culture, and, in some cases, are attempting to renew their ancestral heritage (McLemore, 1983).

Despite having experienced discrimination and internment, the Japanese have done quite well in the United States. Emphasizing the value of hard work and education, they have specialized in such professions as engineering, accounting, and management (Petersen, 1966). But even though they are moving into middle-class economic positions, the economic returns on advanced education and professional and managerial occupations have been consistently lower for Japanese than for white Americans (Woodrum, 1981). And their mobility has been won at high cost and despite considerable hostility and opposition from dominant-group Americans.

American Jews

The first Jews came to North America from Brazil in 1654, but it was not until the 1840s that Jews began arriving in the thousands, fleeing European *pogroms* (periodic massacres of Jews). Today there are more Jews in the United States—about six million—than in any other country in the world. (The Soviet Union is second, Israel a close third.) About a third of American Jews live in or around New York City. Since 1970, more than half a million Jews have settled in the United States, the largest proportion coming from Israel and the Soviet Union. Unlike earlier waves of Jewish immigrants from southern and eastern Europe, the new arrivals are typically highly educated and skilled.

Urbanites and entrepreneurs throughout much of their past, Jews adapted to America with relative ease. This does not mean that they did not encounter discrimination—time and again they have been accused of disloyalty, of participation in international conspiracies, of unscrupulous business practices. Traditionally, many corporations, major law firms, banks, and private clubs did not admit Jews (some still do not), and until World War II many universities maintained strict quota systems. Jews prospered nonetheless—in part, by using Old World skills to start businesses (the garment industry, for example), in part, by taking advantage of public education (today 58 percent of Jews hold college degrees as compared with 29 percent of Americans as a whole), and in part, by continuing to some extent to see themselves as the "chosen people," no matter what the circumstances (a doctrine Jews share with Black Muslims). Of course, most Jews are not wealthy, and many are poor, but as a group, Jews have prospered and are strongly represented in business and the professions. A 1978 survey found that 43 percent of Jews earned $20,000 and over, compared with 21 percent of the total population; and 53 percnt were in business and the professions, compared with 25 percent nationally (Gallup Opinion Index, 1978). Jews are no longer underrepresented on corporate boards of directors, but they are unlikely to be part of the corporate elite in commercial banking and insurance, and they are less likely to be on the boards of the top 100 industrial concerns than on those of the smaller ones (Domhoff and Zweigenhaft, 1983).

Like other minorities, the American Jewish community has a historic connection with its early roots, traditions, and institutions. It has experienced tension between preserving a cultural heritage and gaining success and acceptance in the larger American society. Jewish identity has been preserved by the family, religion, and the vast network of national and community-based organizations. Simultaneously, anti-Semitism from outside the Jewish community has strengthened ingroup feelings and the sense that Jewish survival is at stake. Yet American Jews today confront a new challenge—maintaining their identity in a non-Jewish society where discrimination and prejudice are less pronounced than in the past (Schaefer, 1984).

Other White Ethnics

Besides Jews, a diversity of other white ethnic groups make up American society. (See Table 12.2.) These include Irish, Italians, Poles, and people from other southern and eastern European nations. Many white ethnics are blue-collar workers who work as longshoremen, miners, or mechanics and who own their own homes in communities such as Boston's Charlestown or Cleveland's West Side. Some ethnic groups are concentrated in some regions of the country—Italians and Russians in the Northeast and Norwegians and Czechs in the North Central states.

During the late 1960s, white ethnics acquired a

TABLE 12.2 White Ethnics, 1980

English	49,598,035
German	49,224,146
Irish	40,165,702
French	12,892,246
Italian	12,183,692
Scottish	10,048,816
Polish	8,228,037
Dutch	6,304,499
Swedish	4,345,392
Norwegian	3,453,839
Russian	2,781,432
Spanish-Hispanic	2,686,680
Czech	1,892,456
Hungarian	1,776,902
Welsh	1,664,598
Danish	1,518,273
Portuguese	1,024,351
Swiss	981,543
Greek	959,856
Austrian	948,558
French-Canadian	780,488
Slovak	776,806
Lithuanian	742,776
Ukrainian	730,056
Finnish	615,872
Canadian	456,212
Belgian	360,277
Yugoslavian	360,174
Romanian	315,258

Source: U.S. Bureau of the Census, *Statistical Abstract*, 1980.

reputation for being archconservatives; the term "hard hat" became synonymous with "racist" and "hawk." But this image has proven to be incorrect. In fact, several surveys conducted during the Vietnam War indicated that white ethnics were more likely to be doves than white Anglo-Saxon Protestants. They are more likely than white Protestants to support such liberal causes as a guaranteed annual wage and the fight against pollution. They are more sympathetic toward government efforts to help the poor (45 percent favor aid, as opposed to 19 percent of white Protestants). And a higher percentage of white ethnics than native-born white Protestants are prointegration (Greeley, 1974).

In his analysis of a composite sample of twelve surveys conducted between 1963 and 1974, Andrew Greeley (1976) found that there has been a general integration of many white ethnic groups into the American economy—in fact, Irish, Italian, German, and Polish Catholics have higher family incomes than all groups in American society except for Jews, Presbyterians, and Episcopalians. According to Greeley, the myth that most white ethnics are members of the lower middle class persists because society's elite is not willing to recognize that many members of these groups have indeed "made it."

Over the past decade or so a renewed interest in ethnicity has emerged—what some have termed an "ethnic revival." Some Italians, Poles, Czechs, Irish, and others have sought to revitalize their ethnic heritage and identity. The impulse to recapture the ethnic past was heightened by black cultural nationalism and racial polarization accompanying school desegregation. Yet much of the new ethnicity has proven more symbolic than real (Gans, 1979; Steinberg, 1981). The loss of the mother tongue, the breakup of ethnic enclaves, and the rapid rise of ethnic and religious intermarriage has undercut ethnicity as a significant factor in American life.

Minority Responses to Dominance

We have explored the often devastating consequences that prejudice and discrimination can have for members of a minority group. But how do people react to these consequences? In what ways and under what circumstances do they attempt to fight back?

Trying to become accepted by the majority is one reaction. Some members of a minority will try to "pass"—change their names, their appearances, and their lives, thus shedding their minority identity. Passing means rejecting one's family and origins, and it may leave a person stranded between two worlds, not entirely accepted by either. Mexican-American Richard Rodriguez, highlighted at the beginning of this chapter, was caught in just this dilemma. Other minority group members who are unable to "pass" (because of obvious physical characteristics, for instance) may simply become resigned to their status.

Complete resignation is rare, however. Usually members of an oppressed minority will strike back in some way. When people feel totally powerless to change their treatment (because they are greatly outnumbered, lack access to political channels, do not have the weapons for armed rebellion, and so forth), they may retaliate through *covert aggression*. On the surface, they will appear to accept the role the dominant group assigns to them, obeying the etiquette of racism, deferring to members of the dominant group in most interracial contexts. The classic example of this response is Uncle Tom, who smiled, shuffled, and "yes, ma'am"ed his way through Harriet Beecher Stowe's novel *Uncle Tom's Cabin*. But among themselves, minority group members will show their contempt for the majority. They may call them derogatory names (honky, gringo, paleface), laugh at their arrogance and absurdity, and tell stories about how easily they can be duped. Simpson and Yinger (1972:224) relate one such tale:

> A Negro drives through a red light in a Mississippi town. The sheriff yells, "Where you think you going?" The Negro thinks fast and answers, "Well, boss, when I see that green light come on an' all them white folks' cars goin' through, I says to myself, 'That's the white folks' light!' So I don' move. Then when that ol' red light comes on, I jus' steps on the gas. I says, "That mus' be the niggers' light!'" The sheriff replies, "You're a good boy, Sam, but the next time you kin go on the white folks' light."

It's obvious who had the last laugh here. Flattery, deference, and feigned stupidity can be effective forms of passive aggression—as when a slave pretended he was so simple-minded he couldn't understand a job he didn't want to do. Other forms of covert retaliation include loafing or doing shoddy work, feigning illness, stealing tools and work materials or purposely destroying them, and leaving a job at the worst possible time for the employer (Davis, 1978).

If members of minority groups believe they have some chance of improving their status by working within the existing system, they will often organize various forms of *political and economic protest*. This is what happened in the United States during the early 1960s. Black leaders felt that by publicizing the injustices they suffered through peaceful demonstrations (sit-ins, boycotts, marches, freedom rides, and the like), they could win civil rights through the legislatures and through the courts. During the summer of 1963, some 1,122 demonstrations were recorded, culminating with the "March on Washington." On August 28, 1963, over 200,000 civil rights marchers demonstrated on the Mall between the Washington Monument and the Lincoln Memorial "for jobs and freedom." The wave of demonstrations

Sit-ins were a common form of protest in the South during the 1960s. At a segregated lunch counter in Charlotte, North Carolina, these black men were refused service, and the white waitresses left the serving area. (Bruce Roberts/Rapho-Photo Researchers)

contributed to the passage of the Civil Rights Act of 1964 a year later. Additional demonstrations, particularly those in Selma, Alabama, in the spring of 1965, convinced Congress to strengthen federal law with the Civil Rights Acts of 1965. During this period, the Reverend Martin Luther King, Jr., served as the leader and the symbol of the civil rights movement.

At other times, however, minority group members believe that there is little hope of improving their lot by working within the system. The dominant group, they feel, is unsympathetic or even hostile toward their cause. Such circumstances are often conducive to *violent protest or outright rebellion*. This is especially true when minority group members believe they have enough strength in numbers to inflict substantial injury on the dominant group and when they feel that such injury is justified because of past exploitation and oppression

(Davis, 1978). Sometimes the use of violence is planned in advance as part of a liberation strategy. A number of the slave revolts that took place in the American South before the Civil War are examples of this kind of organized attack on the majority. So is the uprising launched by the Mau Maus against British colonialism in Kenya in the 1950s. At other times, however, minority violence is not so specifically goal-directed. It simply flares up spontaneously, often fanned by a particular event or instance of injustice. The violence that broke out in black ghettos across the United States during the late 1960s was of this type, and such incidents still erupt today. For instance, in May 1980 extensive rioting broke out in a black ghetto in Miami following the acquittal of four policemen accused of beating a black insurance executive to death. Eighteen persons died and about 240 businesses were damaged or destroyed. Reasons given for the violence were anger over the injustices of the American legal system, frustration over an unemployment rate of nearly 70 percent among black youth, and retaliation for a whole array of structured inequities and past wrongs inflicted by whites. The shooting of a black man by police in December 1982 once again sparked an episode of rock throwing and looting by angry blacks (Nazario, 1982; Beck and Sigale, 1983). More will be said about the causes and consequences of riots in Chapter 18.

Violent resistance, of course, almost always means a loss of life and property for the minority as well as the dominant group. This is why it is usually used only as a last resort. One alternative to violence that a minority may have is to minimize contact with the dominant group, thus limiting degradation and abuse. For example, when anti-Chinese sentiment began to increase in the American West, Chinese families withdrew to cities on the Atlantic and Pacific coasts, shutting themselves off from the hostile society around them (Yuan, 1963). At various times since the abolition of slavery, groups of blacks in America have also supported *separatism;* some have even set as their goal the creation of separate black states. Not only does self-segregation provide insulation from aggression and slurs, it also enables members of a minority group to maintain close family ties, to assist one another, to practice their own way of life, and to keep their culture alive. Avoidance of the majority is a two-edged sword, however. While it may give minority group members a sense of solidarity and protection, it may also intensify intergroup prejudice and suspicion and perpetuate discriminatory practices. The line between "we" and "they" becomes all the more heavily drawn.

Efforts to Eliminate Institutional Discrimination

Full equality for racial and ethnic minorities will elude Americans unless institutional discrimination is eliminated. As noted earlier in the chapter, discrimination has become so thoroughly entrenched in our social institutions that it continues, regardless of whether or not people are prejudiced. Special measures are needed to eliminate these institutional arrangements. Busing to achieve educational integration, affirmative action to provide better jobs for minorities, and zoning for low-income housing are among the measures currently being tried in the United States.

Busing

On May 17, 1954, the Supreme Court, in the famous school case *Brown* v. *Board of Education*, held that laws imposing racial separation in the public schools were unconstitutional. A prolonged period of bitter struggle, at times marked by violence and terror, followed. Even so, by October 1970, some 94 percent of the South's 2,702 school districts were estimated by the Justice Department to be in compliance with constitutional and legal requirements for school desegregation. Indeed, as pointed out earlier in the chapter, the South has achieved a better racial mix among its students than has the North. Yet thirty years after the high court's decision, two-thirds of the nation's black children are still in schools attended predominantly by minority students.

In major cities the enrollment of white children in central-city schools is dropping precipitously. Blacks, Hispanics, and Asians outnumber whites in the schools of thirty-three of the fifty biggest cities (see Table 12.3, p. 324). This situation runs counter to the early American ideal of a common school for all children—the notion that bringing together in the schools children of all races, ethnic backgrounds, religions, and classes would produe a single, unified nation. European nations have long operated a two-tiered system: one set of schools for the elite and another set for the masses. Americans, while disavowing such a system, have in effect accomplished a

TABLE 12.3 Minority Enrollments in Big-City Schools

	Total Students	Percent Minority		Total Students	Percent Minority
Washington	104,907	96	Denver	64,274	59
Atlanta	72,295	92	Cincinnati	53,632	58
Newark	59,658	91	Fort Worth	66,170	56
San Antonio	60,695	89	Milwaukee	87,826	55
Detroit	211,886	88	Sacramento	39,873	54
New Orleans	85,707	88	Buffalo	48,236	53
Oakland	48,863	86	Indianapolis	65,958	51
San Francisco	59,385	83	Pittsburgh	46,239	51
Chicago	445,269	81	Albuquerque	78,051	47
Baltimore	129,979	79	Austin	55,369	47
St. Louis	61,474	79	Fresno	47,770	46
Los Angeles	538,038	76	Oklahoma City	41,158	45
Memphis	110,113	76	San Diego	109,793	44
Birmingham	46,523	76	Seattle	49,156	44
Houston	194,060	75	Columbus, Ohio	73,094	41
New York	931,193	74	Tucson	55,654	38
Cleveland	80,074	72	Toledo	45,488	38
El Paso	61,285	72	Akron	38,926	36
Kansas City, Mo.	38,279	72	Tulsa	49,454	31
Corpus Christi	37,383	72	Minneapolis	42,797	31
Philadelphia	224,152	71	Omaha	44,719	30
Dallas	129,305	70	Wichita	44,921	28
Miami	232,951	68	St. Paul	37,051	26
Boston	67,366	65	Portland, Oreg.	52,868	24
Norfolk	37,471	61	Fort Wayne, Ind.	34,716	23

Source: Joint Center for Political Studies, January 24, 1983.

somewhat similar arrangement by sorting themselves out residentially along economic and racial lines and linking school attendance to neighborhood residence (Coleman, 1981).

The nation's courts have devised a variety of remedies to desegregate a community's schools; they include redrawing a school's boundaries, relocating schools, and reassigning students. But of all the remedies, area-wide busing to achieve racially balanced schools has proven to be the most controversial. Because many children do not live within walking distance of a school, busing has been a familiar part of the American school scene since 1919. Today nearly half of the nation's school children are taken to school on buses, though only 4 percent are transported to help achieve desegregation. A 1981 Gallup Poll found that 60 percent of blacks favor busing and 30 percent oppose it; it also found that 78 percent of whites opposed busing and 17 percent favored it (Sheppard, 1981). This evidence suggests that whites are opposed not to busing itself but to busing as a remedy to school segregation. Some black leaders such as the Reverend Jesse Jackson say that for many whites "busing" has become a code word for "desegregation"—"It ain't the bus, it's us."

Research conducted in the 1960s seemed to suggest that the academic performance of black children improved as the proportion of white students in a school increased (Coleman, 1966). This finding led social scientists to hope that desegregation would improve the academic achievement of black students. Although much of the evidence from recent research is inconclusive and even contradictory, it nevertheless seems that when desegregation is begun in the earliest primary grades, it does enhance black achievement (Crain and Mahard, 1983). But there is also more to desegregation than simply sending white and black children to the same school. Children's school experience and what they learn is affected by other factors, including their socioeconomic status and family background, as well as the degree of racial tension and interracial acceptance in the school. In sum, the schools cannot be expected to undo the racism that the larger community continually fashions in the course of its daily activities.

Affirmative Action

The entrenched nature of institutional patterns of racial and ethnic discrimination has led some civil-rights advocates to call for **affirmative action.** This remedy is designed to remove the institutional barriers to the advancement of minorities and women and to redress historic imbalances. In practice it has typically meant setting priorities in the hiring of minorities and establishing timetables for reaching minority employement "target" goals. Critics of affirmative action brand the programs "reverse discrimination" and claim they victimize white males.

The legal foundation of affirmative action is the Civil Rights Act of 1964, which is aimed at eliminating discrimination based on race, religion, ethnic origin, or sex. According to its advocates, attacking job and educational discrimination involves more than just eliminating legal barriers, for if we ignore the deficits in skills and credentials minorities and women suffer, little change is likely. Therefore, affirmative action—special consideration and preferential treatment—is necessary to eliminate the consequences of past discrimination in these areas.

What exactly do affirmative action programs entail? Applied to hiring practices, for example, employers are asked to inventory all employees, and after they have identified areas in which there are proportionately few minorities and women, they are asked to set goals for the employment of members of such groups. Goals are a way of assessing an employer's commitment, but they are not quotas.

> The employer is not compelled to hire unqualified persons or to compromise genuinely valid standards to meet the established goal. If goals are not met, no sanctions are imposed, so long as the contractor can demonstrate that he made good faith efforts to reach them. (U.S. Commission on Civil Rights, 1977:6)

In northern cities, where blacks and whites tend to live in separate neighborhoods, schools have been integrated largely through court-ordered busing. Here, school buses bring black students to a high school in Boston. (Ellis Herwig/Stock, Boston)

One problem, of course, is how to monitor and enforce affirmative action programs. The Equal Employment Opportunity Commission (EEOC) is the main government agency assigned this task. One of its most notable successes was a case in which AT&T agreed to set goals for sexual integration of its jobs and to give $38 million in back pay to women it had channeled into low-paying dead-end jobs. Despite such dramatic cases, however, most complaints to the EEOC languish for years.

Sluggish enforcement may be only a symptom of a greater problem—the feeling on the part of whites, especially white males, that affirmative action puts them at a disadvantage. Just such an issue was presented to the Supreme Court in the recent case of Alan Bakke, a white man who, twice rejected by a California medical school, claimed that less-qualified people had been accepted under a special admissions program that reserved sixteen of the hundred places for minorities. Bakke contended that this policy denied him equal opportunity. In 1978 the Supreme Court ruled that Bakke be admitted. However, they also stated that race or ethnic background could be one—but not the only—factor in assessing applicants.

The Bakke decision left many legal authorities confused regarding the constitutional status of affirmative action programs. However, a year later, the nation's highest court ruled in the case of Brian F. Weber (a white employee at the Kaiser Aluminum plant in Gramercy, Louisiana) that private employers can legally give special preference to black workers to eliminate "manifest racial imbalance" in jobs traditionally restricted to whites. And in 1980 (in the case of *Fullilove* v. *Klutznick*) the Supreme Court for the first time endorsed the power of Congress to set aside a portion of federal contracts for minority firms.

A 1983 study by the Labor Department concluded that affirmative action has been highly effective in promoting the employment of blacks, Hispanics, and women (Pear, 1983). It analyzed employment practices from 1974 to 1980 at 77,000 factories, offices, and work sites. Whereas minority employment grew 20 percent among firms doing business with the federal government, it grew only 12 percent among establishments not covered by affirmative action provisions. The impact was even greater for women: Their numbers increased 15.2 percent in firms covered by affirmative action requirements, and only 2.2 percent in businesses that were not covered.

Zoning

The role of zoning ordinances as a means of excluding the poor and minorities from desirable communities has not yet been addressed at the federal level, but in at least one state, the issue has come before the courts. In a 1983 decision known as Mt. Laurel II, the New Jersey Supreme Court ruled that municipalities must *work actively* to promote housing for the poor. This ruling has the potential to affect zoning laws in every state. It sets a precedent for the courts to mandate zoning laws that would increase the number of low and moderate income housing units in communities throughout America.

EPILOGUE

In this chapter and the previous two chapters dealing with stratification and power, we have emphasized that society is structured in ways that provide more benefits and impose more burdens on some individuals and groups than on others. Consequently, the members of society often find themselves in conflict over the distribution of scarce resources. Moreover, as members of different racial and ethnic groups, they encounter differences in values, norms, beliefs, and, in some cases, language. The determination of which individuals and groups will be able to translate their preferences into the operating realities that will prevail for all members of society is primarily a function of power. And in the last analysis, the state—the political institution—becomes the key vehicle for establishing domination and privilege. This observation in no way negates the importance of economic power. As pointed out in the previous two chapters, economic power can often be "converted" into political power and political power into economic power.

Given the importance of power differentials in contemporary societies, it is easy to understand the concern dominant groups have with those arrangements that allow them to consolidate, protect, and maximize their preferred positions. By the same token, minority groups have sought public policies that reduce or eliminate power differentials and structural inequalities (Blackwell, 1981). Thus the issues of busing and affirmative action have generated considerable controversy in American society.

These issues are closely linked to another matter—the direction in which race relations are currently heading in the United States. More fundamentally, the question is one of why, two decades after the passage of significant civil rights legislation, a large number of blacks still remain at the bottom of the social hierarchy, locked into existences of poverty, chronic unemployment, and despair. Until very recently, the standard explanation for the plight of the so-called black underclass was white prejudice and discrimination. According to this view, racism is so enduring and pervasive in our society that it continues to deny many blacks the opportunity for upward mobility. Yet survey data reveals a substantial decline in traditional race prejudice that would deny blacks legal and social equality, although a substantial minority of Americans still endorse segregationist positions (Kluegel and Smith, 1983). Based upon these shifts in attitudes and other social changes, some white scholars and a small but influential group of black scholars have suggested that new forces have now come to the forefront. While acknowledging that racism still prevails in the United States, these scholars argue that an equally if not more important reason for the conditions faced by underclass blacks is a set of impersonal changes that have taken place in our economic system—changes that make it almost impossible for inner-city blacks to break free from ghetto life. According to this view, therefore, the significance of race as a barrier to economic advancement is declining, and in its place are rising economic and status barriers that our social programs are not yet equipped to handle.

Probably the most widely publicized proponent of this view is William Julius Wilson, a noted black sociologist at the University of Chicago. In *The Declining Significance of Race* (1978), Wilson argues that over the past two decades the rapid growth in the corporate and government sectors of the economy, coupled with affirmative action pressures, has greatly increased the number of white-collar and professional jobs open to well-educated, well-trained blacks. Today, he says, middle-class blacks, especially the younger ones, are enjoying unprecedented job opportunities and salaries—comparable to those of whites. Conditions for poor, inner-city blacks, however, are very different. Ghetto dwellers, Wilson contends, are trapped in a complex web of social and economic circumstances. Because inner-city schools are generally inferior, black youths receive poorer education and poorer training than their white counterparts. This fact puts them at a distinct disadvantage in the competitive job market, especially during economic recessions. At the same time, changing economic conditions have left few jobs for unskilled workers in the central cities. Thus drug dealing, prostitution, and other forms of crime, or dependence on welfare, are among the few means of survival available to many ghetto residents. Although centuries of discrimination and oppression *created* the black underclass in the first place, now, according to Wilson, it is largely economic forces that perpetuate it.

Wilson's ideas have ignited vehement opposition. Many accuse him of wishful thinking regarding the size of the gains made by middle-class blacks. Robert Hill of the National Urban League, for example, argues that the proportion of black families with incomes above the government-established "intermediate budget" level has not increased much at all; it has remained around 25 percent since 1972. What's more, Hill argues, the overall gap between black and white earnings is widening, as pointed out earlier in the chapter. And additional years of schooling, Hill argues, do not do as much for blacks as they do for whites. In fact, over the past decade unemployment rates for white high school dropouts actually have been lower than the rates for black college-educated youths (Hill, cited in Willie, 1979). Others such as Douglas G. Glasgow (1980) contend that the black middle class is a "second class" in the sense that it is usually based on multiple incomes—particularly the earnings of both a husband and wife—and its members have limited opportunities for advancement and personal success. Its members also lack power comparable to that of the white middle class. It is difficult to explain such statistics and facts, Hill, Glasgow, and others say, without concluding that blacks of all classes still face strong and persistent discrimination in our society.

Wilson answers that data like these obscure a vital distinction—the distinction between the effects of *past* economic discrimination against blacks, and the effects of race in *today's* economy. The importance of this distinction becomes clear, he says, when we look not at aggregate income figures, but at income figures for blacks under thirty, who earned close to $1,000 *more* than whites with equivalent education and experience. Today's young middle-class blacks face a much more hospitable economic world than did older college-educated blacks whom past discrimination channeled into dead-end jobs. But this is not the case for underclass blacks. The poverty of poorly educated and poorly trained blacks threatens to become permanent. "Even if all racial discrimination were eliminated today," Wilson writes, "the situation of poor blacks will not be substantially improved unless something is done to remove the structural barriers to decent jobs created by changes in our system of production" (quoted in Willie, 1979:170). This is why Wilson concludes that the black experience in the United States has now moved from racial oppression for *all* blacks to economic subordination for the black underclass.

Critics respond that Wilson's viewpoint is not only wrong but potentially dangerous. They feel it may lead whites to believe that racial prejudice and discrimination is no longer a major problem in our society, thus making further efforts to end discrimination seem unwarranted. This mistaken assumption, Wilson's opponents say, has already helped create a sizable white backlash against affirmative action programs. Without affirmative action and programs like it, these observers contend, full racial equality is unlikely to be achieved. Thus, they insist that race remains a central and important determinant of black life chances and mobility in the United states (Oliver and Glick, 1982).

The debate over the current significance of race in our society has continued. At times it seems as if there is no issue on which there is agreement between those emphasizing racism as the most important factor responsible for the problems of blacks and those who adhere to Wilson's argument. However, both sides strongly desire full racial justice—a goal that both feel is still far from achieved. Both also believe that the existence of a large black underclass in virtually all our major cities is one of the most important problems American society faces. Their differences, therefore, center not on whether racial inequality still exists, but on what its causes are and how it can best be combated.

SUMMARY

Minority groups are people who are singled out for unequal treatment in a society. In many societies, the United States among them, racial and ethnic minorities are subject to widespread social and economic disadvantage.

Race, although commonly a basis for defining minority status, is a slippery concept. With little basis in biology, race is essentially a social construct. The same is true of ethnicity, with the distinction that ethnicity depends on cultural rather than physical differences.

Prejudice is like or dislike of a group of people because of their racial or ethnic characteristics. Discrimination is the favorable or unfavorable treatment of people on the basis of their group membership. The focus of prejudice and discrimination falls on individual racism. But it is also necessary to examine institutional discrimination—how a society's institutions are structured so as to systematically deny opportunities and equal rights to members of particular groups.

Throughout history, when groups of people have come up against one another, the result has been either conflict or accommodation. Sociologists have recognized several common patterns of each: economic and political subjugation, the displacement of a native population, and the creation of racial and ethnic myths that rationalize cruel and unjust treatment of the oppressed.

Sometimes groups meet with a minimum of conflict, as in the melting pot situation, in which the mixing of two or more groups produces a blend of all the biological and cultural traits that go into it. When assimilation occurs, however, the dominant culture incorporates minorities by doing away with their separate identity. In a pluralistic society, several racial or ethnic groups coexist simultaneously, with members of each group interacting socially among themselves.

A number of hypotheses have been advanced to explain racism. One hypothesis, the frustration-aggression thesis, says that people who are frustrated in some sphere of life take out their feelings on others less powerful than themselves, using these individuals as scapegoats. Another hypothesis points to the part that intergroup conflict plays in the generaton of racial antagonisms. And finally, the cultural hypothesis suggests that racism is maintained by becoming embedded in a people's lifeways.

One way in which people respond to prejudice is by attempting to shed minority status. Some people change their names and religion to "pass" into the majority culture. Although some minority group members simply resign themselves to their status, others resist it, either overtly or covertly. Overt resistance may range from peaceful political protest to armed rebellion. Some groups have resisted by separating themselves from the larger society and forming racial or ethnic enclaves.

Blacks, America's largest minority group, have had to combat the legacy of slavery and the belief in black inferiority that developed to justify it. After nearly a century of discrimination following emancipation, the 1960s saw vigorous civil rights protest and a series of legal victories. Blacks today are better off educationally than their parents were, but they are still not even with whites. Moreover, housing is still primarily segregated and in the urban ghettos unemployment is high and poverty the rule.

Hispanic-Americans are the nation's second-largest (and fastest-growing) minority. There are somewhat more than 8.7 million Mexican-Americans, primarily in the Southwest, and 2 million Puerto Ricans, most of whom live in or near New York City. Both groups have been disadvantaged economically.

Native Americans are the poorest American minority. Thirty-eight percent live on reservations; the remainder live throughout the United States, many in urban areas.

Chinese Americans number about 800,000. At one time they were concentrated in Chinatowns, but in recent years many have passed into the mainstream of American life. Japanese Americans, many of whom live on the West Coast, have done well in the United States, despite internment during World War II.

America has more Jews than any other nation in the world. Statistically, Jews rank well above the national average in education and income; despite their achievements, however, some discrimination against them persists.

Other white ethnics such as Italians, Poles, and Irish still are clustered in many urban neighborhoods, but they are increasingly moving into the middle class and out to the suburbs. This movement away from minority group status doubtless reflects the somewhat easier path open to those who, as whites and Christians, are less likely to be the objects of discrimination.

Discrimination is built into our social institutions. Recent efforts have been made to eliminate this kind of discrimination, among them busing to achieve the integration of schools, affirmative action to counterbalance past discrimination in education and employment, and zoning for low-income housing. All of these measures have met with a good deal of opposition, however, and how much impact they will have on reducing discrimination remains to be seen.

GLOSSARY

Affirmative action. A process in which special consideration and preferential treatment are given to members of minority groups to offset the effects of past discrimination.

Assimilation. The incorporation of a minority into the culture and social life of the majority such that the minority eventually disappears as a separate, identifiable unit.

Colonialism. The economic takeover of one nation by another, more powerful one, and the subsequent political and social domination of the native population.

De facto segregation. Segregation by social custom.

De jure segregation. Segregation by law.

Discrimination. The act of disqualifying or mistreating people on ascriptive grounds rationally irrelevant to the situation.

Ethnic group. A category of people who perceive themselves and are perceived by others as possessing shared cultural traits.

Frustration-aggression hypothesis. The theory that people are goal-directed creatures who become angry and hostile when their desires are frustrated and displace their rage upon a scapegoat.

Institutional discrimination. A structuring of policies and programs so as to systematically deny opportunities and equal rights to members of particular groups.

Integration. Ceasing to make distinctions between minority and majority groups in society and assessing individuals according to personal attributes, not race or ethnic background.

Internal colonialism. The economic, political, and social domination of one region of a country (the periphery) by another, more industrialized region (the core).

Jim Crow laws. The legal and social barriers constructed in the South in the late nineteenth and early twentieth centuries to prevent blacks from voting, using public facilities, and mixing with whites. (Jim Crow was the name of a minstrel character who performed in blackface.)

Minority group. People who are singled out for unequal treatment in the society in which they live, and who consider themselves to be victims of collective discrimination.

Pluralism. The coexistence of different racial or ethnic groups, each of which retains its own cultural identity and social structural networks, while participating equally in the economic and political systems.

Prejudice. A categorical like or dislike of a group of people based on real or imagined social characteristics, usually associated with their race, religion, ethnic group, sexual orientation, or perhaps occupation.

Race. Biologically, a population that through generations of inbreeding has developed more or less distinctive physical characteristics that are transmitted genetically. Sociologically, a group of people whom others believe are genetically distinct and whom they treat accordingly.

Racism. The belief that some human races are inherently inferior to others.

Scapegoat. A substitute target on which angry and frustrated individuals displace their hostility.

Segregation. Laws and/or customs that restrict or prohibit contact between groups. Segregation may be ethnic or racial, or based on sex or age.

PART FIVE

SOCIAL INSTITUTIONS

As you learned in Chapter 4, much of the social order revolved around attempts to satisfy fundamental needs. The clusters of roles, statuses, and their associated meanings that develop around these basic needs are called social institutions. They are the topic of Part 5.

Chapter 13 begins with a look at the family. You will discover there are several functions that the family serves in every society. You will also learn that the traditional nuclear family is by no means the only form that families can take. In fact, family life styles in this country have diversified greatly. This chapter discusses how and why.

Chapter 14 turns to another social institution—education. Here you will find that there is more to our educational system than the transmission of knowledge and skills alone. Nor are our schools the unbiased vehicles for social mobility we like to think they are. Throughout a public school education, children from less affluent familes often face discrimination. How such discrimination works is one of many issues we will explore.

Religion is a social institution enjoying renewed importance in recent years. Yet this revival is paradoxical. On the one hand, many of the major religious denominations in our country have been steadily losing members and are currently in states of uncertainty. On the other hand, nonconventional religion, like fundamentalist churches and religious cults, is experiencing new popularity. How can these seemingly contradictory trends be explained? Chapter 15 seeks some answers to this question and others.

CHAPTER 13

The Family

Try to imagine yourself as a young child growing up among the Kikuyu, a people in Kenya. Until you can walk, your mother carries you about most of the day on her back. From this convenient perch you can easily communicate your needs to her and feel comforted by her presence. At night you do not sleep alone but with your mother. There are no cribs, cradles, or carriages to hold you and segregate you from others. Your mother receives considerable help in caring for you since you live in a compound with grandparents, aunts, uncles, cowives (your father may have more than one wife), and many other children of all ages.

When you begin walking, your mother puts you in the care of the older children. You spend your days trailing after siblings, half siblings, and cousins in the courtyard of the family compound. You learn most of your basic skills from these older children. When you need adult assistance or permission, you are as likely to turn to a grandparent or a cowife as you are to your mother. Unlike children reared in the United States, you do not typically seek out an adult simply for praise or approval. Although the Kikuyu make little fuss about your developing self-reliance and independence, you have ample opportunity to do so. Children are not highly dependent upon adults, especially not on one or two adults as they are in Amerian society (Whiting, 1978).

The average middle-class American child seeks out adults for information, entertainment, social interaction, and approval far more than does his or her Kikuyu counterpart.

The differences between Kikuyu and American styles of child rearing reveal how widely patterns of family interaction can vary from one society to the next, and how profoundly these patterns influence children's development. In the first part of this chapter we will examine three major perspectives on the family and then look at ways in which families differ across cultures. We then turn to the subject of marriage, an institution associated with families everywhere. We will explore different forms of marriage and the social forces that affect people's decisions to marry. Next we look more closely at the nature of the American family and at how social class and other factors affect its structure and interaction. Finally, we examine the changing American family and consider current trends and innovations.

THE NATURE OF FAMILY LIFE

What is the family? How do we know who is included in a family and who is not? At first glance these questions may seem easy. Yet when we begin surveying family life across a broad spectrum of the world's cultures, we find a great many different types of arrangements. As our discussion in the following pages will illustrate, this broad range of diversity has proven a challenge to sociologists who study the family. For our purposes, however, let us define the **family** as a group of people who are united by ties of marriage, ancestry, or adoption and who are recognized by the community as constituting a single household and as having the responsibility for rearing children.

Perspectives on the Family

In other chapters of the text we have found that the functionalist, conflict, and interactionist perspectives give us unique and valuable insights into human behavior. Family life is no exception. Each theory calls our attention to dimensions of social experience that the others either slight or entirely neglect. Therefore, we will launch our treatment of family life by considering each of these perspectives.

The Functionalist Perspective

Functionalists say that if a society is to survive and maintain itself across time, certain essential functions must be performed. Their performance cannot be left to chance. If they were, the society would run the risk of their not being carried out, and the society itself would disintegrate. Functionalists view institutions as the principal structures for organizing and directing people's activities so that key tasks are executed. They consider the family to be the institution responsible for the following functions:

The Regulation of Sexual Behavior All societies place limits on the sexual behavior of their members and specify which categories of individuals may mate. Thus every society has an *incest taboo* that bars sexual relations among certain relatives. Societies differ however, as to which relatives are covered by prohibition. For instance, the royal households of ancient Egypt and Hawaii provided for the marriage of brothers and sisters (apparently as a device for keeping power and property within the family). In contrast, traditional Chinese society excluded as sexual partners all individuals bearing the same clan name, even if they were cousins a thousand times removed. Functionalists explain incest taboos as social mechanisms that prevent rivalries and hostilities based upon sexual attraction from arising within families. And the taboos encourage offspring to marry into other family networks, thereby linking together by marriage different families and promoting overall social integration.

Reproduction If a society is to survive from one generation to the next, it must have some arrangement for replacing its members. Since sexual needs can be satisfied in the absence of reproduction, societies must motivate people to have children. They do so in a great many ways. For instance, ancestor worship as practiced in traditional Chinese society encouraged individuals to assure their well-being in the hereafter by having many sons. And in the United States many people feel unfulfilled if they do not have children to link them across time with future generations. The family provides an institutionalized arrangement for replacing a society's members, with men and women occupying the statuses of father and mother and carrying out their associated roles.

Socialization As we pointed out in Chapter 5, children enter society at birth as social blanks. They become social beings as they acquire those elements of culture necessary for competent participation in social life. Throughout most of human history and in most societies today the family is the chief means of transmitting culture. The family functions as an intermediary group between the individual and the larger community.

Care and Protection During infancy and early childhood, human beings are unable to fend for themselves. They must be fed, clothed, and protected from the elements. Similarly, over the course of their lives, individuals experience episodes of illness and disablement, and women undergo extended periods of pregnancy. During these times the family assumes the responsibility for caring for and protecting its dependent members.

Social Placement As functionalists conceive of social life, it consists of social structure—an integrated web of statuses and the distribution of people in them. Individuals must somehow be placed within these statuses and assume their associated roles. Many of our ascribed statuses, including our national, ethnic, racial, reli-

When parents nurture and enjoy their children they provide an environment that allows the children to develop the abilities necessary to function in society. (Hazel Hankin/Stock, Boston)

gious, class, and community identities, derive from our family membership. Even in societies like the United States that stress equality of opportunity and advancement based on merit, the family plays a critical part in facilitating the social mobility of its members (see Chapters 10 and 14).

The Conflict Perspective

Conflict theorists such as Jetse Sprey (1979) agree with the functionalists position that the family institution is essential to the survival of human beings and their societies.. Indeed, these theorists say that groups and societies are organized systems of species survival. But they also point out that human societies operate under conditions of perpetual scarcity for most of the resources that people need or want. Scarcity in turn leads to competition both within and between groups, and people enter a great many relationships as real or potential competitors. Individuals may exploit others or themselves be exploited, but they may also win or lose jointly, often at the expense of outsiders. Viewed from this perspective, families do not differ from one another so much as to the presence or absence of conflict but rather in its forms and intensity.

We often think of conflict behavior as ranging from mild verbal exchanges to physical violence. But much family conflict involves negotiating and bargaining rather than fighting. The terms "negotiating" and "bargaining" imply that some matter is in dispute and that the parties are attempting to reach a collective agreement. Further, family conflict at times may entail litigation, including the filing of charges of abuse, divorce petitions, and child custody demands. For the most part, however, marriages and families, like many other small groups, are survival units, and hence they represent "no-win" combat zones. An awareness that all members must be able to continue living together typically encourages the individuals to temper their actions.

Conflict theorists stress that the family is also a system for regulating conflict (Dahrendorf, 1965; Sprey, 1979). Family and marital life reflect ongoing processes of "give and take," which are necessary to maintain at least a minimal semblance of order and interpersonal harmony. Indeed, confrontations are so much a part of close relationships that family arrangements must incorporate them as part of their structure. Many of these conflicts concern rules and status privileges. Thus family members develop patterns for confronting each other while simultaneously structuring intricate modes of cooperation. For instance, family members create an emotional closeness and interdependence that contribute to situations of joint vulnerability. Viewed in this manner, the love that people feel for each other helps them cope with the underlying competitive quality of their relationships.

The Symbolic Interactionist Perspective

Whereas functionalists direct considerable attention to the structural characteristics of institutions and conflict theorists to the competitive aspects of social life, symbolic interactionists focus their sociological eye on the symbolic environment in which people carry out their daily activities. They point out that human beings differ from lower forms of life in that they have the ability to learn, think, and communicate symbolically (Burr et al., 1979). The symbols that people employ have meaning and allow them to mentally evaluate and formulate various courses of action. As such, individuals fit and align their actions in marital and family relationships by evolving shared definitions of the situation (see Chapters 1 and 4).

Symbolic interactionists stress that a couple's relationship undergoes a continuous process of definition and redefinition. Consider what happens among college students when a man and a woman begin "living together." The sociologists Charles L. Cole (1977:77) observes:

> At the point in the process when the partners move in together, the social reality of their relationship undergoes a significant change that calls for a new subjective assessment of that relationship. They must now redefine their social situation to account for the fact that they are cohabiting. This redefinition frequently is accompanied by a reassessment of their feelings toward their partner as well as their own self-concept.

Hence, marital and family life consists of an ongoing process of attributing meaning to situations and fashioning relationships based on these interpretations.

In sum, from the functionalists perspective, we see society as having an existence of its own—a social structure with distinctive functional requirements. From the conflict perspective we gain an image of society as a setting in which individuals and groups are in competition with one another for scarce resources that people need and want. And finally, from the symbolic interactionist perspective we derive a view of social life as a set of negotiated meanings. Let us now consider how societies vary so that they pose for their individual members somewhat different kinds of reality, including different family realities.

The Wide Variation in Family Form

The family is a conspicuous feature of social organization in all societies. Indeed, it is sometimes termed the most basic social institution. Yet throughout the world societies exhibit quite different patterns for family living. Thus, as we noted earlier in this chapter, the traditional Kikuyu family differs from the typical American middle-class family in important ways. And as we will see later in the chapter, family systems have been subject to continuous social change across history. Even so, it is easy for many of us to take an ethnocentric view and to assume that our own family arrangements are somehow the "best," particularly if we impute moral qualities to them. Accordingly, it is helpful to examine a number of different patterns of marriage, family, and kinship, and to see that in other contexts, other arrangements are appropriate. Indeed, we may find the discussion reassuring, considering the changes our own society's life styles have undergone in recent decades.

The Nayar

One of the more fascinating forms of family life is found among the Nayar of Kerala, India (Gough, 1974). During her adolescence a Nayar girl is encouraged to have several lovers. If she becomes pregnant, one or more of these lovers acknowledges paternity and pays the costs of delivering the baby. Beyond this, however, none of the lovers has any obligations toward the girl or her child. The mother's kin are completely responsible for both care of the child and support of the mother. The Nayar do have a form of marriage, but it is simply a ritual that marks a girl's passage into adulthood; it is not a ceremony that heralds the beginning of a family as we know it. During the ritual marriage, the woman's relatives choose a man to be her husband for three days. Afterward, husband and wife may never see each other again. The wife's only further obligations arise when her husband dies and she must observe his funeral rites.

Once a Nayar woman is ritually married, she is free to take on a series of visiting husbands. If she gives birth to a child, some man of her own rank is assigned the status of father (whether or not he actually is the biological father). But this assigned father has no rights or obligations concerning the child. Thus, among the Nayar, social fatherhood (acknowledged paternity) may be totally unrelated to biological fatherhood. Yet the business of replicating the Nayar culture goes on just as smoothly as it does elsewhere. The mother's brother assumes the male responsibility in rearing the child. The child owes allegiance to the uncle and not to the father. In turn, property and privileged status are transmitted not from father to son but from maternal uncle to nephew. Family life revolves about the brother-sister relationship. Thus children are conceived, born, and socialized in an orderly, socially determined way, and family life is ordered according to regular and predictable expectations and rules.

Life in a nuclear family does not exist for the Dani. This Dani woman rarely sees her husband, who may live in a different compound from hers. When their child is about ten, he too will probably move out of his mother's compound to live with distant relatives. (Malcom S. Kirk/Peter Arnold)

The Dani

The Dani of West Irian, Indonesia, also have a family system that substantially differs from our own. For the Dani, the family is not a particularly meaningful unit; in fact, the Dani language lacks a word meaning "family" (Heider, 1972). Social life is organized not around private, family households but around compounds that continually shift (sometimes as frequently as every three days). While the Dani do have a form of marriage (and one man may marry several women), husbands and wives do not necessarily live in the same compounds. Occasionally spouses cooperate in house building and cooking, but family life is usually short-lived. Children, especially boys, spend much of their time away from their parents, and by the time they are ten years old, they typically move in with distant relatives.

For those of us reared in Western cultures, the most striking feature of Dani life is the seeming indifference to sex. Men and women generally sleep in separate quarters within the Dani compounds. The Dani also observe long periods of ritual sexual abstinence, particularly after the birth of a child. Husbands and wives may abstain from sexual relations for four to five years after a baby is born, and the Dani do not define this abstinence as creating a special hardship (Heider, 1972). Although Dani culture might seem strange to us, it nonetheless functions to produce healthy, socialized children, just as societies do everywhere.

The Israeli Kibbutzim

The collective communes in Isreal, called **kibbutzim**, provide yet another example of a family life style

Family life on an Israeli kibbutz is very different from our own. Children live with their age-mates in children's houses, and are cared for by communal nurses. (Marvin E. Newman/ Woodfin Camp & Associates)

different from ours. On many of these collective farms, the activities we associate with family life are performed by the community as a whole. Cooking, laundry, and recreation are all communally organized. Men are not responsible for the economic support of their wives; both men and women work for the community and are supported by it. The kibbutzim, not the family, is the unit of economic cooperation. Women are not exclusively responsible for the care of their children; child care is the community's responsibility (Talmon-Garber, 1962). A biological mother nurses her child during the first eight months of life, but after this time children are cared for by communal nurses in separate children's houses. Since the children's houses are organized into homogeneous age groups, each child grows up with the same group of peers. This group plays an enormously important role in the child's life.

The experience of the kibbutz has exploded a number of cherished myths about the tight connection between biological and social parenthood. Psychological and sociological studies of kibbutz life have revealed that communal child rearing has many virtues and does in fact provide a viable alternative to the traditional family as we know it (Bettelheim, 1971; Rabin, 1965).

Patterns of Family Organization

Our descriptions of Nayar, Dani, and Israeli kibbutzim practices testify to the great many ways societies have for ordering relationships among men and women. How are we to make sense of these differences? Sociologists and anthropologists have done so by distinguishing among differing patterns of family organization. Let us consider a number of these.

Family Types

In structuring their relationships, a people can assign priority either to marital ties or to blood ties. When priority is given to marital ties, the arrangement is termed a **nuclear family**. The core family consists of the spouses and their offspring; blood relatives are functionally marginal and peripheral. This arrangement is the preferred form of family life in the United States. Normally, during the course of one's life, a person is a member of two different, overlapping nuclear families. The first consists of oneself and one's father, mother, and siblings—the **family of orientation**. The second consists of oneself and one's spouse and children—the **family of procreation.**

When priority is given to blood ties (those between parents and children or between brothers and sisters), the arrangement is termed an **extended family**. The core family consists of blood relatives, with spouses being functionally marginal and peripheral. This arrangement is found among the Nayar, where the role of spouse is virtually nonexistent and family life revolves about the brother-sister relationship. Extended families have continuity across generations. In contrast, the operation of incest taboos makes the nuclear family discontinuous over time. Sons and daughters must secure mates outside the family of orientation, contributing to a break between this nuclear family and the family of procreation. We will contrast the nuclear and extended family arrangements in greater depth later in this chapter.

Rule of Descent

Through the years a good many Americans have taken an interest in their family genealogies, an interest heightened by the television dramatization of Alex Haley's novel, *Roots*. We reckon descent through both our father's and mother's families, a system termed **bilateral descent**. In George Peter Murdock's (1949) survey of some 250 societies, 30 percent of them followed this procedure. Another 42 percent traced their kin only through their father's lineage—**patrilineal descent**—whereas about 20 percent reckoned descent only through their mother's line—**matrilineal descent**. Very often the inheritance of property follows the rules of descent. Such rules define the family as a social group rather than as simply a biological uit.

Rules of Residence

In nuclear family arrangements, the husband and wife typically take up residence together. Because they come from different families of orientation, one or the other or both must move at marriage. The most prevalent arrangment is **patrilocal**—the married couple live with or near the husband's family. In the opposite or **matrilocal** arrangement, the husband leaves his family and sets up housekeeping with or near his wife's family. Finally, a couple may establish a new or **neolocal** residence. This arrangement is the preferred pattern in the United States.

Types of Authority

In theory three types of authority patterns are possible within the family: power may be vested in males, **patriarchy**; in females, **matriarchy**; or relatively equally, **equalitarian**. Throughout most of history the prevalent pattern has been the patriarchal arrangement, the system found among the ancient Greeks, Romans, and Hebrews. In no society has matriarchy been the norm, despite legends of Amazon women. The authority of women typically varies from family to family, depending upon the personalities of the spouses and the nature of their relationship. And where children are born out of wedlock, where a couple divorce, or where the husband dies or deserts, women gain an autonomous position by default. Equalitarian patterns are becoming more prevalent in modern societies. In 1962, for instance, 66 percent of American woman interviewed by University of Michigan researchers said that the major family decisions should be made by the man of the house, but in 1980 only 28 percent felt that way (Klemesrud, 1980).

Sociologists have sought to determine the factors that influence the evolution of various forms of family organization, a matter to which we now turn our attention.

Origins of Different Family Forms

For the most part sociologists have agreed that the form the family takes reflects the principal way in which the members of the society make their living (their predominant subsistence strategy). In agricultural and herding societies, where failure to follow established rules for raising crops and animals could wipe out the entire food supply, families are tightly organized and stratified. In hunting and gathering bands, where food-getting innovations that fail usually affect only a single day's catch, family life is more egalitarian (Barry et al., 1957) Subsistence strategies are related to family size as well. In societies based on agriculture and fishing, family networks are large and cooperative, in an attempt to assure

Among hunter-gathers, like the !Kung Bushmen of the Kalahari Desert, frequent mobility necessitates small families. Similarly, in modern industrial societies where people move often, the nuclear family is highly adaptive. (Top, Irven DeVore/Anthro Photo; bottom, Elliott Erwitt/Magnum)

the survival of all. In hunting and gathering bands, where subsistence depends on individual enterprise and extensive mobility, family units are small and individualistic. These patterns facilitate the group's continual movement and ensure that a limited food supply does not quickly become depleted (Nimkoff and Middleton, 1960).

Until recently, much sociological research seemed to suggest that modern industrial societies resemble hunting and gathering bands rather than settled peasant societies in that they favor the small nuclear family. Both seem to require a high degree of mobility and hence considerable individualism and independence. Robert F. Winch and Rae Lesser Blumberg (1968) conclude that the nuclear family pattern appears in both very simple and very developed societies, whereas the extended family appears in societies of intermediate complexity. The sociologist William Goode (1963) suggests that industrialization undermines extended family arrangements while fostering the nuclear family. He points out that the geographic mobility demanded by modern industrial societies (the demand that people move to areas where work is available) requires a small family unit that can readily move about. When a member of a family must move to increase economic or social opportunities, it is far simpler to take along a small nuclear family than to consult with and accommodate a large number of kin. In addition, the modern occupational system is based on personal achievement rather than family ascription. Individuals who are not tied to the rigid traditions of extended kin are more socially mobile, free from the constraints of established family rules and definitions. Finally, the extended family's hold on its members is weakened as nonkin organizations like schools, corporations, hospitals, nursing homes, welfare agencies, and governments take over many of the educational, economic, health, and welfare functions that it traditionally performed.

Because functional analyses like Goode's are so logical, it is easy to assume that they provide full explanations of why certain social patterns prevail. We must be cautious in making such assumptions, however. Sociologist Peter Laslett (1974) has pointed out that the nuclear family prevailed in England *before* industrialization, so its appearance in modern history cannot be traced solely to industrialism. In this case we probably need to draw the distinction between social patterns that conform to ideal standards and those that reflect everyday realities. Thus the large, extended family may have remained the ideal in preindustrial England, but certain conditions (a high mortality rate, for example) may have forced the majority of people to live in smaller families.

An accumulating body of research also suggests that industrialization and extended family ties are not incompatible (Smelser, 1959). For instance, Tamara K. Hareven (1982) has studied the relationship between family and work in an industrial setting—the Amoskeag Manufacturing Company of Manchester, New Hampshire, a large textile factory founded in 1838. She found that the family, rather than being disrupted by the new industrial order, became its linchpin. The family was the primary unit for supplying a work force for factories, the base for community morality and stability, and the socializer of the young. Nor did migration to a new community necessarily break kinship ties. Rather, the factory system reinforced family ties by permitting grown children to find work in the same community and thus remain near to their parents and their adult siblings. Sons and daughters became fathers and mothers and later, when their aging parents needed assitance, they became sons and daughters again, frequently taking on filial responsibilities. During the transitional period prior to marriage, young adults often lived in their parental households and worked in the mill. And after they married, it was not uncommon for them to continue to live for a time with their spouses in the family home. Thus life in an industrial community offered many opportunities for family interdependence and for overlap among generations within the family. All this suggests that subsistence strategies alone are not always sufficient to explain why particular family structures exist at any given time.

MARRIAGE

Marriage is a socially recognized union between two or more individuals that typically involves sexual and economic rights and duties. It marks the start of a nuclear family or the expansion and continuation of an extended family. In either case, marriage is backed by strong social sanctions. Although we may feel that we are "free" to make our own decisions about whether and whom to marry, there are, in fact, powerful social forces pushing us into marriage and into selection of an "appropriate" partner.

Forms of Marriage

One way societies undertake to regulate marriage is through norms that define the range of potential marriage partners available to an individual. **Endogamy** is a rule that requires a person to marry someone from *within* his or her own group—tribe, nationality, religion, race, community, or other social grouping. **Exogamy** is a rule that requires a person to marry someone from *outside* his or her own group. These regulations frequently operate as a circle within a circle. The rule of exogamy bars marriage within a small inner circle, while the rule of endogamy stipulates the limits of the outer social circle that the individual is not to exceed. Among the early Hebrews, for instance, incest taboos operated as exogamous norms curtailing marriage among close relatives while endogamous norms forbade marriage with non-Jewish outsiders. Within the United States rules of exogamy have extended incest taboos outward roughly to second cousin relationships while rules of endogamy, until loosened in recent decades, served to forbid interracial and in some cases interethnic and interreligious marriages.

Marriage relationships may be structured in four basic ways: **monogamy,** one husband and one wife; **polygyny,** one husband and two or more wives; **polyandry,** one wife and two or more husbands; and **group marriage**, two or more husbands and two or more wives. Although monogamy is found in all societies, only about 20 percent of the 238 societies in Murdock's (1949) cross-cultural sample were strictly monogamous. In contrast, four-fifths of the societies permitted polygyny. But in most of these societies, few married men actually had more than one wife. Typically only economically advantaged men can afford to support more than one family. Thus in China, India, and the Moslem nations, polygyny was usually limited to the wealthy.

Polyandry is quite rare, being found in less than 1 percent of the societies in Murdock's sample. And where it is found, it typically does not allow women free sexual choice of male partners. The most prevalent form of polandry is fraternal, or the sharing of a spouse by brothers, the practice among the non-Hindu Todas of southern India. Apparently few disputes or jealousies arose among Todas brothers because they did not view women as sexual property. Since the biological father of a child remained unknown, the Todas socially established paternity by a ceremony in which one of the husbands would present a toy bow-and-arrow to the mother-to-be. It seems that the polyandrous arrangement evolved among the Todas as an adjustment to poverty. Their subsistence being precarious, a man could have a wife and child only by sharing the burden of their support with other men. Further, polyandry kept the birth rate in check. Since a woman can have only one child a year, it did not matter how many sexual partners she had.

Group marriage also appears relatively rarely and then not as the preferred cultural arrangement. It has been reported among the Kaingang of Brazil, the Dieri of Australia, the Chukchee of Siberia, and the Marquesan Islanders. On occasion it arises out of some combination of polygyny and polyandry or out of the sharing of sexual privileges among couples.

Choosing a Marriage Partner

Good reason exists for the fact that all societies establish laws and customs to guide their members in the choice of a husband or wife. Marriage is seldom a "private" matter involving only two people. When a man and a woman marry, their union binds together many other people as well. Because so many people are involved in the outcome, it is risky to leave such an important decision to the discretion of the young.

Arranged Marriages

Although systems of arranged marriages seem unromantic and constraining to those of us raised with values of individualism and free choice, it is easy to understand why such systems develop and flourish. Think of societies in which newlyweds move into the husband's family's household. In such cases, the family has an important stake in the type of woman the son brings home. Will she share the family's ideas about what is good and worthwhile? Will she readily adjust to the family's codes of behavior? Will she pull her weight in the household? If a new wife is to live in her husband's household forever, it is reasonable for the members of that household to have some say about the new addition. Moreover, in societies where the newlyweds live with either the bride's or the groom's family, it makes sense to avoid matches based entirely on romantic love. In such situa-

Marriage is more than a union of two people. It unites two families, and, sometimes, even two cultures. (Jean-Claude Lejeune/Stock, Boston)

tions an intense emotional attachment could have a disruptive effect. For instance, if the husband were strongly devoted to his wife, he might ally with her against other household members, thereby imperiling customary family relationships and practices. For these reasons, therefore, people in traditional societies will try to control the additions to the family by arranging marriages for the young.

Subsurface Controls

Although marriages in our own society are seldom formally arranged, they are not the acts of spontaneous love we often think they are. Parents and the rest of society shape children's marriage aspirations from a very early age. This shaping process is often very subtle, however.

Parental choices of neighborhoods and school districts influence the kinds of peers children will have to choose from for playmates and later for dates. Such intangibles of family life as the development of a sense of "we" and "they"—of "our kind" and "their kind"—influence young people's ideas concerning whom they will consider attractive. A family's choice of recreational activities and vacation spots and style of celebrating holidays and special occasions will also influence the kinds of potential mates that young people from that family will meet or eventually seek on their own.

These kinds of subsurface controls direct a young person's love interests toward an appropriate pool of eligible mates. And, in fact, the effectiveness of these subtle influences shows up in the marriage statistics. Although religious intermarriage in the United States appears to be increasing, marriages between people of different races and nationalities are relatively rare, particularly among those who belong to the higher strata of the society (Udry, 1974). Only when young people have learned what sorts of people their families consider eligible are they encouraged to let the impulses and emotions of romantic love take over.

Romantic Love

Romantic love is idealized and exalted in American society. It is the theme of most of our popular songs and the subject of many of our movies and television programs. Scores of popular books and magazine articles promise to reveal the secrets of keeping romantic love "alive" in a relationship. No wonder so much of our youthful energy is devoted to the quest for love.

There are good reasons why romantic love has become an important basis for marriage in our society (just as there are good reasons why a system of arranged marriages has developed in more traditional societies). When a man and a woman in the United States marry and set up a new household (as more than 2 million American couples did in 1982), they are relatively independent (at least geographically) of other kin. As a result, they are free to love each other without creating tensions, jealousies, and competition among other household members. Also, since the two will depend on each other for a wide range of emotional and physical supports, they will be better able to meet each other's needs if they are guided by love rather than by strictly defined rights and obligations. Romantic love also helps weaken the strong emotional ties that bind young people to their own families and enables them to move more comfortably into their own independent world.

But as the basis of marriage, romance has its limitations. In some ways romance is completely antithetical to the daily demands of married life. Romance thrives on mystery, distance, and uncertainty, while daily married life is anything but mysterious. When romance fades, all too often the marriage fades with it. Thus, by exalting romance, our society may be simultaneously undermining the very relationship it tries to promote: stable, enduring, child-producing marriages. Marriage is a business partnership as much as a romantic fairy tale; it involves compromises, division of labor, specialization, financial arrangements, and communication systems. To bill it as a flower-strewn paradise is to risk its eventual demise.

STRUCTURE AND INTERACTION IN THE AMERICAN FAMILY

No one pattern typifies the way the American family is set up and interacts. The fact that American society consists of so many different ethnic groups means that different family forms and practices are inevitable. Different social classes also create different kinds of family life, as do changing social conditions (such as the rise in divorce rates and the increasing numbers of women joining the labor force). And as the symbolic interactionist perspective suggests, much of the uniqueness encountered among American families comes about because their members negotiate quite different individual arrangements with one another. Nevertheless, magazine advertisements, novels, and television programs portray the nuclear family consisting of a married couple and their dependent children as the cultural ideal. Although the nuclear structure is no longer the most prevalent family form in our society, it is still considered the most desirable one by a majority of Americans.

The distinction between what people deem desirable and what they actually practice is an extremely important one. Simply because most people label a particular social pattern ideal does not mean that they will follow it. Indeed, the society may operate in ways that preclude their conforming to pevailing norms. Thus, even in a society where individuals prefer the nuclear family arrangements, factors such as high rate of illegitimacy and divorce, widespread poverty and unemployment, or an unbalanced sex ratio may prevent many people from living in a nuclear unit. The contemporary United States provides a good illustration of this situation. A great diversity of family arrangements prevails: many single people living alone, many childless couples, many single-parent families, many families with two breadwinners, and many cohabiting couples. We will consider alternative family forms shortly, but first let us look more closely at the traditional nuclear unit.

Characteristics of the Nuclear Family

What is life like within a nuclear family? How does it differ from extended family arrangements? Table 13.1 summarizes the major differences between the modern nuclear family and the traditional extended form. We will explore two of these: the isolation of the family and the division of labor. It should be remembered, however, that how closely a family conforms to either pattern is influenced by its ethnic group, class, and place of residence and that new social and sexual patterns are evolving in response to divorce, voluntary nonparenthood, and other factors that we will consider later in the chapter.

Isolation of the Family

In the traditional extended family, as we noted earlier in the chapter, married couples from different generations

TABLE 13.1 Traditional Versus Modern in Family Form, Function, and Ideology

Traditional	Modern
1. Kinship is the organizing principle of the society.	1. Kinship is separate from the socioeconomic and political spheres; job recruitment is independent of one's relatives.
2. The extended family is the basic unit of residence and domestic functions.	2. Nuclear family is the basic unit of residence and domestic functions.
3. Most adults work at home.	3. Home and work are separate; the household consumes rather than produces.
4. Low geographic and social mobility; sons inherit their fathers' status and occupation.	4. High geographic and social mobility; individual mobility is based on merit.
5. Parents dominate children; men dominate women.	5. Relations within nuclear family are relatively egalitarian.
6. High fertility rates and high death rates, especially in infancy; population turnover is rapid.	6. Low, controlled fertility rates and low death rates, especially in infancy; death is a phenomenon of old age.
7. Kinship bonds override economic efficiency and individual gain.	7. Advancement and economic gain of individuals prevail over kin obligations.
8. Duty, tradition, and individual submission to authority and fate are valued.	8. Individual rights, equality, freedom, and self-realization are valued.
9. Little emphasis on emotional involvement within the nuclear family; marriage is not based on love; the predominant loyalty of individuals is to blood kin rather than spouse; children are economic rather than emotional assets, but the subordination and dependency of children on their parents may continue as long as the parent lives.	9. Intense involvement of spouses, parents, and children with each other; emphasis on marital happiness and adjustment; great concern with child's development, current adjustment, and future potential. Upon attaining adulthood, children make a sharp break with parental authority.
10. Little or no psychological separation between home and community; broad communal sociability; no large-scale institutions.	10. Sharp line between home and outside world; home is viewed as private retreat and outside world as impersonal, competitive, and threatening.

Source: Adapted from Arlene Skolnick. *The Intimate Environment*. Boston: Little, Brown, 1973, Table 1, p. 97.

—and their children, and often other relatives as well—typically live and work together in the same household. By contrast, the nuclear family is isolated: Each new couple sets up a household independent of the parents' homes. In the absence of large numbers of kin living under the same roof, husband and wife must depend on each other almost exclusively for a sense of emotional well-being and comfort. In addition, they must be self-supporting, and they must take care of all household chores (including child care) by themselves. Thus, whereas the traditional family is knitted together and bound to the larger society by kinship relations, the nuclear family centers on the mutual dependence of husband and wife. It is relatively free of other social bonds. Because mutual dependence is so critical to keeping the nuclear family intact, society has institutionalized love—once an almost irrelevant feature of marriage—as the social glue to replace the structural supports that fastened the traditional family to its social surroundings. Paradoxically, the prevalence of love as a primary bond correlates with high divorce rates, since it justifies breaking up a marriage when the couple is no longer in love.

The Division of Labor

In the isolated nuclear family the division of labor between husband and wife is such that one member must remain home during the child-rearing years or the couple must arrange to pay for child care. In an extended family, other adult relatives typically assist in caring for the children or in performing other important domestic functions. Until recently, the American ideal has been for the husband to earn the money and the wife to maintain the home (although we must remember that between this ideal type and the actual reality, there has always been much disparity).

In a large, extended family, like the Hispanic group shown here, members can help each other and provide the support needed to raise children. The nuclear family, often isolated from relatives, relies on itself to fulfill all of the demands of family life. (Left, Craig Aurness/West Light; below, Susan McCartney/Photo Researchers)

No matter who is the breadwinner and who raises the children, though, the dependency of husband and wife on each other makes the nuclear family extremely fragile. In traditional extended families, for instance, the death or departure of one member was not likely to have a crippling effect on the family. But when an isolated nuclear family loses one member (through death, separation, or divorce), the disruption can be enormous. And even if there are no such disruptions, the nuclear family is still destined to undergo great change once the children leave home. Children used to remain subordinate to, and dependent on, their parents for as long as their parents lived; today, children are encouraged to strike out on their own as soon as they reach maturity. Later, when the parents grow old and are less capable of attending to their own needs, the ideal of the nuclear family inhibits them from moving in with their grown children. They must either manage on their own or be turned over to institutions specifically designed to care for the aged. Thus, the isolated nuclear family may not perform many of the functions traditionally assumed by the extended family.

Variations in Family Patterns

An abiding American myth has been that the vast majority of Americans live in nuclear families. Generations of children learned to read from textbooks describing a married couple and their children, living with their dog Spot in their own home behind a white picket fence. In these books, families with different structures and life styles simply did not exist. The message transmitted was that there was only one desirable type of family in American society: a competent working father and a devoted house-bound mother, both preferably young, native-born, and middle class, and their two or more well-adjusted children. This image became the American ideal, although it does not reflect the American reality (Figure 13.1). In recent years, however, sociologists have increasingly focused on other family types, recognizing that the isolated nuclear model applies to under half of all American families.

Composite Families

One variation in American family structure is the nuclear family embedded in a network of extended kin. (Winch and Blumberg, 1968). This family form is typical in many ethnic enclaves in cities. It may consist of three generations of the same family occupying separate apartments in one building or separate single-family houses located near one another in a neighborhood. The fact that the separate related parts of this family stay in close, day-to-day contact classifies it as extended rather than nuclear. Traditionally, immigrants to urban areas in the United States have made use of this type of extended family. Isolated from the national culture, these immigrants relied on their family bonds for support and identity. Today, however, the second- and third-generation children of the immigrants are finding that the extended family has outlived its usefulness; they feel it restricts their privacy and independence. Consequently, these generations are increasingly forming isolated nuclear families.

Single-Parent Families

Between 1970 and 1981 the number of single-parent families in the United States doubled from 3.3 million to 6.6 million families, constituting 21 percent of all American families. Population experts predict that nearly half of all children born in the 1980s will live in a single-parent home for at least part of their childhood. About 70 percent of one-parent households arise through divorce, 10 percent from the death of a spouse, and 20 percent through the birth of a child out of wedlock. Over 90 percent of one-parent families are headed by women. Of these families, 34.6 percent live below the officially defined poverty level (as against 11.2 percent of all families). In 1981 only 46.7 percent of women who were supposed to receive child-support

FIGURE 13.1 Percentage of U.S. Households with Full-time Working Fathers, Mothers Who Do Not Work Outside the Home, and One or More School-age Children

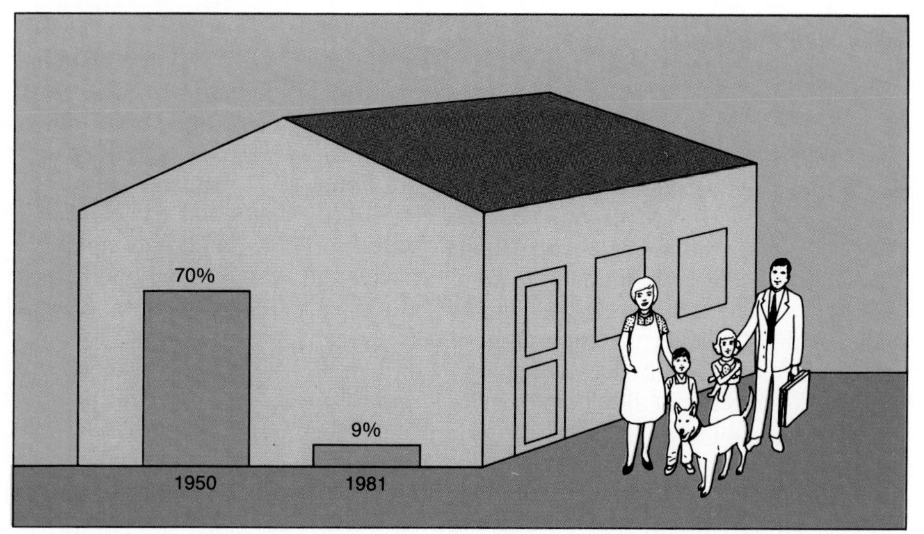

Source: U.S. Bureau of the Census, *Current Population Reports, Population Characteristics*, Series P-20 371, Household and Family, March 1981.

payments from the child's father received the money due them, and this amount was seldom much. Further, women typically are less well-paid than are men (see Chapter 6).

The psychologist Eleanor Maccoby (1978) expresses concern that the rise in single-parent families (especially those headed by women) may pose problems for the socialization of children. A father, she feels, is more effective at commanding obedience than a mother; he is usually adept at engaging the children in play; he can take over child care when the mother is unable to cope for any reason; and he is able to provide important emotional support for his wife. In addition, fathers play an important financial role in intact nuclear families. As noted above, many single mothers receive no financial help from their ex-husbands, or they receive only irregular child support payments. This sudden drop in financial status can drastically change the life style of the single-mother household and give rise to continual worries over money. For all these reasons, therefore, a single mother may undergo a great deal of stress when a father is absent. So may a single father when a mother is absent. Angry outbursts, little affection, poor communication, inconsistent discipline, and irregular meals and bedtimes are indicative of the deterioration of family functioning in the single-parent home. Maccoby (1978:206–207) concludes that child rearing "is something that many people cannot do adequately as single adults functioning in isolation. Single parents need time off from parenting, they need the company of other adults, they need to have other voices joined with theirs in transmitting values and maturity demands to their children."

A study conducted by the Kettering Foundation and the National Association of Elementary School Principals lends support to Maccoby's concerns (Hechinger, 1980). Children from single-parent homes were more likely to do poorly in school and to have behavior and discipline problems than were youngsters who lived with both parents. Yet family income and the child's sex seem to have an even greater effect on achievement than the number of parents in the home. Indeed, girls from high-income homes with only one parent got better grades than did boys from high-income homes with two parents. Further, some researchers find that the performance of one-parent children is improved if the father retains custody of a son and a mother raises a daughter (Santrock and Warshak, 1979).

Maccoby may also be unduly negative in her assessment of the problems single parents face. For instance, in one study based on interviews with twenty single fathers (Orthner, Brown, and Ferguson, 1979), all the men reported close and affectionate relationships with their children, and two-thirds felt that their children were experiencing a normal family life, comparable to that of their peers. Most of the fathers also reported trying to spend as much free time as possible with their children in order to compensate for the absence of a mother. Almost all the men occasionally took their children along with them on dates so that they could experience relationships similar to those existing in a two-parent household. In short, these fathers seemed to be coping quite well with the special demands of single parenthood. What problems they encountered seemed no different from those that arise in any family unit. Perhaps the difference between Maccoby's pessimistic warnings and this study's optimistic findings has to do simply with time. The average father in the sample had been a single parent for almost three years. This period may have been long enough to overcome the initial stresses that the newly divorced or widowed parent faces. Indeed, other research suggests that the high incidence of stress reported by single-parent mothers is primarily a function of the marital disruption process rather than a characteristic of single parenthood (McLanahan, 1983).

Working Parents and Day Care

With more than half of American mothers of preschool children now in the work force, the image of the house-bound, full-time mother no longer conforms to the reality of American practice. This fact, and the surge in single-parent families, has increased the demand for child day-care centers. In 1981, 7 million American children were in some form of day care—5.1 million in private homes other than their own home (half cared for by relatives, especially grandparents) and 1.9 million in organized day-care centers. Many Americans are concerned about this trend. They fear that nonhome care for much of the day during the early years will take its toll on children's later emotional and psychological health. Psychoanalysts such as Selma Fraiberg (1977) claim that children require the continuity and predictability of individual caretakers who show them warmth, love, and understanding. But in day-care centers children must share attention with other youngsters, and problem children—those who are often most in need of loving care—are rarely the favorites of overburdened workers.

Jerome Kagan, a distinguished Harvard developmental psychologist, once took the same position as does Fraiberg. But after he and his colleagues (1978) set up a day-care facility in Boston to investigate its impact on children, he changed his mind. The research revealed that children receiving *high-quality* day-care were not much different intellectually, emotionally, or socially from home-reared children. Other researchers tend to agree with this conclusion (Belsky and Steinberg, 1978). But most of the day care available to parents is not of the quality provided in university-based or university-connected centers. Too often parents must settle for whatever they can find and afford, which frequently is low-quality care. Given this situation, there is ample reason to be concerned about the care many American children are currently receiving.

Social Class Differences

Of all the factors that tend to influence the nature of family life, social class is one of the more important. No matter how social class is defined (by income, occupation, or education), it invariably affects the organization of family life. Of course, on the superficial level, this statement is self-evident. A family's resources clearly influence the quality of the food it consumes, the number and kind of leisure activities it enjoys, the amount of space it has to live in, and the schools its children will attend (see Chapter 10). But beyond these obvious options that money will buy, there are other class differences in family life. We will look at differences in demographic factors, early marital stress, and child-rearing practices.

Demographic Factors

Social class influences the number of children born to each family and its members' death rates. Families lower in the social hierarchy typically have (and desire) more chilren than do those higher in the social hierarchy. The death rate is substantially higher among lower-class families, which means that people in the lower social strata are likely to die at a younger age than people in higher strata. Of course, the death rate is related to such class variables as health care, nutrition, living conditions, and occupational hazards. In addition, lower-class families are more likely than upper-class ones to be disrupted by illness, desertion, and divorce.

Early Marital Stress

The effects of social class differences on the early years of marital and family life are strikingly portrayed in Lillian Rubin's *Worlds of Pain* (1976). Rubin compared fifty white working-class families with twenty-five white professional middle-class families.

As would be expected, economic problems are an enormous source of stress in working-class families, far more so than in professional middle-class families. Quite young when they marry, the working-class men lack the job experience that allows them to count on a steady income. Typically, they must take low-paying, insecure jobs; layoffs are a common problem. Twenty percent of the working-class families Rubin studied had to rely on welfare at some point in the early years of their marriage. It was a struggle just to pay for food and rent. Speaking of these early years, one working-class wife said:

> I don't know how we survived that period. The first thing that hit us was all those financial problems. *We were dirt poor.* Here I'd gotten married with all those dreams and then I got stuck right away trying to manage on $1.50 an hour—and a lot of days he didn't work very many hours. (Rubin, 1976:71)

The usual pattern was for the wife to become frightened and to get angry at the husband, and for the husband to react defensively: "I couldn't figure out what the hell she wanted from me. I was trying, and I didn't like how things were coming out any better than she did" (p. 77). Rubin points out that men and women in the professional middle class have an economic cushion that allows them to gradually work out the problems of entering adulthood, usually before they get married. Working-class couples, often just teenagers when they marry, find themselves catapulted into adult responsibilities.

One responsibility that working-class couples take on very early is parenthood. In the working-class group Rubin studied, the average time between marriage and the first child was nine months. By contrast, the first child of a professional middle-class couple was born, on

Although all couples face an adjustment period during the early years of marriage, working-class families often have economic stresses that professional families do not experience. Adult responsibilities may become overwhelming when very young couples have children early in their marriages. (Peter Menzel)

the average, three years after marriage. Parenthood posed an enormous economic and emotional burden for working-class parents, who shifted roles in a few short months "from girl and boy, to wife and husband, to mother and father" (p. 79). The wife gave up her freedom (and her job in most cases), and the husband yielded his place as the center of his wife's affections while simultaneously assuming responsibility for an infant.

Although acknowledging that such adjustment problems are not class-specific, Rubin believes that the pain of the experience is heightened in working-class families. Many working-class men and women had looked upon marriage as a haven from their own deprived childhood and broken home. A disillusioned and frustrated construction worker, who had married at eighteen and become a father five months later, told Rubin: "There I was, just a kid myself, and I finally had someone to take care of me. Then suddenly, I had to take care of a kid, and she was too busy with him to take care of me. The whole thing didn't make sense" (p. 84). The economic security usually enjoyed by professional middle-class couples allows them to keep their wife/husband roles more central, even in the early years of childbearing.

Relationships with in-laws also proved more troublesome for working-class couples. Half of the working-class wives ranked mother-in-law difficulties second only to financial ones. Wives often complained that their husbands paid more attention to their mothers than to them. In contrast, the middle-class families had fewer dealings with their in-laws. Professional middle-class couples generally did not live near their families, and those that did were usually not in daily contact with them. Thus, by minimizing the ties to in-laws, they also minimized the friction. The working-class couples, on the other hand, tended to live near (or even with) their families, and to see them frequently. For instance, grandmothers were very likely to babysit for the children while the parents worked. In addition, many of the working-class men still had strong ties to their families because they had moved directly from a dependent role in their parents' homes into marriage. The professional middle-class husbands, in contrast, had made a break with their parents long before marriage, for they had all lived away from home while at college.

Rubin's study does not suggest that the early years of marriage are easy for professional middle-class couples. They too have their share of problems. But most escape the chronic unemployment, marginal incomes, early parenthood, and in-law difficulties that distress many working-class couples. As a result, young professional middle-class couples frequently experience less frustration, conflict, and disillusionmnt than do their working-class counterparts.

Child-Rearing Practices

Families from different classes also appear to raise their children in somewhat different ways. The sociologist Melvin H. Kohn (1959, 1977) has argued that in order to understand why different classes raise their children differently, we must know what the parents value and want for their children. Kohn (1974:283) suggests that one of the most significant value differences between middle- and working-class parents finds expression in discipline: "Working-class parents want the children to conform to externally imposed standards, while middle-class parents are far more attentive to . . . internal dynamics." Hence, working-class parents tend to emphasize the *consequences* of children's actions, whereas middle-class parents tend to emphasize children's *intentions*. Middle-class mothers, for instance, are much more likely to punish their youngsters when they "lose their temper" than when they engage in "wild play." They view "temper tantrums" but not "wild play" as a loss of self-control and inner restraint. Working-class mothers, in contrast, punish their children in both situations because they are concerned with the disruptive consequences of the behavior.

Kohn suggests that these differences in values and child-rearing practices stem in large part from differences in occupational conditions. Working-class parents anticipate that as adults their children will have to follow orders. Conformity and obedience, then, become highly valued traits. Middle-class parents tend to envision their children in professional careers, where initiative and self-discipline bring success. Recently, James D. and Sonia R. Wright (1976) carried out a partial replication of Kohn's study and confirmed that the tendency to value self-direction increases with social-class rank. The Wrights argue, however, that Kohn exaggerates the importance of occupation. They say that level of education explains most of the relationship between social class and the values parents transmit to their children.

Social class differences show up not only in child-rearing practices but also in the relationships parents establish with their children. For instance, both middle-class parents are expected to be responsive to the psychological needs of their children. Consequently, the parenting roles of middle-class fathers and mothers are not vastly different: both concentrate their energies and efforts on the inner development of the child.

In working-class families, however, where socialization practices center on constraint and obedience, the mother is more likely to be the supportive parent and the father the constraining parent. In addition, the mother typically takes full charge of the girls, but the father assumes responsibility for socializing the sons into the male role (Le Masters, 1975). Recent forces of social change (for example, the women's liberation movement, increased occupational opportunities for women, and rising levels of education) have begun to influence young working-class people, blurring the traditional division of labor in parenting. How great an impact have these influences had so far? This question was the focus of one recent investigation, which we will now discuss.

Are Class Differences in Family Life Declining?

Some sixty years ago sociologists Robert and Helen Lynd investigated class differences in Muncie, Indiana. They found marked differences in life style between the working- and business-class families in "Middletown" (their fictitious name for Muncie). The sociologists Theodore Caplow and Bruce Chadwick (1979) decided to explore whether these patterns had changed since 1924, the year of the Lynd investigation. So in 1978 they replicated the Lynds' study in Muncie, and discovered some very interesting trends.

The most striking change was in family work patterns. In 1924 most women in Muncie did not seek work outside the home unless their husbands were unemployed. In fact, many more working-class wives held paid jobs because the rate of unemployment was much higher then for working-class men. By 1978, however, nearly as many business-class wives worked outside the home as did working-class wives. From their responses it seems that women of both classes now tend to seek employment not just because they financially have to, but because they want to.

Caplow and Chadwick also found substantial change in work patterns within the home. Most working-class wives still spent relatively more time on housework than did most business-class wives, but the gap between them had narrowed. Also, paid domestic help is now relatively rare. However, in 1924 roughly 90 percent of business-class families had household help, as compared to 5 percent of the working-class families.

Child-rearing approaches have also tended to converge. In 1924 working-class mothers and fathers spent less time with their children than business-class mothers and fathers did. But in 1978 this difference had disappeared. Differences in educational aspirations for children had also changed dramatically. In 1924 only 31 percent of working-class parents expected their children to complete high school and 23 percent expected them to go on to college (compared to nearly all of business-class parents), while in 1978 a high percentage of both working-class (83 percent) and business-class families (90 percent) expected all their children to receive higher education. Finally, there was no longer a great difference between working-class and business-class parents regarding their ideas of desirable behavior for children. In 1924 the most commonly mentioned traits that working-class parents considered desirable were loyalty to the church, strict obedience, and good manners. Business-class parents most frequently mentioned independence, followed by frankness in dealing with others, and only then obedience. In 1978 independence was the most commonly mentioned desirable trait among both working- and business-class parents, although business-class parents tended to list it more often (82 percent versus 68 percent).

In none of the areas investigated by Caplow and Chadwick did the working-and business-class families grow further apart. In some areas the working class moved toward the business-class norms of 1924, while in other areas the business class moved closer to the working-class norms of 1924. In still others a new shared norm seemed to be emerging. In short, Caplow and Chadwick found a partial convergence of family life styles among people of different social classes. We should not conclude, however, that all class-related differences will eventually disappear. If nothing else, the income gap between lower- and upper-class families will inevitably ensure that they generally live in different kinds of housing, engage in somewhat different leisure-time activities, and encounter somewhat different kinds of problems related to family life. The Rubin study described earlier, shows, for example, that the low income and educational attainment of many working-class newlyweds condemns them to stressful experiences that professional couples usually escape. Caplow and Chadwick's findings do not deny that such differences still exist. But they do suggest that social changes over the last fifty years have significantly reduced the even greater disparities that once existed between working-class and business-class family life styles. Other research confirms this conclusion (Gecas and Nye, 1974; Ellis et al., 1978).

Violence in the Family

Although we like to think of the family as a haven from conflict and aggression, unhappily too often this is not the case. The use of physical force is widespread in American families; in fact, there are few groups in American society in which violence is a more frequent everyday occurrence (Steinmetz and Straus, 1974; Gelles, 1983).

The family is vulnerable to violence for a variety of reasons. For one thing, Americans make a large emotional investment in their family relationships, so the words and actions of family members are seldom viewed dispassionately. As a result, small family disagreements can easily escalate into conflicts. Add to this the fact that our culture condones violence—in sports and in movies and television programs—so physical aggression comes to seem less unusual in the family. What's more, the isolation of nuclear families makes violence less visible and less subject to social control. Studies show that when another person, such as a grandparent or a boarder, lives with a married couple and their children, the incidence of violence within the nuclear family is reduced. Finally, our strong belief in the sanctity of the family frequently makes police, social workers, and even well-meaning relatives and friends reluctant to intervene lest they be considered to be invading a family's privacy.

Child Abuse

Violence in American families takes many forms. One prevalent form that we often overlook is the physical punishment of children. Perhaps 93 percent of all parents spank their children in order to discipline them (Stark and McEnvoy, 1974). Young children received the most punishment, but studies reveal that about 50 percent of high school seniors report experiencing or being threatened with physical punishment. Naturally punishment varies from a light tap to a brutal beating, but historically we have granted the parents the right to use physical force against their children. In fact, a law passed in 1696 called for the death penalty for a child of "sufficient understanding" over the age of sixteen who cursed or struck a parent or who was "stubborn and rebellious" in refusing to obey a parent. From interviews with 2,143 married couples constituting a cross-section of American families, sociologists estimate that parents kick, punch, or bite some 1.7 million children a year, beat 460,000 to 750,000 more, and attack 46,000 with guns or knives (Straus et al., 1980).

Today, physical punishment of children that results in injuries requiring medical treatment is generally considered abusive. Most people do not realize, however, that it is the regular use of "ordinary" physical punishment, and the cultural approval it enjoys, that lays the groundwork for child abuse. According to David Gil (1974), "In most incidents of child abuse the caretakers involved are 'normal' individuals exercising their prerogative of disciplining a child whose behavior they find in need of correction." If one adult were to strike another, most people would regard such behavior as abusive.

Most parents use physical punishment in the belief that it will control the aggression in their children and make them obedient. In fact, violence—whether verbal or physical—sets children a poor example. An adult who yells at or slaps a child unwittingly supplies a model for aggression. Studies have found that the frequent use of physical punishment for aggressive acts by a child results in a marked increase in the child's aggression (Walters and Grusec, 1977). Perhaps not surprisingly, an estimated 90 percent of child abusers were themselves abused as children (Reed, 1975). The pattern of abuse is unwittingly transmitted from parent to child and thus from generation to generation.

How can child abuse be checked? Some sociologists maintain that child abuse can end only when the social conditions that bring it about are alleviated (Gelles, 1974; Gil, 1974). In their view violence is used as a resource by those who experience stressful situations and who feel the need to compensate for the lack of such other resources as money, knowledge, and respect. Another proposed solution would be simply to make physical punishment of children illegal as has recently been done in Sweden. By removing the stamp of approval, the propensity to strike a child might be undermined. In the short term, it is important to identify the individual child abusers and attempt to give them treatment. The parent's recognition of the problem is crucial. Psychiatrists estimate that 90 percent of abusing parents are treatable if they receive competent counseling (Helfer and Kempe, 1976). In recent years Parents Anonymous groups have formed across the country so that abusive parents can talk about their problems and give each other support and comfort in a group setting.

Wife Abuse

Force or the threat of force between husband and wife is also common in the American family. The study of 2,143 couples revealed that in any one year 1.8 million wives are beaten two or more times a year (Straus et al., 1980). Research suggests that child and wife abuse is more prevalent in, although not confined to, families of low socioeconomic status. In part, the higher prevalence of violence in these households is due to the more stressful situations and conditions that are present. For instance, unemployment or part-time employment of males increases the incidence of family violence. Child abuse also is more prevalent in single-parent than in two-parent families (Gelles, 1983).

A husband may use force on his wife for several reasons (Whitehurst, 1974). A primary factor derives from the tradition of male superiority that prescribes the husband "should be in control." If he feels he is losing control, he is more likely to strike out. Some men have felt themselves threatened in recent years by the increasing tendency of women to seek equality with men in matters of employment, mobility, decision making, and sexual relations. The tension underlying a relationship may erupt in violence, especially when a spouse is under the influence of alcohol. Complicating matters, Western culture has traditionally approved the use of violence by an aggrieved husband. For instance, for most of recorded

Centers for battered women and "hotlines" for abused wives are becoming more common as public awareness of family violence grows. (Mark Antman/The Image Works)

history the man who killed an adulterous wife had the law on his side. Moreover, males are socialized in ways that reward them for acting tough. And male folklore and poronography portray females as enjoying aggressive treatment by males. Finally, men are permitted and encouraged to give physcial expression to their hostile feelings, whereas women are culturally expected to suppress their anger or to express it in nonphysical forms (taunts, gestures, and arguments).

Divorce

That American society has been successful in promoting marriage as a way of life is clear from American marriage statistics. Nine out of ten people in America get married at least once—and they do it fairly early in life. The median age for marriage among women is between twenty-two and twenty-three years, and for men it is slightly over twenty-five years (U.S. Bureau of the Census, 1983). But what happens to all of those marriages that start out with so much love and so many high hopes? Unfortunately, it is very difficult to know for certain what *does* happen.

To begin, it is almost impossible to come up with a satisfactory definition of what constitutes happy and unhappy marriages. And without such a definition, we cannot expect to come up with figures concerning how many of each kind occur. And even if we rely on information that does seem to be measurable—for instance, the number of marriages that end in divorce—the task remains very complicated.

The Difficulty of Measuring Divorce

Measuring the divorce rate would seem to be an easy job. Just count up the number of divorces granted in any one year and compare that statistic with the number of marriages performed in the same year. For example, in 1982, there were 1.2 million divorces and 2.5 million marriages (U.S. Bureau of the Census, 1983), for a divorce rate of nearly 50 percent.

It seems simple, but the wrong things are being compared and, in fact, we are learning nothing about the *rate* of divorce. A valid divorce rate must compare the number of divorces in one year with the *total number of marriages that exist in that year*. Thus when you compare the more than 50 million marriages existing in 1983, with the 1.2 million divorces in that year, the divorce rate turns out to be only about 2 percent.

Many observers use current divorce statistics and compare them with those of an earlier era (413,000 divorces in 1962, a third of the 1983 total) to show that today marriage is passé and that the institution of the family is in a state of decay. But interpreting divorce statistics is tricky, especially when comparing those of two eras. Say we were to compare the rate of divorce today with that in 1920. One problem would be that divorce rates then were unreliable estimates based on records from less than half the states. Moreover, in 1920 there were more inhibitions about getting a divorce: It was costlier, there were fewer grounds on which to sue for divorce, and there was greater social condemnation of divorce than there is today. Finally, life expectancy was considerably shorter then, which meant that some marriages were dissolved by death before they could be dissolved by divorce. So, for various reasons, there were many couples that stayed married in 1920 that would obtain divorces if they lived today. Hence, divorce rates alone are in inaccurate indicator of the health and happiness of a family life (Crosby, 1980).

Another problem with a general rate of divorce, like our 2 percent figure, is that it reveals nothing about how many marriages do last and for how long. For instance, of the more than 3 million Americans who married in 1952, 29 percent had divorced by their twenty-fifth wedding anniversary. Should current divorce rates continue, another 3 percent will divorce, for a total of 32 percent. In marked contrast, if current divorce rates continue, 19 percent of couples now marrying will end their marriage before the fifth anniversary, 33 percent before the tenth, 40 percent before the fifteenth, 47 percent before the twenty-fifth, and 50 percent before the fiftieth. As these figures reveal, the risk of divorce declines rapidly after the first decade (Weed, 1982).

Explaining Divorce Rates

Over the course of recent decades, divorce rates have been going up (see Figure 13.2). Social factors have played a major part in this trend, all involving change—in values, in institutions, and in the position of women. The major change in values has involved a shift from a philosophy of self-sacrifice to one that emphasizes indi-

FIGURE 13.2 Divorce Rate per 1,000 People in the U.S.

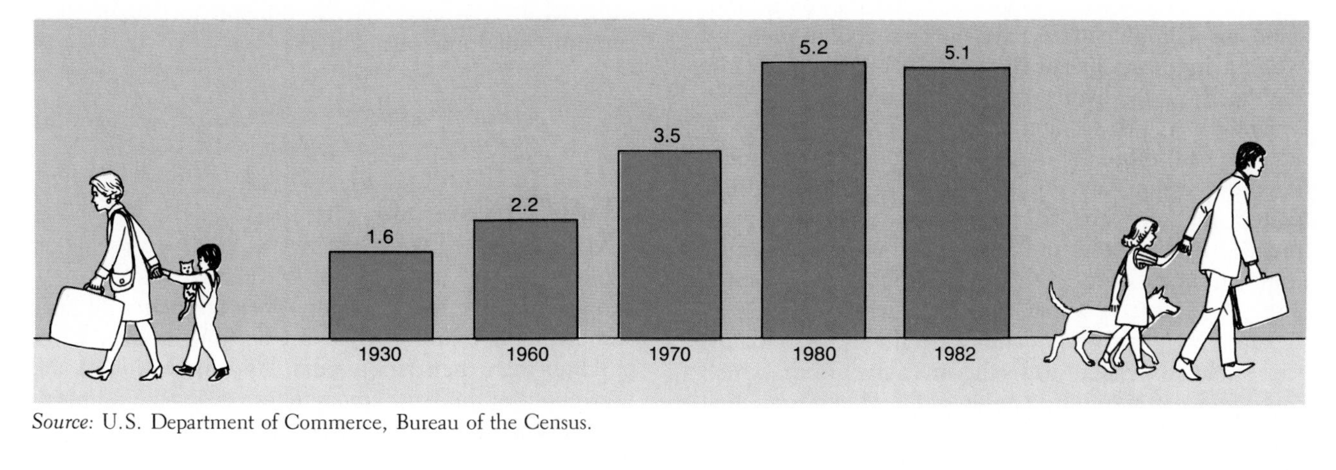

Source: U.S. Department of Commerce, Bureau of the Census.

vidual happiness. The principal reason for getting married today is to satisfy one's personal and psychological needs as these find expression in romantic love. Failure to have these needs met now leads to dissolution of the marriage rather than to an attempt to stay together "for the children's sake." Instead of all divorces being regarded as a sign of personal failure (as in past eras), some divorces today are viewed as "a sign of psychoemotional health, of personal growth, and of the ongoing struggle for personal fulfillment" (Crosby, 1980:57).

Institutions affecting family life have also changed. For instance, most churches now recognize divorce. In addition, the legal apparatus for obtaining divorces has been made less complex; forty-seven states now have some form of no-fault divorce laws, and free legal aid is often available for those unable to afford lawyer fees and court costs (Melville, 1983). Finally, the change in the position of women has contributed to increasing divorce rates. Women have become less economically dependent on men, and therefore freer to opt out of marriage. Further, in promoting the general equality of the sexes, society has made singlehood and single parenthood a more acceptable option.

Who Gets Divorced?

Are some marriages more prone to divorce than others? Certainly, marriages in which there are personal problems, sexual incompatibility, infidelity, excessive drinking, financial difficulties, or difficult in-law relationships are divorce-prone. Less obvious factors also make a marriage prone to divorce. A composite of the findings of sociological studies produces the following profile of a marriage particularly susceptible to divorce:

- The husband and wife live in (and probably grew up in) an urban area.
- They both work, but their incomes are not high.
- They were married early and have not been married long.
- They have a young child.
- The wife has egalitarian attitudes about division of labor in the home and the husband does not.
- Neither husband nor wife has strong religious convictions.
- Both husband and wife are liberal in their attitudes and rather pessimistic about life.
- One or the other has parents who are divorced (Booth and White, 1980; Huber and Spitze, 1980; Yoder and Nichols, 1980).

Of course, none of these factors alone, nor even all of them together, guarantees that a couple will become divorced. But as they accumulate, the statistical likelihood that the marriage will eventually be dissolved increases.

The Personal Costs of Divorce

It is easier to get divorced today than in times past, but it is no less painful. Studies have shown that both men and women suffer significant stress at two key points: before the decision to divorce and at the time of the final separation (Chiriboga and Cutler, 1977; Jacobs, 1982). Poor health, difficulty in sleeping and working, loneliness, depression, anxiety, lowered self-esteem, and impaired memory are all associated with the divorce process. In their study of 252 men and women currently undergoing a divorce, David A. Chiriboga and Loraine Cutler (1977:104) found that "the whole process of separation is highly traumatic, generally more so than is the stress associated with the marriage from which respondents were seeking to escape." They found that men were more vulnerable to stress than women. At the same time, close to 50 percent of both men and women reported that they felt some relief as a result of having initiated the divorce process.

The children of a couple planning to divorce also share in the pain, especially immediately following the separation. In their study of family breakup, Judith S. Wallerstein and Joan B. Kelly (1980) found that parents rarely prepare their children for the coming crisis, nor do they provide them with the necessary assurances that they will be cared for. Preoccupied by their personal problems, the parents are often insensitive to their children's anger, fear, or perplexity. When divorce necessitates that the mother go to work, the child may be placed in unfamiliar child care arrangements, and both mother and father become substantially less available. The first year following a divorce is typically the most stressful for the parents and for the child (Hetherington et al., 1977). In the long run, however, divorce is not necessarily psychologically damaging to children, particularly when both parents remain accessible and loving. (See the box on the effects of divorce on children.)

Whatever the pain that divorce inflicts, it does not seem to sour people on the institution of marriage. A fourth of the people who get divorced are remarried within the year, and 75 percent remarry within nine years of divorce. About five of every six divorced men and three of every four divorced women marry again. One reason that men are more likely to remarry than women is that men typically marry younger women. When we consider that by age twenty-seven women begin outnumbering men, we can see how middle-aged and older men have a larger pool of potential partners from which to choose than do women (Glick, 1984). In sum, while marriage may be difficult to sustain, it is certainly not going out of style.

THE CHANGING AMERICAN FAMILY

People today are living longer. They are marrying later and divorcing more. Couples are deciding to have fewer children than their parents did. And more women are now entering the work force. These changes in mortality, marriage, fertility, and employment patterns are having a profound effect on family life. We will examine two major areas of change—the increasing diversity in family structure and the changing roles of husband and wife.

Alternative Life Styles and Family Structures

One of the most striking aspects of American life over the past two decades has been the expansion in life styles available to its members. As individuals move from youth through old age, they often experience a greater range of household arrangements than did earlier generations of Americans. Even so, public opinion polls show that marriage is by far the preferred life style (see Figure 13.3, p. 358). Only 5 percent favor remaining single and another 3 percent prefer living with someone but not marrying. Let us examine some of these alternative arrangements.

Singlehood

An unmarried life style is becoming increasingly attractive to both men and women for at least a few years of their lives, generally when they are young. However, not too long ago, Americans attached a stigma to the term "spinster." For instance, a 1957 survey found that 80

THE SOCIOLOGICAL EYE ON:

The Effects of Divorce on Children

> I asked Peter when he had last seen his dad. The child looked at me blankly and his thinking became confused, his speech halting. Just then, a police car went by with its siren screaming. The child stared into space and seemed lost in reverie. As this continued for a few minutes, I gently suggested that the police car had reminded him of his father, a police officer. Peter began to cry and sobbed without stopping for 35 minutes (Wallerstein and Kelly, 1980:72)

This interview with a young boy whose parents had separated several years earlier, and who saw his father only once every few months, confirms adult's worst fears about the effects of divorce on children. Conventional wisdom holds that children are usually devastated by the dissolution of their parent's marriage. Often they feel personally abandoned by the parent who has left the home. Confused, grief-stricken, even fearful that the divorce was somehow their fault, the children of separating parents find their world severely shaken.

With the growing incidence of divorce in recent years, social scientist feel an increasing urgency to understand the nature and extent of the impact that divorce has on children. In part, their findings agree with what common sense suggests: Divorce is usually a very painful experience for children. In one study of 131 children of divorcing parents, from nursery school age to adolescence, almost all clung to the hope that their parents would somehow be miraculously reconciled (Wallerstein and Kelly, 1980). Even five years after their parents' separation, over a third of these children remained intensely unhappy with their new family life. Many were moderately to severely depressed and lonely, and a substantial number were angry much of the time.

At times children, particularly sons, pose management problems for single-parent mothers: They become abusive, demanding, and unaffectionate, and their mothers respond with depression, low self-esteem, and a badgering type of parenting. Homes in which mothers lose control are associated with a drop in children's school performance. However, children whose mothers maintain control show no decrease in grades, problem-solving skills, or other measures of academic achievement (Hetherington et al., 1977; Francke, 1983).

But investigation into the effects of divorce on children has also uncovered some encouraging facts. First, the passage of time helps. Within a year after their parents separate, most children no longer experience the intense pain and despondency they felt initially. Instead, they have become resigned to the change in their family structure, even if reluctantly so (Kelly and Wallerstein, 1976). Second, when *both* parents are consistently supportive, understanding, and affectionate, children of divorce adjust much more readily (Clingempeel and Reppucci, 1982). Sometimes one unusually caring parent can make up for another who is uninterested and aloof. But this is relatively rare. Typically, a continuing close relationship with both parents is necessary for good adjustment (Wallerstein and Kelly, 1980). Moreover, if the custodial parent is relatively secure financially and making a healthy psychological transition to his or her new social status, the adjustment of the children is usually even better (Lamb, 1977*a*).

All these findings challenge the popular assumption that divorce is necessarily bad for children. Maintaining a hostile and conflict-ridden marriage can be more damaging to a child than ending that marriage (Kurdek and Siesky, 1980). When a parent is rejecting or abusive toward the children, his or her removal from the home may actually be beneficial, particularly if the remaining parent enjoys a close relationship with the children (Lamb, 1977*a*). On the other hand, it is equally wrong to assume that divorce is necessarily good for the children if it is good for the adults involved. Children of divorce can continue to suffer even when their parents are happy. As one nine-year-old thoughtfully commented a year after her mother and father separated: "Divorce is better for my parents, but not better for me" (Kelly and Wallerstein, 1976:30). In short, the effects of divorce on children are very complex and depend greatly on the individual circumstances. There are no inevitable emotional or psychological consequences of divorce.

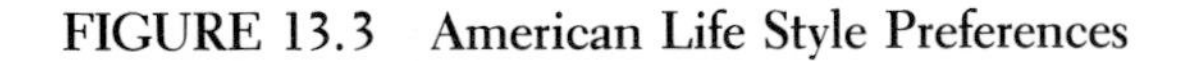

FIGURE 13.3 American Life Style Preferences

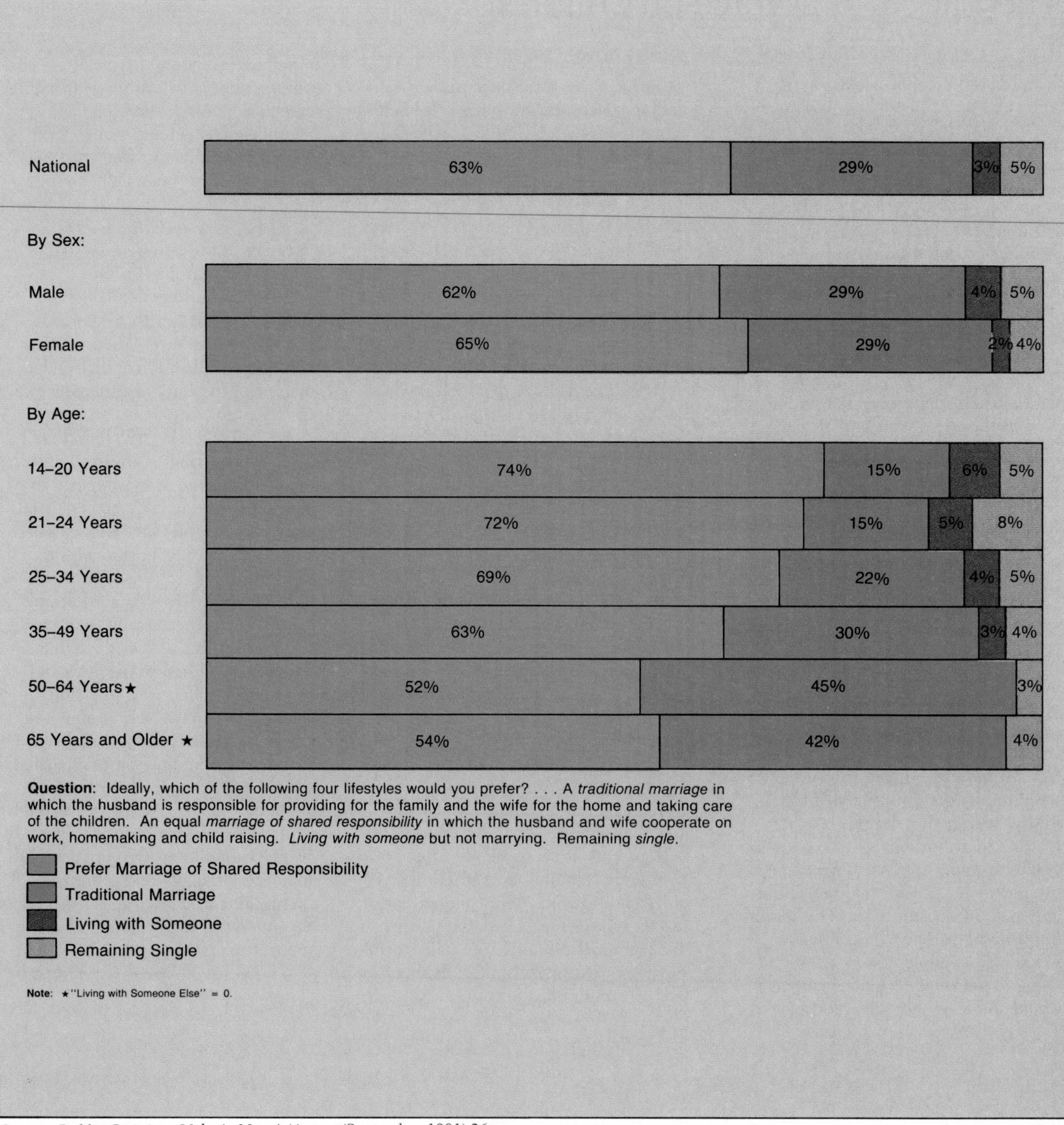

Source: Public Opinion, Vol. 4, No. 4 (August/September 1981):26

percent of Americans believed that a woman must be "sick," "neurotic," or "immoral" to remain unmarried. But by 1978 this proportion had dropped to 25 percent (Yankelovich, 1981). Paralleling these changes in attitudes, singleness among men and women under thirty-five years of age has risen sharply over the past fifteen years. Even so, only one out of every five households in the United States consists of one person living entirely alone (many of whom are widowed). More than two-thirds of the single adults live with a friend, relative, or "spouse-equivalent."

The rapid increase in singlehood can be attributed to a number of coinciding social and economic trends: the postponement of marriage, the rise in the divorce rate (about a fourth of the adults living alone are separated or divorced), career breakthroughs for women, the easing of salary and credit discrimination against women, and the growing independence of young people from their parents. Many young single persons are simply wary of marriage, having seen too many fail, while others are enjoying their independence too much to settle down.

Unmarried Cohabiting Adults of the Opposite Sex

Although unmarried couples living together still account for only about 4 percent of all cohabiting adults, the practice is still on the rise. From 1970 to 1981 the number of such couples more than tripled—from 523,000 to 1.8 million. In particular, the student movements of the late 1960s and early 1970s brought with them a substantial increase in the number of cohabiting college students. It is estimated that during the 1970s about 25 percent of college students lived with a dating partner at some point in their college career, although the trend may now be reversing on some college campuses. Cohabiting students typically view their relationship as part of the courtship process rather than as a long-term alternative to marriage. Of interest, cohabiting couples are no more likely to marry nor to break up than are couples who are simply "going together" (Risman et al., 1981). Although cohabitation has appealed primarily to young adults, it has in recent years become more prevalent among the middle-aged and elderly (Spanier, 1982).

Changing attitudes toward premarital sexual relations and the increasing availability of easy-to-use, effective, and inexpensive contraception has made cohabitation a more acceptable life style. For instance, the use of birth control is now widely accepted, as is making birth control information available to everyone—including unmarried teenagers. This situation is a far cry from the national attitudes that showed up in a Gallup poll in 1936. In that study, 70 percent of the American people opposed the legalization or distribution of birth control information, even to married people (Wattenberg, 1973).

Such enormous changes in attitudes and in sexual behavior make couples feel increasingly free to live with each other before marriage or after a marriage has ended. Adolescents, in particular, are increasingly coming to view marriage "as but one of the relationships in life in which sexual encounter is acceptable. Thus, cohabitation has gained increased acceptance in the views of youth and the urgency for a 'marriage' relationship has lessened" (Walters and Walters, 1980: 191). The law, too, is beginning to catch up with the unmarried who live together. Live-in companions in some cases now qualify for "palimony."

What types of individuals are likely to adopt the pattern of cohabitation? Using Census Bureau data to compare married couples with unmarried adults living together, Paul C. Glick and Graham P. Spanier (1980) found that young cohabiting couples are likely to be more educated than married couples in general, but cohabiting couples over age thirty-five are more likely to be less educated. Cohabiting couples are also more likely to live in urban areas than in rural areas, and more blacks than whites choose to cohabit. Overall, couples living together are characterized by lower income than married couples. Unemployment is more prevalent among cohabiting men than it is among married men, although it is less prevalent among cohabiting women than it is among married women.

Glick and Spanier found that half of the cohabiting men and three-fifths of the cohabiting women had been married previously. They were distributed about equally over young-, middle-, and old-age categories. Evidently those who have been married are somewhat cautious about jumping into marriage again. For cohabiting individuals who have never married, the great majority (85 percent) were concentrated in the under-thirty-five age group. This bears out the increasing acceptance among young people of alternative relationships to marriage.

Marriage Without Children

Childless households include those in which a married couple decide not to have children, those in which the children have grown up and left home, and those headed by a single man or woman with no children present. By 1990 only half of all married couples are expected to have children under age fifteen living at home. And when these couples (25 million) are added to the expected number of female- and male-headed households without children actually living at home (34 million), the total number of households without children (59 million) will constitute about *two-thirds* of the projected number of households in 1990 (Masnick and Bane, 1980).

One reason for the increase in childless households is today's longer life span. In 1920 the average American lived fifty-four to fifty-five years. Today, the average man lives about seventy years, and the average woman seventy-eight years. This means that a couple who marries young and stays married can now expect almost fifty years of togetherness, as compared to only about thirty-five years in 1920. Since married life for those who remain married is now longer than ever before, and since children take approximately the same number of years to raise to adulthood, a much smaller proportion of married life now needs to be child-oriented.

The trend toward fewer households with children is accentuated by the fact that over the past twenty-five years women have been gradually marrying later, having children later, and having fewer children. In fact, the proportion of Americans saying that the ideal number of children in a family is two rose from 41 percent in 1972 to 55 percent in 1982, and the proportion of those favoring four or more children declined from 31 percent to 22 percent (National Opinion Research Center, 1982). Even so, a recent Gallup survey showed that most Americans still regard people who are childless as disadvantaged—45 percent thought them unfulfilled and 64 percent felt they were lonely (Pebley and Bloom, 1982).

While only about 10 percent of women born in 1940 will remain childless, more than 30 percent of those born since 1954 are expected to remain childless. Many factors have contributed to this trend, including the use of effective contraception, the availability of abortion, the two-income household, and changing attitudes toward family life. Women who voluntarily remain childless typically fit the following description: white, living in an urban area, employed, highly educated, not devoutly religious, and separated or divorced. Education has a particularly important role in childbearing decisions. Young couples who have a child in their

These women, out of their twenties, are part of a trend toward delayed motherhood. Postponing childbearing allows many women to complete their educations and pursue careers. (Alan Carey/The Image Works)

teens or early twenties usually are not able to continue in school. In contrast, women who complete college or graduate school not only postpone childbearing during these years but then further delay it to take a job. However, the longer parenthood is postponed, the less likely it is that a woman will bear children (Pebley and Bloom, 1982). Moreover, as childbearing has become more of an issue for women, men too have been forced to articulate and reflect on their own feelings as many did not do before. Increasingly, women are demanding that men not only biologically father a child but also assume a major parenting role (Brozan, 1980).

Stepparenthood

In one out of every three marriages one partner has been previously married. Half of those who are remarrying are parents, which creates a stepparent arrangement. If present trends continue, up to 50 percent of all American children will have experienced divorce and remarriage in their families by 1990. Thus the stepfamily is likely to become common.

Most adults approach stepparenthood seeking to create a traditional nuclear family because it is the only model they have. Yet the complications of a blended family prevent their doing so. Not only are there stepparents, but very often stepbrothers and stepsisters, stepgrandparents, and in-laws from previous marrriages, all of whom present a myriad of complications. Perhaps not surprisingly, some 44 percent of blended families fail within the first five years (Kargman, 1983).

Stepfamilies have special problems (Bohannan and Erickson, 1978; Turnbull and Turnbull, 1983). Stepparents frequently set unrealistically high expectations for themselves. They often expect to be able to relate to their stepchildren as "real" parents do and to find instantaneous love and acceptance. When their hopes and fantasies go unfulfilled, they feel that there is something wrong with themselves and with the children—contributing to anger, guilt, and low self-esteem. And children who are expected to respond to a stepparent as though the person were the child's natural parent often react with hostility, rebellion, and guilt. And some children worry, "If I love my stepparent, will I betray my real dad (mom)?"

Other problems also abound. Frequently there are financial strains, especially if a man must make child-support payments to another household. Differences in food preferences are common. And discipline typically is a touchy matter for the stepparent. However, family counselors have a number of suggestions that can help families deal with the various stresses. These include moving to a new home (rather than living in one or the other's previous homes), setting and enforcing limits on which both the natural parent and stepparent agree, allowing children an outlet for feelings for the absent natural parent, letting time take its course in forging emotional bonds, and maintaining the primacy of the marital relationship (Turnbull and Turnbull, 1983).

The Elderly and the American Family

As we noted earlier, many of the increasing number of childless families in the United States are ones in which the children have grown up and left home. The parents in these households are often nearing retirement age, and many have already retired. In the future the proportion of such older American families is going to increase substantially, as individuals born during the postwar baby boom reach later adulthood. Today, one in nine Americans is sixty-five or older, but between 2010 and 2020 the proportion will be nearly one in six.

What kind of family life can these people expect? Since women will continue to outlive men, at least in the near future, and since women generally select husands several years their senior, there will be more elderly widows in the year 2000 than there will be elderly widowers. Currently three out of four American men sixty-five or over are married and living with their wives, whereas only one out of three women in this age group are married and living with their husbands. It is difficult to say exactly what marriage will be like for these older couples, but some of the current signs are quite positive. Several recent studies suggest that although marital satisfaction often declines after the initial years of marriage, it frequently takes a significant upswing after retirement, when husbands and wives have more time to devote to one another (Rollins and Cannon, 1974; Rollins and Feldman, 1970). This turnabout may be particularly true for professional or managerial couples, probably because their relatively comfortable incomes allow them to escape the financial insecurity that plagues a large number of working-class retirees. A comfortable income also enables a couple to purchase adequate health care, and good health is strongly associated with marital satisfaction (Renne, 1970; Beck, 1982).

Relations with children and grandchildren will

continue to feature prominently in the lives of older Americans during the coming decades. And for older Americans in the year 2000, there will probably be significantly more family members with which to interact. Four- and even five-generation families will be common due to increased longevity. In short, it will no longer be unusual to find children, parents, grandparents, great-grandparents, and great-great-grandparents all living at the same time.

At present, most older Americans want to live as independently as possible, a desire that is likely to continue in the future. This may mean a continuation of the already dramatic trend for older Americans to maintain their own households apart from younger kin (Neugarten, 1978). Most aging parents do not want to be a burden on their children, and they go to great lengths to avoid being so. Yet when they can no longer manage for themselves, most believe that their children should come to their assistance. And most children agree. Even grandchildren feel a strong obligation to help elderly grandparents. The degree to which children and grandchildren *do* assist aging family members is greater than many people think (Shanas, 1980; Quinn, 1983). Currently, about two-thirds of "elderly and frail" Americans are cared for by their own families rather than in nursing homes.

In the future, however, families may want more options regarding care of aging members who find themselves in poor health. Caring for a parent in a son or daughter's home may be increasingly unrealistic as more and more children of the aged are elderly themselves. In addition, economic trends may force many American families to occupy smaller quarters than in the past. For both these reasons, the next several decades may see an increasing demand for community services to care for the elderly in failing health. These services will include not just nursing homes, but day-care centers and home care facilities as well (Johnson and Bursk, 1979). In this and other ways, our burgeoning elderly population will have a significant impact on many of our public policies. The "graying" of the American family may gradually change many aspects of American life.

Changing Roles for Husbands and Wives

With all these changes in family structure, what has happened to the nuclear family of husband, wife, and children? Is it also changing to any significant extent? The answer is a resounding yes. As discussed in Chapter 6, the roles of husband and wife have undergone substantial revision in recent years and will undoubtedly continue to do so in the decade ahead. In part, these changes have been prompted by the women's movement, with its stress on equality between the sexes. In part, they have been prompted by married women entering the labor market in growing numbers. These forces have brought about some innovative alterations in marital arrangments, a matter to which we now turn our attention.

Two-Career Marriages

Marriages in which both husband and wife work have long prevailed among working-class couples, for whom two incomes are often a financial necessity. But the wife's job is usually considered of secondary importance, and she continues to perform most of the household chores. In recent years, however, a new, more egalitarian marital arrangement has been appearing. This is the

This woman is off to work, but she, like most other working mothers, is still responsible for her children's departure for school. (Mark Sherman/Bruce Coleman)

FIGURE 13.4 Percent distribution of individuals responding to the following statement: "A working mother can establish as warm and secure a relationship with her children as a mother who does not work."

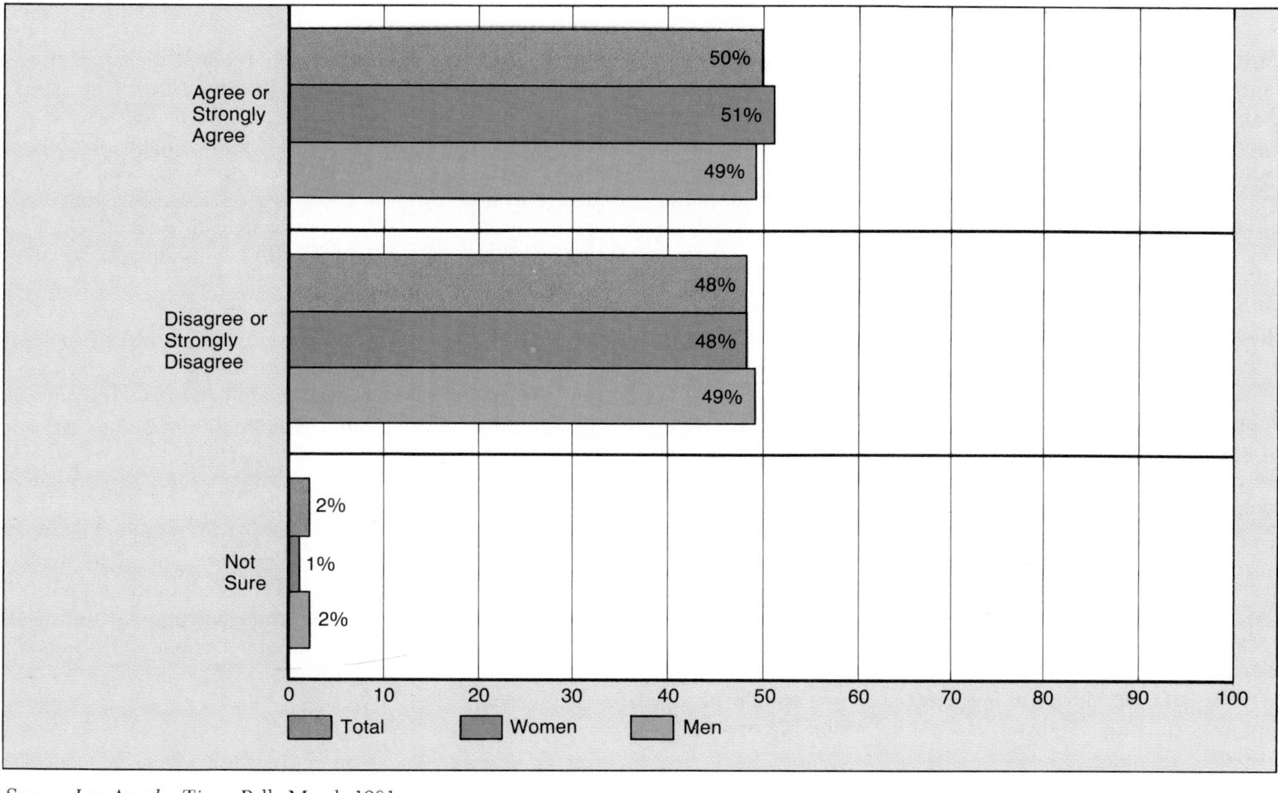

Source: Los Angeles Times Poll, March 1981.

Today, despite women's liberation and the prevalence of working women, about half of all women and men do not think that a woman can both work and have as satisfying a relationship with her children as a nonworking mother.

two-career marriage—typcially, a marriage in which both partners pursue careers and share family responsibilities. The number of two-career or dual-career marriages has grown rapidly in recent years among such middle-class professionals as doctors, lawyers, and academics.

In marriages of this type each partner must somehow mesh the demands of a job with the demands of a family. This is particularly difficult when both husband and wife have rigid (nine-to-five or later) work schedules. If they have children, they must arrange for them to be looked after; they must make sure that necessary domestic tasks get done; and they must also try to set aside time simply for being together. (See Figure 13.4.) Professions in which work schedules are relatively flexible, such as college teaching, make it somewhat easier to juggle a job and a family, but careful organization of tasks and responsibilities is still important.

Even with careful organization, not all conflicts can be predicted or avoided: Husband or wife may have to attend an unexpected meeting or the babysitter may not show up, or vacation schedules may not jibe (Skinner, 1983). How are these conflicts settled? Despite the egalitarian philosophy of the two-career marriage, most household responsibilities are shouldered by women. One survey reveals that in addition to their full-time

THE SOCIOLOGICAL EYE ON CAREERS:
Commuter Marriages

At times a dual-career relationship takes the form of the **two-location** or **commuter marriage**. In this arrangement the partners spend some time living in separate residences—from hundreds to even thousands of miles apart—in order to pursue their separate careers. Such commuters are usually in their thirties or forties, well-educated, and upwardly mobile (Reilly, 1984). The separation typically comes about when one spouse is offered a promotion or new job in another city and neither spouse wishes to jeopardize his or her career advancement. In most cases the couple spend weekends and vacations together. On these occasions they commonly have to spend time (perhaps an evening) getting back on the same wavelength.

Commuter marriages do offer certain advantages. They allow both partners considerable individual freedom and independence. Husbands and wives can also concentrate on their work with fewer obligations to their partners. Commuting arrangements give couples diverse experiences to share, minimize the kinds of trivial conflicts that often arise when people live together day after day, and make the time they do spend together somehow special.

But commuter marriages also have their drawbacks. Couples complain that socializing is difficult (Reilly, 1984). They do not have someone around to share intimacies and to exchange trivia. Occasionally, couples experience sexual problems deriving from the arrangement. Some partners say that they feel neither fish nor fowl —they are not single but they do not experience a sense of being fully married either. Not uncommonly, complications arise from the fact that neither wife nor husband can count on the emotional support and companionship of a full-time partner. At times husbands resent the fact that their wives seem to value their careers over them. And the partner who is left with the children frequently resents the increased responsibility, while the other partner feels guilty about not being with them (Gross, 1980). Finally, commuting is expensive.

The two-location marriage seems to work best for certain kinds of couples: those who are older, have been married longer, are free of child-rearing responsibilities, and are established in their careers (Gerstel, 1977; Gross, 1980). High career motivation, high income, and separation over a small distance also have been found to lessen the strain of a commuter marriage. But few couples are enthusiastic about the arrangement; most justify it by defining it as temporary (Kirschner and Walum, 1978).

---

jobs, wives spend an average of thirty-one hours a week on housework and child care; husbands, twenty-three hours (Shenon, 1983). The same pattern is found among dual-career professional couples. In their study of dual-career couples, in which the wife was a professor, lawyer, or physician, Brian F. Pendleton, Margaret M. Poloma, and T. Neal Garland (1980) discovered that the women tend to agree that the mother has primary responsibility for child care, that the burden of household responsibilities rests primarily on the wife, that work is an enjoyable job rather than a lifelong full-time commitment, and that a woman's career history is different from a man's. But most of these women disagreed with statements that a husband must approve of a wife's employment, that the husband should not be called on to assist in household tasks, and that it was impossible for a married professional woman to combine a full career with family demands. Other research also documents that the dual-career life style produces considerable stress and that the impact falls more heavily on women than on men (Skinner, 1983). Sometimes dual-career partners cannot each find satisfying work in the same location, leading to commuter marriages, a topic discussed in the box.

Job-Sharing Couples

What happens when a dual-career couple in the same profession cannot both get suitable jobs in the same location? Some couples have solved this problem by sharing one job. The advantages of this arrangement are that it provides each partner with more leisure time in which to pursue activities important to him or her; it allows the partners to develop a more intimate relationship; and it enables them to share equally in family responsibilities, including parenting. Women are freed from the stress of a full-time domestic life and men from the stress of a full-time professional life. The disadvantages are that there is a reduction in income from two full-time jobs; there may be problems of competition in the career between husband and wife; and, in reducing his professional workload, the man especially may suffer a loss in self-esteem and in the esteem of his colleagues.

Although job-sharing couples are highly productive and together may put in 50 percent more time than a single individual in the same job, employers are still somewhat suspicious of the job sharing arrangement. The job sharers are suspected of not being serious about their work, or of not wanting to accept full responsibility for it. However, as the benefits of job sharing become more widely recognized, these objections will undoubtedly lessen. It is clear, in any case, that most couples who participate in job sharing are generally pleased with it (Arkin and Dobrofsky, 1978).

Involved Fathering

American society has long regarded the rearing of children as primarily the mother's concern. But as gender roles change and economic requirements are brought to bear, growing legions of fathers are assuming a greater role in child care and rearing. Indeed, an accumulating body of research reveals that men have the potential to be as good caretakers of children as women are (Sawin and Parke, 1979). Indeed, the preponderance of evidence shows that child care is no more compatible with the "natural" inclinations of the one than the other sex (Berman, 1980). Fathers are just as responsive to their infants' vocalizations and movements as are mothers. Fathers look at, talk to, rock, and kiss their babies on hospital maternity wards in much the same way that mothers do. Mothers tend to touch the babies and smile at them more than do fathers, but fathers are likely to pick the babies up and look and talk to them (Sawin and Parke, 1979).

All this does not mean that mothers and fathers are interchangeable; rather, each seems to make a unique and vital contribution to the child's develoment. For instance, American fathers play with babies more than do mothers, encouraging them in the development of curiosity and motor activities. In contrast, American mothers tend to restrict their infants more and to play more verbal games with them (Lamb, 1977*b*). As the children grow older, a positive relationship with their father (especially for sons) seems to facilitate their development of well-internalized moral standards and to promote their academic achievement. Close, loving fathers also seem to help children establish a sense of sexual identity and security (Biller, 1982).

High divorce rates along with changes in child-custody laws have created a growing number of single-parent fathers. Movies such as *Kramer Vs. Kramer* helped to discourage the idea that mothers are always the best parent. Even so, single-parent mothers still outnumber single-parent fathers by a margin of better than

Attitudes toward fathers' involvement in childrearing are changing. Today's fathers are encouraged to start "fathering" while their babies are still in the hospital. Once home with their infants, many men are assuming child-care duties that used to be for mothers only. (Peter Menzel/Stock, Boston)

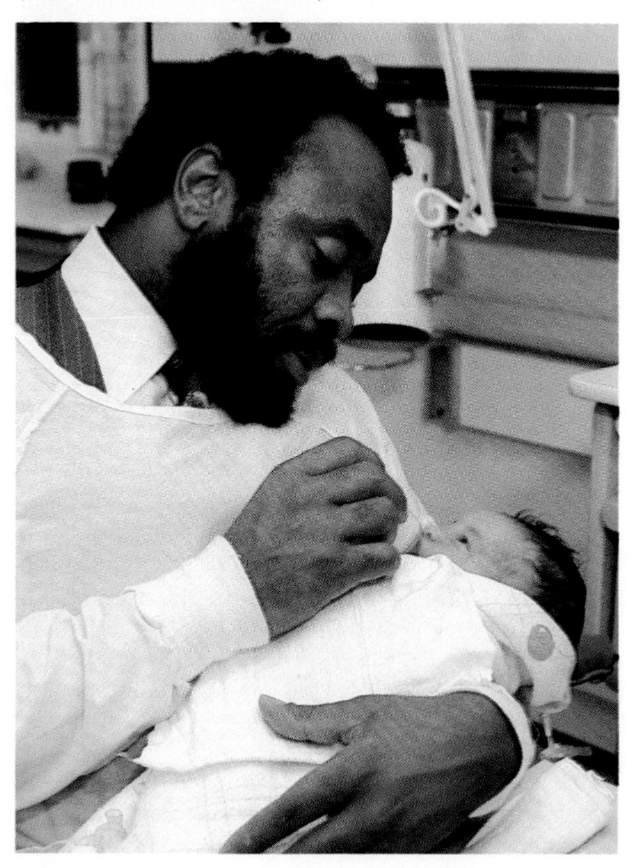

nine to one. And in some marriages the man assumes the role of the primary parent and homemaker. Often these men are educated professionals married to women who earn good salaries. In sum, researchers are increasingly finding that fathers make a difference. They are also finding that being a father frequently improves a man's self-concept, well-being, and life satisfaction (Levinson, 1978).

EPILOGUE

Many innovative family arrangements are attempts to enhance the commitment of marriage while increasing individual freedom and fulfillment. In this way, families are adapting to such broad social trends as delayed marriage, delayed childbearing, greater participation of women in the job market, and a rising rate of divorce. Undoubtedly, the American family will continue to adapt to such pressures, but how rapid and extensive will these future adaptations be? Opinions are mixed. Some observers feel that the changes in family life in the next two decades will be small compared with those in the last two (Glick, 1979). Others predict more fundamental changes in the American family before the year 2000—further changes in child-rearing practices, in division of labor between husbands and wives, in methods of coping with two-career households, and in people's general expectations about marriage and family life (Skolnick, 1978).

Whichever view is correct, the American family is hardly in danger of extinction. Although there are more single people, unmarried couples living together, and single-parent families, these arrangements remain for most individuals merely stopping-off points in their lives. Frequently, they are life styles for particular stages in a person's life. Most individuals will continue to live some part of their lives as a spouse in a nuclear family. Although Americans may be disappointed in their marriage partner, they are not disappointed with marriage itself. If their marriage does not measure up, they are inclined to end it and look for something better. In sum, humankind's most basic and oldest social unit, the family, has taken on many forms and undergone many changes over history, and it will probably continue to change in the future. Increasing diversity in family arrangements will very probably be its hallmark.

SUMMARY

The family is a social construction that varies widely from one society to another. The functionalist, conflict, and interactionist perspectives call our attention to different dimensions of family life. Functionists see the family as an institution performing critical social functions, including the regulation of sexual behavior, reproduction, socialization, care and protection, and social placement. Conflict theorists portray the family as a social arrangement benefiting some people (men) more than others (women). And symbolic interactionists view marital and family life as an ongoing process of imputing meaning to situations and fashioning relationships based on these interpretations.

Our descriptions of Nayar, Dani, and Israeli kibbutzim practices highlighted the great many ways human beings have for ordering relationships between men and women. Its two most common organizational patterns are the nuclear family and the extended family. To a large extent, these patterns reflect a society's primary subsistence strategy.

There is not just one type of family in America, however: Social scientists have discovered important variations, such as the single-parent family and the nuclear family embedded within a network of kin. American families also differ according to social class. A couple's social class affects the number of children they will decide to have, if any, and also the likelihood of disruption to the family because of illness, death, desertion, or divorce. Social class also influences the amount of stress a marriage is likely to undergo and the way parents raise their children. However, American families now seem to differ by social class much less than they did fifty years ago.

The American family has been changing in a number of ways over the past few decades. Many people are marrying later, having children later, and having fewer children or none at all. These social changes have resulted in diverse household patterns, including single-person households, cohabitation without marriage, and childless couples. Role changes are also occurring as more women find satisfying careers outside the home. These changes have led to two-career and two-location marriages as well as job sharing.

Another social change is the increasing incidence of divorce in America. It is difficult to interpret the significance of this trend. A higher divorce rate does not necessarily mean a greater percentage of unhappy marriages. Social reasons for the growing number of divorces include more career opportunities for women, easier divorce procedures, less stigmatization, and a growing belief that a divided family may be better for children than a conflict-ridden one. Still, divorce is a painful procedure for all. It is clear that marriage and family as we know them have been subjected to enormous pressures. These are bound to affect the family of the future.

GLOSSARY

Bilateral descent. The reckoning of descent through both the father's and mother's families.

Endogamy. A rule that requires a person to marry someone from within his or her own group—tribe, nationality, religion, race, community, or other social grouping.

Equalitarian authority. A pattern in which power within the family is vested equally in males and females.

Exogamy. A rule that requires a person to marry someone from outside his or her own group.

Extended family. A household consisting of married couples from different generations, their children, and other relatives; the core family consists of blood relatives, with spouses being functionally marginal and peripheral.

Family. A group of people who are united by ties of marriage, ancestry, or adoption and recognized by community members as constituting a single household and having the responsibility for rearing children.

Family of orientation. A nuclear family consisting of oneself and one's father, mother, and siblings.

Family of procreation. A nuclear family consisting of oneself and one's spouse and children.

Group marriage. Marriage consisting of two or more husbands and two or more wives.

Kibbutzim. Collective settlements in Israel where individuals work for, and children are raised by, the community as a whole.

Marriage. A socially recognized union between two or more individuals that typically involves sexual and economic rights and duties.

Matriarchy. A pattern in which power within the family is vested in females.

Matrilineal descent. The reckoning of descent through the mother's family only.

Matrilocal residence. An arrangement in which the married couple upon marriage sets up housekeeping with or near the wife's family.

Monogamy. Marriage consisting of one husband and one wife.

Neolocal residence. An arrangement in which the married couple upon marriage sets up a new residence.

Nuclear family. A household consisting of spouses and their offspring; blood relatives are functionally marginal and peripheral.

Patriarchy. A pattern in which power within the family is vested in males.

Patrilineal descent. The reckoning of descent through the father's family only.

Patrilocal residence. An arrangment in which the married couple upon marriage sets up housekeeping with or near the husband's family.

Polyandry. Marriage consisting of one wife and two or more husbands.

Polygyny. Marriage consisting of one husband and two or more wives.

Two-career marriage. A marriage in which both partners pursue careers outside the home.

Two-location (commuter) marriage. A marriage in which husband and wife spend some of the time living in separate residences in order to pursue their respective careers.

CHAPTER 14
Education

No nation believes so deeply in education as the United States. Americans feel that education opens opportunity to all, thus allowing all to advance in society according to their abilities. Consequently, Americans have invested huge sums of money in schools and urged more and more students to go on to college.

Yet, despite this commitment to education, problems abound in American schools. Indeed, a 1983 report by the National Commission on Excellence in Education declares:

> Our nation is at risk. Our once unchallenged preeminence in commerce, industry, science, and technological innovation is being overtaken by competitors throughout the world. . . . If an unfriendly foreign power had attempted to impose on America the mediocre educational performance that exists today, we might well have viewed it as an act of war. (National Commission, 1983:1)

The report notes that 23 million American adults are functionally illiterate. Equally disturbing, average student achievement on most standardized tests is now lower than it was a quarter century ago.

The controversies surrounding the nation's schools testify to the important role that education plays in contemporary industrial societies. Elementary schools, high schools, and colleges are formal organizations that carry out important socialization functions. In a formal vs. socialization sense, **education** consists of the organized transmission of a culture's knowledge, skills, and values from one generation to another. Whereas socialization is the broad, overall process by which individuals acquire those modes of thinking, feeling, and acting necessary to participate effectively in society, education is the more deliberate and structured training. In education both the teacher and the student are usually aware that learning is *expected* to occur.

Schools came about several thousand years ago to prepare selected individuals for leadership and professional positions. A century and a half ago public schools evolved as a vehicle for teaching the "three Rs" to the masses and providing them with the literacy essential for employment in an industrial society. For the most part, however, children have traditionally learned by watching their parents—skinning a seal, carving a bowl, cooking a stew—and then trying these activities themselves. Even in our industrialized society, we learn a good deal in this way, but we must also spend many years in school in order to learn the technical skills taught there. Schools also teach much more than the traditional three Rs. Sociologists are reanalyzing the teachings of schools in modern society and are finding that they involve social class, mobility, ethnic relations, sex roles, and group dynamics—virtually all the concepts already discussed in this book.

This chapter opens with the symbolic interaction of the classroom and a sociological analysis of what takes place inside schools. Then, we turn to the classic functions of the school and the conflict theorists' challenge to our traditional ideas about schools. Next, we consider how much real opportunity for mobility schools offer and how opportunity is limited by discrimination. Finally, we take a hard look at colleges and the college experience.

SYMBOLIC INTERACTION INSIDE SCHOOLS

The thirty-one children in Mrs. Bobb's first-grade class are working on their first assignment of the morning. Their task consists of copying onto their papers several sentences from the chalkboard. A few children finish the work promptly, and five of them—Mrs. Bobb's appointed "helpers"—walk up and down the aisles to help other children, several of whom are struggling with the writing. Patricia tries to assist Reginald by guiding his pencil down the page for him. He resists her "help," and Patricia picks up his paper and tears it to pieces. Without reprimanding Patricia, Mrs. Bobb orders Reginald to get up and get a new piece of paper. When Reginald tries to write again with Patricia's "help," the pencil slides off the paper, making a long, jagged line. Patricia blames him for this mistake, and unable to erase the line, she turns his paper upside down and walks away. Nearby, Shirley has given up on her fellow pupil and written the words for him. Another pupil, who has had no "help," has written an unintelligible jumble of letters on the page. Meanwhile, Mrs. Bobb has been correcting papers at her desk in the front of the room.

Classroom Interaction

Clearly pupils like Patricia and Shirley—free to walk around the room and to supervise others—are having a very different experience from that of the Reginalds of the class. Although we might be dismayed at the conduct of this classroom, we would probably assume that Patricia, Shirley, and the other "helpers" are the brightest pupils in the class. But studies of classrooms like Mrs. Bobb's have shown that this is not entirely so. What happens is that through interaction with the students, teachers single out the ones most like themselves—for example, neat, verbal, respectful of school rules—and define them as most promising.

Unfortunately, this discrimination between supposedly bright and slow pupils is usually made very early in a child's school career. In one study by Ray Rist (1970) of an all-black school with black faculty pupils were seated at the first, second, or third table after only eight days in kindergarten. These permanent assignments were based on what the teacher perceived as the students' differing academic ability. In fact, the teacher's decisions were based largely on socioeconomic criteria, with the middle-class pupils placed at Table 1 and the less well-off pupils toward the back of the classroom at Tables 2 and 3. The teacher tended to ignore the students she presumed to be slower and in time they disengaged from classroom activities. When "reading readiness" tests were administered at the end of kindergarten, Table 1 children scored highest. In subsequent years they were placed in the "high" group in first grade, which was called the Tigers. The children at Tables 2 and 3 became Cardinals and Clowns in first grade and had simpler first-grade readers. Cardinals and Clowns were never given the chance to catch up with the Tigers. Yet Rist found that their IQ scores were not significantly lower than those of the "best" students.

The Self-Fulfilling Prophecy

By the time some pupils are classed as Clowns, teachers and other pupils have already formed an idea of how they will behave in school (as the derogatory connotations of the name suggest). Clowns are not expected to do well—and given this expectation, they are unlikely to. This phenomenon is known as a **self-fulfilling prophecy,** which as the sociologist Robert K. Merton (1968:447) put it, "is, in the beginning, a *false* definition of the situation evoking a new behavior which makes the originally false conception come true."

The underlying force behind the self-fulfilling prophecy is labeling (discussed in Chapter 9). When pupils are called Clowns or are recognized by their peers as being in "group three" or "the dumb group," they eventually take on this definition as their own and stop trying to do well. A child like Reginald is punished for his slowness in learning to write by being considered too

Teachers bring to their classrooms knowledge and attitudes that strongly affect their students. When teachers believe their children can learn, the children respond with positive attitudes as well. (Paul Conklin.)

"dumb" even to hold his own pencil—and because he is not allowed to do this, he will have further problems in learning to write. Teachers' attitudes are especially important determinants of pupils' progress. Not only do teachers begin the labeling process by assigning students to different groups in the first few weeks of class, they also act on those initial judgments throughout the school year. Consider the following scene in an elementary school classroom:

> A fourth-grade math teacher writes a half-dozen problems on the board for the class to do. "I think I can pick at least four children who can't do them," she tells the class, and proceeds to call four youngsters to the board to demonstrate, for all to see, how correct the teacher's judgment is. Needless to say, the children fulfill the prophecy. (Silberman, 1971:139)

Does the self-fulfilling prophecy really work? In a famous experiment, Robert Rosenthal and Tenore Jacobson (1968) randomly selected elementary-school students and told their teachers that the tests indicated that these students were "bloomers"—children who would spurt ahead academically in the upcoming year. A year later, retesting showed that the IQ scores of these "bloomers" had risen nearly four points higher than the scores of the rest of the student body had. Rosenthal and Jacobson concluded that the teachers' high expectations had affected their interaction with these randomly selected children in a way that helped raise their IQ scores.

Attempts by other experimenters to replicate these findings have not been successful (Elashoff and Snow, 1971), although a number of field studies of actual interaction in classrooms have supported Rosenthal and

Jacobson's basic premise: Teacher expectations regarding a student's performance can inadvertently be fulfilled.

Other field studies (Leacock, 1969; Gouldner, 1978; Crano and Mellon, 1978) have confirmed the strong influence of a child's social class on teacher expectations and have suggested some factors that may contribute to this bias. For example, Eleanor Leacock found that while teachers delight in the probing questions and ideas of bright students in middle-class schools, they are annoyed by the same behavior among bright students in lower-class schools. They consider these intelligent but underprivileged students to be smart alecks. But low-income children are not just passive victims. From their homes and neighborhoods, boys in particular gain antischool values that belittle intellectual knowledge and emphasize practical skills and "manliness." Their attitudes confirm teachers' stereotypes and set the boys on the road to low achievement.

THE CONFLICTING FUNCTIONS OF SCHOOLS

Learning and job preparation are obvious functions of the school system. But schools have other significant, though less apparent, functions, including socialization and preparation for life in the larger society. Functionalist and conflict theorists interpret these functions differently.

The Functional View of Education

Since the American Revolution, Americans have seen public education as serving a number of functions vital to the preservation of a democracy. Educated citizens, the Founding Fathers believed, would be productive, law-abiding, and slow to embrace monarchs or demagogues. Moreover, they saw education as the key to eliminating poverty and crime—an ideal still widely held today. Other functions of education include political and social integration, talent selection, cultural transmission, skills training, and socialization.

Political and Social Integration

A major function of formal education is to integrate individuals politically and socially within the mainstream culture: teaching students what it means to be American or English or Russian or Chinese. Such socialization is both direct (classes in civics, history, and government) and indirect. Classes are conducted and students are evaluated in ways designed to socialize them to their culture. In the Soviet Union, for example, students are divided into "links" (groups) and are graded on the basis of group performance, not individual effort. An exceptionally bright student is rewarded only for helping less bright group members (Bronfenbrenner, 1970; Daniloff, 1983). The American grading system, in contrast, stresses individuality. Students discovered helping one another solve a math problem during an exam are punished for cheating.

Social integration increases the likelihood that those at the bottom of the social hierarchy will not rebel against the system. This rationale has been offered for public schooling from the revolutionary era to the Great Depression, when school boards were urged to maintain their support for education since it was good insurance against social radicalism. Thus, although public education aims to prepare citizens to participate in a democratic society, it also emphasizes the creation of "good" citizens, that is, citizens who accept the basic rightness of American institutions. Schools try to mold such citizens by emphasizing the merits of the American way of life—our political and economic processes, our form of family life, even our educational system itself.

Selecting Talent

A second function of education is to select and screen talent. Ideally, according to functionalist theory, the school system identifies those students with the particular talents society needs and trains them to fill important positions. However, the idea that schools should screen out individuals with lesser talents goes against the American ideal that all people are created equal. The solution to this conflict is to give every individual an equal opportunity to display his or her talents. Ideally, the right people will be selected for the right jobs, regardless of who they are or where they come from. This idea—that the schools should provide equal opportunity to

In schools, students learn about the kinds of social institutions that exist in the larger society. These students are studying American history in their bilingual classroom. (Cary Wolinsky/Stock, Boston.)

each student and allow able individuals to rise to the top—is a fundamental rationale for American public schooling.

Cultural Transmission

In a society such as the Soviet Union or Cuba, it is easy to see the school's role in transmitting cultural values. Portraits of political leaders adorn classroom walls and students are taught Marxist-Leninist thought—a process usually termed **indoctrination.** In America, we learn about Washington, Jefferson, Lincoln, and the virtues of democracy in a similar—albeit subtler—way. Directly or indirectly, students are taught the values, customs, and traditions of American society. This "melting pot" course of study has been dominant in public education since the mid-nineteenth century. Within the last fifteen years, however, it has been criticized for ignoring the history and contributions of blacks, Native Americans, women, and other minorities.

Teaching Skills

A fourth basic function of schools is to equip individuals with those fundamental social capabilities essential for effective participation in modern societies. This involves teaching basic skills (reading, writing, and arithmetic), developing the ability to think (to apply mental skills to new problems); and providing both general knowledge and specific skills that will be useful in jobs. (see Figure 14.1, p. 374).

A 1983 Gallup poll on the schools reflected these traditional values. Of the respondents, 87 percent favored requiring all high school students to take courses in mathematics and 83 percent favored requiring courses in English. Further, 61 percent believed the schools do not make elementary school children work hard enough. And over three-quarters said that high school students should be required to have instruction on drug and alcohol abuse (Gallup, 1983).

Socialization: The Hidden Curriculum

A fifth function of schools is to wean children from the private world and rules of the family and to socialize them to a public world where impersonal rules and social status replace personal relations. In school, children learn to accommodate themselves to a hierarchical institution in which power and privileges are distributed impersonally and unequally (Parsons, 1959; Apple, 1979).

The **hidden curriculum** is the set of unwritten rules of behavior that prepare children for the world outside

FIGURE 14.1 Responses of 1979 High School Seniors to the Question, "How Important Do You Think the Things You Are Learning in School Are Going to Be for Your Later Life?"

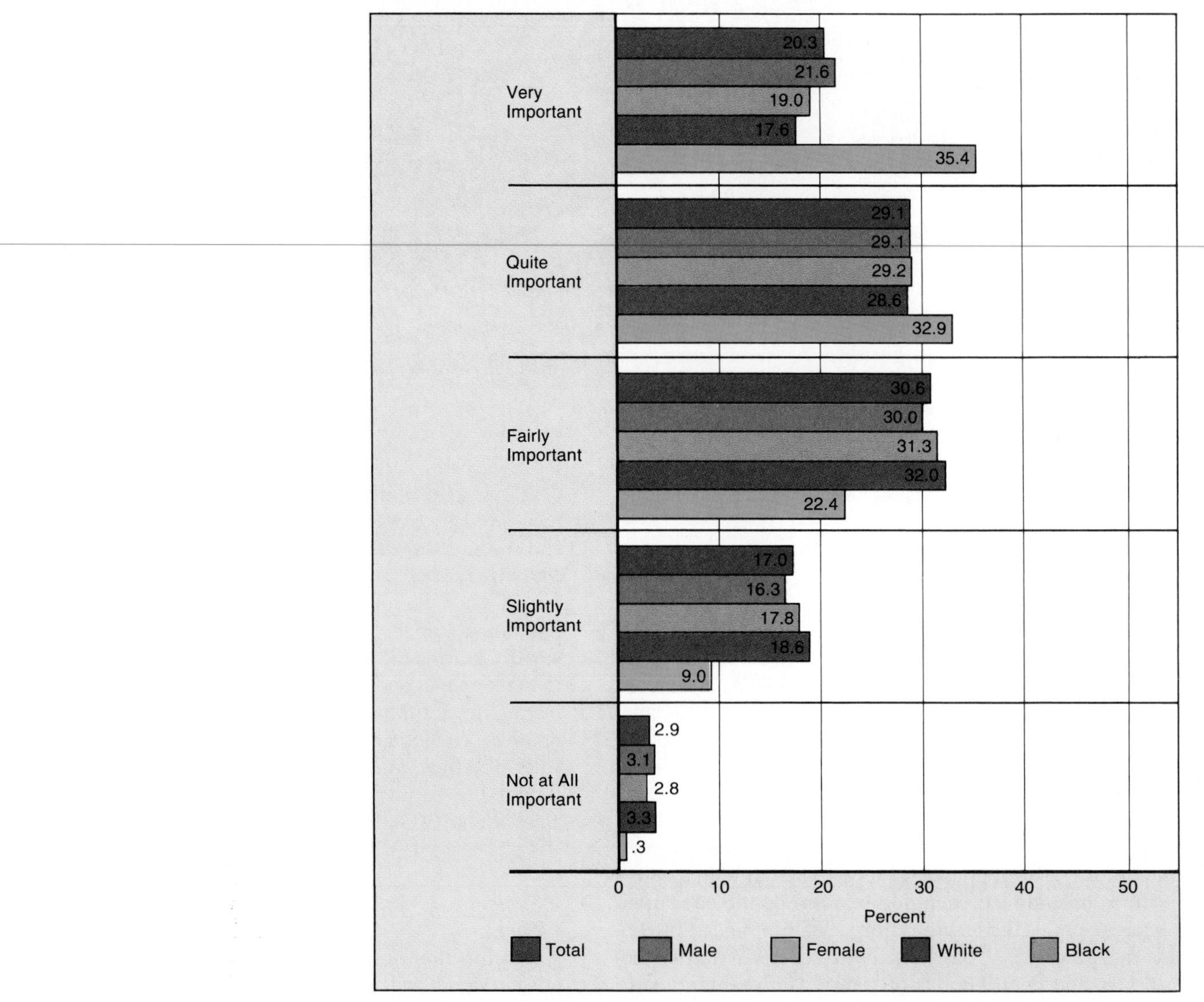

Source: Loyd D. Johnson, Jerald G. Bachman, and Patrick M. O'Malley. *Monitoring the Future: Questionnaire Responses from the Nation's High School Seniors*, 1979. Ann Arbor, Michigan: The University of Michigan Institute for Social Research, 1980, p. 86.

Although a majority of high school seniors questioned in 1979—49.4 percent—felt that their education would be very important or quite important in later life, a sizable percentage—47.6 percent—thought that their education would prove only moderately important. Note that significantly more black students than white students believed that their education would be important to them in later life.

(Jackson, 1968). To advance from grade to grade, to survive academically and socially, youngsters must learn to be quiet, to line up, to wait, to act interested even when they are not, to please their teachers without alienating their peers, to come to grips with the inevitability of school—in short, to play the role of student.

Kindergarten is the child's initiation into the student role. In kindergarten activities the children learn to do what the teacher wants, when the teacher wants it done. There is a story time, a nap time, a pick-up time—an official routine. Day after day, children are taught behavior and attitudes teachers believe to be essential, and they are drilled in these patterns. In some respects, kindergarten resembles boot camp: It is "successful" if youngsters learn to follow routines and obey orders without question, even if the orders are trivial.

The teacher is the child's first boss. Learning to accept orders from a boss, to cope with contradictory evaluations, to tolerate frustrations, and to be one among many are the very qualities people need if they are to function effectively on an assembly line or in a large corporation. In effect, the hidden curriculum is designed to mold students into good workers.

Most Americans apparently agree that the hidden curriculum is necessary and desirable. Asked in 1983 by Gallup pollsters what qualities were important in the development of a child, nearly as many adults responded "the ability to get along with others" as "learning to think for oneself." Asked how to improve the overall quality of education, as many people responded "enforce stricter discipline" as "devote more time to teaching basic skills." Indeed, most Americans consider the lack of discipline the biggest problem in our schools (Gallup, 1983).

Conflict Theories of Education

In examining education according to the functions it serves in society, we are looking at schooling from one limited point of view. Marxists and conflict theorists hold that schooling, in fact, fails to fulfill many of its functions. Instead of offering equal opportunity for all, they argue, schools often restrict opportunity and perpetuate class differences. Let us consider the "functions" of education as viewed from the conflict perspective.

Political and Social Integration

While schools may integrate students from varying backgrounds into American society, conflict theorists point out that Americanism is forced on students with minority backgrounds. Observation of schools in black and Mexican-American communities and on Native American reservations supports this view. For example, approximately one-third of all Native American youngsters attend boarding schools run by the white-dominated Bureau of Indian Affairs. These schools were first instituted in the nineteenth century for the express purpose of separating children from their "savage" parents so that the youngsters might learn to be "Americans." Visits to and from parents are discouraged. The result is that as many as 16,000 Native American children do not go to school at all because their parents refuse to send them away, and every year hundreds more run away from school.

Native Americans are not the only ethnic group whose heritage is ignored or denigrated in school. Until the late 1960s Texas law forbade teaching in any language but English. Most textbooks still give only brief consideration to Indian, Mexican-American, and black history. The assumption in our schools has always been that minorities must be assimilated—for their own good—and that they will not become "Americanized" unless they abandon their different ways. This view, of course, defines their cultural ways as inferior and not worth preserving.

In the past ten to fifteen years, as a result of the civil rights movement, courses geared to minorities—black literature and black history, for example—have been set up, and in some localities, bilingual education is required by law. But these programs may also serve the goals of the dominant culture (Apple, 1979).

Selecting Talent

During the twentieth century average schooling levels have increased dramatically from one generation to the next. However, despite the increasing availability of schooling to all persons, the privileged classes have maintained their advantage over the poorer classes in completing more years of school (Mare, 1981). Thus, while ideally public schools offer equal opportunity to all, there is considerable evidence that equal opportunity

These Navaho boys live at a boarding school in Arizona. Such schools, run by the Bureau of Indian Affairs, were established to train Native Americans to be "Americans." (Jim Cartier/Photo Researchers.)

is not a reality. As we have seen, low-income students are usually assigned to a lower academic track—a placement that is typically permanent. And what is more serious, even those poorer children who later earn high scores on academic aptitude tests are far less likely to go on to college than are more affluent students. Of the brightest 25 percent of the eleventh-grade class, only half of the lowest-income students go to college, while almost 90 percent of the more affluent students do. Among the *weakest* students, 26 percent of those from affluent homes go to college, while only 6 percent of those from poor homes go (Bowles, 1977). Moreover, a relatively high proportion of black and Hispanic youth drop out of school before completing high school (see Figure 14.2).

Although the rapid growth of community colleges since the 1960s has extended opportunity to many students who might not otherwise have gone to college, it has also channeled many working-class students into low-status jobs. Students who attend community colleges are more likely than students at four-year colleges to come from families in which parents have a high school education or less. Many are eager to use the community college as a steppingstone to a four-year institution. But although some make it to senior colleges, community colleges urge many students into vocational programs—a goal that is also supported by business, government, and foundations. Counselors, for example, frequently urge students not to have "unrealistic aspirations," that is, to accept the two-year program as the most they are qualified for. Thus students who enter community college with the hope of becoming managers or professionals often end up as technicians or paraprofessionals. In effect, Marxists and conflict theorists contend, community colleges are merely the upward extension of the public school tracking system, which acts to keep lower- and working-class students at about the same social level as their parents (Karabel, 1977). Marxists argue that these and related patterns show that the purpose of schools in a capitalist society is not to select and train the brightest but to perpetuate class differences and legitimate them with "objective" certificates of educational achievement. It all starts when thousands of teachers like Mrs. Bobb use signs of social class to track students in the first year of school (Apple, 1982).

Cultural Transmission

Conflict social scientists like Samuel Bowles and Herbert Gintis (1976) say that schools are agencies by which capitalist societies reproduce among their young people the existing social and class relations of production. They set forth the **correspondence principle,** which holds that the social relationships governing personal interaction in the work place are mirrored in the social relations fostered by the school. Hence, the authoritarian structure of the school reflects the bureaucratic order found in the corporation. It promotes submissiveness and diligence, characteristics desired by capitalist enterprise. In fact, Michael W. Apple (1979, 1982) and other Marxists contend that the cultural dominance of the capitalist class results in the members of society being saturated with the language, symbols, values, and concepts of a capitalist social order. In this order, they say, there is no room in people's consciousness for alternative languages, symbols, values, and concepts.

The correspondence principle also implies that the schools socialize and reward students from various backgrounds differently, in a way that is consistent with the requirements of their occupational roles later in life. Marxist and conflict theorists point out that different schools teach different "status cultures" (a concept of Max Weber's)—that is, they teach the culture typical of a certain social status. Thus teachers in middle- and upper-class schools stress proper English, while teachers in working-class or slum schools may permit ethnic slang and street grammar in the classroom. Topics brought up for class discussion are also likely to differ, reflecting class differences in leisure-time pursuits, entertainment, and so forth. The result of such differences is that middle-class students will fit more easily into middle- or higher-status positions in society: They will know how to speak and act and will have that important (if intangible) asset, a middle-class "background." Less advantaged students will often be marked by their speech, manners, and past experiences. They will thus be brought into the "status culture" of the blue-collar worker just as more privileged students will be brought into that of the professional or manager. However, the evidence for this argument is in dispute (Olneck and Bills, 1980).

Teaching Skills

Teaching students to read, write, and do mathematics would seem to be the most obvious and necessary

FIGURE 14.2 High School Dropout Rates for Whites, Blacks, and Hispanics, 1980

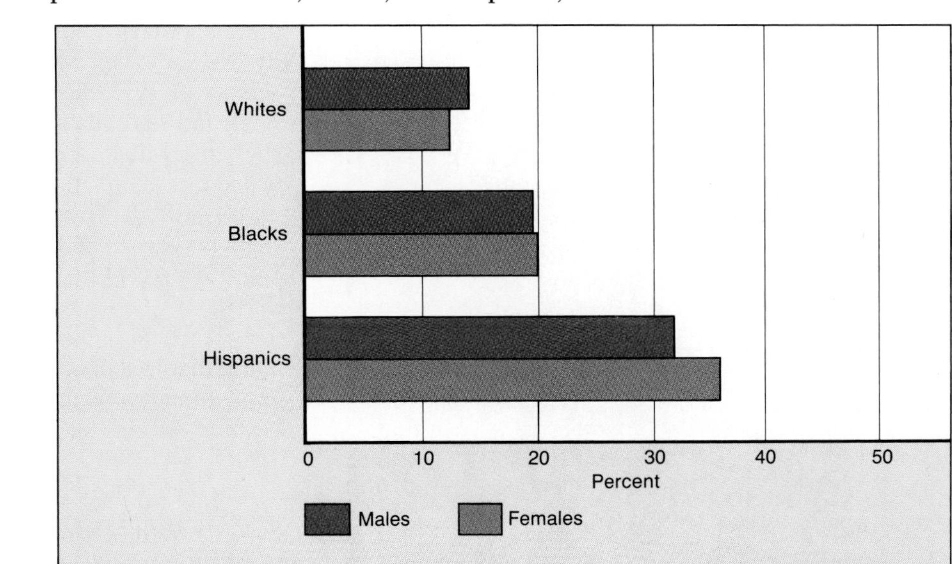

Source: U.S. Census Bureau, 1980.

function of schools. Yet considerable evidence exists that schools are failing in this all-important role, and as a result they are generating sharp conflict with parents. In 1983 about 13 percent of seventeen-year-olds were found to be functionally illiterate: They could not read at a fourth-grade level. Functional illiteracy among minority youth is about 40 percent. Few seventeen-year-olds can express their thoughts effectively in writing. Although their spelling and grammar is adequate, they use short, childlike sentences and cannot organize coherent paragraphs (National Commission, 1983).

A similar pattern is evident in arithmetic skills. Most seventeen-year-olds can perform basic mathematical operations, but they have trouble using them to solve problems. Less than half can figure out the most economical size of a product; only 45 percent can read a federal income tax table; and a mere 1 percent can balance a checkbook (NAEP, 1979). Between 1975 and 1980, remedial math courses in public four-year colleges increased by 72 percent and now constitute a fourth of all math courses taught in these institutions (National Commission, 1983). Overall, American students seem to have trouble applying the skills and facts they know to new situations.

These deficiencies have angered parents. In a 1981 survey, parents listed lack of discipline in the schools as the most important problem, with lack of good teachers a close second (Williams et al., 1981). There is some evidence that many teachers *are* poorly trained and that schools of education admit aspiring teachers with academic deficiencies (Kerr, 1983; Goodlad, 1983). The scores of high school seniors and college students on national tests (SAT, ACT, and GRE) reveal that those who plan to become teachers do not perform as well on average as students entering other fields (Weaver, 1979). Further, as opportunities for women have expanded in other professions and careers, the quality of the applicant pool to teaching programs has declined. Parents also criticize school curriculums. In the same 1981 survey, two-thirds thought their local schools needed more emphasis on reading and writing and more careful monitoring of students' progress. The opinions of parents are supported by those of their children. A comparison of a survey of high school seniors in 1980 with one of seniors in 1972 showed a significant decline in homework and study habits (Wagenaar, 1981). Whereas half the seniors in 1972 said their schools should emphasize academics more, this figure rose to 70 percent for the class of 1980. The percentage of public schools given high ratings (A or B) in annual Gallup polls dropped from 48 percent in 1974 to 31 percent in 1983 (Gallup, 1983).

Teachers, however, see things differently. They admit that lack of order and discipline in the schools is a very serious problem and acknowledge that schools have become settings for much crime and violence. Over 2

Security patrols have become a common sight in many of America's public high schools. Teachers claim that in-school violence results from a lack of parental guidance at home. (Jim Anderson/Woodfin Camp & Associates.)

million thefts and 200,000 assaults occur in American schools every month! In terms of the risk of being robbed or physically attacked, our schools are among the most dangerous places in the country (National Institute of Education, 1978). But teachers are not willing to take the blame for these disturbing statistics. They charge that parents have failed to discipline their children and to teach them respect for authority. Teachers, they argue, cannot compensate for negligent parenting, nor should they be expected to. In addition, teachers and administrators complain bitterly about parents' curriculum demands. They feel that the schools lack both the time and the money to provide the extra courses that parents and special-interest groups want: courses in driver education, sex education, moral education, and so forth. Thus school personnel maintain that unrealistic expectations about what the schools can do, as well as inadequate budgets, hamper academic learning.

In this debate each side sees the other as the major contributor to the declining quality of public education. Thus there is little hope that the conflict will be easily resolved; it will probably rage for many years to come.

Differential Socialization: Class and Tracking

Intertwined with differential cultural transmission is differential socialization. Marxists and conflict theorists agree that school does indeed prepare students for the work world, but they believe that it does so by reproducing traditional class arrangements in each generation of children (Bowles and Gintis, 1976; Apple, 1982). The boxed insert (p. 380) examines how tracking contributes to this outcome. Studies also show that schools in low-income areas and schools in affluent neighborhoods reward very different kinds of behavior (Leacock, 1969; Sharp and Green, 1975; Gouldner, 1978). Because low-income students often bring to the classroom a set of antischool values characteristic of their subculture, the teachers and students often act as adversaries. The teachers expect the students to "act up" and the students expect to be scolded or punished. Not surprisingly, such schools strongly emphasize obedience to rules. In more affluent schools, by contrast, students are more often given academic encouragement and individual attention. The schools emphasize academic performance, not obedience. In addition, the classwork in poor and affluent schools is often different. In middle-class schools students are encouraged to write essays on subjects of their choice. In contrast, in poorer schools students are frequently assigned "multiple-choice" and fill-in-the-blank" tests since teachers often lack the time and energy to evaluate thirty or more individual projects. A middle-class student who has not finished the required work by the end of the term is often given an "incomplete" and extra time to make up the work; a student in a low-income school is more likely to get an F. In similar ways schools socialize girls differently from boys and minorities differently from the dominant group.

In conclusion, the conflicts within the public schools reflect conflicts in the larger society. Like the schools, this society is based on democratic principles that emphasize ethnic integration, equal opportunity, and reward for achievement. Yet ethnic conflict and prejudice persist, and large differences in income make equality of opportunity and reward nearly impossible. This American dilemma finds expression in the debate between Marxists and non-Marxists as to whether track hierarchies and evidence of class bias mean that the schools reproduce social class or whether schools provide students with opportunities for getting ahead on their merits.

EQUALITY OF OPPORTUNITY AND DISCRIMINATION

Equal opportunity, as we noted earlier, has always been a strongly held ideal of American education. But turning this ideal into reality has remained an elusive goal. Those from the lower rungs of the socioeconomic ladder, including many members of racial and ethnic minorities, have a much smaller chance of receiving a quality education than those from the upper social strata. In this section we investigate the extent and roots of discrimination in American education. We begin by exploring the discriminatory practice of labeling and tracking students by means of IQ scores.

Discrimination by IQ

Performance on an Intelligence Quotient (or IQ) test is one of the most common criteria for assigning a student

THE SOCIOLOGICAL EYE ON:

Tracking: Hidden Discrimination in American Schools

One of the guiding ideals of American public education has always been equality of opportunity. It is a familiar notion that in the public schools all students should be provided with a quality education and should be free to advance according to their talents and abilities. What actually happens in school, however, may be a different story.

Perhaps the greatest obstacle to equal opportunity in American schools is **tracking,** the grouping of students according to their perceived abilities and career interests. Sociologist James Rosenbaum (1978) investigated tracking at "Grayton High," located in a white working-class town of about 100,000 people. The school and its administrators claimed to emphasize equal opportunity, allowing students to choose their own curriculum. Grayton High did have three tracks—college, business, and general—but officials said that students had a good deal of flexibility to mingle with those in other tracks and to switch from one track to another.

But when Rosenbaum turned to the actual records of one senior class, he found quite a different picture. First, there were five tracks instead of three: upper *and* lower college, business, and upper *and* lower general tracks. Second, almost all students took courses only in their track—there was almost no mixing. Third, once assigned a track, students rarely left it, except in a few cases to move downward.

Rosenbaum also found that grades and their significance differed substantially from one track to another. In computing overall class standing, for example, an A in the lower-general track was considered equal to a D in the upper-college track. Thus a lower-general student who earned all A's would still be very far from the top of the class. And a low-track student was extremely unlikely to compile a straight-A record; A's were actually *harder* to get in low-track courses than in high-track ones. Apparently, college-track teachers were fairly generous with A's, while business- and general-track teachers were not.

The tracking system at "Grayton High" affected going to college as well. Few students outside the college track went on to college. About half the students in the business track and three-fourths of the students in the general track expected to go to college, even though their chances of actually doing so were slim. One reason was the grading bias just mentioned. Another was that students' grades were weighted by track, so good grades in lower-college and business tracks had less weight than good grades in the upper-college track. A third factor was the inadequate preparation for college that business and general courses offered—which the students were never specifically informed about. For example, a general-track student might elect a chemistry course, but that course would lack a laboratory segment, which leading colleges require. Finally, guidance counselors were so remiss in informing general- and business-track students about college-related matters that some of these students were simply planning to "show up" at the college of their choice in the fall. They had no idea that admissions tests, application forms, and a formal acceptance were required.

The finding that misperceptions are perpetuated among business and general-track students regarding the nature of their education and their likelihood of going to college has also been supported by national, longitudinal data (Rosenbaum, 1980). Marxists would call this false consciousness, the systematically created illusion among the disadvantaged that they have a chance to get ahead. The extent of this false consciousness is shown in a national survey that found that in 80 percent of the schools whose principals said there were no tracks, tracks did exist (Rosenbaum, 1978).

Thus, tracking is a kind of hidden stratification within many public schools that mirrors the stratification in the larger society. Whether educators are really unaware of tracking is questionable. What is not open to question, however, is the fact that many students being "tracked" are genuinely ignorant of a system that will have profound consequences for their future.

---

to a particular track. Even when not used for tracking, a child's score on an IQ test can nevertheless affect a teacher's expectations about his or her ability (Berk et al., 1981). This is because so many people believe that IQ measures innate intelligence—the intellectual capacity with which a person is born. But this belief is mistaken. The abilities that an IQ test measures are the product of both innate intellectual capacity *and* environmental influences (what a person has learned over the years). Yet millions of people continue to believe that a person with a low IQ score is probably innately "slow." This faulty belief is the fundamental basis of discrimination by IQ.

If scores on IQ tests are heavily influenced by environment, it follows that some environments may be more conducive to exceptional performance than others. This is definitely the case. Our IQ tests are biased in favor of those who come from a middle-class, predominantly white, Western, industrialized culture (the same culture that produced the people who devise and administer the tests). Thus the fact that a young black child does not know many of the words on the vocabulary portion of an IQ test may not mean that this child lacks "intelligence." It may simply mean that he or she comes from an environment where these words are seldom if ever used.

It is just such environmental factors that the educational psychologist Arthur Jensen (1969, 1979) deemphasized when he suggested that inheritance in part accounts for the 10- to 15-point difference between the average IQ scores of white and black Americans. As we pointed out in Chapter 12, widespread prejudice against blacks makes it impossible to equate the environmental experiences of white and black children, even when their parents' levels of income and education are similar. And more often than not, these factors are *dis*similar. In almost all the studies comparing the IQs of blacks and whites, the black sample has been drawn from a more socially and economically disadvantaged group than the white sample (Joseph, 1977). Equally significant, when the average IQ scores of white children from privileged and disadvantaged homes are compared, the differences between them are equal to or even greater than those that exist between white and black youngsters (Hurn, 1978).

The most important evidence that IQ is substantially inherited comes from studies of identical twins raised in different families. The idea behind these studies is that since identical twins have exactly the same genetic heritage, close correspondence between their IQ scores even when they have been raised apart would show that intelligence is largely inherited. Jensen, for one, based his controversial hypothesis on just such studies. More recently, however, sociologist Howard Taylor (1980) reanalyzed several twin studies and found many serious flaws in them. For example, two-thirds of the identical twins raised apart nevertheless grew up in similar homes. In addition, there were sample bias, testing errors, and researcher bias in the data. Taylor concluded that most of the twin studies conducted to date tell us nothing about the inheritability of IQ.

What, then, can we say about the relationship between heredity and intelligence as measured by IQ tests? At most, genetic heritage helps establish a rather wide range of "intelligence" that a person can potentially manifest. But precisely where within this range the person will actually score is determined largely by environmental factors. This is why the use of IQ tests to discriminate between "inherently" bright and dull students is so unwarranted. Fortunately, the use of such tests for this purpose is now decreasing.

The Coleman Report

What can be done about inequality in American public schools? Over the last several decades public officials have given serious attention to this important question. One widely publicized effort began as part of the Civil Rights Act of 1964, when a team of sociologists headed by James Coleman (1966) was asked to undertake a nationwide study of inequality in the schools. This study eventually included 570,000 students and 60,000 teachers in 4,000 schools. Halfway through the research, Coleman told an interviewer that "the study will show the difference in quality of schools that the average Negro child and the average white child are exposed to. You know yourself that the difference is going to be striking" (quoted in Hodgson, 1973:37).

The final results were not at all what Coleman had expected. He found relatively little difference between predominantly black schools and predominantly white ones in expenditure per pupil, building age, library facilities, number of textbooks, teacher characteristics, and class size. Even more surprising, he found that modern buildings, up-to-date texts and curricula, and higher expenditures per pupil had *no* discernible effect on achievement test scores. The government and most educators have always assumed a cause-and-effect relationship between school resources and student performance: The more money spent on pupils, the better their education will be. Coleman concluded that

> schools bring little influence to bear on a child's achievement that is independent of his [or her] background and

This little girl's early interest in reading is valued by her family and will have a positive effect on her later performance in school. (Joel Gordon.)

> general social context. . . . This very lack of independent effect means that the inequalities imposed on children by their home, neighborhood, and peer environment are carried along to become the inequalities with which they confront adult life at the end of school. (Coleman, quoted in Silberman, 1971:71)

In other words, schools themselves seemed to have little effect on student achievement with two exceptions. Coleman found that the quality of teachers made a small difference and that low-income blacks who attended middle-class schools performed better than blacks who attended ghetto schools. But mainly Coleman found the family, not the school, to be the major educational institution—even in modern society. Families give children an ascribed status that strongly affects their chances for educational opportunities.

Traditionally, equality of opportunity has meant trying to give all children access to the same kinds of educational *inputs*—teachers, facilities, and so on. This approach is roughly equivalent to giving someone who has never played golf and an experienced player identical sets of clubs and balls and pointing them toward the same tee. There is little doubt as to who will win. Coleman argues that to achieve true equality of opportunity, we must create a situation in which each person has an equal chance of achieving a certain outcome. In golf we accomplish this goal by giving a beginning player a handicap—a number of points to be subtracted from the person's actual score so that the final score is roughly equal to that of an average pro. In much the same way, equal opportunity in education exists when the average scores of graduates from different schools (not per-pupil expenditures, facilities, and the like) are about the same. In order to achieve roughly comparable overall outcomes among students from poor and affluent neighborhoods, the disadvantaged youth would need to receive compensatory education. Such academically enriched programs would help them compete fairly with other students.

The Rutter Report

Not all researchers accept Coleman's conclusion that the nature of a school and the type of teaching found there have little effect on student performance. Critics have contended that the impact of different school environments was masked by Coleman's one-time survey in the mid-1960s. Rather different conclusions emerge from the results of a longitudinal study of inner-city schools in London by Michael Rutter and his colleagues (1979). These investigators criticized Coleman's study for using crude measures and for never finding out what actually went on inside the schools. For example, as a measure of students' academic standing, Coleman used only a single "verbal ability" test score instead of actual measurements of achievement in the various school subjects. And Coleman measured school quality by such variables as expenditure per pupil, which do not capture the quality of school life. Rutter also pointed out that cross-sectional surveys such as Coleman's cannot measure changes over time. What we need, then, is a longitudinal study that measures the progress of students in different types of schools and that gathers firsthand data about the schools, their staffs, and their students.

In their study, Rutter and his colleagues carefully assessed all of the ten-year-olds in an inner London borough, measuring verbal ability, reading achievement, family background, emotional and behavior problems, and so on. They also asked the teachers to report on the children's behavior. Then detailed assessments of the quality of the schools were made, using survey data, classroom observations, and interviews. Finally, this process was repeated four years later to see what changes had occurred. All this careful measurement was designed to assess intake (the character of the students at the start), process (what the schools did to them), and outcome (what changes occurred in the students).

Rutter's findings differed dramatically from those of Coleman's 1966 study. Great differences were found from school to school in attendance, behavior, and academic performance. For example, delinquency at the worst school was three times as high as at the best school, even among matched samples of boys. Students in the highest verbal-ability group at the worst school earned no better grades than students in the lowest verbal-ability group at the best school. Some schools were clearly "better," that is, their students performed and behaved better than students of similar background and ability at other schools. This finding is an interesting confirmation of parents' traditional goal to get their children in "good" schools.

What Makes a Good School?

Exactly what is it about certain schools that makes them encourage high performance? Traditionally, factors such as school size and neighborhood character have been thought to be closely related to the quality of the school. Rutter's research, however, refuted this common-sense notion. What made good schools good was primarily *how teachers taught*. In good schools there was a strong emphasis on academic achievement. Students were given regular homework and their work was carefully checked. They were expected to master the classwork, to turn in their assignments on time, to use the library, and so on. Students were expected to be responsible. Teachers in good schools had a distinctive style of teaching: They interacted with the whole class, had clear standards of discipline and enforced them, and rewarded good work. They made school a comfortable environment for students, decorating their classrooms and urging students to feel free to consult with them about personal problems. Finally, in good schools, the staff was stable and efficiently organized. Rutter's conclusions are supported by a study of effective schools in the United States, conducted by researchers at the Harvard School of Education (Williams et al., 1981). Schools such as Chicago's Beasley Academic Center, Little Rock's Central High, Dayton's Weisenborn Junior High, and Boston's Madison Park High are all employing principles much like those Rutter identified.

Public and Private Schools

More recently, Coleman and his associates (1981) have compared the academic achievement of students in public and private schools. Some of their conclusions parallel those contained in Rutter's research. They found that the average private school is superior to the average public school in many ways. Private school students generally achieve higher levels of academic performance, even when family background and other influential factors are held constant. In addition, private schools generally provide a more disciplined and orderly environment, which is probably related to their overall success. And the traditional criticism that private schools are very elitist does not seem to be true. Although the average private school student is from a somewhat higher income bracket than his or her public school peer, this is due primarily to a relatively few very wealthy students in private schools. The majority of students in private schools, as in public schools, are from middle-class backgrounds. Coleman and his colleagues conclude that policies which facilitate private school attendance (such as tuition tax credits) would increase the proportion of minority and low-income students in the private sector, thus helping to benefit disadvantaged groups.

Discrimination and Busing

Patterns of racial discrimination in the nation's schools have also served as an impediment to equality of opportunity. For decades the South legally mandated separate school systems for black and white children. And in the North a system of neighborhood schools in combination with residential concentrations of minority groups resulted in not too dissimilar patterns of segregation. The Supreme Court's 1954 school desegregation ruling in *Brown* v. *Board of Education* undermined the legal bulwarks of these practices and set in motion a train of events that have substantially challenged traditional American racial barriers in education (Orfield, 1983).

Research indicates that children with middle-class values tend to perform well in the school environment. (Paul Conklin.)

Coleman's 1966 study strongly influenced subsequent desegregation processes and plans. He and his associates had found that low-income black children confined to ghetto schools performed more poorly than low-income blacks who attended largely middle-class schools. Why did the blacks in the middle-class schools do better? Coleman pointed to cultural factors. Immersing a low-income child in middle-class norms and values, he argued, has a positive effect on academic achievement. At the same time, Coleman found that middle-class white children who attended school in a lower-class neighborhood did no worse academically than their middle-class peers anywhere else. These children's middle-class values regarding school and education seemed to stay with them regardless of where they went to school. On the basis of these findings Coleman recommended that metropolitan areas create school districts shaped roughly like the slices of a pie—with the inner tip reaching into the central city and the outer edge extending into the suburbs. Such districts would include both disadvantaged children and more privileged, middle-class ones. The students could then be bused from one part of the district to another in order to achieve a desirable racial and socioeconomic balance in the schools.

The courts have since found busing a very useful approach to school desegregation (Sheppard, 1981). In many cases, no other strategy has proved as effective. The reason has to do with the principal cause of lingering segregation in today's school districts: widespread residential segregation and adherence to the concept of the neighborhood school. Since low-income blacks live in predominantly black neighborhoods, their local schools are also predominantly black. In order to achieve integration, the courts obviously cannot move households, but they *can* move children by busing. Court-ordered busing has prompted a massive reduction in public school segregation, especially in the South. Fewer blacks now attend highly segregated schools in the South than in the North.

Despite its effectiveness in achieving integration, busing has never been popular with middle-class whites. As noted in Chapter 12, a recent Gallup poll (1981) showed that 78 percent of white parents opposed busing, even though the majority claimed they did not object to sending their children to integrated schools (as long as the proportion of black students did not exceed 50 percent). Not surprisingly, black parents largely disagree with the white stance on busing. Sixty percent of them favor it, over three times the proportion of whites. Of interest, a 1981 Harris poll found that parents whose children had *actually* been bused for racial desegregation supported the program: 54 percent said the busing experience had proven very satisfactory; 33 percent indicated it had been partially satisfactory; only 11 percent said it was not satisfactory (Daniels, 1983).

Many of those opposed to busing suggest that the tactic frequently backfires. They argue that court-ordered busing simply encourages white parents to remove their children from metropolitan public schools, either sending them to private schools or moving to a distant suburb not affected by busing. Consequently, busing is said to result in even *more* segregation in city schools as the ratio of white to black students drops sharply. Is this view correct? Fortunately, it does not appear so. Most studies show that "white flight" from the cities is a trend that has been going on for decades. Overall, it does not seem to have been hastened by desegregation of public schools (Pettigrew and Green, 1976; Daniels, 1983).

Clearly, busing has been effective in achieving greater desegregation than is attainable by other means. But has it also resulted in better academic performance in minority group students? The findings on this question are much more mixed. Some research suggests that, by itself, desegregation has not generally increased the achievement scores of disadvantaged children (Rist, 1979; St. John, 1975). Other research finds that minority students' performance in classwork and on standardized tests tends to improve while that of white students is not impaired in desegregated schools (Daniels, 1983). But gains cannot be measured only in terms of academic performance. Black students in desegregated school settings are more likely to be aware of and have a more positive outlook on career opportunities than are black students in segregated schools. And blacks in desegregated schools also have higher levels of educational aspiration. Thus, present-day experiences in desegregated schools may very well lay the foundation for less segregation in adult life and among future generations (Daniels, 1983).

America, of course, is still very far from achieving equality of outcome in public education for all its racial, ethnic, and socioeconomic groups. Blacks and other minorities, however, have made significant gains in their total years of schooling completed, a trend we mentioned in Chapter 12. But educational differences by social class probably will continue as long as there are structured inequalities in society.

Interracial friendships among young people are likely to foster attitudes of social tolerance for a lifetime. (John Lei/Stock, Boston.)

THE SOCIAL STRUCTURE OF HIGHER EDUCATION

Americans, with their great faith in the benefits of education, have idealized the college degree as the surest ticket to the middle class. Only in the past few years have the critics of American education begun to focus on college. Is a college education worth the time and money it takes? If so, why? Just what do we get out of college?

The Declining Value of College

Calculated in terms of the purchasing power of 1981 dollars, the added lifetime value of a college degree versus a high school diploma is $329,000 for men and $142,000 for women. However, even though a college education still has an economic "payoff," it is less than it used to be. In 1970 the median income of men with a college education was 42 percent higher than that of male high school graduates. By 1980 the advantage had fallen to 25 percent. The drop for women was even greater—from 56 percent in 1970 to 31 percent in 1980 (Guinzberg, 1983).

One reason that a bachelor's degree is no longer worth as much in monetary terms is "educational inflation": too many college degrees have been granted for the number of jobs that require a college education. Through the process of educational upgrading, more and more jobs that were once done by high school or technical school graduates are now being done by college graduates (Berg et al., 1978; Rodriquez, 1978; Collins, 1979). Of interest, by 1982 college graduates accounted for nearly one of every four workers age 25 to 64, as compared to about one in seven in 1972 (Ehrenhalt, 1983). As a result many college graduates have had to scramble for any job at all and so are driving taxis, selling shoes, or typing and filing—perhaps temporarily, perhaps permanently. In addition, an economic slowdown that coincided with the last of the baby boom generation's search for jobs has meant that college graduates in the 1970s faced a tight labor market and found their degrees worth less. Any number of observers of the American scene have hypothesized that these trends would result in an increase in job dissatisfaction and political discontent. Yet the sociologist Val Burris (1983) finds little evidence in public opinion polls to support these predictions. It seems that individuals may be overeducated by objective measures, but they do not necessarily view themselves as "overeducated" if norms define them as having the "appropriate" level of education for their occupation.

Of course, the value of a college education cannot be measured solely on the basis of monetary gains to individuals. Howard Bowen (1977) argues that college significantly improves the quality of people's lives. The studies he cites show that college brings about many desirable changes in the individual—for example, increased cognitive abilities through the acquiring of verbal and mathematical skills, more logical thinking, increased knowledge and intellectual curiosity, and increased interest in and responsiveness to the arts. The research of sociologist Herbert H. Hyman and his associates (1975, 1979) in particular has documented the enduring effects of education. It increases receptivity to further learning, stimulates the active seeking of new knowledge, and enhances respect for civil liberties.

The college years are a time to grow socially as well as intellectually. These German law students, like their peers throughout the world, may actually spend more time socializing than studying. (Peter Menzel/Stock, Boston.)

College has an even greater positive impact on the student's emotional and moral development, as we will discuss in the following section.

The Personal Impact of College

To identify the effects of the college experience, sociologist Alexander W. Astin (1977) did a seventeen-year longitudinal study of more than 200,000 college students. Astin has noted that the question "What is the impact of college?" is too simple. There are many different kinds of colleges—two-year and four-year schools, private, public, and religious schools, and so on. And "going to college" may range from living at home and commuting to class to living on a college campus in another state. Moreover, the impact of going to college must be compared with the variety of important experiences noncollege people have. Thus Astin's study had to be designed very carefully. He matched college students against their noncollege peers, and he controlled statistically for fifty-two different variables, including age, sex, race, ethnicity, religion, social background, academic aspirations, choice of major, career plans, and various personality and behavioral factors.

Following his statistical analysis, Astin concluded:

> The longitudinal data . . . show clearly that students change in many ways after they enter college. They develop a more positive self-image as reflected in greater interpersonal and intellectual competence, and they develop more liberal political views and attitudes toward social issues. At the same time, they show less religiousness and altruism and show reduced interest in athletics, business, music, and status. Some of these attitudinal and personality changes are accompanied by parallel changes in behavior. Most dramatic is the decline in religious behavior and the accompanying increase in hedonistic behavior. Freshmen appear to be less studious and to interact less with instructors than they did in high school, but studiousness and interaction with faculty increase with time in college. (1977:212)

Some of these changes, Astin noted, are probably as much related to maturation as to college attendance, and some may be related to changes that were taking place in the larger society during the time his study was conducted (the 1960s and 1970s). Whatever their source, however, Astin found these changes to be lasting.

Junior and Community Colleges

Whereas enrollment in four-year colleges has been dropping, enrollment in two-year institutions for both full-time and part-time students surges ahead year after year. In 1981 two-year colleges enrolled 32 percent of undergraduates, up from 27 percent in 1970 (U.S. Census Bureau, 1983).

The first private junior colleges in this country were designed to provide students who could not get into four-year schools with an opportunity for higher education. The first public community colleges were an extension of the local school system and were intended primarily for students who could not get into or who could not afford four-year schools. Today, both junior and community colleges serve several worthwhile functions. They round out education for students who otherwise would leave school after graduating from high school; they prepare students for enrollment in four-year colleges; they train semiprofessionals; and they provide continuing education for adults.

Junior and community colleges usually offer three types of programs: vocational training (in such areas as health services, mechanics, business skills, computer programming, and police training); "transfer" programs (which emphasize academic subjects to help students transfer to four-year colleges); and community education (special-interest courses in the general areas of civic and cultural affairs and recreational activities). Three out of four students in two-year schools cite getting a better job as their primary reason for attending school (AACJC, 1977).

Most community colleges are oriented toward technical or career education. Students who follow such vocational courses are aiming for semiprofessional jobs in science, health, engineering, and various technical fields. (Such workers make up about 35 percent of the American labor force.) The problem with pursuing such jobs in order to attain higher paying, more prestigious jobs is that most have short career ladders. A nurse, teacher's aide, or laboratory technician, for example, may find little opportunity for advancement. Moreover, many community college graduates cannot find jobs in the fields for which they have trained. For example, only 11 percent of science graduates had science-related jobs in 1976 (Pincus, 1980). Thus, the community college is often of limited help to the student who wants to get a better job. Even so, career education and vocational training have helped move blacks into people-oriented and data-processing occupations (Kerckhoff and Jackson, 1982).

Sociologists like Randall Collins (1971, 1979) also point out that, with the exception of a few highly specialized professions like medicine and engineering, most occupations require little of the kind of skills that schools teach. More often, individuals acquire the necessary skills on the job and not in school. Indeed, employers rely on educational credentials in hiring and promotion not so much because of the technical skills they represent, but because they provide evidence that a potential employee has been properly socialized in the values and norms of the dominant culture and its institutions (Bowles and Gintis, 1976; Burris, 1983). But the sociological perspective differs from the personal one. Even though community college students as a group do not experience significant upward mobility, a community college education often provides rewards of considerable personal significance. For example, community college courses can awaken dormant interests and develop latent talents that enrich students' lives immeasurably. And because community college students are more likely to be older, married, and working than are four-year college students, junior and community colleges have opened up a system of education to millions unable to attend four-year colleges and universities.

EPILOGUE

American education is undergoing great change. Pessimistic observers call this a time of decline and disorder; optimistic ones consider it a period of adaptation and renewal. Whatever view one takes, however, change seems inevitable.

At the very least, changes in the size and composition of our population will affect the shape of American education (see Chapter 16). Elementary school enrollments will continue to decline into the middle of this decade, when the "echo boom" children—those born to the post–World War II baby boom generation—will be reaching school age. High school and college enrollments will follow the same pattern: a continual decline (in this case through the 1990s) followed by a resurgence as the "echo boom" students come of age. This means that for the next decade or so, more American colleges and universities will be forced to shut down, and jobs in the academic world will be scarce (Dearman and Plisko, 1980). It also means that in the short run more and more students will be seeking "practical" training in business and technical fields (see Chapter 19). Further, more than half of today's college students are women and more than half are over age twenty-one (U.S. Census Bureau, 1983). Indeed, one college student in five is a woman aged twenty-five or older (see Chapter 6). Overall, with a growing number of active and healthy older people, and with an increasing number of middle-aged adults forced to train for new careers, continuing (or adult) education will be of even greater importance (see Chapter 5). Until now, most of those taking advantage of continuing education have been middle class. But this may change as adult education programs become more widely publicized.

Demographic trends will not be the only factors shaping the course of American education. Equally important will be pressures to improve the quality of our schools and programs and to give students a greater range of choices in the types of institutions they may attend. New stress is being placed on the teaching of "basics." And many colleges are urging students to take a strong, academically oriented program in high school.

In modern, technologically based societies, knowledge assumes a critical role. The National Commission on Excellence in Education noted in its report, *A Nation At Risk* (1983:6–7):

> The world is indeed one global village. We live among determined, well-educated, and strongly motivated competitors. We compete with them for international standing and markets, not only with products but also with the ideas of our laboratories and neighborhood workshops. . . . Knowledge, learning, information, and skilled intelligence are the new raw materials of international commerce and are today spreading throughout the world as vigorously as miracle drugs, synthetic fertilizers, and blue jeans did earlier. . . . Learning is the indispensable investment required for success in the "information age" we are entering.

Hence, education has strong ties to other social institutions and plays a critical part in contemporary society. Indeed, we find ourselves increasingly turning to the nation's schools and colleges to provide solutions to personal, social, economic, and political problems that the home and other institutions are having difficulty resolving.

SUMMARY

The interaction that takes place between a teacher and a student can greatly shape that student's level of achievement. Within the first few weeks of class, teachers tend to label their pupils "bright" or "dull" and then act toward each student in a corresponding manner. In this way, the initial labels can become self-fulfilling prophecies.

Functionalists argue that schools serve several important functions in American society: political and social integration, talent selection, cultural transmission, skills training, and socialization. They stress the role of schools in providing equal opportunity for all children to develop their abilities. Conflict theorists point out, however, that social integration may mean suppression of class identity, that talent selection is often the rejection of the disadvantaged, that cultural transmission and socialization mean different things depending on social status, and that skills training—ostensibly the school's reason for existing—is often inadequate. Throughout the public school system, conflict theorists argue, children from less affluent families are held back by a track system that is usually based on socially biased intelligence testing.

There has been much debate about why students do well or poorly in school. The influential Coleman report argued in 1966 that family background was the crucial variable, but a more recent study by Rutter and his colleagues has argued that there are such things as good and bad schools. Good schools, according to this research, are characterized principally by good teaching, high expectations for student performance, firm discipline, and consideration for students' needs. Some of our best public and private schools could serve as models for how education in the future might be structured.

For several decades, America has been committed to the desegregation of its public schools. One strategy used to achieve this goal has been busing. Although busing has never been popular with white parents, it has brought about substantial desegregation, especially in the South. Desegregation by itself, however, does not seem sufficient to improve the academic performance of disadvantaged children. Other compensatory programs are needed.

Sociologists question whether getting a college degree is the most important factor determining a person's future success. Still, spending four years at a residential college has been found to yield positive personal returns to most students. Somewhat fewer students are going through four years of college today, however. Great numbers of young people are seeking job preparation in two-year institutions. But these schools may not provide the opportunities for upward mobility that many of their graduates expect.

America's system of education is undergoing much change. In the years ahead, the nature of our schools will be affected by demographic trends, particularly the number of young people seeking an education, as well as by the number of middle-aged and older adults who want to return to school. Our schools will also be shaped by public demands for higher quality education.

GLOSSARY

Correspondence principle. The position advanced by conflict theorists which holds that the social relationships that govern personal interaction in the work place are mirrored in the social relations fostered by the school.

Education. The formal, systematic transmission of a culture's skills, knowledge, and values from one generation to the next.

Hidden curriculum. A set of unwritten rules of behavior taught in school that children must master to succeed there and to be prepared for the world outside.

Indoctrination. The process through which students are taught the values, customs, and traditions of their society.

Self-fulfilling prophecy. An initially false definition of a situation which evokes a behavior that makes the original definition come true.

Tracking. Grouping children according to their scores on aptitude and achievement tests.

HYMNS
267
256
568

CHAPTER 15

Religion

We may think we live in a secular modern world. Yet religion remains a vital force. It pits Jew against Arab in the Middle East; Muslim, Druse, and Christian groups against one another in Lebanon; and Catholic against Protestant in Northern Ireland. Religious fundamentalists in Iran brought about a revolution. Religious fundamentalists in America helped elect a president. Pope John Paul II's visits to America, Africa, and Asia have had an awesome impact on Protestants, Jews, and nonbelievers, as well as on Roman Catholics. Religious cults are able to induce their members to renounce family and friends, donate their wealth, and take a new life.

What do sociologists make of all these forms of religions and their activities? They notice something obvious that is often overlooked by those involved in their particular religion: All religions are social products. They are subject to and shaped by the same social forces that affect nonreligious institutions, including such forces as social roles, social class, ethnic identity, technology, political power, and group dynamics. This is not to say that sociologists consider sacred beliefs false or insignificant. Sociologists cannot assess the truth of religious beliefs. But they recognize that these beliefs and the ways they affect people's lives are related to the social structure and culture in which they occur.

In this chapter we will look at the symbolic meanings of religion, describe its functions as well as its sources of conflict, identify the types of religious institutions, examine the ways religion affects and is affected by social change, describe the widening variety of religious expressions found in modern society, and analyze the dilemmas facing the major churches today.

THE BASIC ELEMENTS OF RELIGION

Although religion means many things to many people, to a sociologist **religion** refers to a set of beliefs and practices that pertain to sacred things among a community of believers. The French sociologist Emile Durkheim identified the four major elements in this definition—sacred objects, beliefs, rituals, community—in distinguishing between the sacred and the profane. He suggested that these opposite categories encompass all aspects of human experience. The **profane** revolves about those human experiences that are mundane, ordinary, and matter-of-fact. Religion is associated with the **sacred,** those experiences that transcend everyday existence; it is extraordinary, powerful, potentially dangerous, and awe-inspiring. People can consider almost anything sacred—a cross, a lizard, an oddly shaped stone. Hence the quality of sacredness is not inherent in the objects. A community *bestows* sacredness on objects, which then serve as symbols of things warranting respect.

But what gave birth to these symbols? In analyzing

To the Hindus, the dominant religious group in India, cows are sacred objects, or totems. Worshiped as sacred beings, cattle cannot be killed, and they are permitted to roam freely in large cities. (Benares.) (Van Bucher/Photo Researchers.)

his thesis further, Durkheim concluded that society itself was symbolized in sacred objects. Among preliterate peoples, this symbolism is frequently expressed in **totem**—an animal or plant that is worshiped as the mystical ancestor of the society. In rituals and dances that center about the totem, the people seek communion with the sacred. But in doing so, Durkheim held, the individuals are really worshiping their society, symbolically. Further, because they do not realize the force of societal pressure, men and women come to think of the intangible forces that guide their conduct and impulses as supernatural, and they venerate them. This idea of Durkheim's suggests, as Guy Swanson (1974:16) has noted, that people "develop a concept of personified supernatural beings directly from the model which their society provides." Let's now examine in greater detail the four elements of religion that Durkheim identified.

Symbols of Sacredness

Because religions are symbolic systems, the range of objects deemed sacred can vary widely. The sacred object can be a supernatural being or force, or a ghost or spirit endowed with supernatural power. It can be a moral principle, or a particular object that symbolizes deep-seated feelings.

The Mbuti Pygmies of the Ituri Forest impute symbolic meaning to the forest by considering it a supernatural being. They personify it as Mother and Father, Life-Giver, and occasionally Death-Giver. In somewhat similar fashion, monotheists, such as the world's 1 billion Christians, 16.8 million Jews, and 548 million Muslims (Littell, 1983) believe in a single deity, or supernatural being, called "God," "Yahweh," or "Allah" (see Table 15.1). Polytheists worship several deities; today's 457 million Hindus, most of whom live in India, have a pantheon of five gods, who are in turn reflections of a higher, more sacred principle of *Brahman*, or "Oneness."

Sometimes the supernatural element is simply a "force." It may reside in a warrior's accurate spear, in a tree growing near a particularly fertile field, in a crucifix, or in a statue of a saint fastened to a car's dashboard.

Sacred ghosts or ancestor spirits, who are imbued with supernatural powers but spring from a human rather than a divine origin, may also be objects of veneration: To the 38 million mostly Japanese followers of Shintoism, family ancestors are sacred beings.

TABLE 15.1 Estimated Membership of the Principal Religions of the World

Religions	North America[1]	South America	Europe[2]	Asia[3]	Africa	Oceania[4]	World
Total Christian	240,745,200	191,046,100	336,868,700	100,975,700	140,013,900	18,520,700	1,028,170,300
Roman Catholic	134,411,300	180,251,200	176,039,500	55,979,100	54,921,400	5,191,300	606,793,800
Eastern Orthodox	5,185,500	408,000	49,946,900	2,784,500	9,131,800[5]	406,600	67,863,300
Protestant[6]	101,148,400	10,386,900	110,882,300	42,212,100	75,960,700[7]	12,922,800	353,513,200
Jewish	7,266,900	699,950	4,470,800	4,096,870	213,530	72,800	16,820,850
Muslim[8]	1,326,200	405,400	20,959,600	375,105,400	150,192,200	86,700	548,075,500
Zoroastrian	2,750	2,600	14,000	236,200	900	1,000	257,450
Shinto[9]	60,000	75,000	–	38,000,000	–	–	38,135,000
Taoist	–	–	–	25,000,000	–	–	25,000,000
Confucian	107,600	69,700	507,000	167,907,800	3,500	19,400	168,615,000
Buddhist[10]	214,100	290,100	188,600	248,833,900	16,600	26,100	249,569,400
Hindu[11]	254,600	673,700	392,500	454,955,800	1,263,800	340,700	457,881,100
Totals	249,977,350	193,262,550	363,401,200	1,415,111,670	291,704,430	19,067,400	2,532,524,600
Population[12]	381,818,000	257,798,000	758,889,000	2,760,514,000	498,080,000	23,427,000	4,680,526,000

[1]Includes Central America and the West Indies.
[2]Includes the U.S.S.R. and other countries with established Marxist ideology where continuing religious adherence is difficult to estimate.
[3]Includes areas in which persons have traditionally enrolled in several religions, as well as mainland China with a Marxist establishment.
[4]Includes Australia and New Zealand as well as islands of the South Pacific.
[5]Includes Coptic Christians, of restricted status in Egypt and precariously situated under the military junta in Ethiopia.
[6]Protestant statistics vary widely in style of reckoning affiliation. See *World Church Membership*.
[7]Including a great proliferation of new churches, sects, and cults among African Christians.
[8]The chief base of Islam is still ethnic, although missionary work is now carried on in Europe and America. In countries where Islam is established, minority religions are frequently persecuted and accurate statistics are rare.
[9]A Japanese ethnic religion, Shinto declined rapidly after the Japanese emperor surrendered his claim to divinity (1947); a revival of cultic participation in the homeland had chiefly literary significance. Shinto does not survive well outside the homeland.
[10]Buddhism has produced several renewal movements in the last century which have gained adherents in Europe and America. Although persecuted in Tibet and sometimes elsewhere in Asia, it has shown greater staying power than other religions of the East. It also transplants better.
[11]Hinduism's strength in India has been enhanced by its connection with the national movement, a phenomenon also observable in the world of Islam. Modern Hinduism has developed several renewal movements that have won adherents in Europe and America.
[12]United Nations, Department of International Economic and Social Affairs; data refer to midyear 1982.

Source: Dr. Franklin H. Littell, *Britannica Book of the Year, 1983*. Chicago: Encyclopedia Britannica, 1983.

Three Asian religions—Buddhism, Confucianism, and Taoism—regard moral or philosophical principles as sacred. The world's 250 million Buddhists, for instance, are less concerned with the Buddha than with achieving the ethical and spiritual ideals that he set forth in his message of the "four noble truths."

In sum, be it a force, a god, a ghost, a moral principle, or a totem, a sacred thing gives the members of a religion a shared sense of the reality of the supernatural, or of what is sometimes called "the holy."

Beliefs

Sacred things derive their meaning from the beliefs that sustain or underlie them. To regard a cross as sacred, for instance, presupposes a belief such as the Christian belief in the Resurrection. By the same token, the Ten Commandments are sacred to Christians and Jews because they are believed to have been given directly by God to Moses atop Mount Sinai.

An underlying set of beliefs unifies a community of worshipers. For example, the members of Christ Communal Organization (CCO), an outgrowth of the Jesus movement of the 1960s, believe that it is possible to achieve a personal relationship with Jesus and that the Bible can be applied to everyday situations. They also believe that prayer is effectual, that an omnipotent God regularly intervenes in human history, and that the second coming of Christ is imminent (Richardson et al., 1979). These beliefs unite the community members in their effort to live as Jesus instructed.

Not all who profess a certain religion accept all its

beliefs unequivocally. Although Gallup polls (1982) have found that about 94 percent of Americans believe in God—a high percentage compared with that in other industrialized nations—there is considerable difference in level of belief within and among religions. For example, only about 12 percent of Americans respond "completely true" to seven items: They say that they accept the divinity of Jesus Christ, claim that their religious beliefs are the most important influence in their lives, indicate that they seek God's will through prayer, believe that God loves them in spite of their frailties, gain comfort and support from their religious beliefs, try to put their religious beliefs into practice in their daily lives, and wish their religious beliefs to grow stronger.

Rituals

Rituals constitute another element of religion. Sociologists regard **rituals** as the visible and symbolic expressions of a religion. The rituals of the CCO provide a good illustration. Within their communal organization the members of CCO lead ascetic lives. They do not use drugs, tobacco, or alcohol, or engage in extramarital sex. They rise early and participate in group prayers before breakfast and before beginning work. While at work (usually in agricultural jobs), they sing spirituals together. Each night they gather for evening prayer and Bible study lasting several hours. In their spare time the members engage in evangelizing (Richardson et al., 1979).

Although the range of possible rituals is vast—from following special dietary laws to using drums, drugs, and magic—ritual activities play a part in every religion. A ritual can recall an aspect of religious belief, honor the sacred, or establish a relationship between the believer and the sacred. Ritual is usually highly symbolic, often condensing several elements of belief into a single activity and striking a responsive chord deep in the participants.

As with levels of beliefs, those who profess a religion do not necessarily observe all its rituals. Not all Protestants who believe in Christ go to church, and not all those who do go to church take communion. A 1982 nationwide survey found that of the 4 percent of the populace who attended religious services regularly, Catholics went most often (53 percent), Protestants next most often (40 percent), and Jews went least often (25 percent) (Gallup Report, 1982). In part these differences reflect the different meanings that the various religious groups attach to church attendance.

Religious Community

Religion is more than just a distinctive cluster of sacred objects, beliefs, and rituals. It also has a unique social character: It is, to use Durkheim's term, a **moral community.** This community is composed of those whose shared common beliefs and practices about the sacred bind them together within a larger social whole. For this reason Durkheim observed, "The idea of society is the soul of religion" (1912/1965:419). He felt community and religion were inseparable for two reasons: Religion both celebrates and creates community.

Like other kinds of communities, religious communities are dynamic—growing or declining, and evolving in response to new circumstances. The CCO, for instance, has undergone continual change. It began as a rescue mission, committed to giving its followers a "way out of chaos" (usually drugs) and providing them with the essentials of life—food, clothing, shelter. Initially, the organization was very dependent on the charity of others and on contributions from members. As its membership grew and its workers became more experienced and enterprising, the CCO began organizing its own service-oriented businesses that both provided for the group's own needs and earned money through serving the general public (Richardson et al., 1979). Thus the religious community embodies the symbols, beliefs, and rituals of religion and serves a number of important functions for its members.

THE FUNCTIONS OF RELIGION

The remains of flowers found among the skeletons of a Neanderthal burial site, the massive stone slabs of Stonehenge in England, the temple ruins of ancient Greece, and the monumental heads carved from volcanic rock on the slopes of Easter Island in the South Pacific attest to the existence of religious behavior among people across the ages. Indeed, there has probably never been a society where religion was altogether absent. From this, any number of sociologists have inferred that religion is a crucial part of social life. But why is it so critical—and so pervasive? What purposes does religion serve for societies and individuals? Functionalist sociologists provide some answers.

Promoting Social Solidarity

Religion promotes social solidarity in the community by acting as a kind of social cement. It provides a context in which relationships develop, establishes norms for "proper" behavior, imposes sanctions against antisocial conduct, and offers ways of atoning for mistakes through prayers, fasting, or penance.

Every week rabbis, priests, and ministers deliver sermons that translate religious themes into guidelines for everyday action. Precepts like "Love thy neighbor," "Thou shalt not steal," and "Turn the other cheek" are more than pious abstractions or sermon topics: They are norms aimed at promoting stability (or discouraging conflict) in the community.

In many less developed societies as well, religion offers a code of conduct. In the Manus society of the South Pacific, families place the skull of an ancestor in a wooden bowl, which they keep and worship in their homes. This ancestor, referred to as "Sir Ghost," is believed to keep a careful eye on the behavior of his descendants. If someone transgresses, particularly through sexual looseness or economic irresponsibility, Sir Ghost may cause a person (not necessarily the offender) to fall ill, have poor fishing, or suffer some other misfortune. The potential intervention of the ancestor functions as a constraint against misbehavior (Pelto and Pelto, 1976).

Legitimation

Religion helps to legitimate the established and dominant groups within a society. In a comparative study of fifty non-Western societies, Guy E. Swanson (1974) found a close relationship between a people's religious practices and the kind of social arrangements that prevailed in their society. For example, in societies where elders occupy key positions, ancestors are typically venerated and worshiped. In societies with large discrepancies of wealth, religious ideas legitimate some people's being much wealthier than others. In a society like ours, which values ambition and individual opportunity, popular television preachers like Reverend Robert Schuller celebrate the potential of every individual and urge everyone to realize his or her potential. With notable exceptions, such as the Latin American priests who declare the dominant regimes to be immoral, religion often serves to reinforce and justify existing social values and arrangements.

Social Adaptation

In the United States, religious groups have helped millions of immigrants adapt to a new land and life (Greeley, 1972*a*). Religion provides a cushion against the rough edges of a different and perhaps suspicious culture, a haven where "back-home" customs and beliefs reaffirm one's roots. It is too simple to regard ourselves as a nation of Protestants, Catholics, and Jews. For example, American religion is made up of *German* Lutherans, *English* Presbyterians, and *Southern* Baptists; *Irish, Italian*, and *Polish* Catholics, *Russian* and *German* Jews. Andrew M. Greeley calls the United States "the denominational society," because the religious practices of each group are distinct and reflect members' ethnic backgrounds.

Besides helping immigrants anchor themselves in a new environment, religion can also influence the ways in which they adapt. For example, religion provided an ethnic cohesion and discipline that helped immigrant Irish Catholics, Polish Catholics, and Jews become upwardly mobile. In some regions of the United States, these groups have surpassed Methodists, Presbyterians, and Episcopalians in income and wealth (Greeley, 1972*b*, 1976). In the case of the Jews, the intellectual and emotional adaptability essential for survival as a persecuted minority in Europe facilitated their ascent in American life.

Consecrating Life Events

Birth, maturity, marriage, and death—universal features of the human life cycle—are celebrated and explained by practically all religions. Many religions have ceremonies to celebrate victory in war or the succession of a new head of state, and many also have puberty rites of one sort or another to mark the transition from childhood to adulthood.

The beliefs and rituals surrounding such important events in life as birth, puberty, marriage, and death illustrate how religion simultaneously provides an interpretation of these events for the individual and links the individual to a larger community. The wedding of Prince Charles of England to Lady Diana Spencer in 1981 consecrated a private decision to marry in such a way as to reaffirm values of church and crown. On a smaller scale every wedding binds a couple and their social group to the laws and values of their own community.

Many cultures have religious ceremonies to mark the passage from childhood to adult responsibilities. The Masai, Catholic, and Jewish ceremonies each reflect the culture from which they arise. (Left, Jen & Des Bartlett/Photo Researchers; top right, Donald C. Dietz/Stock, Boston; bottom right, Eugene Gordon.)

RELIGION: THE CONFLICT PERSPECTIVE

Karl Marx (1844/1964) observed that "Man . . . looked for a superman in the fantastic reality of heaven and found nothing there but the *reflexion* of himself." While this assertion is similar to Durkheim's observation that each society reflects itself in its religion, Durkheim regarded this feature as a legitimate function of religion. In contrast, Marx believed that in each historical era religious ideas evolved that justified the power of the ruling classes and served to pacify the people they oppressed. He thought that once people realized that God was no more than a self-reflecting fantasy, they would see their oppression and revolt (see Chapter 11). As Marx (1844/1964:42) put it:

> Religion is the sign of the oppressed creature, the heart of a heartless world, just as it is the spirit of a spiritless situation. It is the *opium* of the people.

Like opium, Marx felt, religion creates a false consciousness and sense of well-being that keeps workers from seeing that they are being exploited by the capitalists for whom they work.

Sacred Power Versus Secular Order

While Marx was looking at religion from the point of view of the oppressed, other writers have examined it from the perspective of the true believer. The sociologist Peter Berger (1979), reflecting classic religious thought, has observed that the uncompromising, spiritual quality of religious ideas may conflict with a mundane world of compromises. Berger's approach gives a quite different twist to the conflict perspective. It embodies the age-old conflict between the spirit and the flesh, good and evil, and heaven and hell. Berger (1979:49) points out that religious fervor, when allowed full expression, can paralyze everyday activity:

> Religious experience radically relativizes, if it does not devalue altogether, the ordinary concerns of human life. When the angels speak, the business of living pales into insignificance, even irreality. If the angels spoke all the time, the business of living would probably stop completely.

In sum, Berger highlights the powerful force of activities relating to the supernatural or sacred. The lives of saints and many cultists illustrate this point; the power of the sacred can suddenly make all of the things valued in everyday life seem trivial and contribute to a complete change of life. Berger points out that the religious experience can also endanger society because it can threaten the social order, as it recently did in the Iranian Revolution.

Human groups have tried to handle religion's explosive potential by domesticating religious experience. They wrap it in tradition, institutionalize it, and bind it with rituals and laws. Berger (1979:50) points out that "the individual, thanks to religious ritual, can now go about his ordinary business—making love, making war, making a living, and so on—without being constantly interrupted by messengers from another world." Even so, the latent conflict between sacred, otherworldly values and the secular, materialistic world remains constantly beneath the surface of social life.

Fighting Oppression

Often a religious group undertakes a battle against what it considers evil or corrupt in society. In the sixteenth century Martin Luther broke with the Catholic church in Rome because he believed that it was oppressing people by insisting that only priests could interpret God's word and by taking poor people's money for indulgences. The Pilgrims fought the Church of England for years before finally sailing for the New World in the seventeenth century. In modern times Martin Luther King, Jr., and the Southern Christian Leadership Conference spearheaded the civil rights movement in the United States, following the model of another religious crusader against oppression, Mahatma Gandhi. Today, as discussed in the boxed insert, many Catholic bishops and priests see their mission as defending the poor and steadfastly oppose what they consider repressive elite regimes in several Latin American countries (Beaulac, 1981; Hehir, 1981; Smith, 1981). And American Catholic bishops have spoken out strongly against what they deem to be the immorality of nuclear warfare.

These examples show that although religious institutions usually reflect the social structure and values around them, they often embody a vision of what life

THE SOCIOLOGICAL EYE ON:

The Activist Church in Latin America

> SAN SALVADOR, March 24—Archbishop Oscar Arnulfo Romero of El Salvador, one of the most outspoken and respected of Latin America's church leaders, was assassinated tonight as he officiated at a mass here.
>
> Archbishop Romero was killed by a sniper who got out of a small red car, apparently stood just inside the door of the chapel of the Divine Providence Hospital [a hospital Archbishop Romero had established for terminal cancer patients], fired a single shot at the prelate and fled. The bullet struck the Archbishop in the heart. . . .
>
> "His last word was injustice," said Jorge Pinto [a Salvadoran journalist], who said that Archbishop Romero had been talking for about 10 minutes on the theme of justice and peace. (*The New York Times*, March 25, 1980)

What could have motivated such a seemingly senseless murder? Why would a sixty-two-year-old, gentle-mannered Catholic prelate, who repeatedly denounced violence, be a target of attack?

The answer lies in the changing face of the Catholic church in Latin America—in fact, in many parts of the world. Not long ago the Church, if not always the ally of the political and economic establishment, was at least careful to avoid antagonizing those in power. By focusing their primary attention on good works, humility, and salvation in the life hereafter, Church leaders directed the attention of the downtrodden away from the miseries they endured. It was this tendency that prompted Karl Marx to label religion the opium of the people. Today, however, this conservative posture is changing. In countries where poverty abounds and social inequalities are enormous, priests, nuns, and Church officials are increasingly becoming political activists.

The Second Vatican Council (Vatican II) was a moving force in this development. Its assertion that the Church is in and of the world, and that the Church is a community of equals by baptism, laid the foundations for a new direction (Montgomery, 1983).

Archbishop Romero was one of this new breed of Catholic clergy. He was an outspoken critic of the violence, repression, and intimidation carried out by the Salvadoran army, the official government security forces, and right-wing paramilitary groups against workers, peasants, and Catholic nuns and priests. He also deplored the counterviolence on the part of the leftist guerrillas, who are becoming increasingly active in El Salvador. Tragically, he was the victim of the same politically motivated violence he fought to end. His successor, Bishop Arturo Rivera Damas, has had to pursue a more cautious course than did Romero because of the repressive situation in El Salvador and the constraints placed on him by the Vatican (Montgomery, 1983). Even so, Pope John Paul II told the Salvadoran bishops during his visit in 1982: "It is perfectly clear to me that the disagreements and divisions which still rock your country and cause new conflicts and violence find their true and deep roots in situations of social justice" (quoted in Beirne, 1983:190).

What we see in El Salvador, then, is an intense clash between the Church and the reigning political and economic elite. At the root of this conflict is a shift in the way that many Latin American Church officials are interpreting their various roles. The Catholic church, like other religious organizations, has long served both as a preserver of tradition and as an embodiment of social conscience. Today, however, social conscience is taking on much broader meaning. Church leaders increasingly feel that gross inequalities and injustices in society are incompatible with many of the doctrines they preach. As Camilo Torres, a revolutionary Colombian priest, once commented:

> In order to give [the majorities] food, drink, and clothing, basic decisions are necessary, decisions which can only come from the government. Technical solutions we have or we can obtain. But who decides on their application? The minority, against its own interests? It is a sociological absurdity that a group would act against its own interests. . . . The power must be . . . taken so that structural, economic, social, and political reforms benefiting [the] majorities may be realized. This is called revolution, and if it is necessary in order to fulfill love for one's neighbor, then it is necessary for a Christian to be a revolutionary. (Quoted in Beaulac, 1981:422)

Most Catholic church officials are certainly not as radical as this. The majority, in fact, are fervently anti-Marxist. Nevertheless, a large proportion of Catholic clergy in many Latin American countries see a pressing need for widespread social reform, and they are actively working to bring that reform about (Beirne, 1983; Welna, 1983).

should be like and how people should treat one another. Thus religion frequently serves as an important source of social change.

TYPES OF RELIGIOUS INSTITUTIONS

We have seen that a religion is based on a community of believers, and this community generally organizes itself into some type of religious institution. From a sociological point of view these organizations can be studied in the same way that other organizations are studied—in terms of their size, hierarchy, stability, ideologies, and relation to the social environment (see Chapter 8). Sociologists recognize three major forms of religious organizations: church, sect, and cult.

Church and Sect

The sociologist Ernst Troeltsch (1931) viewed religious institutions as typically either churches or sects. For descriptive and analytical purposes he viewed the church and the sect as *ideal types*—conceptual tools or mental constructs that can be used for comparisons and to measure reality (thus a given group does not necessarily conform to the type in every respect). Table 15.2 sets forth some of the ways that Troeltsch and his followers distinguish between churches and sects.

Troeltsch defined the **sect** as a small, exclusive, uncompromising fellowship of individuals seeking spiritual perfection. Members are voluntary converts, and their lives are largely controlled by the sect. Troeltsch found that sects are usually characterized by asceticism—austere, disciplined life styles. They tend to reject the social environment in which they live. Most sects are concerned strictly with religious values and see themselves as a religious elect granted special enlightenment. Often they discourage their members from extensive participation in "worldly affairs" because they consider the world outside the sect to be decadent, corrupt, and sinful.

As the sect grows, Troeltsch believed, it evolves into a **church,** a large, conservative, universalist religious institution. Its growth increasingly comes from those born into the group, not from conversions. Demands on church members diminish, and the church becomes more tolerant of other religious groups. Because it is

TABLE 15.2 Church and Sect

Characteristic	Church	Sect
Size	Large	Small
Relationship with other religious groups	Tolerant	Rejects; feels it has sole truth
Wealth	Extensive	Limited
Religious services	Limited congregational participation; formal; intellectual emphasis	Extensive congregational participation; spontaneous; emotional emphasis
Clergy	Specialized; professional	Unspecialized; little training; part-time
Doctrines	Liberal interpretation of Scriptures; emphasis upon this world	Literal interpretation of Scriptures; emphasis upon other world
Membership	By birth or ritual participation; social institution embracing all socially compatible	By conversion; moral community excluding unworthy
Social class of members	Mainly middle class	Mainly lower class
Relationship with secular world	Endorses prevailing culture and social organization	Renounces or opposes prevailing cultural standards; requires strict adherence to Biblical standards

Source: Adapted from Lifton Pope, *Millhands and Preachers: A Study of Gastonia*. New Haven, Conn.: Yale University Press, 1942.

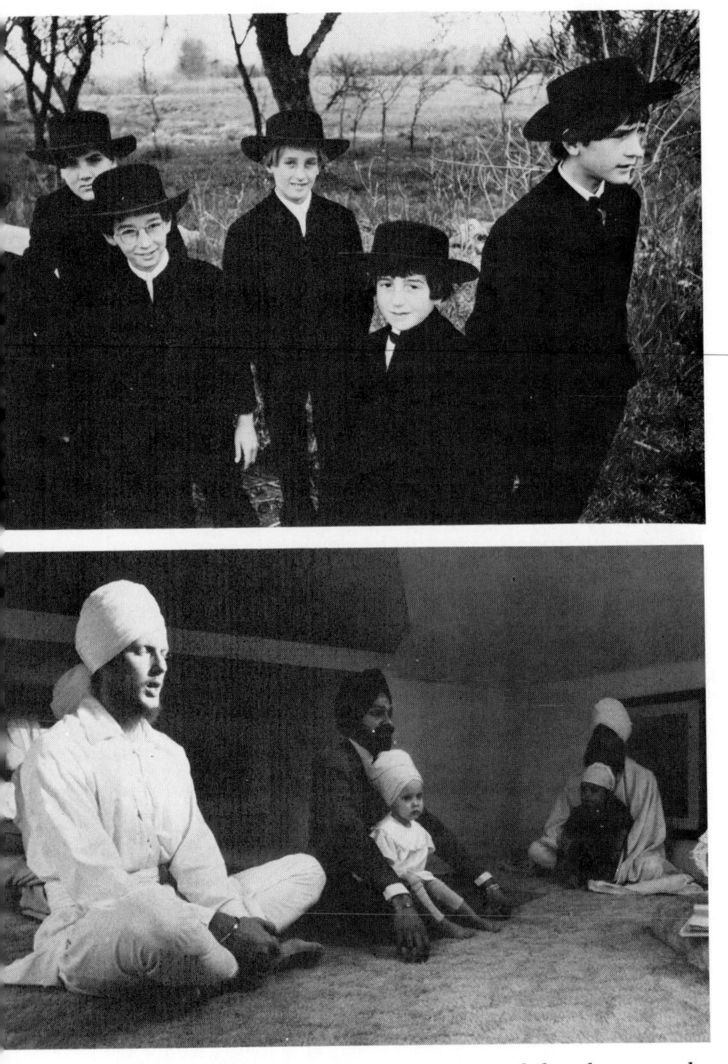

Various American religious groups exhibit the general characteristics of sects, churches, and cults. The Amish can be considered a sect; Episcopalian illustrate a church; and the Ashram have the features of a cult. (Above, John Launois/Black Star; below, Watriss-Baldwin/Woodfin Camp & Associates.)

large, it tends to acquire a certain amount of social and political power, and more often than not it retains that power by becoming associated with the government or the ruling classes. A church thus accommodates itself to the claims of powerful groups and the dominant institutions, and it tends to support the status quo. The Church of England, the Catholic church in Spain, and the Muslim Shiites in Iran come close to fitting this ideal type.

The sociologists Rodney Stark and William Bainbridge (1979) point out that Troeltsch's dichotomy of church and sect, by combining too many dimensions, contributes to sociological confusion. For instance, how does one characterize a religious organization that has some sectlike dimensions, such as small size and limited wealth, and some churchlike dimensions, such as tolerance for other religious groups and a liberal interpretation of the Scriptures? Is it a church or a sect?

Stark and Bainbridge prefer to distribute religious organizations along a single continuum on the basis of their acceptance of the social environment. At one end of the continuum is the church that is at one with its social environment; at the other end is the sect that totally rejects the environment. Most religious groups fall somewhere in between.

This model has the advantage of illustrating the dynamics of an organization as it moves up or down the scale of tension with its environment. For example, as a sect gains stability and respectability, it loses some of the tension with the environment and moves toward the church end of the continuum. This model may have national variations. The Catholic church in the United States, for example, tends to be more sectlike than the Catholic church in Ireland.

Cults

Stark and Bainbridge (1979) actually identify two kinds of religious movements that are at odds with their social environment: **sects,** which arise by *breaking away* from a church, and **cults,** which have *no* prior ties with an established religious body in a given society. For a religious movement to be a sect, it must be founded by individuals who leave one religious body to found a new group. Sects often claim that they are the authentic, cleansed version of the faith from which they split. In contrast, cults represent a new and independent religious tradition.

Stark and Bainbridge describe three types of cults, based on how tightly they are organized. **Audience cults** have practically no formal organization. The "members" are actually consumers of cult doctrines delivered over the airwaves or in books, magazines, and newspaper columns. In **client cults,** the religious leaders offer

THE SOCIOLOGICAL EYE ON:

Explaining Conversion to Unconventional Sects and Cults

While still a graduate student at the University of California at Berkeley during the early 1960s, sociologist John Lofland studied the inner workings of an unconventional religious cult, the Unification Church of the Reverend Sun Myung Moon (Lofland and Stark, 1965). The group was part of a larger movement that centered around a Korean evangelist who proclaimed himself the reincarnation of Christ. This proselytizer warned that the end of the world was approaching and that salvation in heaven could be attained by following him. When Lofland first encountered the movement's adherents, there were only about a dozen of them in the San Francisco Bay area. They devoted most of their time to spreading the group's gospel and attracting converts. What, Lofland wondered, could have prompted these people to forsake conventional norms and values to become the disciples of a self-appointed Korean Christ? More broadly, what factors are involved in developing commitment to *any* religious sect?

Many studies have investigated the psychological makeup of religious converts. Although personality profiles and subconscious needs of converts are important keys to understanding this phenomenon, sociological research shows this approach to be inadequate. Conversion to a religious sect entails both psychological *and* sociological factors.

Like socialization, the process of spiritual conversion begins when people, through social interaction, have the following experiences:

1. Some kind of disruption or strain commonly occurs in the individual's social life. This could be anything from marital problems to conflict with parents to failure in college to prolonged unemployment to a bad experience with drugs (Lofland and Stark, 1965). In a study by Richardson and his colleagues (1979), 54 percent of those interviewed experienced disruptive events immediately prior to joining an unconventional religious sect.
2. A general feeling of unhappiness and disillusionment comes to characterize the individual, which further propels the prospective convert toward a dramatic solution of some kind. He or she almost always believes that traditional social norms and values cannot provide meaningful answers to the important questions of life. As a result, the person frequently feels alienated from conventional society and those who are part of it (Downton, 1980). Fifty-three percent of the sect members Richardson and his colleagues interviewed described themselves as unhappy or very unhappy prior to conversion, and most felt that their past social relationships had not been very rewarding.
3. Interaction with significant others who are religious is typically critical to the conversion process. Through such interaction, potential converts develop a spiritual orientation toward solving the strains and feelings of disillusionment (Lofland and Stark, 1965; Richardson et al., 1979; Downton, 1980). In the process of becoming spiritually oriented, potential converts come to define themselves as religious seekers. Often they experience a deep sense of futility upon discovering that they cannot achieve their spiritual goals alone (Downton, 1980). Such people feel the need for a spiritual community to give them support and guidance. They are now ripe for conversion.
4. The final stage of socialization into a religious sect is conversion itself. Having developed a spiritual orientation from their interaction with members of the sect, potential converts become increasingly dependent on this new group. They loosen or sever old ties with those outside the group. This isolation from nonbelievers continues to be crucial even after the conversion is complete. The new members become totally dependent on the group for the satisfaction of their emotional and social needs. Intense day-to-day interaction with other believers cements their commitment. Thus, the conversion experience involves not just a declaration of religious faith but a process of socialization in which new social bonds and relationships are formed.

specific services to those who follow them. Although the leaders are rather well organized, the clients are not. An example of a client cult is Scientology, which uses an organized network of staff to dispense cult doctrine to groups of clients. Some client cults evolve into **cult movements** as they become larger and more tightly organized; this happened with Scientology, Transcendental Meditation, and Reverend Moon's Unification

Church. In this process of becoming larger and better organized, cult movements often generate opposition in their social environment. Cults that permit their members to pursue normal lives and occupations typically arouse less opposition than do those cults whose members drop their routine activities and become full-time converts. In part, the larger community is hostile to cults that function as total institutions because they rupture the convert's ties to conventional institutions, including the family.

The boxed insert (p. 401) examines the process of conversion to unconventional sects and cults. In Chapter 18, where we consider social movements, we will explore how such groups arise as responses to social change and are sometimes agents of change. Since change is important to religious life, let us now explore some of its ramifications more carefully.

Modernization can take many forms, including special children's masses. (Ellis Herwig/Stock, Boston.)

RELIGION AND SOCIAL CHANGE

A wealthy nation, strategically located, armed with the latest in weapons and tanks, in the process of modernizing at a very rapid pace, governed by a powerful ruler representing a monarchy that stretches back 2,500 years, suddenly undergoes an extraordinary upheaval. The army throws down its weapons, the monarch flees the country, the clock is turned back so that old traditions and customs are revived, and a holy man reigns with seemingly absolute power. To understand such changes as those that took place in Iran, we need a theory explaining how religion and modern society interact.

Modernization and Religious Choice

Modernization has been a major source of social change, and has had far-reaching consequences over the last few centuries. Throughout the world, people have moved from traditional societies where there is usually but one way to do things, to modern societies full of choices. This social change has had a profound effect on religious experience, as people find themselves confronted with dozens of denominations, each claiming to be the one true way. Consequently, people must choose among a multitude of options concerning their religious preferences. As Peter Berger (1979:28) puts it, "Modernity creates a new situation in which picking and choosing becomes an imperative." But in doing so, modernity has plunged religion into a crisis of pluralism. Berger calls this "the heretical imperative" because the very act of choosing which religion to follow throws into question the uniqueness that each faith claims.

In the clash between traditional and modern arrangements, what religious alternatives are available to individuals? Berger suggests that people have three choices:

1. They can affirm traditional religious authority in the face of modern challenges to it. We encounter this approach in the way the old order Amish live, in many Catholics' acceptance of the Pope's pronouncements against the use of contraceptives, and in the authority of religious leaders in Iran. Berger notes that this approach affords the strength associated with traditional authority and uncompromising principles. However, it suffers the weakness of being out of touch with the many changes that have occurred in society since the original principles were enunciated.
2. They can change their religious beliefs by reformulating them in modern terms. The evangelical preachers on television who equate worship of God with being successful (for Him) take this approach, as do many modern churches such as the Unitarians. As Berger points out, this approach offers the benefit of flexibility, but it sacrifices the sacred core of religion.
3. They can try to tap the wellsprings that gave birth and vitality to the original faith and apply them to the modern world. This attempt to capture the original spirit and shape it to the modern situation is the most difficult approach, but Berger believes that it is the most viable one. It retains fundamental religious roots, and simultaneously incorporates aspects of the modern world.

In the next three sections we will take a closer look at these options, examining an example of each: the Iranian Revolution, illustrating the affirming of tradition; the Protestant ethic, an example of secularization; and the fundamentalist revival, an attempt to adapt the original spirit of religion to modern life.

Affirming Tradition: The Iranian Revolution

The Iranian people, faced with the problems that accompanied an influx of Western ideas and economic modernization, chose to reaffirm traditional religious authority by actively supporting the Ayatollah Ruhollah Khomeini. In the nineteenth century and with accelerating speed in the twentieth, traditional Islamic society experienced the secularization that Berger describes as part of modernization (Kedourie, 1980). Islamics increasingly felt the impact of oil installations, Western commerce, and modern schools in Iran's rapidly expanding urban areas (Brown, 1980; Lewis, 1979).

Had the modernizing changes brought about by secularization been highly rewarding, it might have been worth the strain of adjustment, but for thousands it meant dislocation in the cities, unemployment, and a repressive secret police force. Much of the new wealth from oil went to a handful of multimillionaires. The choices offered by modernization seemed more and more undesirable. The real turning point came when Iranians who had imparted hope to modernization lost faith in it. Since more than half of all Iranians were under twenty and, like young people everywhere, were seeking ideals by which to guide their lives, this loss of faith was particularly critical (Lewis, 1979a).

More and more Iranians concluded that westernization was not necessarily best for their country. As they questioned aspects of their lives, they gravitated to the one institution that stood squarely against "Western godlessness and paganism"—their Islamic faith.

Moreover, the mosques of the Muslim sect known as Shiism, which had a long tradition of blending politics and religion, provided readymade sanctuaries for meeting and organizing outside the Shah's control. In these mosques bewildered young Iranians heard idealized accounts of the pristine Islam of old, represented by the exiled leader Ayatollah Khomeini. Writing in the *New York Times Magazine* in 1979, R. W. Apple noted the appeal afforded by the Ayatollah:

> He had suffered like the Shiite leaders of old, having been exiled by the Shah. . . . He stood for traditional values of chastity and honesty and abstinence that were losing ground in modern Iran. He refused to yield to seemingly impossible odds. (p. 106)

As secularization pressures and the abuses of the Shah mounted, plans for the revolution took shape in the mosques. During the revolution that followed, the new leaders affirmed the traditions of early Islam, but not without difficulty and opposition (Kedouri, 1980). On the one hand they found it difficult to turn back the clock on the new freedoms men and women had experienced as a result of modernization. On the other hand, the revolutionaries faced opposition from other religious sects and from the westernized educated class. Hence, the attempt to bridge the gap of 2,000 years had produced new tensions in Iranian society. Iran went through months of bombings, raids, shoot-outs, and assassinations among rival factions. Political arrests and trials have been commonplace. Simultaneously, Iran has undertaken to export radical Islamic revolution to other nations in the Middle East (Rubin, 1983; Smith, 1984).

Secular Change: The Protestant Ethic

According to Berger, another way that people in a modern society can preserve their religious tradition is to secularize it. The German sociologist Max Weber (1904, 1920/1930) found that the seventeenth- and eighteenth-century Calvinists in Europe did something similar in creating the Protestant ethic. And in doing so, they unleashed powerful forces for change.

Struck by the formidable nature of modern industrial society, Weber found one of the sources in what he termed the "Spirit of Capitalism." He began his investigation with an observation: Capitalism had emerged in Europe, not in Asia or Africa. And in the Germany of his day, predominantly Protestant areas were more likely than Catholic areas to be industrialized. And Protestants were more likely than Catholics to be industrial millionnaires. Why was this so? Weber began by examining the Protestant ideals for leading a good Christian life, not as they appeared in abstract theological debates, but as they influenced social and economic behavior. He found himself particularly intrigued by the role of John Calvin (1509–1564) and his followers. At the heart of Calvinist doctrine is the concept of predestination, the idea that a person's fate after death—salvation or damnation—is determined from the very first moment of life. The practical effect of this idea was that the followers of Calvin tried to prove they were among God's chosen people by doing good works, which meant paying meticulous attention to everyday affairs. They believed hard work was a duty to God and was itself intrinsically rewarding.

Thus Calvinism contained a built-in incentive for hard work, self-denial, and deferred gratification, the basis of the **Protestant ethic.** Calvinists, anxious to prove their faith in their own salvation, put aside frivolity and pleasure to pursue that all-important sign of being among God's elect—success. Since profits were not to be spent on pleasurable things, they were reinvested in business or enterprise, or given to the Church. What is more, since Calvinist doctrine held that every individual stood alone before God, hard work and frugality were the means of expressing one's dedication to Him. All these qualities were admirably suited for promoting enterprise and getting modern capitalism under way. In sum, the Protestant ethic contained the spirit of capitalism.

Of course, what Weber had constructed was an ideal type—a standard against which to measure the concrete examples encountered in the real world. His theory has been passionately disputed and defended ever since he first proposed it eighty years ago (Marshall, 1982). Weber's ideal-type Calvinist—sober, unceasingly industrious, and dedicated to the pursuit of profit as a sign of divine favor—could be found in varying degrees in early capitalist societies. The Protestant ethic and its impact on capitalism is an early—perhaps the first—example of **secularization,** which Berger defines as "the process by which sectors of society and culture are removed from the domination of religious institutions and symbols" (1969:107). The rise of a corresponding scientific worldview has led to the interpretation of life in nonreligious terms, and churches now play a much more specific and limited role than they once did.

How much of the Protestant ethic survives today is open to question. In its secularized form it is simply the commitment to work and the drive to succeed. But fewer and fewer people live frugally and deny themselves worldly pleasures as they work to accumulate capital. Weber did not believe that the Protestant ethic was essential to capitalism once capitalism had become rooted in a society. He emphasized that capitalism generated new forces that gave it a momentum of its own.

Transforming Tradition: The Fundamentalist Revival

Faced with the relaxing of religious standards in the major churches, and recognizing the impracticality of turning back the clock, as the Ayatollah has tried to do in Iran, an increasing number of people are making Berger's third choice: They are retrieving the powerful spirit of traditional religion but adapting it to modern life. This fundamentalist revival is taking place both in sects that have spun off from the major churches and in well-

The Pentacostalists are part of the "Back to Jesus" movement that arose in Protestant churches during the 1970s. Baptism by immersion is fundamentalist in its historical biblical links. (Watriss-Baldwin/Woodfin Camp & Associates.)

established denominations, including Methodists, Presbyterians, and Episcopalians. Religious organizations that have stressed evangelism and piety have been growing steadily in recent years. Such groups have typically emphasized the absolute authority of the Bible, the importance of being "born again," and conservative social values. Unlike many mainline churches that in the 1960s preached a "social gospel" of helping the poor and fighting injustice, the fundamentalist movement has focused on personal conversion and salvation.

Through strict standards for behavior and a demand for greater religious commitment, fundamentalist churches and sects give meaning to people's lives. In a survey of a mainline and a fundamentalist Presbyterian congregation, Douglas B. McGaw (1979) found that almost everyone in the fundamentalist congregation interpreted their beliefs in the same way, while fewer than half the members of the mainline congregation did. The fundamentalist congregation also scored much higher than the mainline congregation on measures of communal belonging such as church attendance, donations, hours devoted to parish work, and social ties with other church members.

McGaw identified four aspects of group structure and processes that help explain why meaning and belonging are stronger in the fundamentalist congregation: Potential members are required to have a high level of commitment and preparation before joining; the members reinforce their commitment through a rigorous program of education and mutual support in the faith; they agree on how authority should be distributed; and they have strong social bonds and numerous opportunities for intragroup social contact. Because of these bonds and commitments, members of fundamentalist churches tend to stay with their church longer than do members of mainline churches. Thus conservative churches, particularly the Southern Baptists, Mormons, and Seventh-Day Adventists, have been growing faster than mainline churches not only because they socialize new members and children more intensely, but also because turnover is low (Bibby, 1978; Mann, 1980, 1983).

The resurgence of fundamentalism has led many mainline churches to intensify their efforts to provide their members with a feeling of personal relevance. Yet this turning inward has at times conflicted with the efforts of preachers like the Reverend Jerry Falwell to mobilize fundamentalists into a strong political force. Despite the seeming success of Moral Majority in recruiting members to its cause, the group concedes that it often fights a losing battle against evangelicalism's strong individualistic strain (Kaufman, 1980). Further, so many different kinds of Christians now call themselves evangelical that the term now embraces a great many divergent national organizations and countless local churches and prayer groups (Woodward, 1982).

VARIETIES OF RELIGIOUS EXPRESSION

About 55 percent of Americans report that religion is "very important" in their immediate, day-to-day lives

The percentage of Americans who affirmed that religion was personally important to them declined from 75 percent in 1952 to 52 percent in 1978. Recently, however, the trend has been reversed, with 55 percent of Americans in 1980 asserting that religion is personally important.

FIGURE 15.1 Percentage of Americans Who Believe that Religion Is "Very Important" in Their Personal Life, 1952–1980

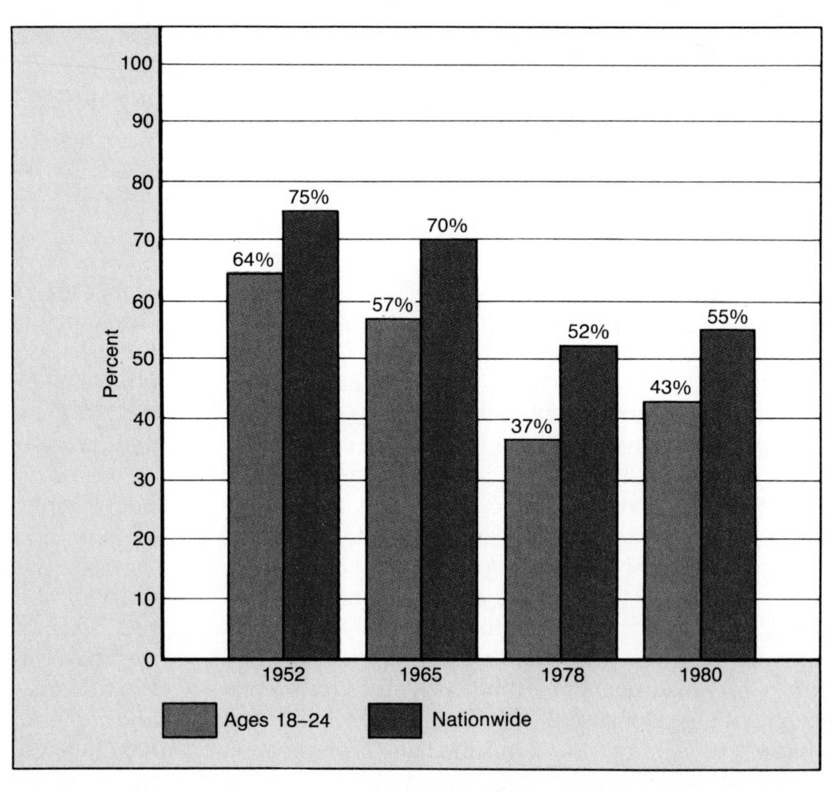

Source: The Princeton Religion Research Center, Inc. *Religion in America, 1981.* Princeton, New Jersey: The Gallup Organization, Inc., 1981.

(see Figure 15.1), and 81 percent of Americans say that they consider themselves religious (among Europeans, only the Italians, with 83 percent, have a higher rating; Gallup Report, 1982). Moreover, 58 percent of American adults say that they have experienced ESP, 27 percent claim they have talked with one or more dead friends, and 6 percent have undergone profound mystical encounters very much like that of St. Paul on the road to Damascus (Hadden and Swann, 1981). This large reservoir of religious feeling has found many outlets, not all of which are within the confines of organized religion. We will now consider some of these.

Mainline Churches: Changes and Trends

Although many Americans have recently sought new avenues of religious expression, for the most part they have not abandoned traditional religion. Instead, they have sought to make the existing churches more responsive to their needs. Some recent developments among American Catholics, Protestants, and Jews illustrate this trend.

Catholics

Over the past twenty years American Catholics have experienced a profound upheaval in their religious lives. In many respects, the reforms instituted by Vatican II marked a turning point for traditional Roman Catholicism in the United States. Vatican II—the Second Vatican Council held in Rome between 1962 and 1965—eliminated the Latin mass and meatless Fridays, allowed laity to receive communion wafers in their own hands and to take wine from the chalice, redefined non-Catholics as no longer heretics and schismatics but separated brothers and sisters, and repudiated anti-Semitism. And after Vatican II, the Church continued to change: Massive numbers of American Catholics came to dissent from papal teachings on birth control and divorce and to act accordingly. A fifth of the priests left the ministry and an even higher proportion of nuns withdrew from religious orders. And increasing numbers of Catholics took to marching and picketing on behalf of social issues and peace (Greeley, 1982).

Other forces of change have also been at work. In a few generations, Catholic immigrants have become well-educated, suburban, middle-class Americans. Success, power, and prosperity have increasingly become the lot of the nation's non-Hispanic Catholics. Simultaneously, the sharp falloff in the ranks of priests has dictated a greater involvement of lay people in local parish affairs, and they have taken on administrative and liturgical duties once reserved to priests, including reading Scripture and distributing communion. And new priorities have been emerging. The welfare of the poor and concerns about peace and the nuclear arms race are moving to the forefront, overshadowing more traditional church and parish preoccupations (O'Rourke, 1983).

Although much has changed from a generation ago when lay people lamented that they were locked in a routine of "pray, pay, and obey," the role of women in the modern church is a source of growing tension. Many Catholic women find themselves deeply troubled by Vatican actions that call upon them to stay in traditional roles. Pope John Paul II has spoken out strongly against birth control, premarital sex, remarriage, optional celibacy, altar girls, and women's ordination. The result has been a mounting strain between the Vatican and the American church. Nuns, who still outnumber priests by two to one, have taken the lead in the movement to change the role of women in the church and have simultaneously assumed a wider and bolder role in American society. Thousands of nuns have remained in their religious orders while serving as lawyers, lobbyists, and political activists, roles sharply different from the traditional teaching and nursing posts.

American Catholics are increasingly concluding that they can disagree with, even criticize, papal teachings and still remain within the church. More than four-fifths of young Catholic adults reject their church's teachings on birth control and remarriage after divorce. Many also do not accept the concept of papal infallibility. Yet they remain solidly Catholic in their fundamental convictions about life and death and about the nature of God, and they say they intend to remain in the church, though on their own terms (Greeley, 1982).

Protestants

In the mid-1960s mainline Protestant denominations began experiencing a drop in membership (although the decline may now be bottoming out) while fundamentalist and evangelical bodies grew. Between 1972 and 1982, membership in the United Methodist Church fell 10 percent; in the Episcopal Church, 15 percent; and in the United Presbyterian Church, 21 percent. During this same period, membership in the Southern Baptist Convention rose 20 percent; in the Seventh-Day Adventists, 36 percent; and in the Assemblies of God, 62 percent. Given these trends, even the more liberal denominations have placed greater emphasis on worship, prayer, religious faith, and spirituality. But one factor holding back a stronger rebound in mainline church memberships is that the birth rate among people who favor these denominations tends to be low (Mann, 1983).

The renewed focus on worship and belief has also given impetus to the ecumenical movement. In 1983 Northern and Southern Presbyterians voted to merge, and a similar movement is underway among three major Lutheran groups. The United Church of Christ and the Disciples of Christ are also discussing union.

A recent survey conducted among Minnesota Christians provides a number of insights into the religious attitudes and practices of Americans (Chittister and Marty, 1983). On the whole, these Christians seem to have evolved a "pick-and-choose" approach to their religion. They take what they want from church traditions and ignore that which does not fit their spiritual needs. Two-thirds of the respondents saw no harm in rejecting some of the doctrines of their church. One woman commented: "I feel that in religious training . . . you are taught the basics. From those basics then, you sort out what you want, or pick it apart as you see fit" (Chittister and Marty, 1983:269).

The Minnesota Christians spoke of suffering and crisis in their lives. Some felt that difficulties were sent by God to test their faith. But others admitted confusion and anger that came with the conviction that they were "good" and yet God had dealt harshly with them. Even so, 88 percent agreed that they became more aware of God through affliction in their lives. And they looked to religion to give meaning to their existence.

Some 71 percent of the respondents described prayer as "very important." But the prayer was not necessarily a literal prayer said on knees with folded hands. It often consisted of "quickies": "Oh God, let us get there," "I hope we have a safe trip," and "Don't let it snow." Overall, they thought of God as a being who walked among them, who helped them, and who intervened in their lives.

Ninety-eight percent of the respondents believed that personal spiritual development requires an awareness of personal sin. Yet only 57 percent considered themselves to be sinful. One respondent expressed the widespread sense of weakness without guilt: "The day I die I should only have to look up at my Maker and say, 'Take me.' Not, 'Forgive me.' I'm not saying that I am perfect . . . but I have led a life that I don't have to be ashamed of" (p. 88). Indeed, 88 percent of the sample credited Jesus with having a compassionate understanding of his followers.

Jews

Denominationalism has been primarily a Protestant phenomenon. American Catholicism has retained its unity, although the recent divergence of Catholic sentiment regarding papal teachings may lead to a denominational expression. Among Jews, a tripartite structure of religious organizations has evolved that in some respects resembles Protestant denominationalism (Harrison and Lazerwitz, 1982). The Jewish denominational bodies differ in their degree of traditionalism, their ethnic loyalties, and their religious observations. Orthodox Jews rank highest on these dimensions and Reform Jews the lowest; Conservative Jews are intermediate in rank. These denominational differences continue to carry over to the younger generation of American Jews. However, in one area denominational differences are absent: concern for world Jewry and Israel. Indeed, even Jews who deem themselves nonreligious express deep attachment and caring for Israel (Cohen, 1983).

Many of the same currents of ferment that characterize American Catholicism and Protestantism also characterize American Judaism. Like their Catholic and Protestant counterparts, many Jews are looking for solace and sustenance in a more personal expression of religion. Some Reform congregations report that members have returned to wearing skull caps and prayer shawls during services. Further, Orthodox Judaism has found new popularity among younger Jews. Of particular interest, attendance at Jewish schools has climbed from 60,000 in 1962 to 110,000 today, despite a decline in Jewish birth rates (Sanoff, 1983).

Many of the nation's nearly 6 million Jews are finding that they want something more in their religious life than passive worship in large and frequently impersonal congregations. They have turned to *havurah*, a movement that aims to make religion more spiritually and personally meaningful (Novak, 1981; Sanoff, 1983). A *havurah* typically consists of a number of families who meet on a regular basis. It may take any number of forms: Some function as study groups, others emphasize social service activities to help the sick and needy, still others attempt to personalize and humanize Judaism by getting families together for worship and the celebration of holidays. *Havurahs* also allow greater participation by women (only the Reform branch ordains women as rabbis).

Like mainline Protestant denominations, many Jewish groups were active in the civil rights and other broad social activist movements of the 1960s and 1970s. But increasingly, many Jews are looking inward and focusing on religious renewal. One problem confronting the American Jewish community has been the steady rise in intermarriage. Some 40 percent of Jews are marrying outside their religion—in some Western communities, the figure is about 60 percent. Yet intermarriage is not proving to be the threat to Jewish survival that some leaders feared it might be. Approximately seven out of ten children in mixed marriages are raised as Jews, and many non-Jewish spouses convert to the Jewish faith. In sum, as with contemporary Protestantism and Catholicism, American Judaism exhibits considerable religious and cultural vitality.

Modernization in Judaism has included the ordination of women as rabbis in the Reform branch of this religion. (Ray Ellis/Rapho-Photo Researchers.)

Invisible or Private Religion

Many people who are highly critical of organized religion or who disclaim any religious affiliation are in fact religious: they practice what Thomas Luckmann (1967) has described as "**invisible**" or **private religion.** Like everyone else, these people must grapple with life's great issues. However, instead of accepting the formulations of established religion, they choose certain themes and private experiences and construct from them an individual "sacred cosmos" that gives meaning to their lives.

Luckmann's formulation has been supported by the work of other investigators. For example, in a study of 208 households in a white working- and middle-class area in the South, Richard Machalek and Michael Martin (1976) found a wide array of "ultimate concerns" and "coping strategies." Only 25 percent of this group had recourse to churchlike coping strategies. Some 67.5 percent relied on private humanistic strategies including informal discussion groups in helping them deal with such ultimate concerns as economic security, survival, happiness, and peace of mind. The issues central to traditional religion—the relationship between human beings and God, life after death, the nature of God—were mentioned by only 18 percent of the people interviewed. Most people's deepest concerns focused on intimacy, work, or peace of mind. We may dismiss these matters as nonreligious, but if people *say* these are ultimate concerns, we must listen. And if large numbers address these concerns by talking to a close friend rather than to a priest, then perhaps we should consider whether these diffuse religious patterns are the modern equivalent, in a transient and fragmented society, of the old village parish.

The Electronic Church

While private or invisible religion is often diffuse and may strain the definition of religion, there is a form of religious expression—religious radio and television programs—that reinforces traditional religious beliefs. In fact, three themes that Luckmann (1967) found characteristic of private religion—autonomy, self-realization, and a sense of family—are served by the messages of religious broadcast. Among the stars of the "electronic church" are Jimmy Lee Swaggart, Oral Roberts, Rex Humbard, Robert Schuller, Jerry Falwell, Jim Bakker, and Pat Robertson.

This new vehicle for religious expression fits modern life well. In a transient world, it is not necessary to be a long-term member of a community, as old-time church membership required. In a fast-paced world, you can "tune in" when it suits you. TV religion is the dramatic opposite of the traditional church. Once an institution that embraced community values, religion now may be an electronic message that is disengaged from the community. Yet one of the striking characteristics of the television ministry is that it gives the illusion of a face-to-face relationship with the performer. In time the viewer may come to view the preacher as a friend, counselor, comforter, and model.

Evangelistic messages on radio and television are frequently parodied and disparaged by critics and the news media. But they have a large audience, and they do bring comfort to many people. The radio programs, in particular, tend to appeal to the poor and less educated segment of society—people who are susceptible to "troubles" and experience a sense of helplessness in coping with them. Television evangelism attracts an audience of some 20 million viewers. Two-thirds to three-quarters of the audiences are fifty years old or over, and of these roughly two-thirds are women (Hadden and Swann, 1981).

Of course, the media preachers do not cast their bread on the waters without expecting some return. Much time is devoted to soliciting funds. But the tube makes up only half of the technology devoted to fund raising. The other half comes from the computer:

> Like an invisible spirit, the computer allows the prime-time preacher to come down out of the television and

Jerry Falwell is perhaps this country's best known minister of the "electronic church." Falwell's followers form a conservative political coalition known as the Moral Majority, which seems to have limited national support even from other fundamentalist religious groups. (Ron Cooper/EKM-Nepenthe.)

> listen to you alone, or seem to, and to pray with you, or seem to, and to call you by name when he holds out the collection plate. . . . It is the thinking machine that plugs in names, thanks Martha or Ray for the $10 contribution, tells John that the Lord will see him through unemployment, and asks Jim one more time if he won't make a special sacrifice for the glory of God. (Hadden and Swann, 1981:104, 107)

Viewers also send money for merchandise promoted by the electronic ministry: calendars, books, magazines, transcripts of sermons, records, tape recordings, religious art, lapel buttons, necklaces, decals, and countless other items. In 1980 the top four programs collectively took in over a quarter of a billion dollars (Hadden and Swann, 1981).

Given the general trend toward rootlessness and disconnectedness caused by moving frequently, concentrating on careers, and remaining single, along with the increasing importance of television in people's lives—especially in light of advances in television technology—it seems likely that the electronic church will continue as a major form of private religion.

The New Christian Right

Until relatively recently, fundamentalists had remained remarkably aloof from American politics, discouraged by their defeat fifty years ago when the Prohibition Amendment was repealed. The New Christian Right, as the movement has been dubbed by the media, has emerged within the context of a broader conservative movement that culminated in the 1980 election of Ronald Reagan. Three major organizations have contributed to the political mobilization of fundamentalists. The first, Christian Voice, was launched on the West Coast in early 1979 and resulted from the merging of several pre-existing antigay, antipornography, and profamily groups. The second, Moral Majority, was founded by the Reverend Jerry Falwell in July, 1979; its strength is centered in the South and Southwest. The third, Religious Roundtable, was set up to attract conservative clergy who were not comfortable with either Christian Voice or Moral Majority (Guth, 1983).

The New Christian Right does not speak with one voice on current issues. Nonetheless, three ideological themes have pervaded the movement: economic libertarianism, social traditionalism, and militant anticommunism (Himmelstein, 1983). The New Right blames economic problems such as inflation, unemployment, high taxes, and high interest rates on government interference. It opposes abortion, school busing, the Equal Rights Amendment, sexual permissiveness, drugs, prohibitions on school prayer, pornography, and gay rights. And it portrays the United States as engaged in a life-or-death struggle with the Soviet Union and world communism. By combining these themes with an organizational strategy featuring extensive networking, up-to-date methods of computerized fund-raising, targeted lobbying, and mass media publicity, the New Christian Right emerged as an important political force on the American scene in the early 1980s.

While many Americans oppose abortion and gay rights and favor school prayer and traditional roles for women, national polls have shown only limited support for Moral Majority itself (Shupe and Stacey, 1983). Its strongest support has come from the ranks of fundamentalists, particularly those who regularly view the Electronic Church. Of interest, however, even conservative and predominantly southern groups like the Southern Baptists are divided in their stance toward Moral Majority. James Guth (1983) finds that support for Moral Majority comes primarily from ministers at the margins of the Southern Baptist Convention: those with rural backgrounds, modest educational accomplishments, and the least involvement in the convention.

Many forces contributed to the recent politicization of American fundamentalists (Wuthnow, 1983). The presidency of Jimmy Carter increased the public's recognition of evangelicals and gave them a strong sense of legitimacy. Other developments of the 1970s, including Watergate and the Supreme Court's ruling on abortion, rearranged many of the symbolic boundaries among religion, morality, and politics. Further, using national survey data, John Simpson (1983) suggests that support for Moral Majority is strongest among devalued groups seeking to enhance their status within American life. Feeling threatened by changing life styles and the mounting secularization of American society, they turned to political action as a mechanism to strengthen their power and increase their prestige.

Whether the New Christian Right signals a religious revival—another Great Awakening—or a passing episode remains to be seen. As we will see in Chapter 18, social movements come and go. Groups and movements that were the center of public attention a decade ago—the Black Panther Party, the Weather Underground, and the Symbionese Liberation Army—are now virtually forgotten. Regardless of the long-term viability of the New Christian Right, it nevertheless has demonstrated the prevalence of unrest among a large segment of the American population.

Civil Religion

Another modern form of religious expression is what the sociologist Robert Bellah (1970) terms national, or **civil religion,** a collection of religious beliefs, symbols, and rituals that exists outside the church and that legitimates civilian institutions. The inauguration of the president provides a good example of civil religion in practice. Bellah has pointed out that at almost every American state or political occasion, God is there. *He* is addressed in the Pledge of Allegiance, in congressional invocations, in all oaths of office, at party conventions, in courtroom procedures, and in political speeches—including every presidential inaugural address but one (Washington's second, which was only two paragraphs long). The nation's currency proclaims "In God We Trust." And the traditional feeling exists in the United States that this nation was established "under God," from whom the government derives its ultimate legitimacy. According to Bellah (1973), the idea of a civil religion embraces the links among religion, morality, and politics that exist in contemporary societies. Civil religion, then, is a vehicle by which modern societies undertake to bind together individual self-interest and the collective good (Bellah and Hammond, 1980).

Civil religion, according to Bellah, is declining and American democratic institutions are in trouble. He finds a general decline of belief in all forms of moral obligation: to one's occupation, family, country, and self (1975). Others also echo the view that civil religion is necessary for the survival of democratic institutions. It provides the foundations for public spirit, public morality, and public virtue by creating a willingness to care for, and sacrifice for, the public good. Hence, civil religion institutionalizes and engenders those patterns of public concern and participation that make for a free citizenry in democratic societies (Coleman, 1983).

Since Bellah first coined the term, there has been continuing interest in civil religion. Sociologist Corwin Smidt (1980) recently studied the influence of civil religion among children. He found that 85 percent of elementary school children believe that America "has been placed on this earth for a special purpose," that America is God's chosen nation, and that America's success is a reward for her goodness.

EPILOGUE

We often think of secularization as leading to a lessening of religious influence and experience relative to other sectors of society. Yet much that is labeled secularization is simply religious change. What is taken to be the decline of religion, upon closer inspection, turns out not to be decline at all. While the link between the church and the state continues to erode in American society, the level of religious belief and participation remains quite high (Greeley, 1972b; Hadden, 1980).

A recent sociological study challenges contemporary doomsayers who claim that religion is becoming irrelevant in the modern age of science and technology. The study's setting was Muncie, Indiana, perhaps better known as "Middletown" since Robert and Helen Lynd did their classic studies of it in the 1920s and 1930s. The most recent investigation, known as the Middletown III Project, was begun in 1976 by Theodore Caplow and his associates (1983), who set out to replicate the Lynds' studies (1929, 1937). To find out what changes have occurred in Muncie over the past fifty years, they put the Lynds' questions to a similar sample of the community's population.

Caplow and his Middletown III colleagues found considerable evidence that religion in Middletown is even stronger now than it was half a century ago. Church attendance has increased dramatically. In 1924 about a quarter of all married couples attended church regularly but in 1978 about half did. In 1978, only a sixth said they had not attended church at all during that year; in 1924 more than half said they had not. Tithing—"a tenth of one's substance to the Lord"—was virtually unknown in the 1920s, but fifty years later nearly a third of the active church members gave a tenth or more of their income. And whereas in 1924 there was one church building for every 870 residents, by 1978 there was one for every 538.

The Middletown III sociologists reject the notion that Muncie is peculiar with respect to the strength of its religious life. They cite data from international Gallup surveys that show the United States to be by far the most religious of the industrialized nations. For instance, 56 percent of Americans say that religion is "very important" to them, while only 27 percent of Western Europeans say the same.

This awareness of the persistence of religion in the United States has emerged so recently that few theories have been advanced to explain it. One theory holds that Americans have returned to religion in flight from other institutions that have deceived and failed them. But Caplow and his colleagues think a more likely explanation is one first advanced in 1835 in *Democracy in America* by Alexis de Tocqueville. The French observer of the American scene suggested that an egalitarian society encourages self-interest and love of pleasure to the point where society is itself jeopardized by selfish individual strivings. Tocqueville noted that the government and the local community lack the moral authority to impose broader norms dictating public duty, responsibility, and service. Consequently, individuals turn to religion because it provides them with those constraints on behavior necessary to commit themselves to long-term undertakings and relationships and to find happiness. Thus an underlying theme in the responses of Middletown residents was that, without religion, they would have no reason not to sin, and their lives would fall apart.

The consideration of religion leads into the material on social change that follows in Part Six. This chapter reminds us that, although the content and particulars of life may change, much of the underlying substance may persist. Even so, social change is a relentless force in human life. The emergence and development of new religious structures such as sects and cults share much in common with collective behavior and social movements, the subjects of Chapter 18. Let us turn our sociological eye, therefore, to an examination of social change.

SUMMARY

The basic elements of religion identified by Emile Durkheim, the first sociologist of religion, are the glorification of sacred beings or sacred things; the affirmation of deeply held beliefs through specific rituals; and a special community of worship.

Religion serves a variety of functions. It creates and reinforces a sense of social solidarity and consensus. It legitimates secular authority. In American society, which is made up of immigrants from many cultures, it helps people adapt to a new way of life. The universal milestones of life—birth, maturity, marriage, death—are also interpreted and celebrated by religion.

Religion is also the source of conflicts. According to Marx, the dominant classes use it to justify the status quo, thereby inhibiting social change by the lower classes. Sometimes religious groups form to oppose corruption in the dominant churches. A religious group may also inititate conflict with what it considers evil or corrupt in society in general. Inherent in religion is a conflict between sacred power and secular order. The power of sacred transcendence must be contained in order to preserve social order.

There are different types of religious institutions. The church is universal and often allied with the status quo. Most people are born into a church, and it places few demands on them. Religious groups that are at odds with the social environment may be divided into sects and cults. Small and exclusive, the sect is composed primarily of converts. It controls members' lives and tends to be either indifferent or hostile to society. Sects arise by breaking away from a church. Cults have no prior ties with an established religious body.

The social change brought by modernization has multiplied our options—both in what we can do and in how we can think about our lives. The pluralism of religious choices has forced many to pick and choose among religious beliefs, rather than accept one religious tradition. People who wish to preserve religious tradition in modern life have three choices, according to Peter Berger. They can affirm religious tradition in the face of modern challenges to it, as the Shiite Muslims in Iran have chosen to do. They can convert religious beliefs to secular form, as the Calvinists in the seventeenth century did when their religious beliefs were incorporated into the Protestant work ethic. Or they can attempt to retrieve the original spirit that established religious tradition and apply that spirit to aspects to their lives. This is the course taken by the fundamentalist sects.

Among the varieties of religious expression today is invisible or private religion, in which individuals choose for themselves the basic life issues that concern them and the ways they will deal with them. Private religion is catered to by the preachers of the airwaves, who promise "healing and blessing" to their listeners and viewers. Robert Bellah believes that the United States has developed a civil religion with its own symbols, hymns, high priests, and martyrs, which binds together our pluralistic society.

America's mainline churches have not been immune to the forces of change within the larger society. Over the past twenty years American Catholics have experienced a profound upheaval in their religious lives. Vatican II marked a turning point for the church in the United States. During this same period mainline Protestant denominations have experienced a drop in their membership while fundamentalist and evangelical bodies have experienced growth. The renewed emphasis on worship and belief that has characterized American Catholicism and Protestantism has also had an impact on Judaism. Many of the nation's six million Jews are finding that they want a more spiritually and personally meaningful religion and have been turning to *havurah* to find it.

A recent sociological study of Muncie, Indiana—"Middletown"—challenges contemporary doomsayers who claim that religion is becoming irrelevant in the modern age of science and technology. They found religion to be even stronger today than it was fifty years ago. The Middletown III sociologists contend that religion plays a particularly important role in an egalitarian and democratic society such as that found in the United States. Individuals turn to religion because it provides them with those constraints on behavior necessary to commit themselves to long-term undertakings and relationships and to find happiness.

GLOSSARY

Audience cults. Religious groups with practically no formal organization; cult doctrine is delivered through the media.

Church. A large, conservative, universalist religious institution, which makes few demands on its members and accommodates itself to the culture of a society (Troeltsch).

Civil religion. Bellah's term for a collection of religious beliefs, symbols, and rituals that exists outside the church and that pervades and helps legitimate a community.

Client cults. Religious movements in which those who offer services are organized but the clients are not.

Cult. A religious group with no prior ties to an established religious body in a society (Stark and Bainbridge).

Cult movements. Religious cults that are intense and tightly organized.

Invisible (private) religion. A set of individual themes and experiences that may substitute for the beliefs of organized religion.

Moral community. A group of people who share common beliefs and practices.

Profane. Human experiences that are ordinary, mundane (Durkheim).

Protestant ethic. A phrase, originally used by Weber, that has come to mean dedication to hard work and the pursuit of profit.

Religion. A set of beliefs and practices that pertain to sacred things among a community of believers.

Ritual. A specific practice that is the visible and symbolic expression of a religion.

Sacred. Human experiences that transcend everyday existence (Durkheim).

Sect. A small, exclusive, uncompromising fellowship that makes heavy demands on its members and sets them apart from the larger society (Troeltsch); a religious group formed by breaking away from an established religious body (Stark and Bainbridge).

Secularization. The process by which sectors of society and culture are removed from religious domination.

Totem. A sacred object, plant, or animal that is worshiped as the mystical ancestor of the society.

PART SIX

CHANGING SOCIETY

To say that society is rapidly changing has become almost a cliché. Yet rapid change *is* occurring and will continue to be a central feature of twentieth century life. Part 6 explores many facets of our changing social order.

Chapter 16 begins with a look at demographic change—overall changes in birth rates, death rates, and net migration. These changes govern the size, composition, and distribution of a population. Indirectly, they also affect many other aspects of social life, such as the kinds of health problems people most frequently face.

We then turn to the subject of how demographic changes are related to changes in the types of communities in which people live. During the twentieth century, the world has become increasingly urbanized. What effect has this had on the way people feel and act? This is one of the intriguing questions we raise in Chapter 17.

Chapter 18 takes up the relationship between social change and collective behavior, those relatively unstructured, unconventional forms of social action like panics, riots, mass hysterias, and the like. Such incidents are usually preceded by some kind of social strain—strain that can be brought about by rapid or unanticipated change. Collective behavior, in turn, sometimes launches other important social changes. In fact, one type of collective behavior, the social movement, is a direct attempt to resist or to precipitate change.

Finally, Chapter 19 shifts to a more general look at the topic of social change. It surveys the major sociological theories about the nature and causes of change. It also explores the consequences of two major social changes occurring in the world today—modernization in developing countries, and the emergence of a post-industrial society in much of the rest of the world.

CHAPTER 16

Population and Health

One way of telling the story of a society is through the numbers, characteristics, and distribution of its people. Population data—information from periodic national censuses and from records of births, marriages, and deaths—are indispensable to an understanding of social life. Population size takes on significance when we appraise the adequacy of a people's environmental resources and the impact that numbers have on an ecological setting. A society's composition—the age, sex, education, income, occupation, marital status, race, and religion of its members—has enormous implications for the nature of relationships among its people. And the distribution of people—their location in world regions, countries, provinces, states, cities, localities, and blocks—has consequences for institutional arrangements (for instance, when many people move into an area, they are likely to increase the demands on its schools, hospitals, shopping centers, and roads; when they move out of an area these facilities may be underused).

Much of our information about a society, including data from opinion and attitude surveys, cannot be usefully interpreted without reference to demographic data. For example, data from current surveys indicate that Americans profess a strong attachment to the institution of marriage. Yet population statistics show that increasing numbers of people are postponing marriage until their late twenties and thirties, remaining single, and getting divorced. Clearly, neither the population statistics nor the survey data tell the whole story. A simple interpretation—either that marriage is in trouble or that it is "alive and well"—is misleading (see Chapter 13). Sociologists, using both kinds of data, make further, more potentially useful inquiries: about why fewer people are choosing to marry or to stay married, about who they are—by age, education, income, and region—and about the economic and social correlates of these statistical patterns.

In this chapter we will look at demographic data and the effects of population changes on society. We will examine what the 1980 census has revealed about population changes in our national life. We will then look at various factors that influence health and the ways in which they in turn affect population. And finally, we will examine the challenges that will confront health care systems in the decades ahead.

SOCIETY AND POPULATION

Demography is the study of how births, deaths, and migration affect the composition, size, and distribution of populations. Although in the short run demographic change is barely perceptible, over a long span of time, demographic change is quite visible. For example, when we return to a city after being away for several years, we may be shocked either by its decline and deterioration or by its growth and development. Although demographic change may occur slowly, over time its effects can be striking: here a booming young city like Houston, Texas, there a shrinking, boarded-up community like Camden, New Jersey; here a housing shortage, there empty apartment buildings. Numbers of people are always a significant correlate of social life, and at times—during famines and epidemics or on frontiers and in newly settled territories—they can become decisive for progress or decline.

The baby boomers who came of age in the 70s were highly political. This May Day demonstration in Washington, D.C. in 1971 was one of the many anti-Vietnam War demonstrations that electrifed the 60s and 70s. (Charles Harbutt/Archive Pictures.)

Population and Social Values

Although population patterns are shaped by social values and sociological forces, they also alter those values and forces. The "baby boom" between 1947 and 1964 provides a good illustration. It was fueled by post–World War II prosperity and people's desire for the "good life"—children and a home in the suburbs. The baby-boom generation accounts for fully a third of the entire American population—74 million men and women. They are sandwiched between two much smaller generations—the children born in the Great Depression of the 1930s and the "baby bust" group of the 1970s. The imbalance in the size of the nation's generations has had and will continue to have long-term implications as each generation moves along its life stages. The baby boomers provided the foundation for the youth culture of the 1960s with its distinctive language, music, and political and social outlooks. And criminologists attribute the record crime rate of the 1970s in part to the vast numbers of youth in the crime-prone ages of fifteen to twenty-four.

The dominant age group in a population tends to set standards governing what is acceptable. The baby boom generation, by its sheer size, has found its every fad adopted (or at least noticed) by the rest of society: Davy Crockett coonskin caps and hula hoops, taken up by the baby boomers, were followed by rock music and blue jeans, which have been followed by roller discos and health foods. The baby boom generation has done much more than launch fads, however. In tolerating or embracing recreational drugs, cohabitation, and homosexuality, and in rejecting traditional ideas about minorities, this generation has redefined deviance, establishing new, more flexible norms for society as a whole. As the baby boomers become middle-aged, they will very likely provide political clout for tax support to day-care centers, expanded maternity and paternity leaves, and more portability in pension benefits from one establishment to another.

Yet the baby-boom generation is hardly uniform. It is divided between younger and older baby boomers (Jones, 1983). Those born before 1955 were on the generation's cutting edge. They were the cultural revolutionaries who gave us rock 'n' roll, went to Woodstock, and mounted student power. In contrast, the younger boomers, those now reaching young adulthood, have had little of their predecessors' ardor for social reform. They are incurring the disadvantages of teeming numbers as they move toward adulthood and are finding the better positions already filled with their older brothers and sisters.

At the other end of the spectrum, society will soon be experiencing the "graying of America." Even now growing numbers of elderly people are significantly affecting the political, economic, and recreational life of the nation. By 1990 the number of people over sixty-five will reach 31 million, up from 20 million a decade ago.

Population and Social Mobility

Most readers of this book are successors to the baby boom, which peaked around 1957 and ended in the early 1960s. This position in the population span will affect many of the opportunities open to your generation. Those about to enter college should find it easier to get into the college of their choice because their **cohort** (the number of people born in the same year) is smaller than the preceding ones. And getting an entry-level job should be easier too. But after the first few promotions, progress up career ladders will become more difficult because the people in the large cohorts born a few years earlier will be occupying the higher level positions. Thus, your position in the population pyramid (see Figure 16.1) affects your prospects for upward social mobility.

Population variables have other, more indirect, effects on economic and social mobility. For example, because the cohorts retiring are larger with each passing year and the cohorts entering the work force are smaller, fewer and fewer workers are available to support more and more retired people. Twenty years ago there were five workers for each Social Security recipient; by 2035 the dependency ratio will have dropped to one worker for every two recipients. Social Security taxes will have to rise, and this will decrease the current generation's take-home pay. Or, more older people will continue to work past the age of sixty-five, which will further block the occupational mobility of those coming up through the ranks. And there may well be another effect—economic necessity may dictate an increase in the percentage of retired and elderly people who live with their sons and daughters.

Population and the Economy

Different sectors of the economy have prospered and then collapsed as the baby-boom generation moved through its life span. Their collective purchasing power has created and supported entire industries—first as their parents moved to the suburbs, bringing a boom in demand for homes and washing machines for their growing families. Then came a boom in the toy industry, as millions of children demanded Slinkys and Barbie dolls; then in records, as the baby boom adolescents discovered the Beatles and all their descendants. As the baby boomers reach thirty to forty-five, they should create a formidable engine of consumption, reinforced by the employment of two of every three baby-boom women. They could do for the housing market and the home-furnishings and appliance industries what they did as teenagers for blue jeans, snack foods, and stereo equipment (Beck, 1981; Jones, 1983).

As the baby boom generation grows older and smaller generations succeed it, the economy will need to adjust to the new demographic realities. Smaller families mean fewer school children and declining college enrollments, which create unemployment for teachers, librarians, and football coaches. And military leaders view with alarm figures that show a 25 percent drop in the number of potential young men available for the armed services by 1992.

New markets are created as well. As baby boomers enter their thirties, companies such as Johnson & Johnson seek to capture their business by promoting Johnson & Johnson baby oil and powder as skin care products suitable for adult use. (And skin care has become a growth industry as baby boomers confront their first wrinkles.) Levi Straus retargeted its clothing toward the adult market, and McDonald's promotes its prework breakfasts-on-the-run. In another two decades the demand for health care services of all kinds is likely to soar as this large generation grows older and falls victim to chronic and debilitating diseases. Currently about one-fourth of the federal budget goes to the elderly, and as their numbers grow, the question increasingly confronting the nation is how much of its resources the elderly should command. In this and many other ways, demographic phenomena are linked to economic upturn and decline, shifts of public opinion, and the extent of opportunity. In assessing these matters, good demographic data are essential. We now turn our attention to how sociologists go about collecting and analyzing such data.

STUDYING POPULATIONS

Demographics entails much more than simply counting heads. It calls for an accurate assessment of a population's composition and distribution to provide a basis for predicting future trends and making informed decisions. And these activities require vast amounts of precise and detailed information from a wide variety of sources. The most important source of such data for the United States is the national **census,** which, in addition to being a count of numbers of people, is a tally of the regional composition and distribution of people by their origins, skills, and activities. To construct a useful census requires a firm grounding in sociology and sophisticated research skills. Let us consider a number of these matters.

The U.S. Census

Article One of the Constitution requires that the population of the United States be enumerated every ten years. Census results provide the basis for the state-by-state allocation of seats in the House of Representatives. With so much at stake in terms of political power, all censuses since the first have been the subject of much controversy. The rapid increase in federal entitlement programs has led to intensified debate in recent years since funds are distributed on the basis of census results. In the early 1980s the allocation of an estimated $100 billion in federal funds was directly tied each year to census figures. Hence, state and local officials have a vital interest in seeing that every individual in their jurisdiction is counted because each person not counted equals hundreds of government dollars lost (Mitroff et al., 1983).

The censuses of 1950, 1960, and 1970 each turned up 5 million fewer people than other calculations had shown were present (Keyfitz, 1981). In 1970, for instance, the Census Bureau used birth and death certificates and immigration, Medicare, and welfare figures to show that the population of the United States was closer to 208.5 million than the 203.2 million figure revealed by the 1970 census. The 1970 census missed about 2 percent of whites, but many more Hispanics were not counted nor were 7.7 percent of the nation's black population.

Even though the 1980 census counted nearly five million more Americans than had been predicted, some groups nonetheless were undercounted (Hauser, 1981; Mitroff et al., 1983). Sociologists and demographers know that immigrants are undercounted, particularly illegal aliens (many of whom are Hispanics). These people are reluctant to answer the census for fear that once their presence in the country is discovered, they will be deported. In addition, many illegal aliens are poor, and undercounts are most prevalent in poor neighborhoods. Overall, the poor, the young, aliens, males, and minorities—the more mobile groups in our society—are more difficult to count than are the middle class, adults, nonaliens, females, and nonminorities.

Problems also exist with the wording of questions, especially among bilingual populations that need bilingual census forms and census takers. And many Americans distrust the entire enterprise and view it an intrusion on their privacy. Many wonder why the government needs so much personal information, and some doubt the information will remain confidential. All of these factors affect the accuracy of the final data.

Recognizing the difficulties inherent in counting the population with a system that relies heavily on voluntary cooperation, the Census Bureau mounted its biggest advertising campaign in its history in 1980. It used actors and actresses, sports heroes, and eye-catching posters to get across two messages: (1) all information is confidential, so we do not care if you are a criminal or an illegal alien, and (2) an accurate census is vital to the nation and to the respondent's share in community resources. Finally, on March 28, 1980, 164 million questionnaires were mailed out. As each return came in, it was checked against a master checklist. Forms that did not come in were followed up by an elaborate system of procedures designed to find everyone. The 1980 undertaking cost more than $1 billion.

Even though the 1980 census was the most accurate in the nation's history, it has given rise to countless lawsuits filed by various groups claiming they were undercounted. However, adjusting the undercount statistically poses many hazards, since the adjustments are only guesses. Moreover, pressure groups could demand that the adjustments be adjusted, and others could demand that the adjusted adjustments be further adjusted. Yet leaving the undercounts of blacks, Hispanics, and others unchanged presents difficulties in a democratic nation. One expert has suggested that the Census Bureau describe all the different ways in which adjustments could be made and their pros and cons and then let the courts choose which (if any) they want to use (Keyfitz, 1981). With the distribution of political power and billions of dollars riding on its work, the Census Bureau can expect to be on the firing line for years to come.

Elements of Population Change

The Census Bureau uses all the information it collects, but its chief goal is to obtain accurate readings on three variables: fertility (births); mortality (deaths); and migration (movement to or away from an area). Demographers often employ the analogy of the bathtub in explaining how these three factors affect population size: Water enters the tub through two faucets, analogous to births and **immigration** (movement to an area). The water leaves through two drains, analogous to deaths and **emigration** (movement out of an area). Let us consider these variables, each in turn.

Birth Rates

The **crude birth rate** is the number of births per 1,000 people during a given year. In 1947, during the baby boom, our crude birth rate was about 27 per 1,000. In

As more Americans choose to limit the number of children they have, large families like this one have become much less common. (David Grossman.)

1982, by contrast, it was about 16 per 1,000 (3.7 million babies). A woman is *fertile* from menarche (first menstruation) to menopause (the permanent cessation of menstruation), a period of about thirty years. But biological potential for reproduction, or **fecundity,** is only one aspect of a society's birth rate at a given time. No society has ever reached, or even come near, its theoretical biological potential for reproduction. The **fertility rate** (often referred to simply as *fertility*) is the number of actual births per 1,000 women between the ages of fifteen and forty-four. In 1982 the fertility rate in the United States stood at 67.8 live births.

A number of factors affect a nation's birth rate. Most important is whether women (or couples) want to have children, and this cultural attitude is strongly influenced by religion and economics. The number of fertile women in the population at any one time also influences the birth rate. And since most babies are born to married parents, the marriage rate and age of marriage are two more factors that influence the birth rate. A final influence is the availability of effective contraceptives. A common myth holds that before the advent of modern methods of contraception people were not very successful at preventing pregnancies. In fact, most of the great decline in the birth rate during the eighteenth and nineteenth centuries was accomplished without modern methods. Nevertheless, effective contraceptive methods further separate sex from conception and fundamentally change the nature of the decision involved. In 1880 a decision not to have children was the exception. Today, many women are interested in having careers and are inclined to delay having children or avoid it altogether.

Death Rates

The **crude death rate** is the number of deaths per 1,000 people during a given year. In 1982 there were just under 2 million deaths in the United States, for a rate of 8.6 deaths per 1,000 population. Death rates vary greatly by age, particularly before age one and after age fifty. The chances of dying in the first year of life are still quite high, but after the first year the mortality rate drops sharply until the later years of life. The **infant mortality rate** is the number of deaths among infants under one year of age per 1,000 live births in a given year. In 1982 there were 11.2 infant deaths per 1,000 live births, the lowest rate ever recorded in the United States. (Fifteen countries report lower infant mortality rates; Sweden, Japan, and Finland have the lowest rates—6.7, 7.4, and 7.7, respectively.)

Life Span, the maximum number of years a human being can possibly live, has not changed substantially over the centuries. But **life expectancy,** the average number of years of life remaining for an individual of a given age, has increased dramatically in the last seventy-five years. With the advances of modern medicine, plus better nutrition and sanitation, life expectancy has approached life span. The life expectancy of Americans now averages about seventy-four years. White females can count on living the longest lives, slightly more than seventy-eight years. Nonwhite women can expect to live 74.5 years. Men have shorter life expectancies than do women: White males can expect to live 70.6 years and nonwhite males about 65.6 years.

Immigration

The movement of people from one country to another is called **international migration.** People migrate for several reasons, among them natural disasters, government and religious persecution, the desire for adventure or improvement in life chances, and—once migration starts—group momentum (Petersen, 1975). All of these reasons have brought people to the United States. The potato famine of the 1840s—a natural force—started a wave of Irish immigration. Political action (genocide) propelled Jewish immigration during World War II. The desire for economic betterment attracted immigrants from southern and eastern Europe in the 1800s. And word of their relative success filtered back to their native lands, creating a social momentum that brought an influx of 6 million of their compatriots by 1910.

Immigration has always been a major source of growth for the United States. Since 1820 more than 50 million people came to live in the United States, including some 3 million slaves who came against their will. Immigration to this country was almost unrestricted until the 1920s, when laws were passed setting limits on the number of immigrants, for all except those from northwestern Europe. Objections to the discriminatory aspects of this immigration policy led to its modification in the Immigration Act of 1965. In the 1970s legal immigration averaged about 420,000 people a year. But in recent years the figure has leaped to 700,000 or more people annually. A good part of these new immigrants come from Latin America, especially Mexico. If immi-

The newest group of immigrants to the United States are Southeast Asians who, like this Laotian family, have fled the wars in their homelands. (Michael O'Brien/Archive Pictures.)

gration continues at its present pace, Hispanics could replace blacks as the nation's largest ethnic minority by the year 2020.

Internal Migration

Movement within a country, or **internal migration,** can have as much impact on a society as movement in or out of that country. Americans have always been a people on the move, and westward migration continues. Today the Sunbelt, Western Mountain, and Pacific states are experiencing the highest growth rates. Good climate and readily available space and resources have drawn new and relocating businesses to southeastern and southwestern states. Political power has also shifted from traditional centers in the Northeast to the Sunbelt. Of the last five presidents, four (Johnson, Nixon, Carter, and Reagan) have been from the South or West.

During the nineteenth century, a different trend emerged: the migration from rural to urban areas. Industrialization, which began in earnest after the Civil War, had a push-pull effect. The mechanization of agriculture pushed farm workers out of rural areas; factories and the demand for industrial labor pulled them to the city. In 1900, 60 percent of the population lived on farms; in 1980 the farm population was only about six million, a 25 percent decline from 1970.

But today many cities in the Northeast and the Midwest are losing population to adjacent suburbs. Demographers first noted this trend around the turn of the century; it accelerated greatly during the 1940s. Because this movement seemed to coincide with an influx of rural blacks from the South, some demographers have described the phenomenon as "white flight." Whether or not such a correlation exists, black Americans are becoming urbanized. In 1900, 90 percent of black Americans lived in the rural South. Today 57.7 percent live in big cities (compared with 24.9 percent of white Americans). However, by 1980 black migration into the central cities had become minimal, and black migration to the suburbs had picked up substantially (Hauser, 1981). But not all urban blacks live in large northern metropolitan areas. New growth in the Sunbelt is drawing blacks to urban areas of the South in increasing numbers.

Another movement away from the cities began in 1970: Not only are people moving to nearby suburbs, they are also moving to smaller towns and rural areas. Two-thirds of all *non*metropolitan counties, which for years had more people moving out than moving in, are now showing gains in net migration (U.S. Census Bureau, 1980). In recent years, for the first time in more than a century, rural areas and small towns are growing faster than are urban areas. Improvements in transportation and communication (easing access to metropolitan economies) and life-style preferences have fed this trend.

The Population Pyramid

The result of these three patterns—births, deaths, and migration—can be seen in the population pyramid (see Figure 16.1). If the birth rate is high, as it was in the United States in 1950, or as it is today in many developing nations, the pyramid will be more triangular because of the large number of babies added to the bottom each year. As the birth rate declines, the pyramid takes on more of a diamond shape. Figure 16.2 shows the pyramids of a developed nation and a developing nation.

A large increase in deaths or migration will also change the shape of the pyramid. Mass immigration will create a big bar of adults in the middle of the population pyramid, as in the case of the postwar population of Israel. From 1948 to 1951, the period immediately after the establishment of Israel, this new country grew in population by 24 percent a year, and 90 percent of this

This figure represents the age structure of the United States in 1980. The longest rectangles in the figure signify the baby boom generation. The size of this cohort will probably diminish the chances for the advancement and prosperity of the cohort that follows.

FIGURE 16.1 Population Pyramid for the United States, 1980

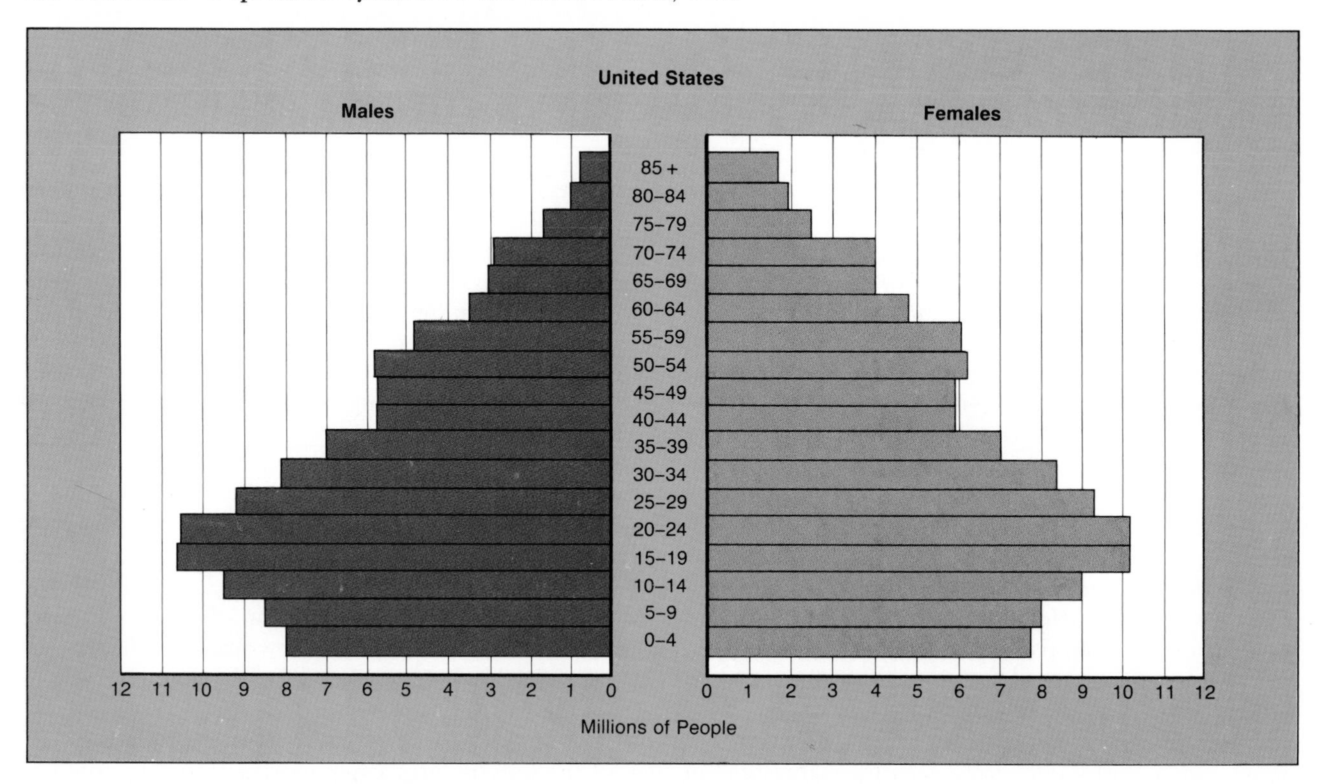

Source: From *Scientific American,* 243 (September 1980): 196.

FIGURE 16.2 Contrasting Population Structures

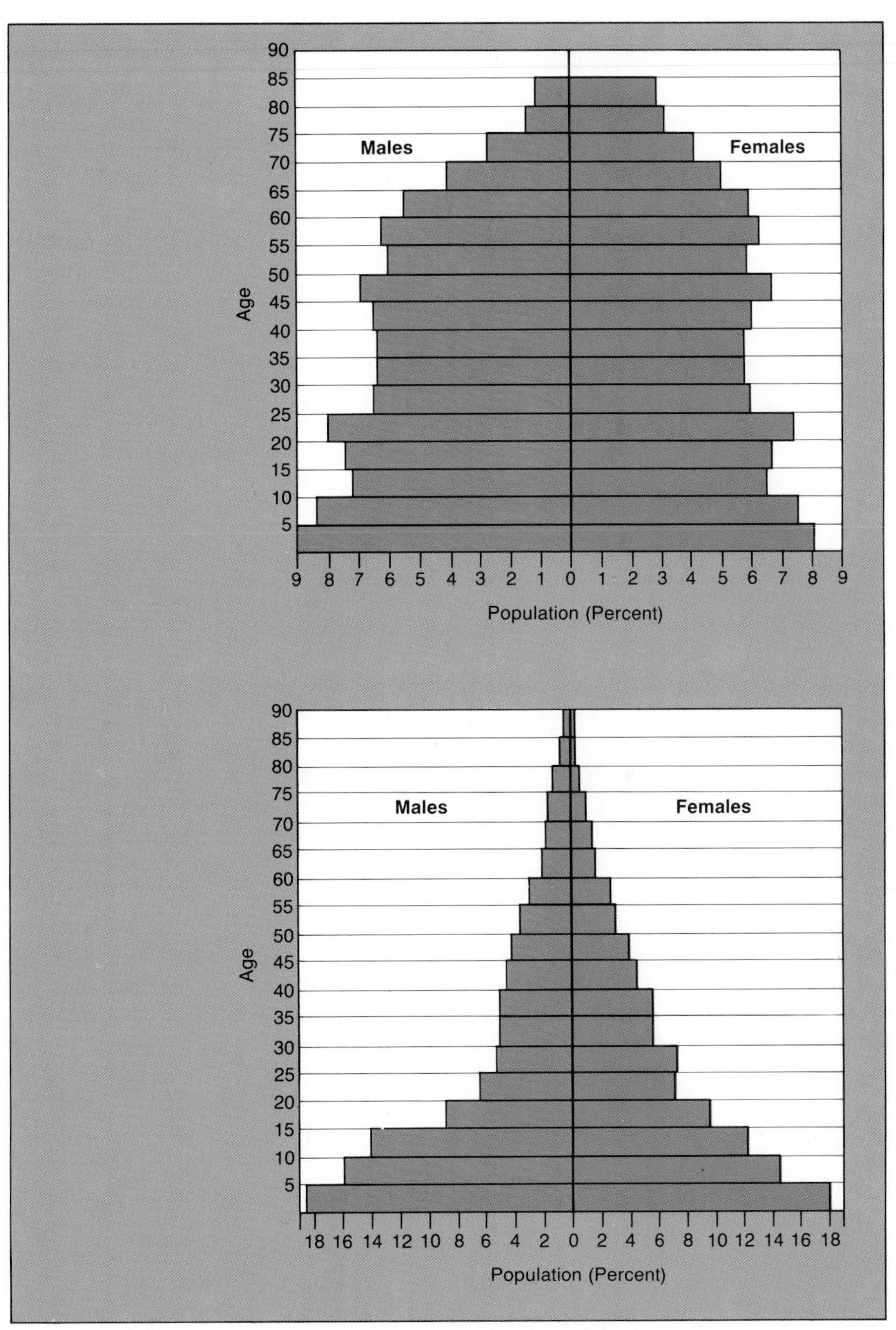

Source: From "Economic Development" by K.K.S. Dadzie. Copyright © 1980 by Scientific American, Inc.

The population pyramid at top depicts the somewhat square structure typical of a developed nation (the population of England and Wales in 1968). The structure at bottom graphically presents the triangular pyramid characteristic of a developing nation (Madagascar in 1966).

growth was due to immigration. On the other hand, mass emigration or a serious war will create a short bar among young adults. For example, the Soviet Union lost 20 million people in World War II and another 15 million to Stalin's purges, leaving a gap in their population pyramid that affected Soviet life profoundly for decades.

WORLD POPULATION GROWTH

The impact of demographic forces does not stop at a nation's boundaries, it has global implications. Overall, the world's population grew slowly until about 1850—so slowly, in fact, that several hundred thousand years were needed for the population of the earth to reach 1 billion (Wilford, 1981). Advances in medicine, farming, and transportation kept many more people alive thereafter, and the earth's second billion were added by 1930. The third billion were added by 1960, and the fourth by 1975 (see Figure 16.3). Although the rate of world population growth has recently begun to decline, there are still 146 new human beings each minute, 8,790 an hour, 210,959 a day, and 77 million a year. Current estimates place the world's population at 4.6 billion people, so that more than 9 percent of everyone who ever lived is currently alive. Unless massive famine, epidemics, or nuclear holocaust intervene, population experts with the United Nations predict that global population will continue to grow, stabilizing at about 10.2 billion toward the end of the twenty-first century (Nossiter, 1983).

Malthus Versus Marx

The rapid increase in the world's population has raised a number of questions. How large can world population ultimately become, and more particularly, how many human beings can the planet feed and the environment sustain? These questions are not new. They haunted the English scholar Thomas Malthus (1766–1834) whose theories appeared in 1798 in "An Essay on the Principle of Population." Malthus took an exceedingly pessimistic view, arguing that human populations are inescapably caught in a conflict between their "need for food" and the "passion between the sexes." Population, he maintained, increases geometrically (2, 4, 8, 16, . . .), while food supplies increase only arithmetically (2, 3, 4, 5, . . .). No population can continue to grow indefinitely, because people will increase their numbers to the limit of subsistence. Since populations increase to the ultimate point of subsistence, low standards of living must prevail. The population will always catch up, "eating" away the higher standards of living.

To Malthus, the only solution to the population problem was for people to marry late and have fewer children (he did not approve of birth control or abortion). Otherwise, population growth would inevitably be checked by drastic means: starvation, pestilence, or war.

Critics have found fault with Malthusian theory. Logically speaking, a population cannot increase more rapidly than food production. If a population is growing, the means to support it must also be growing. Otherwise, mortality would rise and the population would not grow. The world's population can no more "outrun" its food supply than the hind feet of a horse can outrun the front feet (Wrong, 1977). Malthus also failed to anticipate the full possibilities of the Industrial Revolution, and he did not foresee the technological revolution in agriculture. Indeed, in the United States farm machinery, fertilizers, pesticides, irrigation, hybrid plants, and genetically selected animals have contributed to a more rapid growth in the nation's subsistence than in its population. In fact, for the past fifty years the federal government has sponsored farm programs designed to curtail agricultural production.

Karl Marx also took exception to Malthusian doctrine (Grundstaff, 1981). Malthus had placed the blame for "overpopulation" and "poverty" on the individual members of society who succumb to their sexual urges. But Marx saw the matter quite differently. He believed that the problem was not primarily one of population but one of the ownership of the means of production and the inequitable distribution of a society's wealth. Marx depicted capitalism as creating a surplus population so as to drive down wages and maximize profits. He contended that the solution to population problems lay in the establishment of a socialist order. In sum, whereas Malthus focused on the individual and sought the answer to population problems in moral restraint, Marx

FIGURE 16.3 World Population Growth From 8000 B.C. to the Present

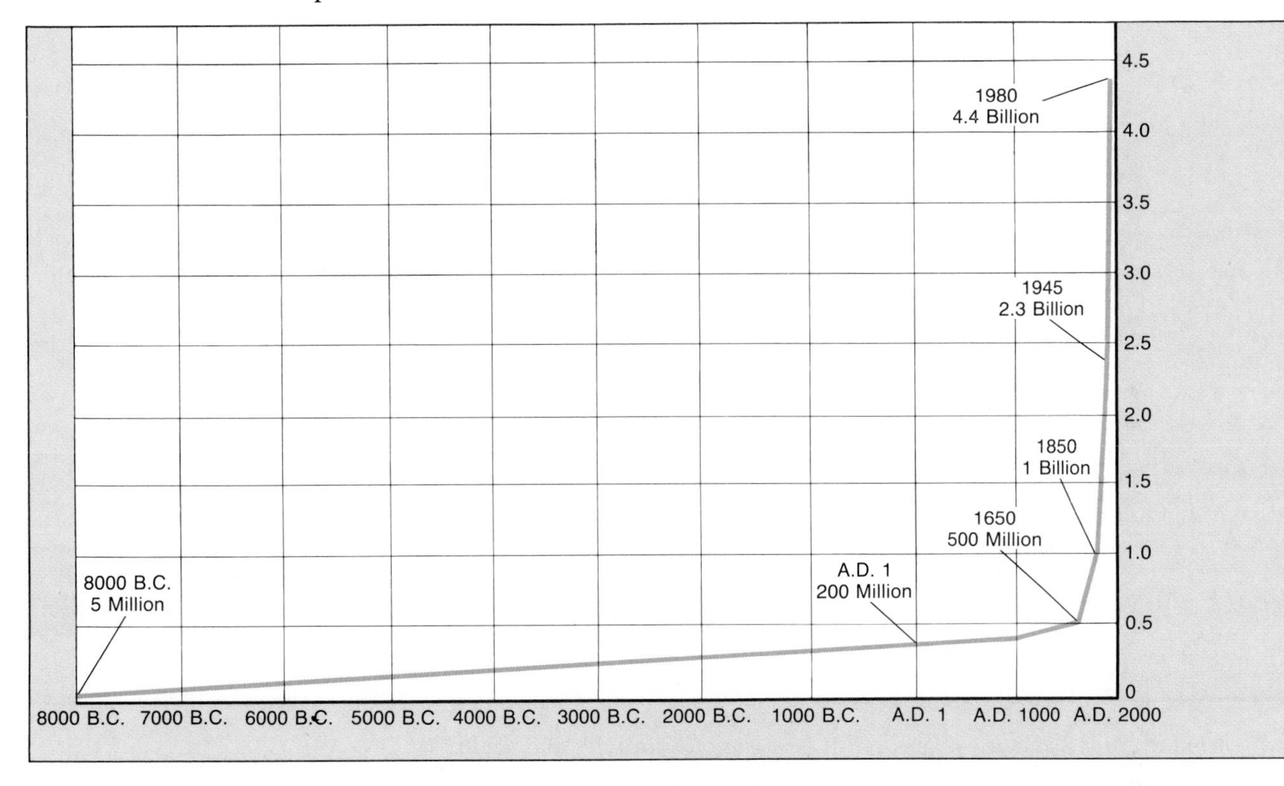

Source: Copyright © 1981 by The New York Times Company. Reprinted by permission.

This figure indicates the growth of the world's population since 8000 B.C. *If stretched all the way back to the emergence of* Homo sapiens, *the line would be a barely visible one starting many feet to the left of the graph.*

highlighted the economic structure of society and sought the solution in a new social order.

As we have repeatedly pointed out throughout the text, the individual and society are interdependent. Hence, social policies must address both the individual and the aggregate if we are to achieve meaningful social change that addresses population problems and poverty. Economic improvement is essential. But programs are also needed that focus on individual belief systems about survival, security in old age, and family size. By the same token, social change in the other areas of life affect population growth, a matter to which we now turn our attention.

The Demographic Transition

Although some demographers continue to be haunted by the Malthusian specter of starvation, plague, and war, others believe that humanity may be able to avert such a disaster. Some evidence suggests that we can achieve a population with low mortality and low fertility, perhaps even zero population growth. In fact, many industrialized countries have brought their rapid rate of population growth down in a process known as the demographic transition.

The concept **demographic transition** refers to the three characteristic stages of the population dynamics for

FIGURE 16.4 The Demographic Transition

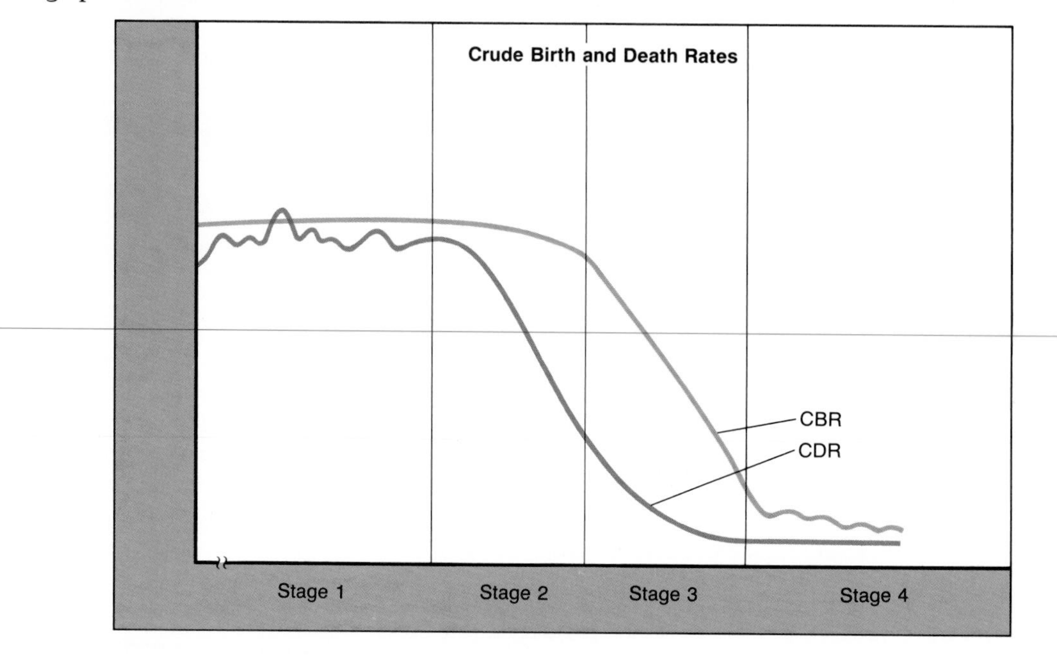

This schematic graph shows the differences in behavior of birth rates and death rates during the demographic transition in the industrialized nations. The gap between births and deaths in stages 2 and 3 produced rapid population growth. Today, the gap has narrowed, although jumps in the birth rate may produce spurts of population growth, as in our postwar baby boom. Even though its population is not growing as fast as that of the developing nations, the industrialized world still must be concerned with population growth because of the heavier demands its people place upon the environment. The United States, for example, has one-sixteenth of the world's population but consumes over one-third of the world's resources.

societies undergoing industrialization (Figure 16.4). In the first stage, which is characteristic of preindustrial societies, both the birth rate and the death rate are high and relatively stable. The second stage is a transitional one: The birth rate remains high but the death rate declines as nutrition, health, and sanitation improve. In particular, as the infant mortality rate is lowered, a larger proportion of the huge yearly crop of babies survives and in due course become parents themselves. Hence, this stage has the potential for explosive population growth. In stage three, both the birth rate and the death rate are low and in balance again. People now bear fewer children because of the dramatic increase in the chances for infant survival. Using this model, most African nations are in stage one, with high birth and death rates. India and most Latin American countries are in stage two, with transitional high growth. The industrialized nations are in the third and final phase, with a low but fluctuating birth rate and low, steady death rate. In some cases, however, births can fall below deaths, as they have in West Germany, causing a nation's population to decline (unless immigration offsets the decline).

The demographic cycle should not be viewed as a fixed sequence inevitably experienced by all countries.

Under some conditions, cultural factors influence fertility patterns more powerfully than do economic development and socioeconomic status. The Netherlands provides an illustration of a nation that contradicts the theory of demographic transition (Petersen, 1960). The Dutch population grew continuously between 1750 and 1850 despite a rising death rate. The Dutch fertility rate *increased* over what it had been in the Middle Ages as the joint-family tradition eroded and young couples set up their own independent households. Similarly, from the twelfth to the eighteenth century the peasants of Saxony (a German province) had relatively few children while the artisan class had many (Tilly, 1978).

Some demographers view demographic transition theory not only as a description of what has happened in the industrialized nations, but also as a theory of what will eventually happen elsewhere. As death rates in the developing countries drop, the population grows dramatically because fertility rates remain high. Such overpopulation creates a tremendous strain on food, health, and spatial resources and great suffering for individuals who cannot find food or work. In the currently developing nations, moreover, the death rate has dropped precipitously not because of indigenous reasons like better nutrition or sanitation, but because of the introduction of vaccinations and pesticides from the West. The words of a man in Calcutta describe this change:

> When I was a boy, they took away forty or fifty bodies after a cholera epidemic. It happened every five or ten years. Now they come and vaccinate our children. I have lived here almost seventy years. The biggest change in my time has been health. We've learned to keep from dying. (quoted in Thomlinson, 1976:29)

Although such public health measures were clearly an advance, they were introduced "overnight" into a culture that had long esteemed large families. People did not have time to adjust their religious and cultural values that shape the birth rate.

In third-world nations the plummeting death rate has not always been accompanied by a shift to an industrial economy, as it has in the West. In rural village life, children are an economic asset: By the age of ten they can care for chickens and livestock, plant seed, and begin to hoe. In a simple farm economy, parents want many children—both to help them produce food now and eventually to produce food for them in their old age. In an industrialized economy, raising many children becomes an economic burden, and with the advent of pensions and Social Security, children are no longer as vital to the care of their elderly parents. Until the people in developing countries lose their *reasons* for producing large families, they are unlikely to limit the number of children they have. Consequently, demographic change does not automatically operate in strict accordance with the demographic transition theory.

The Consequences of Rapid Growth

The rapid population growth of the developing countries accentuates many social and economic problems. The developing countries, burdened with too many people to feed, are falling further behind the advanced industrial nations in their efforts to modernize and to improve the conditions of life for their citizens.

Population and the Food Supply

The Malthusian nightmare is a reality for hundreds of millions of people. For example, of forty-one nations in Africa south of the Sahara, only five are managing to produce enough food to feed their growing populations (Knight, 1983). Further, two billion people in the developing nations—nearly half the world's population—are undernourished to the point of low vitality and high vulnerability to disease, and many millions are near starvation (Green and Fearey, 1978; Crittenden, 1981). Malnutrition predisposes people to disease and death by contributing to prematurity and low birth weight and by impairing immune processes.

Ironically, the world already produces more than enough food to feed its population. About half of it, however, goes to feed animals (some of which are eventually used for food—but mostly in the developed countries). Much food is lost to rot and pests because of poor storage practices. And much of it is wasted or consumed in excess by people in the industrialized nations, who routinely throw away food and eat far more than they need. And although significant advances have been made in food production in recent years—in the so-called green revolution, in which high-yielding grains doubled crop harvests—the new agriculture has had its

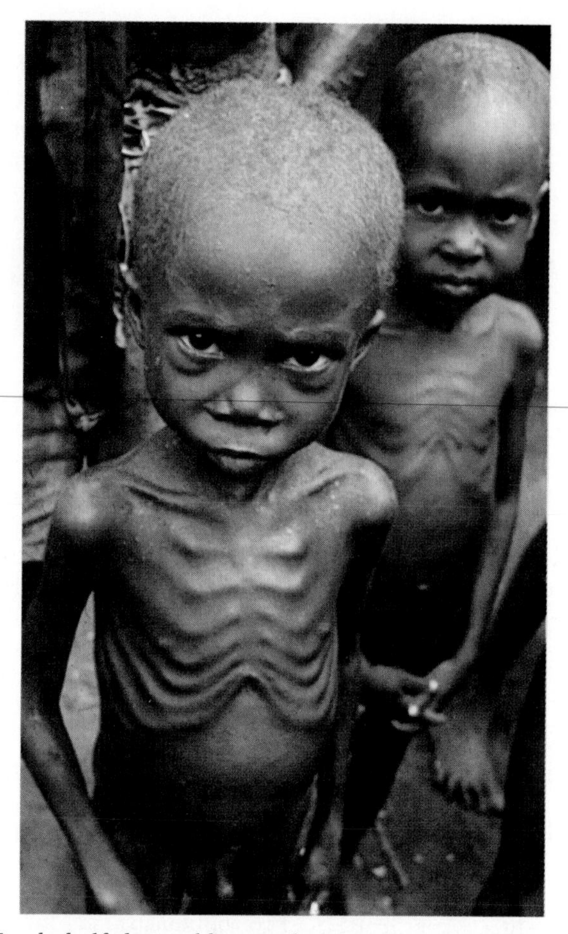

Nearly half the world's population is severely undernourished. Even though the world produces an adequate food supply for all of its inhabitants, much of it is wasted through poor storage or through excessive consumption in industrialized nations. (© S. Heydinger/Woodfin Camp & Assoc.)

costs. First, it requires the intensive use of fertilizers, which are made from oil and thus have become more expensive. Second, larger crops also mean larger crop failures when weather conditions destroy a harvest. Third, the new high-yield grains are genetically more uniform than older stocks, so when a disease attacks them, all may succumb (Enzer et al., 1978; Scrimshaw and Taylor, 1980).

The most practical goal for the future is to reduce population growth and to help the developing nations become more self-reliant (Selim, 1980). Agricultural self-sufficiency has not been easy for developing nations to achieve, however. The irony is that many developing countries must now buy so much food from the United States and other countries with a surplus that they have accumulated massive foreign debts, which leaves them with no funds to spend on their own agricultural development.

Population and Living Standards

When a country has too many people for its resources, most people live in poverty, the resources needed for capital development are used up, and its unemployment is high. In addition, overcrowding occurs, public services are strained, and the environment is polluted.

The social picture in the developing countries is generally bleak. Millions of people unable to find work in the countryside migrate to large cities in the hope of finding work. Unemployment and underemployment trap large segments of the population in poverty. As a result, cities such as Calcutta, Mexico City, and Cairo are becoming vast agglomerations of people surrounded by acres of miserable shantytowns in which residents live in houses made from packing crates and other urban refuse. Living five or six in a room, these people lack clean water, sanitation, decent food, and health care.

With such vast numbers of people cut off from even the rudiments of modern civilization it is little wonder that other urban services are also inadequate. Education and health care are virtually nonexistent in many areas, and entire families live out their lives without ever going to school or seeing a doctor.

An additional misfortune for the developing countries has been environmental destruction. When people need to produce food by any possible method, slash-and-burn agriculture, overcropping, and overgrazing may result in the destruction of farmland. When trees and other vegetation are removed to provide timber, firewood, or farmland the land may be eroded so severely that it turns into desert. None of these problems is caused solely by the demographic surplus, but it aggravates existing economic, political, and social difficulties.

Conflicting Perspectives

A sharp debate has opened in recent years over which way the world's population trends are headed (Holden,

1983). One appraisal is pessimistic; the other optimistic. The gloomy view is reflected in the *Global 2000 Report*, issued in 1980 by the Carter administration. It predicted, "If present trends continue, the world in 2000 will be more crowded, more polluted, less stable ecologically and more vulnerable to disruption than the world we live in now" (quoted by Boffey, 1983:9). This assessment is shared by the Worldwatch Institute, a privately financed research organization. It finds that if the present 2 percent rate of world economic growth continues into the foreseeable future, nearly half of the world's people, primarily in third-world nations, will have lower incomes and declining living standards. Most affected will be those African, Middle Eastern, and Central American nations where populations are expanding at 3 percent or more a year (King, 1983).

Worldwatch analysts say that virtually all the world's productive land is currently under cultivation. As new cropland has become scarce and as fertile topsoils have eroded, the growth in world food output has slowed. A combination of rising energy costs and diminishing returns from the use of chemical fertilizers has contributed to the leveling off of food production. Matters are complicated by increased emissions of environmental pollutants and the buildup of toxic chemicals in food chains. Most of the world's other biological systems—forests, grasslands, and fisheries—are also deteriorating. And essential nonrenewable resources, such as petroleum and natural gas, and nonfuel minerals, such as tungsten, tin, and platinum, are rapidly being depleted. Consequently, a smaller amount of each resource is available for each person. As world population increases, the problem grows. In sum, these investigations contend that the world is on the edge of an environmental crisis that is impairing the global economy.

The pessimistic perspective follows in the Malthusian tradition that portrays the "population problem" as resulting from a rapidly growing population pressing on limited resources. Quite a different view emerges from the highly controversial writings of the futurist Herman Kahn (1979) and the economist Julian L. Simon (1981). Simon rejects the idea that resources are finite. Throughout human history Simon finds that enterprising management and resourceful technicians have discovered new reserves of minerals, have made increasingly efficient use of lower-grade ore, and have found substitutes for many other minerals. Thus, not too long ago ships were dispatched to kill whales for their oil; then blankets were spread over oily pools and the petroleum extracted by wringing the blankets by hand; more recently holes were drilled in the earth to release deposits

As urban areas have expanded, agricultural areas have shrunk. This aerial view of Santa Clara County, California, graphically demonstrates this fact. (Dan McCoy/Rainbow)

of oil. Based on historical trends, Simon expects the future to bring declining scarcity, falling real prices, and increased wealth.

Simon also claims that our water and air are less polluted now than in 1900. In nineteenth-century cities coal smoke, horse manure, and human excrement posed severe health hazards. When these problems were mastered, life expectancies increased. And to nail down the point, he notes that Lake Erie is again teeming with fish.

Simon contends that the key to the recurring problem associated with the depletion of resources is not a lowering of population growth. He sees the human mind as "the ultimate resource," and hence the "amount of improvement depends on the number of people available to use their minds" (1981:197). Wealth is not a fixed quantity; it is produced by people. Thus the more people, the greater the wealth. The human mind gives us technological marvels, which Simon believes will continue to increase yields per acre and will afford humankind ample food. Indeed, he notes that birth rates are falling throughout the world in response to the demographic transition. Simon holds that the world will sort itself out if left to its own devices, a view that many demographers have criticized as naïve if not downright wrong. In sum, pessimistic and optimistic analysts draw on many of the *same* data sources only to arrive at startlingly different conclusions (Holden, 1983).

Women's Status and Reducing Growth

Traditionally, marriage in developing countries has been universal—and early. Women have received little or no formal education and have usually had no alternative to the customary style of motherhood—numerous pregnancies, with several children dying in infancy. A reduction in birth rates in such societies clearly involves a change in women's role (Cramer, 1980; Stevens, 1981).

It has often been noted that families will not change their pattern of childbearing until they are motivated to do so. A reduction in infant mortality can be one important motivating factor. Another is the expansion of basic education, especially for girls (Rindfuss et al., 1980). When girls stay in school longer, they marry later. They may also be able to obtain some kind of work, thus bettering their status. Schooling also presents both young men and young women with the idea of an alternative future. And education helps reduce suspicion of social change, making contraception a less frightening idea. Thus governments in many developing countries seek to expand educational opportunities for women as a means of slowing population growth. Government programs may also encourage women to enter the labor force so that women have other ways than motherhood to gain society's respect. Women with jobs are much less likely to have children than women not working outside the home. The lower fertility rate of employed women reflects the time constraints of coordinating motherhood and employment (U.S. Census Bureau, 1978).

One indication of women's changing status worldwide is the increasing availability of contraceptives, which usually put the ability to control births into the hands of the woman. However, modern contraceptives are still not available to much of the world's population. In the developing countries, nearly 80 percent of couples "at risk" do not have access to (or for other reasons do not use) contraception (Green and Fearey, 1978). Although some couples manage to limit their families by traditional methods (abstinence, withdrawal, rhythm), there is a clear need for the diffusion of contraceptive information and devices. When these are widely available and free, the birth rate can fall dramatically. In China, for example, contraceptives and abortions are free and available to all (and the government has promoted birth control by an array of rewards and penalties). The result, in recent years, has been a drop in the birth rate by approximately 50 percent (Adams and Winston, 1980).

POPULATION AND HEALTH

A basic force underlying the demographic transition has been health. As European populations got healthier, fewer people, especially babies, died. Eventually, people adjusted their habits and responded by having fewer babies. The developing nations that today have a low life expectancy (of forty-five years or so) have populations that suffer from many infectious diseases. In contrast, the populations of nations like ours, with a high life expectancy, have far more of the chronic diseases associated with old age. Thus population and health are intimately and subtly intertwined.

Population and health are also linked to other facets

The Chinese government actively campaigns for birth control with billboards such as this one, which promotes the one-child family. (Owen Franken)

of social life (Russell, 1983). Infectious diseases have shaped history profoundly. When the peoples of Western societies, protected by immunity to diseases endemic in their localities, first came in contact with peoples in the Americas and other parts of the world, the effects were devastating. Smallpox, measles, scarlet fever, tuberculosis, and other infectious diseases spread rampantly among the native populations, contributing greatly to the European conquest of the New World. And until recently, soldiers in war suffered more serious losses from disease than from enemy weaponry. At the turn of the century British deaths from disease in the South African Boer War were five time higher than deaths from combat casualties. Let us consider at greater length some of the social aspects and implications of health.

The Role of Medicine in Health

Medical advances are commonly credited with the tremendous improvement in health experienced by the United States and Western nations in the nineteenth and early twentieth centuries. Vaccines, immunizations, sulfa drugs, the discovery of anesthesia, and modern surgery are widely credited with having eliminated many of the epidemics and diseases that plagued our great-grandparents and their parents.

More careful study of mortality patterns both here and in England, however, shows that the miracles of modern medicine have had little to do with this transformation (McKeown, 1976; McKinlay and McKinlay, 1977). First, most of the decline in the death rate occurred *before* the discovery of effective drugs and vaccinations. For instance, the U. S. death rate from tuberculosis dropped from 200 per 100,000 Americans in 1900 to 70 per 100,000 in the 1930s—*before* lung-collapse therapy or even rest in sanatoriums was widely prescribed. The rate dropped to 30 per 100,000 before effective chemotherapy became available in the 1950s (Mahler, 1980). Second, in many cases the rate of decline did not increase much after the introduction of effective medicine, suggesting that only part of subsequent declines can be credited to medicine. What, then, caused the great decline in death rates and the elimination of most infectious diseases as major killers? In the case of water- and food-borne diseases such as cholera and typhoid, the key was clean water, safe milk, and public sanitation. In the case of air-borne diseases the key was a better-fed, better-housed, better-clothed, and thus stronger and more resistant population.

And what of health today? Modern medicine surely eases the pain and shortens the course of many illnesses. However, the incidence of such illnesses as heart disease, cancer, and stroke are increased by personal habits and environmental factors that are little affected by strictly medical advances. In particular, Americans are harmed by their rich, fatty diet (and the obesity that often accompanies it), their tendency to smoke too much and exercise too little, their polluted environment, and the stresses of modern life. The other major causes of disease, about which we can as yet do little, are genetic, geriatric, and psychiatric.

The Environment and Health

Environmental quality is closely linked to health. Poisons emanating from smokestacks, toxic waste dumps, nuclear reactors, and hazardous products have been implicated in a variety of diseases, including cancer. Indeed, even though many Americans hope that some miraculous new drug will be discovered to cure cancer, many medical researchers have looked to more commonplace solutions. Since up to 80 percent of cancers are tied to environmental factors, they have suggested that many cancers may be preventable by altering environmental conditions, including one's life style.

Perhaps one of the most striking relationships between people's life style and disease is the strong association between cigarette smoking and lung cancer. Lung cancer is also linked with air pollution in cities with high concentrations of industry and vehicular traffic (Hanley, 1982). And lung cancer is higher along the Gulf Coast of

Residents of Times Beach, Missouri were forced to leave their homes in December 1982 when repeated floods revealed the presence of extensive infiltration of the chemical dioxin into the environment. Clean-up crews had to wear special protective suits to prevent contact with the highly toxic substance (Scott Dine/ Picture Group.)

Louisiana and in the Southeast and the Northeast—all areas where chemical, paper, and petroleum industries are dominant. And asbestos workers run a much higher risk for lung cancer and mesotheliona (a rare cancer of the lining of the lung) than do people in the population at large.

The prevalence of the various kinds of cancers differs from one part of the world to another (Maugh, 1982). When people migrate from their home culture to a foreign one—Japanese moving to the United States or European Jews to Israel—they display the cancer patterns of their adopted country within a few generations. For instance, the high amount of animal fat in the diet of Western nations is closely linked with high rates of cancer of the breast, uterus, and large bowel. The rate of uterine cancer in the United States is six times higher than in Nigeria and Japan where average fat consumption is only 40 grams per day (compared with 150 grams per day in the United States).

People's occupations also increase their risk of contracting certain types of cancer. Researchers at the Harvard School of Public Health find that the rate of leukemia is 78 percent higher among shoe-factory workers than in the population at large. Prostate cancer is 156 percent higher among welders; esophagus cancer 97 percent higher among plumbers; oral cavity and pharynx cancer 152 percent higher among workers in printing trades; and multiple myeloma 186 percent higher among carpenters. The environment is implicated in still other occupation-related diseases, including black-lung disease among coal miners and chronic bronchitis and emphysema among textile workers.

Shifts in the environment can also trigger new epidemics. An opportunistic germ may seize on a slight environmental change (Russell, 1983). Toxic shock syndrome is an example of a microbe that adapted itself to a product designed for feminine hygiene—tampons with greater absorbency, which provided a hospitable home for staphylococcus microbes. Similarly, Legionnaire's disease surfaced in 1976 as a puzzling pneumonia epidemic among American Legion conventioneers. The germ had lived harmlessly in soil and water for thousands of years. It found a hospitable new environment in modern plumbing and air-conditioning systems.

The AIDS (Acquired Immune Deficiency Syndrome) epidemic, which began in the United States in 1981, affords still another illustration (Altman, 1983). It was initially identified among homosexuals in a scattering of cities and later among drug addicts and hemophiliacs. The disease wipes out the body's immune system and invites in its wake a rare type of cancer (called Kaposi's sarcoma) and various life-threatening infections. AIDS appears to have taken advantage of changes in technology and life style. It is spread by random sexual activity, the sharing of needles among drug addicts, and the use of blood banks by hemophiliacs. The disease has touched off intense fear and anxiety in homosexual communities and changed the life patterns of countless homosexuals. More recently, the disease has struck other groups so that for many Americans AIDS has come to conjure up the image of something out of *The Andromeda Strain*. These fears have triggered one of the most intensive investigations of an epidemic in medical history.

The World Health Situation

Good health is a fundamental goal of people throughout the world. Indeed, the World Health Organization (WHO) recognizes it as a basic human right. As defined by the WHO, an international health agency made up of 155 nations, health is "a state of complete physical, mental, and social well-being, and not merely the absence of disease or infirmity." Among the countries of the world, there is a strong correlation between a nation's per capita gross national product and such indices of health as its infant mortality and life expectancy. In the more developed nations the infant mortality rate is under 20 per 1,000 infants; in the poorest regions it ranges up to half of all infants (most of these deaths are traceable to malnutrition and diarrheal and infectious disorders). Similarly, life expectancy at birth is about seventy-two years in developed countries, but it is only forty-nine in Africa and fifty-one in southern Asia (Mahler, 1980).

The pattern of disease in underdeveloped nations differs appreciably from that in developed nations. Infectious, parasitic, and respiratory diseases cause more than 40 percent of the deaths in developing nations. By comparison, they cause about 10 percent of deaths in industrialized countries, where the chief causes of death are heart and vascular diseases and cancer. The most widespread diseases in poorer regions are diarrheal ones transmitted by human fecal contamination of food,

THE SOCIOLOGICAL EYE ON:

The Health and Social Costs of the Arms Race

> Every gun that is made, every warship launched, every rocket fired signifies in the final sense a theft from those who hunger and are not fed, those who are cold and are not clothed. This world in arms is not spending money alone. It is spending the sweat of its laborers, the genius of its scientists, the houses of its children.
>
> —President Dwight D. Eisenhower, April 16, 1953

We often ask what could happen to people and the environment should some of the nuclear weapons in the world's arsenals be detonated. In recent years scientists have clearly outlined the catastrophic destruction that nuclear war would entail. However, a related matter that is seldom discussed has enormous implications for the health of people: the ever-growing expenditures for military weapons (Sidel, 1983). Much of the hunger and disease in the world could be prevented were a fraction of the resources now expended on arms redirected to the basic needs of people. One analysis puts the total military expenditures of all nations at over $600 billion a year, more than $1 million a minute (Sivard, 1982).

The arms race has many indirect consequences for people's health (Sidel, 1983). First, massive arms investments divert capital and human resources away from the modernization and development of the productive capacities of civilian economies. Second, large arms expenditures feed inflation, undercutting the purchasing power of people's money. And third, expenditures for military production create fewer jobs than do expenditures for human services. For instance, $1 billion spent on arms generates 76,000 jobs, but the same amount spent on health care generates 138,000 jobs and on education, 187,000 jobs.

When governments spend large sums on arms, revenues are diverted from health and other human services. For instance, for the cost of three Army AH–64 helicopters, the $90 million necessary to return the funding of community health centers to their former level could be restored to the budget. And the cost of two and a half F–15A airplanes is equal to the $75 million in Los Angeles health care cuts that closed eight county health-care clinics. In addition, the arms race diverts highly skilled and trained people away from scientific research and health activities and to military functions. Over half of the federal research and development budget is currently spent for military research. And more than 50 percent of the world's research physicists and engineering scientists work only for the military.

Two of every three nations of the world spend more public funds on arms than on health services. Yet on a world scale, more than 40,000 children die every day from malnutrition and infection. The cost of six hours of arms spending would immunize 100 million newborns each year against childhood diseases. The cost of six months of world arms spending would pay for a ten-year program providing food and health services to underdeveloped nations. Clearly, the health and survival of the peoples of the world is dramatically linked to expenditures for arms (Sidel, 1983).

water, and soil; only about a third of the people in underdeveloped nations have access to safe water. Parasitic diseases such as malaria and schistosomiasis also tend to be widespread, infecting a quarter of the world's population. Malaria, which is transmitted by mosquitoes, is the most prevalent disease worldwide, despite the fact that it can be prevented by the routine administration of inexpensive drugs. Schistosomiasis—caused by a snailborn parasite—infects some 200 million people. Both malaria and schistosomiasis are chronic and debilitating diseases that sap the energy and strength of their victims.

Many underdeveloped countries spend a major portion of their health budgets on establishing medical schools and building hospital complexes. Yet this approach addresses the health problems of only 10 to 15 percent of the population, chiefly members of elites. The resources are used mainly to cure disease with increasingly expensive technology (intensive care units, bypass surgery, "life-support" systems, and whole-body scanners). However, the health needs of the population at large would be better served by an attack on parasitic and infectious agents, programs of preventive medicine, more and better food, and the elimination of contaminated drinking water. Malnutrition and parasitic and infectious diseases continue to be the principal sources of suffering, disability, and death in the poorer nations. Inasmuch as the incidence of most of these conditions can be dramatically reduced at relatively modest cost, the problems they cause are largely unnecessary and preventable. (See the boxed insert on the health and social costs of the arms race.)

Currently, four-fifths of the world's population does not have access to any permanent form of health care. The public health services of the 67 poorest nations, excluding China, spend less on health care than the richer nations spend on tranquilizers alone. Moreover, richer nations (chiefly, Australia, Canada, West Germany, the United Kingdom, and the United States) are attracting physicians from the poorer ones. Although it costs eight times more to train a physician than to train a medical auxiliary, many poorer countries still continue to emphasize training physicians. If the goal of good health is to be achieved for the great masses of the world's population, existing health care strategies will have to be vigorously transformed (Mahler, 1980, 1981).

Poverty and Health

Poverty is linked to poor health throughout the world. The United States is no exception (see Figure 16.5). The medical care received by the rural and urban ghetto poor is often inferior to that received by more advantaged Americans. The health of the poor is often undermined by less adequate diets, poorly heated homes, and the stress of struggling to get by, which weaken them and make them more vulnerable to disease.

Americans spend more on health care than any other nation in the world, yet statistically we are not the world's healthiest nation. Although our overall infant mortality rate has continued to fall, it is edging upward

This figure indicates a relationship between health and income in the United States. The less money people make, the less likely they are to report themselves as having excellent health.

FIGURE 16.5 Self-Assessment of Health by Income, 1976–1977

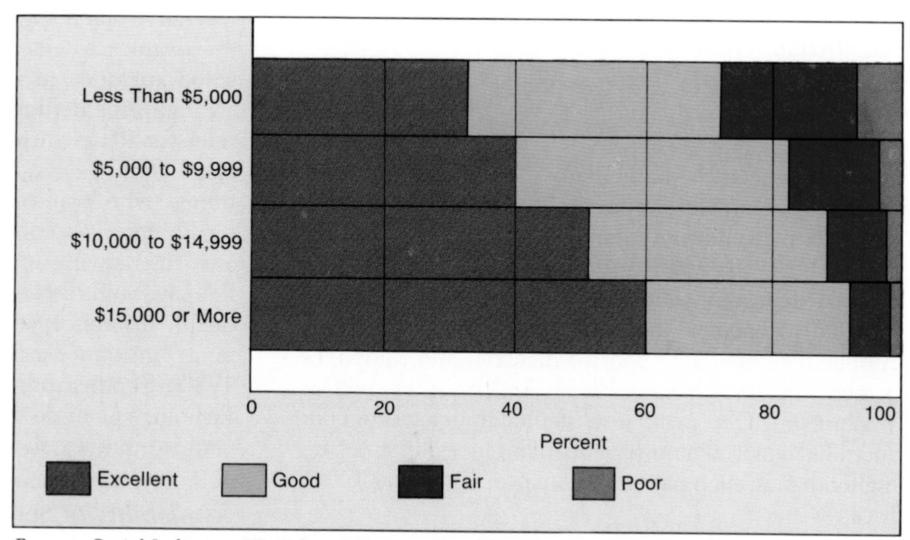

Source: Department of Commerce, Census Bureau, *Social Indicators III: Selected Data on Social Conditions and Trends in the U.S.* (Washington, D.C.: U.S. Government Printing Office (December 1980), p. 64.

This impoverished family in rural Maine show the physical effects of inadequate diets and inferior health care. (Arthur Grace/Stock, Boston.)

again in some areas, particularly in states where reductions in government aid have forced cutbacks in prenatal, maternal, and preventative health services. During the early 1980s when unemployment in Michigan reached depression levels, hard hit cities like Warren reported a 53 percent increase in its infant mortality rate; Pontiac registered a 17 percent increase, and Flint a 12 percent increase (Noble, 1983). And in cities such as Washington, D.C., with a substantial underclass of poor and disadvantaged families, the infant mortality rates are higher than in such nations as Jamaica, Cuba, and Costa Rica.

Unfortunately for the poor, there is a cycle of poverty and illness. The poorer you are, the sicker you are likely to become. And the sicker you are, the poorer you are likely to become. Moreover, the poor not only get the diseases of poverty, such as tuberculosis and other infectious diseases; they also suffer more from the so-called diseases of affluence—cancer and heart disease. Why? Because their diet is more fatty and they are exposed to more pollutants and other cancer-causing agents. And above all, their life is frequently more stressful.

Health Care in America

What actions can be taken to improve America's health? The evidence suggests that we should focus on *prevention*—through cleaning up the environment (much as the public health movement in the nineteenth century cleaned up drinking water and pasteurized milk) and health education. This would include passing regulations to control industrial pollution, adopting safety standards for automobiles, and controlling exposure to toxic and cancer-causing substances, as well as encouraging people to eat a healthful diet, keep their weight down, exercise, and stop smoking. Unfortunately, our nation's health resources are primarily channeled in another direction. Our health care establishment emphasizes high-technology medical intervention *after* we get sick.

Traditionally, individual doctors in the United States have been highly independent, choosing their specialty, practicing where they want to in the manner they want, and charging whatever they want to patients who want (and can afford) to see them. This freedom has created some desirable diversity, but it also has its dark side, for it has meant that such sociological factors as class, family background, and education have determined who could get good health care. Essentially, health care is a commodity that can be purchased like any other—with unfortunate results for those who cannot pay. Some 20 to 25 million Americans currently lack health insurance, and another 19 million have inadequate insurance against large medical bills (Mahler, 1980). In other industrialized countries, national health insurance plans do much to ensure that adequate health care is more widely available.

Availability of Service

Physicians in America are unevenly distributed, both geographically and professionally. There is no doctor at all in 135 counties and 5,000 towns in America. There are 260 doctors for every 100,000 people in Westchester County, New York, but only 82 per 100,000 in Mississippi. The shortage of doctors is as acute in urban ghettos as it is in rural areas. Some 49 million Americans live in areas officially designated as medically underserved—22 million in urban areas and 27 million in rural areas (Mahler, 1980). The reason is obvious: Doctors would rather practice among the affluent. As a result, poor Americans and those who live in rural areas have a much harder time finding doctors than other Americans do. Rather than lose working time, many pay no attention to health problems until they become acute.

Doctors are also unevenly distributed professionally. Seventy-four percent of the nation's physicians are specialists. This country needs an estimated 133 general practitioners per 100,000 population for quality medical care, but the national average is about 26 per 100,000 (AMA, 1980). As a result, even middle-class families in affluent communities have trouble obtaining personalized care for general medical problems.

Another problem is that American medicine emphasizes treatment more than prevention. In recent years, health maintenance organizations (HMOs) have been set up in an effort to solve this problem. In an HMO, doctors are paid a flat sum per patient for the year, which motivates them to keep patients out of the office (or hospital) rather than in it. Since 1973, enrollment in HMOs has quadrupled from 3 million to 12 million members (Trafford, 1983).

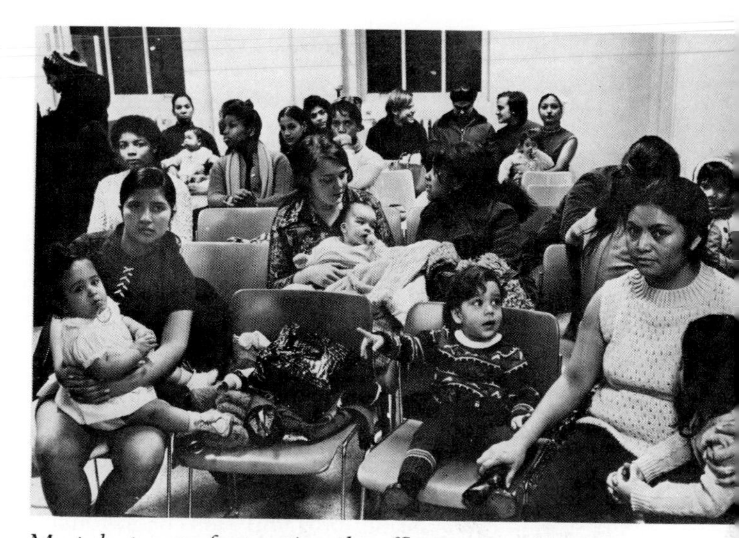

Most doctors prefer treating the affluent to working in an urban ghetto. Consequently, hospitals in poor urban neighborhoods are often understaffed, and people may have to wait hours to see a doctor. (Barbara Pfeffer/Photo Researchers.)

Neglect of Preventive Medicine

Until recently, preventive medicine has been neglected in America. The drama of open-heart surgery gets more attention than the practicality of a low-fat diet that may lower the risk of heart disease. The absence of adequate prevention takes its greatest toll with children. A 1975 survey found one-fourth of the children in the United States to be anemic (Kennedy, 1976). Only about 10 percent of children with mental health problems receive care, and child abuse was legally unrecognized until just a few years ago. As a nation, we spend less on pediatrics than on any other medical speciality, and fewer children are covered by health insurance than are members of any other age group.

The children of the poor suffer the most. The infant mortality rate for blacks, more of whom are poor, is twice that for whites. One-third of the women who give birth in public hospitals receive no prenatal care, and many are malnourished. Low birth weights are linked to various birth defects, including mental retardation (Holmes et al., 1982). Poor children grow up malnourished, and they are exposed to special environmental dangers as well, such as lead poisoning, worms, and rat bites (*America's Children*, 1976, 1978; Sidel, 1983). Low birth weight, malnutrition, disease, and lack of care eventually take their toll—often showing up as behavior problems and low school achievement. Thus health problems contribute to educational deficiencies, which reduce potential—and the cycle of poverty begins again.

New Concepts in Health Care

The inadequacies of the American health care system have brought the practice of medicine under increasing scrutiny (McDermott, 1980). The current arrangement, centered on a personal encounter with the physician, has served Americans well in meeting health problems that require a direct one-to-one relationship with a doctor. However, many of the nation's health problems are so closely related to the environment and to people's life styles that they can be addressed only by new alternative strategies.

Community Health Programs

There is a growing recognition in medical circles that any attempt to improve the health status of a population requires the active participation of people themselves. Good health care requires more than medical professionals and high technology. People are the ones who must decide whether they will utilize particular services. And people must have an informed basis for making appropriate decisions concerning their own health on a day-by-day basis. This awareness has brought to the forefront the importance of community health programs. Such programs are based on the notion that people are not simply passive recipients of health services but active agents in promoting healthful practices and in preventing and treating illness.

Community health programs aim to encourage health habits—diet, exercise, and life style—that result in significantly longer and healthier lives. They can also play a part in preventing some types of illness. Rheumatic fever is a case in point. Once contracted, the disease tends to recur or to leave lifelong damage. Its prevention depends on the prompt and adequate treatment of streptococcal infections. Rheumatic fever has decreased 60 percent in those areas of Baltimore that have had comprehensive community care programs, but it has remained unchanged in other areas (McDermott, 1980).

Hospice Programs

The humane care of the dying has long represented another neglected area in our medical system. The void has existed in part because hospitals are geared to curing patients and sending them home as quickly as possible. Incurable cases, particularly terminally ill cancer patients, are viewed as an embarrassment to institutionalized medicine, evidence of its failure. Indeed, modern medicine is often perceived to be the enemy rather than the friend of the terminally ill. "Aggressive" medical care in an era of advanced technology prevents many people from dying quickly and naturally and compromises basic human considerations and sensitivities.

The hospice movement has sprung up over the past two decades to provide an alternative care arrangement for the dying (DuBois, 1980). It originated in England and has since spread to the United States. Hospice programs are designed to allow the terminally ill to live with as little pain as possible and to provide them and their loved ones with emotional support.

Hospice care can be given in a variety of settings. A hospice may be an independent facility or a unit attached to a hospital. The center is made as homelike as possible. Family members may stay overnight and pets are not excluded. However, the emphasis of most hospice programs is on maintaining the patient at home. Indeed, some hospices exist solely as medical vans that make regular rounds, with visiting physicians, nurses, social workers, and volunteers available to assist with a patient's emotional and physical care.

The hospice and hospital differ in their attitude toward pain control. In hospitals the basic expectation is that every patient should get better. Thus the relief of pain is weighed against its long-term consequences. Morphine is administered with the thought that the patient should not be allowed to become addicted to it. But the hospice provides round-the-clock doses of whatever medication works best in dosages that not only relieve pain but also prevent it from occurring. The emphasis of hospice programs falls on giving comfort and care rather than on prolonging life. And a follow-up program maintains contact with family members after a loved one's death to assist them in their bereavement. In the last analysis, hospice care is geared to restoring dignity to the dying process.

This terminally ill patient is in a hospice, a homelike setting where the staff is trained to provide comfort and support for the dying. (Abraham Menashe/Photo Researchers.)

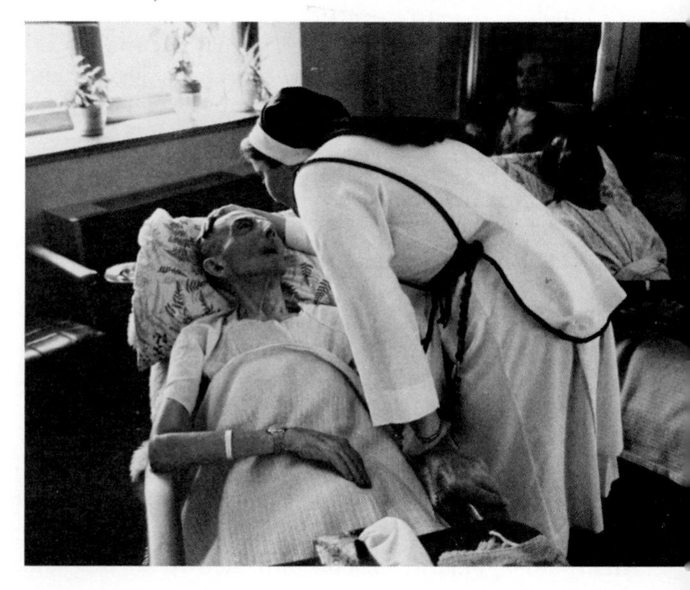

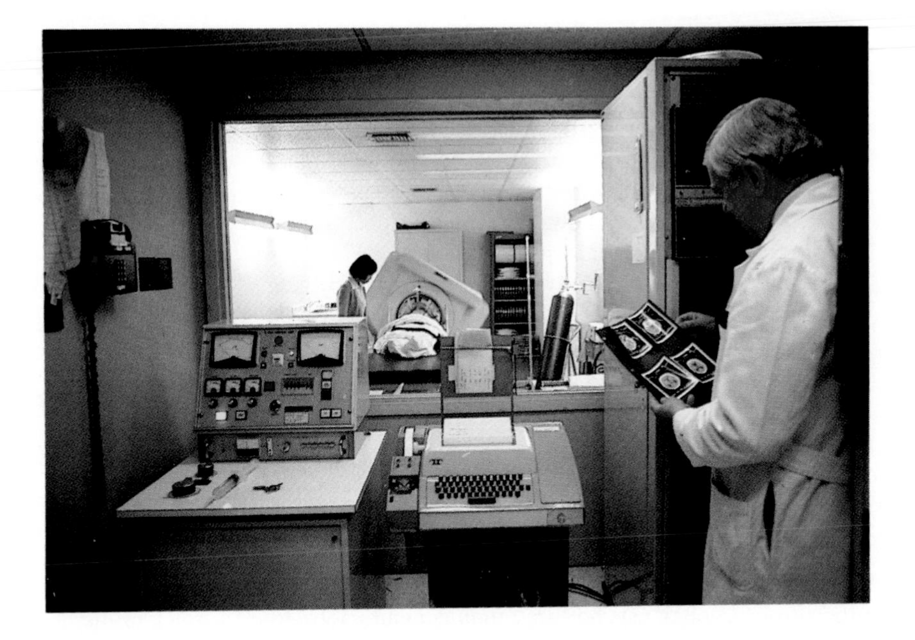

Advanced medical equipment, such as this CAT scanner, has brought benefits to many patients. But it has also caused a steep rise in health care costs. (Bill Gallery/Stock, Boston.)

Future Trends in American Health Care

Depending on what aspects of American life you examine, you can find reason to be either optimistic or pessimistic about our national health. On the positive side, people are increasingly aware of what they eat. More people are reading food labels and are trimming excess fat and sugar from their diets. More people are exercising regularly, as the number of joggers, bicyclists, and roller skaters attests. Concern for improving health extends beyond the individual; large corporations are beginning to take an interest in preventive medicine, in large part to cut their medical benefit programs. Some have provided their employees with exercise facilities or time off for exercise, for example. And health insurance companies are beginning to sponsor health maintenance organizations.

On the environmental front, however, the future looks somewhat bleaker. A good many industrial chemicals and synthetic substances released into the environment in large quantity have been found to be carcinogenic. Toxic agents—pesticides and other chemicals—are beginning to be found in sources of drinking water. And even after a decade of effort aimed at cleaning up the air, it remains unhealthful in many urban areas. With cutbacks in federal enforcement agencies, such as the Occupational Safety and Health Administration, these problems are likely to worsen.

The central reason why United States life expectancy and infant mortality statistics are worse than those of most industrialized nations is that we have far more people living in poverty than they do. If, for example, the infant mortality rate of the poor was the same as that of the middle-class, college-educated population, then the United States would have one of the lowest infant mortality rates. Most industrialized nations have welfare systems that virtually eliminate poverty, and none of them has a history of discrimination against such a large percentage of the population. The drastic effects of poverty on the people and the nation can be seen in the fact that when the infant mortality rates of America's poor and blacks are separated out from those of whites, the United States gets a high health rating.

Opposition to the rising costs of medical care is triggering major changes in the American health-care system (Trafford, 1983). Hospital-room costs have risen by about 14 percent every year since 1970. Spending on overall health care has more than tripled over the past decade to $362 billion; by 1993 the figure is expected to top $1 trillion. Roughly a third of the increase in cost over the past two decades has resulted from new medical technology, including such items as computerized axial tomography, nuclear-magnetic resonance, and CAT scanners. Physicians have also acquired new skills. Coronary-bypass surgery for heart disease was unknown fifteen years ago; today it is the most frequently performed heart operation, at a total cost of about $4 billion a year. Another factor in the rising costs of health care has been the increasing number of elderly, who typically have more complicated and severe diseases. And finally, since doctors and hospitals have traditionally been paid for their services whether or not patients benefit from them, few incentives have existed for not using all available medical techniques (estimates vary as to how many procedures are actually performed unnecessarily, but 30 percent is a generally accepted figure).

The mounting cost of medical service is bringing about growing pressure to cap the rising spiral. Since 1983, Medicare has paid hospitals a predetermined amount based on each patient's diagnosed problem. Previously, hospitals were reimbursed for itemized daily charges. With a fixed price per patient, hospitals are exerting pressure on physicians to prescribe only essential care and to cut down on unnecessary diagnostic tests. Medical-care experts also are looking to new ways to keep people out of hospitals, including expansion of health maintenance organizations (HMOs) and hospice programs and provision for kidney dialysis at home. If present trends are not reversed, by the year 2000 one dollar out of every seven dollars of the gross national product will be spent on medical care (Trafford, 1983).

EPILOGUE

Population and health touch all aspects of social life. Take population size. Explosive population growth in many third-world nations compels their leaders to divert funds from capital expenditures that generate jobs to population maintenance—food, housing, and health care (Chapter 11). Even moderate success in economic development cannot be translated into an improved quality of life for the citizens of these countries. At the same time rapid population growth overtaxes educational institutions and contributes to a rising tide of illiteracy (Chapter 14). And health and medical systems cannot cope with the malnutrition and infectious diseases found in crowded and improverished environments. In many countries population pressures are intensifying internal tensions and contributing to political instability (Chapter 18 and 19). These problems often spill over into neighboring nations, which are seen as sancturaries for insurgents and refugees (Chapter 12).

The distribution of people within a country also has far-reaching consequences. The massive exodus of middle-class Americans from the nation's central cities to the suburbs is undermining the tax base of the cities and in many cases speeding their economic decline (Chapter 17). Simultaneously, the clustering of poorer Americans in the central cities has intensified many of the nation's welfare and housing problems (Chapter 10). The clustering of people and industries also has consequences for the environment, often leading to the pollution of the air, land, and water of the localities. Nationally the migration of Americans from Mid-Western states troubled by the decline of their smokestack industries to the South and West is contributing to major dislocations in the use and availability of major services. And internationally a brain drain is drawing professionals, technicians, and skilled workers who are desperately needed by their home countries in Africa and Asia to the United States and other developed nations.

Changes in the composition of a population similarly have implications for a society. The steep rise in the proportion of elderly Americans is placing severe strains on the support and care systems for older citizens. A proportionately smaller work force is paying Social Security taxes, while growing numbers of people collect benefits over a longer span of time. This shift has also had political consequences, with older Americans emerging as a vocal and effective interest group (Chapter 11). The combined membership of the American Association of Retired Persons, the National Retired Teachers Association, and the National Council of Senior Citizens now exceeds 12 million. By the same token the growing proportion of Americans in their middle years is structuring "roadblocks" to the occupational mobility of younger Americans (Chapter 10). In the chapters that follow on urban life, collective behavior, and social change we follow up on some of the ramifications of these demographic forces.

SUMMARY

Demography is the study of how births, deaths, and migration affect the composition, size, and distribution of populations. The *census* is a periodic counting of the population and a collection of data about it. This compilation of vital statistics is the demographer's major source of data.

Population growth depends on the relationship between three demographic variables: births, deaths, and net migration. The rate of population growth is the extent to which births and immigration exceed deaths and emigration.

Thomas Malthus was the first scholar to analyze population growth and to worry about its consequences for humankind. He felt that increases in food supply could never keep pace with population growth. Malthus thought that the only way to halt population growth was by voluntary abstinence from sexual relations; otherwise, population would be checked drastically by war, pestilence, or starvation. Karl Marx took exception to Malthusian doctrine, believing that the problem was not primarily one of population but one of the ownership of the means of production and the inequitable distribution of the world's wealth.

The basic model of population change in the West over the past two centuries is known as the *demographic transition*. In stage one, a high, steady birth rate and an equally high death rate, which shot up during epidemics and famines, kept the rate of population growth low. In the second phase, the death rate began to decline as public hygiene and sanitation improved, and better food supplies became available. Populations grew rapidly. Finally, as in the industrialized nations of today, the death rate is low and steady, while the birth rate is low but fluctuates with social trends.

Malthusian growth still haunts the developing parts of the world. There, the demographic transition has taken a different form as more advanced medical practices, better hygiene, and increased agricultural productivity greatly reduced the death rate within just a few years. The birth rates in these countries, however, have remained high, as has population growth. As population growth strains available resources, hunger, unemployment, overcrowding, and other social ills result. Birth control programs are effective only if they reinforce cultural trends toward smaller families.

Population patterns and a nation's health are intimately related. The leading causes of death in this country are, in large measure, the so-called diseases of affluence—although they afflict the poor as well. America has fallen behind other industrialized nations in health care. High costs, uneven distribution, and poor-quality care all affect medical services. The poor and the young in particular are not getting the care that is theoretically available. There is some hope for improvement in the nation's health, however: More people are watching their diets, exercising, and stopping smoking. People seem more health-conscious than ever before in our nation's history. As a result, more people are likely to live longer, and the ratio of older to younger people in the population will increase, leading to many changes in social and economic conditions.

GLOSSARY

Census. A periodic counting of the population, in which facts on age, sex, occupation, and so forth, are also recorded. In the United States the census is taken every tenth year and provides a wealth of statistical data for both demographers and social planners.

Cohort. Those people born in the same year.

Crude birth rate. The number of births per 1,000 people in a given year.

Crude death rate. The number of deaths per 1,000 people in a given year.

Demographic transition. A three-stage process in which a population shifts from a high birth rate and a high death rate to a low birth rate and a low death rate.

Demography. The statistical study of changes in population and the effects of these changes on society.

Emigration. The movement of people out of an area.

Fecundity. The biological potential for reproduction.

Fertility rate. The number of births per 1,000 women between the ages of fifteen and forty-four.

Immigration. The movement of people into an area.

Infant mortality rate. The number of deaths to infants in their first year of life per 1,000 live births in a given year.

Internal migration. The movement of people from one place to another within the same country.

International migration. The movement of people from one country to another.

Life expectancy. The average number of years of life remaining to a person of a given age.

Life span. The maximum number of years of a human life.

CHAPTER 17
Urban Life

In many ways the city has become the hallmark of modern society. Its teeming populace has inspired both wonder and aversion. When the German sociologist Max Weber visited Chicago at the turn of the century, he found it "incredible." He wrote that the city seemed "like a man whose skin has been peeled off and whose entrails one sees at work" (Gerth and Mills, 1958:15). Indeed, the city is an extraordinary human creation whose impact reaches far and wide. Whether individuals live near or far away from an urban center, its existence has profound effects on their behavior and life style.

Within cities people express their character and reveal their way of life in a striking and intense form. Since cities compress countless people and activities into a relatively small territory, they have provided poets, novelists, and chroniclers with a wealth of material for portraying human life. Charles Dickens's portrait of London, James Joyce's depiction of Dublin, and Honoré Balzac's representation of Paris have had a powerful influence on contemporary literature. And sociologists find in cities wonderful laboratories for studying the diversity of social life and the many forms in which it is contained.

In this chapter, we will explore the evolution of cities from the earliest historic times to the present. We will consider the dynamics of urban life. We will examine the problems cities confront and proposals to deal with them. And we will look into the future and examine significant trends for urban living.

THE URBAN TRANSFORMATION

Throughout history, cities have been characterized by certain features. One is their dependence on agricultural goods grown in outlying areas. Another is their social heterogeneity—the fact that residents of cities do not all belong to the same economic class or practice the same occupations. The residents distribute themselves within the city's confines according to income, social status, subculture, recency of arrival, and style of life. All these characteristics create a special urban culture that gives each city a special ambience and symbolism. And although cities are, richer in political, organizational, cultural, and human resources than villages, towns, and rural settlements, nonetheless they depend on the countryside for their basic subsistence. Hence, cities are powerful but dependent, a fact any definition must recognize. One widely used definition of a **city** depicts it as a relatively large, dense, and permanent settlement of socially diverse people who do not directly produce their own food (Wirth, 1938). This definition includes not only central cities like downtown New York or London but also the many suburban communities that typically surround them.

Cities are such a familiar part of our social landscape that we often forget how much they have shaped human culture. The formation of cities contributed to the development of writing, the calendar, and organized scientific inquiry. Complex stratification systems, institutionalized religions, and the centralized state are also associated with the emergence of cities. In short, modern civilization is very much a product of cities and the urban societies they spawned.

The Evolution of the City

For thousands of years, humans were nomadic creatures who traveled about in small families or bands, hunting, fishing, and foraging for food. Because the bounty of nature in most parts of the world was not plentiful enough to support more than a few persons in any one spot, humans would settle in one place for only a short time, and then move on. Without adequate means of storing supplies, people were unable to accumulate a surplus of food and therfore led a precarious existence (Childe, 1952).

The Neolithic Revolution

At the dawn of the Neolithic period, some 10,000 years ago, people discovered ways of cultivating plants and domesticating animals. They also developed simple tools for gardening and made pots for storage. These technological innovations allowed them to increase their food supply enough to abandon wandering for a permanent residence. The earliest villages were small by today's standards, housing only 200 to 400 people. These small villages were typical for the next 4,000 to 5,000 years (Childe, 1952).

The First True Cities

Sometime between 6000 and 5000 B.C., in the basins of the Nile, Tigris-Euphrates, and Indus river valleys, there emerged settlements more than ten times the size of any earlier ones. Housing between 7,000 and 20,000 persons, these first true cities developed largely because innovations in agriculture and transportation enabled people to take advantage of the valleys' exceptionally fertile soils. Thus the domestication of new, higher-yield grains and the development of the ox-drawn plow, irrigation, and metallurgy allowed the production of a very large food surplus. This surplus permitted some portion of the working population to take up occupations other than farming—artisan, trader, teacher, religious leader, lawmaker, soldier, and so forth. But this specialization of labor required that people live in close proximity to others on whom they depended. Relatively densely populated areas therefore became necessities, and cities began to increase in size and number.

Yet the emergence of cities cannot be explained strictly in economic terms. A centralized power structure is also needed for cities to grow and flourish (Sjoberg, 1960). A central "government" is essential so that diverse social and economic activities can be coordinated effectively. In addition, as populations become more heterogeneous, the need for formal law enforcement becomes more acute. Diverse urban groups have different, often competing interests, and their disputes and conflicts must be settled. The authority vested in lawmakers and judges is effective for this purpose. Thus it is no accident that the development of the first great cities coincided with the emergence of powerful political kingdoms. The city of Rome, for example, reached its zenith at about the same time the Roman Empire did. At its peak, life in Rome was remarkably sophisticated, from magnificent public architecture to such technological conveniences as aqueducts to transport the city's water. The grandeur of Rome was made possible in part by the collection of taxes from citizens of its Empire, which once covered most of Europe and much of northern Africa. When the military power of the Roman Empire was no longer sufficient to guarantee the payment of these taxes, its capital city collapsed. During most of the Middle Ages, from the fall of Rome in A.D. 500 until A.D. 1350, urban expansion and development in Europe were at a virtual standstill.

The Preindustrial City

Feudal technology in the Middle Ages typically limited the population in cities to no more than about 100,000 persons, although a few cities were much larger (see Table 17.1). Transportation methods were poorly developed, and it was difficult to bring in the bulky goods needed for construction and manufacturing. Without large-scale manufacturing, job opportunities were limited. Poor transportation systems also made it difficult to move food from farms to the city, a problem that was compounded by the lack of adequate means to store large

TABLE 17.1 Largest Cities Across Time

1360 B.C.	
Thebes (Greece)	100,000
Memphis (Egypt)	74,000
Babylon (Iraq)	54,000
Chengchow (China)	40,000
Khattushas (Turkey)	40,000
A.D. 1000	
Cordoba (Spain)	450,000
Constantinople (Turkey)	450,000
Kaifeng (China)	400,000
Sian (China)	300,000
Kyoto (Japan)	200,000
A.D. 1600	
Peking (China)	706,000
Constantinople (Turkey)	700,000
Agra (India)	500,000
Cairo (Egypt)	400,000
Osaka (Japan)	400,000
1925 A.D.	
New York	7,774,000
London	7,742,000
Tokyo	5,300,000
Paris	4,800,000
Berlin	4,013,000
Chicago	3,564,000
Ruhr	3,400,000
Buenos Aires	2,410,000
Osaka	2,219,000
Philadelphia	2,085,000
Vienna	1,862,000
Boston	1,773,000
Moscow	1,764,000

Source: United Nations data.

quantities of perishable goods. Poor communication methods made it hard to govern large regions outside the city. Sanitation methods and medical techniques were so primitive that dense urban settlements bred disease and epidemics. Thus the limited technology of the Middle Ages greatly restricted the size to which cities could grow. It was not until the early Renaissance, around the middle of the fourteenth century, that urban expansion resumed, spurred by an improved technological base and increased travel and trade.

During the Middle Ages, urban growth was limited by poorly developed methods of transportation, communication, and sanitation. As a result, preindustrial cities rarely had populations of more than 100,000. (Art Resource)

The Industrial Revolution and the Urban Explosion

A true explosion in urban development did not occur until the mid-eighteenth century with the Industrial Revolution. The Industrial Revolution brought with it technological innovations that reduced the constraints on the size and density of cities. New farming implements, new plant strains, and new ways of raising livestock increased food production dramatically. Because of increased productivity, far fewer workers were now needed on the farms. Displaced farmers and their families streamed into the cities in search of jobs, and the number of urban jobs was increasing due to the growth in factory production made possible by new machinery. New transportation systems also aided the explosive growth of cities. The spread of railroads allowed the city to reach faraway resources needed for growth. The development of cheap steel and the invention of the elevator made it possible for urban architects to build the cities higher, thus meeting the residential and office needs of an increasingly dense urban population. Innovations in public hygiene and in medical facilities cut the health risks that had plagued preindustrial cities. And under the impetus of nationalism, large territories were consolidated, making for larger internal markets, common coinage and weights, and an absence of domestic tariffs and duties on goods.

Within the United States, economic institutions played a powerful role in shaping urban growth (Powell, 1962). A business ideology contributed to a municipal organization that favored low taxes and minimal controls, providing a climate favorable to emerging enterprises. As the chief employer of the community, the industrial corporation fashioned a life style that favored submissiveness and the subordination of people to the goal of profit. And the progressive accumulation of capital in urban centers functioned as a powerful impetus for industrial and commercial growth that in turn served as a magnet to rural and foreign migrants.

Within a matter of decades, America became an urban nation. In 1850 we were a rural society, with only 15 percent of the population living in urban areas; by 1900 the proportion had increased to almost 40 percent. The turning point came around 1920, when more than half of all Americans were urban dwellers. Sixty years later, more than three-fourths of the population lived in towns or cities of more than 2,500 persons. Thus, within a few generations, America had shifted from a rural to an urban base (see Figure 17.1).

The Metropolis

By the turn of the twentieth century, American cities had extended their reach, and many became sprawling giants with indistinct edges. The central hub was a business and administrative center. Industrial areas were usually located outside this core and farther out were the residential areas. Beyond the political boundaries of the central city, suburbs arose. Simultaneously small neighboring towns and cities were brought within the social and economic orbit of the central city. These areas linked, forming the modern **metropolis.** The rise of such metropolitan areas has led the federal government to view as a metropolitan entity "a geographical area with a large population nucleus together with adjacent communities which have a high degree of economic and social integration with that nucleus" (Herbers, 1983d).

The growth of the metropolis has had far-reaching consequences for urban life (Ekerstein and Frisbie, 1982). Sub-areas specialize, becoming primarily residential, commercial, or industrial communities. These satellite communities are typically interdependent. They rely on other sectors for at least a portion of their needs, such as their working force, food, clothing, entertainment, hospitalization, and newspapers. Highway beltways and expressways interlink the various areas. Many of them are in their own right the sites of industrial parks, shopping malls, corporate headquarters, superhotels, and big-league stadiums.

The Megalopolis

Urban areas that are expanding can run into one another, giving rise to yet another form, the supercity or megalopolis. The term **megalopolis,** which literally means "great city," refers to the fact that many cities and their outlying suburbs are growing so large that they are merging into one another (Gottman, 1964). This trend is especially prominent in the United States which has taken a more laissez-faire approach to urban development than have many European nations. Indeed, the most prominent megalopolis exists along the northeastern seaboard of the United States, from Boston to Washington, colloquially referred to as Boswash. Municipalities having more than 100 people per square mile are stretched along a continuous 500-mile belt from Kittery, Maine, to Quantico, Virginia, producing a megalopolis that includes the major urban centers of Boston, New York, Philadelphia, Baltimore, and Washington. Over 40 million people (a fifth of the nation's population) live in this sprawling belt. Over the past fifteen years, demographic growth on the fringe of the urban settlements continued in Boswash, but most of its central cities lost population (Long and De Are, 1983). Other megalopolises are also emerging: Los Angeles–San Diego; Palm Beach–Miami; Dallas–Fort Worth; Pittsburgh–Youngstown–Canton–Akron–Cleveland; Milwaukee–Chicago–Detroit; and perhaps even Seattle–Tacoma.

FIGURE 17.1 Growth of U.S. Urban Areas, 1850–1980

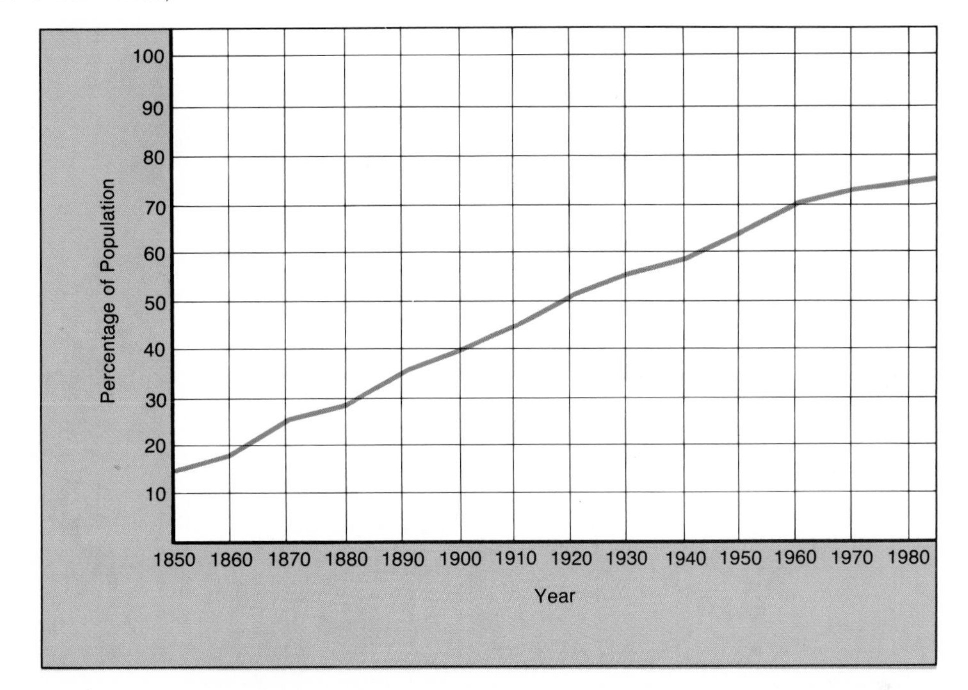

Source: U.S. Department of Commerce, Census Bureau. *Statistical Abstract of the United States, 1980*. Washington, D.C.: U.S. Government Printing Office, 1981, p. 16; A *Statistical Abstract Supplement: Historical Statistics of the United States Colonial Times to 1957*. Washington, D.C.: U.S. Government Printing Office, 1980.

The percentage of Americans living in urban areas (with 2,500 or more people) steadily climbed from 1850 to 1980. In the past decade, however, the country experienced the smallest gain in urban population for this 130-year period.

There are now twenty-nine urban centers in the United States with a population of a million or more. About half of them arose from the fusion of two or more preexisting cities. This trend toward supercities underlines the fact that we can no longer conceive of the city as a tightly settled and organized territory in which people and activities are crowded into a small area distinctly separate from its nonurban surroundings. The unplanned growth that has created these megalopolises —called **urban sprawl** by some—continues unabated (see Figure 17.2, p. 450). Indeed, this is an essential part of what is often called the crisis of the cities, a topic we will take up later.

The spread of cities has caused some striking changes. Shopping malls now stand on fields where corn grew only two decades ago. Row upon row of tract houses cover the ground where cows used to graze, and six-lane highways bisect once-deserted marshlands. Ugliness and pollution have made their appearance now that more than a third of suburban communities have become industrial. The desire for better services and low tax rates is being thwarted by the ever-increasing cost of schooling and other municipal services. In many suburbs rising crime rates, juvenile delinquency, and other social disorders typical of the cities make the suburbanite's dream of personal safety and security seem increasingly remote. Attempts have been made to find some solution to these problems, but while common to the megalopolis as a whole, typically they are dealt with only by local governments separately administering tiny seg-

FIGURE 17.2 America's Supercities

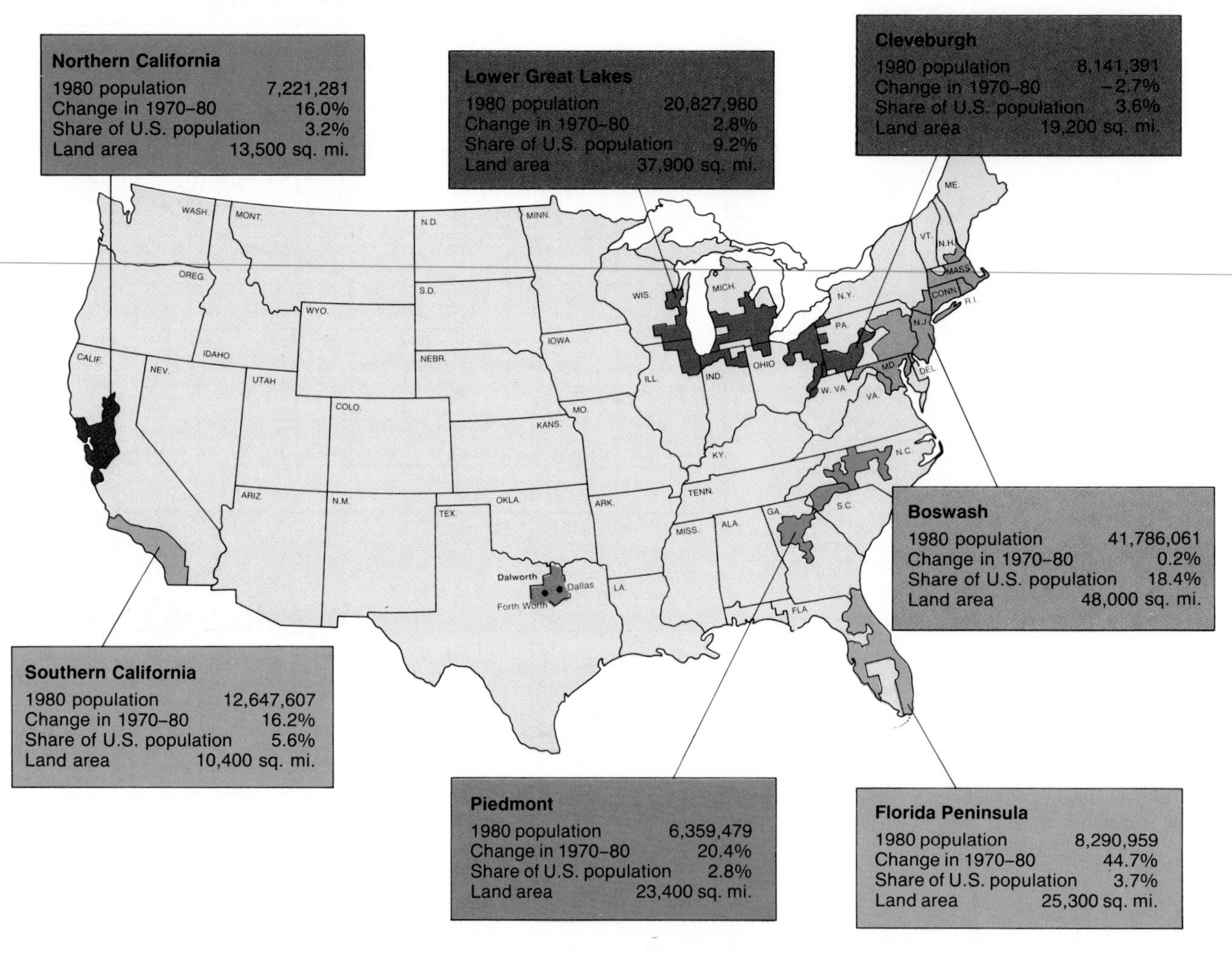

Source: Reprinted from U.S. News & World Report issue of October 3, 1983, pp 54-55. Copyright, 1983, U.S. News & World Report, Inc.

ments of a huge metropolitan area. For instance, in the four counties closest to New York City—Nassau, Suffolk, Rockland, and Westchester—there are 548 governmental units, each of which is administratively and fiscally independent.

In some instances, large central cities have attempted to annex adjoining suburban areas in an attempt to widen their tax base and thus to provide more funds with which to attack problems common to both cities and suburbs. Such moves, however, have usually resulted only in legal battles between suburban and city governments. The numerous communities that make up a megalopolis are usually adamant about protecting their own special prerogatives and interests. Moreover, the expansion of urban areas has created struggles between environmentalists, who want to preserve open "greenspace" near densely populated city centers, and developers, who want to profit from building homes and office buildings in the countryside. Without some regional government that has jurisdiction over cities and suburbs —in effect, over all parts of the megalopolis—the problems that beset these areas may be very difficult to solve.

The problems associated with urban growth are tied to population growth and the search for space in which to live and work. Persistent human multiplication invariably frustrates many programs set up to deal with urban problems. Demographers such as Kingsley Davis (1968:45) argue that the only way to stop urban crowding is to reduce the overall rate of population growth: "Urban planners continue to treat population growth as something to be planned for, not something to be itself planned. Any talk about applying brakes to city growth is therefore purely speculative, overshadowed as it is by the reality of uncontrolled population increase." Hence, the problems associated with urban living are linked to many other spheres of social life.

World Urbanization

The tremendous growth of cities in the United States during the last hundred years has been part of a worldwide phenomenon of **urbanization,** the movement of increasing numbers of people from rural villages to metropolitan areas. Between 1800 and 1982, a period in which the total population of the world expanded about 5.3 times, the number of people living in its cities swelled about 84 times from about 21.7 million to about

TABLE 17.2 Biggest Urban Centers: 1980 and 2000

	Population (estimates)	
	1980	2000
New York–Northeast New Jersey	20.4 million	22.8 million
Tokyo–Yokohama	20.0	24.2
Mexico City	15.0	31.0
São Paulo	13.5	25.8
Shanghai	13.4	22.7
Los Angeles–Long Beach	11.7	14.2
Peking	10.7	19.9
Rio de Janeiro	10.7	19.0
London	10.2	9.9
Buenos Aires	10.1	12.1
Paris	9.9	11.3
Osaka–Kobe	9.5	11.1
Rhein–Ruhr	9.3	9.2
Calcutta	8.8	16.7
Seoul	8.5	14.2
Bombay	8.3	17.1
Chicago–Northwest Indiana	8.3	9.4
Moscow	7.8	9.1
Cairo–Giza–Imbaba	7.5	13.1
Djakarta	7.3	16.6
Milan	6.6	7.7
Manila	5.7	12.3
Bogotá	5.5	11.7

Source: United Nations, Population Reference Bureau.

1.8 billion people. In 1980, 26 cities had 5 million or more residents, with a combined population of 252 million (see Table 17.2, p. 451). By 1990, United Nations demographers estimate that the number of cities with a population over 5 million will reach 60, with an estimated total of nearly 650 million people (Lewis, 1982). Mexico City will have the world's largest urban population, with an estimated 31 million people.

What caused this great demographic shift? First, the increase in population must be taken into account; cities grew, at least in part, because of a growth in population as a whole. A more significant influence, however, was the change in patterns of employment we discussed earlier. Agriculture can absorb only a finite amount of labor, and as the population grew beyond this point, unemployment and underemployment in rural areas became severe. At the same time, an enormous expansion in the number of industrial and service jobs took place, and since these jobs were located chiefly in the cities, they tended to draw large numbers of people to the metropolitan areas.

In many ways, the cities have grown too fast—particularly in the developing countries, where too many people crowd into cities that lack sufficient employment opportunities, services, and facilities to sustain them. Calcutta, India's largest city, is an excellent example of such a "premature metropolis" (Bose, cited in Schwirian et al., 1977). Most Calcuttans live in slums and many of the poor exist on the streets. Sanitation, health conditions, and transportation are all inadequate, and unfortunately the primitive, disorganized urban economy shows little sign of generating the necessary capital to effect significant change. Nevertheless, the population of Calcutta—and the populations of similar urban centers in most of the developing countries—continues to grow, often at a rate exceeding that of cities in the industrialized world. Such bulging centers will increasingly become fertile fields for social unrest. Larger numbers of young people in urban clusters will be better educated, unemployed, and demanding a better life.

Why does the rural-to-urban migration in third world countries of Asia and Latin America continue? Why should millions of people flock to cities that offer only poverty, unemployment, overcrowding, and other adverse living conditions? Part of the answer lies in the alternatives offered by rural life. In a comparison of twenty-seven third world nations, Glenn Firebaugh (1979) discovered that high rates of rural-to-urban migration are associated with adverse conditions in the countryside, conditions such as high agricultural density (many people per acre) and a plantation system of land ownership (where very few people own the land that they farm). The conditions of rural life in third world countries often "push" people to the cities, although they may also be "pulled" there by the often vain hope of steady jobs and improved living conditions.

Mexico provides a good illustration of these processes (Exter, 1982). Its population is projected to reach at least 104 million by the year 2000, up from 67 million in 1980. Over the past decade Mexico's average annual growth rate was an enormous 3.3 percent—more than three times the rate of the United States. Fifty years ago, two-thirds of the Mexican population lived in rural areas and only a third in urban places. Today the percentages have been reversed. For the most part, the rural-to-urban migration has flowed toward the largest cities. For instance, in 1980 the population of Mexico City stood at 15 million, fully 22 percent of the Mexican population. Consequently, Mexico is suffering from *primacy*, the concentration of a nation's population in one or more large cities. Mexico's high degree of primacy is the product of settlement patterns dating from the colonial period, from an export-oriented economy, from political and cultural centralization, and from the transportation networks that have emerged to service these patterns.

Urban Ecology

In all urban areas—the city, the metropolis, and the megalopolis—people distribute themselves spatially in recognizable patterns. These patterns can be graphically represented, as is done in Figure 17.3, but the neatness of the images conceals the complexity of the forces that create them. Urban spatial patterns develop out of an ongoing competition for land and resources among groups and classes and lead to a functional differentiation in land use and patterns of social domination. For instance, present-day Calcutta is an area of confrontation between the enduring institutions of old India—its caste communities and diversity of ethnic heritages—and the pressures and values associated with urbanization that have accompanied the nation's industrial

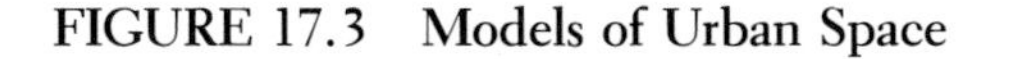
FIGURE 17.3 Models of Urban Space

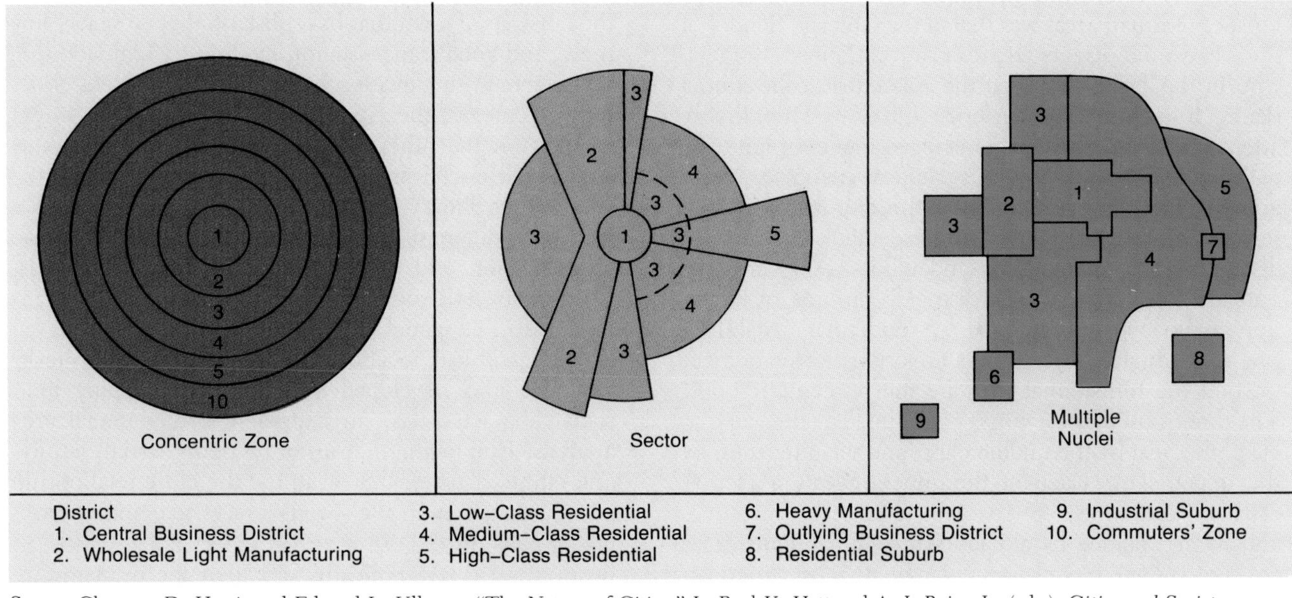

Source: Chauncy D. Harris and Edward L. Ullman. "The Nature of Cities." In Paul K. Hatt and A. J. Reiss, Jr. (eds.), *Cities and Society* (Glencoe, Ill.: Free Press, 1957). Courtesy of Professor Harris.

Attempts to describe the structure of cities have produced the three alternative models shown here: Burgess's concentric zone model, with the business district at the center and other districts radiating out from it; Hoyt's sector model, emphasizing transportation routes; and Harris and Ullman's multiple nuclei model, organized around land uses, costs, and interests. A newer approach to the analysis of urban structure is called social area analysis. Analysts, using the census and other social indicators, attempt to explain residential patterns by correlating broad social categories, such as social rank, family structure, and ethnicity. With the advent of the computer, even more factors are being taken into account in models of urban land use and social structure.

revolution (Bose, 1968; Berry and Kasarda, 1977). Traditionally, some 12,000 caste communities, each identified with a particular occupation, monopolized certain locales of the cities. The ranking of these caste communities resulted in a spatial ordering according to the relative social desirability of the various castes. Although the social worlds of the privileged and lower castes were separated by space, their activities nonetheless did interconnect in the larger economic and political web of urban life.

Urban ecology is concerned with the configurations and relationships that occur among people, their activities, and the land they occupy. The ecological analysis of urban communities provides us with valuable insights regarding the social division of labor and the resulting patterns that surround the collective use of space and resources. By studying urban ecology, we learn about the ongoing accommodations that human beings evolve as they pursue their social goals within a physical environment.

The Shape of Cities

The classic American attempt to map the spatial characteristics of urban areas was that of the Chicago School of Sociology and its key representative, Ernest Burgess, who in the 1920s proposed the **concentric zone model** (Park, Burgess, and McKenzie, 1925). This theory attempted to formulate a generalized model of land use patterns in cities and to link ecological change to urban growth. The approach depicted the city in terms of a series of zones (Figure 17.3). At the center is the business district, made up of shops and offices. Adjacent and outward from the business district is an area of transition, which is characterized by residential instability, low rents, high crime rates, and various forms of vice. Beyond the transitional ring are the residential zones. The innermost of these zones is inhabited by the working class, the next by the middle class, and the outermost by the upper class. Each of the zones reflects a group's capacity to compete for space in terms of its resources and its acceptance by already settled inhabitants. The concentric zone model does not apply to most American cities. It is most characteristic of cities like Chicago, which developed very rapidly in the period after the Industrial Revolution and before the development and widespread introduction of the automobile.

In the 1930s, Homer Hoyt (1943), in response to Burgess's work, proposed a different system of urban patterning, one that emphasized the importance of transportation routes—highways, railroad lines, and waterways—in shaping the growth of cities. Hoyt's scheme features the same type of outward movement as Burgess's did, but in sectors rather than concentric zones (Figure 17.3). According to Hoyt's **sector model,** a business district occupies the center of the city. Beyond it, development occurs in sectors that tend to be distributed along major transportation routes radiating out from the city's center. As land uses expand, they tend to remain within their respective sectors, but extend outward toward the edge of the metropolis. An example is the recent development of "Silicon Valley" in California. Here, a number of manufacturers of computer equipment have settled along freeways running south out of the central cities of Oakland and San Francisco.

Yet another model of urban ecological development, the **multiple nuclei model,** was proposed by Chauncy D. Harris and Edward L. Ullman (1945). According to this theory, land uses, costs, and interests cause a city to develop in a series of nuclei, each with its specialized activities (Figure 17.3). For example, a nucleus of car manufacturing might develop in an area on the outskirts of town that has substantial open space, low rents, and good transportation facilities. Manufacturing interests requiring less space might form a nucleus closer to the center of the city, while residential areas might develop on the other side of town. The city grows as specialized nuclei proliferate.

Eshref Shevky and Marilyn Williams (1949) took a somewhat different approach to the city. The concentric circle, sector, and multiple-nuclei models seek to discern the overall social organization of the city as it is reflected in its spatial patterns. Rather than focusing on the geographical locations of particular areas, Shevky and Williams developed a measure for tapping their social characteristics, an approach termed **social area analysis.** Employing indexes of residents' social, family, and ethnic statuses, they examine the close relationship between changes in the society as a whole and changes taking place in the use of urban space. For instance, in business areas one typically finds that the residents are unmarried, childless, and low in socioeconomic status. In contrast, people in suburban neighborhoods tend to score high on both social and family dimensions. By periodically restudying an area and computing its scores on these key indexes, sociologists can determine the changes that are taking place and the patterns they reveal in broad social trends.

Sociologists have traditionally portrayed the processes shaping land use within the city as deriving from a free market in which thousands of persons follow their individual tastes and interests. Conflict theorists dispute this image (McAdams, 1981). They say that American urban form reflects the priorities of the capitalist economy. Rather than being patterned as evolutionary adaptations that insure human survival, cities reflect the profit-oriented purposes of the capitalist class. Local real estate interests, construction firms, utilities, industries, businesses, homeowners, and government agencies are all land-interested parties pursuing power and gain. As an example, they point out that nearly 70 percent of the dwelling units condemned for urban renewal projects have been ones housing black residents. In many cities such programs have operated to remove blacks from the vicinity of central business districts so that large businesses that wished to could establish their offices or retail stores in the area (Greer, 1966). Likewise, large regional, national, and international organizations, including governments, banks, insurance companies, real-estate investment trusts, and major corporations, impose their requirements on the local community and shape its environment. Decisions about where to locate or relocate offices, plants, and shopping malls have vast ramifications for employment opportunities and the urban tax base. Hence, conflict theorists conclude that modern cities are fashioned by powerful interests and not primarily by impersonal ecological and market forces.

Clearly, a great many factors influence land use patterns, including the workings of various economic processes and groups. But they are also influenced by the values and personal preferences of the people who live and work in the city. The historic Boston Commons, a forty-eight-acre park in the middle of the downtown business area, is a good example of sentimental attachment overriding economic considerations. The Commons, which in colonial days served as a grazing area for livestock, continues to be protected by a special provision of the city charter even though it occupies extremely valuable land and causes significant traffic delays (Firey, 1961). Other examples include New York City's Central Park, San Francisco's Golden Gate Park, Mexico City's Chapultepec Park, and London's Regency Park. Hence, the use of urban space is governed not only by utilitarian factors but by emotional and symbolic ones as well.

Ecological Succession

That city neighborhoods undergo change is obvious to anyone who frequents a city. One year a street is lined with dilapidated brownstones; the next, glass and concrete skyscrapers rise in their place. New clusters of shops appear. Industries move to the suburbs; their abandoned factories are converted into residential lofts. Even in long-time residential neighborhoods, change is often evident. Some residential neighborhoods are allowed to deteriorate, while others are maintained or renovated. Such changes are visible enough. But is there any pattern to them?

Urban ecologists believe there is. For instance, Robert E. Park, Ernest W. Burgess, and Roderick D. McKenzie (1925) described a general pattern called the **invasion cycle.** The invasion cycle begins imperceptibly. For example, one brownstone or decaying urban mansion in a rundown area is bought and refurbished by an architect. Next, more professionals and other middle-

Philadelphia's Society Hill district was extremely rundown only a few years ago. Now, very few buildings remain that have not been renovated, and succession is virtually complete. (Cary Wolinsky/Stock, Boston)

class singles and couples buy houses nearby, and the area's long-time residents, who belong to a much lower socioeconomic class, become concerned about the change. As land values, taxes, and rents go up, these older and poorer inhabitants protest that they can no longer afford to live there and have nowhere else to go. If opposition is unsuccessful, a general influx of newcomers into the area begins. A turning point is reached as the old inhabitants are forced out or no longer wish to remain. The invasion reaches the climax stage when the new inhabitants completely occupy the area. At this point, **succession** is said to have taken place.

Zoning

The processes of invasion and succession pose a threat to groups who currently occupy an area, and at the same time, present opportunities for various real estate and other interests. And undeveloped areas beckon entrepreneurs who see favorable conditions for making profits through their development. Consequently, it is not surprising that land use should become involved in the political process. It does so through **zoning,** a procedure by which land parcels are designated by law for specific purposes and the size of lots and the structures on them are regulated.

As a means for organizing land use, zoning affects the life chances of many individuals since it influences available jobs, housing, safety, police protection, and garbage removal. For example, a Chicago study (Shlay and Rossi, 1981) found that zoning influences the type of housing development that occurs in both the city and the suburbs. It operates to separate the rich from the poor, homeowners from renters, and single-family dwellers from apartment residents. As an economic policy, zoning commonly distributes land use so that property will have maximum value on the market and property values will be protected. In practice, it serves to create an "invisible wall" that restricts the shifting of low-income and minority families from older, central-city neighborhoods to newer suburbs.

All this suggests that the city is an evolving, dynamic system. Population and activities are not simply distributed by ecological processes such as invasion and succession but also by political decisions regarding the use of land. Thus sociological models of the city must continually change to depict and anticipate the city's spatial and social form.

MODERN URBAN LIFE

Life in American cities offers an unprecedented range of opportunities: diversity in jobs, cultural attractions, housing, and values. But this specialization has its costs: It sometimes leads to a destruction of community, a loss of the sense of belonging, and an increase in feelings of alienation (Haworth, 1963).

Gemeinschaft and Gesellschaft

The contrast between traditional communities and modern societies was highlighted by Ferdinand Tönnies (1855–1936), a German sociologist. He (1957) noted that in a small isolated village, relationships tend to be intimate and enduring and life highly integrated, a type of community he termed **Gemeinschaft.** In contrast, in a large urban center, relationships tend to be impersonal and transitory and life is segmented, a type of society he termed **Gesellschaft.** Tönnies, along with virtually all of the nineteenth-century social thinkers, made the polar distinction between *Gemeinschaft* and *Gesellschaft* types of social organization because of the profound social dislocations of the time. Much of the world was undergoing dramatic change as a result of industrialization, urbanization, and bureaucratization. The movement of people from stable, intimate villages to fragmented, heterogeneous cities was often accompanied by considerable personal and social upheaval.

Characteristics

In a *Gemeinschaft*, such as an agrarian or tribal village, all members typically interact on a daily basis. They share a common ancestry, as well as common goals, values, aspirations, and traditions. Everyone in the village is involved with the survival and welfare of the whole. There are relatively few specialized roles; social bonds develop because people have many activities and roles in common. In addition, each member of the community has a fixed position in the social order, one usually assigned at birth. Geographic mobility is as limited as social mobility; a person often lives and dies in a very restricted geographic area. Such expressions of individuality as distinctive clothing, work aspirations, leisure activities, and friendship circles are all highly circumscribed by the rights and obligations of others in the village. The entire web of each person's relationships is interconnected and predetermined at birth. Since every aspect of an individual's life meshes with every other aspect (family, coworkers, neighbors, and friends are all the same people), a person's entire social identity is involved in each relationship. Personal, social, and economic life are all rolled up in one, and the notion of self fuses with the individual's identification with the village or little society.

The characteristics of a *Gemeinschaft*, then, are:

1. Common values and norms
2. Common ancestry
3. Common and fixed roles, positions, and functions
4. Close-knit network of friends and relatives
5. Geographical and social stability; long-term face-to-face relations.

Our urban, industrial *Gesellschaft* society presents dramatic differences. Social life is much more fragmented. Relatives may live far away, friends may live across town, fellow workers may live in a different town altogether, and we may not know any of our neighbors. With no one group, except perhaps the immediate nuclear family, do we have regular, continuous, face-to-face interaction. Many of the people we encounter—shopkeepers, service people, civil servants—we deal with in very impersonal, superficial ways. Those who live around us may come from very different backgrounds and have very heterogeneous histories, so we do not necessarily share with them common goals, values, aspirations, traditions, or ancestry. Nor do we share roles and functions with many other people. Tasks in our society are highly specialized. People have diverse and complementary roles that mesh into an interdependent whole. And unlike people in rural villages who spend their entire lives in the same community, we are extremely mobile; one out of every ten Americans moves each year. We also move socially, leaving old friends behind as we make new ones.

The characteristics of a *Gesellschaft* are in direct contrast to those of a *Gemeinschaft:*

1. Diverse values and norms
2. Diverse ancestry
3. Complementary roles, positions, and functions
4. Loosely linked networks of friends across several groups
5. Geographical and social mobility; transient relations

Consequences

Each type of society has its functions and dysfunctions. Village life is intimate and secure, but as the French sociologist Emile Durkheim noted, life there is also confining. The number of roles one can play and the kinds of social bonds one can make are limited.

City dwellers must deal with different rules in different groups and adjust to continually changing norms. Moreover, the variety of people they are so dependent on can lead to a sense of fragmentation and impersonality. On the other hand, they have more freedom in deciding whom to associate with and how to spend their time (Durkheim, 1947).

The consequences of the shift in human relations brought about by modernization have both fascinated and frightened many social observers. But while no one would deny that the shifts from farm to factory and from village to city have brought about great changes in human social organization, the initial alarm has been tempered by the discovery that modern relationships are not wholly isolating and alienating. Even when families are separated by great distances and different value systems, they still stay in contact and help one another (think of how many college students go home for vacation; receive gifts on holidays; keep their parents informed of their whereabouts). Even in large urban centers, people still make friends at work, in their neighborhood, through their children's schools (see Chapter 7). And even in the most bureaucratic organizations, work groups and friendship cliques form (see Chapter 8). While these relationships are clearly not as all-consuming as the relationships in a tribal or agrarian village, they do have merits of their own. Let us consider these matters at greater length.

Alienation or Community?

The striking contrasts between the intimacy and neighborliness of rural village life and the anonymity and self-interestedness of city life not only impressed European sociologists but also provided the initial focus for American sociologists. Much of the pioneering work in this field was done during the 1920s and 1930s by social scientists at the University of Chicago. Migration to the cities was particularly heavy during this period, and it seemed that Americans by the hundreds of thousands, seeking to make their fortunes, were giving up the close social relationships of their rural lives for the impersonality of existence in a large city.

A classic study that reflects these assumptions about life in large and small communities is Louis Wirth's "Urbanism as a Way of Life" (1938). Like many of us, Wirth saw the city as the prototype of mass society, in which the traditional bases of social solidarity and control—kinship and the neighborhood—are undermined. Wirth suggested that urban life led to atomized and depersonalized social relations, with the result that people who live in cities are more likely to suffer from mental breakdown or suicide. Moreover, an indifference to the welfare of others permits increases in rates of crime, delinquency, corruption, and disorder. Wirth maintained that the peculiar kind of social relationship fostered by city living is determined by three factors: the size, the density, and the heterogeneity of city populations. And since larger populations tend to be more diversified and heterogeneous than small ones, they have more isolation and anonymity. Although a city dweller may have an enormous number of encounters with others, these encounters are likely to be segmented and superficial, impersonal and transitory. In place of sustained and intimate relations with relatives and close neighbors, a person encounters the butcher, the taxicab driver, the waitress, the news vendor, the accountant, the sales clerk. In other words, a person's social relations are secondary rather than primary (see Chapter 7).

These impersonal and anonymous social relations do increase the city dweller's sense of personal freedom. Such freedom, however, can mean that some people feel free to prey on others—con artists or muggers, for example. With the waning of traditional social constraints, urban society must maintain order through formal mechanisms of control—law and its supporting agencies, the police and the courts. But because these mechanisms of control are rarely as effective at keeping order as tradition and custom, the urban society is more prone to personal and social disorganization, more prone to alienation.

Wirth's description of urban life was based on his study of Chicago during the 1920s and 1930s. A great influx of immigrants from many nations, coupled with a severe economic depression, created a city far removed from the small, intimate village so many of these new Americans had left behind. But what about today? Does the large size, density, and heterogeneity of contemporary American cities erode a sense of community and thus breed alienation, as Wirth suggested?

Recent studies suggest that intimate bonds often persist despite urbanization, and a strong sense of community is possible in urban settings (Sennett, 1971; Fischer, 1981, 1982). (See the box on alienation and city life.) A sense of community may emerge among city dwellers who do the same kind of work or who have lived in the same neighborhood for a long period of time. John Esposito and John Fiorillo (1974) investigated several working-class neighborhoods in New York City and found that residents in defined areas tended to hold jobs in the same industry—construction, textiles, transportation, public administration, insurance, and so forth. This pattern helped generate a neighborhood cohesiveness that cut across ethnic divisions. In a study of rural and urban residents in Great Britain, researchers asked people such questions as: How many people do you know in your neighborhood? How many friends and relatives live within a ten-minute walk from your home? How glad or sorry would you be if you had to move away from your neighborhood? The responses showed that regardless of the size and density of the community in which a person lived, those who had spent a longer time in a neighborhood tended to have more primary relationships there (Kasarda and Janowitz, 1974).

Perhaps the closest-knit communities in urban areas are those linking people of the same ethnic group. From Herbert Gans's (1962) classic study of Italians in the North End of Boston to Gerald Suttles's (1968) study of the Addams area of Chicago (one of the city's oldest slums), the findings suggest that a common ethnic heritage can reduce the alienating effects of city life. Rather than the normlessness that Wirth had predicted would characterize slums, Suttles found that residents reinterpreted traditional norms to fit their own special needs.

Research by the sociologist James Christenson (1979) has shown that residents of sparsely populated areas generally have more favorable attitudes toward their communities than do residents of densely popu-

THE SOCIOLOGICAL EYE ON:

Alienation and City Life

City life, as everyone knows, is impersonal, lonely, alienating, and emotionally stressful. Or is it? On this subject as on others, sociological research often discovers that what "everyone knows" is not exactly the truth. In a study conducted among northern California residents, the sociologist Claude S. Fischer (1981, 1982) explored the "urban alienation" thesis—and reported some interesting findings.

According to this thesis, the stresses of city life are destructive to people and to social interaction. People in cities avoid one another and are indifferent, suspicious, or even hostile to others—with resulting damage to their psyches and to their social relationships. Fischer, however, found this picture to be painted with far too broad a brush. First of all, he found no evidence that city life imposed particular strain on the personality: City dwellers showed no more symptoms of stress, psychological disorder, or estrangement than did people who lived in smaller communities. Second, although city dwellers in some circumstances are less helpful to others (a third of those whom Fischer's team approached were reluctant to allow an interviewer into their home), this can largely be ascribed to fear of crime. Those city dwellers who admitted the interviewer were as helpful in responding to the survey as were the people who lived in smaller communities. Third, urban residents were generally found to have extensive networks of friends and associates; most were not socially isolated or alienated. The urban residents were as socially integrated as were inhabitants of rural areas. However, higher-income and highly educated individuals were more likely to have broader, deeper, and more enriching networks than were lower-income and less well-educated individuals.

These findings should not be taken to say that there are no differences between people who live in cities and those who live in small communities. Fischer found several differences. City dwellers were somewhat more distrustful of others and tended to experience their communities as more anonymous than did small-town residents. They were also more likely to express fears of crime and feelings that their neighborhoods were unsafe.

What, then, of urban alienation? Fischer says that there actually is such a thing, but that it exists in the public sphere of city life, not in the private sphere. He suggests that urban life requires people to develop a special etiquette: In the presence of so many strangers, city dwellers must learn to be reserved, detached, nonintrusive, and impersonal. Thus, in public, people often display a kind of withdrawn, or alienated, behavior: They ignore others, avoid eye contact with them, and may not reply if spoken to. This kind of behavior is likely to be strongest when strangers appear threatening or are racially, ethnically, or culturally different. These mannerisms, however, are apparently confined to the public sphere: with family and friends urbanites are not withdrawn. As Fischer concludes, "Urbanism does not produce estrangement from close associates, or from familiar groups, such as neighbors. It does seem to produce estrangement from . . . the socially dissimilar and potentially threatening people and subcultures who make up the city—the inhabitants of the 'world of strangers'" (1981:315).

lated ones. This finding is in keeping with Wirth's theory that high population density encourages anonymity, impersonality, and a general social malaise. However, Christenson also found that the provision of good public services such as excellent schools, libraries, cultural opportunities, and recreational facilities can prompt people to view their communities more positively. Since such services are more likely to be found in large cities than in small towns, the negative forces Wirth associated with the city may sometimes be offset.

Thus, while urban life may be alienating for some, it manages to provide a sense of community for others. Paradoxically, this sense of community often stems from the very diversity that also fragments city dwellers to a great extent. Large, heterogeneous populations breed a diversity of subcultures, each with its own rich social life and strong cohesion among members. Consequently, people in cities can usually find others with similar values, backgrounds, and tastes. As a result, urban residents can sometimes enjoy the intimacy, loyalty, and cooperation of a close-knit community regardless of how large a city they live in (Fischer, 1975; 1982).

Not all aspects of city life are alienating. These people share a sense of community within the larger city of Boston. (Elizabeth Hamlin/Stock, Boston)

The Suburbs

Although suburbs are distant and distinct from central cities, they are nonetheless part of the larger urbanization process, an offshoot of the expansion of city into metropolis and megalopolis. Initially, suburbs were on the fringes of urban settlements and their residents remained connected with the central city through work and play. Gradually, however, suburbs diversified and became part of the expanding urban core. Commercial and industrial activities moved out to what previously had been primarily residential enclaves, thereby increasingly blurring the distinction between city and suburb.

The Variety of Suburbs

Suburbs have a long history in the United States. However, they grew most rapidly in the years following World War II. By 1980 some 45 percent of the American population lived in communities adjoining central cities. Over the century, the trend has been for the urban fringe areas to grow more rapidly than the central cities (see Table 17.3).

As suburbs multiplied, they developed different social characteristics and activity patterns. Two broad types emerged: residential suburbs and employing suburbs (Schwab, 1982). **Residential suburbs** (also known

TABLE 17.3 Population Increase, 1900–1980

Population Status	1970–1980	1960–1970	1950–1960	1940–1950	1930–1940	1920–1930	1910–1920	1900–1910
Total United States	11.3	13.4	18.5	14.5	7.2	16.1	14.9	21.0
Nonmetropolitan	3.4	5.8	8.1	6.1	6.5	6.0	6.7	13.6
Metropolitan	14.5	28.8	47.5	22.0	8.4	27.5	25.9	32.5
Central City	4.8	9.0	20.8	13.8	5.5	24.2	27.9	37.1
Urbanized Fringe	18.2	45.0	81.0	26.0	8.0	42.6	35.9	49.2

Source: U.S. Bureau of Census data.

as dormitory suburbs) consist of homeowners and breadwinners who commute to their jobs in cities or other suburbs. Residentials suburbs typically want to keep out manufacturing and industry so as to preserve the residential character of their neighborhoods. For the most part, the only economic activities within their borders are retail and personal services, including supermarkets, service stations, dry cleaners, and drug stores. Frequently, these activities are concentrated in shopping malls. **Employing suburbs,** in contrast, include manufacturing or industrial operations that are centers of employment for their own residents and also for those from other communities. Many of the suburbs around the nation's older cities, such as Cleveland, are of this type.

In the 1950s and early 1960s the suburban population profile was one of largely white, married, well-educated, and relatively highly-paid people. But in the past two decades, this picture has changed. Suburbs now have a variety of economic classes and racial and ethinic groups. For instance, over the 1960s and 1970s the number of blacks living in suburbs grew by 72 percent, to about 5 million, while the number of whites grew by 38 percent. However, blacks have moved largely from black city neighborhoods to suburbs that are primarily black or rapidly becoming so. In large measure, black suburbanites have settled in formerly white neighborhoods where the physical condition and market value of housing has deteriorated (Lake, 1981).

Clearly, suburbs differ from one another in their history, wealth, ethnic and racial composition, and relation to central cities. Internally, however, each suburb tends to be rather homogeneous. Take the matter of status level or prestige. Compared with low-status suburbs, high-status ones are much more likely to attract adults who have had some college education, who are employed in white-collar occupations, and who earn over $40,000 a year. And the status level of a suburb tends to persist for a long time. One reason for this status continuity is that each suburb fills a particular "ecological niche" (Stahura, 1979). For example, if a certain suburb initially emerges as a residential center for affluent, white-collar commuters, the type of housing affordable there will tend to preclude a subsequent influx of blue-collar families. Similarly, if a suburb initially emerges as an industrial center with surrounding homes for factory workers, the nature of the housing will tend to ensure that only working-class families are attracted there. Thus the character of a suburb depends on the specialized economic role it plays in the larger metropolitan area.

Many suburbs also consciously attempt to cultivate and maintain their homogeneity. Because most suburbs are politically autonomous, they can exert considerable influence over the composition and life style of their residents. By means of zoning laws, licensing, school boards, business associations, and the local police department, a suburban community can effectively dictate who may live in it, as well as set general guidelines on how those people must conduct their lives. The conformity fostered by these means tends to be self-perpetuating, since individuals who migrate to the suburbs are usually those who already approve of and share suburban values. Thus, while there are socioeconomic differences *between* suburbs, within each one there is considerable homogeneity.

Explaining Suburban Growth

The explosive growth of the nation's urban fringe since World War II can best be explained in terms of four elements: population, organization, environment, and technology (POET) (Duncan, 1959, 1961). The most obvious factor contributing to suburbanization has been population growth, particularly the baby boom (see Chapter 16). Young parents and children accounted for much of the demographic increase. Organizations also fueled suburban growth. The federal government subsidized fringe development with its FHA (Federal Housing Administration) and VA (Veterans Administration) loan programs, its grants to suburbs for water and sewer construction, and its massive highway construction programs. Banking and lending institutions, large-scale developers, and the real-estate industry equally promoted development outside the central city. Further, the environment of the core city was such that the only available land for expansion was on the fringe. And technology, especially efficient electrification and the automobile, made the modern suburb a reality. The elements in the POET framework influence one another and have shaped the pattern of suburbanization (Schwab, 1982).

Americans are both drawn to the suburbs by their yearning for a home of their own in a green and pleasant land and pushed from the central cities by such undesirable features as noise, pollution, crime, and periodic strikes. But most middle-class whites who settle in the suburbs are not just fleeing central-city life. Instead, they are drawn to the suburbs because of special opportunities they find there. The high density of many central cities puts limits on the amount and quality of housing and jobs. In the suburbs, where land is more plentiful, businesses can readily expand and builders can construct new homes by the thousands. The lure of jobs and housing is a principal factor encouraging city dwellers to relocate in the suburbs. Negative features of city life—crime, high taxes, civil disorders, strikes by municipal workers—seem to play only a small part in suburbanization. The rate of white outmigration to the suburbs is essentially the same in central cities that have experienced prolonged strikes, severe riots, and record-breaking crime rates as it is in far more peaceful urban areas (Marshall, 1979). In short, the great exodus of white Americans to the suburbs has been more a quest than a flight.

Historically, urban growth and industrialization have been closely connected. Initially, factories were built in or near urban centers. But in recent years industrial plants and corporate headquarters have increasingly been located in rural settings. For instance, when Volkswagen decided to set up a plant in the United States, it went to New Stanton, Pennsylvania, rather than to Detroit. Corporations move to avoid the high costs and taxes in core-city locations; they have been attracted to the suburbs because of the availability of land and transportation, advances in communication, new methods of production, and a work force potential beyond the city. As the corporations move, so do workers, followed by retail shops and services. In many cases, suburban workers have the kind of training required in modern industry or are professionals (Long and DeAre, 1983). In the New York metropolitan area, for example, 80 percent of the main wage earners in suburban households do not work in one of the city's five boroughs. Half of the suburbanites make fewer than five nonbusiness visits a year to the city, and a quarter of them say they have not been to one of the boroughs in at least a year (Madden, 1978).

THE URBAN CRISIS

Many American central cities are losing population and their economies are floundering. St. Louis provides a good illustration of this process (Long and DeAre, 1983). Over the past twenty-five years its population loss has been so great that the city currently has about the same number of residents as it had in 1890. The population of its inner suburbs began to drop slightly in the 1960s. In the 1970s the decline accelerated, and the inner suburbs lost about 15 percent of their population. Beyond the inner ring of suburbs, the population has continued to grow, but at a sharply diminishing rate. The outer suburbs grew by 103 percent in the 1950s, by 55 percent in the 1960s, and by 17 percent in the 1970s.

Demographers have used the metaphor of the doughnut to describe the pattern that has unfolded in St. Louis and many other midwestern cities. The "hole" in the doughnut represents the inner region where population and economic shrinkage has been greatest. As the inner suburbs start losing population, the "hole" expands outward. In many of the old and ailing industrial cities of the Midwest, housing, stores, and even factories have been abandoned. The declining economies have severely strained municipal finances, and several cities were near bankruptcy. What has been responsible for these events? How do sociologists explain the population shifts seen in many urban centers? It is to these matters that we now turn our attention.

Population and Economic Shifts

Katharine Bradbury and her colleagues (1982) distinguish between descriptive and functional decline in an urban area. *Descriptive decline* refers to the loss of population and jobs. *Functional decline* describes the deterioration in the social amenities a city provides. Both descriptive and functional decline are associated with the "hole-in-the-doughnut" pattern and the urban crisis. As we noted earlier, people are leaving the cities for better opportunities in the suburbs. Between 1980 and 1981, central cities in the United States lost a net of 2.2 million people; the suburbs gained 2 million of these city migrants and nonmetropolitan areas gained 200,000.

At first glance, a drop in population in the inner cities might seem like cause for rejoicing. Fewer people should mean more housing, more room on public transportation, and a less burdened municipal bureaucracy. But the cities' loss of population is having anything but a positive effect. A primary reason is that most of the

Since the 1960s, Midwestern cities like Detroit have been losing population. One result has been the decay and abandonment of houses, stores, and factories. (Robert Eckert/EKM-Nepenthe)

people moving out of the inner cities are white and in the middle and upper income brackets, while most of those who remain are nonwhite and poor. As a result, the core of the city is left to those who can least afford to finance its upkeep. Moreover, most of the new migrants to the city are relatively poor, and their arrival does little to pull the city out of its downward spiral.

In 1970, the median household income in American cities was 80 percent of that in the suburbs (Herbers, 1983a). But by 1980 it was 74 percent. The difference was even greater in old industrial cities; Baltimore, for example, had a median income just 58 percent of the median income of its suburbs. Further, in the past many poor city residents entered the labor market through blue-collar jobs. Yet in the 1970s city dwellers holding blue-collar jobs declined by 5 percent while suburban dwellers holding such jobs increased by 20 percent. And although the percentage of households headed by married couples with children declined during the 1970s in both central cities and suburbs, the drop was more abrupt in central cities. By 1980 one in three households in the suburbs consisted of a married couple with children as against one household in five in central cities.

It is not just people who are abandoning the cities. Businesses are leaving too. Forty percent of America's fifty-seven largest central cities lost jobs during the 1970s. In many of these cities, the rate of job loss was more than twice that experienced during the previous decade, and it usually exceeded the rate at which population was declining (Department of Housing and Urban Development, 1980). One of the most important factors in the job drain from the central cities is the tremendous economic expansion of suburban areas. As we discussed earlier in the chapter, no longer are suburbs strictly "bedroom" communities. There has been a marked shift in business activity outward from the urban core. This shift, in fact, is one of the principal factors drawing middle- and upper-class whites to the suburbs: They prefer to live near where they work.

Despite the acceleration of black suburbanization over the last decade (Lake, 1981), blacks remain vastly underrepresented in suburbia. Of the 200 or so suburbs that ring Chicago, for example, only 15 have a substantial black population.

The long-term shift to the suburbs has had detrimental effects on central cities throughout America, but urban centers in the Northeast and North Central regions have faced a double handicap. In the last several decades, these older cities have been losing jobs and people to metropolitan areas in the South and Southwest. For instance, in the 1970s there was a slight increase in the population of the urbanized areas of the North Central states: from 31.5 to 31.9 million. During the same period, however, the population of urbanized areas in the South increased from 29 to 36 million.

To make matters worse, jobs also have been moving in the same direction (Herbers, 1983*b*). Between 1970 and 1980 the number of people in blue-collar jobs in northern cities declined by 63 percent, a loss of 1.64 million jobs. But southern and western cities gained 253,000 blue-collar employees, for a 22 percent increase over 1970. (Nationally, the gain in blue-collar jobs averaged 11 percent.) A somewhat similar pattern has emerged for white-collar jobs: Northern cities experienced a 3 percent loss in white-collar employment, and southern and western cities showed a gain of 37 percent. Likewise, household income in 1980 was almost $2,000 higher on the average in southern and western cities than in northern cities. Particularly victimized by these trends have been the poor and minorities who have been abandoned in northern central cities and inner suburbs when the white population and business move to the outer suburbs and the Sun Belt. Nor has the growth of Sun Belt cities offered the promise of improving the social and economic well-being of the poor, since these cities increasingly duplicate the patterns of Snow Belt cities.

The reasons for the population and economic growth in the Sun Belt are very much the same as the reasons for the movement of jobs from central cities to suburbs. Land for expansion is more readily available in many parts of the South and West, taxes there are frequently lower, and labor is often cheaper than in the North. Assembly-line jobs can be filled by unskilled workers, in many cases by the migrant work force arriving daily from Mexico. And western communities have proven themselves well-versed in the use of industrial development bonds, tax-increment financing, low tax rates, minimal development restrictions, and other incentives to lure industry (Butler and Chinitz, 1982). Such factors are attractive to businesses, especially when transportation facilities no longer demand that firms be located near principal markets and sources of raw materials (Department of Housing and Urban Development, 1980). The result is that many older cities of the North are experiencing an unprecedented decline.

Declining Older Central Cities

To understand how serious the current plight of many older cities is, it is useful to look more closely at a number of their key problems. Consider urban poverty and unemployment in the North. Whereas poverty is generally declining in rural areas, in the suburbs, and in the economically expanding cities of the South and West, it is increasing in many of our largest northern cities. In Chicago, for example, the proportion of residents living in poverty rose from 14.3 percent to 1969 to 21 percent less than ten years later. Other large northern cities, such as New York, Philadelphia, and Baltimore, have faced similar sharp increases in their poverty rates. In economically prosperous cities such as Dallas and Houston, in contrast, the poverty rate has dropped several percentage points during the same period (Department of Housing and Urban Development, 1980).

A decline in employment opportunities is closely related to central-city poverty in the North. The cities in which poverty is increasing are also those in which the number of jobs is shrinking faster than the population. Unemployment rates in cities such as Detroit, New York, and Philadelphia have been running about twice as high as those in cities such as Houston and Dallas. And there is no doubt that black residents of the northern cities are bearing the brunt of this economic decline. In Chicago over 35 percent of the black population is now poor! Significantly, in economically declining cities, nearly 60 percent of blacks living in poverty do not participate in the labor force, and many others can find only intermittent work (Department of Housing and Urban Development, 1980). As discussed in Chapter 12, such statistics give sociologists reason to fear that poor blacks in many of the nation's oldest cities are becoming a permanent underclass with very little chance of ever finding jobs that can pull them out of poverty.

Besides the individual suffering that central-city poverty causes, it has broader effects. For one thing, it has contributed to a crisis in the housing market. Residents have difficulty meeting the mortgage payments, and renters cannot keep up their rent. Large banks and other lending institutions then pull out of the market. Homeowners and landlords who wish to sell their properties cannot locate buyers. Some find it easier to set them on fire and claim insurance as a way of cutting their losses. Hence, in sections of Manhattan, the Bronx, and Brooklyn, entire neighborhoods have been firebombed, abandoned, and reduced to rubble.

Poverty has an additional consequence. Cities raise money for public services through taxes, and poor populations yield relatively few tax dollars. Yet, paradox-

The rubble of the South Bronx in New York City has resulted, in part, from landlords who walked away from buildings that were no longer profitable. (Barbara Alper/Stock, Boston)

ically, widespread poverty often means that cities must *increase* their expenditures. More must usually be spent on unemployment benefits, on welfare, and on public health care services. And because poverty is closely related to crime, more must usually be spent on law enforcement and the courts. In addition, many of the facilities in older northern cities—the roads, the subways and buses, the water and sewage lines, the schools and other public buildings—are antiquated and deteriorating fast. The financial crisis many cities face boils down to this: Existing municipal taxes simply cannot provide enough money to pay for needed services. And the basic problem is extremely widespread. A congressional survey of 275 American cities showed that 70 percent of those with populations over 250,000 had budget deficits in 1980 and 89 percent expected to have deficits in 1981 (Herbers, 1981). Thus in cities such as New York, subway trains and streets are not maintained, garbage collections become less frequent, more fire stations close, police patrols are reduced, and social services are cut.

As social problems consume larger shares of city resources, life there becomes less agreeable and more costly. People with higher incomes can afford to leave for the suburbs or for Sun Belt cities where the quality of life is better and where more amenities are available. But as those with greater resources escape the central city, the city poor are left even worse off (Bradbury et al., 1982).

One solution that would substantially alleviate the financial burdens of the cities would be to tax suburbanites. Although suburban residents use the central-city services—shopping, entertainment, education, and the like—they seldom contribute a fair share to the city's maintenance. But a city government usually lacks control over an entire metropolitan region. Consequently, it cannot impose taxes on suburbanites even though they benefit from what the city has to offer. For this reason, among others, many sociologists believe that cutting state and federal aid to cities is a step in the wrong direction. Such cuts move away from the goal of distributing financial responsibility for cities across a broader population. In addition, decreases in aid leave city governments with only a few short-run solutions to their financial problems: substantial cutbacks in municipal services, significant increases in taxes, or some combination of the two. Both prospects are highly unpopular with city residents, so hard choices must be made. Since most cities cannot substantially raise their taxes without losing even more revenue-producing businesses and upper-income families, many are opting for moderate tax hikes coupled with very sharp cutbacks in public services.

THE FUTURE OF URBAN AMERICA

Changing and intensified urban patterns require new and innovative social responses. Sociological inquiry into urban life gives us useful insights that can help us adapt to modern living and improve the quality of our environment. Because urbanized societies are large and dynamic, programs to deal with urban problems must be societal in scope while their implementation is shaped by the dictates of the local situation. A comprehensive urban policy must address both the physical and social aspects of urban life and decline.

Revitalizing the Cities: Innovations and Programs

Some observers contend that the recent decline of older northern cities is an inevitable development of a free-market system. Because business firms seek to maximize profits, they will locate wherever land, labor, and other costs of production are cheapest. Eventually, the argument goes, costs of production will equalize in America's different regions, making it no longer so profitable for firms to move to the South and West. This equalization process, although temporarily painful for the North, will presumably usher northern cities into a new prosperity—one based not on the heavy industry that dominated during the nineteenth and early twentieth centuries, but rather on service jobs, light manufacturing, and high technology. Observers who hold this optimistic view often point to signs that many once blighted cities are finally "turning the corner." In recent years there has been a flurry of office and hotel construction in New York City. Renovation has produced thriving commercial districts and tourist attractions such as Ghirardelli Square in San Francisco, the Inner Harbor in Baltimore, and Quincy Market in Boston. And an impressive amount of housing in places like Philadelphia's Queen Village and Washington's Adams-Morgan section is undergoing a process of "gentrification," in which young, relatively affluent people move back into the central city to buy and refurbish run-down townhouses.

Others, however, feel that this optimism is premature. While gentrification has increased property values of certain inner-city neighborhoods, it has displaced less affluent residents who can no longer afford to meet the increasing rents. Many of these families are forced to move into public housing, which creates a further demand on the city's scarce financial resources. Urban finance and policy specialists Richard Nathan and James Fosset report that construction in many urban centers is still too modest to boost the overall level of prosperity. What it provides instead are "pockets of plenty" in the midst of continued decline (quoted in Herbers, 1981). For example, the number of central-city houses currently being renovated usually amounts to less than 2 percent of the community's total housing stock (Clay, 1978). And for every neighborhood that is being improved, usually several others are slipping into abandonment or decay. What's more, many of the recent development projects in older American cities seem to benefit primarily the wealthy. Renaissance Center in Detroit is a good example. These magnificent new towers house executive offices, expensive shops, and fashionable restaurants, but the surrounding neighborhoods remain poor, crime-ridden, and deteriorating. Thus, revitalization efforts in older northern cities frequently do very little to improve conditions for many of the poor.

What, then, can be done to rebuild these cities into economically viable centers? One step is to stop viewing cities as isolated districts and to see them instead as parts of larger metropolitan regions. As we have already mentioned, older cities have been severely handicapped by their inability to annex the flourishing suburban communities around them, which would greatly expand their shrinking tax bases. Imposing a regional tax on the suburbs remains an unlikely prospect, but increased regional planning and policy making would be a positive step. Overall, metropolitan regions need coordinated public policies that enable communities to adjust to population and economic change. If cities are to continue one of their historic functions—helping society upgrade its poorer citizens and assimilate its immigrants—then sustained infusions of outside resources will be required.

One frequently heard proposal for urban revitalization centers on involvement of the private sector. In countless cities throughout the United States, local officials and private sector groups, including developers, planners, bankers, property owners, and retailers, have forged sophisticated central-city programs. Main-street malls, skywalks, civic and cultural centers, architectural restorations, Dial-A-Bus systems, and downtown improvement districts have been among their products.

Downtown redevelopment programs have operated on the assumption that without a strong urban core, it is next to impossible to revitalize surrounding neighborhoods. Indeed, some urban planners have argued that the abandonment of slum dwellings actually speeds up

The renovation of Inner Harbor in Baltimore has turned this area into a thriving tourist attraction. However, it is doubtful that this type of redevelopment project yields much benefit to the poor. (Frank Fisher/Gamma-Liaison)

the revival of a slum neighborhood because it gives developers an opportunity to acquire property cheaply and to consolidate land parcels. The property can then be used for office buildings and high-income apartments (Huth, 1980). But these programs have typically not benefited low-income groups, they have simply moved the poor outward toward the inner suburbs.

Another proposal for dealing with the problems of unemployment, abandonment, and crime that have plagued American cities is the *urban enterprise zone* (Haar et al., 1982). At a time when budget cuts have curtailed many government programs to aid cities, the urban enterprise zone is designed as a laissez-faire approach that will encourage industry and business to locate in the inner-city. Proponents have noted that "free zones" such as Hong Kong and Singapore in Asia have prospered, serving as centers for the employment of unskilled workers. They suggest that American cities can regenerate by providing zones in which government regulations are reduced and firms locating there are allowed substantial tax breaks. But critics claim that such programs are unlikely to succeed because quality-of-life considerations play a more important role than do tax incentives in corporate plant-location decisions.

While some look to the private sector for programs to revitalize the cities, others look to government. They say that decisions affecting the fortunes of millions of Americans cannot be left to corporate decision makers. Indeed, they believe it is futile to expect private enterprise to find the will or capacity to halt—much less reverse—the decline of northeastern and midwestern cities. Moreover, Katherine Bradbury and her colleagues (1982), among others, hold that it is only equitable that those people and firms who worsen urban poverty by fleeing the city should bear the costs of remedying it. They see federal programs as necessary because local governments lack the financial base to deal with the deepening problems of the inner cities.

Among federal programs designed to meet the urban crisis have been those of the Housing and Urban Development Department (HUD). For instance, in coorporation with a number of other agencies, it has sponsored the Neighborhood Reinvestment Corporation (Clay, 1978). The Neighborhood Reinvestment Corporation has sought to improve the physical environment and the quality of urban living by making loans to homeowners who want to renovate their dwellings but who have difficulty meeting commercial credit standards. And it has promoted capital improvement in street surfacing, street lighting, drainage, landscaping, and parks.

Another approach to urban problems has centered on neighborhood groups (Herbers, 1983*c*). Where once such groups demanded better services from city halls, they are now increasingly providing the services for themselves. Local governments are finding that they can often reduce costs by hiring civic groups to perform services that have traditionally been carried out by public employees. For instance, in Portland, Oregon, neighborhood organizations are repairing streets; in Louisville, Kentucky, they are constructing sidewalks; in Jacksonville, Florida, such groups are operating shelters for the poor; in Baltimore, they are maintaining parks; in Woodbury, New Jersey, they are rehabilitating housing; and in Canton, New York, they are assisting children and disabled people.

In sum, as cities grapple with the loss of people, industries, and jobs and with the breakdown of services and amenities, they must look to new avenues and approaches for regenerating urban life. And since urban problems are deep, pervasive, and complex, a many-pronged attack will be needed. All this offers ample opportunities for imaginative and innovative thought and programs.

Beyond the Megalopolis

The city of the future will be far different from the nineteenth- and twentieth-century industrial city, which was a center for manufacturing. Increasingly, people and businesses will be able to take many of the economic functions out of the city (Beale and Fuguitt, 1978). However, some firms, particularly those in banking, insurance, finance, and business services, will maintain offices in large cities because only there can they have ready links to foreign-trade partners and customers. Thus cities like New York and London should remain viable urban giants well into the next century. Cities are also increasingly likely to become the focus for political, cultural, recreational, and service functions. The city of the future will be seen primarily as a center of administration and consumption, and not as a center of industry.

Cities will also become less congested. In the United States a significant change is already under way. The 1980 census showed that many small towns are experiencing dramatic growth (Dionne, 1980). Underlying this shift seems to be a belief that small, sparsely settled communities offer a less hectic, more satisfying way of life. But it has only been in the last several decades that economic trends have allowed an increasing number of people to earn a living in rural areas. Some rural residents are employed in outlying suburbs and commute from their homes to work. Others are finding jobs in the growing number of industries locating their production facilities outside the metropolitan rings, where taxes are usually low and labor relatively cheap. Many people who want to run their own small businesses are establishing them in less congested areas. Finally, modern communication and transportation systems have led to a revival of "cottage industries," in which individuals produce goods or offer services from their homes. With all these factors at work, it seems likely that people will continue to spread out across the American countryside for many years.

As people spread out and many businesses decentralize, satellite centers around the largest cities will offer many of the advantages of big-city living: quality entertainment, cultural attractions, fine restaurants, and top-grade shopping areas. Emphasis will fall on the quality of life that such communities provide. Some satellite communities will evolve as specialized centers for higher education, medical care, and high technology. Indeed, one possibility is that there will be less need for central cities as urbanization spreads to megalopolis.

Even so, the poor, minorities, and new immigrants will continue to be concentrated in America's central cities in the foreseeable future. Although some inner-city neighborhoods will undergo "gentrification," others will remain repositories for those whom the prevailing economic and social order deems unemployable or expendable (see Chapter 12). Thus without considerable ingenuity and governmental help, the problems of many central-city peoples—upgrading skills, finding jobs, and obtaining adequate housing and health care—are likely to persist.

Some individuals who are concerned about the future of urban life in industrialized nations have turned their attention and talents toward redesigning human living space. They have championed the idea of building **new towns,** carefully and comprehensively planned communities usually located near a larger metropolis, which would take care of urban growth in a systematic fashion. Many new towns design their use of land to allow for small neighborhoods clustered into larger communities, high degrees of social interaction, and attractive open spaces. The communities are conceived as total environments. Ebenezer Howard created the English new town of Letchworth in 1902, and according to its 1966 census, Great Britain had over 150,000 people living in such developments (Schaffer, 1970). In the United States, Columbia, Maryland; Greenhills, Ohio; Greendale, Wisconsin; and Reston, Virginia, are well publicized new towns, but there are hundreds of other less well-known efforts throughout the country.

Some day, however, there will probably be very little land surface left to settle. Where will the human population then be housed? Futurists are already proposing many possibilities (Estes, 1979). Whole cities of people may occupy overground **megastructures**—acres of living, working, and recreational space supported high above the earth's surface on giant vertical pillars. Megastructures would be designed to allow maximum sunlight to strike the land below, thus allowing agriculture for food production right beneath the city. Millions of other people may occupy floating cities—massive structures on flotation platforms that could be anchored on large bays or along protected coastlines. Still others may move underground into huge networks of housing, offices, commercial districts, and entertainment facilities that reach deep into the earth. And some could even inhabit cities beneath the surface of the sea.

This planned development in Montgomery County, Maryland, combines clustered housing with open recreational areas. (Frank Fisher/Gamma-Liaison)

Although some of these ideas may seem remote at present, we already have the technology to make them possible. In fact, the prototype of a floating city, built by the Japanese for an international exposition, is now at anchor off the coast of Okinawa. Similarly, deep inside the Cheyenne Mountains in Colorado, the American government has built a gigantic air defense center that consists of eleven interconnected structures and over 18,500 square meters of floor space. And marine scientists have already created permanent undersea laboratories off the coasts of Texas, Florida, and the Bahamas. Tomorrow's cities as depicted by futurists promise to alter the urban landscape.

Of course, the future of the city is still open. The city provides a complex, dynamic, and continually evolving environment. The characteristics of urban life in the future will become evident only as the years unfold. Even so, the challenge confronting us is that we inhabit a finite planet. Our common fate is tied up with how we treat our environment and one another. Ideally, the knowledge we gain from sociological research will allow us to shape urban living so as to create safer, healthier, and more beautiful cities. Such planning must not only address land use but must also consider the health, educational, social, and cultural life of urban inhabitants (Murphy, 1982).

EPILOGUE

For the foreseeable future, we can identify forces at work to accelerate the spread of urban and metropolitan forms away from core cities to far-flung urban regions. But we also see forces at work to retard the outward migration and revitalize the core cities. These forces link to elements and processes that we have considered in other chapters. Economic changes have contributed to the flow of people outward toward rural areas and away from the Snow Belt to the Sun Belt (Chapter 16). Technological innovations (Chapter 19), foreign competition, and changing corporate interests and structures (Chapter 11) have devastated many "smokestack" industries and led to the exodus of Americans from northeastern and midwestern manufacturing cities dependent on these industries. The declining tax base of central cities has aggravated the problems of their minority populations and deepened the urban crisis, accelerating the movement of upper-income groups and whites to urban fringes (Chapter 12).

Other forces have slowed the outward shift of people to the suburbs, small towns, and rural areas. Rising divorce rates and the explosive growth of households headed by single persons have undermined the ability of many Americans to afford single-family homes in the suburbs (Chapter 13). Economic difficulties associated with sharp swings in the business cycle during the 1970s and 1980s have placed many traditional types of housing beyond the financial reach of many individuals (Chapter 11). High costs of commuting from outlying areas and office- and service-job opportunities in revitalized downtowns have also helped slow the outflow. And in two-earner households, both parties may prefer to live in the city, close to urban amenities.

All these changes have had wide-ranging consequences. For instance, shifting life styles and lower birth rates have left many once-proud central-city and suburban schools ailing and empty (Chapter 14). Even schools that remain open are subject to financial troubles and place a tax burden on an increasingly aging and disgruntled population (Kowinski, 1980). Further, as the scale of modern urban life has expanded—reaching dimensions of the metropolis, megalopolis, and beyond—the self-determination of local communities has been progressively undermined. Increasingly, decisions that vitally affect the community's well-being are being made in remote political capitals or in the home offices of giant conglomerates (Chapter 11). All the while, the underclasses, particularly minorities, have been progressively rendered unemployable and expendable (Chapters 10 and 12). It is not surprising that changes of this magnitude have produced many social dislocations and problems to which people have responded by collective behavior and social movements. It is to these latter matters that we turn our attention in the next chapter.

SUMMARY

Cities are relatively large, dense, and permanent settlements of socially diverse people who do not produce their own food. The first true cities developed about 6000 to 5000 B.C. in the great river valleys of the Near East. The modern city emerged only with the coming of the Industrial Revolution in the mid-eighteenth century. Since then, urbanization has been a worldwide phenomenon.

In America, cities began to develop rapidly after the Civil War. By 1950 more than 70 percent of the United States population was urbanized. Since this time, some cities have merged into *megalopolises*, huge urban areas including two or more cities and their outlying suburbs.

Although city life can be rich and interesting, it can also be impersonal and alienating. City dwellers may have few close friends among their neighbors (unless they have lived in the same place for a long time); however, they often have close personal ties with family members who live nearby or with those who do the same kind of work.

The development of suburbs—primarily since World War II—has had a great impact on American life. It appears that rather than fleeing the problems of the cities, many of those who choose to settle in the suburbs go in search of the special opportunities to be found there: good schools, homes with yards, and so on. Although suburbs are often thought of as all alike, they actually differ considerably—by social class, in particular. Many are fairly homogeneous in population.

City neighborhoods evolve; some improve, some decline. An "invasion" by a new group, for example, can change the character of a neighborhood and move property values up or down. Several models of the development of cities as a whole have been proposed, among them the concentric zone model, the sector model, and the multiple nuclei model. A newer approach to studying the structure of cities is social area analysis.

America's older cities, particularly those in the Northeast and upper Midwest, are currently facing massive problems. With a large population of poor people, such cities lack the tax revenue to provide city services and to repair and maintain decrepit public facilities. Not only have many middle-class residents left for the suburbs; so too have many businesses, taking with them thousands of jobs. This has increased inner-city unemployment and made the cities' problems worse. Most cities have had little choice in recent years but to increase taxes and decrease public services.

Although there have been some striking efforts at urban redevelopment in recent years, unless cities can regain some of the jobs and wealth that have moved to the suburbs, it is difficult to see how revitalization can be widespread.

One interesting finding of the 1980 census is that many Americans have moved to small towns. Some of these people commute to work in outlying suburbs; others are finding work with manufacturing firms that have relocated outside the cities; and still others have devised ways of working at home. Given developments in communications technology, it seems likely that this movement of people to smaller communities will continue.

GLOSSARY

City. A relatively large, dense, and permanent settlement of socially diverse people who do not directly produce their own food.

Concentric zone model. A model of urban structure proposed by Burgess; according to it, cities develop with a business district at the core, surrounded by an area of transition characterized by residential instability and high crime rates, beyond which are the various residential zones.

Employing suburbs. Communities that are centers of manufacturing or industrial operations and of employment for their own residents and also for those from other communities.

Gemeinschaft. Tönnies's term for small traditional communities characterized by common values, norms, and ancestry; shared roles, positions, and functions; a close-knit network of friends and relatives, and geographical and social stability.

Gesellschaft. Tönnies's term for societies characterized by diverse values, norms, and ancestry; complementary roles, positions, and functions; a loosely linked network of friends; and geographical and social mobility.

Invasion cycle. A process of change in urban land use in which new users drive out earlier users.

Megalopolis. A developing urban form in which separate cities grow together, forming an interdependent entity.

Megastructure. A type of futuristic urban architecture in which acres of living, working, and recreational space are supported high above the earth's surface.

Multiple nuclei model. A model of urban structure proposed by Harris and Ullman; according to it, land uses, costs, and interests cause a city to develop a series of nuclei, each with specialized activities.

New town. A comprehensively planned settlement, usually near a larger metropolis, built to absorb urban growth in a systematic fashion.

Residential suburbs. Communities that consist of homeowners and breadwinners who commute to their jobs in cities or other communities.

Sector model. A model of urban structure proposed by Hoyt; according to it, cities are composed of sectors around a central business district, distributed along major transportation routes radiating outward from the center.

Social area analysis. The use of indexes of residents' social, family, and ethnic statuses to examine changes taking place in urban space and in society as a whole.

Succession. The climax stage in the process of invasion, when the new inhabitants completely occupy an area.

Urban ecology. The configurations and relationships that occur among people, their activities, and the land they occupy.

Urban sprawl. The unplanned growth that has accompanied the emergence of megalopolises.

Urbanization. The increase in the percentage of a population that lives in urban settlements and the consequent extension of influence of urban ways over the populace.

Zoning. A procedure by which land parcels are designated by law for specific purposes and the size of lots and the structures on them are regulated.

CLUB KOKOMO
adidas
10,000 METER SERIES
USA

CHAPTER 18

Collective Behavior and Social Movements

In late September 1982 seven Chicago-area residents died suddenly and mysteriously. All seven had taken Extra-Strength Tylenol capsules. Days before, someone had laced capsules of the popular painkiller with cyanide, a deadly poison. The culprit then returned the capsules to their containers and placed the now-deadly bottles, looking good as new, in Tylenol displays in a number of supermarkets and drug stores. Within a day or so of the deaths, fear gripped Chicago and spread to communities throughout the United States. Citizens flooded poison-control centers and hotlines with calls. Rumors abounded, including one that terrorists were at work to destroy the United States. Public officials warned people not to flush Tylenol down their toilets lest it get into the sewage system and ultimately contaminate the water supply. Feelings of unease and anxiety radiated across the nation at the prospect of a "madman" at large who struck at innocent people, bringing death via substances designed to heal.

On March 23, 1954, Seattle newspapers carried the first of several stories about damage to automobile windshields in a town eighty miles to the north of the city. The windshields had small pit marks and bubbles in them, and car owners occasionally found tiny, metallic-looking particles embedded in the glass. The cause of this curious damage was unknown, but police suspected vandals. Then on the evening of April 14, the mysterious destructive agent appeared to hit Seattle itself. During the next two days, nearly 250 people called the Seattle police department, reporting windshield damage to over 3,000 cars! By this time, the people of Seattle had begun to attribute the windshield pits to a variety of causes—meteoric dust, sand flea eggs hatching in the glass, high-frequency waves from a recently installed regional radio transmitter. But by far the most frequent "cause" cited was radioactive fallout from H-bomb tests in the north Pacific earlier that year. As this rumor swept the Seattle area, frightened citizens tried desperately to devise protective shields. On the evening of April 15, the mayor of Seattle appealed to the governor and to the President for emergency help. But then, as quickly as it had arisen, the hysteria died down. Later, a team of experts determined that the pit marks had always been there. But people hardly ever noticed them before because drivers customarily look *through* their windshields, not *at* them (Medalia and Larsen, 1958).

These bizarre episodes of mass hysteria illustrate what sociologists call collective behavior. **Collective behavior** refers to relatively nonroutine actions that engage large, often anonymous, groups of people. It entails episodes of behavior that differ from the more habitual, repetitive behaviors that characterize our daily lives and that primarily follow established norms and patterns (Rose, 1982). Collective behavior encompasses a wide range of activities, including fads, fashions, crazes, mass hysteria, panics, crowds, and riots.

Another form of social behavior also occurs outside the institutional framework of everyday life—social movements. A **social movement** is "a conscious, collective, organized attempt to bring about or resist large-scale change in the social order by non-institutionalized means" (Wilson, 1973:8). For many years sociologists grouped social movements with collective behavior. They did so because both break with the familiar web of ordered expectations and because large-scale social movements are often accompanied by gatherings of insurgents and outbursts of volatile behavior. However, more recently sociologists like Mark Traugott (1978) have argued that collective behavior and social movements are separate phenomena. Whereas collective behavior is characterized by spontaneity and the lack of internal structure, social movements have a high degree of internal order and a sustained, purposeful orientation. Thus many social movements—including the women's liberation, the environmental, and the antinuclear movements, which we will consider later in the chapter—are highly structured, have well-defined statuses and norms, endure for many years, and have well-established goals. In this chapter we will regard collective behavior and social movements as distinct types of social behavior, although they share some common elements.

We begin with a look at the preconditions and determinants of collective behavior, then turn our sociological eye on crowd behavior, especially that of volatile and potentially violent crowds. Next we examine some explanations of why people act as they do in crowd settings.

We then turn our attention to social movements. We consider various types of social movements, the sources of social movements, and some recent efforts to bring about social change by means of organized, conscious action. Finally we will see that whatever the forms they take, collective behavior and social movements are highly dependent on the nature and speed of the means of communication. Effective communication creates coherent collectivities out of disparate individuals and groups. For this reason access to mass media such as radio, television, films, and the press is crucial for many contemporary forms of collective behavior and social movement.

PRECONDITIONS FOR COLLECTIVE BEHAVIOR

Because some forms of collective behavior, particularly panics, crowds, and mass exuberances, are highly charged and emotional, at first sight they seem to be irrational and unpredictable. Yet when we subject them to sociological scrutiny, we discover much that belies such interpretations. Indeed, collective behaviors typically reveal continuities with everyday behaviors (Oberschall, 1973). For example, the survivors of sudden

Collective behavior often proceeds in a very orderly way. After a severe earthquake, for example, these people in Managua, Nicaragua, set up an orderly system to distribute food. (Hank Morgan/Rainbow.)

disasters, such as fires, tornadoes, or flash floods, do not always act in a dazed and aimless fashion. Frequently, despite their shock and their grief, they are able to behave in surprisingly level-headed and coherent ways—forming search and rescue parties, providing emergency medical care to the injured, setting up temporary shelters and food distribution centers, and so forth.

Even acts that appear to outsiders to be largely irrational may in fact have a great deal of rationality to them. For instance, during the 1960s, while many whites saw riots in black ghettos as totally senseless, the rioters saw such civil disorder as an effective way to make known their anger over white oppression. And they did not attack haphazardly. In most cases it was only white-owned ghetto businesses that were burned and looted. The point is that to analyze collective behavior sociologically, we must look beyond the impressions of unbridled emotionalism, irrationality, and total unpredictability that many people hold. These popular assumptions are seldom true, as you will see more clearly later in this chapter.

Further, sociologists find that collective behavior does not simply spring up at any time, in any place. There are a variety of preconditions that make events like the Seattle windshield-pitting hysteria not as unpredictable as they may at first seem. One influential view of the preconditions for collective action is that of the sociologist Neil Smelser (1962). According to Smelser, six conditions typically precede an episode of collective behavior: structural conduciveness, social strain, a generalized belief, precipitating events, the mobilization of participants, and social control. These conditions or determining factors occur in sequence so that each one creates a social environment that helps make the next one possible. Smelser does not say that collective behavior will always occur when a few or even all of these conditions are present. But as each one is added, the likelihood of alternative responses decreases, until eventually some kind of collective action is virtually inevitable.

Structural Conduciveness

By **structural conduciveness,** Smelser means that social conditions must favor collective action. In Seattle, for instance, the fact that the people lived in or near a densely populated urban center, where rapid communication via radio, newspapers, and neighborhood gossip took place, made widespread collective behavior possible. Moreover, the complexity of the nation's military establishment, coupled with a high level of technological development, had created a weapons climate so awesome that it was beyond most people's ability to comprehend. These conditions, of course, are very general and in no way necessitate collective behavior. But they do set a stage that at least makes possible certain forms of collective action.

Social Strain

Social strain can arise from various sources. For instance, it can spring from a sudden disruption of the existing social order, as in disastrous floods or tornadoes, or from long term social change, such as those dislocations leading to the medieval witch craze (see boxed insert, p. 476). Strain can also arise from persistent and increasingly intense value conflicts between different segments of society—for example, incompatible religious groups, hostile political camps, or widely disparate economic classes. Finally, strain can result when the culture offers inadequate guidelines for responding to an event or experience. This last situation seems to have been at work in the Seattle windshield-pitting case. The culture offered little information about what to expect from nuclear fallout. Consequently, people living relatively close to nuclear test areas were anxious about their safety but did not know what to do. Such anxiety can be a powerful source of social strain. In sum, collective behavior typically derives from the failure of some aspect of the social system to function effectively (Rose, 1982).

Generalized Belief

Before people organize for action, a generalized belief usually develops to explain the strain they are experiencing and to describe its consequences. Frequently, this only heightens the tension by better "defining" a formerly vague threat and making it seem more imminent. In Seattle such a generalized belief was fostered by the

THE SOCIOLOGICAL EYE ON:

The European Witch Craze

In one of the most bizarre and macabre episodes of human history, between 200,000 and 500,000 European women were executed for witchcraft during the fourteenth and fifteenth centuries. When we consider such strange episodes of collective behavior, we might well conclude that they are the work of some malevolent person who has succeeded in stirring people to an irrational frenzy. At times this may be a factor. Yet deeper social forces are also at work, which some leaders may seek to exploit and turn to their advantage. According to the sociologist Nachman Ben-Yehuda (1980), the European witch craze was not simply an irrational outburst; it was also a response by established institutions and their elites to the social changes taking place at the end of the Middle Ages.

Fomenting the persecutions were the Church and its Inquisition, which had earlier focused its energies on fighting heretics. Why did the medieval Church, particularly its branches in Germany, France, and Switzerland, feel itself threatened? And why did it choose to strike out against "witches," most of whom were apparently ordinary women? To answer these questions, we must consider a number of social, economic, and demographic changes that were occurring in these countries.

First of all, economic development was accelerating and eroding the traditional medieval order. Under feudalism, social and economic life were strictly ordered. From the king and top Church officials down to the most impoverished peasant, each member of society occupied a "place." The family was tightly ordered, with a clearly defined role for each member in a structure centered on household production. In the fourteenth century, this structure began to break down. Economic development meant more trade, industry, and urbanization. With the rise of industries, the family began to lose its importance as a productive unit: Manufacturing was increasingly carried on in workshops and factories. The new urban order of cities, factories, and a secular life did not fit into the feudal scheme. As people moved from being peasants to being workers, they lost the security of a life in which their role and tasks were clearly defined. As more single men and women moved into the cities to seek work, women became more visible. Often unable to find jobs as spinners and weavers, many women were reduced to prostitution to eke out a livelihood.

All these changes produced a mood of insecurity and uneasiness. To many, society seemed to be coming apart—particularly as the influence of the Church slipped. To make matters worse, the fourteenth century saw the devastating Black Death, the plague that eventually killed between one-third and one-half of Europe's population. This calamity created a sense of pervasive doom and decline.

The witch craze was a reaction to these developments, an attempt to "counteract and prevent change and to reestablish traditional religious authority . . . . By persecuting witches, this society, led by the Church, attempted to redefine its moral boundaries," (Ben-Yehuda, 1980:14). "Witches" served as convenient symbols of all that was wrong: As the position of women changed, they became prime targets for the fears and anxieties that change engenders.

The witch hunts were a means (brutal to be sure) of coping with crisis and disorganization at both an institutional and an individual level. The witch-hunters' attempts to purify the faith, redefine moral boundaries, and halt the tide of change obviously failed. These desperate efforts at cleansing society represented attempts to forestall the death of institutions by destroying the lives of thousands of individuals. Here, then, is a dramatic example of the elaborate strategems to which dominant elites may resort in order to protect their hold on social order.

---

local press. For several months before the windshield-pitting incident, newspapers had published a variety of stories about recent H-bomb tests in the Pacific. "Atomic Energy Commission Discloses Blast Amid Mounting Concern" announced one headline; "Witness Says Hydrogen Test Out of Control" warned another; "Three H-Bomb Victims Face Death" declared a third. Such unnerving reports helped provide a basis for people's vague anxieties.

Precipitating Events

Often episodes of collective behavior emerge when something happens to confirm people's generalized belief. In Seattle the precipitating events were the reports of a few pitted windshields, for which police had no definite explanation. Given the widespread fears over nuclear testing, these discoveries provided concrete "evidence" that the terrible consequences of nuclear fallout were at hand.

Mobilization of Participants

When the "evidence" is in and "interpreted" for them by leaders, people begin acting on their beliefs. Mass hysteria breaks out, panic erupts, mobs form, social movements are organized, or some other form of collective behavior occurs. In Seattle this mobilization was spurred both by the front-page news coverage of the windshield "emergency" and by the rapid spreading of rumors among the area's residents.

Social Control

Governing elites often attempt to stop or deflect the collective activity, or to eliminate its major causes. Their measures influence the timing, content, direction, and outcome of incidents of collective behavior. The results are not always what the agents of social control intended. In Seattle, for instance, the mayor's appeal for assistance from the governor and the president did not help to restore calm—it only fueled the hysteria.

Smelser's six preconditions highlight for us how social strain and conflict are mediated and filtered through intervening processes before being activated in episodes of collective behavior. But his approach also has shortcomings. Critics point out that he defines his determinants so broadly that they cannot be used to predict when collective behavior will occur or in what form it will appear. And critics fault Smelser for overemphasizing the differences and discontinuities between collective behavior and everyday behavior while overlooking their similarities and continuities (Oberschall, 1973). For instance, athletic competitions, elections, and the daily clashes of political life have elements in common with riots, peaceful demonstrations, and spontaneous clashes. Nevertheless, Smelser's model is a useful way to begin thinking about the causes of collective action. As you will see, it can be applied to many of the incidents discussed in the remainder of the chapter.

CROWD BEHAVIOR

Crowds are temporary collections of people, gathered around a person or an event, who are conscious of and influenced by one another's presence. Crowds differ from other social groups primarily in that crowds are short-lived, lack a past and future, are relatively unstructured, and use convential spatial areas or buildings for unconventional purposes (Snow, Zurcher, and Peters, 1981). For example, the people who collect around an accident stop interacting as soon as they leave the scene. Beyond the specific moment of their common focus, they typically have no other exchanges. In his classic essay "Collective Behavior," sociologist Herbert Blumer (1939/1951:178) called such spontaneous congregations **casual crowds** whose "members come and go, giving but temporary attention to the object which has awakened the interest of the crowd, and entering into only feeble association with one another." Blumer also identified three other types of crowds: conventional, expressive, and acting crowds.

Passengers on a plane, shoppers in a store, the audience at a concert, are illustrations of **conventional crowds.** These people are gathered for a specific purpose and behave according to established norms. For example, although booing is expected at a football game, it is considered quite inappropriate at a concert of classical music or at a funeral. Relatively little interaction occurs in a conventional crowd. Its members individually pursue a common goal, a destination, a bargain, or an entertainment. Exchanges among such people are usually highly routinized and impersonal.

The people at rock festivals, revival meetings, and exuberant carnivals (such as those held in New Orleans and Rio de Janeiro in Brazil) are **expressive crowds:** Members behave in ways they would consider unacceptable in other settings. Expressive crowds are emotionally charged. Members are carried away by their enthusiasm and other intense feelings. The expression of these feelings becomes their primary aim. The legendary Woodstock Music and Art Fair, held in New York's Catskill Mountains in August, 1969, is an example of such a crowd. An impressive array of rock stars drew over 300,000 young people to the farm where the festival was held. The mood of the crowd became increasingly joyous, and today the event is remembered as much for this experience and expression of good feeling as for the concert itself.

An **acting crowd** is an excited, volatile collection of

All crowds are temporary collections of people, but all such collections are not alike. In a casual crowd, such as the gathering at a New York City street fair, members have little association with each other. In a conventional crowd, such as the group at a Democratic fund-raising banquet, people gather for a specific purpose and behave according to specific norms. (Above, Harvey Stein; below, Owen Franken/Stock, Boston.)

people who focus on a controversial event that provokes their indignation, anger, and desire to act—a gang roughing up a youth, for example, or an incident of police brutality. Thus both expressive crowds and acting crowds are emotionally charged, but there is a difference between the two. Whereas members of an expressive crowd see release of their feelings as an end in itself, members of an acting crowd see redress of the perceived wrong as their ultimate goal. When members of an acting crowd are engaged in or ready to engage in violence, they are often referred to as a **mob** (Hoult, 1969). Because the social effects of mob action can be so far-reaching, we will examine it in some detail.

Profile of Mob Action

Mass uprisings and destructive orgies have for centuries been the nightmare of people in power. Mob action was common in eighteenth- and nineteenth-century Europe. In town and country, throngs of armed men and women took over markets and warehouses, demanding the rollback of prices and sometimes seizing goods. In England angry bands of craftspeople burned factories and destroyed the machines that threatened their livelihood. On July 14, 1789, Parisians stormed the ancient Bastille prison in the most famous confrontation of the French Revolution.

Violent, unruly crowds have also figured importantly in American history. The nineteenth century was marked by farmers' revolts, miners' rebellions, bloody battles between unions and police, lynchings, and urban riots. The Civil War Draft Riot of 1863, which raged for four days, was probably one of the worst in this country's history. Mob action has also arisen in the twentieth century, one of the most recent examples being the civil disorders of the 1960s. The following brief account of the Detroit riots of July 1967 is based on the *Report of the National Advisory Commission on Civil Disorders* (1968). Although the report falls short of completely explaining the disorders, it does portray in concrete terms the dimensions of the Detroit uprising.

The Detroit Riots

In the summer of 1967 black ghettos in twenty-three cities exploded in violent public disturbances. Civil rights legislation had raised hopes but delivered little in the way of concrete improvements. Many blacks were frustrated and disillusioned. The National Advisory Commission on Civil Disorders (also known as the Kerner Commission), which had been appointed by President Johnson, found that 70 percent of the rioters believed they deserved better jobs and blamed their problems on racism, not on lack of training, ability, or ambition. In short, ghetto dwellers were subject to substantial social strain. In addition, ghettos are structurally conducive to mass action. Residents live in close proximity, and substandard housing encourages many to spend a great deal of time outdoors, especially during the hot summer months. As a result, the streets are normally filled with bystanders. Such conditions increase the possibility that collective behavior will arise.

Still, even when faced with social strain in a conducive social setting, people do not necessarily engage in mob violence. Usually they must first develop a generalized belief about the people or forces responsible for their plight (Smelser, 1962). The sources of anger and frustration must be identified. In the ghetto, stores tantalize residents with the goods America seems to promise. And police harass and sometimes abuse ghetto dwellers, although often appearing unable to protect them. Property and the police functioned as ever-present reminders of white dominance. Resentment was widespread. All that was needed was a spark to set off an explosion—a precipitating incident, to use Smelser's term.

That incident occurred on Saturday night, July 22, when the Detroit vice squad conducted gambling raids on five social clubs frequented by blacks. These mass arrests provided a focus for the ghetto dwellers' discontent. By the time police hauled the last of the participants away on Sunday morning, a crowd of 200 had gathered on the street. A bottle hurled from the crowd crashed through the window of the last retreating patrol car. This act triggered other outbreaks, mobilizing the participants for action.

By 8:00 A.M., the crowd on 12th Street had grown to 3,000. Finding themselves outnumbered, the police withdrew. For a few hours a carnival mood prevailed among crowd members. By noon the police had positioned themselves on surrounding streets. Rumors rapidly passed among the crowd. One reported that a police officer had bayoneted a black just blocks away.

As police reinforcements mounted and rumors spread, the crowd's mood shifted from revelry to anger.

People began stoning police and setting fire to stores. Firefighters tried to control the fires, but at 4:30 on Sunday afternoon, exhausted, they abandoned the area. At this point, the mayor proclaimed a curfew and summoned the National Guard.

The number of fires and lootings declined. However, reports of sniper fire increased, reaching a peak of 534 reports on Wednesday, July 26. Panic and confusion spread among ghetto residents. Police actions compounded the fright. They broke into homes on the slightest excuse and arrested anyone found to have a weapon. These frantic efforts to reimpose order intensified the violence and exacerbated the problem. Thus, as Smelser argues, social control can be a powerful determinant of the direction that collective behavior takes.

Before the end of the week, the police had arrested 7,200 people. Forty-three people had been killed, thirty or more by police and soldiers, two by store owners, and two or possibly three by rioters. Included among the dead were one National Guardsman, one firefighter, and one police officer (killed accidentally by a fellow officer). Thirty-three of the victims were black, ten white. Property damage was estimated at $22 million.

Researchers found that the 1960s riots were not instigated or carried out by criminals or outside agitators. Property, not people, was the focus of crowd members. They sought to benefit from, not overthrow, the American social system (Allen, 1970). In short, the riots were "spontaneous protests against unjust social conditions" (Campbell and Schuman, 1968). They also proved effective as a means of protest. As one observer put it: "Reporters and cameramen rushed into ghettos; elected and appointed officials followed behind; sociologists and other scholars arrived shortly after. The President established a riot commission; so did the governors" (Fogelson, 1970:146). Thus the riots brought immediate, if not long-term, results that decades of peaceful protest had not (Button, 1978).

The Role of Rumor in Collective Action

A **rumor** is an unverified story that circulates from person to person and is accepted as fact, although its sources may be vague or unknown. Rumors proliferate in tense and ambiguous situations, when people are unable to learn the facts or when, for one reason or another, they distrust the information they receive. Hence, rumors entail a process of dispersing information, although the information is unproven and suspect. Rumors differ from gossip in that in some cases gossip involves known fact. Further, gossip deals with the personal affairs of individuals whereas rumors typically deal with events and issues of greater importance and magnitude (Rosnow and Fine, 1976).

Rumor mongering is not simply a response to idle curiosity. It reflects people's desire to find meaning in events, and thus it represents a form of group problem solving. Recall the 1967 Detroit story that a black man had been bayoneted by police, which helped blacks define the events of the morning and changed the early carnival mood of the crowd. And in the Seattle windshield pitting epidemic of 1954, residents came to interpret the "pittings" as caused by radioactive fallout from the Eniwetok H-bomb tests.

Competitiveness and secrecy encourage rumors. Thus, war and politics give rise to rumors, and events surrounding financial and corporate happenings are constant sources of rumor mongering on various stock exchanges. The competitiveness and secrecy that surrounds critical examinations make college students receptive to rumors. (Indeed, some students have been known to float false information to mislead their unsuspecting peers and to give themselves a competitive edge.) Similarly, in the Soviet Union, where an authoritarian political climate prevents a free flow of reliable information, the people come to rely heavily on word-of-mouth hearsay to make sense out of what otherwise constitute unfathomable events (Rosnow and Fine, 1976).

Most rumors are born, live, and die within a relatively short time. After studying the transmission of rumors in the laboratory and in the field, the psychologists Gordon W. Allport and Leo Postman (1947) discovered a basic pattern to them. A person hears a story that seems interesting and repeats the story—or what is remembered of it—to a friend. Gradually, the original story is reduced to a few essential details that are easy to tell. This is what Allport and Postman call **leveling:** "As a rumor travels, it tends to grow shorter, more concise, more easily grasped and told. In successive versions, fewer words are used and fewer details are mentioned" (p. 75). As a result of leveling, certain details gain in importance, and the rumor is *sharpened*—people remember and pass on only part of the original story.

As a rumor circulates, people also tend to "correct" details so as to make the story more plausible and more coherent. In one of Allport and Postman's experiments, for instance, a story about an ambulance carrying explosives was changed in the retelling to a story about an ambulance carrying medical supplies. The latter version conformed to people's common expectations. Similarly, during the Detroit riots, ghetto residents embellished reports of police brutality because they had come to *expect* the police to be brutal; police and National Guardsmen created rumors about snipers because they *expected* sniping during a riot. In short, rumors tend to confirm people's preconceptions and stereotypes.

Alone on a muddy field, few people would indulge in a mud bath. Yet, as Le Bon noted, people in a crowd behave quite differently than they would if they were alone. (Peter Menzel.)

Explaining Crowd Behavior

Why do riots break out? Why do people abandon the routines of daily life and become participants in hostile crowds? One popular explanation is the riffraff theory. It holds that only criminal types (hoodlums, drifters, bums, drug addicts) participate in riots, and that a hard core of agitators incites violence against the strong disapproval of an area's residents. However, the National Advisory Commission on Civil Disorders disproved this and other myths. Thus, in Detroit, nearly 40 percent of ghetto residents either participated in the 1967 riot or identified themselves as bystanders—hardly a deviant minority. And average Detroit rioters were better educated, better informed, and more involved in the community than were the nonrioters, and they had jobs (albeit ones they thought beneath them). So why, then, did these people become involved in violent mob action?

Emotional and Social Contagion

One view depicts crowd members as losing their individuality and their normal reasoning capabilities. This notion was first proposed by French sociologist Gustave Le Bon (1841–1931) in his book *The Psychology of Crowds* (1895/1960). Le Bon argued that the transformation of individuals into a crowd "puts them in possession of a collective mind" that makes people think, feel, and act quite differently from the way they would if they were alone. Being part of a crowd gives people a sense of invincible power: they "will undertake . . . certain acts with irresistible impetuosity," wrote Le Bon. Crowds gain control over the individual much as hypnotists gain control over their subjects. Individuals become highly suggestible; they are no longer conscious of their actions. Waves of emotion sweep through the crowd, infecting one person after another, much as a highly contagious disease spreads. The thin veneer of civilization falls away, allowing primitive motivations and antisocial impulses to rise to the surface. "The age we are about to enter," Le Bon wrote, "will be in truth the *era of crowds*." He meant this as a dire warning.

In the 1950s, the sociologist Herbert Blumer (1939) refined Le Bon's ideas. He traced contagion to an "exciting event" that creates unrest in a suggestible crowd. People begin milling about, "as if seeking to find or avoid something, but without knowing what it is they are trying to find or avoid" (p. 173). As people search for clues, excited behavior or rhetoric catches their attention. Instead of interpreting and judging these actions, as they ordinarily would, they respond impulsively by modeling their own behavior after them. This reaction reinforces the original actors, making them still more excited (what Blumer called the **circular reaction**). As excitement builds, people become more and more inclined to act on their mounting feelings of agitation. In Blumer's view, this tendency explains "the relatively rapid, unwitting and nonrational dissemination of a mood, impulse or form of conduct" through a crowd (p. 176). Like Le Bon, Blumer emphasized the importance of group pressure for collective behavior.

Emergent Norms and Social Relationships

Few contemporary sociologists dispute the observation that emotions and behavior sometimes spread through crowds as if they were contagious. However, most contemporary sociologists reject the idea that people in crowds necessarily behave in an unreflective, irrational way. It is simplistic, they argue, to view crowds as little more than impulsive, unpredictable creatures who can no longer control their own behavior. The sociologists Ralph Turner and Lewis Killian (1972) are forceful proponents of this view. They question the implicit assumption that social conformity no longer operates in a crowd. They say that in situations lacking firm guidelines for coping, people evolve new social norms as they interact with one another. These norms then exert a powerful influence on their behavior. Turner and Killian's view is called **emergent norm theory.**

The new norms evolve through a gradual process of social exploration and testing. One or more innovators may suggest a course of action, for instance, by shouting obscenities or hurling bottles. Others follow. The crowd begins to define the situation, to develop a justification for acts that would in other circumstances seem questionable. In this way new norms emerge that, although they may condone violent and destructive actions, still impose some limits on crowd behavior.

Turner and Killian argue that the emergence of new norms does not mean that members of a crowd come to think and feel as one. Although it may appear to outsiders that a crowd is a unanimous whole, some participants may just be going along to avoid disapproval and ridicule. Unlike Le Bon and Blumer, Turner and Killian believe that "crowd unanimity" is little more than an illusion. Hence, crowd members not only formulate a new norm and convert others to it. They also exact conformity to the norm and punish dissenters.

Extending Turner and Killian's ideas, other sociologists have argued that an adequate theory of collective behavior must take into account not only the emergence of new norms, but also the emergence of new social relationships (Weller and Quarentelli, 1973). Consider the lynch mob, a fairly common form of crowd violence in the early American West and until recent decades in the South. Here, conventional norms of trial by jury, rule of law, and execution only by the state are replaced with the norms of a vigilante trial and punishment by mob consensus. But new social relationships develop too. Participants improvise a division of labor—informally designating such roles as prosecutor, witnesses, jury members, and executioners. The important point in all such analyses is that crowds are neither normless nor totally lacking in social organization. Collective behavior often originates with an established group, usually involves the emergence of new norms and social relationships, and almost always reflects efforts to deal with strains in the larger society.

Crowd Behavior as Rational Decision Making

One problem with Turner and Killian's view is that it fails to explain why the new norms that emerge in a crowd are often so extreme. Why is it that crowds can endorse arson, looting, and personal assault—behaviors strongly condemned under normal social circumstances? The sociologist Richard Berk (1974) suggests one answer. He says the crowd members calculate that in the current situation such behaviors will "pay off." As portrayed by Berk, people are essentially rational decision makers, and they do not suspend this rationality when they participate in crowd behavior. They intuitively weigh the probable costs and rewards of their actions. The costs associated with rioting revolve around the risk of personal injury and the likelihood of being arrested. The rewards may be tangible, such as looted merchandise, or intangible, such as the psychological gratification of releasing pent-up frustrations. In any case, Berk sees people in mobs as typically selecting behaviors that offer the greatest possible reward at the least possible price. He suggests that crowd actions are often extreme because of the reduction of individual risk when large numbers of people are involved.

Not all sociologists, especially followers of Le Bon's theory of contagion, agree that crowd action is indeed this calculated. But the fact that the ghetto riots of the late 1960s did gain for dissatisfied blacks renewed attention from white America seems to lend some support to Berk's hypothesis. From the perspective of rioters, violent action may in fact offer some benefits.

SOCIAL MOVEMENTS

Thus far we have focused primarily on relatively transitory forms of collective behavior. Mass hysterias flare up and then quickly wither away; crowds gather and soon disperse; even episodes of rioting triggered by deep-seated social strains typically run their course over a relatively brief time. But collective action is not always short-lived. At times people organize long-term social movements to encourage or prevent social change. These movements are signs that some aspect of the social order is not meeting people's needs, and so they actively organize to do something about it. Thus social movements are often catalysts for revolutions, be they great or small.

As we pointed out earlier, a social movement entails an organized effort on the part of people to bring about or resist change through noninstitutionalized means. Indeed, participants in movements often attempt to achieve their goals through *anti*-institutionalized means, including mass demonstrations, boycotts, and occasionally even violence, sabotage, and other illegal acts (especially when agents of social control try to suppress them). Such tactics go beyond conventional procedures for airing grievances, just as panics, mass hysterias, and riots are not conventional ways of coping with strain (Traugott, 1978). Yet social movements also differ from other forms of collective behavior in their degree of organization. While panics, mass hysterias, and riots involve fairly amorphous collectivities of people, participants in social movements typically devise some hierarchy of authority and a division of labor in order to pursue social change effectively. Social movements, therefore, lie somewhere between the formally organized and highly institutionalized aspects of social life and the more loosely structured, noninstitutionalized ones.

Types of Social Movements

Given the great variety of social movements, a number of sociologists have tried to classify them. David Aberle (1966) groups social movements on the basis of two criteria: the *type* of change their sponsors seek (either a change in individuals or a change in the social order) and the *amount* of change they seek (either partial or total). This approach creates four types of movements: alterative, redemptive, reformative, and transformative.

Alterative movements aim to achieve some limited but specific change in individuals. Their participants view human beings as essentially good, but they believe that character flaws or societal pressures can lead people astray. A good alterative movement example is the Women's Christian Temperance Union during its early years when it sought to teach people about the evils of alcohol and to discourage their consumption of it.

Redemptive movements also focus on the individual, but they seek total, not partial, change. Participants believe that the majority of people require conversion to arrive at an entirely different inner state. Most redemptive movements are religious. For example, the evangelical Christian movement sees most individuals as racked with sin and able to redeem themselves only by accepting the teachings of Christ.

Reformative movements differ from both alternative and redemptive movements in that they emphasize changing society rather than individuals. Their aim is partial change since they view the present social order as basically workable. However, their members are dissatisfied with policies in one, or at most a few, specific areas of social life. Civil rights movements of various kinds (for blacks, other racial and ethnic minorities, women, and homosexuals) are examples of reformative movements. They seek not to overturn society as a whole, but to change certain aspects of it. Hence, the aim of such groups is not to destroy the prevailing system but to share in its benefits.

Moderate change is not the goal of **transformative movements,** which aim at total change in the social order. Transformative movements are true revolutions. The changes they endorse are all-embracing; nothing of the old order is to survive. The Bolshevik movement in Russia in the early twentieth century is one example. Followers sought a complete overthrow of the traditional ruling class. Clearly, the results of such movements can be cataclysmic.

Redemptive movements, such as the evangelical Christian movement, see humanity as sinful and open to salvation only through adopting Christ's teachings. (Tim Eagan/Woodfin Camp & Associates.)

The Causes of Social Movements

Regardless of the type of social movement being considered, one of the questions sociologists ask is why these forms of collective action arise in the first place. Under what conditions are people most likely to organize an effort to bring about change? Researchers have proposed two basic answers. Some claim that social movements arise from social and economic deprivation. When discontent with existing institutional arrangements becomes deep and broad enough, people will join together and fight back, or so this argument goes. Other sociologists see things differently. They contend that some level of discontent always exists in a society, so discontent alone cannot explain the creation of social movements. The key factor in precipitating social movements, they say, is a group's ability to mobilize resources in support of its cause. Without sufficient resources, even the most aggrieved members of society cannot launch an organized demand for change. Both these explanations of social movements seem highly persuasive. In the following sections we will explore them in more detail.

Social and Economic Deprivation

The most basic form of deprivation is a lack of life's necessities: inadequate food, shelter, and clothing. Such conditions seem likely precursors of revolution, and sometimes they are. The French Revolution, for instance, was preceded by a sharp increase in the price of bread (the highest price in seventy years) due to poor harvests in 1787 and 1788. Workers in the cities and even residents in rural areas faced severe hunger. In 1789 they rebelled.

The argument that revolutionary movements spring up when people are deprived of their most fundamental needs was basic to Marx's theory of revolution. Marx held that the ever-increasing use of machinery and assembly-line production would condemn workers to more and more menial tasks, thus continually depressing their wages and feeding their sense of alienation. The economic cycle of boom and bust that characterizes capitalist societies would only aggravate and compound the misery of the working class. Eventually, workers would be cast into a state of such intolerable exploitation that they would organize to overthrow their oppressors.

But not all sociologists agree with the view that progressive impoverishment puts people in a revolutionary frame of mind. Over a hundred years ago the French observer Alexis de Tocqueville (1856) studied economic and social decline in the seventeenth century and renewed advancement in the eighteenth. He concluded that revolutionary movements generally occur not when conditions are most hopeless, but after they have begun to improve. During periods of improvement, de Tocqueville argued, people begin to realize that abject deprivation is not inevitable. A better life is suddenly seen as possible, and the downtrodden react by reaching for it. "Evils which are patiently endured when they seem inevitable," wrote de Tocqueville, "become intolerable when once the idea of escape from them is suggested" (p. 214). Sociologists call this gap between people's expectations and their actual conditions **relative deprivation** (Gurr, 1970).

Relative deprivation occurs under a variety of circumstances. De Tocqueville identified one condition, that of *rising expectations*. It was this sense of rising expectations that some sociologists say bred the black protest movement and the ghetto outbreaks of the 1960s (Geschwender, 1964; Abeles, 1976). The economic prosperity of the 1950s and the early gains of the civil rights movement led blacks to believe that their circumstances would substantially improve in the foreseeable future. But the new civil rights legislation and President Lyndon Johnson's "War on Poverty" program delivered little. Dreams of a "Great Society" faded as the United States became increasingly preoccupied with Vietnam. To raise people's expectations for a new day and then to deliver crumbs is to create socially explosive conditions. Not surprisingly, ghetto riots and the Black Power movement followed.

The sociologist James Davies (1962, 1974) identified another condition that fosters feelings of relative deprivation: a "rise-and-drop," or "J-curve," situation. He bases his observation on an analysis of such events as Dorr's Rebellion in Rhode Island in 1782, the Pullman Strike of 1894, the Russian Revolution of 1917, and the Egyptian Revolutiuon of 1953. Davies concludes that revolutionary movements are most likely when a prolonged period of economic and social improvement is followed by a drastic reversal in people's fortunes. The first period presumably creates an expectation that things will steadily get better; the second period creates a terrible fear that all past progress will be suddenly and irretrievably lost. Davies believes that the actual conditions prevailing in the period of reversal are less important than the psychological state they foster. People may even be objectively better off than they were before the economic and social downturn began. But they *feel* deprived in relation to their expectations. They feel robbed of what they thought they should receive. Consequently, they experience intense frustration. Figure 18.1 (p. 486) summarizes Davies's theory. As you can see, revolutions flare up when the gap between what people expect and what they actually receive suddenly widens.

The approaches of Marx, de Tocqueville, and Davies to the role of deprivation in revolution seem on the surface quite different. In the first, progressive impoverishment is said to cause rebellion; in the second, revolution is said to spring from rising hopes for a better life; in the third, social and economic improvement followed by a sharp decline are said to be the necessary ingredients for popular uprising. But a closer look reveals that, despite their obvious differences, a common psychological process underlies all these views. In all cases people are experiencing intense dissatisfaction over their current share of valuable rewards. It may not be crucial whether that current share is steadily declining, taking a temporary downturn, or actually gaining slightly. What may be most important is that people *perceive* themselves to be targets of injustice. They perceive themselves to be deprived—economically or socially, or both—in relation to what is available to others. As a result, they are frustrated and their frustration causes them to launch an organized, often violent demand for change.

Resource Mobilization

Other sociologists argue that perceived deprivation is only one factor precipitating a social movement. To change existing values or norms, they say, people must mobilize resources in support of their cause. Without resources, even the most aggrieved group will not be able to bring about change (Jenkins and Perrow, 1977; Snow et al., 1981). Thus, sociologists such as Charles Tilly (1973, 1978) argue that political violence and revolution occur only when aggrieved groups have the resources and organization to take significant actions.

The resources capable of being mobilized in sup-

FIGURE 18.1 Davies' Theory of Revolution

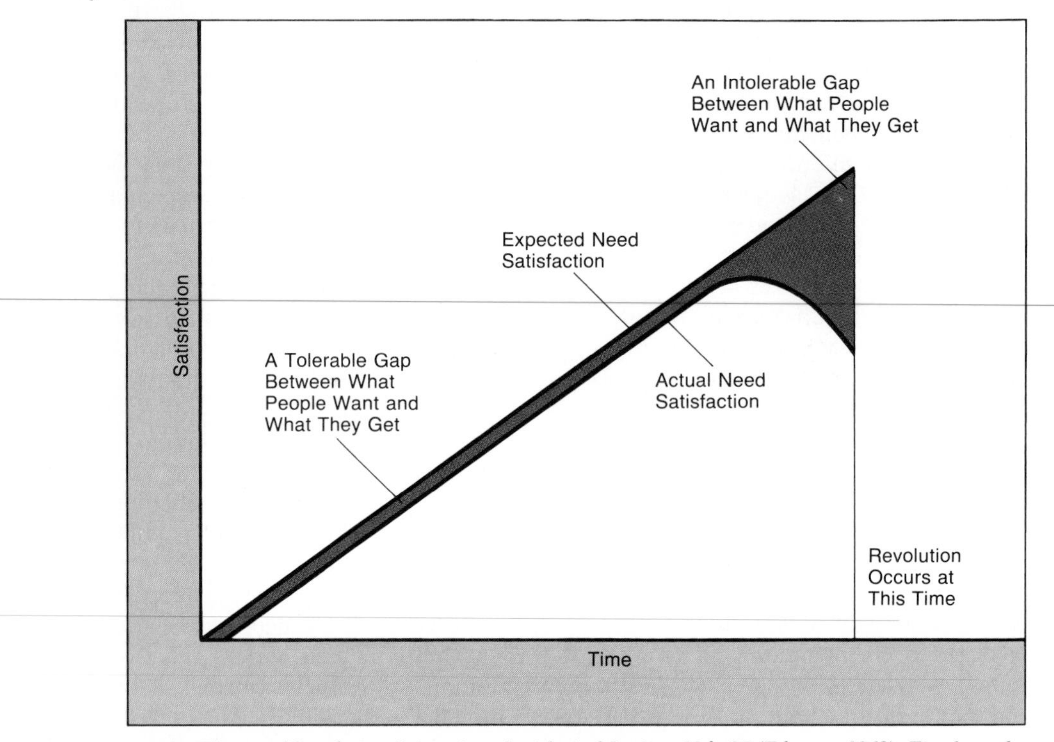

Source: Adapted from James C. Davies, "Toward a Theory of Revolution." *American Sociological Review*, Vol. 27 (February 1962), Fig. 1, p. 6.

This graph illustrates Davies' theory that revolutions are most likely when a period of economic and social progress is succeeded by sharp reversals, fueling fears that all gains will be lost.

port of a social movement include both human skills and tangible assets (Freeman, 1979). Among the primary tangible resources are money (which can purchase a variety of other things), channels of mass communication (leaflets, radio, and television broadcasts, which can publicize a movement's goals), and space to house a movement's headquarters. Human skills are equally important resources. They include leadership, organizational talent, personal prestige (which is helpful in attracting followers and in gaining social acceptance), and in-depth knowledge about the people or institutions the movement hopes to change. Time to devote to movement activities and commitment to movement causes (meaning willingness to endure risk and inconvenience so that movement goals can be achieved) are also critical. For example, in its early years, the civil rights movement depended heavily on the mobilization of supporters' time and commitment. Students in particular, both black and white, were mobilized for sit-ins, marches, and voter registration drives. In this way, the movement achieved a great deal of national attention and sympathy at relatively low cost. Additionally, black urbanization and the growth of black churches and colleges in the post–World War II South increased black group solidarity and facilitated the emergence of the movement (McAdam, 1982).

Resource mobilization theorists assert that the factors causing a social movement often do not originate within the aggrieved group. Support from "outsiders"—from people who do not stand to gain directly from the changes the movement seeks—is critical. For instance, the success of many of the civil rights efforts of the NAACP (National Association for the Advancement of Colored People) during the 1960s derived in part from its ties to a variety of nonmovement organizations, including churches, labor unions, businesses, government agencies, and civic groups (Aveni, 1978). The resources of the poor are often insufficient to launch a successful social movement. Movements by people who themselves lack wealth, power, and prestige usually require a large and sustained influx of outside resources if they are to succeed.

A social movement commonly owes much of its success to its leadership. Sociologists have identified several types of leaders, ranging from the "agitator" or "prophet," whose skills at articulating some demand compel public attention, to the "administrator," who puts together the "nuts and bolts" of an organized campaign (Wilson, 1973). Sometimes a single leader exerts several kinds of leadership simultaneously. Martin Luther King, Jr., and Betty Friedan were both influential "prophets," voicing the concerns of blacks and women, and both functioned as administrators—King as spokesperson for the Southern Christian Leadership Conference and Friedan for the National Organization for Women. More often, however, a movement develops a division of labor among several types of leaders.

Recently, the sociologists John McCarthy and Mayer Zald (1973, 1977) have proposed that the creation of many modern-day social movements is largely the work of "outside" leadership. They say that a groundswell of discontent among aggrieved individuals is of secondary importance in generating a social movement. Skilled leaders can take weak and ill-defined discontent and broaden its base. For this reason grass roots support for some social movements actually comes *after* the movement is under way. For example, the movement to provide federally funded health care for the elderly in America did not initially derive from an outcry among senior citizens. Instead, the movement's principal organization, the National Council for Senior Citizens for Health Care through Social Security (NCSC), was staffed primarily by young and middle-aged professionals and funded by the AFL-CIO. Organizers staged rallies across the country and encouraged mass petitioning. Later, when the movement encountered opposition from the American Medical Association, the NCSC began to use its resources to mobilize a large membership base among the elderly. Thus active support from the aggrieved group was sought *after* the movement was in full swing. Far from involving a popular outcry of discontent, this social movement was professionally planned and directed by outsiders (Rose, 1967).

This view regarding the emergence of social movements is very different from the one that focuses on discontent and protest among members of a deprived group. The social and economic deprivation perspective looks to the internal frustrations and feelings of injustice that spur people to rise up and seek change. The resource mobilization perspective looks to the external conditions that make organized protest possible. Yet the two views are not mutually exclusive. Both provide important insights and neither is completely adequate by itself. Only by considering both the social forces that underlie discontent *and* the process by which resources are mobilized can we fully understand how social movements arise, develop, and decline. The sociologist Theda Skocpol (1979) has made a notable contribution along these lines in her work dealing with social revolutions.

Many modern social movements are begun by outside organizers and only later acquire the support of the people they are meant to help. The movement for federally funded health care, for example, was funded by the AFL-CIO before it attracted support among the elderly (Elizabeth Crews.)

Theda Skocpol and Social Revolution

Skocpol (1979:4) defines **social revolution** as "rapid, basic transformations of a society's state and class structures . . . accompanied and in part carried through by class-based revolts from below." The coincidence of class upheaval and sociopolitical transformation distinguishes a social revolution from a rebellion (which does not result in structural change), from political revolution (which involves no change in social structure), and from such "revolutionary" processes as industrialization (which involves no change in political structure).

Skocpol proposes an approach for explaining social revolution that combines aspects of Marxist and resource-mobilization theories. She finds that although underlying class conflict is fundamental to revolution, it is also necessary to consider how the class members are organized and what their resources are. Based on her careful study of the French, Russian, and Chinese revolutions, Skocpol highlights three factors that tend to be ignored in other theories of revolution: (1) Revolutions are rarely started intentionally; they generally emerge from crisis situations; (2) revolutions are not purely products of internal forces; international relations and developments, particularly a long, drawn-out war and military defeat, contribute to the emergence of crises and thus help shape the course of revolution by undermining old political regimes; and (3) states have an existence of their own as potentially coercive organizations that are not necessarily dependent on the interests and structure of the dominant class. Skocpol does not attempt to create a general theory of all revolutions. She simply proposes that revolution be analyzed from a structural perspective, "with special attention devoted to international contexts and to developments at home and abroad that affect the breakdown of the state organizations of old regimes and the buildup of new, revolutionary state organizations" (1979:5).

Other studies have focused on the economic consequences of revolution. In an examination of the aftermath of the Cuban Revolution led by Fidel Castro in 1961, Michael S. Lewis-Beck (1979) found that in the short-run the revolution had positive effects on the Cuban economy, as measured by an increase in per capita Gross National Product (GNP) growth. However, these positive effects were short-lived. Because of trade difficulties, a scarcity of managers and materials, and administrative errors, the Cuban economy soon began to suffer a decline in per capita GNP growth. Lewis-Beck calls this a "euphoric" pattern: Initial prosperity immediately following the revolution creates a feeling of unequivocal success, but it is not sustained for long. This study, however, looked only at the effects of the Cuban Revolution on the nation's economy. The changes in social organization that the revolution brought about may have been more substantial and more enduring.

Profile on Contemporary Social Movements

The appearance in recent decades of so many social movements has made modern life an era of protest. The antiwar movement, the ecology movement, the antinuclear movement, the gay rights movement, the women's liberation movement, the civil rights movement, the farm workers' movement, the prison reform movement, the zero population growth movement, the right-to-life movement, the evangelical Christian movement—all these and many others arose or were renewed during these decades. What can sociologists learn from studying such social movements? Are there similarities in the ways various movements have evolved? What success have they had in the long run? Perhaps the best way to begin answering these questions is with an in-depth look at a number of contemporary social movements. We have selected the struggle for women's liberation, the environmental movement, and the antinuclear campaign.

The Women's Liberation Movement

In 1963 the publication of Betty Friedan's *The Feminine Mystique* helped launch an era of change in America. The book brought to public attention the private grievances of women whose careers had been thwarted, of women isolated at home with children, and of abandoned mothers with no means of supporting themselves or their children. Homemakers across the country became aware of their shared discontent. Trained from childhood to relinquish self-reliance, careers, and personal autonomy and to dedicate their lives to serving others, many women found themselves dependent, isolated, and beset by "the problem that has no name" (Friedan, 1963). Friedan's book heightened women's consciousness and helped them to identify the feeling

The women's liberation movement, sparked in part by The Feminine Mystique, *has appealed to dissatisfactions experienced by women of diverse ages and backgrounds. (Paul Conklin.)*

that they were somehow superfluous despite having children, husbands, and suburban "dream" houses.

The movement also appealed to women who were not happy with full-time domesticity and opted for careers in fields marked "for men only," and to women who struggled to combine home and work. Women who worked outside the home typically confronted an invisible barrier of prejudice and discrimination in the "man's world" (Bird, 1971). Regardless of their personal qualifications, they found themselves relegated to routine, low-paying, and dead-end jobs.

During 1963, commissions to investigate the status of women were organized in the fifty states. These commissions brought together large numbers of knowledgeable and politically active women. But they did more; they created a climate of expectation (Freeman, 1973). Three years later, on June 29, 1966, a small group of women attending the Third National Conference of Commissions on the Status of Women met in Betty Friedan's hotel room and founded the National Organization for Women (NOW). With Friedan as president, NOW began to attract women in the professions, labor, government, and the communications industry. The organization received a major impetus in 1969 when the mass media began to carry national news stories on women's liberation.

NOW's goal, stated in 1966, is "to bring women into the mainstream of society." Through its national board and 800 or more local chapters, NOW has used legal suits, lobbying, demonstrations, boycotts, and other methods to press for such goals as educational reform, nonstereotyped protrayal of women in the media, repeal of antiabortion laws, lesbians' rights, enhanced roles for women in religion, politics, and sports, and passage of the Equal Rights Amendment (ERA) to the Constitution. In addition, a number of other organizations of professional women have been formed, such as WEAL (Women's Equity Action League), which focuses on legal questions, and the NWPC (National Women's Political Caucus), which focuses on electing more women to public office.

NOW arose initially as a national structure with few community-based chapters. Simultaneously, at the grassroots level, many younger women also began organizing. The student, civil rights, and peace movements of the time had attracted thousands of women. However, more often than not, they found themselves relegated to traditional female roles such as typing, answering telephones, making coffee as they confronted the contradiction of working in "freedom movements" without themselves being "free." Consequently, they became deeply disillusioned with the male-dominanted movements. At the same time they rejected "top-heavy" and highly structured organizations, believing that they inevitably stifled those at the bottom of the hierarchy, and instead created highly egalitarian women's groups. They sought not only to increase opportunities for women within the existing system but to change the entire structure of human relations. Many of the groups emphasized consciousness-raising: Through sharing their ideas and experiences, women attempted to identify their previously unconscious attitudes and behaviors in dealing with both males and females—and through this new awareness, to change these attitudes and behaviors to foster more egalitarian human relations. In addition, they undertook a variety of local educational and service projects—establishing women's centers, abortion-counseling clinics, centers for rape victims and battered wives, feminist bookstores and publications, and day care facilities.

Sociologists ask why the women's movement reemerged at the particular time in history that it did. Certainly women in the 1940s and 1950s faced similar inequalities. Several factors were operating. First, the civil rights movement stimulated increased awareness of injustice and oppression in a number of other groups, including women. Second, increasing numbers of women were entering the paid workforce in the 1960s and encountering negative male attitudes that severely hurt their financial opportunities. Finally, many well-educated wives and mothers were becoming increasingly dissatisfied with their domestic confinement. In earlier times, housekeeping was a skilled and socially valued occupation centered in the production of household necessities. With the development of appliances that simplified housework and with fewer children, modern homemakers often felt that they had little socially useful work to do (Dixon, 1971). All these factors contributed to a growing sense of deprivation among women.

But resource mobilization was important, too. The sociologist Jo Freeman argues that the women's movement would not have materialized without the communications network developed through the commissions on the status of women and the student and civil rights movements. Women's opportunities in this country were as limited in 1945 or 1955 as they were in 1965. "What changed was the organizational situation. It was not until a communications network developed between like-minded people beyond local boundaries that the movement could emerge and develop past the point of occasional, spontaneous uprising" (1973:804).

Although the women's liberation movement did not succeed in winning passage of ERA, it can count many successes. Since 1966 when NOW was founded, women have made great strides in moving into the mainstream of our society. Chapter 6 details many of these changes. But as Chapter 6 also points out, institutionalized arrangements still operate to the detriment of women in many areas of American life.

The Environmental Movement

Much in the fashion of Friedan's *The Feminine Mystique,* Rachel Carson's *Silent Spring* (1962) gave a powerful impetus to the environmental movement. In her book, Carson described a future in which the indiscriminate use of pesticides would "still the songs of birds and the leaping fish in the streams." Her warning led President John F. Kennedy to direct federal agencies to take a close look at the issue. The book also contributed to the enactment of a spate of local and state laws regulating the use of pesticides, helped make ecology a popular cause, and began a groundswell of support that led to the creation of the Environmental Protection Agency (McDowell, 1982).

Why was Carson's work necessary for the emergence of a movement when the evidence for the dangers of pollution daily confronted smog-plagued residents of large cities and when countless communities could no longer use their rivers and lakes for drinking water and recreation? For one thing, Carson provided a rather sinister view in which the forces underming the world's ecosystem operated less dramatically but with greater impact than most individuals had previously appreciated. She exposed some of the vested interests in the business and scientific communities that knowingly engaged in environmental degradation. In so doing, Carson aroused a constituency who recognized the importance of the quality of the environment for their health and welfare. A concerned chorus of experts, authors, and media commentators rapidly joined Carson, warning of the imminent decline of civilization if our environmental problems were not solved.

But resource mobilization was also required. And again, the young people who had taken part in the civil rights campaigns of the early 1960s had a powerful impact on the environmental movement. The movement for black rights involved large numbers of individuals in a cause that went beyond their immediate economic concerns and led to a confrontation with established power centers. The movement also developed new techniques for mass participation, including sit-ins, mass demonstrations, marches, picketing, writing and distributing leaflets, and staging media events. These same techniques were refined in the course of the anti–Vietnam War movement. In this way the process of *participatory mobilization* was thereby generalized to other arenas, including ecological concerns (Schnaiberg, 1973). Moreover, the communications networks established by the civil rights and peace movements were already available and could be used for other political concerns.

Nearly a quarter of a century after Carson's book ushered in an era of environmentalism, we see some encouraging signs. The quality of air in twenty major American cities is measurably cleaner than it was before the passage of the Clean Air Act in 1970. Fish swim in rivers and lakes that several years ago were devoid of life. Moreover, in 1983 government and industry spent an estimated $50 billion—$220 for every man, woman, and child in the United States—to reduce pollution (Taylor, 1983). Of equal significance, environmental protection has emerged as a mainstream issue. Thus a 1983 New York Times/CBS News Poll found that 58 percent of the nationally polled respondents agreed that "protecting the environment is so important that requirements and standards cannot be too high and continuing environmental improvements must be made, regardless of cost" (Shabecoff, 1983). This support for environmentalism is reflected in the growing political power and activism of such organizations as the Sierra Club and the Wilderness Society and the proliferation of local groups.

Yet the United States still confronts major problems and obstacles in cleaning up the environment. In 1983 the Environmental Protection Agency reported that 111 of the nation's 3,000 counties—most of them large metropolitan centers with a total of more than 50 million people—were not in compliance with federal air-pollution standards. And acid rain produced by sulfur dioxide and nitrogen oxides released by midwestern power plants, factories, and automobiles falls on the Northeast, poisoning fish in Adirondack lakes, killing spruce trees in Vermont's Green Mountains, and eating away bronze statues in downtown Boston. Further, many communities had failed to attain fishable, swimmable waters by July 1983, the goal set by the 1972 Clean Water Act. Complicating the problems, municipal treatment plants can clean and recycle biologically polluted water, but they can do little to remove chloroform, benzene, PCBs, and other chemical pollutants believed to be carcinogens (Taylor, 1983; Beck, 1983*b*).

Frightening incidents like that at Niagara's Love Canal area and at Times Beach, Missouri, have also focused attention on the deadly menace of hazardous wastes. Chemical and radioactive wastes are by-products of modern societies. American industries produce an estimated 40 to 60 million tons of contaminated oil, solvents, acids, and sludge each year. Experts estimate that toxic chemical wastes fester in some 50,000 dumps and 180,000 open pits, ponds, and lagoons. Officials of the Environmental Protection Agency say that at least 17,000 of the sites are potentially dangerous, yet fewer than 3 percent of the sites are slated for cleanup. Industry, electric-power plants, and hospitals annually produce another 100,000 tons of radioactive waste. It is little wonder that some environmentalists warn that the dangers that toxic wastes pose to this nation's land,

At Love Canal, a community near New York's Niagara Falls, the dumping of toxic chemical wastes resulted in tragic health problems. Because of chemical contamination, many residents had to abandon their homes, leaving jobs and community ties behind. (Cynthia Johnson/Contact Press Images.)

water, air, and public health are second only to the threat of nuclear war (Beck, 1983*a*).

The Antinuclear Movement

Given the terrifying prospect of nuclear conflagration arising from the arms race, much of the energy and many of the resources that have gone into the environmental movement have in recent years been shifting to the antinuclear movement. In the 1980s the numbers of Americans enlisted in the campaign to end the nuclear arms race has steadily grown. Thousands of groups have sprung up, producing a loosely linked and diverse movement. Some, like the War Resisters League, Women Strike for Peace, and the National Committee for a Sane Nuclear Policy (SANE), are long-time fixtures of the American peace movement. But most of the antinuclear groups are relatively new. Moreover, by early 1983 voters in nine states, several dozen cities, and more than 500 small towns had endorsed freeze resolutions. And public opinion polls have shown that about 70 percent of Americans who are familiar with the nuclear freeze proposal favor it (Alpern, 1982; Wallace, 1983).

A review of American opinion on nuclear weapons and war reveals that it has scarcely changed during the past four decades (Ladd, 1982). Americans continue to believe that a nuclear war would entail a staggering loss of life, and they indicate support for efforts to contain its destructive potential. But they have also steadfastly deemed the Soviet Union to be an untrustworthy adversary that would use its military advantage against the vital interests of the United States if it could.

Given the pervasive and long-term American concern with nuclear war, why did the antinuclear movement begin to flourish only in recent years? The resource mobilization perspective affords one answer. But first it is necessary to distinguish between two roots of the antinuclear movement: the opponents of nuclear power and the opponents of nuclear weapons (Nelkin, 1981).

Until the Three Mile Island accident (see Chapter 2), the two movements remained distinct and attracted different constituencies. Many of those who viewed the proliferation of nuclear power plants and their attendant hazards with alarm were located in the academic and scientific communities. They were drawn into the movement primarily out of a concern for public health and the environment. Many of them had participated in the student movements of the 1960s. Strategic considerations had encouraged them to focus almost exclusively on nuclear power and to avoid the weapons issue. They believed that it would be difficult to mobilize people around issues relating to national defense, but that corporate policy was open to attack.

The 1979 accident at the Three Mile Island nuclear plant extended the support for the anti–nuclear power movement. Many peace activists entered the campaign, since they too shared a concern about radiological hazards and nuclear wastes, and some saw it as an opportunity to broaden the base of the peace movement as public opposition to nuclear energy mounted (Rothman and Lichter, 1982). At the same time, many anti–nuclear power activists believed that Three Mile Island had created a climate in which more substantial cooperation with peace activists would be strategically useful. Thus, increasingly, the issues of nuclear power and nuclear weapons have been joined.

Meanwhile, veteran antiwar activists were carefuly sowing and cultivating the seeds of a grassroots anti–nuclear weapons movement. The structures put in place by the peace movement during the Vietnam War years remained, although the organizations limped along for a period in the aftermath of the war. Then as the nation entered the 1980s, the rhetoric and policies of the Reagan administration focused public attention on issues surrounding national defense. President Reagan proposed a substantial increase in defense spending, the deployment of MX, Trident 2, and Pershing missiles, and the development of a new generation of doomsday weapons.

Many Democratic party leaders rallied their constituencies in opposition to the president's programs and to his tightening of social welfare budgets. Dramatic antinuclear demonstrations in Western Europe provided cogent examples for the mobilization of Americans. The widespread participation of church leaders also fueled the movement. America's Roman Catholic bishops, for example, firmly positioned themselves in favor of a bilateral nuclear freeze by the United States and the Soviet Union and forthrightly condemned the morality of nuclear war. Thus church groups that have normally shunned overly partisan politics—as well as women's and civic organizations—provided an existing infrastructure for organizing opponents to the arms race. As yet the antinuclear movement has not achieved its primary

The anti-nuclear weapons movement in America has been fueled in part by demonstrations in Western Europe. (Regis Bossu/Sygma.)

objectives. However, within the United States nuclear power plants are being more closely monitored and construction has been halted on many facilities (in part due to their extraordinary cost).

COLLECTIVE BEHAVIOR AND THE MEDIA

Collective behavior and social movements depend heavily on communication among many people. Daily newspapers became available early in the eighteenth century while radio and television have been products of the twentieth century. The emergence of the mass media has greatly increased the number of people exposed to collective action, and the amount of information (or misinformation) conveyed to them.

A historic example demonstrates the powerful impact that radio can have on collective behavior. On Halloween evening, 1938, CBS stations carried Orson Welles's dramatic broadcast *War of the Worlds,* a fictitious account of what an invasion from Mars might be like. The program started innocuously enough with what appeared to be an interlude of music. Suddenly the music was interrupted by a bulletin about atmospheric disturbances. Shortly thereafter, a special news bulletin reported that a strange spacecraft had been spotted in a New Jersey field. Highly dramatic announcements came in quick order reporting that a Martian army was launching an all-out attack. As the broadcast continued, many people panicked. They jammed telephone lines with calls to bid loved ones farewell. Some rushed into the streets for help or gathered in bars and other public places. Others took to their cars to drive as far as possible from the site of the invasion. After a few hours, however, the confusion died down (Cantril et al., 1947).

The mass hysteria can be attributed to the skill of the dramatists and to the use of "expert testimony," which lent credibility to the terrifying descriptions. Yet how could so many people believe, even briefly, that Martians were climbing out of a spaceship on a New Jersey farm? Part of the answer is that people are generally prepared to believe the media and the accuracy of what they report.

In choosing to headline or report some stories instead of others, newspaper publishers and television news editors affect the flow of information. Everyday life does not come broken down and neatly packaged in distinct events that people simply mirror (Schoenfeld et al., 1969; Lester, 1980). News does not simply describe reality; media personnel in a very real sense create reality, in that they select the happenings that they will portray and in doing so they transform them into public events. Accordingly, many news items never come to public attention, not because reporters and editors deliberately suppress them, but because in their eyes these events are unimportant and uninteresting.

Since groups often have competing interests, they have different and conflicting definitions of what is and is not newsworthy. However, critics of American mass media point out that most newspapers and TV networks usually have the same "establishment" bias and so edit the news in very much the same way. This bias arises from the fact that the owners, executives, and financial backers of the media are by and large well-to-do people with a vested interest in the status quo. What is more, media staff members, like most Americans, have been indoctrinated into establishment ideology and myths. They too accept existing social arrangements as the taken-for-granted ways for ordering human affairs. They also view government statistics and indices like the GNP as reliable measures of American life. And, like most Americans, they believe that there is something slightly deviant about people who picket and march, angrily shout their grievances, or riot in the streets.

Such underlying assumptions subtly shape the "angles" reporters take when covering incidents of collective behavior. For example, activists in the women's movement were initially portrayed in the media as bra-burning malcontents who were hostile toward men. Why, it was implied, should women complain when they enjoyed so many privileges? Were not women freed from the daily toils and worries of forging a career? Were they not protected from having to make most of life's troublesome decisions? Similarly, activists in the student movement were often cast in the media as spoiled children from affluent, overly permissive homes—kids who enjoyed the luxury of "playing" at protest. Why else would young people who apparently had "everything" behave in this fashion? As a result of such biases, participants in the women's liberation and student movements found it very difficult to get accurate and thorough news coverage of the issues they considered important. Reporters were too busy probing into their backgrounds to find out where and how they "went wrong" (Molotch, 1979).

If the media are indeed biased, an important question is: How much influence do they actually exert on public opinion? To the extent that they are the only source of information, their influence is bound to be considerable. But when we ask whether they can literally *change* people's opinions, the picture becomes more complex. Summarizing the research on opinion change, Raymond Bauer (1972:235) states:

> The audience selects what it will attend to. Since people generally listen to and read things they are interested in, these usually are topics on which they have a good deal of information and fixed opinion. Hence the very people most likely to attend to a message are those most difficult to change; those who can be converted do not look or listen.

Moreover, a good many interpersonal and situational factors affect the effectiveness of media communications. People's social networks play a particularly critical role. Studies indicate that the mass media influence people *if* their social background predisposes them to accept a report as fact and a particular course of action as legitimate; *if* one viewpoint or another is associated with groups they consider significant (their reference groups); and *if* individuals they respect (that is, opinion leaders) call their attention to the issue (Katz and Lazarsfeld, 1955; Piepe et al., 1978).

The media's ability to influence public opinion, then, may reside primarily in their ability to amplify already existing viewpoints rather than to create new ones. But this capacity in itself can have far-reaching consequences. For example, in the latter years of the Vietnam War, the media gradually moved from a posture favoring the war to one of opposition. The dominant newspapers and TV networks in the United States began to talk less about preserving freedom in Southeast Asia and more about the corruption of the South Vietnamese government. And the daily body counts of enemy dead in their reports gave way to dollar counts of the war's cost to Americans (Molotch, 1979). These shifts in media coverage increased antiwar sentiment among many Americans who at first were only vaguely tired of and frustrated with the confrontation.

Thus for a time the dominant American media and an "antiestablishment" movement became allies. The importance of favorable coverage to achieving movement goals is one reason social movement leaders are concerned about their relationships with the press. It is no exaggeration to say that the media can make or break a social movement.

EPILOGUE

Like other aspects of social life, collective behavior consists of group-shared attitudes and actions that find expression in people's social relationships. In this chapter we have looked at the diverse roots of collective action and social movements. One source we considered is social or structural strain. Breakdowns in the functioning of the social system leave people frustrated and susceptible to courses of action that are not ordinarily indicated by their culture (Chapter 3). In an attempt to achieve some level of stability and find some way out of their difficulties, people are prone to accept new forms of behavior. Inequitable institutional arrangements, discrimination, and unemployment are examples of these types of strain (Chapters 6, 10, 11, and 12).

Yet some degree of disorder, confusion, and inadequate functioning seems to be present in all societies. Social institutions do not function perfectly or in accordance with utopian conceptions. Moreover, human beings have demonstrated remarkable resilience throughout history in adjusting themselves to and coping with objectively abominable circumstances. Hence, how disruptive social strain will be depends on subjective factors, including people's definition of the situation (Chapter 4). Individuals assign meaning to the objects, events, and persons that make up their environment. The relative deprivation thesis captures this element in focusing on the disparity between what people perceive they have and what they believe they deserve.

But the underlying structural strains and people's definitions of the situation merely provide the raw materials that may or may not find expression in collective action. Although societal malfunctioning and feelings of relative deprivation often provide the fuel for collective behavior, people must translate their sentiment into overt action. More important, they must link their actions together to arrive at patterned interactions that manifest themselves in mass hysterias, fads, crowds, and movements. In recognition of this fact, contending groups may seek to exploit the discontent endemic to society by mobilizing people as one means to attain collective ends. Institutional malfunctioning, then, may enbolden groups to demand various outcomes by providing them with the resources necessary for popular mobilization (Chapter 11).

Collective behavior contributes to the complexity of modern life while simultaneously deriving from this very complexity. It typically alters or supplants some aspect of the existing social order and culture. Collective action and social movements are both manifestations and agencies of social change. It is to this matter of social change that we turn our attention in the next chapter.

SUMMARY

Collective behavior refers to relatively nonroutine actions that engage large, often anonymous, groups of people. It entails episodes of behavior that differ from the more habitual, repetitive behaviors that characterize our daily lives. Some examples of collective behavior include panics, riots, mass hysterias, crazes, and exuberant crowds.

Although incidents of collective behavior often

appear to erupt suddenly and for no apparent reason, sociologists have found that certain preconditions make their occurrence much more likely. These include structural conduciveness, social strain, generalized belief, precipitating events, mobilization of participants, and social control.

Crowds are temporary collections of people, gathered around a person or event, who are conscious of and influenced by one another's presence. Crowds, unlike other social groups, are ephemeral and unstructured.

The actions of violent, unruly crowds have been important in human history. A recent example in America was the series of riots that occurred in major cities in the summer of 1967. In analyzing these disturbances, sociologists have focused on their preconditions as well as on the role of rumor in spurring mob action.

A number of different theories have attempted to account for the behavior of crowds. The French sociologist Gustave Le Bon argued that the crowd possesses a "collective mind" that makes people act differently than they would if alone or in smaller groups. Later sociologists have developed explanations for how a crowd becomes active. For example, the emergent norm theory suggests that the people in a crowd develop new social norms. Some sociologists have pointed out that seemingly bizarre crowd behavior—looting, for example—can actually be the result of a rational decision.

A social movement is a type of collective behavior that is relatively organized and that persists in time. Behind it is an attempt to bring about or resist change in the social order. The tactics of those involved may include mass demonstrations, boycotts, violence, and sabotage. Social movements are thought to arise as a result of social and economic deprivation and resource mobilization. For example, the women's movement grew out of the grievances of women shut out from full participation in society; but without leaders and organization, the grievances would not have produced a movement.

Collective behavior of any kind is greatly influenced by the kinds of communications available to people. Mass media have increased the number of people who can be caught up in collective behavior and the speed with which mass behavior can spread. The media also can choose what information is spread and thus can affect collective behavior. Favorable media coverage is important to the development of any modern social movement.

GLOSSARY

Acting crowd. Blumer's term for an excited, volatile group of people who are focused on a controversial event that provokes their indignation, anger, and desire to act.

Alterative movement. A social movement that aims at partial change in individuals.

Casual crowd. Blumer's label for a spontaneous gathering whose members give temporary attention to the object that attracted them and then go their separate ways.

Circular reaction. Blumer's term for a phenomenon of crowd behavior in which people react immediately and directly to an action, thereby encouraging the original actors to continue their behavior.

Collective behavior. Relatively routine actions that engage large, often anonymous, groups of people.

Conventional crowd. Blumer's term for people who gather for a specific purpose and behave according to established norms.

Crowd. A temporary collection of people, gathered around some person or event, who are conscious of and influenced by one another.

Emergent norm theory. The principle that crowds develop norms in order to define an ambiguous situation.

Expressive crowd. Blumer's label for a crowd that gives members license to express feelings and behave in ways they would not consider acceptable in other settings.

Leveling. The reduction of a complex story to a few simple details, as with rumors.

Mob. A crowd whose members are emotionally aroused and are engaged in, or are ready to engage in, violent action.

Redemptive movement. A social movement that aims at total change in individuals.

Reformative movement. A social movement that aims at partial change in the social structure.

Relative deprivation. The gap between people's expectations and their actual conditions.

Rumor. An unverified story that circulates from person to person and is accepted as fact, although its sources may be vague or unknown.

Social movement. An organized effort to bring about or resist large-scale social change through noninstitutionalized means.

Social revolution. A rapid and basic transformation of the state and of the class structures.

Structural conduciveness. The principle that preconditions for collective behavior are built into a society's social structure.

Transformative movement. A social movement that aims at total change in the social structure.

CHAPTER 19

Social Change and Technology

We live in what is aptly called the computer age. In less than forty years many aspects of our lives have been dramatically transformed by these remarkable machines. Consider how they have affected American businesses, for instance. During the 1940s even the largest corporations had to compute all their data with only simple adding machines. Imagine the staff and filing space needed just to keep the payroll records for a company the size of General Motors! The modern computer, with its thousands of microscopic circuits etched into tiny silicon chips, has totally changed all that. Today, vast quantities of information are easily and economically stored on magnetic tapes or discs, and thousands of paychecks are computer-processed with the mere press of a button.

Even though most of us are not accountants with General Motors, computers have affected our lives as well. Many bills we receive each month are prepared entirely by computer—which is why it is often so difficult to get an error corrected. We are sometimes surprised at how much information about us is stored in various computers. When you register for classes, for example, the bursar's office may know from the campus computer that you have a library book overdue. But computers can also save us time and money. Those in modern supermarkets can check out groceries in a matter of seconds. And the tiny computers in late-model cars automatically adjust the engine to improve the gas mileage. Scientists foresee the day when computers will virtually run our homes: The machines will plan meals, order groceries, pay bills and balance checkbooks, and even remember to lock the doors at night.

The many transformations in human life brought about by computers are just one example of the social changes that sociologists study. What, they ask, causes a major change in society, like the computer revolution? And what are the sources of resistance to change? Finally, sociologists wonder whether the future direction of change is predictable. To what extent can we foresee what life will be like in 10, 20, 50, 100 years? These are some questions we will be raising later in this chapter. But first, we begin by asking the very basic question: What does social change entail?

SOCIAL CHANGE AND THE COMPUTER REVOLUTION

Social change refers to basic alterations, over time, in the behavior patterns, culture, and structure of society. Clearly, this is a broad definition, and not all changes are social changes. For instance, the socialization we experience as children creates a profound effect in our personal lives, but it does not alter the basic organization of the family and, therefore, is not social change. On the other hand, the creation of communal child-care centers in Israeli kibbutzim, where the young are housed, fed, and taught, constitutes a major social change in that country. The child is socialized in a way that differs from traditional family organization. Similarly, inventions that never catch on may be interesting, but they do not represent social change. They constitute social change only when their widespread use affects our patterns of daily life or the structure of our institutions.

Social change occurs in all aspects of the social order. It affects both our everyday patterns of social interaction and the larger structures of our social institutions. The American family provides an excellent example of how patterns of social interaction have changed over the years. Three centuries ago, in colonial times, relationships between parents and children differed significantly from those that prevail today. The Puritans of the Massachusetts Bay Colony, for instance, prescribed a strict code for raising children. Unquestioned obedience to the parents' wishes was considered a great virtue, and in many families, parents struggled to "break" a self-willed child. Thus a properly reared child would be submissive to parental authority, quiet and well-mannered, and inclined at an early age toward spiritual rather than earthly matters (Greven, 1979). Certainly this presents a sharp contrast to patterns of interaction within today's American family, where independence, self-expression, and material success are often emphasized.

Equally important as changes in patterns of social interaction are changes in the structure of social institutions. To give just one example, consider how technology and the organization of work have transformed our occupational structure. Over a hundred years ago the changes in production methods that launched the first Industrial Revolution began turning American farmers into factory workers. In 1820 about 70 percent of all Americans worked on farms; by 1900 this figure had fallen to 40 percent and it is now a mere 3 percent (Ginzberg, 1982). Moreover, today we are on the threshold of a new phase in human history: the second Industrial Revolution. Central to this development is the restructuring of America from an industrial to an information society. Just as the steam engine transformed agricultural society, the computer is transforming contemporary society. Simultaneously, we are increasingly shifting from a national to a global economy. Various metaphors have been applied to the new industrial revolution, including Alvin Toffler's (1980) "third wave" and John Naisbitt's (1982) "megatrends."

Two events in the mid-1950s signaled this transformation (Hallblade and Mathews, 1980). First, the balance of the American work force shifted from manufacturing goods to delivering services. Second, the computer became more than simply a scientific tool and entered the commercial and industrial sectors. The first Industrial Revolution freed people from the land and created a largely human-devised or artificial envionment. The computer-induced revolution promises to free the human mind and lead to equally staggering social change. Let us examine these matters more carefully.

Computers and Social Change

Like other aspects of institutional life, developments in technology and the organization of work take place within a social context (Stern and Stern, 1983). They are responses to social forces, and in turn they act upon these same forces in a dynamic and reciprocal relationship. Consider computers. The notion of a programmable computer dates back to the first half of the nineteenth century. A well-known English inventor of the time, Charles Babbage, employed the technology of the Industrial Revolution to develop ideas for the building of a computer. But the technology of the time—cogs, wheels, and axles—did not permit him to construct a practical instrument.

By the early 1940s certain elements had appeared within the cultural repertory that made the time ripe for the development of electronic digital computers, particularly advances in radar, electronic counters, and vacuum-tube technology. Further, during World War II, the United States government brought together scientists in physics, mathematics, astronomy, and related fields and put them to work on a series of computer projects. The first modern-day computer dates to this period when two University of Pennsylvania engineers, John W. Mauchly and J. Presper Eckert, created a machine that employed electronic language to calculate the trajectories of bombs. That the computing field received a major impetus during World War II is not surprising (Stern and Stern, 1983). Wartime tends to make nations receptive to inventions that will give them an advantage over their enemies. And individuals and organizations are often prepared to exert themselves in a spirit of wartime cooperation.

Since World War II, new generations of computers

have been designed and manufactured. The first four computer generations are typically distinguished by their constituent technologies: vacuum tubes, transistors, integrated circuits, and very large-scale integration (VLSI). Today, fifth-generation supercomputers are under development in the hope that the new technologies will result in computers capable of using superspeed symbol manipulation to simulate human thought processes.

The computer revolution is transforming the ways Americans live and work. Indeed, a study commissioned by the National Science Foundation speculates that by the year 2000 the electronic information revolution will have appreciably transformed American home, business, school, and political life (Institute for the Future, 1982). It suggests that one-way and two-way home information systems—termed teletext and videotext—will penetrate far into the fabric of people's daily lives, with an impact rivaling that of the automobile and television.

The report estimates that by the turn of the century some 40 percent of American homes will have two-way videotext service. Such systems will permit individuals to exercise greater choice over the information they receive, enabling them to create their own newspapers, compile their own consumer guides, design their own educational curricula, and shop and pay their bills electronically. Videotext systems will also carry information about people's preferences and activities out of the home, a development that could create new dangers to individual freedom and privacy. We will consider these matters later in the chapter.

The new technology will touch many areas of social life. For example, rather than traveling to their places of employment each day, many men and women may be able to do much of their work at a home computer terminal, a way of working termed **telecommuting** (Kingston, 1983). In the early 1980s some 10 million office employees were already using visual display terminals (VDTs) to do word processing, prepare reports, file information, and calculate statistical data. Many of these operations can be performed at home because it matters little whether the link between the computer and the visual display terminal is 40 feet, 40 miles, or 4,000 miles away.

Telecommuting is likely to have both positive and negative effects. On the positive side, workers may have more control over their time. Parents can also work at home while caring for children. And the handicapped and the elderly may find new job opportunities open to them. Further, employees can save the time and expense

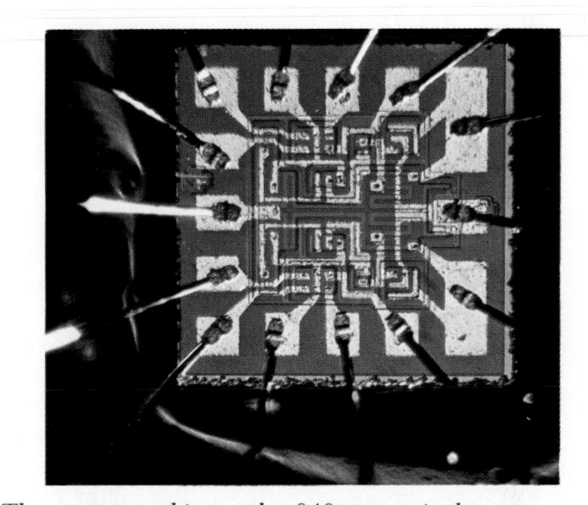

The computer chip—only .040 square inches—revolutionized computer technology. It allowed for integrated circuitry, making the small-scale home computer not just a futuristic dream. (Erich Hartmann/Magnum.)

of commuting to work, and employers can save on office space allocations. But the blessings will not be unmixed. Telecommuting can cut workers off socially and psychologically from one another, producing a sense of isolation and estrangement. And although it may reduce conflicts among coworkers, it may create new and deeper strains among family members, who will be spending more time interacting with one another. Finally, although telecommuting may increase a worker's physical privacy, it will decrease privacy surrounding the work pace and quality of output since the work can be centrally monitored by computer.

The electronic revolution could also transform the home. In electronic homes, a central computer may monitor and control the temperature in each room, sense and adjust light levels, raise and lower blinds according to the position of the sun and the weather, and turn appliances on and off. This introduction of computers within the home and the workplace has given impetus to a new field and profession, **ergonomics.** Its purpose is to design environments based on the ways people think and move so that users of products can employ them safely, efficiently, and comfortably. For instance, to help reduce the physical stress of working at computers, ergonomists have designed glare-reducing hoods, adjustable screen units, and detachable keyboards for the machines.

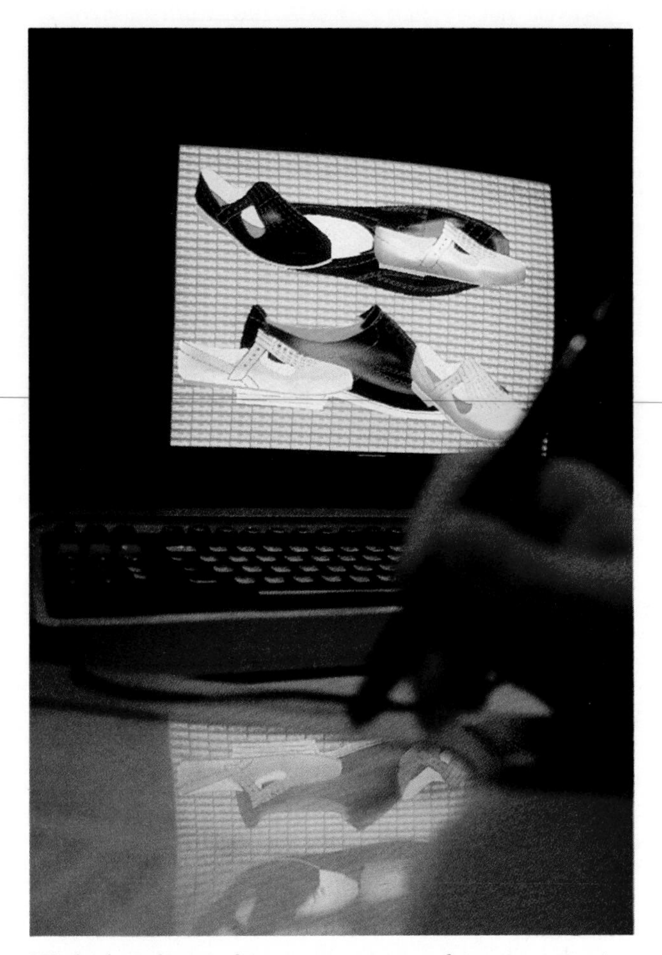

With the advent of computer-generated imagery, engineers can design everything from shoes to planes on a video screen. Here, a computer graphics design for Clark's shoes is displayed. (Jerry Mason/Science Photo Library–Photo Researchers.)

Design itself is becoming the province of computers. Computer-generated imagery (CGI) has been made possible by "raster scan" displays—the electron gun that lights up a video screen fires in such a manner that lifelike images instead of mere line drawings appear. Computer graphics permit engineers to design everything from shoes to planes. The computer can remember previous sketches and calculate various time-consuming essentials, including the amount of leather needed for a sole or the aerodynamics of a wing. Biochemists rely on CGI to produce images of DNA molecules. And artists are using it to make television commercials (Begley, 1982).

Computers are making their mark on vast areas of American life. In Chapter 15 we noted how the electronic church uses computers for fund-raising and related activities. Similarly, computerized devices permit physicians to take blood counts and carry out other diagnostic procedures in an office setting. And new generations of plastic credit cards, which can be verified electronically, are making completely automated, self-service gasoline stations possible. Sociologists expect such changes to have far-reaching social consequences. It is to this matter that we now turn our attention.

Social Effects of Computers

Social change confronts individuals with new situations and compels them to construct new forms of action. They must alter the ways in which they relate to one another and carry on their daily activities. Thus sociologists and futurists anticipate that the computer revolution will have major social implications, a number of which we consider below.

Distribution of Social Power

Information is a source of power in organizations, and computers are a means of gaining information (Hallblade and Mathews, 1980) (see Chapter 8). As information accumulates in massive, centralized data banks, those with access to it gain enormous power for dictating public tastes, policies, and behavior. Such information already plays an important role in marketing products, candidates, and the electronic church. And the gap between information-rich and information-deprived people will very likely widen, with consequences for stratification systems (see Chapters 10 and 12).

Privacy and Individual Rights

The growing use of computers to collect data and handle information raises the issue of individual privacy and the confidentiality of personal data. Increasingly the Social Security number is becoming a "single identifying" number for keeping track of people and developing individual "data images" of them. For instance, credit bureaus and local police departments have progressivly come to rely on centralized computers as sources of information. Many civil libertarians fear the instrusive or "big brother" potential for electronic snooping, endangering individual freedom in democratic societies.

Social Relationships

As already noted earlier in the chapter, telecommuting can leave workers socially and psychologically isolated. In fact, some "hackers," or computer enthusiasts, seem to form their most meaningful relationships with the computer and may have difficulty relating to people. But communicating by computer can also break down social barriers. Students, for example, appear less hesitant to ask their professors questions through computer networks than they do in person (Goleman, 1983). Computers tend to overcome status biases, enabling people of lower status to participate more fully and get a better hearing. Hence, in some instances, computers allow for a more egalitarian interchange. Further, machines help many individuals to communicate without embarrassment, stimulating human contact rather than reducing it. By the same token, however, computer networks often become "gripe-nets" and sources of electronic graffiti.

Decision Making

The computer's ability to substitute hard decision rules for the guesswork of individual judgment has been highly touted (Goleman, 1983). The computer can dictate when to buy or sell stock, when to make adjustments in a jetliner's flight pattern, and whether to make a bank loan. In effect, it removes decision making from the human sphere, which has consequences for how people view themselves and their work. Further, many individuals find it difficult to challenge a computer's decisions. This factor tends to insulate decision making from the kind of debate and confrontation that often ensures its quality. And decision making by computer works to preserve the authority of those who design computer-based models and develop computer programs.

Electronic Sweatshops

Computer-based automation has reached into countless offices, producing what some critics label "electronic sweatshops" (Andrew, 1983). With computer systems employers have been able to increase productivity and reduce labor costs. But simultaneously, critics charge, such systems have increased the employer's control over employees and created mounting pressures for productivity—the electronic equivalent of the moving assembly line. Automation often makes work more monotonous and more highly scrutinized. Many who regularly work at VDTs report high levels of physical and mental stress. And some claim they experience a high incidence of headaches, eye problems, and backaches from sitting in front of a terminal for long hours.

New Images of Humankind

Researchers are expending considerable energy and resources to develop **artificial intelligence**—computers that can think and reason in somewhat the same fashion as humans do and that can understand and utilize information that is conveyed by use of symbols. As yet, nobody has demonstrated any intrinsic limits to what the computer can do in this area. But like major scientific breakthroughs in the past, developments in artificial intelligence will have substantial implications for how human beings perceive themselves. Copernicus removed humankind from the center of the universe; Darwin removed it from a place separate from the animals; and Freud showed human rationality to be illusion. Similarly, the computer revolution is likely to have consequences for humankind's view of itself, for its view of the universe, and for its place in the universe (Simon, 1981).

Vulnerabilities

As computers take on more roles in business, medicine, education, and defense, society finds itself more vulnerable to computer failures and errors (Pollack, 1983). For instance, in 1979 an Air New Zealand jetliner crashed into a mountain in Antarctica, killing 257 people, because the computerized flight plan fed into the plane's automatic pilot system had been changed without the pilot's knowledge. And in 1983 one or more individuals gained access to and reprogrammed a computer that contained patients' radiation-therapy records at Manhattan's Memorial Sloan-Kettering Cancer Center. Other types of risks are associated with computer dependence, including the halting of critical activities in banking, electrical, and transportation services when a central computer goes down. Perhaps most alarming of all, national defense computers have repeatedly provided erroneous reports that the United States was under attack. Fortunately, the errors were quickly discovered.

In sum, the computer revolution is contributing to many technological and social gains. But, like most social change, the new patterns are not an unmixed blessing. The proliferation of computers has also brought new problems. It is little wonder that the computer has been portrayed in the media as both monster and messiah—both a dehumanizing and troublesome machine and the munificent genie in Aladdin's magical lamp (Laurenzo, 1980). These counterforces are highlighted by the impact high technology has upon job opportunities and employment prospects.

High Technology and Jobs

High technology is the application of electronics to industry, communications, medicine,and other spheres of life. High technology is even now transforming the job market. And some futurists predict that, by the year 2000, manufacturing will account for about 11 percent of the jobs, down from 28 percent in 1980. The remaining 89 percent of jobs will be in the service sector, up from 68 percent in 1980. Probably half of the service jobs will relate to collecting, managing, and disseminating information (Cetron, 1983). Yet experts admit that their predictions are at best educated guesses and that they should be received warily (Boffey, 1983). Overall, expert opinion about the impact high technology will have on employment divides into two viewpoints: a pessimistic scenario and an optimistic scenario.

The Pessimistic Scenario

At a time when many communities and areas are troubled by high levels of unemployment and a cloudy economic future, high-technology industries seem to offer much promise. Yet many experts believe that a high-technology strategy to solving such problems is unlikely to be successful. Three considerations prompt this conclusion (Serrin, 1983). First, applying advanced technology may decrease rather than increase jobs. Second, the communities that are losing jobs in smokestack industries are unlikely to attract new high-technology industries. And third, most of the new high-tech jobs do not pay as well as old production jobs. Let us look at each of these arguments more closely.

Pessimists say that high technology will never replace the number of jobs that it eliminates. They cite figures from the U.S. Bureau of Labor Statistics that show only 600,000 jobs were created in the United States from 1972 to 1982 by firms in such high-technology areas as computers and robots; they accounted for no more than 5 percent of the nation's job growth during this period (Serrin, 1983). By the same token, the pessimists point to Congressional Budget Office estimates that a combination of automation and cutbacks in basic industries will eliminate 3 million manufacturing jobs in the 1980s (Austin and Beazley, 1983). Some experts predict that by the year 2000, factory robots will be doing what 7 million human beings were doing in 1980.

The Big Three auto makers are said to foretell this trend. By the year 1990 they are expected to have 21,000 robots in place. The big attraction is economics: A robot costs about $6 an hour to operate and can do the jobs of two workers who each cost their employer about $20 an hour (Buss, 1983). Likewise, a study of 654,000 mill workers laid off in Massachusetts between 1957 and 1975 revealed that only 18,000, or about 3 percent, found jobs in fields that were technology related (Bluestone and Harrison, 1982). And currently workers laid off from jobs in heavy industry are about five times more likely to end up working for businesses like McDonald's or K-Mart than in high-technology fields.

Many white-collar jobs, which could be an alternative to blue-collar jobs, are also likely to be sharply reduced by office automation. Computers already handle much of the "paper shuffling" between individuals and organizations. Paychecks are typically prepared by computers and are generated by a computer recordkeeping and accounting system. Banking and other financial institutions have computerized many of their operations. And even in the local supermarket, electronic scanners automatically read and record product/price codes, producing a printed bill for the customer and inventory data for the firm.

Although the auto and other heavy industries are the primary areas in which robots are used extensively, other uses for robots are being developed as well. (Cary Wolinsky/Stock, Boston.)

Jobs of white-collar workers will also change dramatically. For example, machines will be able to take dictation, then type much of the material without human transcription. Some experts predict that such machines will eliminate 50 percent of all clerical and stenographic jobs (Cetron, 1983). Of equal importance, advances in computers and telecommunicating will allow some companies to farm out office work, employing workers in countries where lower wages prevail. Magazines are already frequently using foreign facilities to enter subscriptions into computerized mailing lists (Pollack, 1982).

Pessimists also claim that midwestern states and cities like Detroit, Cleveland, and Buffalo will not be able to attract substantial numbers of high-technology firms. Companies specializing in high technology have generally avoided older manufacturing centers and sought sites near universities. Examples include California's Silicon Valley, adjacent to Stanford University, Route 128 near Boston and its numerous universities, and Research Triangle near North Carolina, North Carolina State, and Duke universities. In these localities high-technology firms find the highly skilled workers they need without having to contend with strong union traditions. In contrast, in Michigan, Ohio, and other Great Lake states, unions like the United Auto Workers have strong roots. Firms are reluctant to hire laid-off auto and steel workers, pay them minimum wages, and then confront a union election a few months down the road (Serrin, 1983).

Finally, pessimists say that most high-technology jobs require little skill and hence do not pay high wages. They contend that high technology produces a two-tier labor force. At the top, highly skilled computer and engineering jobs offer exhilarating and mind-challenging tasks that command good pay. But the vast majority of jobs are mind-dulling and menial. They resemble assembly work and are paid routine wages. For example, whereas a steelworker may earn $12 to $15 an hour, a computer operator often makes little more than the minimum wage of $3.35. Thus pessimists allege that the growth of computer and high-technology industries decreases the skill level of the average worker and results in lower pay.

Moreover, since many technology jobs are simple and repetitive, they can readily be exported to nations where wages are low. Thus in 1983 Atari announced that it would shift most of its manufacturing operations from California to Hong Kong and Taiwan, idling some 1,700 American workers who assembled home computers and video games. And companies like Intel, National Semiconductor, Apple Computer, and Wang Laboratories have turned to the Far East for substantial preliminary work on computer components. Further, when engineers at General Motors began developing their own manufacturing robots, the company contracted with a Japanese firm to produce them—ironically, with American-licensed technology (Peterson, 1982).

The pessimists contend that minorities will be particularly victimized by high technology. Blacks and women will face growing competition for jobs from Hispanic workers, illegal immigrants, and foreign workers in wage-sensitive manufacturing industries. Because

THE SOCIOLOGICAL EYE ON CAREERS: Jobs with a Future

Students are concerned with selecting careers that hold promise for the decades ahead. Yet the task of identifying growth industries and jobs is a risky venture. Labor economists and futurists have not had the best track records in forecasting and labor market (O'Toole, 1983). Indeed, some were still predicting teacher shortages in the late 1960s when demographic trends foreshadowed the impending "baby bust" and declining school enrollments. One error that forecasters make is to assume that they can gauge the future by simply extrapolating current trends. Thus in the 1970s forecasters at the U.S. Bureau of Labor Statistics assumed that high levels of employment, cheap sources of energy, and the prevailing pace of federal expenditures would persist in the decades ahead. They did not foresee the surge in unemployment, oil prices, or defense expenditures. Thus the future is always full of surprises.

Nor do economists and futurists necessarily agree on the growth occupations of the future. For example, government labor economists predict a substantial increase in the need for computer programmers in the years ahead. Yet some independent experts disagree. They say that new generations of computers will be directly accessible to users and that computers will program other computers. Likewise, demographers disagree about whether a new baby boom is under way, a matter of no small significance to students contemplating careers in elementary-school teaching. And although defense expenditures have substantially increased in recent years, aerospace and other defense industries have been notorious for their boom-bust record of employment (Nicholson, 1982).

Although job forecasting is admittedly a risky venture, most experts predict that the major new areas of growth will be in the fields of information and conservation (see table). Information includes jobs in computers, robotics, biotechnology, and transmission technologies (for instance, laser and fiber optics). Conservation includes jobs in both human and ecological fields, ranging from health care to solar energy and waste disposal. As Americans live longer and become more health-oriented, experts anticipate appreciable growth in such areas as occupational and physical therapy and speech pathology. But more conventional jobs will also abound. Even though robots may replace people on the assembly line, machines are unlikely to eliminate such basic service jobs as janitors, sales clerks, and waiters. And people with administrative and managerial skills will still be needed.

In assessing career opportunities, young people would be well advised to keep in mind a point emphasized by James O'Toole (1983), a professor of management in the University of Southern California's Graduate School of Business Administration. He notes that in addition to appraising the general opportunities likely to be available, individuals should consider two other factors in mapping their work futures: what they enjoy doing and what they are good at. O'Toole observes that even a job as a blacksmith is not out of the question if a person is willing to go where there are horses. If people are willing to devote themselves singlemindedly to a field, and if they demonstrate convincing evidence of their talent, they can often secure a job.

O'Toole (1983:25) advises:

> Remember: for any given job, most people don't want it, most don't have the talent for it, and even fewer are willing to make an effort to obtain it. Thus, if you have am-

wage scales are so much lower in some nations, communications so cheap, and the diffusion of technology so rapid, not enough labor-intensive industry can afford to remain in the U.S. to absorb unemployed workers and a growing labor force. Historically, unskilled and semiskilled jobs have been an important channel for immigrants and for internal migrants from economically depressed or less-developed regions in the nation.

The Optimistic Scenario

Optimists reject these conclusions. They emphasize that high technology permits the production of low-cost, high-quality goods of enormous variety with equipment that need not be replaced, only reprogrammed. Consequently, automation can improve the competitive position of the United States and forestall the migration of jobs overseas. If firms fail to automate, they find themselves at a competitive disadvantage in the world market. Automation, therefore, becomes a matter of survival for

THE SHIFTING JOB MARKET

Jobs in the smokestack industries will continue to decline, but there will be new opportunities in service and high-tech sectors.

Some jobs are going . . .		*Others are growing . . .*		*But the future is here.*	
Occupation	Percent decline in employment	Occupation	Percent growth in employment	Occupation	Estimated employment by 1990
Shoemaking-machine operators	−19.2	Data-processing-machine mechanics	+157.1	Industrial-robot production	800,000
Farm laborers	19.0	Paralegal personnel	143.0	Geriatric social work	700,000
Railroad-car repairers	17.9	Computer-systems analysts	112.4	Energy technicians	650,000
Farm managers	17.7	Midwives	110.0	Industrial-laser processing	600,000
Graduate assistants	16.7	Computer operators	91.7	Housing rehabilitation	500,000
Housekeepers, private household	14.9	Office-machine servicers	86.7	Handling new synthetic materials	400,000
Child-care workers, private household	14.8	Tax preparers	77.9	On-line emergency medical	400,000
Maids and servants, private household	14.7	Computer programmers	77.2	Hazardous-waste management	300,000
Farm supervisors	14.3	Aero-astronautic engineers	74.8	Genetic engineering	250,000
Farmers, owners and tenants	13.7	Employment interviewers	72.0	Bionic medical electronics	200,000
Timber-cutting and logging workers	13.6	Fast-food restaurant workers	69.4	Laser, holographic and optical-fiber maintenance	200,000
Secondary-school teachers	13.1	Child-care attendants	66.5		
		Veterinarians	66.1		

bition and talent the odds are almost always in your favor for any career. With the exception of most professional organizations, few employers will turn down an applicant who persistently and convincingly says, "This is the job I want; I'm willing to work for it, even if I have to start at the bottom and work up.

In sum, there is more to appraising a career prospect than merely identifying likely job opportunities in the future.

companies. And to the extent that this occurs, technology actually saves jobs that would otherwise have been eliminated.

Moreover, optimists contend that the jobs lost through automation are partly offset by new jobs created in automated factories. Additionally, by lowering the prices of goods so that people can afford more of them, technology will increase total production, creating more jobs among suppliers. Finally, should the net rates of growth of the labor force decline in the 1980s and 1990s, as some futurists predict, then the problem of job displacement by robots could be taken care of by attrition as older workers retire.

Optimists point out that workers' fears of being displaced by machines are hardly new. In the early nineteenth century, the Luddites in England smashed the machines they believed were destroying their jobs. Yet the advances brought by the Industrial Revolution, although contributing to unemployment among specific individuals, resulted in the overall increase of employment and real income. Bruce Barlett (1983:16) contends that the arguments of the pessimists, like those of the

Luddites, are based on a static analysis. They assume, he says, that the economy will continue to produce the same goods in the same quantities using less labor. He challenges this perspective:

> One might respond by asking what our economy would look like without rising productivity. In 1910 the Bell System had 121,310 employees. Approximately 7 million calls were placed that year, or 57 per employee. In 1981 the Bell System had 874,000 employees, who served over 219 billion calls. Had there been no increase in productivity since 1910 it would have required close to 4 billion employees to service that many calls. The result, of course, has been that telephones are widely available and calls can be made at very modest cost compared with 1910. This has given rise to vast numbers of jobs in every industry which simply couldn't exist without efficient, inexpensive telephone service.

In sum, optimists say that the labor force has a remarkable capacity to absorb rapid technological change.

As in most other situations, both pessimists and optimists tend to overstate their cases. Pessimists focus on the short-term dislocations associated with the demise of old industries and the birth of new ones while tending to neglect the long-term benefits associated with new technology. Optimists emphasize long-term trends while tending to overlook the fact that displaced workers find little comfort in expanding job opportunities twenty or thirty years down the road. All this leads to the question of which jobs are likely to hold the most promise in the foreseeable future. In brief, where will those entering the job market find work in the years ahead? The box on careers (p. 506–507) examines this matter.

Programs to Handle Unemployment

It is clear from our discussion of high-technology jobs that some individuals come out the losers. The demise of America's smokestack industries has been particularly devastating to blue-collar workers in the auto, steel, aluminum, glass, and rubber industries. The effects of foreign competition and high technology take a severe economic, social, and psychological toll on displaced workers. In many respects, the impact of massive change requires responses that are beyond the abilities of any union, company, industry, or even state to carry out alone. In some nations, such as West Germany, Austria, Norway, and Japan, government and industry cooperate in reducing the work force when necessary. They do so either by retraining workers for other jobs or shifting workers to related industries (Marcus, 1983). Such programs are currently only in their infancy in the United States and are inadequate to deal with the

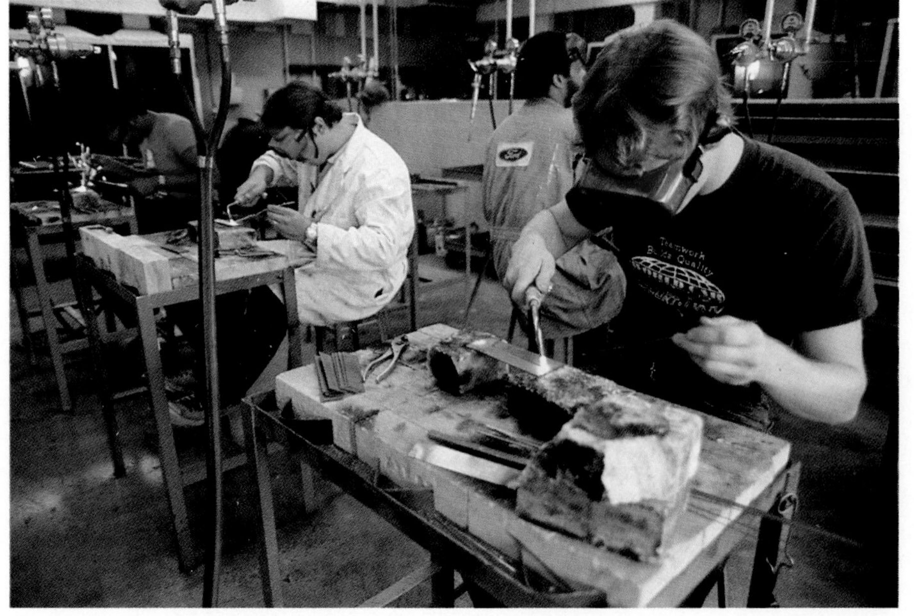

These men, at Henry Ford Community College, are learning new skills as part of a retraining program for laid-off auto workers. (Andrew Sacks/Black Star.)

anticipated impact of the computer and technological revolution. In 1982 the United Auto Workers negotiated in its contract with Ford a program by which the company offers job counseling and tuition payments to laid-off workers looking for jobs outside the industry.

A short-term solution to the problems associated with automation would be to find ways to pace the introduction of new technology. But there is a long-term need to rethink and restructure the educational system so that new generations of workers will have those skills essential for finding employment. Of course, not all students will need to be adept at micro-electronics or biogenetics. Even so, the consequences of shifts in technology dictate that our society not move blindly and unprepared into the world that is rapidly unfolding (Byrne, 1983). If we neglect the long-range needs of members of our society, we will have a population that is out of touch with social realities and occupational needs. Clearly, human and social factors have to be considered in designing change and planning for the future.

MACROPERSPECTIVES ON SOCIAL CHANGE

Our discussion of computers and technological change highlights the significance of social change for our lives. One of the realities of social life is that change is endemic, a permanent feature of society despite our periodic yearning for stability and permanence. There is a rhythm of stability and change that runs through all social arrangements, from small groups to major institutions to the all-embracing social system we call society.

Sociologists, of course, study contemporary social change not simply to monitor the transformations of our society but also to understand why such transformations occur and what their consequences are. In addition, they want to know if any broad, recurring patterns underlie the general phenomenon of social change.

Sociological theories of social change are concerned both with short-run trends and with changes and trends that affect an entire civilization over centuries. They address such concerns as why agriculture replaced hunting and gathering, and why industrial production superseded a system based on individual artisans. Are there any overriding factors that, throughout history, have repeatedly prompted social change? And what can we say about the direction of change? Do trends from the past suggest where social change is leading? No single perspective can adequately explain the causes and direction of social change. However, there are four major perspectives that give us insight into these matters. Let us consider each in turn.

The Evolutionary Perspective

The **evolutionary perspective** of social change flourished during the latter half of the nineteenth century. Virtually all the founders of sociology, in one way or another, maintained that society progresses from simple beginnings to more complex forms. This, they believed, was the inevitable long-run direction of social change.

Even Emile Durkheim (1858–1916) proposed an evolutionary scheme in his famous discussion of *The Division of Labor in Society* (1893/1947), in which he contrasted societies according to their type of solidarity. As we saw in Chapter 1, he pointed out that simple societies have a relatively undifferentiated structure, with a minimal division of labor. People share a common set of values, and these values provide the chief source of solidarity for society's members. Durkheim called this moral cohesion "mechanical solidarity." But as population grows, pressures build on the available resources and a greater division of labor is needed to use these scarce resources efficiently. Society becomes differentiated into increasingly specialized units, which are more dependent upon each other—Durkheim called this kind of cohesion "organic solidarity." Social differentiation multiplies, common values decrease, and the fragmented social order then requires more formal means to hold it together. Civil law and a central government are among the institutions that evolve in the face of growing change and diversity.

Herbert Spencer (1820–1903), writing a number of decades before Durkheim, attributed even greater significance to social evolution. He drew elaborate parallels between the evolution of biological organisms and the evolution of human societies. According to Spencer (1974), the driving force behind all evolution was a struggle for existence in a world of competition and scarcity. Only the "fittest," in his view, would eventually survive. Thus, the social forms that naturally prevailed,

Spencer believed, must have features that made them "superior."

It is easy to understand why, in an age of expansionist imperialism, such ideas would be greeted with enthusiastic approval and used to justify further colonial expansion. Europeans were coming into contact with very distant, seemingly exotic cultures. And with predictable ethnocentrism they generally concluded that their own beliefs and practices were more "advanced" than were any others. If the colonial powers did not have a divine right to rule the world, in the popular view they at least had an "evolutionary prerogative."

In the decades that followed, however, the nineteenth-century view of social evolution began to come under heavy attack. One obvious weakness was its undercurrent of enthnocentrism. As knowledge about non-Western societies increased, it became clear to sociologists that these societies were not inferior from a human standpoint. In fact, some of the most "primitive" societies turned out to be the most peaceful, the most capable of offering a sense of community, and the most likely to provide their members with ample leisure time.

Classical evolutionary theories were also found wanting for their implicit assumption that all societies follow the same uniform developmental course. This notion, called **unilinear evolution,** holds that all societies pass through a single line of successive stages until they ultimately reach the same end. The evidence gathered in this century does not support a unilineal view. For instance, many African and Asian nations have not undergone the same kind of industrial revolution as occurred in Western Europe. In some cases, they have achieved the fruits of "modern society"—higher standards of living, increased literacy rates, improved health care—without massive investment in a wide range of highly specialized industries. Finally, classical evolutionary theories were justly criticized because they did not really *explain* social change; they merely described its general patterns. At best, the early evolutionists pointed to a single factor that presumably propelled societies from one evolutionary stage to the next. Most modern sociologists believe that this approach is a gross oversimplification.

All these criticisms have not brought about the death of evolutionary theory, merely its transformation. Modern evolutionists, such as Leslie White, Julian Steward, and Gerhard Lenski, reject the assumption that technological modernization creates a society that is better in all ways. They also argue that evolution is **multilinear:** the stages of development in Western civilization are not inevitable; other societies may follow different routes. Granted, some contemporary theorists maintain that certain developmental patterns are common. For instance, Neil Smelser (1973) believes that cultures undergoing modernization have a tendency to shift from traditional technology (based on folklore or trial and error) to the application of scientific knowledge; from subsistence agriculture to cash crops; from human and animal power to fossil fuels; from rural life to urban settlements. But it is widely recognized now that there are exceptions to these trends. Finally, modern evolutionary theories appeal to a broader range of factors in attempting to explain social change. Anthropologist Marvin Harris (1974), for example, suggests that technological innovation was not the only reason that societies moved from hunting and gathering to agriculture. Ecological limitations, such as overpopulation, were also relevant. With these new realizations, the evolutionary perspective is enhancing our understanding of how societies change and where they may be headed.

The Cyclical Perspective

As we suggested earlier, part of the criticism of nineteenth-century evolutionary theory arose from a growing acknowledgment that our own way of life was far from ideal. In this century, the decimation of life in two world wars, the degradation of the environment by industrialization, and the social strife caused by gross inequities in the distribution of wealth have led people to question the assumptions that modernization is "progress," and that our civilization has eliminated the savagery committed by our ancestors. The question is often asked: Are societies in fact advancing? Or are they experiencing stagnation, and perhaps even decline? The **cyclical perspective** on social change provides an intriguing answer. It argues that every society has a natural life cycle: birth, adolescence, maturation, decay, and eventual death, followed by the birth of some new social order. A graph of the history of societies would thus show a continual series of waves, rising and falling, rising again and falling again.

Perhaps the most famous exponent of the idea that just as Western culture could rise to the pinnacle of civilization, so too could it fall, was Oswald Spengler. In his widely read book *The Decline of the West* (1926–1928), Spengler argued that all cultures are destined to follow a course of growth and decay in much the same ways as do individuals. In its youth a society is most creative and most idealistic. As it matures, society becomes less flexible, more materialistic, and more prone to decay in the form of war and social disintegration. Spengler was convinced that Western society had reached its "golden years" and was on the point of decay. Few contemporary sociologists share Spengler's pessimism, in part because his theories tend to be more poetic than scientific, appealing to a cosmic destiny rather than observable causes.

Arnold Toynbee (1946), a British historian, has offered a more optimistic cyclical theory of change. Central to his theory are the concepts of "challenge and response": the measure of a civilization's success is found in its responses to specific challenges posed by its physical and social environment. All civilizations, in his view, rise and fall according to their ability to meet these challenges, although later civilizations have the benefit of learning from the mistakes of civilizations before them.

Cyclical approaches to social change have an intrinsic appeal. They seem to cover all eventualities (the rise *and* fall of civilizations). But they rarely explain the causes of change. Why, for example, does a society that has successfully responded to social and physical challenges suddenly become rigid? For an answer, one must turn to other theoretical perspectives.

The Equilibrium Perspective

The **equilibrium perspective** on social change views society as tending toward a state of stability or balance. Thus, when sudden changes cause disruption, those disruptions are only temporary. Society's institutions will eventually adapt, achieving a new stability.

Many social changes and their aftermaths seem to confirm the predictions of equilibrium theory. Consider the disaster at Buffalo Creek in 1972, for instance (Erikson, 1976). When a collapsed dam released a torrent of water that wiped out the community of Buffalo Creek, West Virginia, the social order there was suddenly thrown into chaos. Many friends and family members were dead or missing; most houses and buildings were totally destroyed. Survivors were dazed and disoriented. But in time, the devastated victims managed to piece the fragments of their lives back together. The result bore little resemblance to the happy, neighborly way of life they once enjoyed. But some kind of social order was again established. A new equilibrium was achieved.

Of course, there is often a significant time gap between change in one part of a social system and change in other, related parts. William F. Ogburn (1964) coined the term **culture lag** to describe the problems that arise when one aspect of society changes so rapidly that other aspects do not have enough time to adapt, thus creating disequilibrium. In particular, material culture (technology, medicine, and other material *things*) changes far more readily than does nonmaterial culture (beliefs and values). A situation that took place in Australia provides a classic example. Gifts of steel axes to aborigines greatly disrupted their culture because their entire network of social relationships centered around the ceremonial exchange of stone axes. The aborigines' belief system, in short, did not have time to adapt to these new material objects (Arensberg and Niehoff, 1964:50). Culture lag also abounds in societies such as ours. For instance, many believe that we have the technology to perform genetic engineering but are neither morally nor socially prepared to tamper with life on this level. Ogburn suggests that major social change occurs when leaps in technology, or in other material factors, force us to adjust our beliefs and values; this change in turn lays the foundation for further changes in material culture. This process can be viewed as a striving toward equilibrium.

Equilibrium theory does not exclude acceptance of other perspectives on social change. For instance, Talcott Parsons (1951, 1966) has combined aspects of evolutionary and equilibrium theory in his view of where change is leading. Parsons maintains that the long-run evolutionary direction of a society is toward greater differentiation in function of its major cultural, economic, social, and political subsystems. But binding these increasingly differentiated parts are new forms of integration, such as new value and belief systems.

In spite of its appeal to many sociologists, equilibrium theory has serious limitations. It implicitly likens a society to a biological organism that can automatically correct deviations (a drop in temperature, a rise in blood sugar) from its normal physical state. But in societies such adjustment processes are difficult to measure. Although we know what constitutes a healthy, balanced physical body, how do we identify a healthy, balanced

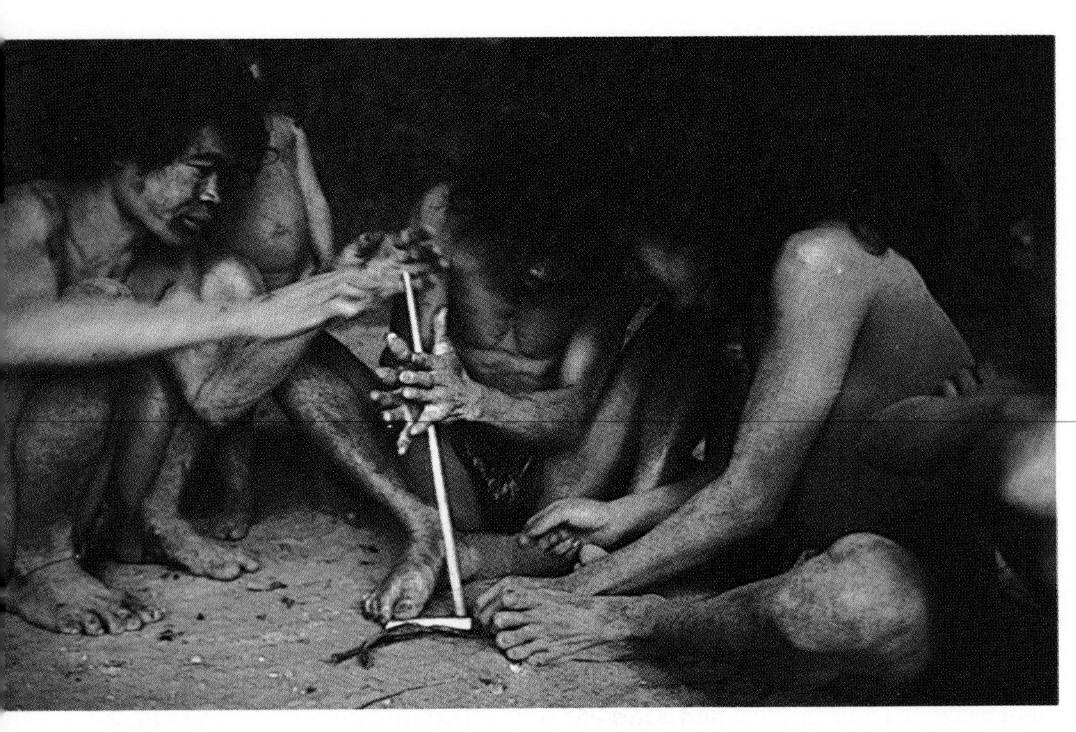

A group of Tasaday in the Philippines builds a fire. When discovered about a decade ago, the Tasaday were a forest people who lived in caves and had been isolated from their neighbors for centuries. Such societies are likely to be affected profoundly by culture lag: The introduction of modern technology could seriously disrupt age-old beliefs and values. (John Nance/Magnum.)

social system? Thus, the usefulness of the equilibrium perspective is curtailed by the fact that we have no reliable indicators of balanced and imbalanced social states.

The Conflict Perspective

The equilibrium perspective emphasizes the integrative and stabilizing processes at work in social systems. The directly opposing view is the **conflict perspective,** an orientation based on the belief that all societies are fraught with conflict and are, therefore, inherently unstable. Accordingly, struggle and conflict among groups is the cause of major social change.

By far the most articulate and influential advocate of the conflict perspective was Karl Marx. "Without conflict," Marx wrote, "there is no progress: this is the law which civilization has followed to the present day" (Quoted in Dahrendorf, 1959:27). In particular, Marx focused on class struggle, as we have seen in earlier chapters. He postulated that with the advent of capitalism, society would begin to break up into two classes: the exploiters (the bourgeoisie), who owned the means of production, and the exploited (the proletariat), who sell their labor in order to survive. These two classes would become increasingly polarized, until eventually the conflict between them would boil over. The oppressed would seize power, and a new society would emerge. Marx went on to predict that the revolution of the proletariat would ultimately create a classless society, eliminating the sources of conflict.

Social change in capitalist societies this century has not followed the course hypothesized by Marx. The expected revolt of the working class has not come to pass, partly because society has not polarized into two hostile camps. Rather, society has become increasingly differentiated, with countless factions and interest groups. This indicates that significant social conflict is not limited to struggles between economic classes. In fact, there have been conflicts between racial groups, age groups, religious groups, and, most recently, between men and women over legal, economic, and institutional rights. All these conflicts and many others can be important catalysts of change.

Ironically, however, a great diversity of conflicts may actually prevent cataclysmic social change. Marx himself recognized this when he pointed out that in some countries divided antagonisms might pose a serious obstacle to the ultimate class revolution. Analyzing why the British proletariat had not yet organized to overthrow the bourgeoisie, Marx proposed that hostile competition between English and Irish workers hindered the unity of the working class. Similarly in our society, crosscutting conflicts between whites and blacks, men and women, old and young may dilute the single-minded unity of any one group, thus weakening its potential to bring about change. The modern conflict perspective, therefore, is complex and multifaceted.

SOURCES OF CHANGE

The evolutionary, cyclical, equilibrium, and conflict perspectives provide only a general idea of the sources of social change. We must also consider more specifically where change comes from. To take an example, what forces contributed to the rapid transformation of Japan following World War II? Clearly, there was no one cause. One must take into consideration the population pressures on a small island, the rapid introduction of technological changes, and the radical difference to be found in values that derive from a militaristic orientation as opposed to an economic orientation. Each of these sources of change has some relation to the others, and they all worked together to thoroughly transform Japanese society. Still, some aspects of traditional Japan were preserved in the midst of this transformation. As we saw in Chapter 8, Japanese workers have not given up their familylike relationship with their work organization. Thus, any factor that is a potential source of change may also encourage *resistance* to change, depending on the circumstances. Bear this in mind as we examine the more important sources of change below.

Population Changes

One cannot overestimate the importance of population trends in promoting social change. Increasing or decreasing numbers and changes in the numbers and proportion of young and old, male and female, urban and rural dwellers, all significantly affect social organization. Some anthropologists suggest that sharp rises in population size forced the shift 10,000 years ago from hunting and gathering subsistence strategies to simple agriculture (gardening and raising animals).

We still feel the effects of shifting populations. Between the years 1946 and 1964 women in America gave birth to what is now referred to as the baby boom generation. In 1940 there were fewer than 11 million children under the age of five, but by 1960 that figure had risen to 20 million. In 1964 out of every 10 persons

In modernized Japan, a mother who dresses her child in Western-style clothes may herself continue to wear the traditional kimono. (Allen Green/Photo Researchers.)

in the United States, 4 were under twenty years of age (Jones, 1980). After that year the birth rate fell off markedly, producing what has been called a baby bust.

What social changes have resulted from the boom and bust? We saw in Chapter 16 that the boom affected the need for services (such as schools), the size and shape of the labor force, the demand for consumer goods (creating the "youth market"), and even traffic flow and settlement patterns. As the baby boom generation has aged, it has taken with it the power that goes with numbers. The youth market has yielded to a market catering to young adults in their late twenties and thirties. Motorcycles are being superseded by mopeds, tennis by cross-country skiing, sock hops by aerobic dancing. Even bowling, which was nearly phased out when the baby boom cohorts were teenagers, is now making a comeback. And leisure-time industries are not alone in feeling the effects of the maturing baby boom generation. The labor market is experiencing strain as well. Too many baby boom cohorts are bunched together at the lower levels of management, angling for promotion. The climb to the top will take much longer than many of them had anticipated (Jones, 1980).

There is one other radical shift in population taking place now, the full effects of which will not be felt until early in the next century. That shift is the aging of our population. Between 1980 and 2040 the number of Americans over sixty-five will more than double. The elderly may be neglected to some extent today, but it is certain that a great deal of political, social, cultural, and economic attention will have to be focused on the final bulge of the baby boom generation next century.

The prospect of a horse population large enough to serve a city of one million people caused many turn-of-the-century New Yorkers considerable concern. The advent of the automobile eliminated the horse problem, however, and the city quickly grew beyond any contemporary projections. (The Bettmann Archive.)

Technological Innovation

Predictions about demographic patterns may be undone by unanticipated technological change. For instance, at the turn of this century it was commonly assumed that New York City could not grow to 1 million people because there would not be room to stall all the horses (Jones, 1980). The invention of the "horseless carriage" quickly eliminated this restriction, showing that technological innovation can be an important source of social change. Innovation in the realm of ideas, such as new views on liberty, equality, or community, can also produce social change.

Sociologists differ in their view of the relative importance of *technology*, or knowledge applied in practical ways to the material aspects of life, and *ideas*, or cultural values, in determining the course of history. Auguste Comte, the eighteenth-century social thinker who gave sociology its name, took an **idealist view of change.** For him, social change was largely prompted by new ideas and outlooks—especially by the replacement of religious and metaphysical beliefs with scientific ones. Karl Marx, on the other hand, espoused a **materialist view of change.** He believed that the development of society is directed less by new ideas than by new means of producing goods and services—that is, by new technology. We will consider these sources of social change.

We tend to think that the current age of technology is a fairly recent event in the course of history. But technological innovation leading to social change has gone on from the beginning of human history. Even such a relatively simple invention as the stirrup, which allowed the rider of a horse to maintain a firm seat in the saddle, produced a major social change. This medieval innovation led to a completely new form of attack—mounted shock combat—in which a rapidly moving warrior could slash and jab at his opponent without fear of tumbling unchivalrously to the ground. This new mode of fighting, in turn, placed new demands on soldiering. No longer could a freeman simply take up arms and declare himself fit for battle. The new technique of mounted combat required many years of training, not to mention the great expense of horses, attendants, and equipment. Thus, a whole new social aristocracy was inevitably born—the knightly class—and with it a new set of social patterns attuned to the needs of a mounted warrior's way of life. "Few inventions have been so simple as the stirrup," writes Lynn White, Jr. (1962:38), "but few have had so catalytic an influence on history."

In our own times a number of technological changes have had equally profound effects. Consider the automobile. On a personal level it has had an enormous impact on our everyday patterns of social life. It has allowed us great mobility in visiting friends and relatives, participating in community organizations, engaging in sports and other leisure-time pursuits, and even conducting activities as intimate as dating and courtship. Stepping back and viewing society as a whole, the vast influence of the automobile is also apparent. The car has encouraged the development of many major industries, in addition to car manufacturing, shipping, and marketing—supplying materials to auto makers, seeing that their products are cared for and serviced, producing the fuels to run automobiles, and providing the roads they drive on. In this way, the automobile directly or indirectly employs many millions of American workers. The car has greatly affected our settlement patterns as well. Without the car, it is unlikely that today's sprawling suburbs would have evolved as they have. Accompanying these changes in residence patterns are other transformations. For instance, the car has promoted great change in retail distribution: the small, main-street merchants are being replaced by huge shopping malls located on the outskirts of town. The car, in short, has virtually revolutionized the American way of life.

As this example of the car's social impact illustrates, most technological innovations involve not only the creation of a new physical object but also a managerial and support system to control and exploit that product (Brooks, 1980). The car has brought with it a vast economic, social, and political complex: assembly lines, service stations, oil companies and refineries, automobile insurance, highways and highway lobbyists, driving laws, licenses and regulations, and the police, courts, and bureaucracies to enforce them. Similarly, elaborate support systems have grown up around all our major technological developments—from atomic weapons to spacecraft to television to techniques of modern brain surgery.

New Ideas

What is the effect of innovative ideas or values on social change? As we saw in Chapter 15, the seventeenth-century ideals of hard work, frugality, and self-denial (known as the Protestant Ethic) established certain behavior patterns that were consistent with the requirements of a capitalist market economy. As a set of values, the Protestant Ethic facilitated the development of modern industrial capitalism.

Ronald Inglehart (1977) maintains that in our day certain people in advanced industrial societies are experiencing a shift in values that involves a new definition of progress. Inglehart suggests that highly developed countries are moving into an era of post-Materialism: our present emphasis on consumption of goods and services is giving way to an emphasis on the *quality* of human life. While traditional societies have mostly been concerned with satisfying economic wants and assuring physical security against enemies, the post-Materialist society will largely concern itself with questions of relativism, such as the relative benefits of continued economic growth and the relative costs of polluted environments. While only about 12 percent of the American population is currently involved in promoting these new concerns, these people are generally well-educated and politically active. They are also predominantly young. Thus, the values that they advocate have a reasonably good chance of spreading and ultimately changing other aspects of our culture.

Sometimes, however, values and ideas have an opposite effect: They *resist* social change rather than promoting it. Such resistance has occurred throughout human history. For instance, nineteenth-century England saw periodic episodes of rioting, arson, and machine-wrecking among both rural and industrial workers. Part of the reason for this behavior was the abject poverty to which the new industrial capitalism was condemning workers. Technological innovations, such as the threshing machine, were widely viewed as a direct cause of unemployment and so were angrily attacked. But the workers were also protesting a decline in their dignity and sense of self-worth that the machines seemed to have brought. In short, their desire to maintain traditional norms and values caused strong, if futile, resistance to technological change.

There are many examples of similar resistance in our own era. Consider the storm of protest that arose when biologists first announced that they could recombine molecules of DNA. (DNA is the basis of an organism's genes—that is, the chemical blueprints for its physical makeup.) In simple terms, the new recombinant techniques allowed scientists to splice the DNA from one living creature onto the DNA of another, thus giving the "host" organism new features. The potential value of this process is enormous. For instance, scientists might some day be able to alter genetically our agricultural crops so as to greatly increase their yields. Or they might be able to correct genetic defects in humans by providing afflicted persons with the proper DNA code. Many observers, however, have serious reservations. For one thing, they fear that new microorganisms, against which humans have no immunities, might accidentally escape from laboratories, thus causing epidemics of new diseases. In response, strict regulations have been imposed regarding safety procedures in recombinant DNA labs. But still, critics have not been silenced. To some, tampering with life on this level does not seem morally right. Where will the lines be drawn, they ask, in creating new traits and new creatures? And perhaps more important, who will draw those lines? Will it be the biologists? And if so, what gives them the right to play God (Goodfield, 1977)? Again we see an intense clash between traditional beliefs and values and the direction that a new technology is taking.

Thus, ideas and values can both cause (or facilitate) social change and constrain (or at least resist) its rate and direction. Sometimes it is necessary to wait for cultural values to catch up with the changes in material culture, as we saw in our discussion of Ogburn's "culture lag."

Diffusion

Human beings have always been on the move, making a totally isolated society extremely rare. Direct or indirect contact between members of two different cultures often leads to change in one or both societies. The process by which such change comes about is called **diffusion,** because it entails a gradual dissemination of cultural traits. Soldiers, colonial administrators, missionaries, migrants, traders, visiting scholars and artists, exchange students, and even tourists are all potential agents of diffusion (An "invasion" of free-spending tourists who dress and act as they would at home can have as much impact on their hosts as an invading army.)

The extent to which diffusion actually occurs will vary. At one extreme, contact between societies may result in a cultural "takeover." For example, the Dutch colonials transformed Indonesian society from a group of subsistence horticulturists who lived in small, egalitarian villages into a competitive, stratified society oriented toward the world market (Plog, Jolly, and Bates, 1976). At the other extreme, contact may prompt people to withdraw and cling to their traditions. Although the Sumu Indians of Nicaragua have been trading with neighboring groups for centuries, until recently they shut their doors when strangers entered their villages, kept their ways secret, and married only among themselves.

Between these two extremes are numerous examples of societies borrowing foreign traits selectively. For instance, Marco Polo introduced his Italian countrymen to the long, thin, round noodles eaten by the Chinese. They soon became popular in Italy, where they were called spaghetti. Italian immigrants later brought spaghetti to America. Similarly, the Incas of Peru discovered quinine and passed it along to their Spanish conquerors, who then shared it with other Europeans, who in turn used it in Africa to offset malaria attacks. (Thus, were it not for the Incas, Europeans might never have colonized Africa.)

Although material objects and technology spread more readily than do systems of beliefs and values or

The selective effects of diffusion may lead to some surprising cultural practices. (Robert Azzi/Woodfin Camp & Associates.)

forms of social organization, these too may widely diffuse. Examples are the missionary religions, Buddhism, Christianity, and Islam. The Napoleonic Code, the basis for law in France and all its former colonies, was adopted by many other societies.

Sometimes in the process of being diffused, a cultural idea or technology gets modified to suit the needs of the society adopting it. For instance, the Haitians wove together myths and rituals from Catholicism and West African religions into a new religio-magical system, voodoo. This process of modification can even mean that the original trait gets totally transformed. Such a transformation occurred in the so-called cargo cults that emerged on several South Pacific islands, where the U.S. Air Force established resupply bases, during World War II. Many of these islands were inhabited by peoples barely out of the Stone Age. What were they to make of these huge silvery birds dropping from the sky into their midst? White-skinned men wearing bizarre clothes moved about in strange vehicles, coaxing these enormous birds open, taking out fantastic things. One day these white-skinned men suddenly left, and the gift-bearing birds flying overhead never descended again. Not surprisingly, cults developed to try to lure the birds and their cargo back. Thus, the arrival of the Americans deeply affected the ancient society of Tana, and it led to the development of a new religion that integrated disturbing new elements by reinterpreting them as signs of redemptive hope for the islanders (Worseley, 1958).

MODERNIZATION AND WORLD-SYSTEMS

In the last fifty years, societies around the globe have been swept up in the process of modernization. **Modernization** means change in values, institutions, and outlook that moves traditional societies toward industrialization and urbanization. Diffusion, new technology, sharp economic inequalities, new ideologies, and demographic shifts all contribute to this wave of social change.

In all but the most remote corners of the world, people are hungry for the fruits of an industrial economy, and they are pushing for a rapid—even revolutionary—transformation of their society. Until the past few centuries, hundreds, and perhaps thousands, of local societies went about their business pretty much the same way day after day. Most of these societies had subsistence economies, living either by nomadic hunting and gathering or by sedentary agriculture. But the societies created in North America and Western Europe have been expansive ones. In their desire for prestige, their search for resources to fuel their economic development, and their sense of mission in spreading "civilization," they have penetrated these once-traditional and isolated societies and have introduced them to the trappings of modern life.

In doing so they have brought much of the non-Western world into the world-wide market system as suppliers of raw materials for Western industrial development. Although those who lived in the colonies (mostly former colonies now) managed to hold on to many of their traditional ways, colonization and modernization in general have had profound social, political, and psychological implications.

Patterns of Modernization

Social researchers and theorists have recently paid a great deal of attention to different patterns of modernization. While sociologists agree that most societies are modernizing, they have not yet reached agreement on what forms this modernization will take (Meyer et al., 1975). Are the modernizing societies showing a pattern of *convergence*, moving toward greater similarity in social, political, and economic institutions? Or is it a pattern of *divergence*, moving toward greater differences among societies?

Sociologists who support the convergence view suggest that the less-developed nations will copy the social and economic structures of successfully modernized nations. They point to the role of multinational corporations in setting up essentially similar political and economic contexts in whatever country they choose to do business. The sociologists who support the divergence view, in contrast, suggest that distinctive cultural and political traditions will shape different patterns of modernization. They bolster their argument by pointing to the fact that late-industrializing nations (for example, those of the Third World) are following different paths to modernity than did nations that industrialized in the eighteenth and nineteenth centuries.

World-System Approaches

Immanuel Wallerstein, among others, attempts to explain patterns of modernization through **world-system** (or *dependency*) theory. Instead of viewing individual modernizing nations as units isolated from the rest of the world, undergoing a largely *intra*national process, Wallerstein (1974) suggests that modernization must be seen as an *inter*national phenomenon. The development of any particular nation is basically determined by its role in the world-system. This system includes core and peripheral nations linked in "dynamic and exploitative ways" in an international division of labor (Snyder and Kick, 1979). Most political and economic power is centered in the *core* nations, such as the United States, whose residents typically enjoy high standards of living. The core nations provide the management and much of the essential machinery for production of the world's goods, and they also reap most of the profits. The natural resources and sometimes the cheap labor of the nations on the *periphery* of the world-system (such as third world nations) are typically exploited by core nations. The standard of living in peripheral nations is far lower than that in the core—and so is the rate of economic growth (Snyder and Kick, 1979). Some nations on the periphery will not experience full modernization of their social institutions.

One economist—André Gunder Frank (1972)—

American manufacturers find they can cut production costs by setting up factories in Third World countries, where labor is cheap. Here, Cabbage Patch dolls, which sold for $25 and up in American stores, are being packaged in a Hong Kong factory. (Stuart Franklin/Sygma.)

thinks that instead of undergoing "modernization," many nations on the periphery are submitting to the "development of underdevelopment." In these nations, underdevelopment was not the original state. It was only as they became colonized and dependent on the economies of core nations that pre-existing subsistence strategies lost viability and the countries became underdeveloped. **Underdevelopment** may be characterized by a nation's support coming from a small number of primary exports (often linked to a plentiful natural resource, such as copper or tin), the absence of different types of industries, and dependency on other nations for basic goods and services. Chronic balance-of-payments deficits have led to the encouragement of increased foreign investment, which means that these underdeveloped nations are gradually losing control over their own economies.

These new theories suggest that complete modernization—whereby African and Asian nations would soon resemble the political, economic, and social structure of the United States or European nations—is not inevitable. Patterns of development are affected by a nation's position in the world-system as well as by its own cultural or political heritage.

EPILOGUE

It is fitting that we should conclude a sociological textbook with a consideration of social change and a look into the future. Much of our concern in the preceding chapters has been with social structure and institutional arrangements, those aspects of social life that are relatively patterned, recurrent, and orderly. Thus we have examined groups and organizations, structural patterns of inequality, and specific institutions. We gain a sense of continuity from viewing the stable components of social life. Yet the social world is hardly static. Instead, it is dynamic and ever-changing. This realization leads us to ask, what lies ahead? Where are global modernization and related changes in politics, social forms, and individual psychology taking us? Different prophets provide somewhat different answers and foresee somewhat different futures.

Daniel Bell (1973) believes that we have entered the postindustrial age. Whereas early inventions of the Industrial Revolution were typically produced by craftsmen, new technologies increasingly depend upon specialized knowledge. The development of the machine was the central force in industrial society. In **postindustrial society,** the central force is the organization of theoretical knowledge. Energy production drove industrial society; information production drives the postindustrial one. Economic growth was the goal of the industrial age; advancement of theoretical knowledge is the new goal. Thus, the class structure of postindustrial society will be based on access to information and control of decision making rather than on ownership of property. The lower class will be defined not by their poverty but by a lack of knowledge that would give them access to dominant organizations. The primary value of postindustrial society is efficiency, which means greater output for less cost. In order to promote efficiency, Bell argues, human activities will be more bureaucratized. Postindustrial society will not be without its conflicts, Bell contends. The political system will stress the values of equality and popular participation, which run counter to the values of hierarchy and subordination found in bureaucratic organizations.

The French sociologist Jacques Ellul (1964) believes that postindustrial society is doomed if we allow technological progress to be our overriding concern. Technology, writes Ellul, is like a virus. A virus perpetuates its strain by invading a cell, taking over its chemistry of reproduction, and causing it to stop producing its own kind and begin producing viruses. Similarly, "technique," or technology, takes over society and "dissociates the sociological forms, destroys the moral framework, . . . explodes social and religious taboos, and reduces the body social to a collection of individuals" (1964:126).

This occurs because those who use technology always seek the most efficient way of performing tasks, not taking into consideration that it might make work less satisfying to the individual or foul the environment or disrupt the social fabric. Trying to curb pollution (or to correct other defects of technological progress) with new technology only compounds the problem. According to Ellul, the criterion is still efficiency, and the new technology has its own imperatives that may lead to equally unfortunate side effects. One of these imperatives is a tendency toward self-perpetuation and immunity from human control.

Because efficiency in a technological society is so important, Ellul maintains that techniques will be developed to manipulate behavior through education, propaganda, and psychology. Ellul suggests that although people will be unhappy about these encroachments on their freedom, they *won't* revolt. Instead, technology will devise one last ignominy, the manipulation of people into happiness—or at least complacency. Technology will become a tyrant, ruling human society with absolute power.

Willis W. Harman's analysis (1977) is less dramatic, but no less sobering. Harman believes the problems we are experiencing today derive from the *successful* solution of problems we faced in the past. Modern societies are struggling with four basic dilemmas:

1. *The growth dilemma* Unless we continue to grow economically, unemployment and alienation will rise to intolerable levels. But the environmental costs of continued growth are unacceptably high.
2. *The control dilemma* We need to control technological development. Technology has reached the point where *everything* in our environment, physical makeup, and behavior is subject to human intervention. (Just think about genetic engineering.) The dangers are enormous unless

there is some kind of guiding intelligence.

3. *The distribution dilemma* The gap between the rich nations and the poor ones is widening at a dangerous rate. Yet we have no suitable mechanism, no philosophy, for distributing wealth. The problem cannot be solved through the development of the poor nations. The planet simply could not support all the people alive today if they were to consume and pollute at the level the United States does.

    These dilemmas all relate to what Harman calls the "new scarcity" (of fossil fuels and minerals, of fresh water, of productive land, of living space, and of places to dispose of waste), and the limits of the earth's life-support ecosystems. Our modern problems are the product of technological solutions for the problems of the "old scarcity" (of food, clothing, shelter, and the like). We cannot resolve them through more of the same.

4. *The work-role dilemma* Modern societies are increasingly unable to provide meaningful social roles. The only legitimate roles in our society are work-related: holding a job, being married to someone who holds a job, or studying in preparation for a job. Yet millions are unemployed. Being jobless means being useless in our society: Individual self-respect, effective citizenship, and ultimately even national security are endangered. Creating make-work jobs won't solve the problem of self-respect. (Harman considers this perhaps the most serious dilemma, because for the most part we try to ignore it.)

Harman believes the future is indeed bleak *unless* we reexamine the premises on which we now operate, including each and every one of the following ideas: Any technology that can be developed should be; the sum total of the knowledge of specialized experts is wisdom; people can be treated in dehumanizing ways; individuals are essentially separate, and so have little responsibility for faraway people or future generations; nature is to be controlled and exploited rather than cooperated with; ever-increasing economic growth is possible and desirable; the future can be left safely in the hands of autonomous nation-states; "the disbelief that 'what ought to be' is a meaningful and achievable concept" (1977:8).

For Harman, the main hope lies in massive and effective reeducation for the values of frugal living so that microdecisions (what to buy, who to hire) add up to sensible macrodecisions (a controlled rate of growth, clean air). Treading the line between optimism and pessimism, Harman concludes that "industrial society . . . will transform itself into something different, probably involving a wrenching and traumatic transition period" (1977:11).

Sociologists may disgree on the kind of future human society will follow, but there is widespread consensus on another point: anticipating and planning for the future is full of hazards and bound to be imprecise. One common tendency is to focus on obviously desirable consequences and to ignore others that may eventually turn out to thwart our original intentions (Merton, 1976). For example, a decision to cut back on government spending for the poor may certainly help balance the budget, but it may also increase anger among poor groups who suffer most from the cutbacks. They may take violent action that could well end up costing almost as much as the short-term savings from the budget cut.

Many social scientists today are emphasizing the importance of educating people about future trends and possibilities, and especially of widening the horizons in our world view. We must come to realize that all who live on this planet are interdependent. But as George W. Bonham (1980:3) notes, "old ways of thinking die slowly with nations, as they do with individuals. We only seem sensitive to the unpleasant facets of an interdependent world, a circumstance unprecedented in the American experience. It is difficult for the mind to adapt to new systems of which we may be but a small part."

SUMMARY

Social change refers to basic alterations over time in the behavior patterns, culture, and structure of society. Sociologists want to know what causes social changes, what impact they have, and what they tell us about the future.

Technological developments take place within a

social context. They are responses to social forces and in turn act back on these same forces. Computers are no exception. The computer revolution is appreciably transforming the American home, business, school, and political life.

High technology is bringing about major shifts in employment. The pessimistic scenario sees high technology decreasing rather than increasing jobs. The optimistic scenario says that, over the long run, high technology will save and expand jobs. However, job forecasting is a risky venture. One error that forecasters commonly make is that they assume that they can gauge the future by simply extrapolating current trends.

Computers will have effects beyond the workplace. They will influence the distribution of power within society. They will have consequences for individual rights and privacy. They will alter the way individuals relate to one another. They will take over many decision-making tasks. They will have consequences for physical and mental stress on the job. And they will foster new images of humankind.

General perspectives on social change fall into four main categories. Those who see social change from the point of view of the modern *evolutionary perspective* stress the progressive differentiation and complexity of social structures, while recognizing that there is more than one possible line of development. Those who adopt a *cyclical perspective,* in contrast, view societies and civilizations as passing through stages of development and decay. Theorists who view social change from the *equilibrium perspective* stress the adjustments that restore social stability; social change is generally seen as involving temporary disruptions. Directly opposed to this point of view is the *conflict perspective,* which stresses that social conflict and resulting pressures toward change are ubiquitous in all societies.

The sources of (as well as limits to) social change may be found in population shifts, innovative technology and ideas, and *diffusion* (the spread of cultural traits from one society to others).

Most societies have been or are involved in the process of *modernization:* change toward the type of society found in the urbanized and industrialized nations. Modernization affects politics, social forms, and even individual psychology. Social scientists today are interested in the patterns of modernization: whether there is a trend toward *convergence* (greater similarity among nations in their institutions) or *divergence* (greater differences); and what effect the position of a nation in the world economy has on its modernization effort *(world-system theory).*

Looking ahead, all forecasters see dramatic change for society as a whole. Harman sees our current problems (the growth, control, distribution, and work-role dilemmas) as the product of successful solutions to the problems of the past. He believes that we cannot resolve these dilemmas with more of the same, but that we must reexamine the basic premises of modernization and industrialism. Most social scientists agree that it is difficult to foresee the full consequences of planning for the future, but that it is vitally important to educate people about future possibilities.

GLOSSARY

Artificial intelligence. Machines that can think and reason in somewhat the same fashion as humans do and that can understand and utilize information that is conveyed by use of symbols.

Conflict perspective. The view that all societies are fraught with conflict and are, therefore, inherently unstable.

Culture lag. Ogburn's term for the discontinuity that occurs when one part of the culture changes more rapidly than another.

Cyclical perspective. The view that every society has a natural life span: It grows and develops then eventually decays; it is followed by a new social form.

Diffusion. The spread of cultural traits from one society to another.

Equilibrium perspective. The view that regardless of what changes might upset the balance of society, subsequent changes will restore the society to its original condition.

Ergonomics. A field concerned with designing environments based on the ways people think and move so that users of products can employ them safely, efficiently, and comfortably.

Evolutionary perspective. The view that societies evolve from simple, traditional structures into increasingly complex and differentiated forms.

High technology. The application of electronics to industry, communications, medicine, and other spheres of life.

Idealist view of change. The belief that social change is prompted largely by new ideas and outlooks.

Materialist view of change. The belief that social change is prompted largely by innovations in technology and other aspects of material culture.

Modernization. Change toward the type of society found in urbanized and industrialized nations; it has profound social, political, and psychological implications.

Multilinear evolution. The notion that societies pass through different stages of development and follow different routes of growth.

Postindustrial society. An advanced society marked by new forms of technology.

Social change. Basic alterations in the behavior patterns, culture, and structure of society that occur over time.

Telecommuting. Working at home using a computer terminal linked to an office.

Underdevelopment. The condition of a nation, marked by poverty, that is dependent on a small number of primary exports, that lacks a variety of industries, and that relies on other nations for vital goods and services.

Unilinear evolution. The notion that all societies pass through a single line of successive stages until they ultimately reach the same end.

World-system theory. A view of modernization as an international phenomenon, holding that the development of a particular nation is largely determined by its role or function in the world economy.

REFERENCES

CHAPTER 1

American Sociological Association. *Careers in Sociology*. Washington, D.C.: American Sociological Association, 1977.

Arnold Arluke, Louanne Kennedy, and Ronald C. Kessler. "Reexamining the Sick-Role Concept: An Empirical Assessment." *Journal of Health and Social Behavior* 20 (1979):30–36.

Peter L. Berger. *Invitation to Sociology: A Humanistic Perspective*. Garden City, N.Y.: Anchor Books, 1963.

Randall Collins. *Conflict Sociology: Toward an Explanatory Science*. New York: Academic Press, 1975.

Auguste Comte. *The Positive Philosophy* (Harriet Martineau, trans. and ed.). London: Bell, 1915.

Lewis Coser. *Masters of Sociological Thought: Ideas in Social and Historical Context* (2nd ed.). New York: Harcourt Brace Jovanovich, 1977.

Emile Durkheim. *The Rules of Sociological Method*. Chicago: University of Chicago Press, 1938.

Pamela Fishman. "Interaction: The Work Women Do." *Social Problems* 25 (1978): 387–406.

Ronald Fletcher. *The Making of Sociology: A Study of Sociological Theory* (vol. 1). New York: Scribner's, 1973.

Alvin W. Gouldner. *The Coming Crisis of Western Sociology*. New York: Basic Books, 1970.

Alvin W. Gouldner. *The Two Marxisms: Contradictions and Anomalies in the Development of Theory*. New York: Seabury Press, 1980.

Jürgen Habermas. *Antworte auf Herbert Marcuse*. Frankfurt: Suhrkamp, 1968.

Jürgen Habermas. *Theorie und Praxis* (4th enl. ed.). Frankfurt: Suhrkamp, 1971.

Jürgen Habermas. *Legitimation Crisis* (Thomas McCarthy, trans.). Boston: Beacon, 1975.

Jürgen Habermas. *Zur Rekonstruktion des Historischen Materialismus*. Frankfurt: Suhrkamp, 1976.

Louis Harris and Associates, Inc. *A Study of Attitudes Toward Racial and Religious Minorities and Toward Women*. November 1978.

Irving Louis Horowitz and James Everett Katz. *Social Science and Public Policy in the U.S.* New York: Praeger, 1975.

E. Gartley Jaco (ed.). *Patients, Physicians, and Illness* (3rd ed.). New York: Free Press, 1979.

Karl Marx. *Capital* (Friedrich Engels, ed.). New York: International, 1967.

Karl Marx and Friedrich Engels. *The Communist Manifesto* (Samuel H. Beer, ed.). New York: Appleton, 1955.

George Herbert Mead. "Mind, Self and Society." In Charles W. Morris (ed.), *From the Standpoint of a Social Behavioralist*. Chicago: University of Chicago Press, 1934.

C. Wright Mills. *The Power Elite*. New York: Oxford University Press, 1956.

C. Wright Mills. *The Sociological Imagination*. New York: Oxford University Press, 1959.

Gunnar Myrdal. *An American Dilemma*. New York: Harper & Row, 1944.

National Academy of Sciences. *Behavioral and Social Science Research: A National Resource*. Washington, D.C.: National Academy Press, 1982.

David E. Rosenbaum. "The Myths of Welfare." *The New York Times*, May 22, 1977, Section 4, p. 3.

Peter H. Rossi. "The Challenge and Opportunities of Applied Social Research." *American Sociological Review* 45 (1980):889–904.

Bradley R. Schiller. *The Economics of Poverty and Discrimination*. Englewood Cliffs, N.J.: Prentice-Hall, 1980.

Bradley R. Schiller. "Welfare: Reforming Our Expectations." *The Public Interest* 62 (1981):55–65.

Robert A. Scott and Arnold R. Shore. *Why Sociology Does Not Apply: A Study of the Use of Sociology in Public Policy*. New York: Elsevier, 1979.

Theda Skocpol. *States and Social Revolutions: A Comparative Analysis of France, Russia, and China*. New York: Cambridge University Press, 1979.

Max Weber. *The Theory of Social and Economic Organization* (A. N. Henderson and Talcott Parsons, trans.). New York: Free Press, 1964.

William Foote Whyte. *Street Corner Society: The Social Structure of an Italian Slum* (rev. ed.). Chicago: University of Chicago Press, 1955.

William Foote Whyte. "Social Inventions for Solving Human Problems." *American Sociological Review* 47 (1982):1–13.

Everett K. Wilson and Hanan Selvin. *Why Study Sociology? A Note to Undergraduates*. Belmont, Calif.: Wadsworth, 1980.

CHAPTER 2

Elliot Aronson and J. Merrill Carlsmith. "Experimentation in Social Psychology." In G. Linzey and E. Aronson (eds.), *The Handbook of Social Psychology* (2nd ed., vol. 2). Reading, Mass.: Addison-Wesley, 1968.

Elliot Aronson and J. Mills. "The Effect of Severity on Liking for a Group." *Journal of Abnormal and Social Psychology* 59 (1959):177–181.

J. Maxwell Atkinson. *Discovering Suicide: Studies in the Social Organization of Sudden Death*. Pittsburgh: University of Pittsburgh Press, 1978.

Earl R. Babbie. *The Practice of Social Research*. Belmont, Calif.: Wadsworth, 1979.

Bernard Barber. *Informed Consent in Medical Therapy and Research*. New Brunswick, N.J.: Rutgers University Press, 1980.

Bruce P. Dohrenwend et al. "President's Commission on the Accident at Three Mile Island: Report of the Task Force on Behavioral Effects." Unpublished report, October 1979*a*.

Bruce P. Dohrenwend. *Report of the Public Health and Safety Task Force to the President's Commission on Three Mile Island: 1979*. Washington, D.C.: U.S. Government Printing Office, 1979*b*.

Jack D. Douglas. *The Social Meaning of Suicide*. Princeton, N.J.: Princeton University Press, 1967.

Arthur Conan Doyle. *The Annotated Sherlock Holmes* (vol. II). New York: Clarkson N. Potter, 1967.

Emile Durkheim. *Suicide: A Study of Sociology* (John A. Spaulding and G. Simpson, trans.). New York: Free Press, 1951. (Originally published in 1897.)

Alvin W. Gouldner. "Anti-Minotaur: A Myth of a Value-Free Society." *Social Problems* 9, No. 3 (Winter 1962):199–213.

Alvin W. Gouldner. *The Coming Crisis of Western Sociology*. New York: Basic Books, 1980.

Bradford Gray. "An Assessment of Institutional Review Committees in Human Experimentation." *Medical Care* 13, No. 4 (April 1975):318–328.

Peter S. Houts and Marilyn K. Goldhaber. "Psychological and Social Effects on the Population Surrounding Three Mile Island after the Nuclear Accident on March 28, 1979." In S. Majumdar (ed.), *Energy, Environment and the Economy*. Pennsylvania Academy of Sciences, 1981.

Robert S. Laufer and Vern L. Bengtson. "Generations, Aging, and Social Stratification: On the Development of Generational Units." *Journal of Social Issues* 30 (1974):181–205.

Robert S. Lynd. *Knowledge for What?* Princeton, N.J.: Princeton University Press, 1946.

John McCarthy and Mayer Zald. "Resource Mobilization and Social Movements: A Partial Theory." *American Journal of Sociology* 82, No. 6 (May 1977):1212–1241.

Karl Mannheim. "The Problem of Generations." In K. Mannheim, *Essays on the Sociology of Knowledge*. London: Routledge and Kegan Paul, 1952.

Robert K. Merton. "Preface: 1970." In *Science, Technology and Society in Seventeenth Century England*. Atlantic Highlands, N.J.: Humanities Press, 1970.

Robert K. Merton. *The Sociology of Science: Theoretical and Empirical Investigations*. Chicago: University of Chicago Press, 1973.

C. Wright Mills. *The Sociological Imagination*. New York: Oxford University Press, 1959.

Ian I. Mitroff. "Norms and Counter-Norms in a Select Group of the Apollo Moon Scientists: A Case Study of the Ambivalence of Scientists." *American Sociological Review* 39 (August 1974):579–595.

Gunnar Myrdal. "How Scientific Are the Social Sciences?" *Bulletin of Atomic Scientists* 29 (January 1973):31–37.

John Naisbitt. *Megatrends*. New York: Warner Books, 1982.

Alberta J. Nassi and Stephen I. Abramowitz. "Transition or Transformation? Personal and Political Development of Former Berkeley Free Speech Movement Activists." *Journal of Youth and Adolescence* 8 (1979):21–35.

F. J. Roethlisberger and William Dickson. *Management and the Worker*. Cambridge, Mass.: Harvard University Press, 1939.

William B. Sanders. *The Sociologist as Detective*. New York: Praeger, 1974.

Leon Shaskolsky. "The Development of Sociological Theory in America—A Sociology of Knowledge Interpretation." In Larry T. Reynolds and Janice M. Reynolds (eds.), *The Sociology of Sociology: Analysis and Criticism of the Thought, Research, and Ethical Folkways of Sociology and Its Practitioners*. New York: David McKay, 1970.

Theda Skocpol. *States and Social Revolutions: A Comparative Analysis of France, Russia, and China*. New York: Cambridge University Press, 1979.

Edward J. Walsh. "Resource Mobilization Theory and the Dynamics of Local Anti-Nuclear Coalition Formation in the Wake of the Three Mile Island Accident." Paper presented at ASA meeting, New York, August 1980.

Edward J. Walsh. "Resource Mobilization and Citizen Protest in Communities Around Three Mile Island." *Social Problems* 29 (1981):1–21.

Edward J. Walsh. "Three Mile Island: Meltdown of Democracy?" *Bulletin of Atomic Scientists* (March 1983):57–60.

William Foote Whyte. *Street Corner Society: The Social Structure of an Italian Slum* (rev. ed.). Chicago: University of Chicago Press, 1955.

Everett K. Wilson and Hanan Selvin. *Why Study Sociology? A Note to Undergraduates*. Belmont, Calif.: Wadsworth, 1980.

Emily Yoffe. "John Naisbitt's Clip Joint." *Harper's*, September 16, 1983, pp. 16, 18–22.

J. M. Ziman. *Public Knowledge–An Essay Concerning the Social Dimension of Science*. Cambridge, England: Cambridge University Press, 1968.

CHAPTER 3

Alexander Alland, Jr. *Evolution of Human Behavior* (rev. ed.). Garden City, N.Y.: Doubleday Anchor, 1973.

Conrad M. Arensberg and Arthur H. Niehoff. *Introducing Social Change*. Chicago: Aldine, 1964.

Alexander W. Astin. *The American Freshman: National Norms for Fall 1983*. Los Angeles: Cooperative Institutional Research Program, Graduate School of Education, University of California (Los Angeles), 1983.

David P. Barash. *Sociobiology and Behavior*. New York: Elsevier, 1977.

Ruth Benedict. *Patterns of Culture*. New York: Mentor Books, 1946.
Eric Berne. *Games People Play: The Psychology of Human Relationships*. New York: Grove Press, 1964.
Bruno Bettelheim. *Children of the Dream*. New York: Macmillan, 1969.
Kenneth Bock. *Human Nature and History: A Response to Sociobiology*. New York: Columbia University Press, 1980.
Kenelm O. L. Burridge. "A Tangu Game." *Man* 57 (1957):88–89.
Ian A. Canino, Brian F. Earley, and Lloyd H. Rogler. *The Puerto Rican Child in New York City: Stress and Mental Health*. New York: Fordham University Hispanic Research Center, 1980.
Edmund Carpenter. "Comments." *Current Anthropology* 6 (1965):55.
Carlos E. Cortés. "Mexicans." In Stephan Thernstrom (ed.), *Harvard Encyclopedia of American Ethnic Groups*. Cambridge, Mass.: Harvard University Press, 1980.
Alan Dundes (ed.). *Every Man His Way: Readings in Cultural Anthropology*. Englewood Cliffs, N.J.: Prentice-Hall, 1968.
C. M. Eastman. *Aspects of Language and Culture*. San Francisco: Chandler and Sharp, 1975.
Carol R. Ember and Melvin Ember. *Anthropology* (2nd ed.). Englewood Cliffs, N.J.: Prentice-Hall, 1977.
Joseph P. Fitzpatrick. *Puerto Rican Americans: The Meaning of Migration to the Mainland*. Englewood Cliffs, N.J.: Prentice-Hall, 1971.
Robin Fox. "The Cultural Animal." *Encounters* 35 (July 1970):31–42.
Sigmund Freud. *Civilization and Its Discontents*. New York: Norton, 1961.
Katherine George. "The Civilized West Looks at Primitive Africa: 1400–1800." In Alan Dundes (ed.), *Every Man His Way: Readings in Cultural Anthropology*. Englewood Cliffs, N.J.: Prentice-Hall, 1968.
Arthur S. Golden. "Group Think in Japan, Inc." *New York Times Magazine*, December 5, 1982, pp. 133–140.
Milton M. Gordon. *Assimilation in American Life*. New York: Oxford University Press, 1964.
Edward T. Hall. *The Hidden Dimension*. Garden City, N.Y.: Doubleday, 1966.
Marvin Harris. *Cultural Materialism*. New York: Random House, 1979. (Vintage edition, 1980.)
John Langton. "Darwinism and the Behavioral Theory of Sociocultural Evolution: An Analysis." *American Journal of Sociology* 85, No. 2 (September 1979):288–309.
Christopher Lasch. *The Culture of Narcissism*. New York: Norton, 1978.
Ralph Linton. *The Study of Man*. New York: Appleton, 1947.
Charles J. Lumsden and Edward O. Wilson. *Genes, Mind, and Culture: The Coevolutionary Process*. Cambridge, Mass.: Harvard University Press, 1981.
George Peter Murdock. "The Common Denominator of Cultures." In Ralph Linton (ed.), *The Science of Man in World Crisis*. New York: Columbia University Press, 1945.
Cheryl Russell. "The News about Hispanics." *American Demographics* 5 (March 1983):15–25.
Marshall Sahlins. *The Use and Abuse of Biology*. Ann Arbor: University of Michigan Press, 1981.
Edward Sapir. *Selected Writings in Language, Culture, and Personality*. Berkeley: University of California Press, 1949.
Georg Simmel. *Conflict* (Kurt Wolff, trans.). New York: Free Press, 1955.
Philip E. Slater. *The Pursuit of Loneliness: American Culture at the Breaking Point* (rev. ed.). Boston: Beacon Press, 1976.
Joseph Veroff, Elizabeth Douvan, and Richard A. Kulka. *The Inner American: A Self-Portrait from 1957 to 1976*. New York: Basic Books, 1981.
Ken Wells. "Togan Chic in Utah is Horsemeat in Luau and Kava and Rugby." *Wall Street Journal*, May 13, 1983, pp. 1, 10.
Benjamin L. Whorf. *Language, Thought, and Reality*. Cambridge, Mass.: MIT Press, 1956.
Robin Williams. *American Society* (3rd ed.). New York: Knopf, 1970.
Edward O. Wilson. *On Human Nature*. Cambridge, Mass.: Harvard University Press, 1978.
Daniel Yankelovich. *Yankelovich Youth Study*. Copyright 1973 by the JDR, 3rd Fund.

CHAPTER 4

Elijah Anderson. *A Place on the Corner*. Chicago: University of Chicago Press, 1978.
Peter L. Berger. *Invitation to Sociology*. New York: Doubleday, 1963.
Peter Blau. *Exchange and Power in Social Life*. New York: Wiley, 1964.
Peter Blau. *Inequality and Heterogeneity: A Primitive Theory of Social Structure*. New York: Free Press, 1977.
Herbert Blumer. *Symbolic Interactionism: Perspective and Method*. Englewood Cliffs, N.J.: Prentice-Hall, 1969.
Andrew Cherlin. "Remarriage as an Incomplete Institution." *American Journal of Sociology* 84 (November 1978):634–650.
Randall Collins. "On the Microfoundations of Macrosociology." *American Journal of Sociology* 86 (1981):984–1014.
Herbert Gans. *More Equality*. New York: Pantheon, 1973.
Harold Garfinkel. *Studies in Ethnomethodology*. Englewood Cliffs, N.J.: Prentice-Hall, 1967.
Erving Goffman. *Presentation of the Self in Everyday Life*. New York: Doubleday, 1959.
Erving Goffman. *Frame Analysis: An Essay on the Organization of Experience*. Cambridge, Mass.: Harvard University Press, 1974.
Erving Goffman. *Forms of Talk*. Philadelphia: University of Pennsylvania Press, 1981.
William J. Goode. "A Theory of Role Strain." *American Sociological Review* 25 (1960):483–496.
John P. Hewitt. *Self and Society: A Symbolic Interactionist Social Psychology* (2nd ed.). Boston: Allyn & Bacon, 1979.
George C. Homans. *Social Behavior: Its Elementary Forms* (rev. ed.). New York: Harcourt Brace Jovanovich, 1974.
Richard B. Lee. *The Kung San: Men, Women and Work in a Foraging Society*. New York: Cambridge University Press, 1979.
Elliot Liebow. *Tally's Corner: A Study of Negro Streetcorner Men*. Boston: Little, Brown, 1967.
Ralph Linton. *The Study of Man*. New York: Appleton-Century-Crofts, 1947.
S. L. A. Marshall. *Man Against Fire*. New York: Morrow, 1947.
Robert Merton. "Social Structure and Anomie." *American Sociological Review* 3 (1938):672–682.
Robert Merton. *Social Theory and Social Structure*. New York: Free Press, 1968.
J. Clyde Mitchell. *Social Networks in Urban Situations*. Manchester: Manchester University Press, 1969.
W. I. Thomas. *The Unadjusted Girl*. Boston: Little, Brown, 1937.

William I. Thomas and Dorothy Swaine Thomas. *The Child in America*. New York: Knopf, 1928.

James W. Vander Zanden. *Social Psychology* (3rd ed.). New York: Random House, 1984.

James W. Vander Zanden. *American Minority Relations* (4th ed.). New York: Knopf, 1983.

Mark L. Wardell and Ellsworth R. Fuhrman. "Controversy and Ideological Hegemony in Sociological Theory." *Sociological Quarterly* 22 (1981):479–493.

CHAPTER 5

Gordon W. Allport. *The Nature of Prejudice*. Reading, Mass.: Addison-Wesley, 1954.

Philippe Ariès. *Centuries of Childhood* (R. Baldick, trans.). New York: Random House, 1962.

Robert C. Atchley. *The Social Forces in Later Life: An Introduction to Social Gerontology* (3rd ed.). Belmont, Calif.: Wadsworth, 1980.

Diana Baumrind. "Effects of Authoritative Parental Control on Child Behavior." *Child Development* 37 (1966):887–907.

Diana Baumrind. "New Directions in Socialization Research." *American Psychologist* 35 (1980):639–652.

Peter L. Berger and Brigitte Berger. "Becoming a Member of Society." In Peter Rose (ed.), *Socialization and the Life Cycle*. New York: St. Martin's Press, 1979.

Augusto Blasi. "Bridging Moral Cognition and Moral Action: A Critical Review of the Literature." *Psychological Bulletin* 88 (1980):1–45.

Pierre Bourdieu and Jean-Claude Passeron. *Reproduction in Education, Society and Culture*. Beverly Hills, Calif.: Sage, 1977.

John Bowlby. *Separation: Anxiety and Anger*. New York: Basic Books, 1973.

Arthur L. Caplan (ed.). *The Sociobiology Debate*. New York: Harper & Row, 1979.

Douglass Cater and Stephen Strickland. *TV Violence and the Child: The Evolution and Fate of the Surgeon General's Report*. New York: Russell Sage Foundation, 1975.

S. Chess, A. Thomas, and H. G. Birch. "Behavioral Problems Revisited." In S. Chess and H. Birch (eds.), *Annual Progress in Child Psychiatry and Development*. New York: Brunner/Mazel, 1968.

Victor G. Circirelli. "A Comparison of College Women's Feelings Toward Their Siblings and Parents." *Journal of Marriage and the Family* 42 (1980):111–118.

Anne Colby, Lawrence Kohlberg, John Gibbs, and Marcus Lieberman. "A Longitudinal Study of Moral Judgment." *Monographs of the Society for Research in Child Development* 48, No. 200 (1983).

Glenn Collins. "The Childhood 'Industry': Conflicting Advice." *New York Times*, March 16, 1981, p. 17.

Charles Horton Cooley. *Social Organization: A Study of the Larger Mind*. Glencoe, Ill.: Free Press, 1956.

Charles Horton Cooley. *Human Nature and the Social Order*. New York: Schocken, 1964.

Joan Davidson. "Vietnam's Sad Legacy: Vets Living in the Wild." *U.S. News & World Report*, March 12, 1984, pp. 38–39.

Mark Davies and Denise B. Kandel. "Parental and Peer Influences on Adolescents' Educational Plans: Some Further Evidence." *American Journal of Sociology* 87 (1981):363–387.

Fred Davis. "Professional Socialization as Subjective Experience: The Process of Doctrinal Conversion Among Student Nurses." In Howard S. Becker et al. (eds.), *Institutions and the Person*. Chicago: Aldine, 1968.

Kingsley Davis. *Human Society*. New York: Macmillan, 1948.

L. Richard Della Fava. "The Meek Shall Not Inherit the Earth: Self-Evaluation and the Legitimacy of Stratification." *American Sociological Review* 45 (1980):955–971.

Lloyd deMause. *The History of Childhood*. New York: Harper & Row, 1974.

Glen H. Elder, Jr. "Adolescence in the Life Cycle: An Introduction." In Sigmund E. Dragastin and Glen H. Elder, Jr. (eds.), *Adolescence in the Life Cycle: Psychological Change and the Social Context*. New York: Halsted Press, 1975.

Frederick Elkin and Gerald Handel. *The Child and Society* (3rd ed.). New York: Random House, 1978.

Erik Erikson. *Childhood and Society*. New York: Norton, 1950.

Erik Erikson. *Identity: Youth and Crisis*. New York: Norton, 1968.

Susan L. Farber. *Identical Twins Reared Apart*. New York: Basic Books, 1981.

Robert R. Faulkner and Douglas B. McGaw. "Uneasy Homecoming, Stages in the Reentry Transition of Vietnam Veterans." *Urban Life* 6 (1977):303–325.

Lucille K. Forer. *The Birth Order Factor—How Your Personality Is Influenced by Your Place in the Family*. New York: David McKay, 1976.

Sigmund Freud. *Five Lectures on Psychoanalysis: The Standard Edition* (James Strachey, ed.). New York: Norton, 1977.

Sigmund Freud. *A General Introduction to Psychoanalysis* (Joan Riviare, trans.). New York: Washington Square Press, 1960. (Originally published in 1939.)

Viktor Gecas. "Contexts of Socialization." In Morris Rosenberg and Ralph H. Turner (eds.), *Social Psychology*. New York: Basic Books, 1981.

Carol Gilligan. *In a Different Voice: Psychological Theory and Women's Development*. Cambridge, Mass.: Harvard University Press, 1982.

Peggy Golde and Nathan Kogan. "A Sentence Completion Procedure for Assessing Attitudes Toward Old People." *Journal of Gerontology* 14, No. 3 (1959):355–363.

Emily Greenspan. "Little Winners." *The New York Times Magazine*, April 26, 1981, pp. 59–74.

Harry F. Harlow and R. Z. Zimmerman. "Affectional Responses in the Infant Monkey." *Science* 130 (1959):421–432.

Adella J. Harris and Jonathan Feinberg. "Television and Aging: Is What You See What You Get?" *The Gerontologist* 18, No. 5 (1978).

Louis Harris and Associates. *The Myth and Reality of Aging in America: A Study for the National Council on Aging*. Washington, D.C.: National Council on Aging, 1975.

Louis Harris. *Aging in the Eighties: America in Transition*. Washington, D.C.: National Council on Aging, 1981.

Constance Holden. "Twins Reunited." *Science 80*, No. 1 (November 1980):55–59.

J. Kagan and H. A. Moss. *Birth to Maturity*. New York: Wiley, 1962.

Richard A. Kalish. "Death and Dying in a Social Context." In Robert Binstock and Ethel Shanas (eds.), *Handbook of Aging and Social Sciences*. New York: Van Nostrand Reinhold, 1976.

Lawrence Kohlberg. "Moral Stages and Moralization." In T. Lickona

(ed.), *Moral Development and Behavior: Theory, Research, and Social Issues*. New York: Holt, Rinehart & Winston, 1976.
Lawrence Kohlberg. *The Development of Sociomoral Knowledge*. New York: Cambridge University Press, 1980.
Lawrence Kohlberg and Carol Gilligan. "The Adolescent as a Philosopher: The Discovery of the Self in a Postconventional World." *Daedalus* 100 (Fall 1971):1051–1086.
Melvin L. Kohn. "Occupational Structure and Alienation." *American Journal of Sociology* 82 (July 1976):111–130.
Jon A. Krosnick and Charles M. Judd. "Transitions in Social Influence at Adolescence: Who Induces Cigarette Smoking?" *Developmental Psychology* 18 (1982):359–368.
Elisabeth Kübler-Ross. *On Death and Dying*. New York: Macmillan, 1969.
Robert S. Laufer et al. *Legacies of Vietnam: Comparative Adjustment of Veterans and Their Peers*. Washington, D.C.: U.S. Government Printing Office, 1981.
E. E. LeMasters. *Blue-Collar Aristocrats*. Madison: University of Wisconsin Press, 1975.
Nona Plessner Lyons. "Two Perspectives: On Self, Relationships, and Morality." *Harvard Educational Review* 53 (1983):125–145.
David C. McClelland. "Making It to Maturity." *Psychology Today* 12 (June 1978): 12+.
Karl Marx. *Capital* (vol. 1). New York: Modern Library, 1906.
Karl Marx. "Critique of the Gotha Program." In L. S. Feuer (ed.), *Marx and Engels: Basic Writings on Politics and Philosophy*. Garden City, N.Y.: Doubleday, 1959.
Karl Marx. *The Poverty of Philosophy*. New York: International Publishers, 1963.
George Herbert Mead. *Mind, Self and Society*. Chicago: University of Chicago Press, 1934.
Jeylan T. Mortimer and Roberta G. Simmons. "Adult Socialization." In R. H. Turner, J. Coleman, and R. C. Fox (eds.), *Annual Review of Sociology* (vol. 4). Palo Alto, Calif.: Annual Reviews, 1978.
National Institute of Mental Health. *Television and Behavior: Ten Years of Scientific Progress and Implications for the Eighties* (vols. 1 and 2). Washington, D.C.: U.S. Government Printing Office, 1982.
Bernice L. Neugarten. "Adult Personality: Toward a Psychology of the Life Cycle." In E. Vinacke (ed.), *Readings in General Psychology*. New York: American Book Co., 1968.
Erdman Palmore. *The Honorable Elders*. Durham, N.C.: Duke University Press, 1975.
Talcott Parsons. *Social Structure and Personality*. New York: Free Press, 1964.
J. L. Phillips, Jr. *The Origins of the Intellect: Piaget's Theory*. San Francisco, Calif.: Freeman, 1969.
Jean Piaget. *The Child's Conception of the World*. London: Routledge and Kegan Paul, 1971.
Jean Piaget. *The Moral Judgment of the Child*. London: Routledge and Kegan Paul, 1932.
Jean Piaget and Bärbel Inhelder. *The Psychology of the Child*. New York: Basic Books, 1969.
Maya Pines. "Behavior and Heredity: Links for Specific Traits Are Growing Stronger." *New York Times*, June 29, 1982, pp. 19, 22.
Robert Plomin and Terryl T. Foch. "A Twin Study of Objectively Assessed Personality in Childhood." *Journal of Personality and Social Psychology* 39 (1980):680–688.
Richard A. Price, Steven G. Vandenberg, Hariharan Iyer, and James S. Williams. "Components of Variation in Normal Personality." *Journal of Personality and Social Psychology* 43 (1982):328–340.
Morris Rosenberg. *Conceiving the Self*. New York: Basic Books, 1979.
C. S. Russell. "Transition to Parenthood: Problems and Gratifications." *Journal of Marriage and the Family* 36 (1974):294–302.
Arnold J. Sameroff. "Transactional Models in Early Social Relations." *Human Development* 18 (1975):65–79.
John W. Santrock. *Life-Span Development*. Dubuque, Iowa: Wm. C. Brown, 1983.
Sandra Scarr. "Development is Internally Guided, Not Determined." *Contemporary Psychology* 27 (1982):852–853.
Edgar H. Schein. *Career Dynamics: Matching Individual and Organizational Needs*. Reading, Mass.: Addison-Wesley, 1978.
Paul F. Secord and Carl W. Backman. *Social Psychology*. New York: McGraw-Hill, 1964.
Tom Sheehan. "Senior Esteem as a Factor of Socioeconomic Complexity." *The Gerontologist* 16, No. 5 (1976):433–440.
Charles E. Silberman. *Crisis in the Classroom*. New York: Random House, 1971.
Ida Harper Simpson. *From Student to Nurse: A Longitudinal Study of Socialization*. New York: Cambridge University Press, 1979.
Dorothy G. Singer. "A Time to Reexamine the Role of Television in Our Lives." *American Psychologist* 38 (1983):815–816.
Jerome L. Singer and Dorothy G. Singer. *Television, Imagination, and Aggression: A Study of Preschoolers*. Hillsdale, N.J.: Erlbaum, 1981.
Jerome L. Singer and Dorothy G. Singer. "Psychologists Look at Television." *American Psychologist* 38 (1983):826–834.
Margaret E. Snow, Carol Nagy Jacklin, and Eleanor E. Maccob. "Birth-Order Differences in Peer Sociability at Thirty-Three Months." *Child Development* 52 (1981):589–595.
Dava Sobel. "Siblings: Studies Find Rivalry, Dependency Revive in Adulthood." *New York Times*, October 28, 1980, p. Cl.
R. D. Spitz. "The Psychogenic Diseases of Infancy: An Attempt at Their Etiological Classification." *Psychoanalytic Study of the Child* 6 (1951):255–275.
Harry Stack Sullivan. *The Interpersonal Theory of Psychiatry*. New York: W. W. Norton, 1953.
Maurice K. Temerlin. *Lucy: Growing Up Human*. Palo Alto, Calif.: Science and Behavior Books, 1975.
Lillian E. Troll and Vern Bengtson. "Intergenerational Relations Throughout the Life Span." In B. B. Wolman (ed.), *Handbook of Developmental Psychology*. Englewood Cliffs, N.J.: Prentice-Hall, 1982.
Jacob Tuckman and Irving Lorge. "Attitudes Toward Old Workers." *Journal of Applied Psychology* 35, No. 3 (1952):149–153.
George E. Vaillant and Caroline O. Vaillant. "Natural History of Male Psychological Health, X: Work as a Predictor of Positive Mental Health." *American Journal of Psychiatry* 138 (1981):1433–1440.
James W. Vander Zanden. *Social Psychology* (3rd ed.). New York: Random House, 1984.
John Van Maanen. "Breaking-in: Socialization to Work." In R. Dubin (ed.), *Handbook of Work, Organization and Society*. Indianapolis: Bobbs-Merrill, 1976.
Harry F. Waters. "Life According to TV." *Newsweek*, December 6, 1982, pp. 136–140.
John B. Watson. *Behaviorism*. New York: Norton, 1970. (Originally

published in 1925.)

Linda E. Weinberger and Jim Millham. "A Multidimensional Multiple Method Analysis of Attitudes Toward the Elderly." *Journal of Gerontology* 30, No. 3 (1975):343–348.

Stanton Wheeler. "The Structure of Formally Organized Socialization Settings." In O. G. Brim and S. Wheeler (eds.), *Socialization After Childhood*. New York: Wiley, 1966.

Burton L. White, Barbara T. Kaban, and Jane S. Attanucci. *The Origins of Human Competence*. Lexington, Mass.: D.C. Heath, 1979.

C. B. White, N. Bushnell, and J. L. Regnemer. "Moral Development in Bahamian School Children: A 3 Year Examination of Kohlberg's Stages of Moral Development." *Developmental Psychology* 14 (1978):58–65.

Norbert Wiley. "Notes on Self Genesis: From Me to We to I." *Studies in Symbolic Interaction* 2 (1979):87–105.

L. Willerman and R. Plomin. "Activity Level in Children and Parents." *Child Development* 44 (1973):854–858.

Edward O. Wilson. *On Human Nature*. Cambridge, Mass.: Harvard University Press, 1978.

Marie Winn. *Children Without Childhood*. New York: Pantheon, 1983.

Dennis H. Wrong. "The Oversocialized Conception of Man in Modern Sociology." *American Sociological Review* 26 (1961):183–193.

James Youniss. *Parents and Peers in Social Development*. Chicago: University of Chicago Press, 1980.

CHAPTER 6

Aniceto Aramoni. "Machismo." *Psychology Today* 5 (January 1972):69–72.

M. A. Baker. *Women Today: A Multidisciplinary Approach to Women's Studies*. Monterey, Calif.: Brooks/Cole, 1980.

Judith M. Bardwick and Elizabeth Douvan. "Ambivalence: The Socialization of Women." In Vivian Gornick and Barbara K. Moran (eds.), *Women in Sexist Society*. New York: Basic Books, 1971.

Camilla Benbow and Julian Stanley. "Sex Differences in Mathematical Ability: Fact or Artifact?" *Science* 210 (1980):1262.

Jessie Bernard. *Women and the Public Interest: An Essay on Policy and Protest*. Chicago: Aldine-Atherton, 1971.

Josephine V. Brown, Rober Bakerman, Patricia A. Snyder, and others. "Interactions of Black Inner-City Mothers with Their Newborn Infants." *Child Development* 46 (1975):677–686.

Harlan S. Byrne. "Firms Are Adding Female Directors More Slowly than During the 1970s." *Wall Street Journal*, April 7, 1982, p. 27.

Glenn Collins. "Unforeseen Business Barriers for Women." *New York Times*, May 31, 1982, p. 18.

Glenn Collins. "The Stress in Doctors' Families." *New York Times*, March 8, 1982, p. 20.

Nicholas Daniloff. "For Russia's Women, Worst of Both Worlds." *U.S. News & World Report*, June 28, 1982, pp. 53–54.

Doris R. Entwisle and David P. Baker. "Gender and Young Children's Expectations for Performance in Arithmetic." *Developmental Psychology* 19 (1983):200–209.

Beverly I. Fagot. "Consequences of Moderate Cross-Gender Behavior in Preschool Children." *Child Development* 48 (1977):902–907.

Beverly I. Fagot. "The Influence of Sex of Child on Parental Reactions to Toddler Children." *Child Development* 49 (1978):459–465*a*.

Beverly I. Fagot. "Reinforcing Contingencies for Sex-Role Behaviors: Effect of Experiences with Children." *Child Development* 49 (1978):30–36*b*.

Barbara L. Forisha. *Sex Roles and Personal Awareness*. Chicago: Scott, Foresman, 1978.

Betty Friedan. *The Feminine Mystique*. New York: Norton, 1963.

Irene H. Frieze, J. E. Parsons, P. B. Johnson, Diana N. Ruble, and Gail L. Zellman. *Women and Sex Roles: A Social-Psychological Perspective*. New York: Norton, 1978.

Terry Fruch and Paul E. McGhee. "Traditional Sex Role Development and Amount of Time Spent Watching Television." *Developmental Psychology* 11, No. 1 (1975):109.

Ted Gest. "Battle of the Sexes over 'Comparable Worth.'" *U.S. News & World Report*, February 20, 1984, pp. 73–74.

Roger L. Gould. *Transformations*. New York: Touchstone Books, 1978.

Walter R. Gove and Jeannette F. Tudor. "Adult Sex Roles and Mental Illness." In Joan Huber (ed.), *Changing Women in a Changing Society*. Chicago: University of Chicago Press, 1973.

Margaret Hennig and Anne Jardim. *The Managerial Woman*. Garden City, N.Y.: Anchor Press/Doubleday, 1977.

Jennifer Bingham Hull. "Female Bosses Say Biggest Barriers Are Insecurity and 'Being a Woman.'" *Wall Street Journal*, November 2, 1982, p. 29.

Janet S. Hyde. "How Large Are Cognitive Gender Differences?" *American Psychologist* 36 (1981):892–901.

Judy Klemesrud. "Voice of Authority Still Male." *New York Times*, February 2, 1981, p. 16.

Lawrence Kohlberg. "A Cognitive-Developmental Analysis of Children's Sex Role Concepts and Attitudes." In E. E. Maccoby (ed.), *The Development of Sex Differences*. Stanford, Calif.: Stanford University Press, 1966.

Gina Bari Kolata. "Math and Sex: Are Girls Born with Less Ability?" *Science* 210 (1980):1234–1235.

Michael E. Lamb, M. Ann Easterbrooks, and George W. Holden. "Reinforcement and Punishment among Preschoolers: Characteristics, Effects, and Correlates." *Child Development* 51 (1980):1230–1236.

Judith H. Langolois and A. Chris Downs. "Mothers, Fathers, and Peers as Socialization Agents of Sex-Typed Play Behaviors in Young Children." *Child Development* 51 (1980):1237–1247.

Gerda Lerner. *The Majority Finds Its Past: Placing Women in History*. New York: Oxford University Press, 1979.

Tamar Lewin. "A New Push to Raise Women's Pay." *New York Times*, January 1, 1984, pp. F1–F15.

David B. Lynn. "Fathers and Sex-Role Development." *Family Coordinator* 25 (1976):403–409.

Eleanor E. Maccoby and Carol N. Jacklin. *The Psychology of Sex Differences*. Stanford, Calif.: Stanford University Press, 1974.

Eleanor E. Maccoby and Carol N. Jacklin. "Sex Differences in Aggression: A Rejoinder and Reprise." *Child Development* 51 (1980):964–980.

Neil J. MacLusky and Frederick Naftolin. "Sexual Differentiation of the Central Nervous System." *Science* 211 (1981):1294–1303.

Jack Magarrell. "Female Professors Average 15 Pct. Less Pay than Males." *The Chronicle of Higher Education*, November 25, 1981, p. 8.

Sharon S. Mayes. "Women in Positions of Authority: A Case Study of

Changing Sex Roles." *Journal of Women in Culture and Society* 4, No. 3 (1979):556–568.

Margaret Mead. *Sex and Temperament in Three Primitive Societies*. New York: Morrow, 1963. (Originally published in 1935.)

Judith L. Meece, Jacquelynne Eccles Parsons, Caroline M. Kaczala, Susan B. Goff, and Robert Futterman. "Sex Differences in Math Achievement: Toward a Model of Academic Choice." *Psychological Bulletin* 91 (1982):324–348.

John Money and Patricia Tucker. *Sexual Signatures: On Being a Man or a Woman*. Boston: Little, Brown, 1975.

New York Times. "Poll Finds Women Perceive Job Bias." August 15, 1982, p. 19.

Jacquelynne Eccles Parsons, Terry F. Adler, and Caroline M. Kaczala. "Socialization of Achievement Attitudes and Beliefs: Parental Influences." *Child Development* 53 (1982):310–321.

Joan Daniels Pedro, Patricia Wollcat, Elizabeth Fennema, and Ann Devaney Becker. "Election of High School Mathematics by Females and Males: Attributes and Attitudes." *American Education Research Journal* 18 (1981):207–218.

Elizabeth Pleck. "Sex Roles in Transition: The Historical Perspective." In Dorothy G. McGuigan (ed.), *New Research on Women and Sex Roles*. Ann Arbor: University of Michigan Center for Continuing Education of Women, 1974.

Joseph Pleck. "Male Sex Role and Personality: Toward a Research and Clinical Perspective." Paper given at Harvard University, Cambridge, Mass., February 1972.

Robert Plomin and Terryl T. Foch. "Sex Differences and Individual Differences." *Child Development* 52 (1981):383–385.

Frank J. Prial. "More Women Work at Traditional Male Jobs." *New York Times*, November 15, 1982, pp. 1, 22.

Mary Lou Randour, Georgia L. Strasburg, and Jean Lipman-Blumen. "Women in Higher Education: Trends in Enrollments and Degrees Earned." *Harvard Educational Review* 52 (1982):189–202.

David Reuben. *Any Woman Can!* New York: McKay, 1972.

Harriet L. Rheingold and Kaye V. Cook. "The Contents of Boys' and Girls' Rooms as an Index of Parents' Behavior." *Child Development* 46 (1975):459–463.

Stephanie Riger and Margaret T. Gordon. "The Fear of Rape: A Study in Social Control." *Journal of Social Issues* 37 (1981):71–92.

Roper Organization, Inc. The 1980 Virginia Slims American Women's Opinion Poll.

Sarah Rosenfield. "Sex Differences in Depression: Do Women Always Have Higher Rates?" *Journal of Health and Social Behavior* 21, No. 1 (March 1980):33–42.

Sheila M. Rothman. *Women's Proper Place*. New York: Basic Books, 1978.

Debra Kaplan Rubin. "Fifth Annual Salary Survey." *Working Woman*, January 1984, pp. 59–63.

J. Z. Rubin, F. J. Provenzano, and Z. Luria. "The Eye of the Beholder: Parents' Views on Sex of Newborns." *American Journal of Orthopsychiatry* 44 (1974):512–519.

Lillian Rubin. "Changing Expectations: New Sources of Strain." In *Worlds of Pain: Life in the Working-Class Family*. New York: Basic Books, 1976.

Lillian B. Rubin. "Women of a Certain Age." *Society* 17 (March–April 1980):68–76.

Robert T. Rubin, June M. Reinisch, and Roger F. Haskett. "Postnatal Gonadal Steroid Effects on Human Behavior." *Science* 211 (1981):1318–1324.

Maggie Scarf. "He and She: The Sex Hormones and Behavior." *New York Times Magazine*, May 7, 1972.

Maggie Scarf. *Unfinished Business: Pressure Points in the Lives of Women*. Garden City, N.Y.: Doubleday, 1980.

Alice Schlegel (ed.). *Sexual Stratification, A Cross-Cultural View*. New York: Columbia University Press, 1977.

Joan Wallach Scott. "The Mechanization of Women's Work." *Scientific American* 247 (September 1982):167–187.

Lisa A. Serbin. K. Daniel O'Leary, Ronald N. Kent, and Illene J. Tonick. "A Comparison of Teacher Response to the Preacademic and Problem Behavior of Boys and Girls." *Child Development* 44 (1973):796–804.

Julia Sherman. *Sex-Related Cognitive Differences*. Springfield, Ill.: Charles C. Thomas, 1978.

David Shribman. "Study Finds Women 'Systematically Underpaid.'" *New York Times*, September 2, 1981, p. 9.

Ronald G. Slaby and Karin S. Frey. "Development of Gender Constancy and Selective Attention to Same-Sex Models." *Child Development* 46 (1975):849–856.

Margaret Ellis Snow, Carol Nagy Jacklin, and Eleanor E. Maccoby. "Sex-of-Child Differences in Father-Child Interactions at One Year of Age." *Child Development* 54 (1983):227–232.

Joyce N. Sprafkin and Robert M. Liebert. "Sex Typing and Children's Television Preferences." In Gaye Tuchman, Arlene Kaplan Daniels, and James Benét (eds.), *Hearth and Home: Images of Women in the Mass Media*. New York: Oxford University Press, 1978.

Robert Stoller. *Sex and Gender*. New York: Science House, 1968.

Carol Tavris and T. Jayaratne. "How Do You Feel About Being a Woman: The Results of a *Redbook* Questionnaire." *Redbook*, 1972.

Spencer K. Thompson. "Gender Labels and Early Sex Role Development." *Child Development* 46 (1975):339–347.

Todd Tieger. "On the Biological Basis of Sex Differences in Aggression." *Child Development* 51 (1980):943–963.

Sheila Tobias. *Overcoming Math Anxiety*. New York: Norton, 1978.

Leonore J. Weitzman and Deborah Eifler. "Sex Role Socialization in Picture Books for Preschool Children." *American Journal of Sociology* 77 (May 1972):1125–1144.

Kendall J. Wills. "Losing the Salary Game." *New York Times*, February 20, 1983, p. 27.

World Book Encyclopedia, 1981 Edition, Vol. 21, p. 321.

CHAPTER 7

Solomon E. Asch. *Social Psychology*. Englewood Cliffs, N.J.: Prentice-Hall, 1952.

Robert F. Bales and Fred L. Strodtbeck. "Phases in Group Problem Solving." *Journal of Abnormal and Social Psychology* 46 (1951):485–495.

Theodore Caplow. *Two Against One: Coalition in Triads*. Englewood Cliffs, N.J.: Prentice-Hall, 1969.

Dorwin Cartwright and Alvin Zander (eds.). *Group Dynamics: Research and Theory* (3rd ed.). New York: Harper & Row, 1968.

Charles H. Cooley. *Social Organization*. New York: Scribner's, 1929. (Originally published in 1909.)

Lewis Coser. *The Functions of Social Conflict*. New York: Free Press, 1956.

Kay Deaux and Lawrence S. Wrightsman. *Social Psychology in the 80s* (4th ed.). Monterey, Calif.: Brooks/Cole, 1983.

Robert A. Dentler and Kai T. Erikson. "The Functions of Deviance in Groups." *Social Problems* 7 (1959):98–107.

Thomas L. Friedman. "Living with the Violence of Beirut." *New York Times Magazine*, July 17, 1983, pp. 12–18+.

William Golding. *Lord of the Flies*. New York: Coward-McCann, 1954.

A. Paul Hare. *Handbook of Small Group Research* (2nd ed.). New York: Free Press, 1976.

Fritz Heider. *The Psychology of Interpersonal Relations*. New York: Wiley, 1958.

Irving L. Janis. *Victims of Groupthink: A Psychological Study of Foreign-Policy Decisions and Fiascos*. Boston: Houghton Mifflin, 1972.

Norris Johnson, James G. Stemler, and Deborah Hunter. "Crowd Behavior as 'Risky Shift': A Laboratory Experiment." *Sociometry* 40 (1977):183–187.

H. G. Kalven, Jr., and H. Zeisel. *The American Jury*. Boston: Little, Brown, 1966.

Mirra Komarovsky. *The Unemployed Man and His Family: The Effect of Unemployment Upon the Status of the Man in Fifty-nine Families*. New York: Arno, 1971. (Originally published in 1940.)

Manford H. Kuhn. "Self-Attitudes by Age, Sex, and Professional Training." *Sociological Quarterly* 1 (1960):39–55.

James Mann. "Behind the Explosion in Self-Help Groups." *U.S. News & World Report*, May 2, 1983, pp. 33–35.

Stanley Milgram. *Obedience to Authority*. New York: Harper & Row, 1974.

David G. Myers and G. D. Bishop. "Discussion Effects on Racial Attitudes." *Science* 169 (1970):778–789.

David G. Myers and Helmut Lamm. "The Group Polarization Phenomenon." *Psychology Bulletin* 83 (1976):602–627.

Theodore Newcomb. "Attitude Development as a Function of Reference Groups: The Bennington Study." In G. E. Swanson, T. M. Newcomb, and E. L. Hartley (eds.), *Readings in Social Psychology*. New York: Holt, Rinehart & Winston, 1958.

Theodore Newcomb et al. *Persistence and Change: Bennington College and Its Students, Twenty-five Years*. New York: Wiley, 1967.

Paul F. Secord and Carl W. Backman. *Social Psychology* (2nd ed.). New York: McGraw-Hill, 1974.

Muzafer Sherif. *The Psychology of Social Norms*. New York: Harper & Row, 1936.

Georg Simmel. *The Sociology of Georg Simmel* (Kurt W. Wolff, ed. and trans.). New York: Free Press, 1950.

Philip E. Slater. "Contrasting Correlates of Group Size." *Sociometry* 21 (1958):129–139.

William Graham Sumner. *Folkways*. Boston: Ginn, 1906.

Tom R. Tyler and David O. Sears. "Coming to Like Obnoxious People When We Must Live With Them." *Journal of Personality and Social Psychology* 35, No. 4 (1977):200–211.

CHAPTER 8

Karen W. Arenson. "Management's Ranks Grow." *New York Times*, April 14, 1983, p. 31.

Judith R. Blau. "Prominence in a Network of Communication: Work Relations in a Children's Psychiatric Hospital." *Sociological Quarterly* 23 (1982):235–251.

Peter M. Blau and Marshall W. Meyer. *Bureaucracy in Modern Society* (2nd ed.). New York: Random House, 1971.

Barry Bluestone and Bennett Harrison. *The Deindustrialization of America*. New York: Basic Books, 1982.

Samuel Bowles, David M. Gordon, and Thomas E. Weisskopf. *Beyond the Wasteland*. New York: Anchor Press, 1983.

Harry Braverman. *Labor and Monopoly Capital: The Degradation of Work in the Twentieth Century*. New York: Monthly Review Press, 1974.

Michael Burawoy. *Manufacturing Consent: Changes in the Labor Process under Monopoly Capitalism*. Chicago: University of Chicago Press, 1979.

Terrence E. Deal and Allan A. Kennedy. *Corporate Cultures: The Rites and Rituals of Corporate Life*. Reading, Mass.: Addison-Wesley, 1982.

Paul Dickson. *The Future of the Workplace*. New York: Weybright and Talley, 1975.

Peter F. Drucker. "Squeezing the Firm's Midriff Bulge." *Wall Street Journal*, March 25, 1983, p. 14.

Amitai Etzioni. *Modern Organizations*. Englewood Cliffs, N.J.: Prentice-Hall, 1964.

Amitai Etzioni. *A Comparative Analysis of Complex Organizations* (rev. ed.). New York: Free Press, 1975.

Olive Evans. "Friendship: On the Job and After 5." *New York Times*, August 1, 1983, p. 18.

William E. Geist. "Princeton Reunion Hails '73 Women." *New York Times*, June 6, 1983, p. 13.

H. H. Gerth and C. Wright Mills (eds.). *From Max Weber: Essays in Sociology*. Oxford: Oxford University Press, 1946.

George Gilder. "Built upon Bankrupt Theories." *New York Times*, July 24, 1983, p. F2.

Erving Goffman. *Asylums*. Garden City, N.Y.: Doubleday, 1961.

William J. Goode. "The Protection of the Inept." *American Sociological Review* 32 (February 1967):5–19.

Barry Gruenberg. "The Happy Worker: An Analysis of Educational and Occupational Differences in Determinants of Job Satisfaction." *American Journal of Sociology* 86 (1980):247–271.

Richard H. Hall. "The Concept of Bureaucracy: An Empirical Assessment." *American Journal of Sociology* 69 (1963–1964):32–40.

Richard C. Hollinger and John P. Clark. "Formal and Informal Social Controls of Employee Deviance." *Sociological Quarterly* 23 (1982):333–343.

Hem C. Jain and Genevieve L. Jain. *Worker Participation: Success and Problems*. New York: Praeger, 1980.

Rosabeth Moss Kanter. *Men and Women of the Corporation*. New York: Basic Books, 1977*a*.

Rosabeth Moss Kanter. "Some Effects of Proportions on Group Life: Skewed Sex Ratios and Responses to Token Women." *American Journal of Sociology* 82 (1977):965–990*b*.

David Knoke. "Commitment and Detachment in Voluntary Associations." *American Sociological Review* 46 (1981):141–158.

Steve Lohr. "Japan's Trade Ministry Draws Praise and Ire." *New York Times*, May 17, 1983, pp. 1, 33*a*.

Steve Lohr. "How Japan Helps Its Industry." *New York Times*, May 18, 1983, pp. 25, 41*b*.

J. Miller McPherson. "A Dynamic Model of Voluntary Affiliation." *Social Forces* 59 (1981):705–728.

Robert Merton. *Social Theory and Social Structure*. Glencoe, Ill.: Free Press, 1968.

Robert Michels. *First Lectures in Political Science* (Alfred de Grazia,

trans.). Minneapolis: University of Minnesota Press, 1949. (Originally published in 1915.)
Amal Nag. "High New-Car Prices Keep Many Lookers Looking, Not Buying." *Wall Street Journal*, August 3, 1983, pp. 1, 13.
William G. Ouchi. *Theory Z*. New York: Avon Books, 1982.
C. Northcote Parkinson. *Parkinson's Law*. Boston: Houghton Mifflin, 1957.
Charles Perrow. *Complex Organizations: A Critical Essay* (2nd ed.). Glenview, Ill.: Scott, Foresman, 1979.
Laurence F. Peter and Raymond Hull. *The Peter Principle*. New York: Morrow, 1969.
Philip H. Pollock, III. "Organizations and Alienation: The Mediation Hypothesis Revisited." *Sociological Quarterly* 23 (1982):143–155.
Robert Presthus. *The Organizational Society* (rev. ed.). New York: St. Martin's, 1978.
David Rothman. *The Discovery of the Asylum*. Boston: Little, Brown, 1971.
David Rothman. *Conscience and Convenience*. Boston: Little, Brown, 1980.
Roy Rowan. "'How Harvard's Women MBA's Are Managing." *Fortune*, July 11, 1983, pp. 58–64+.
Murray Sayle. "The Yellow Peril and the Red Haired Devils." *Harper's*, November 1982, pp. 23–35.
David L. Sills. "The Succession of Goals." In Amatai Etzioni (ed.), *Complex Organizations: A Sociological Reader*. New York: Holt, Rinehart & Winston, 1961.
Michael Sosin. "Organizational Maintenance, Sensitivity to Clients, and Vulnerability: Some New Suggestions about a Traditional Concept." *Sociological Quarterly* 22 (1981):347–358.
Evelyn Huber Stephens. *The Politics of Workers' Participation: The Peruvian Approach in Comparative Perspective*. New York: Academic Press, 1980.
Shelby Stewman and Suresh L. Konda. "Careers and Organizational Labor Markets: Demographic Models of Organizational Behavior." *American Journal of Sociology* 88 (1983):637–685.
Anselm Strauss et al. *Psychiatric Ideologies and Institutions*. New York: Free Press, 1964.
Arnold S. Tannenbaum et al. *Hierarchy in Organizations: An International Comparison*. San Francisco: Jossey-Bass, 1974.
Stanley H. Udy, Jr. "'Bureaucracy' and 'Rationality' in Weber's Organizational Theory: An Empirical Study." *American Sociological Review* 24 (December 1959):791–795.
Ezra F. Vogel. *Japan as Number 1: Lessons for America*. New York: Harper Colophon Books, 1980. (Originally published by Harvard University Press, 1979.)
Carol Weiss. "Myths about Women 'and Men' Managers." *Radcliffe Quarterly*, June 1983, pp. 4–7.
William Foote Whyte. "Social Inventions for Solving Human Problems." *American Sociological Review* 47 (1982):1–13.
William Foote Whyte and Joseph R. Blasi. "From Research to Legislation on Employee Ownership." *Economic and Industrial Democracy* 1 (1980):395–415.
Warner P. Woodworth. "Tearing Down the Pyramids." *Contemporary Sociology* 11 (1982): 173–175.
Gerald Zeitz. "Structural and Individual Determinants of Organization Morale and Satisfaction." *Social Forces* 61 (1983):1088–1108.
Mary Zey-Ferrell. "Criticisms of the Dominant Perspective on Organizations." *Sociological Quarterly* 22 (1981):181–205.

CHAPTER 9

Albert Bandura. "The Role of Modeling Processes in Personality Development." In W. W. Hartup and N. L. Smothergill (eds.), *The Young Child: A Review of Research*. Washington, D.C.: National Association for the Education of Young Children, 1967.
Albert Bandura. *Aggression: A Social Learning Analysis*. Englewood Cliffs, N.J.: Prentice-Hall, 1973.
Albert Bandura. *Social Learning Theory*. Englewood Cliffs, N.J.: Prentice-Hall, 1977.
Albert Bandura and Richard H. Walters. *Adolescent Aggression*. New York: Ronald Press, 1959.
Howard S. Becker. *Outsiders: Studies in the Sociology of Deviance*. New York: Free Press, 1963.
Piers Beirne. "Empiricism and the Critique of Marxism on Law and Crime." *Social Problems* 26 (1979):373–385.
Michael Burawoy. *Manufacturing Consent*. Chicago: University of Chicago Press, 1979.
William J. Chambliss. "The Saints and Roughnecks." *Society* 11 (December 1973):24–31.
William Chambliss. "The State, the Law and the Definition of Behavior as Criminal or Delinquent." In Daniel Glaser (ed.), *Handbook of Criminology*. Indianapolis: Bobbs-Merrill, 1974.
Marshall B. Clinard and Peter C. Yeager. *Corporate Crime*. New York: Free Press, 1980.
Albert K. Cohen. *Deviance and Control*. Englewood Cliffs, N.J.: Prentice-Hall, 1966.
Albert K. Cohen. "The Sociology of the Deviant Act: Anomie Theory and Beyond." *American Sociological Review* 30 (February 1965):5–14.
Peter Conrad and Joseph W. Schneider. *Deviance: From Badness to Sickness*. St. Louis: Mosby, 1980.
Crime in the U.S., 1981. Washington, D.C.: U.S. Department of Justice, Federal Bureau of Investigation, 1982.
Criminal Victimization in the U.S., 1980. Washington, D.C.: U.S. Department of Justice, Bureau of Justice Statistics, 1982.
Emile Durkheim. *Suicide: A Study in Sociology* (J.A. Spaulding and G. Simpson, trans.). New York: Free Press, 1951. (Originally published in 1897.)
Robert B. Edgerton. *The Cloak of Competence*. Berkeley: University of California Press, 1967.
Lee Ellis. "Toward Neurologically-Specific Theories of Criminal Behavior." *Contemporary Sociology* 8 (1979):372–376.
Kai T. Erikson. *Wayward Puritans*. New York: Wiley, 1966.
Malcolm M. Feeley. *The Process Is the Punishment: Handling Cases in a Lower Criminal Court*. New York: Russell Sage, 1979.
Erving Goffman. *Behavior in Public Places*. New York: Free Press, 1963*a*.
Erving Goffman. *Stigma: Notes on the Management of Spoiled Identity*. Englewood Cliffs, N.J.: Prentice-Hall, 1963*b*.
Erving Goffman. *Interaction Ritual: Essays on Face-to-Face Behavior*. Garden City, N.Y.: Anchor, Doubleday, 1967.
Charles Goring. *The English Convict*. London: His Majesty's Stationery Office, 1913.
Walter R. Gove (ed.). *The Labelling of Deviance: Evaulating a Perspective*. New York: Sage, 1975.
Walter R. Gove. "The Labeling Versus the Psychiatric Explanation of Mental Illness: A Debate That Has Become Substantially Irrelevant." *Journal of Health and Social Behavior* 20 (September 1979):301–303.

Travis Hirschi. *Causes of Delinquency*. Berkeley: University of California Press, 1969.

Orr Kelly. "Corporate Crime." *U.S. News & World Report*, September 6, 1982, pp. 25–29.

Edwin M. Lemert. *Human Deviance, Social Problems, and Social Control*. New York: McGraw-Hill, 1951.

Sasha Gregory Lewis. *Sunday's Women: A Report on Lesbian Life Today*. Boston: Beacon, 1979.

Judith Lorber. "Good Patients and Problem Patients: Conformity and Deviance in a General Hospital." *Journal of Health and Social Behavior* 16 (June 1975):213–225.

Ross L. Matsueda. "Testing Control Theory and Differential Association: A Casual Modeling Approach." *American Sociological Review* 47 (1982):489–504.

Robert K. Merton. *Social Theory and Social Structure*. Glencoe, Ill.: Free Press, 1957. (Originally published in 1938.)

Richard J. Michalowski and Edward W. Bohlander. "Repression and Criminal Justice in Capitalist America." *Sociological Inquiry* 46 (1976):96–106.

Walter B. Miller. "Lower-Class Culture as a Generating Milieu of Gang Delinquency." *Journal of Sociological Issues* 14 (Summer 1958):5–19.

C. Wright Mills. *The Sociological Imagination*. New York: Oxford University Press, 1959.

Gaylen Moore. "The Beast in the Jungle." *Psychology Today* 17 (November 1983):38–45.

Aric Press. "How the Mob Really Works." *Newsweek*, January 5, 1981, pp. 34–43.

Richard Quinney. *Criminology* (2nd ed.). Boston: Little, Brown, 1979.

Sir Leon Radzinowicz and Joan King. *The Growth of Crime: The International Experience*. New York: Basic Books, 1977.

Roger Ricklefs. "Executives and General Public Say Ethical Behavior is Declining in U.S." *Wall Street Journal*, October 31, 1983, p. 23.

Lee N. Robins and Eric Wish. "Childhood Deviance as a Developmental Process: A Study of 223 Urban Black Men From Birth to 18." *Social Forces* 56, No. 2 (December 1977):448–471.

Edwin M. Schur. *The Politics of Deviance: Stigma Contests and the Uses of Power*. Englewood Cliffs, N.J.: Prentice-Hall, 1980.

Clifford R. Shaw and Henry D. McKay. *Juvenile Delinquency and Urban Areas*. Chicago: University of Chicago Press, 1969.

Charles E. Silberman. *Criminal Violence, Criminal Justice*. New York: Vintage, 1980.

William Simon and John H. Gagnon. "On Being in the 'Community.'" In Jack D. Douglas (ed.), *Observations of Deviance*. New York: Random House, 1970.

James S. Slotkin. *Social Anthropology*. New York: Macmillan, 1950.

Sourcebook of Criminal Justice Statistics, 1981. Washington, D.C.: U.S. Department of Justice, 1982.

Leo Srole and Anita K. Fisher (eds.). *Mental Health in the Metropolis*. New York: New York University Press, 1978.

Statistical Abstract of the U.S., 1982–1983. Washington, D.C.: U.S. Department of Commerce, Bureau of the Census, 1983.

Edwin Sutherland. *White Collar Crime*. New York: Dryden, 1949.

Edwin H. Sutherland and Donald R. Cressy. *Principles of Criminology* (6th ed.). Philadelphia: Lippincott, 1960.

Philip Taubman. "Faking of College Credits for Athletes Is Under Inquiry." *New York Times*, January 9, 1980, pp. 1, 8.

Katherine Teilmann Van Dusen, Sarnoff A. Mednick, William F. Gabrielli, Jr., and Barry Hutchings. "Social Class and Crime in an Adoption Cohort." *The Journal of Criminal Law and Criminology* 74 (1983):249–269.

Harrison M. Trice and Paul Michael Roman. "Delabeling, Relabeling, and Alcoholics Anonymous." *Social Problems* 17 (Spring 1970):538–547.

Vera Institute of Justice. *Felony Arrests: Their Prosecution and Disposition in New York City's Courts*. New York: Vera Institute of Justice, 1977.

Ezra F. Vogel. *Japan as Number 1: Lessons for America*. New York: Harper & Row, Harper Colophon Books, 1980.

Paul H. Wender and Donald F. Klein. "The Promise of Biological Psychiatry." *Psychology Today* 15 (February 1981):25–41.

Leslie Maitland Werner. "Do Lower Statistics Mean Less Crime?" *New York Times*, September 18, 1983, p. E4.

James Q. Wilson. *Crime and Public Policy*. New York: ICS Press, 1983.

Herman A. Witkin et al. "Criminality in XYY and XXY Men." *Science* 193 (August 1976):547–555.

CHAPTER 10

Wendell Bell and Robert V. Robinson. "An Index of Evaluated Equality: Measuring Conceptions of Social Justice in England and the United States." *Comparative Studies in Sociology* 1 (1978):235–270.

Richard A. Berk, Kenneth J. Lenihan, and Peter H. Rossi. "Crime and Poverty: Some Experimental Evidence from Ex-Offenders." *American Sociological Review* 45 (1980):766–786.

Peter M. Blau and Otis Dudley Duncan. *The American Occupational Structure*. New York: Wiley, 1967.

T. B. Bottomore. *Classes in Modern Society*. New York: Pantheon Books, 1966.

Gail Bronson and Robert Morse. "How the Boss's Paycheck Weathered Recession." *U.S. News & World Report*, May 30, 1983, pp. 59–61.

M. Burawoy. "Introduction: The Resurgence of Marxism in American Sociology." *American Journal of Sociology* 88 (1982) Supplement:S1–S29.

Fox Butterfield. "China, for a Fortunate Few at the Top, Is Paradise of Privilege and Perquisites." *New York Times*, January 2, 1981, p. 5.

Frank Ching. "As Confucius Say, People's Impostor Unfortunate Cookie." *Wall Street Journal*, December 18, 1979, pp. 1, 14.

Richard D. Coleman and Lee Rainwater. *Social Standing in America: New Dimensions of Class*. New York: Basic Books, 1978.

Walter D. Connor. *Socialism, Politics, and Equality*. New York: Columbia University Press, 1979.

John Cratsley. "The Crime of the Courts." In Bruce Wasserstein and Mark J. Green (eds.), *With Justice for Some*. Boston: Beacon Press, 1972.

Kingsley Davis and Wilbert E. Moore. "Some Principles of Stratification." *American Sociological Review* 10 (April 1945):242–249.

Kingsley Davis and Wilbert E. Moore. "Replies to Tumin." *American Sociological Review* 18 (1953):394–396.

L. Richard Della Fave and George A. Hillery, Jr. "Status Inequality in a Religious Community: The Case of a Trappist Monastery." *Social Forces* 59 (1980):62–84.

G. William Domhoff. *Who Rules America?* Englewood Cliffs, N.J.: Prentice-Hall, 1967.

Greg J. Duncan. "Who Gets Ahead? And Who Gets Left Behind?" *American Demographics* 4 (July–August 1982):38–41.

William W. Eaton. "A Formal Theory of Selection for Schizophrenia." *American Journal of Sociology* 86 (1980):149–158.

David L. Featherman. "Opportunities Are Expanding . . ." *Society* 16, No. 3 (March–April 1979):4, 6–11.

Anthony E. Gallo, James A. Zellner, and David M. Smallwood. "The Rich, the Poor, and the Money They Spend for Food." In Consumer Research, *National Food Review*, Summer 1980, 16–18.

Herbert J. Gans. *More Equality*. New York: Random House, Pantheon Books, 1973.

William J. Goode. *The Celebration of Heroes: Prestige as a Control System*. Berkeley: University of California Press, 1978.

Ann B. Goodman, Carole Siegel, Thomas J. Craig, and Shang P. Lin. "The Relationship between Socioeconomic Class and Prevalence of Schizophrenia, Alcoholism, and Affective Disorders Treated by Inpatient Care in a Suburban Area." *American Journal of Psychiatry* 140 (1983):166–170.

Steven L. Gortmaker. "Poverty and Infant Mortality in the U.S." *American Sociological Review* 44 (April 1979):280–297.

Robert M. Hauser, Archibald O. Haller, David Mechanic, and Taissa S. Hauser (eds.). *Social Structure and Behavior*. New York: Academic Press, 1982.

Robert M. Hauser, Shu-Ling Tsai, and William H. Sewell. "A Model of Stratification with Response Error in Social and Psychological Variables." *Sociology of Education* 56 (1983):20–46.

Beth B. Hess. "New Faces of Poverty." *American Demographics* 5 (May 1983):26–31.

Robert W. Hodge, Donald J. Treiman, and Peter H. Rossi. "A Comparative Study of Occupational Prestige." In Reinhard Bendix and Seymour Martin Lipset (eds.), *Class, Status, and Power* (2nd ed.). New York: Free Press, 1966.

Doris B. Holleb. "Housing and the Environment: Shooting at Moving Targets." *Annals* 453 (January 1981):180–222.

August Hollingshead and Frederick Redlich. *Social Class and Mental Illness*. New York: Wiley, 1958.

George C. Homans. *Social Behavior: Its Elementary Forms* (rev. ed.). New York: Harcourt, 1974.

Keith Hope. "Vertical and Nonvertical Class Mobility in Three Countries." *American Sociological Review* 47 (1982):99–113.

Carol Hymowitz. "Culture Shock Affects Steelworker Who Switched to White-Collar Job." *Wall Street Journal*, June 1, 1983, p. 31.

Christopher Jencks. *Who Gets Ahead? The Determinants of Economic Success in America*. New York: Basic Books, 1979.

Christopher Jencks et al. *Inequality: A Reassessment of the Effect of Family and Schooling in America*. New York: Basic Books, 1972.

Christopher Jencks, James Crouse, and Peter Mueser. "The Wisconsin Model of Status Attainment: A National Replication with Improved Measures of Ability and Aspiration." *Sociology of Education* 56 (1983):3–19.

Theodore D. Kemper. "Marxist and Functionalist Theories of the Study of Stratification." *Social Forces* 54, No. 3 (March 1976):559–578.

Ronald C. Kessler. "A Disaggregation of the Relationship Between Socioeconomic Status and Psychological Distress." *American Sociological Review* 47 (1982):752–764.

Ronald C. Kessler and Paul D. Cleary. "Social Class and Psychological Distress." *American Sociological Review* 45 (1980):463–478.

Gerhard E. Lenski. *Power and Privilege: A Theory of Social Stratification*. New York: McGraw-Hill, 1966.

Seymour Martin Lipset. "Social Mobility in Industrial Societies." *Public Opinion* 5 (June–July 1982):41–44.

George Cabot Lodge and William R. Glass. "The Desperate Plight of the Underclass." *Harvard Business Review* 60 (1982):60–71.

Arthur M. Louis. "The New Rich of the Seventies." *Fortune* 88 (September 1973):170–175.

Ira C. Magaziner and Robert Reich. *Minding America's Business*. New York: Vintage Books, 1983.

Martin N. Marger. *Elites and Masses*. New York: D. Van Nostrand, 1981.

Roderick Martin. *The Sociology of Power*. London: Routledge and Kegan Paul, 1977.

Karl Marx. *The Eighteenth Brumaire of Louis Bonaparte*. New York: International Publishers, 1963.

C. Wright Mills. *The Power Elite*. New York: Oxford University Press, 1956.

Jerome K. Myers, Jacob J. Lindenthal, and Max P. Pepper. "Social Class, Life Events and Psychiatric Symptoms: A Longitudinal Study." In B. P. and B. S. Dohrenwend (eds.), *Stressful Life Events*. New York: Wiley, 1974.

Benjamin I. Page. *Who Gets What from Government*. Berkeley: University of California Press, 1983.

Talcott Parsons. *Sociological Theory and Modern Society*. New York: Free Press, 1967.

Robert Pear. "Most of Those Taken Off Welfare Are Said Not to Leave Their Jobs." *New York Times*, April 29, 1983, pp. 1, 8.

David Riesman. *The Lonely Crowd*. New York: Doubleday, 1953.

Dennis W. Roncek. "Dangerous Places: Crime and Residential Environment." *Social Forces* 60 (1981):74–96.

William H. Sewell and Robert M. Hauser. "Causes and Consequences of Higher Education: Models of the Status Attainment Process." In W. H. Sewell and R. M. Hauser (eds.), *Schooling and Achievement in American Society*. New York: Academic Press, 1976.

Timothy M. Smeeding. *Alternative Methods for Valuing Selected In-Kind Transfer Benefits and Measuring Their Effect on Poverty*. U.S. Bureau of the Census, Technical Paper No. 50. Washington, D.C.: U.S. Government Printing Office, 1982.

Kevin B. Smith. "Class Structure and Intergenerational Mobility from a Marxian Perspective." *The Sociological Quarterly* 22 (1981):385–401.

Albert J. Szymanski and Ted George Goertzel. *Sociology: Class, Consciousness and Contradictions*. New York: D. Van Nostrand, 1979.

Randall J. Thomson and Matthew T. Zingraff. "Detecting Sentencing Disparity: Some Problems and Evidence." *American Journal of Sociology* 86 (1981):869–880.

Melvin M. Tumin. "Some Principles of Stratification: A Critical Analysis." *American Sociological Review* 18 (August 1953):387–393.

Melvin M. Tumin (ed.). *Readings on Social Stratification*. Englewood Cliffs, N.J.: Prentice-Hall, 1970.

Melvin M. Tumin. *Patterns of Society*. Boston: Little, Brown, 1973.

Andrea Tyree, Moshe Semyonou, and Robert W. Hodge. "Gaps and Glissandos: Inequality, Economic Development, and Social Mobility in 24 Countries." *American Sociological Review* 44 (June 1979):410–424.

W. Lloyd Warner, Paul S. Lunt, Marchia Meeker, and Kenneth Eels. *Social Class in America*. Chicago: Science Research, 1949.

Sidney M. Willhelm. "Opportunities Are Diminishing . . ." *Society* 16, No. 3 (March–April 1979):5, 12–17.

Myron Winick. "Nutrition and Brain Development." *Natural History* 89, No. 12 (December 1980):6–13.

Erik Olin Wright, David Hachen, Cynthia Costello, and Joey Sprague. "The American Class Structure." *American Sociological Review* 47 (1982):709–726.

CHAPTER 11

Kenneth L. Adelman. "Non-voting: A Sign of Decay or Health?" *Wall Street Journal*, October 15, 1980, p. 20.

Herbert E. Alexander and Brian Haggerty. *The Federal Election Campaign Act*. Citizens Research Foundation, University of Southern California, 1981.

Charles F. Andrain. *Political Life and Social Change: An Introduction to Political Science* (2nd ed.). Belmont, Calif.: Duxbury, 1975.

Paul A. Beck and M. Kent Jennings. "Political Periods and Political Participation." *The American Political Science Review* 73 (1979):737–750.

Adolph A. Berle, Jr., and Gardiner C. Means. *The Modern Corporation and Private Property* (rev. ed.). New York: Harcourt, Brace & World, 1968. (Originally published, New York: Macmillan, 1932.)

Barry Bluestone and Bennett Harrison. *The Deindustrialization of America*. New York: Basic Books, 1982.

Volker Bornschier and Thanh-Huyen Ballmer-Cao. "Income Inequality: A Cross-National Study of the Relationships Between MNC-Penetration, Dimensions of the Power Structure and Income Distribution." *American Sociological Review* 44 (June 1979):487–506.

Volker Bornschier and Jean-Pierre Hoby. "Economic Policy and Multinational Corporations in Development: The Measurable Impacts in Cross-National Perspective." *Social Problems* 28 (1981):363–377.

Gail Bronson and Robert Morse. "How the Boss's Paycheck Weathered Recession." *U.S. News & World Report*, May 30, 1983, pp. 59–61.

Walter D. Burnham. *Critical Elections and the Mainsprings of American Politics*. New York: Norton, 1970.

Christopher Chase-Dunn. "The Effects of International Economic Dependence on Development and Inequality: A Cross-National Study." *American Sociological Review* 40 (December 1975):720–738.

Adam Clymer. "Displeasure with Carter Turned Many to Reagan." *New York Times*, November 9, 1980, p. 19.

Adam Clymer. "Poll Finds Nation Is Becoming Increasingly Republican." *New York Times*, May 3, 1981.

Adam Clymer. "Jobless Were More Likely to Vote in '82 Than in Previous Off Years." *New York Times*, April 18, 1983, pp. 1, 8*a*.

Adam Clymer. "Campaign Costs Soar as Median Spending for Senate Seat Hits $1.7 Million." *New York Times*, April 3, 1983, p. 20*b*.

Robert Dahl. *Who Governs?* New Haven: Yale University Press, 1961.

R. W. Davies and Dennis J. B. Shaw (eds.). *The Soviet Union*. London: George, Allen, and Unwin, 1978.

G. William Domhoff. *The Powers That Be*. New York: Random House, 1978.

Robert E. Dowse and John A. Hughes. *Political Science*. New York: Wiley, 1972.

Maurice Duverger. *Political Parties* (Barbara North and Robert North, trans.). New York: Wiley, 1954.

Maurice Duverger. *Modern Democracies: Economic Power Versus Political Power*. Hinsdale, Ill.: Dryden Press, 1974.

Amitai Etzioni. "Making Interest Groups Work for the Public." *Public Opinion* 5 (August–September 1982):52–55.

G. Lowell Field and John Higley. *Elitism*. Boston: Routledge & Kegan Paul, 1980.

John Kenneth Galbraith. *The New Industrial State* (3rd rev. ed.). New York: New American Library, 1979.

Davita Silfen Glasberg. "Corporate Power and Control: The Case of Leasco Corporation Versus Chemical Bank." *Social Problems* 29 (1981):104–116.

Robert Gogel and Thomas Koenig. "Commercial Banks, Interlocking Directorates and Economic Power: An Analysis of the Primary Metals Industry." *Social Problems* 29 (1981):117–128.

Thomas M. Guterbock. "Social Class and Voting Choices in Middletown." *Social Forces* 58 (June 1980):1044–1056.

Amos H. Hawley. "Community Power and Urban-Renewal Success." *American Journal of Sociology* 68 (1963):422–431.

Robert L. Heilbroner. *Business Civilization in Decline*. New York: Norton, 1976.

Edward S. Herman. *Corporate Control, Corporate Power*. New York: Cambridge University Press, 1981.

Brooks Jackson and John J. Fialka. "New Congressmen Get Many Offers of Money to Cut Campaign Debt." *Wall Street Journal*, April 21, 1983, pp. 1, 29.

David R. James and Michael Soref. "Profit Constraints on Managerial Autonomy: Managerial Theory and the Unmaking of the Corporation President." *American Sociological Review* 46 (1981):1–18.

Suzanne Keller. *Beyond the Ruling Class: Strategic Elites in Modern Society*. New York: Random House, 1963.

David Kipniz. *The Powerholders*. Chicago: University of Chicago Press, 1976.

William Kornhauser. "'Power Elite' or 'Veto Groups'?" In Seymour Martin Lipset and Leo Lowenthal (eds.), *Culture and Social Character*. Glencoe, Ill.: Free Press, 1961.

Everett Carl Ladd. "Politics in the 80's: An Electorate at Odds with Itself." *Public Opinion* 5 (January 1983):2–5.

Everett Carl Ladd, Jr., and Charles D. Hadley. *Transformation of the American Party System*. New York: Norton, 1975.

Howard Lasswell. *Politics: Who Gets What, When, How?* New York: McGraw-Hill, 1936.

Gerhard Lenski. *Power and Privilege*. New York: McGraw-Hill, 1966.

Seymour Martin Lipset. *Political Man*. New York: Doubleday/Anchor, 1963.

Seymour M. Lipset and William Schneider. *The Confidence Gap*. New York: Free Press, 1983.

Robert Lynd and Helen Lynd. *Middletown*. New York: Harcourt, Brace, 1929.

Robert Lynd and Helen Lynd. *Middletown in Transition*. New York: Harcourt, Brace, 1937.

Thomas William Madron. "Political Parties in the 1980s." *The Futurist* 12, No. 6 (December 1979):465–475.

Ira C. Magaziner and Robert B. Reich. *Minding America's Business*.

New York: Vintage Books, 1982.

Karl Marx and Friedrich Engels. *Communist Manifesto.* New York: Pantheon, 1967. (Originally published in 1848.)

Robert Michels. *First Lectures in Political Science* (Alfred de Grazia, trans.). Minneapolis: University of Minnesota Press, 1949. (Originally published in 1915.)

C. Wright Mills. "The Structure of Power in American Society." *British Journal of Sociology* 9 (March 1958):29–41.

C. Wright Mills. *The Power Elite.* New York: Oxford University Press, 1959.

Beth Mintz and Michael Schwartz. "Interlocking Directorates and Interest Group Formation." *American Sociological Review* 46 (1981*a*):851–869.

Beth Mintz and Michael Schwartz. "The Structure of Intercorporate Unity in American Business." *Social Problems* 29 (1981*b*):87–103.

John J. Molloy. *Dress for Success.* New York: Warner Books, 1975.

Gaetano Mosca. *The Ruling Class.* New York: McGraw-Hill, 1939.

Norman H. Nie et al. *The Changing American Voter.* Cambridge, Mass.: Harvard University Press, 1976.

Marvin E. Olsen (ed.). *Power in Societies.* New York: Macmillan, 1970.

Vilfredo Pareto. *The Mind and Society* (A. Bongiorno and A. Livingston, trans.). New York: Harcourt, Brace, 1935. (Originally published in 1916.)

Nelson W. Polsby. *Community Power and Political Theory.* New Haven: Yale University Press, 1980, pp. 112–121.

Gerald M. Pomper. *Voter's Choice.* New York: Dodd, Mead, 1975.

Gerald M. Pomper. "The Decline of the Party in American Elections." *Political Science Quarterly* 92 (Spring 1977):21–41.

David Riesman, with Nathan Glazer and Reuel Denney. *The Lonely Crowd.* New Haven: Yale University Press, 1951.

Arnold M. Rose. *The Power Structure.* New York: Oxford University Press, 1967.

David Satter. "Soviet Threat is One of Ideas More than Arms." *Wall Street Journal*, May 23, 1983, p. 22.

Arthur Schlesinger, Jr. "Crisis of the Party System." *Wall Street Journal*, May 10, 1979, p. 22.

Lester C. Thurow. *The Zero-Sum Society.* New York: Basic Books, 1980.

U.N. Commission on Transnational Corporations. "Transnational Corporations in World Development: A Re-examination." Fourth session, New York, May 15–26, 1978.

U.S. Bureau of the Census. *Statistical Abstract of the United States, 1982–1983.* Washington, D.C.: U.S. Government Printing Office, 1983.

Michael Useem. "The Social Organization of the American Business Elite and Participation of Corporation Directors in the Governance of American Institutions." *American Sociological Review* 44 (1979):553–572.

Michael Useem. "Corporations and the Corporate Elite." *Annual Review of Sociology* 6 (1980):41–77.

Charles Wagley and Marvin Harris. *Minorities in the New World.* New York: Columbia University Press, 1964.

Anise C. Wallace. "The New Activists: Big Investors." *New York Times*, June 12, 1983, p. F4.

Max Weber. *From Max Weber: Essays in Sociology* (2nd ed., Hans H. Gerth and C. Wright Mills, trans.). New York: Oxford University Press, 1949. (Originally published in 1918.)

Robert P. Weber. "Society and Economy in the Western World System." *Social Forces* 59 (1981):1130–1148.

J. Allen Whitt. "Toward a Class Dialectical Model of Power: An Empirical Assessment of Three Competing Models of Political Power." *American Sociological Review* 44 (February 1979):81–100.

CHAPTER 12

Ernest A.T. Barth and Donald L. Noel. "Conceptual Frameworks for the Analysis of Race Relations: An Evaluation." In Norman R. Yetman and C. Roy Steele (eds.). *Majorities and Minorities.* Boston: Allyn & Bacon, 1975.

Melinda Beck and Merwin Sigale. "A Racial Outburst in Miami." *U.S. News & World Report*, January 10, 1983, p. 23.

Brewton Berry and Henry L. Tischler. *Race and Ethnic Relations.* Boston: Houghton Mifflin, 1978.

James E. Blackwell. "Persistence and Change in Intergroup Relations: The Crisis upon Us." *Social Problems* 29 (1982):325–346.

Robert Blauner. *Racial Oppression in America.* New York: Harper & Row, 1972.

Edna Bonacich. "A Theory of Ethnic Antagonism: The Split-Labor Market." *American Sociological Review* 37 (1972):547–559.

Edna Bonacich. "Abolition, the Extension of Slavery, and the Position of Free Blacks: A Study of Split-Labor Markets in the United States, 1830–1863." *American Journal of Sociology* 81 (1975):601–628.

William C. Boyd. *Genetics and the Races of Man.* Boston: Little, Brown, 1950.

Stokely Carmichael and Charles V. Hamilton. *Black Power.* New York: Random House, 1967.

Kenneth B. Clark. *Youth in the Ghetto.* New York: Haryou Associates, 1964.

Kenneth B. Clark. *Dark Ghetto.* New York: Harper & Row, 1965.

James Coates. "Study: Whites to Be in Minority." *Columbus Dispatch*, September 12, 1982, p. 2.

James S. Coleman. *Equality of Educational Opportunity.* Washington, D.C.: U.S. Government Printing Office, 1966.

James S. Coleman. "The Role of Incentives in School Desegregation." In Adam Yarmolinsky, Lance Liebman, and Corinne Schelling (eds.), *Race and Schooling in the City.* Cambridge, Mass.: Harvard University Press, 1981.

Robert Crain and Rita Mahard. "Desegregation and Academic Achievement." In M. Friedman, R. Meltzer, and C. Miller (eds.), *New Perspectives on School Integration.* Philadelphia: Fortress Press, 1979.

F. James Davis. *Minority-Dominant Relations.* Arlington Heights, Ill.: AHM, 1978.

Theodosius Dobzhansky. *Genetic Diversity and Human Equality.* New York: Basic Books, 1973.

G. William Domhoff and Richard L. Zweigenhaft. "Jews in the Corporate Establishment." *New York Times*, April 24, 1983, p. F2.

Raymond S. Franklin and Solomon Resnik. *The Political Economy of Racism.* New York: Holt, Rinehart & Winston, 1973.

Samuel Friedman. "How Is Racism Maintained?" *Et Al.* 2 (1969):19–20.

Gallup Opinion Index. *Religion in America, 1977–78*, Report No. 145, May 1978.

Herbert J. Gans. "Symbolic Ethnicity: The Future of Ethnic Groups and Cultures in America." *Ethnic and Racial Studies* 2 (1979):1–20.

William E. Geist. "New Land, New Hope." *New York Times*, August 17, 1982, p. B2.

Herbert P. Ginsburg and Robert L. Russell. "Social Class and Racial Influences on Early Mathematical Thinking." *Monographs of the Society for Research in Child Development* 46 (1981), Serial No. 193.

Douglas G. Glasgow. *The Black Underclass*. San Francisco: Jossey-Bass, 1980.

Milton M. Gordon. *Assimilation in American Life*. New York: Oxford University Press, 1964.

Milton M. Gordon. *Human Nature, Class, and Ethnicity*. New York: Oxford University Press, 1978.

Andrew M. Greeley. *Ethnicity, Denomination, and Inequality*. Beverly Hills, Calif.: Sage Publications, 1976.

Michael Hechter. *Internal Colonialism*. Berkeley: University of California Press, 1975.

Harold R. Isaacs. *Idols of the Tribe: Group Identity and Political Change*. New York: Harper & Row, 1975.

Arthur R. Jensen. "How Much Can We Boost IQ and Scholastic Achievement?" *Harvard Educational Review* 39 (Winter 1969):1–123.

Leon J. Kamin. *The Science and Politics of IQ*. Hillsdale, N.J.: Erlbaum, 1974.

Charles B. Keely. "Illegal Migration." *Scientific American* 246 (March 1982):41–47.

James R. Kluegel and Eliot R. Smith. "Affirmative Action Attitudes." *Social Forces* 61 (1983):797–822.

Stanley Lieberson. *A Piece of the Pie*. Berkeley: University of California Press, 1980.

Elliot Liebow. *Tally's Corner: A Study of Negro Streetcorner Men*. Boston: Little, Brown, 1967.

S. Dale McLemore. *Racial and Ethnic Relations in America* (2nd ed.). Boston: Allyn & Bacon, 1983.

Douglas S. Massey. "Dimensions of the New Immigration to the United States and the Prospects for Assimilation." *Annual Review of Sociology* 7 (1981):57–85.

Robert K. Merton. *Social Theory and Social Structure* (rev. ed.). New York: Free Press, 1957.

Bloke Modisane. *Blame Me on History*. New York: Dutton, 1963.

Sonia L. Nazario. "Site of 1980 Miami Riot Is Still Down and Out, Despite a Cash Infusion." *Wall Street Journal*, December 30, 1982, pp. 1, 6.

William M. Newman. *American Pluralism: A Study of Minority Groups and Social Theory*. New York: Harper & Row, 1973.

Donald L. Noel (ed.). *The Origins of American Slavery and Racism*. Columbus, Ohio: Charles E. Merrill, 1972.

Melvin L. Oliver and Mark A. Glick. "An Analysis of the New Orthodoxy on Black Militancy." *Social Problems* 29 (1982):511–523.

Robert E. Park, Ernest W. Burgess, Roderick D. McKenzie (eds.). *The City*. Chicago: University of Chicago Press, 1925.

Robert Pear. "Study Says North Lags in Integration." *New York Times*, September 8, 1982, p. 8.

Robert Pear. "Administration Balks at Cost of Amnesty for Illegal Aliens." *New York Times*, April 30, 1983, p. 8.

Robert Pear. "Study Says Affirmative Rule Expands Hiring of Minorities." *New York Times*, June 19, 1983, p. 12.

William Petersen. "Success Story, Japanese-American Style." *New York Times*, January 9, 1966. Section 6, p. 20.

Michael Reich. *Racial Inequality: A Political-Economic Analysis*. Princeton, N.J.: Princeton University Press, 1981.

John Reid. *Black America*. New York: Population Reference Bureau, 1982.

Richard Rodriguez. *Hunger of Memory: "The Education of Richard Rodriguez."* New York: Bantam Books, 1983.

Cheryl Russell. "The News about Hispanics." *American Demographics* 5 (March 1983):15–25.

Sandra Scarr and Richard A. Weinberg. "When Black Children Grow Up in White Homes." *Psychology Today* 9 (December 1975):80–82.

Sandra Scarr and Richard A. Weinberg. "IQ Test Performance of Black Children Adopted by White Families." *American Psychologist* 31 (1976):726–739.

Sandra Scarr. *Race, Social Class, and Individual Differences in I.Q.* Hillsdale, N.J.: Erlbaum, 1981.

Richard T. Schaefer. *Racial and Ethnic Groups* (2nd ed.). Boston: Little, Brown, 1984.

Timothy D. Schellhardt. "Data on Average Wealth of Blacks Suggest Economic Gap with Whites Is Widening." *Wall Street Journal*, June 20, 1983, p. 12.

Nathaniel Sheppard, Jr. "Rights Activists Fear Integration Will Be Slowed." *New York Times*, July 18, 1981, p. 6.

Tamotsu Shibutani and Kian M. Kwan. *Ethnic Stratification: A Comparative Approach*. New York: Macmillan, 1965.

George E. Simpson and J. Milton Yinger. *Racial and Cultural Minorities: An Analysis of Prejudice and Discrimination* (4th ed.). New York: Harper & Row, 1972.

Edward H. Spicer. "American Indians." In Stephan Thernstrom (ed.), *Harvard Encyclopedia of American Ethnic Groups*. Cambridge, Mass.: Harvard University Press, 1980.

Stephan Steinberg. *The Ethnic Myth: Race, Ethnicity, and Class in America*. New York: Atheneum, 1981.

Melvin Tumin. *Patterns of Society*. Boston: Little, Brown, 1973.

U.S. Bureau of the Census. *Statistical Abstract of the United States: 1980*. Washington, D.C.: U.S. Government Printing Office, 1980.

U.S. Commission on Civil Rights. *Statement on Affirmative Action, for Equal Employment Opportunities*. Clearinghouse Publication 54. Washington, D.C.: U.S. Government Printing Office, 1977.

Pierre Van den Berghe. *Race and Racism: A Comparative Perspective* (2nd ed.). New York: Wiley, 1978.

James W. Vander Zanden. "The Klan Revival." *American Journal of Sociology* 65, No. 5 (March 1960):456–462.

James W. Vander Zanden. *American Minority Relations* (4th ed.). New York: Knopf, 1983.

Sidney M. Willhelm. *Who Needs the Negro?* Cambridge, Mass.: Schenkman, 1970.

Sidney M. Willhelm. "Can Marxism Explain America's Racism?" *Social Problems* 28 (1980):98–112.

Charles Vert Willie. *The Caste and Class Controversy*. Bayside, N.Y.: General Hall, 1979.

William Julius Wilson. *The Declining Significance of Race: Blacks and Changing American Institutions*. Chicago: University of Chicago Press, 1978.

Bernard P. Wong. *Chinatown: Economic Adaptation and Ethnic*

Identity of the Chinese. New York: Holt, Rinehart & Winston, 1982.

Eric Woodrum. "Japanese American Social Adaptation over Three Generations." Ph.D. dissertation, University of Texas at Austin.

Eric Woodrum. "An Assessment of Japanese American Assimilation, Pluralism, and Subordination." *American Journal of Sociology* 87 (1981):157–169.

D. Y. Yuan. "Voluntary Segregation: A Study of New York Chinatown." *Phylon* 24 (Fall 1963):255–265.

Israel Zangwill. *The Melting Pot*. New York: Jewish Publishing Society of America, 1909.

CHAPTER 13

William Arkin and Lynne R. Dobrofsky. "Shared Labor and Love: Job-Sharing Couples in Academia." *Alternative Lifestyles* 4 (November 1978):492–512.

H. Barry, Margaret K. Bacon, and I. L. Child. "A Cross-Cultural Survey of Some Sex Differences in Socialization." *Journal of Abnormal Psychology* 55 (1957):327–332.

Scott H. Beck. "Adjustment to and Satisfaction with Retirement." *Journal of Gerontology* 37 (1982):616–624.

Jay Belsky and Laurence D. Steinberg. "The Effects of Day Care: A Critical Review." *Child Development* 49 (1978):929–949.

Phyllis W. Berman. "Are Women More Responsive than Men to the Young? A Review of Developmental and Situational Variables." *Psychological Bulletin* 88 (1980):668–695.

Bruno Bettelheim. *Children of the Dream*. New York: Avon, 1971.

Henry B. Biller. "Fatherhood: Implications for Child and Adult Development." In B. B. Wolman (ed.), *Handbook of Developmental Psychology*. Englewood Cliffs, N.J.: Prentice-Hall, 1982.

Paul Bohannan and Rosemary Erickson. "Stepping In." *Psychology Today* 11 (January 1978):11+.

Alan Booth and Lynn White. "Thinking About Divorce." *Journal of Marriage and the Family* 42, No. 3 (August 1980):605–616.

Nadine Brozan. "New Marriage Roles Make Men Ambivalent about Fatherhood." *New York Times*, May 30, 1980, p. B5.

Wesley R. Burr, Geoffrey K. Leigh, Randall D. Day, and John Constantine. "Symbolic Interaction and the Family." In Wesley R. Burr, Reuben Hill, F. Ivan Nye, and Ira L. Reiss (eds.), *Contemporary Theories about the Family* (Vol. 2). New York: Free Press, 1979.

Theodore Caplow and Bruce A. Chadwick. "Inequality and Life-Styles in Middletown, 1920–1978." *Social Science Quarterly* 60, No. 3 (December 1979):367–386.

David A. Chiriboga and Loraine Cutler. "Stress Responses Among Divorcing Men and Women." *Journal of Divorce* 1, No. 2 (Winter 1977):95–106.

W. Glenn Clingempeel and N. Dickon Reppucci. "Joint Custody after Divorce: Major Issues and Goals for Research." *Psychological Bulletin* 9L (1982):102–127.

Charles L. Cole. "Cohabitation in Social Context." In Roger W. Libby and Robert N. Whitehurst (eds.), *Marriage and Alternatives: Exploring Intimate Relationships*. Glenview, Ill.: Scott, Foresman, 1977.

John F. Crosby. "A Critique of Divorce Statistics and Their Interpretation." *Family Relations* 29 (January 1980):51–58.

Ralf Dahrendorf. *Gesellschaft und Demokratie in Deutschland*. Munchen: Piper Verlag, 1965.

Godfrey J. Ellis, Gary R. Lee, and Larry R. Petersen. "Supervision and Conformity: A Cross-Cultural Analysis of Parental Socialization Values." *American Journal of Sociology* 84 (1978):386–403.

Selma H. Fraiberg. *Every Child's Birthright*. New York: Basic Books, 1977.

Linda Bird Francke. "The Sons of Divorce." *New York Times Magazine*, May 22, 1983, p. 40+.

Viktor Gecas and F. Ivan Nye. "Sex and Class Differences in Parent-Child Interaction: A Test of Kohn's Hypothesis." *Journal of Marriage and the Family* 36 (1974):742–749.

Richard J. Gelles. "Violence in the Family." In David H. Olson and Brent C. Miller (eds.), *Family Studies Review Yearbook* (Vol. 1). Beverly Hills, Calif.: Sage Publications, 1983.

Richard J. Gelles. "Child Abuse as Psychopathology: A Sociological Critique and Reformulation." In Suzanne K. Steinmetz and Murray A. Straus (eds.), *Violence in the Family*. New York: Harper & Row, 1974.

Naomi R. Gerstel. "The Feasibility of Commuter Marriage." In Peter J. Stein, Judith Richman, and Natalie Harmon (eds.), *The Family*. Reading, Mass.: Addison-Wesley, 1977.

David G. Gil. "Helping Parents and Protecting Children." In Suzanne K. Steinmetz and Murray A. Straus (eds.), *Violence in the Family*. New York: Harper & Row, 1974.

Paul C. Glick. "The Future of the American Family." *Current Population Reports Special Studies*, Series P-23, No. 78. Washington, D.C.: U.S. Government Printing Office, 1979.

Paul C. Glick and Graham P. Spanier. "Married and Unmarried Cohabitation in the United States." *Journal of Marriage and the Family* 48, No. 1 (February 1980):19–30.

Paul C. Glick. "How American Families Are Changing." *American Demographics* 6 (January 1984):21–25.

William J. Goode. "The Role of the Family in Industrialization." In *Social Problems of Development* (Vol. 7). The U.S. Papers Prepared for the UN Conference on the Application of Science and Technology for the Benefit of the Less Developed Areas. Washington, D.C.: U.S. Government Printing Office, 1963.

E. Kathleen Gough. "Nayar: Central Kerala." In David Schneider and E. Kathleen Gough (eds.), *Matrilineal Kinship*. Berkeley: University of California Press, 1974.

Harriet Engel Gross. "Dual-Career Couples Who Live Apart: Two Types." *Journal of Marriage and the Family* 42, No. 3 (August 1980):567–576.

Tamara K. Hareven. *Family Time and Industrial Time*. New York: Cambridge University Press, 1982.

Fred M. Hechinger. "Is One-Parent Household a Handicap for Pupils?" *New York Times*, September 30, 1980, p. C1.

Karl G. Heider. *The Dani of West Irian*. Andover, Md.: Warner Modular, 1972.

Ray E. Helfer and C. Henry Kempe. *Child Abuse and Neglect*. Cambridge, Mass.: Ballinger, 1976.

E. Mavis Hetherington, Martha Cox, and Roger Cox. "Divorced Fathers." *Psychology Today* 10 (April 1977):42–46.

Joan Huber and Glenna Spitze. "Considering Divorce: An Expansion of Becker's Theory of Marital Instability." *American Journal of Sociology* 86, No. 1 (1980):75–89.

John W. Jacobs. "The Effect of Divorce on Fathers: An Overview of the Literature." *American Journal of Psychiatry* 139 (1982):1235–1241.

Elizabeth S. Johnson and Barbara J. Bursk. "Relationships Between the Elderly and Their Adult Children." In Gladys K. Phelan (ed.), *Family Relationships*. Minneapolis: Burgess, 1979.

Jerome Kagan, Richard B. Kearsley, and Philip R. Zelazo. *Infancy: Its Place in Human Development*. Cambridge, Mass.: Harvard University Press, 1978.

Marie Witkin Kargman. "Stepchild Support Obligations of Stepparents." *Family Relations* 32 (1983):231–238.

Joan B. Kelly and Judith S. Wallerstein. "The Effects of Parental Divorce: Experiences of the Child in Early Latency." *American Journal of Orthopsychiatry* 46 (1976):20–32.

Betty Frankle Kirschner and Laurel Richardson Walum. "Two-Location Families: Married Singles." *Alternative Lifestyles* 1, No. 4 (November 1978):513–525.

Judy Klemesrud. "A Wife's Role in Big Decisions." *New York Times*, November 13, 1980, p. 68.

Melvin L. Kohn. "Social Class and Parental Values." *American Journal of Sociology* 64 (January 1959):337–351.

Melvin L. Kohn. "Social Class and Parent-Child Relationships: An Interpretation." In Robert F. Winch and Louis W. Goodman (eds.), *Selected Studies in Marriage and the Family* (4th ed.). New York: Holt, Rinehart & Winston, 1974.

Melvin H. Kohn. *Social Competence, Symptoms and Underachievement in Childhood: A Longitudinal Perspective*. Washington, D.C.: Winston, 1977.

Lawrence A. Kurdek and Albert E. Siesky. "Children's Perception of Their Parents' Divorce." *Journal of Divorce* 3 (Summer 1980):339–378.

Michael E. Lamb. "The Effect of Divorce on Children's Personality Development." *Journal of Divorce* 1 (Winter 1977):163–174*a*.

Michael E. Lamb. "Father-Infant and Mother-Infant Interaction in the First Year of Life." *Child Development* 48 (1977):167–181*b*.

Peter Laslett. "Introduction." In Peter Laslett (ed.), *Household and Family in Past Time*. Cambridge, Mass.: Harvard University Press, 1974.

E. E. LeMasters. *Blue-Collar Aristocrats*. Madison: University of Wisconsin Press, 1975.

Daniel J. Levinson. *The Seasons of a Man's Life*. New York: Knopf, 1978.

Eleanor E. Maccoby. "Current Changes in the Family and Their Impact upon the Socialization of Children." In J. Milton Yinger and Stephen J. Cutler (eds.), *Major Social Issues*. New York: Free Press, 1978.

Sara S. McLanahan. "Family Structure and Stress: A Longitudinal Comparison of Two-Parent and Female-Headed Families." *Journal of Marriage and the Family* 45 (1983):347–357.

George Masnick and Mary Jo Bane. "The Nation's Families, 1960–1990." Cambridge, Mass.: Joint Center for Urban Studies of MIT and Harvard University, 1980.

Keith Melville. *Marriage and Family Today*. New York: Random House, 1980.

George Peter Murdock. *Social Structure*. New York: Macmillan, 1949.

Bernice L. Neugarten. "The Future and the Young-Old." In J. Savells and L. Cross (eds.), *The Changing Family: Making Way for Tomorrow*. New York: Holt, Rinehart & Winston, 1978.

M. F. Nimkoff and Russell Middleton. "Types of Family and Types of Economy." *American Journal of Sociology* 66 (November 1960):215–225.

Dennis K. Orthner, Terry Brown, and Dennis Ferguson. "Single-Parent Fatherhood: An Emerging Lifestyle." In Gladys K. Phelan (ed.), *Family Relationships*. Minneapolis: Burgess, 1979.

Anne R. Pebley and David E. Bloom. "Childless Americans." *American Demographics* 4 (January 1982):18–21.

Brian F. Pendleton, Margaret M. Poloma, and T. Neal Garland. "Scales for Investigation of the Dual Career Family." *Journal of Marriage and the Family* 42, No. 2 (May 1980):269–275.

William H. Quinn. "Personal and Family Adjustment in Later Life." *Journal of Marriage and the Family* 45 (1983):57–73.

Albert I. Rabin. *Growing Up in the Kibbutz*. New York: Springer, 1965.

Judith Reed. "Working with Abusive Parents." *Children Today* 4, No. 3 (May 1975):6–9.

John Reilly. "Loneliness of Long-Distance Marriage." *USA Today*, January 11, 1984, p. B-1.

Karen S. Renne. "Correlates of Dissatisfaction in Marriage." *Journal of Marriage and the Family* 32, No. 1 (November 1970):54–67.

Barbara J. Risman, Charles T. Hill, Zick Rubin, and Letitia A. Peplau. "Living Together in College: Implications for Courtship." *Journal of Marriage and the Family* 43 (1981):77–83.

Boyd C. Rollins and Kenneth L. Cannon. "Marital Satisfaction over the Family Life Cycle: A Reevaluation." *Journal of Marriage and the Family* 36, No. 2 (May 1974):271–283.

Boyd C. Rollins and Harold Feldman. "Marital Satisfaction over the Family Life Cycle." *Journal of Marriage and the Family* 32, No. 1 (November 1970):20–28.

Heather L. Ross and Isabel V. Sawhill. *Time of Transition: The Growth of Families Headed by Women*. Washington, D.C.: Urban Institute, 1975.

Lillian Breslow Rubin. *Worlds of Pain: Life in the Working-Class Family*. New York: Basic Books, 1976.

John W. Santrock and Richard A. Warshak. "Father Custody and Social Development in Boys and Girls." *Journal of Social Issues* 35 (1979):112–125.

Douglas B. Sawin and Ross D. Parke. "Fathers' Affectionate Stimulation and Caregiving Behaviors with Newborn Infants." *Family Coordinator* 28 (1979):509–513.

Robert R. Sears et al. "The Sources of Aggression in the Home." In Suzanne K. Steinmetz and Murray A. Straus (eds.), *Violence in the Family*. New York: Harper & Row, 1974.

Ethel Shanas. "Other People and Their Families: The New Pioneers." *Journal of Marriage and the Family* 42 (1980):9–15.

Philip Shenon. "What's New with Dual-Career Couples." *New York Times*, March 6, 1983, p. F29.

Denise A. Skinner. "Dual-Career Family Stress and Coping." In David H. Olson and Brent C. Miller (eds.), *Family Studies Review Yearbook* (Vol. 1). Beverly Hills: Sage, 1983.

Arlene S. Skolnick. *The Intimate Environment: Exploring Marriage and the Family*. Boston: Little, Brown, 1978.

Neil J. Smelser. *Social Change in the Industrial Revolution*. Chicago: University of Chicago Press, 1959.

Graham B. Spanier. "Living Together in the Eighties." *American Demographics* 4 (November 1982):17–23.

Jetse Sprey. "Conflict Theory and the Study of Marriage and the Family." In Wesley R. Burr, Reuben Hill, F. Ivan Nye, and Ira L. Reiss (eds.), *Contemporary Theories About the Family* (Vol. 2). New York: Free Press, 1979.

Rodney Stark and James McEvoy III. "Middle Class Violence." In Suzanne K. Steinmetz and Murray A. Straus (eds.), *Violence in the Family*. New York: Harper & Row, 1974.

Suzanne K. Steinmetz and Murray A. Straus (eds.). *Violence in the*

Family. New York: Harper & Row, 1974.

Murray A. Straus, Richard J. Gelles, and Suzanne K. Steinmetz. *Behind Closed Doors: Violence in the American Family*. Garden City, N.Y.: Doubleday, 1980.

Y. Talmon-Garber. "Social Change and Family Structure." *International Social Science Journal* 14, No. 3 (1962):468–487.

Sharon K. Turnbull and James M. Turnbull. "To Dream the Impossible Dream: An Agenda for Discussion with Stepparents." *Family Relations* 32 (1983):227–230.

J. Richard Udry. *The Social Context of Marriage* (3rd ed.): New York: Harper Colophon, 1974.

U.S. Bureau of the Census. *Current Population Reports*, Series P-20, No. 349, "Marital Status and Living Arrangements: March 1979." Washington, D.C.: U.S. Government Printing Office, 1980.

U.S. Bureau of the Census. News Release, June 30, 1983.

Judith S. Wallerstein and Joan Berlin Kelly. *Surviving the Breakup: How Children and Parents Cope with Divorce*. New York: Basic Books, 1980.

Judith S. Wallerstein and Joan B. Kelly. "California's Children of Divorce." *Psychology Today* 13, No. 8 (January 1980):67–76.

Gary C. Walters and Joan E. Grusec. *Punishment*. San Francisco: W. H. Freeman, 1977.

James Walters and Lynda Henley Walters. "Trends Affecting Adolescent Views of Sexuality, Employment, Marriage, and Child Rearing." *Family Relations* 29, No. 2 (April 1980):191–198.

Ben J. Wattenberg. "A Family Survey: Is the Family Really in Trouble?" *Better Homes and Gardens* 51 (March 1973):2, 30, 31, 33.

James A. Weed. "Divorce: Americans' Style." *American Demographics* 4 (March 1982):13–17.

Robert N. Whitehurst. "Violence in Husband-Wife Interaction." In Suzanne K. Steinmetz and Murray A. Straus (eds.), *Violence in the Family*. New York: Harper & Row, 1974.

Beatrice B. Whiting. "The Dependency Hang-Up and Experiments in Alternative Life Styles." In J. Milton Yinger and Stephen J. Cutler (eds.), *Major Social Issues*. New York: Free Press, 1978.

Robert F. Winch and Rae Lesser Blumberg. "Societal Complexity and Familiar Organization." In Robert F. Winch and Graham B. Spanier (eds.), *Selected Studies in Marriage and the Family* (3rd ed.). New York: Holt, Rinehart & Winston, 1968.

James D. Wright and Sonia R. Wright. "Social Class and Parental Values for Children." *American Sociological Review* 41 (June 1976):527–548.

Daniel Yankelovich. "New Rules in American Life." *Psychology Today* 15 (April 1981):35–91.

Jan D. Yoder and Robert C. Nichols. "A Life Perspective Comparison of Married and Divorced Persons." *Journal of Marriage and the Family* 42, No. 2 (May 1980):413–419.

CHAPTER 14

AACJC (American Association of Community and Junior Colleges). "Students in Two-Year Colleges." May 1977.

Michael W. Apple. *Ideology and Curriculum*. London: Routledge & Kegan Paul, 1979.

Michael W. Apple. *Education and Power: Reproduction and Contradiction in Education*. London: Routledge & Kegan Paul, 1982.

Alexander W. Astin. *Four Critical Years*. San Francisco: Jossey-Bass, 1977.

Ivar Berg, Marcia Freedman, and Michael Freeman. *Managers and Work Reform*. New York: Free Press, 1978.

Richard A. Berk, William P. Bridges, and Anthony Shih. "Does IQ Really Matter? A Study of the Use of IQ Scores for the Tracking of the Mentally Retarded." *American Sociological Review* 46 (1981):58–71.

Howard R. Bowen. *Investment in Learning: The Individual and Social Value of Higher Education*. San Francisco: Jossey-Bass, 1977.

Samuel Bowles. "Unequal Education and the Reproduction of the Social Division of Labor." In Jerome Karabel and A. H. Halsey (eds.), *Power and Ideology in Education*. New York: Oxford University Press, 1977.

Samuel Bowles and Herbert Gintis. *Schooling and Capitalist America*. New York: Basic Books, 1976.

Urie Bronfenbrenner. *Two Worlds of Childhood*. New York: Russell Sage Foundation, 1970.

Val Burris. "The Social and Political Consequences of Overeducation." *American Sociological Review* 48 (1983):454–467.

James S. Coleman. "Equal Schools or Equal Students?" *The Public Interest* 4 (Summer 1966):70–75.

James Coleman, Thomas Hoffer, and Sally Kilgore. *Summary of Major Findings for Public and Private Schools of High School and Beyond*. Washington, D.C.: National Center for Educational Statistics, March 1981. Mimeograph.

Randall Collins. "Functional and Conflict Theories of Educational Stratification." *American Sociological Review* 36 (December 1971):1002–1018.

Randall Collins. *The Credential Society*. New York: Academic Press, 1979.

William D. Crano and Phyllis M. Mellon. "Causal Influence of Teachers' Expectations on Children's Academic Performance: A Cross-Lagged Panel Analysis." *Journal of Educational Psychology* 70 (1978):39–49.

Lee A. Daniels. "In Defense of Busing." *New York Times Magazine*, April 17, 1983, pp. 34–37+.

Nicholas Daniloff. "Are Soviet Schools as Good as They Look?" *U.S. News & World Report*, March 28, 1983, pp. 33–34.

Nancy B. Dearman and Valena White Plisko. *The Condition of Education*. Washington, D.C.: National Center for Educational Statistics, 1980.

Samuel M. Ehrenhalt. "What Lies Ahead for College Graduates?" *American Demographics* 5 (September 1983):29–33.

J. D. Elashoff and R. E. Snow. *Pygmalion Reconsidered*. Worthington, Ohio: Charles A. Jones, 1971.

George H. Gallup. "Whites, Blacks in Sharp Disagreement on Busing." *The Gallup Poll*, February 5, 1981.

George H. Gallup. "The 15th Annual Gallup Poll of the Public's Attitudes toward the Public Schools." *Phi Delta Kappan* 65 (1983):33–47.

John I. Goodlad. *A Place Called School*. New York: McGraw-Hill, 1983.

Helen Gouldner, with the assistance of Mary Symons Strong. *Teacher's Pets, Troublemakers and Nobodies*. Westport, Conn.: Greenwood Press, 1978.

Suzanne Guinzburg. "Education's Earning Power." *Psychology Today* 17 (October 1983):20–21.

Godfrey Hodgson. "Do Schools Make a Difference?" *Atlantic Monthly* 213 (March 1973):35–46.

Christopher J. Hurn. *The Limits and Possibilities of Schooling: An*

Introduction to the Sociology of Education. Boston: Allyn & Bacon, 1978.
Herbert H. Hyman and Charles R. Wright. *Education's Lasting Influence on Values*. Chicago: University of Chicago Press, 1979.
Herbert H. Hyman, Charles R. Wright, and John Shelton Reed. *The Enduring Effects of Education*. Chicago: University of Chicago Press, 1975.
Philip W. Jackson. *Life in Classrooms*. New York: Holt, Rinehart & Winston, 1968.
Arthur Jensen. "How Much Can We Boost IQ and Scholastic Achievement?" *Harvard Educational Review* 39 (1969):273–314.
Arthur Jensen. *Bias in Mental Testing*. New York: Free Press, 1979.
André Joseph. *Intelligence, IQ and Race—When, How and Why They Became Associated*. San Francisco: R. & E. Research Associates, 1977.
Jerome Karabel. "Community Colleges and Social Stratification: Submerged Class Conflict in American Higher Education." In Jerome Karabel and A. H. Halsey (eds.), *Power and Ideology in Education*. New York: Oxford University Press, 1977.
Alan C. Kerckhoff and Robert A. Jackson. "Types of Education and the Occupational Attainments of Young Men." *Social Forces* 61 (1982):24–45.
Donna Kerr. "Teaching Competence and Teacher Education in the United States." *Teachers College Record* 81 (1983):525–552.
Eleanor Leacock. *Teaching and Learning in City Schools*. New York: Basic Books, 1969.
Robert D. Mare. "Change and Stability in Educational Stratification." *American Sociological Review* 46 (1981):72–87.
R. K. Merton. "Social Problems and Social Theory." In R. Merton and R. Nisbet (eds.), *Contemporary Social Problems*. New York: Harcourt, Brace & World, 1968.
NAEP (National Assessment of Educational Progress). *Changes in Mathematical Achievement, 1973–1978*. Denver: Educational Commission of the States, 1979.
National Commission on Excellence in Education. *A Nation At Risk*. Washington, D.C.: U.S. Government Printing Office, 1983.
National Institute of Education. "Violent Schools—Safe Schools." Washington, D.C.: U.S. Department of Health, Education and Welfare, 1978.
Michael R. Olneck and David B. Bills. "What Makes Sammy Run? An Empirical Assessment of the Bowles-Gintis Correspondence Theory." *American Journal of Education* 89 (1980):27–61.
Gary Orfield. *Public School Desegregation in the United States, 1968–1980*. Washington, D.C.: Joint Center for Political Studies, 1983.
Talcott Parsons. "The School Class as a Social System: Some of Its Functions in American Society." *Harvard Educational Review* 29 (Fall 1959):297–318.
Thomas F. Pettigrew and Robert L. Green. "School Desegregation in Large Cities: A Critique of the Coleman 'White Flight' Thesis." *Harvard Educational Review* 46 (1976):1–53.
Fred L. Pincus. "The False Promises of Community Colleges: Class Conflict and Vocational Education." *Harvard Educational Review* 50 (August 1980):332–361.
Ray C. Rist. "Student Social Class and Teacher Expectations: The Self-Fulfilling Prophecy in Ghetto Education." *Harvard Educational Review* 40 (1970).
Ray C. Rist (ed.). *Desegregated Schools: Appraisals for an American Experiment*. New York: Academic Press, 1979.
Orlando Rodriguez. "Occupational Shifts and Educational Upgrading in the American Labor Force Between 1950 and 1970." *Sociology of Education* 51 (January 1978):55–67.
James E. Rosenbaum. "The Structure of Opportunity in School." *Social Forces* (September 1978):236–256.
James E. Rosenbaum. "Track Misperceptions and Frustrated College Plans: An Analysis of the Effects of Tracks and Track Perceptions in the National Longitudinal Survey." *Sociology of Education* 53 (April 1980):74–88.
R. Rosenthal and L. Jacobson. *Pygmalion in the Classroom: Teacher Expectation and Pupils' Intellectual Development*. New York: Holt, Rinehart & Winston, 1968.
Michael Rutter et al. *Fifteen Thousand Hours*. Cambridge, Mass.: Harvard University Press, 1979.
Nancy St. John. *School Desegregation: Outcomes for Children*. New York: Wiley, 1975.
Rachael Sharp and Anthony Green. *Education and Social Control*. London: Routledge & Kegan Paul, 1975.
Nathaniel Sheppard, Jr. "Schools Ending Chapter in U.S. Desegregation Saga." *New York Times*, June 10, 1981, p. A28.
Charles E. Silberman. *Crisis in the Classroom*. New York: Vintage, 1971.
Howard F. Taylor. *The IQ Game*. New Brunswick, N.J.: Rutgers University Press, 1980.
U.S. Bureau of the Census. *School Enrollment—Social and Economic Characteristics of Students: October 1981* (Advance Report). Current Population Report Series P-20, No. 373. Washington, D.C.: U.S. Government Printing Office, 1983.
Theodore C. Wagenaar. "High School Seniors' Views of Themselves and Their Schools." *Phi Delta Kappan* (September 1981):29–32.
W. Timothy Weaver. "In Search of Quality." *Phi Delta Kappan* (September 1979):29–46.
D. A. Williams, E. Gelman, S. Monroe, J. Huck, V. Coppola, and P. King. "Hope for the Schools." *Newsweek*, May 4, 1981, pp. 66–72.
D. A. Williams, J. Huck, C. Ma, and S. Monroe. "Why Public Schools Fail." *Newsweek*, April 20, 1981, pp. 62–73.

CHAPTER 15

R. W. Apple, Jr. "Iran: Heart of the Matter." *New York Times Magazine*, March 11, 1979.
Willard L. Beaulac. "The Latin American Church: Marxist Inroads." *National Review*, April 17, 1981, pp. 422–423.
Charles J. Beirne. "Return to El Salvador." *America* 149 (October 8, 1983):188–190.
Robert N. Bellah. *Beyond Belief*. New York: Harper & Row, 1970.
Robert N. Bellah. "American Civil Religion in the 1970s." Unpublished paper delivered at Drew University, March 1973.
Robert N. Bellah. *The Broken Covenant*. New York: Seabury Press, 1975.
Robert N. Bellah and Phillip E. Hammond. *Varieties of Civil Religion*. New York: Harper & Row, 1980.
Peter L. Berger. *The Sacred Canopy*, New York: Doubleday, 1969.
Peter L. Berger. *The Heretical Imperative: Contemporary Possibilities of Religious Affirmation*. Garden City, N.Y.: Doubleday, Anchor Press, 1979.
Reginald W. Bibby. "Why Conservative Churches are *Really* Growing: Kelley Revisited." *Journal for the Scientific Study of Religion* 17 (1978):129–137.

L. Carl Brown. "Ayatollahs and Abracadabra." *Princeton Alumni Weekly*, October 6, 1980, pp. 22–28.

Theodore Caplow, Howard M. Bahr, and Bruce A. Chadwick. *All Faithful People: Change and Continuity in Middletown's Religion.* Minneapolis: University of Minnesota Press, 1983.

Joan D. Chittister and Martin E. Marty. *Faith & Ferment.* Minneapolis: Augsburg Publishing House, 1983.

Steven M. Cohen. *Attitudes of American Jews Toward Israel and Israelis.* New York: Institute on American Jewish-Israeli Relations, 1983.

John A. Coleman. "The Christian as Citizen." *Commonweal* CX (1983):457–462.

James V. Downton, Jr. "An Evolutionary Theory of Spiritual Conversion and Commitment: The Case of Divine Light Mission." *Journal for the Scientific Study of Religion* 19, No. 4 (1980):381–396.

Emile Durkheim. *The Elementary Forms of Religious Life* (Joseph Ward Swain, trans.). New York: Free Press, 1965. (Originally published in 1912.)

Gallup Report. *Religion in America.* Report Nos. 201–202 (June–July), 1982.

Andrew M. Greeley. *The Denominational Society.* Glenview, Ill.: Scott, Foresman, 1972*a*.

Andrew M. Greeley. *Unsecular Man: The Persistence of Religion.* New York: Schocken Books, 1972*b*.

Andrew M. Greeley. "Going Their Own Way." *New York Times Magazine*, October 10, 1982, pp. 28–29+.

James L. Guth. "The New Christian Right." In Robert C. Liebman and Robert Wuthnow (eds.), *The New Christian Right.* New York: Aldine, 1983.

Jeffrey K. Hadden and Charles E. Swann. *Prime Time Preachers: The Rising Power of Televangelism.* Reading, Mass.: Addison-Wesley, 1981.

Michael I. Harrison and Bernard Lazerwitz. "Do Denominations Matter?" *American Journal of Sociology* 88 (1982):356–377.

J. Bryan Hehir. "The Bishops Speak on El Salvador." *Commonweal*, April 10, 1981, pp. 199, 223.

Jerome L. Himmelstein. "The New Right." In Robert C. Liebman and Robert Wuthnow (eds.), *The New Christian Right.* New York: Aldine, 1983.

Jonathan Kaufman. "Old-Time Religion." *Wall Street Journal*, July 11, 1980, pp. 1, 11.

Elie Kedourie. "Islam Resurgent." *Britannica Book of the Year, 1980.* Chicago: Encyclopedia Britannica, 1980.

Flora Lewis. "Basis of the New Moslem Fervor Seen as Rejection of Alien Values." First article in a series: "Upsurge in Islam." *New York Times*, December 28, 1979, pp. A1, A6. (a)

Flora Lewis. "Students and the Young Leading Moslem Fundamentalist Revival." Second article in a series: "Upsurge in Islam." *New York Times*, December 29, 1979, pp. A1, A4. (b)

Dr. Franklin H. Littell. *Britannica Book of the Year, 1983.* Chicago: Encyclopedia Britannica, 1983.

John Lofland and Rodney Stark. "Becoming a World-Saver: A Theory of Conversion to a Deviant Perspective." *American Sociological Review* 30 (1965):865–875.

Thomas Luckmann. *The Invisible Religion.* New York: Macmillan, 1967.

Robert S. Lynd and Helen M. Lynd. *Middletown: A Study in American Culture.* New York: Harcourt and Brace, 1929.

Robert S. Lynd and Helen M. Lynd. *Middletown in Transition: A Study in Cultural Conflicts.* New York: Harcourt and Brace, 1937.

Douglas B. McGaw. "Commitment and Religious Community: A Comparison of a Charismatic and a Mainline Congregation." *Journal for the Scientific Study of Religion* 18 (1979):146–163.

Richard Machalek and Michael Martin. "'Invisible' Religions: Some Preliminary Evidence." *Journal for the Scientific Study of Religion* 15 (December 1976):311–321.

James Mann. "Old-Time Religion on the Offensive." *U.S. News & World Report*, April 7, 1980, pp. 40–42.

James Mann. "Protestants Shift from Issues to Prayer." *U.S. News & World Report*, April 4, 1983, pp. 36–38.

Karl Marx. *Selected Writings in Sociology and Social Philosophy* (T. B. Bottomore and Maximilian Rubel, eds.). Baltimore: Penguin, 1964. (Originally published in 1848.)

Tommie Sue Montgomery. "The Church in the Salvadoran Revolution." *Latin American Perspectives* 10 (1983):62–87.

William Novak. "From Somerville to Savannah . . . and Los Angeles . . . and Dayton." *Moment* 6 (January–February 1981):17–24.

David K. O'Rourke. "Revolution and Alienation in the American Church." *Commonweal* CX (1983):76–79.

Gretel H. Pelto and Pertti J. Pelto. *The Human Adventure.* New York: Macmillan, 1976.

James T. Richardson, Mary White Stewart, and Robert B. Simmonds. *Organized Miracles: A Study of a Contemporary, Youth, Communal Fundamentalist Organization.* New Brunswick, N.J.: Transaction Books, 1979.

Barry Rubin. "Iran's year of turmoil." *Current History*, (January 1983):28–31.

"Salvador Archbishop Assassinated by Sniper While Officiating At Mass." *New York Times*, March 25, 1980, pp. 1, 8.

Alvin P. Sanoff. "Jews Find New Solace in the Old Traditions." *U.S. News & World Report*, April 4, 1983, pp. 43–44.

Anson Shupe and William Stacey. "The Moral Majority Constituency." In Robert C. Liebman and Robert Wuthnow (eds.), *The New Christian Right.* New York: Aldine, 1983.

John H. Simpson. "Moral Issues and Status Politics." In Robert C. Liebman and Robert Wuthnow (eds.), *The New Christian Right.* New York: Aldine, 1983.

Simon E. Smith. "San Salvador: A Chronicle of Intimidation." *America*, March 28, 1981, pp. 250–251.

Terrence Smith. "Iran: Five Years of Fanaticism." *New York Times Magazine*, February 12, 1984, pp. 21–32.

Rodney Stark and William Sims Bainbridge. "Of Churches, Sects, and Cults: Preliminary Concepts for a Theory of Religious Movements." *Journal for the Scientific Study of Religion* 18 (1979):117–133.

Guy E. Swanson. *The Birth of the Gods.* Ann Arbor: University of Michigan Press, 1974.

Alexis de Tocqueville. *Democracy in America.* Garden City, N.Y.: Doubleday, 1969. (Originally published in 1835.)

Ernst Troeltsch. *The Social Teaching of the Christian Churches.* New York: Macmillan, 1931.

Ernst Troeltsch. "Church and Sect." In Milton J. Yinger (ed.), *Religion, Society, and the Individual: An Introduction to the Sociology of Religion.* New York: Macmillan, 1957.

Max Weber. *The Protestant Ethic and the Spirit of Capitalism.* (1904, 1920) London: Allen & Unwin, 1930.

David Welna. "Argentina's Bishops and the Disappeared." *Christianity and Crisis* 43 (June 27, 1983):252–253.

Kenneth L. Woodward. "The Split-Up Evangelicals." *Newsweek*, April 26, 1982, pp. 88–91.

Robert Wuthnow. "The Political Rebirth of American Evangelicals." In Robert C. Liebman and Robert Wuthnow (eds.), *The New Christian Right*. New York: Aldine, 1983.

CHAPTER 16

C. T. Adams and K. T. Winston. *Mothers at Work*. New York: Longman, 1980.

Lawrence K. Altman. "AIDS Now Seen as a Worldwide Health Problem." *New York Times*, November 29, 1983, pp. 13, 19.

AMA (American Medical Association). "Physician Distribution and Medical Licensure in the U.S., 1979." Chicago: American Medical Association, 1980.

America's Children 1976. Washington, D.C.: National Council of Organizations for Children and Youth, 1978.

Melinda Beck. "The Baby Boomers Come of Age." *Newsweek*, March 30, 1981, pp. 34–37.

Philip M. Boffey. "Panel of Experts Challenges Gloomy Forecast for 2000." *New York Times*, May 30, 1983, p. 9.

A. J. Coale and N. W. Rives, Jr. "A Statistical Reconstruction of the Black Population of the United States, 1880–1970." *Population Index* 39 (January 1973):3–36.

James C. Cramer. "Fertility and Female Employment: Problems of Causal Direction." *American Sociological Review* 45 (1980):167–190.

Ann Crittenden. "Demand Outpaces World Food Supply." *New York Times*, August 16, 1981, pp. 1, 12.

Paul M. DuBois. *The Hospice Way of Death*. New York: Human Sciences Press, 1980.

Selwyn Enzer, Richard Drobnick, and Steven Alter. "World Food Prospects: The Next 20 Years." *The Futurist* 12 (October 1978):283–288.

Marshall Green and Robert A. Fearey. *World Population: Silent Explosion*. Washington, D.C.: U.S. Department of State, 1978.

Carl F. Grundstaff. *Population and Society: A Sociological Perspective*. West Hanover, Mass.: Christopher Publishing House, 1981.

Robert Hanley. "Study Finds Airborne Carcinogens in Newark, Camden, and Elizabeth." *New York Times*, May 14, 1982, p. 18.

Philip M. Hauser. "The Census of 1980." *Scientific American* 245 (November 1981):53–61.

Constance Holden. "Simon and Kahn Versus Global 2000." *Science* 221 (1983):341–343.

Deborah Holmes, Jill N. Nagy, and Frank Slaymaker. "Early Influences of Prematurity, Illness, and Prolonged Hospitalization on Infant Behavior." *Developmental Psychology* 18 (1982):744–750.

Landon Y. Jones. "The Baby Boomers." *Money* (March 1983):57–64.

Herman Kahn. *World Economic Development*. New York: Morrow, 1979.

Edward M. Kennedy. Address to the National Council of Organizations for Children and Youth, Bicentennial Conference on Children. Washington, D.C., February 3, 1976.

Nathan Keyfitz. "Statistics, Law, and Census Reporting." *Society* (January–February 1981):5–12.

Seth S. King. "Birth Rates Called Key to Hope in Third World." *New York Times*, April 3, 1983, p. 4.

Robin Knight. "Another Deadly Famine Stalks Black Africa." *U.S. News & World Report*, August 22, 1983, p. 27.

Walsh McDermott. "Medicine: The Public Good and One's Own." *World Health Forum* 1 (1980):123–132.

Thomas McKeown. *The Role of Medicine*. Nuffield Provincial Hospitals Trust, 1976.

John B. and Sonja M. McKinlay. "The Questionable Contribution of Medical Measures to the Decline of Mortality in the United States in the Twentieth Century." *Health and Society* 53, No. 3 (1977):405.

Halfdan Mahler. "People." *Scientific American* 243 (September 1980):67–77.

Halfdan Mahler. "The Meaning of 'Health for All by the Year 2000.'" *World Health Forum* 2 (1981):5–22.

Thomas Robert Malthus. *Essay on the Principle of Population* (Gertrude Himmelfarb, ed.). New York: Modern Library, 1960. (Originally published in 1798.)

Thomas H. Maugh II. "Cancer Is Not Inevitable." *Science* 217 (1982):36–37.

Ian Mitroff, Richard Mason, and Vincent Barabba. *The 1980 Census: Policymaking Amid Turbulence*. Lexington, Mass.: Lexington Books, 1983.

Kenneth A. Noble. "Are Program Cuts Linked to Increased Infant Deaths?" *New York Times*, February 13, 1983, p. E6.

Bernard D. Nossiter. "U.N. Study Predicts Slower Population Gains." *New York Times*, June 19, 1983, p. 4.

William Petersen. "The Demographic Transition in the Netherlands." *American Sociological Review* 25 (1960):334–347.

William Petersen. *Population* (3rd ed.). New York: Macmillan, 1975.

Ronald R. Rindfuss, Larry Bumpass, and Craig St. John. "Education and Fertility: Implications for the Roles Women Occupy." *American Sociological Review* 45 (1980):431–447.

Cristine Russell. "Infectious Diseases Rage on." *Washington Post*, April 28, 1983, p. E1.

Nevin S. Scrimshaw and Lance Taylor. "Food." *Scientific American* 243 (September 1980):78–88.

Robert Selim. "The 1980s: A Decade of Hunger?" *The Futurist* 14 (April 1980):29–38.

Victor W. Sidel. "Destruction before Detonation." *Health and Medicine* (Winter/Spring 1983):6–15.

Julian L. Simon. *The Ultimate Resource*. Princeton, N.J.: Princeton University Press, 1981.

Ruth Leger Sivard. *World Military and Social Expenditures 1982*. Leesburg, Va.: World Priorities, Inc., 1982.

Gillian Stevens. "Social Mobility and Fertility." *American Sociological Review* 46 (1981):573–584.

Ralph Thomlinson. *Population Dynamics* (2nd ed.). New York: Random House, 1976.

Charles Tilly (ed.). *Historical Studies of Changing Fertility*. Princeton: Princeton University Press, 1978.

Abigail Trafford. "Soaring Hospital Costs." *U.S. News & World Report*, August 22, 1983, pp. 39–42.

U.S. Bureau of the Census. *Statistical Abstract of the United States, 1980*. Washington, D.C.: U.S. Government Printing Office, 1980.

U.S. Department of Commerce, Bureau of the Census. "A Statistical Portrait of Women in the United States." In *Current Population Reports*, Series P-23, No. 100, 1978, p. 30.

John Noble Wilford. "9 Percent of Everyone Who Ever Lived Is Alive Now." *New York Times*, October 6, 1981, pp. 13, 14.

Dennis H. Wrong. *Population and Society*. New York: Random House, 1977.

CHAPTER 17

Calvin Beale and G. V. Fuguitt. "The New Pattern of Nonmetropolitan Population Change." In Karl Taeuber (ed.), *Social Demography*. New York: Academic Press, 1978.

Brian J. L. Berry and John D. Kasarda. *Contemporary Urban Ecology*. New York: Macmillan, 1977.

Nirmal Kumur Bose. *Calcutta, 1964: A Social Survey*. Calcutta: Lalvani Publishing House, 1968.

Katharine L. Bradbury, Anthony Downs, and Kenneth A. Small. *Urban Decline and the Future of American Cities*. Washington: Brookings Institution, 1982.

Kathleen Butler and Ben Chinitz. "Urban Growth in the Sunbelt." In Gary Gappert and Richard V. Knight (eds.), *Cities in the 21st Century*. Beverly Hills, Calif.: Sage Publications, 1982.

V. Gordon Childe. *Man Makes Himself*. New York: New American Library, 1952.

James A. Christenson. "Urbanism and Community Sentiment: Extending Wirth's Model." *Social Science Quarterly* 60 (December 1979):387–400.

Phillip Clay. "Neighborhood Revitalization: The Experience and the Promise." Center for Community Economic Development *Newsletter*, August–October 1978, pp. 1–9.

Kingsley Davis. "The Urbanization of the Human Population." In Sylvia F. Fava (ed.), *Urbanism in World Perspective*. New York: Thomas Y. Crowell, 1968.

Department of Housing and Urban Development. *The President's National Urban Policy Report*, 1980.

E. J. Dionne, Jr. "Small Towns and Rural Areas Grow, Census Finds." *New York Times*, September 30, 1980.

Otis Dudley Duncan. "Human Ecology and Population Studies." In P. M. Hauser and O. D. Duncan (eds.), *The Study of Population*. Chicago: University of Chicago Press, 1959.

Otis Dudley Duncan. "From Social System to Ecosystem." *Sociological Inquiry* 31 (1961):140–149.

Emile Durkheim. *The Division of Labor in Society* (George Simpson, trans.). Glencoe, Ill.: Free Press, 1947. (Originally published in 1893.)

Issac W. Eberstein and W. Parker Frisbie. "Metropolitan Function and Interdependence in the U.S. Urban System." *Social Forces* 60 (1982):676–700.

John Esposito and John Fiorillo. "Who's Left on the Block? New York City's Working Class Neighborhoods." In Hans Spiegel (ed.), *Citizen Participation in Urban Development*. Fairfax, Va.: Learning Resources Corporation/NTL, 1974.

Kirby L. Estes. "The Extra Dimension: Urban Architecture for Tomorrow." *The Futurist* 13 (December 1979):439–446.

Thomas G. Exter. "Demographics of Mexico." *American Demographics* 4 (February 1982):22–27.

Glenn Firebaugh. "Structural Determinants of Urbanization in Asia and Latin America, 1950–1970." *American Sociological Review* 44 (April 1979):199–215.

Walter Firey. "Sentiment and Symbolism as Ecological Variables." In George A. Theodorson (ed.), *Studies in Human Ecology*. Evanston, Ill.: Row, Peterson, 1961.

Claude S. Fischer. "Towards a Subcultural Theory of Urbanism." *American Journal of Sociology* 80 (May 1975):1319–1341.

Claude S. Fischer. "The Public and Private Worlds of City Life." *American Sociological Review* 46 (1981):306–316.

Claude S. Fischer. *To Dwell Among Friends: Personal Networks in Town and City*. Chicago: University of Chicago Press, 1982.

Herbert J. Gans. *The Urban Villagers*. New York: Free Press, 1962.

Hans H. Gerth and C. Wright Mills. *From Max Weber: Essays in Sociology*. New York: Oxford University Press, 1958.

Jean Gottman. *Megalopolis: The Urbanized Northeastern Seaboard of the United States*. Cambridge, Mass.: MIT Press, 1964.

Scott Greer. *Urban Renewal and American Cities*. Indianapolis: Bobbs-Merrill, 1966.

Charles M. Haar, Michael Allan Wolf, Sarah L. Sheon, and Jill Friedlander. *Urban Enterprise Zones: Inner City Panacea or Supply-Side Showpiece?* Land Policy Roundtable, Lincoln Institute of Land Policy, No. 105, 1982.

Chauncy D. Harris and Edward L. Ullman. "The Nature of Cities." *Annals of the American Academy of Political and Social Science* 242 (November 1945):12.

Lawrence Haworth. *The Good City*. Bloomington: Indiana University Press, 1963.

John Herbers. "Study Finds Aid Cuts Threaten Cities with Fiscal Crisis." *New York Times*, May 17, 1981.

John Herbers. "Census Data Reveal 70's Legacy: Poorer Cities and Richer Suburbs." *New York Times*, February 27, 1983, pp. 1, 14. (a)

John Herbers. "Cities Data Show Wide Differences in the Sun Belt and Industrial North." *New York Times*, February 28, 1983, p. 10. (b)

John Herbers. "Cities Turn to Private Groups to Administer Local Services." *New York Times*, May 23, 1983, pp. 1, 8. (c)

John Herbers. "Large Cities and Suburbs Giving Way to the Sprawl of Small Urban Areas." *New York Times*, July 8, 1983, p. 1. (d)

Homer Hoyt. "The Structure of American Cities in the Post-War Era." *American Journal of Sociology* 48 (January 1943):475–492.

Mary Jo Huth. "New Hope for Revival of America's Central Cities." *The Annals, ASPSS* 51 (1980):118–129.

John D. Kasarda and Morris Janowitz. "Community Attachment in Mass Society." *American Sociological Review* 39 (June 1974):328–339.

William S. Kowinski. "Suburbia: End of the Golden Age." *New York Times Magazine*, March 16, 1980, pp. 16–19+.

Robert W. Lake. *The New Suburbanites: Race and Housing*. New Brunswick, N.J.: Rutgers University Press, 1981.

David B. Lewis. "International Demographics: The Meaning Behind the Numbers." *American Demographics* 4 (February 1982):17–21.

Larry Long and Diana DeAre. "The Slowing of Urbanization in the U.S." *Scientific American* 249 (July 1983):33–41.

D. Claire McAdams. "A Power-Conflict Approach to Urban Land Use: Toward a New Urban Ecology." *Urban Anthropology* g (Fall 1981):295–318.

Richard L. Madden. "Poll of Suburbanites Shows a Growing Sense of a Separate World." *New York Times*, November 14, 1978, p. B3.

Harvey Marshall. "White Movement to the Suburbs: A Comparison of Explanations." *American Sociological Review* 44 (December 1979):975–994.

Earl Finbar Murphy. "Effects of Structure and Organization of Human Settlements on Health, Productivity, and Quality of Life." *Ekistics* 49 (1982):369–372.

Robert E. Park, Ernest W. Burgess, and Roderick D. McKenzie (eds.). *The City*. Chicago: University of Chicago Press, 1925.

Elwin H. Powell. "The Evolution of the American City and the Emergence of Anomie: A Culture Case Study of Buffalo, New York: 1810–1910." *British Journal of Sociology* 13 (1962):156–166.

Frank Schaffer. *The New Town Story*. London: MacGibbon & McKee, 1970.

William A. Schwab. *Urban Sociology: A Human Ecological Perspective*. Reading, Mass.: Addison-Wesley, 1982.

Kent P. Schwirian et al. *Contemporary Topics in Urban Sociology*. Morristown, N.J.: General Learning Press, 1977.

Richard Sennett. *Uses of Disorder: Personal Identity and City Life*. New York: Random House, 1971.

Eshref Shevky and Marilyn Williams. *The Social Areas of Los Angeles*. Berkeley: University of California Press, 1949.

Anne B. Shlay and Peter H. Rossi. "Putting Politics into Urban Ecology: Estimating Net Effects of Zoning." In Terry Nichols Clark (ed.), *Directions for Future Research*. Beverly Hills, Calif.: Sage Publications, 1981.

Gideon Sjoberg. *The Preindustrial City: Past and Present*. Glencoe, Ill.: Free Press, 1960.

John M. Stahura. "Suburban Status Evolution/Persistence: A Structural Model." *American Sociological Review* 44 (December 1979):937–947.

Gerald D. Suttles. *The Social Order of the Slum*. Chicago: University of Chicago Press, 1968.

Ferdinand Tönnies. *Community and Society* (Charles A. Loomis, ed. and trans.). East Lansing: Michigan State University Press, 1957. (Originally published in 1887.)

Louis Wirth. "Urbanism as a Way of Life." *American Journal of Sociology* 44 (July 1938):1–24.

CHAPTER 18

Ronald P. Abeles. "Relative Deprivation, Rising Expectations, and Black Militancy." *Journal of Social Issues* 32 (1976):119–137.

David Aberle. *The Peyote Religion Among the Navaho*. Chicago: Aldine, 1966.

Vernon L. Allen. "Toward Understanding Riots: Some Perspectives." *Journal of Social Issues* 26 (Winter 1970):1–18.

Gordon W. Allport and Leo Postman. *The Psychology of Rumor*. New York: Holt, 1947.

David M. Alpern. "A Matter of Life and Death." *Newsweek*, April 26, 1982, pp. 20–25.

Adrian F. Aveni. "Organization Linkages and Resource Mobilization." *Sociological Quarterly* 19 (Spring 1978):185–202.

Raymond Bauer. "The Obstinate Audience." In Alan Wells (ed.), *Mass Media and Society*. Palo Alto, Calif.: National Press Books, 1972.

Melinda Beck. "The Toxic-Waste Crisis." *Newsweek*, March 7, 1983, pp. 20–24. (a)

Melinda Beck. "The Bitter Politics of Acid Rain." *Newsweek*, April 25, 1983, pp. 36–37. (b)

Nachman Ben-Yehuda. "The European Witch Craze of the 14th to 17th Centuries: A Sociologist's Perspective." *American Journal of Sociology* 86, No. 1 (July 1980).

Carolyn Bird. "The Invisible Bar." In Elsie Adams and Mary Louise Briscoe (eds.), *Up Against the Wall, Mother. . . .* Beverly Hills, Calif.: Glencoe, 1971.

Herbert Blumer. "Collective Behavior." In Alfred McClung Lee (ed.), *New Outline of the Principles of Sociology*. New York: Barnes & Noble, 1951. (First published in 1939.)

James W. Button. *Black Violence*. Princeton, N.J.: Princeton University Press, 1978.

A. Campbell and H. Schuman. "Racial Attitudes in Fifteen American Cities." In *Supplementary Studies for the National Advisory Commission on Civil Disorders*. Washington, D.C.: U.S. Government Printing Office, 1968.

Hadley Cantril, with Hazel Gaudet and Herta Herzog. *Invasion from Mars*. Princeton, N.J.: Princeton University Press, 1947.

Rachel Carson. *Silent Spring*. Boston: Houghton Mifflin, 1962.

James C. Davies. "Toward a Theory of Revolution." *American Sociological Review* 27 (1962):5–19.

James Davies. "The J-Curve and Power Struggle Theories of Collective Violence." *American Sociological Review* 39 (1974):607–619.

Marlene Dixon. "Why Women's Liberation?" In Elsie Adams and Mary Louise Briscoe (eds.), *Up Against the Wall, Mother. . . .* Beverly Hills, Calif.: Glencoe, 1971.

Robert M. Fogelson. "Violence and Grievances: Reflections on the 1960s Riots." *Journal of Social Issues* 26 (Winter 1970):141–163.

Jo Freeman. "The Origins of the Women's Liberation Movement." *American Journal of Sociology* 78 (1973):792–811.

Jo Freeman. "Resource Mobilization and Strategy." In Mayer N. Zald and John D. McCarthy (eds.), *The Dynamics of Social Movements*. Cambridge, Mass.: Winthrop, 1979.

Betty Friedan. *The Feminine Mystique*. New York: Dell, 1963.

James A. Geschwender. "Social Structure and the Negro Revolt: An Examination of Some Hypotheses." *Social Forces* 43 (1964):248–256.

Ted Robert Gurr. *Why Men Rebel*. Princeton, N.J.: Princeton University Press, 1970.

Thomas Ford Hoult. *A Dictionary of Modern Sociology*. Totowa, N.J.: Littlefield, Adams, 1969.

J. Craig Jenkins and Charles Perrow. "Insurgency of the Powerless: Farm Worker Movements (1946–1972)." *American Sociological Review* 42 (1977):249–268.

Elihu Katz and Paul Lazarsfeld. *Personal Influence*. New York: Free Press, 1955.

Everett Carll Ladd. "The Freeze Framework." *Public Opinion* 5 (August–September 1982):20, 41.

Gustave Le Bon. *The Crowd: A Study of the Popular Mind*. New York: Viking, 1960. (Originally published in 1895.)

Marilyn Lester. "Generating Newsworthiness: The Interpretative Construction of Public Events." *American Sociological Review* 45 (1980):984–994.

Michael S. Lewis-Beck. "Some Economic Effects of Revolution Models, Measurement and the Cuban Evidence." *American Journal of Sociology* 84 (March 1979):1127–1149.

Doug McAdam. *Political Process and the Development of Black Insurgency*. Chicago: University of Chicago Press, 1982.

John D. McCarthy and Mayer N. Zald. *The Trend of Social Movements in America*. Morristown, N.J.: General Learning Press, 1973.

John D. McCarthy and Mayer N. Zald. "Resource Mobilization and Social Movements: A Partial Theory." *American Journal of*

Sociology 82 (1977):1212–1241.
Edwin McDowell. "'Silent Spring,' 20 Years a Milestone." *New York Times*, September 27, 1982, p. C16.
Nehum Z. Medalia and Otto N. Larson. "Diffusion and Belief in a Collective Delusion: The Seattle Windshield Pitting Epidemic." *American Sociological Review* 23 (1958):221–232.
Harvey Molotch. "Media and Movement." In Mayer N. Zald and John B. McCarthy (eds.), *The Dynamics of Social Movements*. Cambridge, Mass.: Winthrop, 1979, pp. 71–93.
Dorothy Nelkin. "Anti-Nuclear Connections: Power and Weapons." *The Bulletin of the Atomic Scientists* 37 (1981):36–40.
Anthony Oberschall. *Social Conflicts and Social Movements*. Englewood Cliffs, N.J.: Prentice-Hall, 1973.
Joseph B. Perry, Jr., and Meredith Pugh (eds.). *Collective Behavior: Response to Social Stress*. New York: West, 1978.
Anthony Piepe, Sunny Crouch, and Miles Emerson. *Mass Media and Cultural Relationships*. Farnborough, England: Saxan House, 1978.
Frances Fox Piven and Richard A. Cloward. *Poor People's Movements: Why They Succeed, How They Fail*. New York: Pantheon Books, 1977.
Report of the National Advisory Commission on Civil Disorders. Washington, D.C.: U.S. Government Printing Office, 1968.
Arnold M. Rose. *The Power Structure*. New York: Oxford University Press, 1967.
Gerry B. Rose. *Outbreaks*. New York: Free Press, 1982.
Ralph L. Rosnow and Gary Alan Fine. *Rumor and Gossip: The Social Psychology of Hearsay*. New York: Elsevier, 1976.
Stanley Rothman and S. Robert Lichter. "The Nuclear Debate: Scientists, the Media and the Public." *Public Opinion* 5 (August–September 1982):47–52.
Allan Schnaiberg. "Politics, Participation, and Pollution: The 'Environmental Movement.'" In John Watson and Donald E. Carns (eds.), *Cities in Change: Studies on the Urban Condition*. Boston: Allyn & Bacon, 1973.
A. Clay Schoenfeld, Robert F. Meier, and Robert J. Griffin. "Constructing a Social Problem: The Press and the Environment." *Social Problems* 27 (1979):38–55.
Philip Shabecoff. "Politics and the E.P.A. Crisis: Environment Emerges as a Mainstream Issue." *New York Times*, April 29, 1983, p. 13.
Theda Skocpol. *States and Social Revolutions: A Comparative Analysis of France, Russia, and China*. New York: Cambridge University Press, 1979.
Neil J. Smelser. *Theory of Collective Behavior*. New York: Free Press, 1962.
David A. Snow, Louis A. Zurcher, Jr., and Robert Peters. "Victory Celebrations as Theater: A Dramaturgical Approach to Crowd Behavior." *Symbolic Interaction* 4, No. 1 (May 1981).
Ronald A. Taylor. "Cleaner Air and Water." *U.S. News & World Report*, February 28, 1983, pp. 27–28.
Charles Tilly. "Revolutions and Collective Violence." In Fred I. Greenstein and Nelson W. Polsby (eds.), *Handbook of Political Science*. Reading, Mass.: Addison-Wesley, 1973.
Charles Tilly. *From Mobilization to Revolution*. Reading, Mass.: Addison-Wesley, 1978.
Alexis de Tocqueville. *The Old Regime and the French Revolution* (John Bonner, trans.). New York: Harper & Brothers, 1856.
Mark Traugott. "Reconceiving Social Movements." *Social Problems* 26 (1978):38–49.
Ralph H. Turner and Lewis M. Killian. *Collective Behavior* (2nd ed.). Englewood Cliffs, N.J.: Prentice-Hall, 1972.
James Wallace. "Nuclear Freeze Crusade." *U.S. News & World Report*, April 25, 1983, pp. 18–21.
Jack M. Weller and E. L. Quarantelli. "Neglected Characteristics of Collective Behavior." *American Journal of Sociology* 79 (November 1973):665–685.
John Wilson. *Introduction to Social Movements*. New York: Basic Books, 1973.

CHAPTER 19

John Andrew. "Terminal Tedium." *Wall Street Journal*, May 6, 1983, pp. 1, 16.
Conrad M. Arensberg and Arthur H. Niehoff. *Introducing Social Change*. Chicago: Aldine, 1964.
Danforth W. Austin and J. Ernest Beazley. "Struggling Industries in Nation's Heartland Speed up Automation." *Wall Street Journal*, April 4, 1983, pp. 1, 11.
Bruce Bartlett. "The Luddite Answer to Unemployment." *Wall Street Journal*, July 18, 1983, p. 16.
Sharon Begley. "The Creative Computers." *Newsweek*, July 5, 1982, pp. 58–62.
Daniel Bell. *The Coming of the Post-Industrial Society*. New York: Basic Books, 1973.
Barry Bluestone and Bennett Harrison. *The Deindustrialization of America*. New York: Basic Books, 1982.
Phillip M. Boffey. "Job Impact of Robots Debated at Hearing." *New York Times*, March 19, 1983, p. 21.
George W. Bonham. "Education and the World View." *Change* 12, No. 4 (May–June 1980):2–7.
Harvey Brooks. "Technology, Evaluation and Purpose." *Daedalus* 109, No. 1 (Winter 1980):65–81.
Dale D. Buss. "Retraining of Workers for Automated Plants Gets Off to Slow Start." *Wall Street Journal*, April 13, 1983, pp. 1, 19.
Edmund Byrne. "Robots and the Future of Work." In Howard F. Didsbury, Jr. (ed.), *The World of Work*. Bethesda, Md.: World Future Society, 1983.
Marvin J. Cetron. "Jobs with a Future." In Howard F. Didsbury, Jr. (ed.), *The World of Work*. Bethesda, Md.: World Future Society, 1983.
Ralf Dahrendorf. *Class and Class Conflict in Industrial Society*. Stanford, Calif.: Stanford University Press, 1959.
John Diebold. "Innovation and New Institutional Structures." In Howard F. Didsbury, Jr. (ed.), *The World of Work*. Bethesda, Md.: World Future Society, 1983.
Emile Durkheim. *The Division of Labor in Society* (George Simpson, trans.). Glencoe, Ill.: Free Press, 1947. (Originally published in 1893.)
Jacques Ellul. *The Technological Society*. New York: Knopf, 1964.
Kai Erikson. *Everything in Its Path*. New York: Simon & Schuster, 1976.
André Gunder Frank. "The Development of Underdevelopment." In James P. Cockcraft, André Gunder Frank, and Dale L. Johnson (eds.), *Dependence and Underdevelopment*. Garden City, N.Y.: Doubleday, Anchor Books, 1972.
Eli Ginzberg. "The Mechanization of Work." *Scientific American* 247 (September 1982):67–75.

Daniel Goleman. "The Electronic Rorschach." *Psychology Today* 17 (February 1983):36–43.

June Goodfield. *Playing God.* New York: Harper & Row, 1977.

Philip Greven. *The Protestant Temperament.* New York: Knopf, 1979.

Shirley Hallblade and Walter M. Mathews. "Computers and Society: Today and Tomorrow." In Walter M. Mathews (ed.), *Monster or Messiah? The Computer's Impact on Society.* Jackson: University Press of Mississippi, 1980.

Willis W. Harman. "The Coming Transformation." *The Futurist* 11 (February 1977):5–12.

Marvin Harris. *Cows, Pigs, Wars, and Witches.* New York: Random House, 1974.

Ronald Inglehart. *The Silent Revolution.* Princeton, N.J.: Princeton University Press, 1977.

Institute for the Future. *Teletext and Videotext in the United States.* New York: McGraw-Hill, 1982.

Landon Y. Jones. *Great Expectations: America and the Baby Boom Generation.* New York: Coward, McCann, and Geoghegan, 1980.

Jane Kingston. "Telecommuting: Its Impact on the Home." In Howard F. Didsbury, Jr. (ed.), *The World of Work.* Bethesda, Md.: World Future Society, 1983.

Frederick E. Laurenzo. "Computers and the Idea of Progress." In Walter H. Mathews (ed.), *Monster or Messiah? The Computer's Impact on Society.* Jackson: University Press of Mississippi, 1980.

Steven J. Marcus. "As Computers Eliminate Jobs." *New York Times,* June 2, 1983, p. 28.

Robert K. Merton and Robert A. Nisbet (eds.). *Contemporary Social Problems* (4th ed.). New York: Harcourt Brace Jovanovich, 1976.

John W. Meyer, John Boli-Bennet, and Christopher Chase-Dunn. "Convergence and Divergence in Development." *Annual Review of Sociology* 1 (1975):223–246.

John Naisbitt. *Megatrends.* New York: Warner Books, 1982.

Tom Nicholson. "Growth Industries of the Future." *Newsweek,* October 18, 1982, p. 83.

William F. Ogburn. *On Culture and Social Change.* Chicago: University of Chicago Press, 1964.

James O'Toole. "How to Forecast Your Own Working Future." In Edward Corhish (ed.), *Careers Tomorrow.* Bethesda, Md.: World Future Society, 1983.

Talcott Parsons. *The Social System.* New York: Free Press, 1951.

Talcott Parsons. *Societies: Evolutionary and Comparative Perspectives.* Englewood Cliffs, N.J.: Prentice-Hall, 1966.

Ivor Peterson. "Is Talk of High Tech Jobs More Political than Real?" *New York Times,* October 24, 1982, p. E3.

Fred Plog, Clifford J. Jolly, and Daniel G. Bates. *Anthropology: Decisions, Adaptation, and Evolution.* New York: Knopf, 1976.

Andrew Pollack. "Latest Technology May Spawn Electronic Sweatshop." *New York Times,* October 3, 1982, p. 17.

Andrew Pollack. "Trust in Computers Raising Risk of Errors and Sabotage." *New York Times,* August 22, 1983, p. 25.

William Serrin. "'High Tech' Is No Jobs Panacea, Experts Say." *New York Times,* September 18, 1983, pp. 1, 16.

Herbert A. Simon. "The Social Impact of Computers." In Tom Forester (ed.), *The Microelectronics Revolution.* Cambridge, Mass.: MIT Press, 1981.

Neil Smelser. "Toward a Theory of Modernization." In Amitai Etzioni and Eva Etzioni-Halevy (eds.), *Social Change: Sources, Patterns, and Consequences.* New York: Basic Books, 1973.

David Snyder and Edward L. Kick. "Structural Position in the World System and Economic Growth, 1955–1970: A Multiple-Network Analysis of Transnational Interactions." *American Journal of Sociology* 84 (May 1979):1096–1126.

Herbert Spencer. *The Evolution of Society: Selections from Herbert Spencer's 'Principles of Sociology'*" (Robert L. Carniero, ed.). Chicago: University of Chicago Press, 1974.

Oswald Spengler. *The Decline of the West.* New York: Knopf, 1926–1928.

Nancy Stern and Robert A. Stern. *Computers in Society.* Englewood Cliffs, N.J.: Prentice-Hall, 1983.

Alvin Toffler. *The Third Wave.* New York: Morrow, 1980.

Arnold Toynbee. *A Study of History.* New York: Oxford University Press, 1946.

Immanuel Wallerstein. *The Modern World-System.* New York: Academic Press, 1974.

Lynn White, Jr. *Medieval Technology and Social Change.* New York: Oxford University Press, 1962.

Peter Worseley. *The Trumpet Shall Sound.* New York: Schocken Books, 1958.

GLOSSARY

Institutional discrimination, 329
Integration, 329–330
Interactionist perspective, 24
Interest group, 293
Interlocking directorates, 293
Internal colonialism, 330
Internal environment, 199
Internalization, 129, 227
Internal migration, 441
International migration, 441
Invasion cycle, 471
Invisible (private) religion, 414
Iron law of oligarchy, 293

Jim Crow laws, 330

Kibbutzim, 367

Labeling, 227
Laboratory experiment, 51
Language, 74
Latent function, 24, 96
Laws, 74
Legal-rational authority, 293
Leveling, 496
Life chances, 259
Life expectancy, 441
Life span, 441
Linguistic relativity hypothesis, 74
Looking-glass self, 129

Machismo, 154
Macrosociology, 96
Manifest function, 24, 96
Marital assimilation, 74
Marriage, 367
Master status, 96
Materialist view of change, 523
Matriarchy, 367
Matrilineal descent, 367
Matrilocal residence, 367
Mean, 51
Median, 51
Megalopolis, 471
Megastructure, 471
Microsociology, 96
Minority group, 330
Mob, 496
Mode, 51
Modernization, 523
Monogamy, 367
Moral community, 414
Mores, 74
Mortification, 199
Motor intelligence, 129
Multilinear evolution, 523
Multinational corporation, 293
Multiple nuclei model, 471

Natural selection, 74
Negotiated order, 199
Neolocal residence, 367
New town, 471
Norm, 51, 74
Norm of reciprocity, 96
Nuclear family, 367

Object permanence, 129
Oligarchy, 293
Oligopoly, 293
Open class system, 259
Operational definition, 51
Opportunity structure, 96
Organized crime, 227
Organized skepticism, 51
Out-group, 175

Parkinson's law, 199
Patriarchy, 367
Patrilineal descent, 367
Patrilocal residence, 367
Peter principle, 199
Plea bargaining, 227
Pluralism, 293, 330
Political party, 293
Polyandry, 367
Polygyny, 367
Postindustrial society, 523
Power, 259, 293
Power elite, 259, 293
Prejudice, 330
Prestige, 259
Primary deviance, 227
Primary group, 175
Private religion, 414
Profane, 414
Progressive tax, 259
Proletariat, 24, 259
Protestant ethic, 414

Protest movement, 293

Race, 330
Racism, 330
Random sample, 51
Rebellion, 227
Redemptive movement, 496
Reference group, 175
Reformative movement, 496
Regions, 96
Regressive tax, 259
Relative deprivation, 497
Reliability, 51
Religion, 414
Residential suburbs, 471
Resocialization, 129
Retreatism, 227
Ritual, 414
Ritualism, 199, 227
Role, 96
Role conflict, 96
Role set, 96
Role strain, 97
Rumor, 497

Sacred, 414
Sample, 51–52
Sanctions, 74, 227
Scapegoat, 330
Scientific method, 52
Secondary analysis, 52
Secondary deviance, 227
Secondary group, 175
Sect, 414
Sector model, 471
Secularization, 414
Segregation, 330
Self, 129
Self-fulfilling prophecy, 389
Semistructured interview, 52
Sex, 154
Sexism, 154
Sex role, 154
Sex role stratification, 154
Sharing, 52
Significant others, 129
Significant symbols, 129
Social area analysis, 471
Social change, 523
Social control, 227
Social dynamics, 25
Social exchange, 97
Social facts, 25
Social group, 97, 175
Social interaction, 97
Socialist command economy, 293
Socialization, 129
Social mobility, 259
Social movement, 497
Social revolution, 497
Social statics, 25
Social structure, 97
Society, 97
Sociobiology, 74
Sociocultural selection, 74
Socioemotional leadership, 175
Sociological imagination, 25
Sociology, 25
State, 293
Status, 97
Stratification, 259
Structural assimilation, 74–75
Structural conduciveness, 497
Structured interview, 52
Subculture, 75
Succession, 471
Superego, 129
Survey, 52
Symbol, 75
Symbolic interaction, 25
System, 25

Task leadership, 175
Telecommuting, 523
Theory, 25, 52
Thomas theorem, 97
Total institution, 199
Totalitarian state, 293
Totemism, 414
Tracking, 389
Traditional authority, 293
Transfer payments, 259
Transformative movement, 497
Triad, 175
Two-career marriage, 367
Two-location (commuter) marriage, 367

Underdevelopment, 523
Unilinear evolution, 523
Unstructured interview, 52
Urban ecology, 471
Urbanization, 471

Urban sprawl, 471

Validity, 52
Values, 75
Variable, 52
Verstehen, 25
Vertical mobility, 259

Victimless crime, 227
Voluntary association, 199

White-collar crime, 227
World-system theory, 523

Zoning, 471

NAME INDEX

SUBJECT INDEX

ABOUT THE AUTHORS

Donald Light is Professor of Sociology at Rutgers University and Professor of Social and Behavioral Medicine in the Department of Psychiatry at the University of Medicine and Dentistry of New Jersey, School of Osteopathic Medicine. Born and raised in Massachusetts, Professor Light went to college at Stanford and completed his graduate work in sociology at the University of Chicago and Brandeis University. Along the way, he helped to implement President Kennedy's Equal Employment Opportunity Program for minority workers and became increasingly interested in the field of education and health. He is now conducting research on the sociological changes taking place in the American health care system.

Professor Light's first appointment was to the faculty of Princeton where he taught the introductory course in sociology as well as courses in education, deviance, and the professions. It was there he met and became friends with Suzanne Keller and subsequently developed the first edition of this text. He has published a well-known study of medical training entitled *Becoming Psychiatrists: The Professional Transformation of Self* (Norton, 1980), and his new book on how political values affect health care services will be published by the M.I.T. Press in 1985. He is the author of numerous articles, which have appeared in *The American Journal of Sociology, The Hournal of Health and Social Behavior, The Administrative Science Quarterly, Daedalus,* and *The New England Journal of Medicine.*

Suzanne Keller is currently Professor of Sociology at Princeton University, where she has served as Chairperson of the Department of Sociology. She was born in Vienna, Austria, and came to the United States as a child. After college she spent several years in Europe, mainly in Paris and Munich, where she worked as a survey analyst and translator. She received a Ph.D. in sociology from Columbia University in 1953. In 1957, she became an Assistant Professor at Brandeis University, where she taught courses in social theory, stratification, and the sociology of religion. A Fulbright Lectureship in 1963 at the Athens Center of Ekistics marked the beginning of her interest in architecture and community planning. At the completion of her Fulbright in 1965, Professor Keller joined the Center, where she remained until 1967. That year she came to Princeton University as a Visiting Professor, and in 1968 she was the first woman to be appointed to a tenured Professorship there. She has held several elective offices in the American Sociological Association, including that of Vice-President, and served a three-year term as editor of the Rose Series in sociology.

Today, Professor Keller is pursuing her interests in teaching, writing, research, public lectures, and world-wide travel. She is currently completing a book on the creation of a community and is embarking on a study of contemporary elites. The author of numerous articles and several books, Suzanne Keller has also helped to launch the new program in Women's Studies at Princeton. A consultant to many corporations, universities, and government agencies, Professor Keller has received a number of fellowships and honors, including a Guggenheim award.

A NOTE ON THE TYPE

This book is set in Electra, a typeface designed by W.A. Dwiggins. This face cannot be classified as either modern or old-style. It is not based on any historical model, nor does it echo any particular period or style. It avoids the extreme contrasts between thick and thin elements that mark most modern faces, and attempts to give a feeling of fluidity, power, and speed.